Border Lines

DIVINATIONS: REREADING LATE ANCIENT RELIGION

Series Editors
Daniel Boyarin
Virginia Burrus
Charlotte Fonrobert
Robert Gregg

A complete list of books in the series is available from the publisher.

Border Lines

The Partition of Judaeo-Christianity

Daniel Boyarin

PENN

University of Pennsylvania Press
Philadelphia

10   9   8   7   6   5   4   3   2   1

Published by
University of Pennsylvania Press
Philadelphia, Pennsylvania 19104-4011

Library of Congress Cataloging-in-Publication Data

Boyarin, Daniel.
    Border lines : the partition of Judaeo-Christianity / Daniel Boyarin.
        p. cm. — (Divinations: Rereading Late Ancient Religion)
    Includes bibliographical references and index.
    ISBN 0-8122-3764-1 (cloth : alk. paper)
    1. Christianity—Origin. I. Title: Border lines. II. Title. III. Series.

BR129.B69 2004
296.3'96'09015—dc22

                                                2003065753

Ghermii pel crine il desiderio alato!

Arrigo Boito

Contents

Preface: Interrogate My Love   ix

List of Abbreviations   xvii

1   Introduction   1

Part I   Making a Difference: The Heresiological Beginnings of
Christianity and Judaism

2   Justin's Dialogue with the Jews:
The Beginnings of Orthodoxy   37

3   Naturalizing the Border:
Apostolic Succession in the Mishna   74

Part II   The Crucifixion of the Logos: How Logos Theology
Became Christian

4   The Intertextual Birth of the Logos:
The Prologue to John as a Jewish Midrash   89

5   The Jewish Life of the Logos:
Logos Theology in Pre- and Pararabbinic Judaism   112

6   The Crucifixion of the Memra:
How the Logos Became Christian   128

Part III   Sparks of the Logos: Historicizing Rabbinic Religion

7   The Yavneh Legend of the Stammaim:
On the Invention of the Rabbis in the Sixth Century   151

8   "When the Kingdom Turned to *Minut*":
The Christian Empire and the Rabbinic Refusal
of Religion   202

Concluding Political Postscript: A Fragment   227

Notes   229

Bibliography   333

Index   361

Acknowledgments   373

Preface
Interrogate My Love

As long as I can remember I have been in love with some manifestations of Christianity (not always ones that my Christian friends would themselves love or even approve). Tennessee Ernie Ford singing on television the hymn "The Garden" moved me to tears when I was a child. For an oddly gendered teenager, St. Francis, the Sissy, proved an incredibly tantalizing figure of a man. Later on it was medieval Christian art and architecture, the cathedrals of Europe, the spirituality of Meister Eckhart and Jakob Böhme. Still later, and most significantly, it has been the writings of the Fathers of the Church (and their excluded others, the Christian heretics) that have been most riveting for me, pulling me into a world so close to that of my own beloved Rabbis of late antiquity and yet so foreign as well, a world in which oceans of ink (and rivers of blood) could be spilt on questions of detail in the description of the precise relationships between the posited persons of a complex godhead, a world, as well, in which massive numbers of men and women could choose freely and enthusiastically to live lives without the pleasures of sex and the joys of family. I find this world endlessly moving and alluring, even when at its most bizarre to me. For the last decade or so I have devoted much of my time and spirit to learning the languages of and understanding something of the inner and outer worlds of those early Christian men and women who wrote such texts and lived such lives.

Some Jews, it seems, are destined by fate, psychology, or personal history to be drawn to Christianity.[1] This book won't let me be done with it, or so it seems, until I come clean and confess that I am one of those Jews. I cannot, of course, deny the problematic aspects of that desire; desire is frequently unruly and problematic. Christians, of course, have been bloody rotten to Jews through much of our histories, and Jews, when occasionally given the chance, have taken their turn at being rotten to Christians. This desire seems sometimes to be not entirely unlike the "love" that binds an abusive couple to each other. Nevertheless, it is there. The question is, then, what creative use can be made of problematic desire—not only what pleasures can it engender but also what *utile* can it be in the world?

Some Jews who are so absorbed by Christianity have been induced by that affection to convert and become Christians. I have not, held back by an even more powerful libidinal commitment to the religion, the memories, the thick history, the literature and liturgy of diasporic rabbinic Judaism as practiced for nearly the last two millennia. In earlier work, I have attempted to express and make some sense of that greater love.[2] In this preface, I want to make some sense of my other love and show how it drives the text that follows. Perhaps, better than "greater" or "lesser" in characterizing these investments, I should distinguish between a love of who I am, diasporic rabbinic Jew, and a desire for a different other, the subject of Christianity.

Years have gone into the making of this book (more, indeed, than any of my other books), and during those years the work has been presented in many venues. On one occasion, when I had delivered a lecture based on some of the work below on the Gospel of John, a very upset undergraduate arose from the audience to inquire: Who are you and why are you trying to take our Gospel away from us? On another occasion, a group of Christian ministers asked me why I was not a Jew for Jesus (not in an effort to convert me to that movement but rather to understand what it is that makes me not one). At still another time, in Jerusalem on one memorable occasion, I was asked explicitly by the organizer of a conference, Dr. Alon Goshen-Gottstein, to reflect on the implications of this work for the present and future. On all of those occasions, I disengaged from the question that was being asked, falling on the last resort of the scholarly scoundrel: "I'm just trying to figure out what really happened!" In a more ongoing sense, I have experienced the work on this book as a pleasing withdrawal from cultural wars in which I have been engaged for so long, for once not seeking (so I thought) to defend or attack, to apologize or polemicize, but simply to describe and analyze. But the book would not get done; it would not let me finish. In particular, certain parts of the writing felt, even more than usual, peculiarly unsatisfying, feeble and flabby in their rhetoric, even, oddly, when I was more or less pleased with what I had to say. The penny dropped when my dear colleague Chana Kronfeld observed that this was the first of my books that did not begin with a personal letter, as it were, to the readers and the first, as well, in which I, at least occasionally, lapsed into a first-person plural subject, not quite an authorial *we* but still a voice that was seeking to distance myself from what I was saying. Overnight it became clear to me that I could not evade the good and hard questions that the undergraduate at Grinnell asked, that the ministers asked, that Alon had asked of me. The book is, once again, an attempt to justify my love, to explain it, to ask that it be understood by others, but also, once again, to make it just, just to the Jews and Christians and their discourses that are its subjects. But I have allowed myself to see my investment in this book, let alone reveal it, only in extremis, at the end of the writing, at the eleventh hour and even then with more of a sense of having been constrained to do this by the language, the text, the parts that would not come alive without this energy than by a desire for self-exposure. Something seems to frighten me here, either some boundary that I am afraid, for myself, that I am threatening to breach or perhaps a fear that I will be perceived to have breached such a boundary and be marginalized or excluded from a community to which I still fervently desire to belong. But there's no way out of this now other than to go right through the middle of it.

Why does my book want me to "come out?" Why do I need to tell about the love that (almost) would not dare to say its name, the love of this Orthodox Jew for Christianity? Even more grandiosely, I could pose the question (but very hesitantly, almost taking it back as I ask it), What purpose might this strange attraction play? Perhaps it has led me to uncover something: Implicitly through this scholarship and explicitly right here, I suggest that the affiliation between what we call Judaism and what we call Christianity is much more complex than most scholars, let alone most layfolk, imagine and that that complexity has work to do in the world, that we can learn something from it about identities and affiliations. The world that I have found in this research is one in which identities were much less sure than they have appeared to us until now, in which the very terms of identity were being worked on and worked out. Not only had there not been the vaunted "parting of the ways," but Christianity was deeply engaged in finding its identity, its boundaries, and even busily and noisily sorting out what kind of an entity it would be, what kind of an identity it would form. There was no telling yet (or even now) what the telos of the story would be. Non-Christian Jews, and especially an important group of Jewish religious elites, were busy as well, working hard to discover how to define their own borders in a discursive world being dramatically changed by the noise that Christians were making, soundings of "New Israels," "true Jews," and "heretics." "Judaism"—an anachronism—was up for grabs as well, by which I don't mean only the by-now well-accepted notion that there was no normative Judaism, only Judaisms, but something more. Even rabbinic Judaism was struggling to figure out for itself what a "Judaism" is and who, then, could be defined as in and out of it. My book is a narrative of that period of struggle, of false starts and ruptures and abandoned paths during the initial phases of this site under construction.

I am arguing in this book that "heresiology," the extraordinary practice of anatomizing, pinning down, making taxonomies of Christians who are not somehow "in," was an integral part of the answer to the question, What kind of a thing will Christianity be? Integral to that heresiological answer as well was a response to Jews who would not be Christians, or, better put (in a way that I hope will become clearer as you read this book), a response to the question of how the mapping of a border with something that Christianity will call Judaism will make the new Christian self-definition as a "religion" work. As an important, even vital part, of the answer to these questions, Christian discourse from the second through the fifth centuries—the centuries that are the object of this book—kept producing a species of heretics called "Jews" and "Judaizers," hybrids, "monsters" to use the terminology of one of the earliest of Christian writers, Ignatius of Antioch: "It is monstrous to talk of Jesus Christ and to practice Judaism" (Magnesians 10:3). These very monsters were to appear as a heresiological topos of the orthodox Christian writers who almost constantly figured heresy as a hydra. The Rabbis, in those same centuries, produced an analogous response, a discourse as well of the pure and the authentic opposed to the impure, the contaminated, the hybrid, the *min*.

I speak here, then, for the monsters. But why? What right do I have to do so? I am not, after all, a heretic from either the orthodox Christian or orthodox Jewish point of view, neither a Judaizing Christian nor a Christian Jew (a *min*), for all my attraction to Christianity and Christians. I do not choose, in any way, to be a Messianic Jew, a Jew for Jesus, or anything of that sort, but actually, to be just a Jew, according to the flesh and according to the spirit. Let me state here the obvious, the simple, the straightforward and definitive: I do not believe that Jesus the son of Joseph of Nazareth was (or is) the Messiah, let alone do I subscribe to even higher christological glories ascribed to him as "Son of God." I am not, I think, a Jew *against* Jesus but there is no credible sense in which I could be construed as a Jew *for* Jesus either. I do not seek, of course, covertly (as sometimes Jews for Jesus do) or overtly, to convert myself or any other Jew to Christianity, nor claim that Christianity is the true Judaism, nor preach that somehow Jews must accept John as gospel truth.

There is, therefore, a conundrum here. On the one hand I occupy an "orthodox"—or at least quite conventional—form of Jewish identification, belief, and practice, but on the other hand, I find myself driven to write a history that calls the very terms of that orthodox identity into question. I need to figure out in what way the position of monster, of heretic, calls me in order to discover the meaning of my work *to me*. I think I read the record, in some sense, from the point of view of the hybrids, the heretics, not because I wish, then, to revive their particular religious modality, whether we call it Jewish Christian or find some other name for it, but because there is some other sense in which the position of those "monsters" is close enough to my own to call me to it, to identify with it, as my place. My first apparent apologia must, it seems, give way to another, deeper one.

For all the conventionality of my self-identification as orthodox Jew, I am seriously out of step with my community at this moment, in a position of marginality that is frequently very painful to me. The present is a time in which Jewish orthodoxy has been redefined as including the unquestioning support for a political entity, the State of Israel, and all of its martial adventures. My own vaunted "love" for Christianity has become suspect to me at this moment, for I am writing at a time (2003) in which Jews and Christians (millennial enemies) are suddenly strange bedfellows, collectively engaged in a war or wars against Muslims. Ariel Sharon's war of ethnic cleansing against the Palestinians is applauded by fundamentalist Christians, and American president George W. Bush's crusade against Iraq is cheered by most Jews in the name of a battle against Muslim terrorists. (Ironically—but not accidentally—just as in the first Crusades, Arab Christians are assimilated to Muslims by the discourse of both the Jewish and American Christian anti-Muslim campaigns.)[3] Already I have heard rumblings, ominous warnings, that the import of my critical work is precisely that, of aiding and abetting in the forging of a new identity of Jews and Christians against the Muslims. Perhaps my transgressive love is not transgressive enough, maybe even, in the current social-political context, not transgressive at all but the enactment, or potential enactment, of a dangerous liason.

I have been repeatedly asked in the last year or so why my book does not engage the history of Islam as part of the history of Judaism in the same way that it engages Christianity. Once again, I have until now taken the easy way out: It is not in my period of research. I cannot continue to evade the hard question at this time of crisis, but I am hoping that there is at least the embryo of an answer in this book itself. Indeed, in some sense my book can only be justified to me now, via an allegorical reading of it. I think that while the historical sense of the book concerns Christians and Jews in late antiquity, its moral sense lies elsewhere, paradoxically in an interrogation of the easy and terrible alliances between most Jews and many Christians against Muslims in the present.

I and all of us (especially Jews) who dissent from a version of a Jewish-Christian alliance that brands the Palestinians, Saddam Hussein, and Osama bin-Laden as equally and demonically Islamic terrorists are labeled by both Jews and Christians as Jewish antisemites. This is powerfully reminiscent to me of a Jerome, many centuries before, stigmatizing Jews who were Christians and Christians who were Jews as heretics and declaring them confidently "neither Jews nor Christians." The mind boggles and the imagination is beggared at the spectacle of right-wing Protestant presidents, Southern Baptist fundamentalist preachers (historically no friends of the Jews), and the Jewish president of Harvard University, speaking from the (Christian) pulpit at Harvard Memorial Church (historically no site for the championing of Jews), making common cause in demonizing those, Jews and others, who dissent radically from Israeli policy and practice toward the Palestinians. How bitterly ironic to find the latter pulpit being used to label Jewish and other signers of a petition calling on universities to divest from apartheid Israel as "antisemites!" I and other Jews who dissent from Jewish support of Israel are being labeled heretics.

On the stairs of my synagogue, in Berkeley, on Rosh Hashanah this year, I was told that I should be praying in a mosque, and versions of this, less crude perhaps, are being hurled at Jews daily by other Jews. I don't wish to romanticize my situation. It is not I who is suffering; my only personal pain is the pain of living on the margins, and that, too, has its privileges. More piercing to me is the pain of watching a tradition, my Judaism, to which I have dedicated my life, morally disintegrating before my eyes. It has been said by many Christians that Christianity died at Auschwitz, Treblinka, and Sobibor. I fear—G–d forbid— that my Judaism may be dying at Nablus, Daheishe, Beteen (Beth El), and al-Khalil (Hebron.)[4] The violent actions taken in the name of defense *may* help some Jewish bodies survive (and even that only dubiously, temporarily, momentarily), but they threaten to empty Jewish existence of all meaning, to make hollow the resistance for two thousand years to being dissolved into the majority. If we are not for ourselves, other Jews say to me, who will be for us? And I answer, but if we are for ourselves alone, what are we?

In this book, I am suggesting that the borders between Judaism and Christianity have been historically constructed out of acts of discursive (and too often actual) violence, especially acts of violence against the heretics who embody the instability of our constructed essences, of our terrifying bleedings into each other. I ask whether we can transform transgressive desires for the proscribed other, for proscribed otherness, from a phobic moment within ourselves that produces ever more violent attempts to repress them and insist on purity into something like what the best love should be, a psychic (in the allegorical instance, social) situation in which one seeks the good of another out of the autonomy and security of a self. Can observing the processes through which a self (two selves) were formed enable a rewriting of the story of self, of Jewish self and Christian self, not only with respect to each other but also, or perhaps especially, as each separately and both together encounter new others? Paradoxically, it is my transgression of that unholy alliance of Jews and so many Christians (but not, indeed, all Christian groups, let alone all Christians)—a transgression born paradoxically at least in part of my attraction to Christianity and with it my interest in the time of blurred identity—that constitutes my monstrosity, my heresy.

Seeing the complexities of identification and desire, the roads crissing and crossing through which identities, entities, ultimately Christianity and Judaism, were forged in late antiquity might help, a bit, in the greatest, most acutely emergent task with which Jews (in the end it comes to this for me) are faced right now, once again to maintain our existence, our cultural, religious memory without sacrificing the very meanings of that existence, continuity, and memory on their own altar, without fetishizing borders and boundaries in the enactment of an ethnic cleansing that finally, in my view, negates the very meaning of Jewish survival until now. If we have been for only ourselves, what are we? As I write, in occupied Palestine literal physical boundaries of barbed wire and electrified fencing are being raised to separate violently one "people" from another. In the process of maintaining our own identities (and now I address Christians—and, indeed, Muslims—as well), can we learn the lessons of the past and prevent ourselves at the eleventh hour from the path of new and even more violent heresiologies? Jews and Christians are called upon at this moment to learn from our own difficult histories, without in any way rendering those histories equivalent phenomenologically or morally, and do something different now. The Prophet teaches: Zion will be redeemed only through justice.

This book may not wear its heart on its sleeve like its elder siblings; I hope to have gotten a little more blood pumping through its arteries.

Abbreviations

Ant.	Antiquities
BT	Babylonian Talmud
Ap.	Apology
C. Ap.	*Contra Apionem*
c. Ar.	Orations against the Arians
Conf. Ling.	*De confusione lingnarum*
CTh	Code of Theodosius
DD	Damascus Document
E.H.	Ecclesiastical History
Ep. ad Africanum	*Epistula ad Africanum*
Frag.	Fragment
Her.	*Quis rerum divinarum heres*
Hom. Jer.	*Homilies on Jeremiah*
Hom. Ps.	*Homilies on Psalms*
Mart. Poly.	*Martyrdom of Polycarp*
Migr.	*De migratione Abraham*
Mut.	De Mutatione nominum
Opif.	De opificio mundi
Pan.	Panarion
P.G.	Patrologia Graecae
PT	Palestinian Talmud

Chapter 1

Introduction

Every day for thirty years a man drove a wheelbarrow full of sand over the Tijuana border crossing. The customs inspector dug through the sand each morning but could not discover any contraband. He remained, of course, convinced that he was dealing with a smuggler. On the day of his retirement from the service, he asked the smuggler to reveal what it was that he was smuggling and how he had been doing so. "Wheelbarrows; I've been smuggling wheelbarrows, of course."

This humorous anecdote functions for me on several levels at once. First of all, I will insist that the borders between Christianity and Judaism are as constructed and imposed, as artificial and political as any of the borders on earth. I shall propose in this book that just as the border between Mexico and the United States is a border that was imposed by strong people on weaker people, so too is the border between Christianity and Judaism. Rather than a natural-sounding "parting of the ways," such as we usually hear about with respect to these two "religions," I will suggest an imposed *partitioning* of what was once a territory without border lines, much as India and Pakistan, and Israel and Palestine were artificially partitioned by colonial power. A wonderful simile of Jacques Derrida's based on such a partitioning may help develop the power of this metaphor here. Derrida wrote: "Like Czechoslovakia and Poland, [speech and writing] resemble each other, regard each other; separated nonetheless by a frontier all the more mysterious . . . because it is abstract, legal, ideal."[1] We would not be wrong, I think, in appropriating this figure for another figure and applying all of these terms to the imagined frontier between Judaism and Christianity.

Second, the Tijuana border is a space for the crossing of contraband humans and contraband goods and services. Similarly, the border space between the juridical and abstract entities Judaism and Christianity, throughout late antiquity and even beyond, was a crossing point for people and religious practices. Religious ideas, practices, and innovations permeated that border crossing in both directions. There were people, as well, who simply didn't recognize the legitimacy or even the existence of the border. The Chicanos and Tejanos say: We didn't cross the border; the border crossed us. Furthermore, there were customs inspectors at the frontiers of this Christianity and Judaism. They inscribed the border lines in texts that we know of now as heresiologies. Finally, I will suggest that those very inspectors of religious customers, in their zeal to prevent any contraband from crossing the borders that they sought to enforce by fiat, were, themselves, the agents of illicit interchange of some of the most important contraband, the wheelbarrows—in this case, the very ideas of heresiology themselves.

How and why that border was written and who wrote it are the questions that drive this book. Once I am no longer prepared to think in terms of preexistent different entities—religions, if you will—that came (gradually or suddenly) to enact their difference in a "parting of the ways," I need to ask who it was in antiquity who desired to make such a difference, how did they accomplish (or seek to accomplish) that making, and what was it that drove them? (And also, where possible, who and what resisted them?) Answers (not the answers) to these questions will be essayed in this book. My proposal here is that the discourse we know of as orthodoxy and heresy provides at least one crucial site for the excavation of a genealogy of Judaism and Christianity. The idea of orthodoxy comes into the world some time in the second century with a group of Christian writers called "heresiologists," the anatomizers of heresy and heresies, and their Jewish counterparts, the Rabbis. "Heresiology"—the "science" of heresies—inscribes the border lines, and heresiologists are the inspectors of religious customs. Ancient heresiologists tried to police the boundaries so as to identify and interdict those who respected no borders, those smugglers of ideas and practices newly declared to be contraband, nomads who would not recognize the efforts to institute limits, to posit a separation between "two opposed places," and thus to clearly establish who was and who was not a "Christian," a "Jew."[2] Authorities on both sides tried to establish a border, a line that, when crossed, meant that someone had definitively left one group for another. They named such folk "Judaizers" or *minim*, respectively, and attempted to declare their beliefs and practices, their very identities, as out of bounds.

Groups that are differentiated in various ways by class, ethnicity, and other forms of social differentiation become transformed into "religions" in large part, I would suggest, through discourses of orthodoxy/heresy.[3] Early Christian heresiology, whatever else it is, is largely the work of those who wished to eradicate the fuzziness of the borders, semantic and social, between Jews and Christians and thus produce Judaism and Christianity as fully separate (and opposed) entities—as religions, at least in the eyes of Christianity.[4]

For nearly two decades now, scholars of early Christianity have been building toward a major revision of the history of Christian heresiology. The work of much of the scholarship of the first half of the twentieth century consisted of dislodging the traditional "Eusebian" account of the origins of orthodoxy and heresy, within which orthodoxy was simply the teaching of Jesus as communicated to the apostles and passed down to bishops, while heresy was the later incursion of false and wicked error into Christian tradition under the influence of the Devil or his later secularized counterpart Greek philosophy. Scholars throughout the twentieth century demonstrated that in many cases "heretical" ideas and practices were coeval—at least—with those that came to be defined as orthodox. The culmination of the scholarly direction was in the work of Walter Bauer, which had enormous impact twice, once when it was published in German in the 1930s and once again after being published in English in 1971.[5] Bauer's work has remained, however, problematic in some respects, notably in his strange ascription of essence to heresy and orthodoxy, such that he could state that in many places, "heresy preceded orthodoxy." Working within a Foucauldian paradigm, Alain Le Boulluec has completely shifted the research strategy.[6] Apart from his specific historical achievements and insights, Le Boulluec's most important move has been to shift the scholarly conversation away from the question of orthodoxy and heresy understood as essences and to move the discussion in the direction of a history of the representation of orthodoxy and heresy, the discourse that we know of as heresiology, the history of the idea of heresy itself. From this perspective, it will be seen that orthodoxy cannot precede heresy (the traditional account), nor can heresy precede orthodoxy (Bauer); *orthodoxy* and *heresy* must, of necessity, come into the world of discourse together. *Orthodoxy* and *heresy* are decidedly not things, but notions that must always be defined in each other's context.[7] In this book, "orthodoxy" means those church writers, whatever the specifics of their own doctrines, who promulgate the notion of orthodoxy, and the opposite of *orthodoxy* in terms of the scholarly discourse adopted here is not *heresy* but rather something like *heterodoxy*, represented by religious writers, thinkers, practitioners who do not operate with a notion of orthodoxy. This means, inter alia, that some writers defined by the Church as *heretics* belong to the camp of orthodoxy, insofar as they promulgate such a notion of Christian truth.

The Greek term *hairesis* earlier meant just a "choice," that is an affinity group joined by common ideas, theories, and practices, without any pejorative overtones at all. Le Boulluec found that Justin Martyr, a "pagan" convert who lived in Asia Minor and Rome through the first two thirds or so of the second century, was a crucial figure (if not the crucial figure) in the Christian shift from understanding *hairesis* to be a "group of people, a party or sect marked by common ideas and aims" to being "a party or sect that stands outside established or recognized tradition, a heretical group that propounds false doctrine in the form of a heresy."[8] As Le Boulluec himself puts it, the result of his research is that "Il revient à Justin d'avoir inventé l'hérésie."[9] Le Boulluec has been, perhaps, at more of a loss to explain the causes and functions of this invention, largely attributing them to the influence of "Judaism" and the challenge of "Gnosticism," neither of which turns out, on balance, to be a very compelling explanation. The very practices of the Rabbis that Le Boulluec identifies as models for Christian orthodoxy are only attested—as is all of rabbinic Judaism—later than Justin, and, as Elaine Pagels has recently made clear, Justin hardly seems to know of "gnostics" at all.[10] Other explanations, other ways of relating rabbinic to Christian orthodoxy, need to be sought.

Building on Le Boulluec's work, I shall argue in this book that at least a significant part of the function of heresiology, if not its proximate cause, was to define Christian identity—not only to produce the Christian as neither Jew nor Greek but also to construct the whatness of what Christianity would be, not finally a third race or *genos* but something entirely new, a religion.[11] It is no accident, I will suggest, that the alleged "inventor of heresy" is also the author of "one of the earliest texts [*The Dialogue*] which reflects a self-consciously independent Christianity,"[12] or, as I would prefer to put the same point, one of the earliest texts that is self-consciously engaged in the production of an independent Christianity.

Similarly, where scholars of rabbinic Judaism have looked for evidence of response to Christianity at specific points within rabbinic texts, either as denunciation in the form of *minut* or as imitation of or polemic against certain Christian practices and ideas, I can follow Le Boulluec's lead in taking up Foucault's notions of discourse and shift my investigation from the specifics of what was thought or said to the *episteme* or universe of possible knowledge within which they were said and thought. Matching, then, Le Boulluec's transformation of the study of heresiology from the reconstruction of heresies to the history of the notion of heresy in Christianity, I can try for a similar transformation in the history of Judaism, transforming my inquiry from the identification of *minim* to the history of the notion of *minut* in rabbinic texts.

To come back to my allegory one more time (perhaps to belabor it): Where till now, it might be said, scholarship has been looking for what is hidden in the sand (with more success than the customs inspector), I prefer to look at smuggled wheelbarrows as the vehicles of language within which identities are formed and differences made.[13] A very sophisticated recent effort in the former direction has been made by Israeli historian Israel Yuval.[14] It is a measure, however, of our different approaches that Yuval can write: "Whenever we find a similarity between Judaism and Christianity, we must assume that we have a case of influence by the Christian surroundings on the Jews, not the opposite, unless it can be proven that the Jewish sources are ancient and earlier than [the Christian ones]."[15] While Yuval seems absolutely correct in taking cognizance of the enormous asymmetry in power between Jews and Christians in the late Roman world (as Heine famously wrote, *wie es sich christelt, so jüdelt es sich*), his formulation of the problematic is dependent on the assumption that there are already fully formed, bounded identities (both social and cultural) of Christianity and Judaism already in late antiquity, rather than seeing the processes of formation. This is in part, I think, an artifact of looking for goods smuggled in the sand and not the wheelbarrows. I agree completely with Yuval's claim that there is something fundamentally upside down in looking within rabbinic sources for "background" to the New Testament.[16] Judaism is not the "mother" of Christianity; they are twins, joined at the hip. I am also in total agreement with his insistence that the frequently expressed scholarly notion that Jews were not concerned with Christianity until the Middle Ages is a serious error.[17] Here's an example of the difference between us: Yuval provides an illuminating discussion of the rabbinic legends of the death of the Messiah, the son of Joseph. He finds remarkable parallels between the Passion midrash of the Gospels and these midrashic texts, insisting, however, that they must reflect Christian influence on Jews.[18] I have no doubt that the Rabbis were aware of the use of Psalm 22 in the construction of the death of the Messiah in the Gospels and that they sometimes reflected it and even parodied it.[19] It is hard for me to imagine, however, that a whole rabbinic narrative of a suffering and dying Messiah arose in response to and in a polemic against the Gospel midrash. I would prefer to think about a theme common to the two Judaic dialects, inflected differently for each, including the different weights that it received there.[20] This view is to be contrasted, also, with the view of Jacob Neusner who would limit such responses to the fourth century.[21]

According to the readings proposed here, in the tannaitic period (roughly equivalent to the period of ante-Nicene Christianity), rabbinic texts project a nascent and budding heresiology, different in content (in some ways complementary in content) but strikingly similar in form to that of the second-century Fathers. In their very efforts to define themselves and mark themselves off from each other, Christian writers of orthodoxy and the Rabbis were evolving in important and strikingly parallel ways. Shaye Cohen has already noticed this and wondered how and by what means were the rabbinic and Christian developments connected. In a very lucid programmatic exploration of scholarship on heresy, Michel Desjardin articulated the following desiderata for Jewish scholarship: "To what extent was the Jewish concern for heresy early, and what explains the striking overlap in heresiological perspectives between the rabbis and the fathers? The term *minim* has to be thrown into the heretical pot, and its use

compared in detail to *haretikoi*. Could the Jewish treatment of Christians perhaps have led to a Christian devaluation of others as 'heretics?' "[22] I hope to be
addressing some of these questions in this book. My suggestion is that it was in
large part the very discursive effect of the mutual efforts to distinguish Judaism
from Christianity that provided the major impetus for the development of heresiology in its different forms among the second-century church writers and the
Rabbis. (Note that this is a very different formulation from Desjardin's.) Little
did they suspect, I warrant, that in struggling so hard to define who was in and
who was out, who was Jewish and who was Christian, what was Christianity and
what was Judaism, it was they themselves who were smuggling the wheelbarrows, the very discourses of heresiology and of religion as identity.

One of the scholars who has been most active in the study of the history of
the complex interactions and negotiations out of which Judaism and Christianity were formed is Judith M. Lieu. In a recent paper, she has set the question elegantly:

Both "Judaism" and "Christianity" have come to elude our conceptual grasp; we feel sure
that they are there, and can quote those "others," outsiders, who were no less sure. How
else are we to understand the *fiscus judaicus*, how else to make sense of the death, if not
of the myriads of whom Eusebius speaks, at least of some who would not let go of their
conviction about Jesus as they understood it? Yet when we try to describe, when we seek
to draw the boundaries which will define our subject for us, we lack the tools, both conceptual and material. It seems to me equally justifiable to "construct" "Christianity" in
opposition to "Judaism" at the moment when Jesus "cleansed the Temple," at least in the
literary representation of that event, and to think of that separation only in the fourth
century, stimulated by dramatic changes in access to power—and I could call to my de-
fence advocates of both positions, no doubt determined by their own starting-points and
definitional frameworks.[23]

I think that Lieu has hit the nail precisely on the head. The question of when
Christianity separated from Judaism is a question whose answer is determined
ideologically. We need always to ask: Whose Judaism; whose Christianity? Shall
we make the determining point an act of inner-Jewish hostility to certain authorities that we choose now to name "the Jews," or are we looking for something
else, and if so, what? What is revealed and concealed in this or that way of framing or defining the issues, in seeing Christianity as separate from Judaism *ab ovo*
or in claiming that "it takes an army" to separate them? I am interested in the dis-
closures that await us when we take something like the second position enumer-
ated by Lieu, that sometime around the fourth century we can begin to speak of
Judaism and Christianity as separate "religions,"[24] and, even then, as I shall try to
show, primarily (if not exclusively) when speaking from a Christian location. But
a partial answer to the paradox that, as early as the first century, Christians were,

nevertheless, recognizable at least in some places as not-Jews (Tacitus, the *fiscus judaicus*, other evidence) is to note that whether or not there were Christianity and Judaism, there were, it seems, at least some Christians who were not Jews, and, of course, many Jews who were not Christians, and the distinctions of identity/identification would, ultimately, make a difference. They hadn't, however, yet. There seems to be no absolute point, theological or otherwise, at which we could say for this early period: It is this that marks the difference between Judaism and Christianity. I don't wish to argue that this position is correct but rather consciously to make it the starting point in a search for "the boundaries that were also crossing points," and for more glimpses of the folks, "even perhaps the majority," who dwelt in the interstices of the texts and objected to or simply ignored the work of the religious customs officers. Moreover, adopting such a perspective—a perspective that refuses the option of seeing Christian and Jew, Christianity and Judaism, as fully formed, bounded, and separate entities and identities in late antiquity—will help us, I hope, to perceive more fully the work of those early Christian and Jewish writers as they were making the difference. Accordingly, rather than attempting (even if that were possible) a complete coverage of the texts of my period, looking for the voices and texts of the suppressed versions of Judaeo-Christianity in hopes of discovering diversity there, I choose to look at the ideological work being done by some of our most canonized and central of texts—Justin Martyr, Jerome, Athanasius, the Mishnah, the Tosefta, the Talmuds—looking for the interstices internal to the "orthodox" canons and what these texts are trying to hide and suppress there.

The problem, then, of how my texts relate to reality, that is, the methodological problem of how one moves from the legendary and legal texts of the Talmud to some understanding of the lives of Jews in late antiquity, is, in a sense, solved by revealing it as an instance of a theoretical problem of the relation of language in general to social practice in general. "Discourse in this sense is a whole field or domain within which language is used in particular ways. The domain is rooted (as is Gramsci's or Althusser's notion of ideology) in human practices, institutions and actions."[25] Analysis of discourse in this sense, whatever its other theoretical and political virtues and defects, is ideally situated for constructing the past with greater complexity, depth, and nuance than might otherwise be attempted or thought possible, since—adapting words of Ania Loomba—"It seeks to widen the scope of studies [of religious history] by examining the intersection of ideas and institutions, knowledge and power."[26]

In the end, I will argue that there is a real dissymmetry between a reading of that difference from within Christianity or from within Judaism. While Christianity finally configures Judaism as a different religion, Judaism itself, I suggest, at the end of the day refuses that call, so that seen from that perspective

the difference between Christianity and Judaism is not so much a difference between two religions as a difference between a religion and an entity that refuses
to be one.

In Western languages one habitually speaks—in both the scholarly and the
quotidian registers—of "Judaism" and "Christianity" (and, for that matter, Islam,
Buddhism, Taoism, Confucianism, and Hinduism) as members of a single category: (names of) religions, or even—faiths. This scholarly and popular practice,
as the last term particularly reveals, involves the reproduction of a Christian
worldview. The questionable appropriateness of projecting a Christian worldview
or a Christian model upon peoples and practices who don't quite fit, or even don't
wish to fit that model and worldview should be evident. Indeed, speaking for Judaism, it seems highly significant that there is no word in pre-modern Jewish parlance that means "Judaism." When the term *Ioudaismos* appears in non-Christian
Jewish writing—to my knowledge only in 2 Maccabees—it doesn't mean Judaism
the religion but the entire complex of loyalties and practices that mark off the
people of Israel; after that, it is used as the name of the Jewish religion only by
writers who do not identify themselves with and by that name at all, until well into
the nineteenth century.[27] It might seem, then, that Judaism has not, until some
time in modernity, existed at all, and that whatever moderns might be tempted to
abstract out or to disembed from the culture of Jews and call their religion was not
so disembedded nor ascribed particular status by Jews until very recently.

Until our present moment, it could be defensibly argued, Judaism both is
and is not a "religion." On the one hand, for many purposes it—like Hinduism—operates as a religion within multireligious societies. Jews claim for
their religion a semantic, cultural status parallel to that of Christianity in the
West. We study Judaism in programs of religious studies, claim religious freedom, have sections on Judaism at the American Academy of Religion—even
one on comparative Judaism and Hinduism—and in general function as members of a "faith" (or system of ultimate meaning or whatever) among other
faiths. On the other hand, there are many ways that we continue to be uncom-
fortable and express our discomfort with this very definition. For both Zion-
ists and many non-Zionist Jews (including me), versions of description or
practice with respect to Judaism that treat it as a faith that can be separated
from ethnicity, nationality, language, and shared history have felt false. Precisely that very position of Judaism at the American Academy of Religion has
been experienced by us, sometimes, as in itself a form of ambivalently capitu-
lating behavior (which is not, I hasten to add, altogether unpleasurable). Something about the difference between Judaism and Christianity is captured
precisely by insisting on the ways that Judaism is not a religion.[28] This ambivalence has deep historical roots.

The theory of interpellation, inter alia, the calling of names is relevant here. As Judith Butler has remarked, "To be called a name is one of the first forms of linguistic injury that one learns. But not all name-calling is injurious. Being called a name is also one of the conditions by which a subject is constituted in language; indeed, it is one of the examples Althusser supplies for an understanding of 'interpellation.'" Butler goes further than this, however. She discerns that the injurious and the noninjurious moments of calling a name can be one and the same moment. Hailing is recognition. "In being called an injurious name, one is derogated and demeaned. But the name holds out another possibility as well: by being called a name, one is also, paradoxically, given a certain possibility for social existence, initiated into a temporal life of language that exceeds the prior purposes that animate that call."[29] As a surprising instance of this phenomenon, one might refer to the apparent invention of the term *rhetoric* by Plato as a term of reproach, "as part of an effort to limit the scope and popularity of Sophistic teaching, particularly that of his rival Isocrates." The term, however, quickly became an empowering one "for organizing thought and effort around a specific set of problems—those of being a persuasive *rhētor*." Indeed, "Plato may have helped to empower a discipline that his philosophical outlook found repugnant."[30] *Rhetoric*, oddly, has a history similar to *Christianity*. Or as the Rabbis put it: He came to curse, and in the end blessed.

Recently Virginia Burrus has mobilized the Althusser/Butler theory as a way of articulating the possible effect of one Christian heresiologist, Athanasius, on Jewish history. Burrus argues, following Butler and Althusser, that Athanasius's "hate-speech," although directed at "Arians" and, therefore, seemingly having nothing to do with Jews, is nevertheless well worth attending to, because Athanasius's heretics are so often named as Jews, and indeed may be supremely relevant for the history of Judaism, because "injurious address may, in the very act of inflicting pain, give rise to an 'other' agency within language, summon a [Jewish] subject into existence."[31] Once again, as Butler has put it: "If to be addressed is to be interpellated, then the offensive call runs the risk of inaugurating a subject in speech who comes to use language to counter the offensive call."[32] If, for example, to be called the name "queer" in a powerful sense is not only to be injured but also to be called into being, then to be called "Jew" or "heretic" is similarly so to be interpellated. Indeed, as David Brakke has shown, at the time that Athanasius was active, there was a kind of Jewish revival in Alexandria itself.

A historically close analogy may help to clarify matters here. A leading historian of Christianity in late antiquity, Robert Markus, has argued (partially following Momigliano) that "paganism" also became a religion through the discourses of Christian orthodoxy: "The image of a society neatly divided into 'Christian' and 'pagan' is the creation of late fourth-century Christians, and has been too readily taken at its face value by modern historians. Unlike Christianity, with its growing world-wide cohesiveness, 'paganism' was a varied group of cults and observances. It never constituted a single coherent religious movement analogous to either Christianity or Judaism. It existed only in the minds, and, increasingly *the speech habits* of Christians. Insofar as a particular section of Roman paganism acquired some sort of homogeneous identity—as did that of some groups of Roman aristocrats in the last decades of the fourth century— it was a response to the growing self-confidence and assertiveness of a Christian establishment."[33] The hailing of the "pagan" subject via the hate speech of the Christian thus produced this subject and her religion (just as, earlier, one could say it was the hate speech of the crowd in Antioch that produced "Christian" as a separate identity, if not religion; what goes around, comes around).

What about Jews and Judaism? Did the hailing of Judaism as religion call forth a response similar to that of the "pagans" of whom Markus speaks, those upper-class Romans who adopted this interpellation/appellation as a name for a religion? The argument of this book is that the answer to this question has to be disclosed diachronically, that, at the first stage of its existence, at the time of the initial formulation of rabbinic Judaism, the Rabbis, at least, did seriously attempt to construct Judaism (the term, however, is an anachronism) as an orthodoxy, and thus as a "religion," the product of a disembedding of certain realms of practice, speech, and so on from others and identifying them as of particular circumstance. If you do not believe such and such or practice so and so, you are not a Jew, imply the texts of the period. At a later stage, however, according to my hypothesis, that is, at the stage of the "definitive" formulation of rabbinic Judaism in the Babylonian Talmud, the Rabbis rejected this option, proposing instead the distinct ecclesiological principle that "an Israelite, even if he [*sic*] sins, remains an Israelite." The historical layering of these two ideologies and even self-definitions by the Rabbis themselves of what it is that constitutes an Israel and an Israelite provide for the creative ambivalence in the status of Judaism today. Christianity, it would seem, or rather, the Church, needed "Judaism" to be a religious other, and some maintained and reified this term as the name of a religion.

That Judaism is both interpellated as a religion and partly accepts and partly evades that position is perhaps an artifact of the Christian invention of religion, to start with. According to Rowan Williams, "Orthodoxy" is a way that a "religion"—disembedded from ethnic or geocultural self-definition, as Christianity had made itself—asks itself: "How, if at all, is one to identify the 'centre' of [our] religious tradition? At what point and why do we start speaking about 'a' religion?"[34] I choose to understand these questions as historical rather than methodological ones, temporal rather than spatially located queries. At what point in history, and why, did *they* begin speaking about a religion, an orthodoxy, a heresiology? As I shall attempt to show, heresiology plays a powerful role within Judaism precisely in the period of mutual differentiation, yet once that border is (more or less) firmly inscribed, heresiology virtually drops out of Judaism, leaving in its wake Judaism's equivocal status as a "religion." It is not a trivial but a very interesting fact that as the history moved on, heresiology remained a living, vital, and central part of Christianity, while in rabbinic Judaism, eventually Judaism *tout court*, heresiology was to wither and (almost) die out,[35] leaving in its wake the ambiguity that marks Judaism till this day as sometimes a religion, sometimes not.[36]

This book thus seeks to locate the roots of this ambiguity about being a religion in a time long before the present moment by examining the "postcolonial" situation of Judaism at the time of the invention of religion. It has become a truism that religion in its modern sense is an invention of Christians. This argument has been made by several theoreticians/historians, notably Wilfred Cantwell Smith and Talal Asad.[37] These scholars have claimed that "religion" in the sense in which we use the term today is a post-Enlightenment concept and category produced within Protestant Christianity.[38] Other scholars locate the "invention of religion" not in the Enlightenment but during the time of the very formation of Christianity at the dawn of late antiquity. This historical production does not belong to the eighteenth century but was in process from nearly the beginning of certain parts of the Jesus movement and was largely complete—whatever that might mean—by the beginning of the fifth century. Supporting the notion of a late ancient epistemic shift that we might call the invention of religion, Maurice Sachot has argued that the term *religio*, in the sense in which we use it, is entirely the product of Christianity.[39] This view has been maintained as well by historian of late ancient Judaism Seth Schwartz, who has phrased this point strikingly by referring to "Christianization, and what is in social-historical terms its sibling, the emergence of religion as a discrete category of human experience—religion's *disembedding*."[40] Schwartz is claiming that the production of Christianity is, itself, the invention of religion as such—a discrete category of human experience. The production of this category does not imply that many elements of what would form religions did not exist before this time, but rather that the particular aggregation of verbal and other practices that would now be named as constituting a religion only came into being as a discrete category as Christianization itself.[41] In this sense, one cannot speak of Judaism as existing before Christianity but only as part of the process of the invention of Christianity. "Religion," Denis Guénoun has recently pointed out, "is constituted as the difference between religions."[42] Christianity, in its constitution as a religion, therefore needed religious difference, needed Judaism to be its other—the religion that is false.

I hope in this book to add several new perspectives to this theme by asking and attempting to answer several new questions, questions that are generated out of new ways of understanding difference that I will elaborate below. How was heresiology implicated in the Christian invention of religion? How did these Christian inventions interact with and affect the developments taking place among non-Christian Jews at the same time? Heresiology, I will argue, was the technology, as well, for the initial rabbinic acceptance of membership in the category of "religion," while the end of rabbinic heresiology constituted an ultimate refusal of that membership. The self-definition by certain Christians of Christianity over and against Judaism and the self-definition of orthodoxy as opposed to heresy are closely linked, for much of what goes under the name of heresy in these early Christian centuries consists in one variety or another of Judaizing, or, sometimes the opposite, as in the case of Marcion, of denying any connection with the Bible and the "Jewish" God.[43] Heresy, then, is always defined with reference to *Judaism*. The rise to power of the Rabbis, I will suggest, is deeply dependent on the impact of the notion of orthodoxy on rabbinic Jewish discourse: that is, the autonomy brought by the self-definition of an "orthodox" Judaism vis-à-vis an "orthodox" Christianity, or Judaism as a religion.

Schwartz has written that the disembedding of religion that constitutes the invention of religion per se "had a direct impact on the Jewish culture of late antiquity because the Jewish communities *appropriated* much from the Christian society around them."[44] In other words, when Christianity separated religious belief and practice from *Romanitas*, cult from culture, Judaism as a religion came into the world. The Rabbis articulated their own sense of identity and definition in part through "appropriation" of the question of identity asked by at least some early Christians. This partial "appropriation" referred to by Schwartz is not, on the interpretation to be offered here, the product of the influence of Christianity on Judaism but is an exercise of agency in a "colonial" situation by non-Christian Jews.[45] It should be read, I will argue, as a kind of mimicry in the technical postcolonial sense and thus as an act of resistance. As Homi Bhabha writes: "Resistance is not necessarily an oppositional act of political intention, nor is it the simple negation or exclusion of the 'content' of another culture, as a difference once perceived. It is the effect of an ambivalence produced within the rules of recognition of dominating discourses as they articulate the signs of cultural difference and reimplicate them within the deferential relations of colonial power—hierarchy, normalization, marginalization and so forth."[46]

In the end—at least in the end of late antiquity—rabbinic Judaism refused the option of becoming a religion, another species of the kind that Christianity offered. At the final stage of the development of classical rabbinism, a reassertion of the "locative" of identity as given and not as achieved—or lost—came to be emblematic of Judaism. One might say, adopting the language of Schwartz, that what made Judaism and Christianity different in the end, different products of the history of post-Israelite religious culture, was the re-embedding of the former, the sub/mergence of religion as a discrete category of human experience, the refusal by the Jews of their interpellation as a religion. A fascinating modern instantiation and even proof for this proposition can be discovered, I think, in the fate of the Jewish sect known as Lubavitch Hasidim in the last decades. Certain groups within this sect have held that their deceased Rabbi was the Messiah, that his death is only temporary, as it were, and that he will soon return, a set of religious ideas strikingly reminiscent of Christianity. Demonstrating the heterodox nature of these notions, Orthodox scholar David Berger has vigorously argued that these radical Hasidim should be declared heretics.[47] The logic of Berger's position cannot be gainsaid. What he misses, however, in my opinion, is precisely that Judaism is not and has not been, since early in the Christian era, a "religion" in the sense of an orthodoxy whereby heterodox views, even very strange opinions, would make one an outsider. This is the force of the historical reconstruction attempted here.

In the end, it is not the case that Christianity and Judaism are two separate or different religions, but that they are two different kinds of things altogether. From the point of view of the Church's category formation, Judaism and Christianity (and Hinduism later on) are examples of the category *religions,* one a bad example and the other a very good one, indeed the only prototype. But from the point of view of the Rabbis' categorization, Christianity is a religion and Judaism is not. Judaism remains a religion for the Church because, I will suggest, it is a necessary moment in the construction of Christian orthodoxy and thus Christian religion, whereas occasional and partial Jewish appropriations of the name and status of religion are strategic, mimetic, and contingent. Like the layerings of the unconscious or the interpenetrating stratifications of Roman material culture that so inspired Freud, however, the vaunted ambivalence of Judaism is, I suggest, a product of that history, of that partial acceptance and then almost total refusal of the option of orthodoxy and heresy as the Jews' mode of self-definition—the refusal, that is, finally to become and be a religion. Reading the archaelogical record given by that stratification is the work of this book.

Hybrids and Heretics

A recent writer on the history of comparative religion, David Chidester, has developed the notion of an "apartheid comparative religion." By this (working out of the southern African situation as a model for theorization), Chidester means a system that is "committed to identifying and reifying the many languages, cultures, peoples, and religions of the world as if they were separate and distinct regions."[48] The point of such a knowledge/power regime is that "each religion has to be understood as a separate, hermetically sealed compartment into which human beings can be classified and divided." I locate the beginnings of such ideologies of religious difference in late antiquity. Following Chidester's descriptions, I want to suggest that the heresiologists of antiquity were performing a very similar function to that of the students of comparative religion of modernity, conceptually organizing "human diversity into rigid, static categories [as] one strategy for simplifying, and thereby achieving some cognitive control over, the bewildering complexity of a frontier zone."[49] Heresiology is, I might say, a form of apartheid comparative religion, and apartheid comparative religion, in turn, is a product of late antiquity.

Generally, the orthodox topos that Christian heretics are Jews or Judaizers is seen as a sort of sideshow to the real heresiological concern, the search for the Christian doctrine of God, to put it in Hanson's terms.[50] According to this view, heresiology is primarily an artifact of the contact between biblical Christian language and Greek philosophical categories which forced ever more detailed and refined definitions of godhead, especially, in the early centuries, in the face of the overly abstract or philosophical approaches of the "Gnostics." The naming of heretics as Jews or Judaizers is treated, on such an account, as a nearly vacant form of reprobation for reprobation's sake. Without denying that interpretation's validity for the history of Christian theology, I nonetheless hypothesize that it is not epiphenomenal that so often heresy is designated as "Judaism" and "Judaizing" in Christian discourse of this time,[51] nor that a certain veritable obsession with varieties of "Jewish Christianity" (Nazoreans, Ebionites) became so prominent in some quarters precisely at the moment when Nicene orthodoxy was consolidating.[52] Furthermore, it is not a necessary outcome for even a very refined theological discourse and controversy on such issues as the relations of the persons of the Trinity to have produced a structure of orthodoxy and heresy, without some other cause or function intervening.[53] At least one major impetus for the formation of the discourse of heresiology, on my reading, is the construction of a Christianity that would not be Judaism. The "Jews" (for this context, heretics so named), the Judaizers, and the Jewish Christians—whether they existed or to what extent is irrelevant in this context—thus mark a space of threatening hybridity, which it is the task of the religion police to do away with.[54]

Note that these religion police, the border guards, were operating on both sides; hybridity was as threatening to a "pure" rabbinic Judaism as it was to an orthodox Christianity. An elegant example is the fair of Elone Mamre, which, according to the church historian Sozomen, attracted Jews, Christians, and pagans, who each commemorated the angelic theophany to Abraham in their own way: the Jews celebrating Abraham; the Christians the appearance of the Logos; and the pagans, Hermes.[55] Here is, perhaps, the very parade instantiation of Bhabhan "interstitial" spaces that bear the meaning of culture. The Rabbis prohibited Jews from attending at all (PT Avoda Zara 1.5. 39d), thus reinscribing the hybridity as something like what would later be called "syncretism," and banishing it from their orthodoxy. We will see that this is an oft-repeated phenomenon at this particular time.[56]

One of the most important themes of postcolonial theorizing is the hybridity of cultural identifications and the instability of dominating cultural paradigms, which necessitate their constant reproduction and the constant assertion of their naturalness and of hybridity as unnatural and monstrous.[57] Homi Bhabha has written that cultures interact, not on the basis of "the exoticism of multiculturalism or the *diversity* of cultures, but on the inscription and articulation of culture's *hybridity*." Bhabha concludes, "it is the 'inter'—the cutting edge of translation and negotiation, the *in-between* space—that carries the burden of the meaning of culture."[58] The instability of colonial discourse makes possible the subaltern's voice, which colonizes, in turn, the discourse of the colonizer. As Bhabha puts it, "in the very practice of domination the language of the master becomes hybrid—neither the one thing nor the other."[59] Robert Young glosses Bhabha: "Bhabha shows that [the decentering of colonial discourse from its position of authority] occurs when authority becomes hybridized when placed in a colonial context and finds itself layered against other cultures, very often through the exploitation by the colonized themselves of its evident equivocations and contradictions."[60] Bhabha focuses on the fault lines, on the border situations and thresholds, as sites where identities are performed and contested.[61] Borders, I might add, are also places where people are stripsearched, detained, imprisoned, and sometimes shot. Borders themselves are not given but constructed by power to mask hybridity, to occlude and disown it. The localization of hybridity in some others, called the hybrids or the heretics, serves that purpose.

I thus argue that hybridity is double-edged. On the one hand, the hybrids "represent . . . a difference 'within', a subject that inhabits the rim of an 'in-between' reality,"[62] but on the other hand, the literal ascription of hybridity on the part of hegemonic discourses to one group of people or one set of practices disavows the very difference within by externalizing it. Hybridity itself is the disowned other. It is this very disowned hybridity that supports the notion of purity. Talal Asad clarifies this operation: "The claim of many radical critics that hegemonic power necessarily suppresses difference in favor of unity is quite mistaken. Just as mistaken is their claim that that power always abhors ambiguity. To secure its unity—to make its own history—dominant power has worked best through differentiating and classifying practices. . . . In this context power is constructive, not repressive. Furthermore, its ability to select (or construct) the differences that serve its purposes has depended on its exploiting the dangers and opportunities contained in ambiguous situations."[63] Following this mode of analysis, the commonplace that orthodoxy needs heresy for its self-definition can be nuanced and further specified. "Heresy" is marked not only as the space of the not-true in religion but also as the space of the syncretistic, the difference that enables unity itself. A similar point has been made in another historical context by Young, who writes: "The idea of race here shows itself to be profoundly dialectical: it only works when defined against potential intermixture, which also threatens to undo its calculations altogether."[64] Young helps us see that it is not only that "white" is defined as that which is "not-black," but that the very system of race itself, the very division into white and black as races, is dependent on the production of an idea of hybridity, against which the notion of the "natural" pure races comes into discourse. This way of thinking about hybridity in the classification of humans into races can be mobilized in thinking about heresy and the classification of people and doctrines into religions as well. This provides a certain corrective, then, to those versions of a postcolonial theory that would seem to presuppose pure essences, afterward "hybridized," thus buying into the very activity of an apartheid they would seek to subvert.[65]

As Schwartz, providing us with a model for a non-essentialist way of thinking about this question, has urged: "We should not be debating whether some pre-existing Jewish polity declined or prospered, or think only about relatively superficial cultural borrowing conducted by two well defined groups. In my view, we should be looking for *systemic change*: the Jewish culture which emerged in late antiquity was radically distinctive, and distinctively late antique—a product of the same political, social and economic forces which produced the no less distinctive Christian culture of late antiquity."[66] By systemic change, Schwartz means changes in entire systems of social, cultural, and, in this case, religious organization that affect Jews, Christians, and others equally, if not identically. This seems just right to me, but calls for a bit more of an emphasis on the differentiating factors in that very same productive process, in addition to highlighting the forces tending toward similarity.

In looking at that differentiating process within the context of a shared systemic change, I may be able to suggest at least a tentative hypothesis as to one of the factors that set this systemic change in motion, or in other words to begin to suggest an answer to the question of "why that was border written." In my historical construction, a serious problem of identity arose for Christians who were not prepared (for whatever reason) to think of themselves as Jews, as early as the second century, if not at the end of the first. These Christians, whom I will call by virtue of their own *self*-presentation, Gentile Christians ("The Church from the Gentiles, *ek tôn ethnôn*"), were confronted with a dilemma: Since we are no longer "Greeks" and not "Jews," to what kind of a group do we belong? We are told that it was in Antioch that the disciples were first named "Christians" (Acts 11:26).[67] I think it no accident that this act of naming occurs in a context where the entry of "Greeks" into the Christian community is thematized. Nor is it an accident that Justin is our earliest source for both heresiology and the notion that the Gentile church has replaced the Jews as Israel.

These Christians had to ask themselves: What is this *Christianismos* in which we find ourselves? Is it a new *gens*, a new *ethnos*, a third one, neither Jew nor Greek,[68] or is it an entirely new something in the world, some new kind of identity completely? For one important strand of early Christianity, beginning with Justin Martyr, the option of seeing *Christianismos* as an entirely novel form of identity was chosen. Christianity was a new thing, a community defined by adherence to a certain canon of doctrine and practice. For these Christian thinkers, the question of who's in and who's out became the primary way of thinking about Christianicity. The vehicle to answer that question was, again for these Christians, orthodoxy and heresy. "In" was to be defined by correct belief; "out" by adherence via an alleged choice to false belief. This notion that identity is achieved and not given by birth, history, language, and geographical location was the novum that produced religion, having an impact, I suggest, on the whole semantic system of identities within the Mediterranean world. Exploring this impact on Jews and on the formation of Judaism within these same centuries and thus the ambiguous production of Judaism and Christianity as separate (and politically unequal but semantically equal members of a paradigm) is a large part of this book. I shall argue that the question raised by Justin and his fellows became an important question for the Rabbis as well and, moreover, that for a crucial moment in history, they adopted a similar answer and a similar technique for answering—namely, heresiology.

Thinking Hybridity in Language

In my 1999 work, *Dying for God*, I suggested that we might think of Christianity and Judaism in the second and third centuries as points on a continuum from the Marcionites, who followed the second-century Marcion in believing that the Hebrew Bible had been written by an inferior God and had no standing for Christians, and who completely denied the "Jewishness" of Christianity, on one end, to many Jews on the other end for whom Jesus meant nothing. In the middle, however, there were many gradations which provided social and cultural progression across this spectrum.[69] In other words, to use a linguistic metaphor, I proffered a wave theory account of Christian-Jewish history to replace the older *Stammbaum* (family tree) model. Wave theory posits that linguistic similarity is not necessarily the product of a common origin but may be the product of convergence of different dialects spoken in contiguous areas, dialects that are, moreover, not strictly bounded and differentiated from each other but instead shade one into the other. Innovations at any one point spread like the waves created when a stone is thrown into a pond, intersecting with other such waves produced in other places and leading to the currently observed patterns of differentiation and similarity. The older theory, the *Stammbaum* model, presumed that all similarity between languages and dialects is the product of a shared origin, while differentiation is produced after the languages no longer have contact with each other. It will be seen that the older model corresponds with descriptions of the history of Judaism and Christianity that talk of a "parting of the ways" and assume that all that is shared between the two is a product of their common origins, while the wave theory model leads us to think of much more fluid and not strictly defined borders on the ground, with partitioning taking place well above the ground.[70] To put the same point in terms drawn from postcolonial studies, we must imagine, I think, a "contact zone," a space of "transculturation," where, as Mary Louise Pratt defines it, "disparate cultures meet, clash, grapple with each other, often in highly asymmetrical relations of domination and subordination."[71] The advantage of the wave theory model for my purposes here is that it does not presuppose an originary separatedness of the two cultures in question, which the colonial description sometimes tends to.[72] Thus, to put one possible point on this, I and many if not most scholars of Judaism currently do not operate with an opposition between Judaism and Hellenism, seeing all of Jewish culture in the Hellenistic period (including the anti-Hellenists) as a Hellenistic culture.[73] Rabbinic Judaism can be seen as a nativist reaction, a movement that imagines itself to be a community free of Hellenism, and therefore it is itself no less Hellenistic precisely because of its reaction.[74] Inscriptions of purity against some "other" hybridity are the bread and butter of heresiological discourses.

The religious dialect map is a hybridized one, and the point is that that hybridity extends even to those religious groups that would consider themselves "purely" Jewish or "purely" Christian in their self-understanding. This shift in model is significant, not only for scholarly reasons, by which I mean that it provides a better, "truer" description of "facts," but also because it represents a shift in fundamental understandings of human difference and its meanings. Writing in an analogous context, Robert Young has said: "We may note here the insistently genetic emphasis on the metaphor of 'families' of languages, and the oft-charted language 'trees' which were to determine the whole basis of phylogenetic racial theories of conquest, absorption and decline—designed to deny the more obvious possibilities of mixture, fusion and creolization."[75] It is, then, no minor matter to revise our basic metaphors for understanding how "religions"—Christianity, Judaism, and Paganism—came into being. According to the new way of thinking, these entities are not natural kinds that have somehow split off from each other or been born of each other but are distinctions produced (and resisted) for particular purposes by particular people.

Jonathan M. Hall has undertaken a critical rethinking of the use of ancient genealogical texts for the reconstruction of archaic Greek history.[76] Among the other issues and methods that Hall has employed in his investigation are linguistic ones, in particular *Stammbaum* versus wave theory. Traditional historiography of Greek ethnicity has assumed that the various Greek groups, as well as their dialects—Ionian, Dorian, and so forth—derived from a once unified proto-Greek. Assuming this original unity and subsequent divergence has enabled historians to construct narratives of tribal migrations and invasions in the pre-archaic period. Hall mounts a critique of this methodology. Hall's argument, however, could have been enhanced by a sharper articulation of wave theory itself. Clarifying the difference between his and my understanding may prove an effective way for me to propose a first rough draft of the theory that I am developing in my work. Hall believes that wave theory, just as much as *Stammbaum* theory, presupposes primal linguistic (cultural) uniformity and merely explains the differences between dialects as owing to diffusion of innovations over various parts of the language area.[77] However, it is the virtue of wave theory, as usually understood by historical linguists, that it does *not* presuppose a unified protolanguage at any point in time and imagines dialects in contiguous geographical areas becoming more like each other than previously, not less, and thus producing dialect groups. Wave theory is thus more akin to the situation that Hall himself imagines as the historical origin of groupings such as Dorian in archaic Greece, where once unrelated groups became more like each other, linguistically and otherwise, and agglomerated into the "ethnic" groups known from the archaic period.

This is a model to which I appeal as well. I am not claiming an undifferentiated "Judaism" that formed itself into Judaism and Christianity through the "borrowing" of various religious traits but rather an assortment of religious "dialects" throughout the Jewish world that gradually developed structure as clusters through diffusion and were eventually organized as "languages" (religions) through processes very much analogous to those juridical processes by which national languages, such as French and Italian were also formed. In other words, I am not denying that in the second, third, and fourth centuries, there were religious groups that were more Christian than others (I shall immediately below be talking about what this comparative might mean). I am also not, of course, claiming that there were no Jewish groups that were not Christian at all, but rather that the various Christian groups formed a dialect cluster within the overall assortment of dialects that constituted Judaism (or perhaps better Judaeo-Christianity) at the time.

It is important, however, in this context to understand that "dialect" itself, as much as language, is a social construct. More accurately we might speak of clusters of particular linguistic (or in our case religious) practices. Hall himself argues that "the clustering of dialects within dialect groups is 'a scholars' heuristic fiction.'" Linguist William Labov has also written: "But in regard to geographical dialects, it has long been argued that such gradient models are characteristic of the diffusion of linguistic features across a territory and the challenge has been to establish that boundaries between dialects are anything but arbitrary." But Labov goes on to state: "Nevertheless, even in dialect geography, most investigators agree that properties do bundle, and that is possible to show boundaries of varying degrees of clarity even when all variable features are superimposed upon a single map."[78] In other words, one can model a situation in which there will be persons or groups who will clearly be "Christian" or "non-Christian Jewish," that is form definable clusters of religious features, while the boundaries between the two categories will remain undefinable. The eventual triumph (or even partial triumph) of orthodoxies in defining a separate identity for the two religions is much like the formation of national languages. Remarking that many dialects of Italian are more understandable by French speakers than by other Italians, and other similar phenomena, Hall writes: "What allows for this at first sight surprising phenomenon is the fact that a 'national language' is seldom a higher order linguistic category which embraces and subsumes its constituent dialects. It is, rather, an invention which rarely precedes the nineteenth century and which owes its existence to reasons 'that are as much political, geographical, historical, sociological and cultural as linguistic.' From a linguistic point of view, there is little or no difference between a standardized national language and a dialect in terms of their hierarchical ranking within the historical structure of a language."[79]

Adding only the proviso, following Labov, that dialects do group eventually into dialect clusters, analogous to Judaism and Christianity in formation, I suggest, once more, that this provides a powerful analogy for thinking about the history of these nascent "religions." "What an ethnic group does is actively and consciously to select *certain artefacts from within the overall material cultural repertoire* which then act as emblemic indicia of ethnic boundaries. In the words of Catherine Morgan, 'ethnic behaviour affects only those categories of artefact selected to carry social or political meaning under particular circumstances, rather than the totality of a society's material culture.'"[80] In this case, religious ideas and practices are the equivalent of artefacts. The crucial example of this process that will be developed in this book is the issue of belief in or rejection of the concept of God's Logos. A distinction that once did not divide between followers of Jesus and Jews who were not Jesus-folks, this was eventually chosen as the most significant of indicia for Christian and Jewish separate religious identity. Jews who continued to believe in the Logos and Christians who denied it were no longer Jews or Christians but heretics by decision of the "legislative" bodies, the metaphorical parliaments of religious power. Not via a separation, a parting of the ways, but by a dialect clustering through the choice of specific indicia of identity and the diffusion and clustering of such indicia (such as circumcision/not circumcision) were groups gradually congealing into Christianity and Judaism. But it was only with the mobilizations of temporal power (via ideological state apparatuses and repressive state apparatuses[81]) in the fourth century that the process can be said to have formed "religions," and even then only lopsidedly, as I shall try to show further on. One might say that Judaism and Christianity were invented in order to explain the fact that there were Jews and Christians.

In suggesting that Judaism and Christianity were not separate entities until very late in late antiquity, I am, accordingly, not claiming that it is impossible to discern separate social groups that are in an important sense Christian/not-Jewish or Jewish/not-Christian from fairly early on (by which I mean the mid–second century). In order to make the opposite claim, even if I believed it, I would have to do a very different kind of historical research from what I am doing here. Indeed, although I do not know quite how one would show this, such "separatist" groups may have been statistically dominant much earlier than the fifth century. Thus I cannot answer empirical questions such as: How much were Christian and other Jewish congregations mixed at any given time or place? Or, What was the social status of Jewish-Christian groups? Were they accepted as Jews, as Christians (by whom?), or neither at any given time?

Instead, the question that I pose is a theoretical one, or at least an interpretative one: Even if we grant the statistical dominance (and perhaps a certain power dominance, although, once more, I don't know how we would show or know this) of the separatists, in terms of the semantics of the cultural language, the discourse of the time, are there sets of features that absolutely define who is a Jew and who is a Christian in such wise that the two categories will not seriously overlap, irrespective of the numbers of members of the blurring sets? I think not.

The perspective adopted here is not unlike that of Beard, North, and Price, who write: "[This section] does investigate the degrees of religious continuity in these cults traceable across the Roman world. By and large, however, in discussing the religions of the empire we have tried to avoid thinking in terms of uniformity, or in terms of a central core 'orthodox' tradition with its peripheral 'variants'; we have preferred to think rather in terms of different religions as clusters of ideas, people and rituals, sharing some common identity across time and place, but at the same time inevitably invested with different meanings in their different contexts."[82]

The Semantics of Orthodoxy

Another body of theory (closely related to Labov's[83]), prototype semantics, may help me make progress in understanding a situation in which there are recognizably separate entities within a given field but no way to articulate the borders between them. It may also help me to some clearer thinking on the constructed oppressiveness of the very borders themselves. These theories begin with Wittgenstein's notion of family resemblance in the formation of semantic fields.[84] In Chana Kronfeld's succinct formulation: "Members of one family share a variety of similar features: eyes, gait, hair color, temperament. But—and this is the crucial point—there need be no one set of features shared by all family members."[85] There is, perhaps, one feature that constitutes all as members of the Judaeo-Christian semantic family—appeal to the Hebrew Scriptures as Revelation—but in all other respects, the category of Jews/Christians constitutes a family in which any one subgroup might share features with any other (on *either* side of that supposed divide) but not all features with any, and there is no one set of features that uniquely determines a Christian group (except, of course, for some appeal to Jesus, which is simply an analytic statement and therefore tautologous) over against a non-Christian Jewish group.

Kronfeld's work, of course, has been devoted to an entirely different classificatory problem, namely the description of modernism as a literary movement, but it is a relevant one for my inquiry in that it has to do with groups of people and their practices and the ways that they and others (including scholars) array the people and the practices into named categories (as opposed, for example, to the ways that people, including scholars or scientists, categorize plants, animals, or colors).[86] The problems and solutions that she has envisioned will therefore be useful for me. Kronfeld has written:

Despite the overwhelming evidence that modernism defies reduction to simple common denominators, one study after another, after asserting the complexity and heterogeneiety of the various manifestations of modernism, proceeds to attempt the impossibly positivist task of providing a definition of modernism; and this usually means, explicitly or tacitly, an attempt at what logicians call an *intensional definition*—namely, a list of necessary and sufficient conditions for all modernist trends. . . . While it would be nice for a theory of modernism to have the explanatory power that an intensional definition can facilitate (by showing clearly what makes all the branches of modernism part of one distinctive movement or trend), such an approach would force us to restrict severely the extension of what we could term modernist. Many important works, authors, and even entire groups that identified themselves as modernist and that are commonly perceived to be subsumed under this admittedly tattered and oversized umbrella would have to be kept out. There simply is no set of distinctive features that can apply to all the subgroupings of modernism (from futurism to surrealism) and separate them from all nonmodernist groupings (classicism, baroque, romanticism, and so forth).[87]

The problem with Judaism/Christianity is somewhat different, but analogous enough for this statement of the issue to be useful for me. While, as I have said, there is one (analytic) feature that could be said to be common to all groups that we might want to call (anachronistically) "Christian," namely some form of discipleship to Jesus, this feature hardly captures enough richness and depth to produce an interesting category, for in so many other vitally important ways, groups that follow Jesus and groups that ignore him are similar to each other, or put another way, groups that ignore (or reject) Jesus may have some highly salient other religious features (for instance, Logos theology) that binds them to Jesus groups and disconnects them from other non-Jesus Jews, or some Jesus Jews may have aspects to their religious lives (to wit, following Pharisaic halakha) that draws them closer to some non-Jesus Jews than to other Jesus people.[88] Moreover, some Jesus groups might relate to Jesus in ways phenomenally more similar to the ways that other Jewish groups relate to other prophets, leaders, or messiahs than the ways that other Jesus groups are relating to Jesus; and the reverse, some non-Jesus Jews might very well have had in their religious lives elements similar to the belief in an incarnated or present mediator from God.[89] The model of family resemblance that Kronfeld develops for talking about modernism seems, therefore, apt for talking about Judaeo-Christianity as well. "[Judaeo-Christianity] can remain one clear category even though no two subtrends within it may share the same features."[90]

Kronfeld's version of semantic categorization can crucially help with the theoretical problem that I have been exposing, namely how to indicate (at least nascent) articulation within a "family." I am not only trying to describe a category called *Judaeo-Christianity,* but also to account for a division within this category that will ultimately produce a binary opposition between categories, namely between Christianity and Judaism. This is, as we have seen, an issue only partly addressed by the linguistic theories discussed so far. The part of the the-

ory of family-resemblance semantics that seems relevant for this is called the
"prototype theory of categorization."[91] The "*prototype*, in the technical sense developed by Rosch and others,[[92]] is a member of the category (for example,
birds) which is considered a 'best example' of that category (sparrow, swallow,
or robin, but not turkey, penguin, or chicken)."[93]

Prototype semantics makes, moreover, distinctions between categories,
however family-resemblance-like, that have clear boundaries and categories that
don't. Some things may be prototypical birds, and indeed different birds can be
more or less central to the category—this is called the *centrality gradience*—but
in the end, a given object is either a bird or it isn't. The category *bird* is not,
seemingly, one with "extendable boundaries" like the categories *number* or
game. Thus, George Lakoff has written with respect to Eleanor Rosch's work:

> For example, take her results showing prototype effects within the category *bird*. Her ex-
> perimental rankings show that subjects view robins and sparrows as the best examples
> of birds, with owls and eagles lower down in the rankings and ostriches, emus, and pen-
> guins among the worst examples. In the early to mid 1970's . . . such empirical goodness-
> of-example ratings were commonly taken as constituting a claim to the effect that
> membership in the category *bird* is graded and that owls and penguins are less members
> of the *bird* category than robins. . . . It later became clear that that was a mistaken inter-
> pretation of the data. Rosch's ratings . . . are consistent with the interpretation that the
> category *bird* has strict boundaries and that robins, owls, and penguins are all 100 per-
> cent members of that category. However, that category must have additional internal
> structure of some sort that produces these goodness-of-example ratings.[94]

Similarly, there may be "best examples" (prototypes) of *Jew* and *Christian* already in the second or third century with, however, an internal structure to the
category that will allow other than best examples to be members of the group as
well.[95] This is the semantic analogue of Labov's point about dialect grouping in
language geography: Are there or are there not "objective" criteria with which
such distinctions can be made? This is particularly relevant, I think, when there
are different political actors in antiquity and in the present as well (both in
scholarship and outside of it) attempting to make such determinations. *Best example* is, itself, a context-bound,[96] historically shifting, and, therefore, political
category. In a situation such as the one under investigation, moreover, it can be
(and is) a contested one. Another way of putting this is to say that I am inquir-
ing whether an emu would have a different sense of what the best example of a
bird is than a robin would, and, moreover, do robins get to judge what a bird is?
We must all, I think, be careful when writing history to avoid simply reproducing the position of the Rabbins.

There is, moreover, a further wrinkle. While some birds are more birdy than others in our experience and categorization, the category itself has definite borders. One is either a bird or not. Another kind of category has "unclear boundaries," and then, in addition to a typicality gradience, there is a *membership gradience* as well. *Judaism* and *Christianity*, I want to claim, are categories more like *red* and *tall* than like *bird*: "It seems to me that (modernism) [Judaism/Christianity] present(s) so many difficulties for the (literary theorist) [historian of religions] partly because in its different constructions it involves both centrality and membership gradience."[97] As Lakoff has argued, "Prototype effects are superficial. They may result from many factors. In the case of a graded category like *tall man*, which is fuzzy and does not have rigid boundaries, prototype effects may result from degree of category membership, while in the case of *bird*, which does have rigid boundaries, the prototype effects must result from some other aspect of internal category structure."[98] There is an important consequence of this difference between types of categories. One cannot be both a *bird* and a *fish*, but one can be both a *tall* man and a *short* man. (On this last point, see already Plato *Republic* 479b6-8). Moreover, I suspect that this latter form of category is typically the case for the human construction of categories of the human and that much human violence is generated simply by resisting the fuzziness of our own categories of sociocultural division. Just as certain entities can be more or less tall or red, I wish to suggest they can be more or less Christian (or Jewish) as well. And just as certain entities can be tall and short given different perspectives, so too can certain people or groups be Christian or Jewish from different perspectives, or both.[99] Indeed, the determination itself will be a matter of contention. Jerome's very important notice that the sect of Nazoreans are to be found "in all of the synagogues of the East among the Jews" and that they consider themselves both Christians and Jews but are really "neither Christians nor Jews," is a case in point.[100]

Let us imagine that *Jew* and *Christian* are both categories with gradation of membership. Moreover, while both have central members (which can be different at different times and even at the same time for different groups), there will be a semantic (and in this case, therefore, social[101]) chain that connects the most central and salient members to others: "Another case is where I call *B* by the same name as *A*, because it resembles *A*, *C* by the same name because it resembles *B*, *D* . . . and so on. But ultimately *A* and say *D* do not resemble each other in any recognizable sense at all. This is a very common case: and the dangers are obvious when we search for something 'identical' in all of them!"[102] The net result will be that there might indeed be people who are prototypes of *Jew* but are also *Christian* (say a Pharisee who observes all of the Pharisaic laws and rules but believes that Jesus is the Messiah), and, moreover, that the "best example" of *Jew* and *Christian* would almost definitely be both a politically charged and a diachronically varying category. Further, while there would be Jews who would not recognize certain other Jews as such, there might be ones whom they would recognize as Jews who would recognize in turn those others as Jews, setting up the possibility of chained communion or communication. This would then be an example of a family resemblance with the additional element of agency among members of the family itself. An example of this phenomenon (from the other side) would be Justin who recognizes as Christians precisely those Jewish Christians to whom Jerome, much later of course, would deny the name *Christian*, but Jerome would certainly recognize Justin as Christian. Those so-called Jewish Christians surely thought of themselves as both Jews and Christians, and some non-Christian Jews may have recognized them as Jews as well.

Therefore, with respect to religious history we must add yet another factor, which may be less relevant to a literary movement like modernism (although probably equally salient for something like Marxism), to wit the activities of certain writers/speakers who wish to transform the fuzzy category into one with absolutely clear borders and the family resemblance into a checklist of features that will determine an intensional definition for who is in and who is out of the group as it defines itself and, therefore, its others. Insofar as this attempt to transform may serve the interests of particular power centers within the society or culture (as they did the nascent "Church," for instance), the intensional definitions may be imposed on the "folk" through the operations of hegemony.[103] Note the contrast between this account and Lakoff's statement that "we even have a folk model of what categories themselves are, and this folk model has evolved into the classical theory of categorization. Part of the problem that prototype theory now has, and will face in the future, is that it goes beyond our folk understanding of categorization. And much of what has given the classical theory its appeal over the centuries is that it meshes with our folk theory and seems like simple common sense."[104] I am suggesting that for the categories *Jew* and *Christian* it is distinctly possible that "folk models" worked more like prototype or experiential real categories for centuries, while it was precisely the work of certain "experts" to attempt to impose "traditional" or "objective" categorization upon them.[105] Returning to the wave theory metaphor, these are the legislators who wish, as well, to determine and enforce clear boundaries between languages, to decide what is orthodox French and what is orthodox Italian. These are the writers whom we know of now as heresiologists.

Heresiology as Ideological Church Apparatus

I shall be studying the forces that wish to draw such clear distinctions, the Christian and the rabbinic heresiologists, as well as looking for the forces that resist the production of an episteme of religions as a disembedded category of human experience and, even more to the point, of human naming and group identification. The point is, and I cannot emphasize this enough, *not* that "religion" actually *is* such a disembedded category but that it is projected as such by the ideological church apparatuses of orthodox Christianity. I shall return to this point toward the end of the book.

The interests that are served by the ideological discourse (by ideological non-state apparatuses, to adapt Althusser) can be investments in other sorts of power and satisfaction for elites of various types within a given social formation. The discourses of orthodoxy/heresy, and thus, I will argue, of religious difference, of religion as an independent category of human identification, do not necessarily serve the interests of an economic class (it would be hard to describe the Rabbis of late Roman Palestine or Sassanid Babylonia or the bishops of Nicaea as an economic class), but they do serve in the production of ideology, of hegemony, the consent of a dominated group to be ruled by an elite (hence "consensual orthodoxy," that marvelous mystification). This makes an enormous difference, for it leads to the Althusserian notion of ideology as having a material existence, as having its own material existence in that it "always exists in an apparatus, and its practice, or practices."[106] Ania Loomba's statement of the current theoretical position that "no human utterance could be seen as innocent," that, indeed, "any set of words could be analysed to reveal not just an individual but a historical consciousness at work,"[107] is crucial for me, for it is this postulate that enables my work as historian. This set of notions, to which I can more or less only allude in this context, does not quite dissolve completely (as sometimes charged) but surely renders much more permeable any boundary between linguistic (or textual) practice and "the real conditions" of life within a given historical moment and society, thus empowering the study of texts not as reflective of social realities but as social apparatuses that are understood to be complexly tied to other apparatuses via the notion of a discourse or a *dispositif.*

The Argument of This Book

The argument of the book proceeds through three parts.

The first part is entitled "Making a Difference: The Heresiological Beginnings of Christianity and Judaism." Here I shall be reading texts of the second and third century, attempting to show that they can be construed as engaged in a process of creating a difference between Judaism and Christianity. I wish to make a case, moreover, that the production of the difference was intimately connected with and implicated in the invention of the notion of heresy during these centuries. My goal will be to show that both Christian writers of the tendency that would ultimately be classified as orthodox and the Rabbis are invested in the model of orthodoxy/heresy as their favored mode of self-definition in these two centuries.

In the first chapter of the section, "Justin's Dialogue with the Jews: The Beginnings of Orthodoxy," I will read Justin Martyr with an ear out for echoes of the role that a construction of *Judaism* was playing in his efforts to produce Christian identity and, in particular, the nexus between these efforts and the nascent heresiological project of this author, all the while skating fairly lightly over the question of how realistic this construction was. Even the attention paid in these early heresiologies to the gnosticism, falsely so-called, can be read in this context, as Karen King has suggested, that is, in the context of the determination of the placement of Christianness with respect to a constructed Judaism, which it must both be and not be at the very same time. This section of the chapter is a prefiguration in two senses of the major arguments of the book. On the one hand, I suggest that Justin prefigures discourses that were to become dominant within the Christianity of a couple of hundred years later; on the other hand, my discussion of this figure outlines analyses and claims that will be more fully developed in the rest of the book. In my discussion of Justin Martyr—the originator, according to Le Boulluec, of the discourse of heresiology—I suggest a revision of our understanding of what it is that Justin means by *Judaism* in the *Dialogue*. Judaism is, for Justin, not a given entity to which he is opposed and which he describes accurately or not, or to which he addresses an apologetic, but an entity that he is engaged in constructing in the textual process. Note that this does not constitute the familiar question of whether or not Justin's description is reliable or ignorant—it is, in fact, an independent variable of that question—but rather an argument for the discursive force of the *Dialogue with Trypho*. Rather than disputing with anyone or producing a genuinely apologetic text, on my reading Justin is working out in the dialogue form the whatness of Christianity as he would see it. In essence, the *Dialogue* is part of Justin's overall project of inventing orthodoxy as the form and structure of Christianity and, as such, demonstrates the intimate role that producing a non-Christian Judaism plays in the project. To exemplify this take on the *Dialogue*, I present a sketch of what will be a major argument of the book as a whole, namely the case of Logos theology. Justin repeatedly presents himself in the *Dialogue* as attempting to prove to Trypho that God has a second person distinct in number from him, and Trypho, of course, argues against him. We are used to reading this as a straightforward theological disputation between Judaism and Christianity, but I propose that Logos theology is not an essential and aboriginal distinguishing mark of Christianity as opposed to Judaism but rather a common theological inheritance that was construed and constructed as such a distinguishing mark via a virtual conspiracy of orthodox theologians on both sides of the new border line—Justin and followers on one side, the Rabbis on the other. The Logos becomes a virtual shibboleth for the production, then, of both orthodoxies. It was this invention, essentially the production of the idea of religion as separable from "ethnicity,"[108] I shall argue, that produced a powerful corresponding effect in the history of Judaism also. The invention of heresy and the invention of a Christian religion that is clearly distinct from a Jewish religion are thus shown to go intimately together, part and parcel of the very production of the discursive institution of orthodoxy itself.

In the second part of this chapter I turn a similar spotlight on the earliest of the rabbinic writings, the Mishna, apparently edited at the beginning of the third century, and the Tosefta, toward the middle of that century. On the one hand, I hypothesize that it was the challenge of Gentile Christianity, in the manner that I have interpreted this term above, as represented by figures such as Justin, that led the Rabbis to begin to transform Judaism into a Church (in a modified version of the Weberian [Troeltschian] sense) with its orthodoxy and its heresy, supported in large part by rules of faith, that is, practices of discourse expressed both in language and in action that serve to set the bounds of who is in and who is out of the religious group. I should emphasize that I employ *Gentile Christianity* in a sort of subtechnical sense to refer to Christian converts from among non-Jews (and their descendants) who have neither a sense of genealogical attachment to the historical, physical people of Israel (Israel according to the flesh), nor an attachment (and frequently the exact opposite of one) to the fleshly practices of that historical community. It is my strong intuition that it was this formation, Gentile Christianity, that first presented the structural irritant around which the notion of belonging by virtue of faith would arise.

In order to make this claim, earlier versions of Israelite religion, including Josephus and the Dead Sea Scrolls, will be analyzed in order to establish a difference between their structure and self-definition and that of the later Rabbis. On the other hand, it seems at least plausible to imagine that the notion of orthodoxy/heresy that manifests itself at the beginnings of the rabbinic movement in the guise of the Hebrew neologism *minut*, first attested at this time, is itself the appropriation of a Christian notion, a wheelbarrow smuggled across the border, precisely in service of the establishment and naturalization of the border and of the human kinds that it serves to identify.

Thus, after presenting arguments that the situation of the Jewish sects in the first century does not constitute a structure of orthodoxy/heresy, a structure

that needs to be distinguished from sectarianism, I attempt to delineate the rabbinic concept of *minut* and show that it is a close cognate semantically with
Christian *heresy*. I suggest that while the development of this concept is a complex response to the challenge of a Christianity (the very line of Justinian discourse of "orthodoxy" discussed in the first part), this does not mean that the
minim are actually a representation of Jewish Christians. They are, rather, a
rhetorical construct for the production of a Jewish religion or church, functioning in this sense much as *gnostikoi* does for Christian orthodoxy—as argued
by Karen King—and as *Ioudaioi* does for these same Christian writers. I read in
this chapter the earliest rabbinic text, the Mishna, looking for the beginnings of
rabbinic heresiology there and suggesting that this rudimentary heresiological
project represents a dual response of the Rabbis to nascent Christian orthodoxy.

The second chapter of this section, "Naturalizing the Border: Apostolic
Succession in the Mishna," continues this line of thinking by exploring yet another technology for the establishment of orthodoxy that seems to appear in Judaism at about the same time as (or slightly later than) its appearance in
Christianity, *apostolic succession,* the claim to an unbroken chain of tradition
from a foundational moment of revelation and a founding figure of the religious group. In addition to the hypothesis of influence from a nascent Christianity on an equally nascent Judaism (which should, in any case, also not be
read as "influence" so much as appropriation; there is agency here), I also consider the possibility of a suppler, less definable, common historicocultural environment and situation leading to these joint (and mutually supporting) projects
of religious identity formation through heresiology. Heresiology emerges at the
moment when sectarian/school structure is becoming less viable everywhere.
The transformation of both nascent Christianity and nascent Judaism from
groups of sects—collections of philosophical schools, as Josephus had described
Judaism and Allen Brent third-century Christianity[109]—into orthodox churches
with their heretical others would be seen on this reading as part of the same sociocultural process and practice. Theological discourse was the major discursive
vehicle for the making of this difference.

The second part of the book is entitled "The Crucifixion of the Logos." The
work of this section is to narrate, through readings of various sorts of texts, the
transmutation, adumbrated above, of Logos theology from a doctrine of God
commonly held (and as commonly contested) by non-Christian and Christian
Jews to the essence of the theological difference between the two. *Logos theology,*
in the sense in which I use it here, is constituted by several variations of a doctrine that between God and the world, there is a second divine entity, God's
Word (Logos) or God's Wisdom, who mediates between the fully transcendent
Godhead and the material world. This doctrine was widely held by Jews in the

pre-Christian era and after the beginnings of Christianity was widely held and widely contested in Christian circles. By the fourth century, Jews who held such a doctrine and Christians who rejected it were defined as "neither Jews nor Christians" but heretics. In the first chapter of this section, "The Intertextual Birth of the Logos: The Prologue to John as a Jewish Midrash," I undertake a close intertextual reading of the Prologue to the Fourth Gospel. Rather than seeing in the Logos of John a parthenogenetic birth from a Greek mother-father, foisted illegitimately on a "Jewish" Christianity, I read a legitimate Hebrew birth in the intertextual matrix of early midrash. On the basis of this reading, arguing the specifics of the derivation of the Prologue from midrashic sources, it becomes, I think, highly conceivable to see this Prologue, together with its Logos doctrine, as a Jewish text through and through rather than, as it has often enough been read, a "Hellenized corruption" of Judaism.

The second chapter of this section is entitled "The Jewish Life of the Logos: Logos Theology in Pre- and Pararabbinic Judaism." In this chapter I propose to show how widespread Logos theology was in the versions of Judaism that preceded the Rabbis and even coincided with them, and also how rich and vibrant it was, thus rendering stronger the argument that Logos theology is native, as it were, to Judaism. That said, I can go back and think further about the *Dialogue* of Justin, reading it more strongly as part of a dual-faced strategy to render binitarianism (the ante-Nicene predecessor to trinitarianism) orthodox for Christians and heretical for Jews. Non-binitarian Christians are effectively and simply named as "Jews." This leads neatly into the third chapter, "The Crucifixion of the Memra: How the Logos Became Christian." In this chapter I will try to show how the Rabbis, like Justin mutatis mutandis, also took a significant inner theological difference between Jews who held versions of Logos theology and those who didn't, and rendered it a difference between Jews and Others, to wit, *minim* or heretics, thereby excluding Christians from Judaism via heresiological means. In an interesting kind of complicity, the Rabbis agree, as it were, to cede traditional Jewish Logos theology to Christianity, declaring it and its once orthodox holders (symbolized by no less than Rabbi Akiva) as members of an imagined heretical group, "Two Powers in Heaven." On this reading, crucifying the Logos means giving it up to the Christians, complying with the work of heresiologists such as Justin who regard belief in the Logos as the very touchstone of Christian orthodoxy, and the modalism of many once acceptable Christian thinkers and of Rabbis alike, as heresy. The two heresiological projects form, therefore, a perfect mirror in which the Rabbis construct (as it were) Christianity, while the Christian writers, such as Justin, construct (as it were) Judaism. If my readings are cogent, we can observe within rabbinic texts the process so well documented for other moments in Christian history when an older form of "orthodox" belief is rendered heresy.[110] The net result of this virtual conspiracy between Christian and Jewish would-be orthodoxies is a redistribution of both modes of identity and of identity itself, so that by the end of the process Judaism and Christianity had been more or less definitively divided on theological grounds, with both "religions" crucifying the Logos, that is, on my conceit, identifying Logos theology so thoroughly with Christology that the Logos became Christian and the rejection of binitarianism the very touchstone of Judaism.

In the last section of the book, "Sparks of the Logos: Historicizing Rabbinic Religion," I aim to account for what happens in the two new entities thus formed (especially in Judaism) following in the wake of the consolidation of orthodox Christian theology in the fourth and fifth centuries, including finally the ultimate rejection by the Rabbis of the category of religion, Judaism, as a name for Jewishness. Attention to particular developments within the history of rabbinic Judaism at this juncture plays an important role in the discussion.

Rabbinic Judaism is no longer understood, at least not by most American scholars and some Europeans and Israelis too, as a single organic entity that gradually evolved out of biblical religion; nor are its texts understood to be a slow and gradual accretion of earlier "sources." We see, rather, a series of breaks, near ruptures that lead to the identification of distinct strata of development within the tradition and the texts, with the texts themselves and their earlier matter being significantly reworked and recontextualized at the various stages. Surely, when conceived in this way, one of the most important of these passages is the one from everything that had come before to the particular social, cultural, and textual world of the Babylonian Talmud. The culture of the scholars who produced the Babylonian Talmud was significantly different from the rabbinic cultures that produced the other texts of classical rabbinic literature. The first is apparently in their social organization as members of formally organized academies (distinct from each other not in terms of philosophical approach but in geographical location). As Jeffrey Rubenstein has pointed out, this resulted in "new issues and tensions, including competition for rank, pursuit of status and protocol for selecting leaders. Scholastic values including skill in debate and the ability to construct hypothetical arguments increased in importance."[111] These discursive characteristics that emerge with the redaction of the Babylonian Talmud in the late fifth and sixth centuries, in the end, produce a great deal of the sense of how different rabbinic Judaism is from Christianity. At the same time, I shall argue that Judaism and Christianity, as they finally emerged from late antiquity, were not in the end two species of the same genus, but that the difference between them consists in their assymetrical understandings of what Judaism is.

Chapter 7 thus intends to lay out the ways in which at this very end of late antiquity, at the end of late ancient Judaeo-Christianity, rabbinic Judaism undergoes what is a virtual revolution in consciousness. In the process, the most salient phenomenal differences between the Judaism and the Christianity of the end of late antiquity are put into place, including the highly salient difference between their two major textual corpora, the Babylonian Talmud and the "Fathers of the Church," respectively. This chapter consists largely, therefore, in extended readings of deeply interconnected talmudic narratives of Yavneh as produced in the post-amoraic phase of the final anonymous redaction of the Talmud in the context of patristic scholarship and the ways in which these indicate responses to the epistemological crisis that visited the entire Mediterranean thought-world, rendering in the end Judaism and Christianity both very different and oddly the same.[112]

In the final chapter of the book, turning again to some exemplary instances of fourth- and early fifth-century Christian discourses, notably heresiology and the Law, and then reading some narratives of the Talmud in their context, I try to show the asymmetry of the developments of the notion of religion in the Christian empire, with the Church (and its "secular" ally) defining Judaism as a religion, whereas the Rabbis (the Jews?) refuse this interpellation and re-ethnicize their distinction from the Christians, as simply now an instance, the exemplary instance of Gentiles.

PART I

Making a Difference:
The Heresiological Beginnings
of Christianity and Judaism

Chapter 2

Justin's Dialogue with the Jews: The Beginnings of Orthodoxy

Religion is inseparable from the idea of a Church.
—Emile Durkheim

In this chapter, I will be looking at the inscription of border lines between Christianity and Judaism from the points of view of the cartographers on both sides. Looking at the earliest of rabbinic texts, the Mishna, with eyes trained as well on the broader (here read Christian) discursive contexts within which the Mishna was produced enables us to uncover the beginnings of heresiological discourse among the Rabbis. Reading Justin's *Dialogue*, I find there discursive work engaged in constructing a Judaism with which to contrast Christianity, and the use of heresiology in that project. Then, when I transpose to rabbinism the theme of Le Boulluec's study, the question addressed to the rabbinic texts will no longer be, as it has been in most research, Who were the *minim*?, but instead, When and why did the discourse of *minut* (heresiology) arise in Judaism? And how does *that* compare with and relate to Christianity? How, in short, does what we might call rabbinic ecclesiology develop alongside of and in possible interaction with Christian discourse about religion, identity, exclusion, and inclusion?

Justin Makes a Difference

Justin Martyr, a "pagan" born at Neapolis (modern Nablus) in Palestine and converted to Christianity, wrote his *Dialogue with Trypho* in the second half of the second century (although large parts of the *Dialogue* may have been written two decades earlier[1]). According to tradition, the text, written in Rome in the 160s, presents itself as the record of a conversation that Justin held with a Jew in Ephesus, Trypho by name, some time in the late 130s. The reality or fictionality of this conversation is much disputed and shall not concern me here. Justin is a writer fighting, as it were, on two fronts, against heresy and against Judaism. Arguably in his writing as well, these two battles are deeply implicated in one another.[2] Justin is obsessed with the question of those who call themselves Christians and are not (*Dialogue* 35:80). This work of self-definition is carried out through a contrast with something called *Ioudaismos*.

Throughout the *Dialogue*, Justin is very concerned to define the Jews as those who do not believe in the Logos. This permits me to introduce here one of the major axes of my argument. Belief in the Logos of God as a second divine person is taken by most authorities, ancient and modern, as a virtual touchstone of the theological difference of Christianity from Judaism. In contrast to this consensus, a major part of the argument of this book is that prior (and even well into) the rabbinic period, most (or at any rate many) non-Christian Jews did see the Logos (or his female alter ego, Sophia) as a central part of their doctrines about God (Chapters 4, 5, and 6 in this book). I suggest that an important motivation for Justin's expenditure of discursive energy is not so much to convince the Jews to accept the Logos, but rather to *deny* the Logos to the Jews, to take it away from them, in order for it to be the major theological center of Christianity, with the goal of establishing a religious identity for the believers in Christ that would, precisely, mark them off as religiously different from Jews. This enterprise, I shall also be proposing, was ultimately shared by the Rabbis, such that for them, the primary definition of heresy was belief in the Logos (Two Powers in Heaven). Justin, accordingly, is seen as a key figure in the theological definition of Judaism as well as Christianity, while the Rabbis play a major role in the ultimate definition of Christianity too.

Justin articulates his identity crisis through the medium of Trypho's challenge: "You do not distinguish yourselves in any way from the Gentiles" (*Dialogue* 10:3). This provides the justification for the *Dialogue* as an attempt by a Gentile Christian to distinguish himself as such.[3] There is more, however. Justin tells us that he has been accused of ditheism from within the "Christian" world, because of his Logos theology. By making those who deny the Logos theology into Jews, Justin is protecting himself from being called a heretic. That the *Dialogue* is aimed in two directions is supported from another important passage of Justin. Near its end, Justin writes of those who would dispute his distinction that Father and Son are separate persons and repeats arguments that he has earlier mobilized against Trypho: "Then I proceeded to relate again all that I had even already written from Exodus, both about the vision at the bush, and the surnaming of the name of Joshua (Jesus), and I continued: Yet do not think, Sirs, that I am speaking superfluously when I repeat these words frequently.[4] It is because I know that there are even some who wish to anticipate my explana-

tion, and to assert" that although they too recognize that He is called "Angel,"
"Man," "Son of Man," and "Word," they nevertheless maintain "that this power
can never be cut off or separated from the Father, in the same way, as they say,
the light of the sun on earth cannot be cut off or separated, though the sun is in
heaven. And when the sun sets the light is borne away with it. So the Father,
makes, when He will, His power to spring forward, and, when He will, He draws
it back into Himself" (*Dialogue* 128: 2–3).[5] By contrast to the image of the sun,
in order to argue that the second person is an entity distinct in number, Justin
draws on the metaphor of fire, which can produce another fire without itself
being diminished or changed in any way. He then goes on to repeat the very
words of proof that he has used previously against Jews. It seems clear from
his rhetoric that Justin is addressing Christians who hold to a "dynamic
modalism"—though the term is admittedly anachronistic—that is, a theory that
God produces the other "persons" of the Trinity only at such time as they are
needed for a particular purpose, and, even then, only as appearances of different persons.[6] Indeed, these others say that "the Power is called *Angel* when He
came forth unto men," called "*Glory* since He appears sometimes in an appearance that cannot be reckoned by space; and was called sometimes *a man* and *a
human being*, since He makes His appearance in the fashion of such forms as the
Father wills. And they call Him *Word (Logos)*, since He also bears to men the discourses that come from the Father." Justin's explicit thematization of this argument, for instance, the argument from "Lest the man become as one of us," as a
repetition—with a difference—discloses unambiguously that the very same reasons that are used against the Jews, who ostensibly reject a distinction of persons, can also be mobilized against Christian "heretics" who similarly, but
differently, reject such a distinction.[7]

The *Dialogue*, by establishing a binary opposition between the Christian
and the Jew over the question of the Logos, accomplishes two purposes at once.
First, it articulates Christian identity as theological. Christians are those people
who believe in the Logos; Jews cannot, then, believe in the Logos. Second, Christians are those people who believe in the Logos; those who do not are not Christians but heretics. The double construction of Jews and heretics—or rather, of
Judaism and heresy—effected through Justin's *Dialogue* thus serves to produce
a secure religious identity, a self-definition for Christians.[8] It should be clear
why for Justin the discourse about Judaism and the discourse about heresy
would have been so inextricably intertwined. If Christian identity is theological,
then orthodoxy must be at the very center of its articulation, and for Justin belief in the Logos as a second divine person is the touchstone of that center, the
very core of his religion. I am not claiming either that Justin invented "heresy"
in order to make a difference between Christianity and Judaism or that he pur-

sued Jewish difference (via the *Dialogue*) in order to condemn heretics, but rather that these two projects overlapped and were imbricated on each other— like tiles on a Mediterranean roof—so as finally to be, if not indistinguishable, impossible without each other. The case of Justin is, thus, particularly instructive in that it almost explicitly makes manifest the powerfully imbricated roles of heresy and Judaism in the construction of orthodox Christian identity. The hybridity of Christianity is managed by a double construction: by identifying some Christians as heretics and then showing that their views are "really" Judaism. Never mind, of course, that the "orthodox" theologoumena are Jewish ones as well.

Justin's Jewish Heresiology

One telling piece of evidence that the very notion of heresy was so significant in making and defending borders is that it is in Justin Martyr that we find for the first time *hairesis* in the sense of "heresy" attributed to Jewish usage as well. In the *Dialogue*, Justin addresses the Jew Trypho, attempting to convince him of the existence of the Logos:

I will again relate words spoken by Moses, from which we can recognize without any question that He conversed with one different in number from Himself and possessed of reason. Now these are the words: *And God said: Behold, Adam has become as one of Us, to know good and evil.* Therefore by saying *as one of Us* He has indicated also number in those that were present together, two at least. *For I cannot consider that assertion true which is affirmed by what you call an heretical party among you, and cannot be proved by the teachers of that heresy,*[9] that He was speaking to angels, or that the human body was the work of angels. (*Dialogue* 62:2)[10]

Justin quotes Genesis 3:22 to prevent the Jewish teachers' "distortion" of Genesis 1:26, "let us make," since in the later verse it is impossible to interpret that God is speaking to the elements or to Godself. In order to demonstrate that the only possible interpretation here is his own—that God is speaking to the Logos—Justin must discard another reading that some Jewish teachers, those whom Trypho himself would refer to as an *hairesis*, have offered but cannot prove: God is speaking to angels.

The text is extremely difficult, and the Williams translation does not seem exact, though it periphrastically captures the sense. A more precise translation, although still difficult, would be: "For I cannot consider that assertion true which is affirmed by what you call an *hairesis* among you, or that the teachers of it are able to demonstrate."[11] "It" in the second clause can only refer to *hairesis*. Justin cannot consider the assertion true, nor can he consider that the teachers of the *hairesis* can prove it. There are two reasons for reading *hairesis* here as "heresy." First, this is consistent with the usage otherwise well attested in Justin with respect to Christian dissident groups, and therefore seems to be what Justin means by the term in general; and second, the phrase "what you call" strongly implies a pejorative usage.

This interpretation is consistent with the view, to be defended below in this chapter, that a major transition took place within Judaism from a sectarian structure to one of orthodoxy and heresy and that this took place between the time of Acts and that of Justin.[12] As Marcel Simon comments: "When this passage, written in the middle of the second century, is compared with the passage in Acts, it seems that the term *hairesis* has undergone in Judaism an evolution identical to, and parallel with, the one it underwent in Christianity. This is no doubt due to the triumph of Pharisaism which, after the catastrophe of 70 C.E., established precise norms of orthodoxy unknown in Israel before that time. Pharisaism had been one heresy among many; now it is identified with authentic Judaism and the term *hairesis*, now given a pejorative sense, designates anything that deviates from the Pharisaic way."[13]

There is a noteworthy (if somewhat later) rabbinic parallel to this passage, that, to my knowledge, has not been noted in the literature.[14] According to Justin, those whom the "Jews" denominate a heresy interpret God as speaking here to the angels.[15] In the Mekhilta d'Rabbi Ishmael, a late third-century or early fourth-century midrash, we find recorded the following dialogue: "Papos [mss. Papias] expounded: 'Behold, Adam has become as one of Us,' *like one of the serving angels*. Rabbi Aqiva said: Shut up, Papos! Papos said to him, and how will you interpret 'Behold, Adam has become as one of Us'? [Aqiva answered] Rather the Holy, Blessed One gave before him two ways: one of life and one of death, and he chose the way of death."[16]

Although much about this text and its context remains obscure, it is clear that a marginal, even heretical figure, Papos, is being ascribed a view very close to the one Justin is claiming for the *hairesis* among the Jews.[17] Rabbi Akiva's response—"Shut up"—represents the intensity of the response that the alleged Papos's interpretation aroused and thus its apparently heterodox nature. Justin does seem to have accurate information about a Jewish sectarian interpretation of the verse and asserts that the "Jews" refer to it as *hairesis*, presumably in Hebrew, *minut*. The Mekhilta text therefore provides evidence—albeit somewhat ex post facto—for the authenticity of Justin's information and its richness of detail. At least, we might see in the Justin text a sort of *terminus post quem* for this contestation in Rabbi Akiva's second century, very close to the time that Justin was beginning to confront (construct) his gnostics as well.[18]

For Marcel Simon, it is obvious that when Justin refers to "your teachers" here the Pharisees are the object, while the *hairesis* in question "designates anything that deviates from the Pharisaic way." There is, however, another important wrinkle that Simon has seemingly overlooked, for in another passage in Justin "Pharisees" are named as one of the heresies, not as "authentic Judaism":[19]

> For I made it clear to you that those who are Christians in name, but in reality are godless and impious heretics, teach in all respects what is blasphemous and godless and foolish. . . . For even if you yourselves have ever met with some so-called Christians, who yet do not acknowledge this, but even dare to blaspheme the God of Abraham, and the God of Isaac, and the God of Jacob, who say too that there is no resurrection of the dead, but that their souls ascend to heaven at the very moment of their death—do not suppose that they are Christians, any more than if one examined the matter rightly he would acknowledge as Jews those who are Sadducees,[20] or similar sects of Genistae, and Meristae, and Galileans, and Hellelians,[21] and Pharisees and Baptists[22] (pray, do not be vexed with me as I say all I think), but (would say) that though called Jews and children of Abraham, and acknowledging God with their lips, as God Himself has cried aloud, yet their heart is far from Him. (*Dialogue* 80:3–4)[23]

Significantly, the Rabbis themselves, as Shaye Cohen has emphasized, never understand themselves to be Pharisees, which explains how for them, too, "Pharisee" could designate a sect or even heresy: "The tannaim refused to see themselves as Pharisees."[24] Indeed, as I shall show in the next chapter, in the Tosefta, a rabbinic text approximately a century later than Justin, "Pharisees" are associated with *minim*, as precisely heretics to be anathematized. Those whom we (and other Jewish texts, such as Josephus and Acts) call Pharisees, were, for the Rabbis, simply Rabbis. Cohen captures the import of this passage: "This rabbinic ideology is reflected in Justin's discussion of the Jewish sects: there are Jews, i.e., the 'orthodox,' and there are sects, among them the Pharisees, who scarcely deserve the name Jew."[25] Indeed, Justin testifies that the name *Jew* would be denied to any of these sectarians, including Pharisees. It is not that the Rabbis would deny the legitimacy of "historical" Pharisees such as Rabban Gamaliel. Nothing could be more implausible. Rather—I suggest, following Cohen—that they would not use the name *Pharisees* for their legitimated ancestors.

Matthew Black, followed by L. W. Barnard, explains away the references to Sadducees and Pharisees as heresies in Justin by virtual sleight of hand.[26] Such a notion that both Sadducees and Pharisees were sects, and therefore "heretics," could very well have been characteristic of a second-century Judaism moving toward a notion of orthodoxy in which all *named* sects are ipso facto heresies. There are Jews, and there are *minim* (kinds), a usage that can perhaps be compared with that of Athanasius, for example, for whom there are Christians and there are Arians.[27] Even more appositely, one might quote Justin himself: "And there shall be schisms and heresies . . . many false christs and many false apostles shall arrive, and shall deceive many of the faithful, . . . but these are called by us after the name of the men from whom each false-doctrine and opinion had its origin. . . . Some are called Marcionites, some Valentinians, some Basilideans and some Saturnalians and some others by other names" (*Dialogue* 35). "We," of course, are called "Christians."[28] Assuming the same topos, the Rabbis, therefore, as Catholic Israel, could hardly recognize a named sect, the Pharisees, as their predecessors, whatever the historical "reality."[29] The Rabbis are just "Israel."

In the second half of the chapter, I pursue the notion that the Rabbis themselves were developing a heresiological discourse and ecclesiology in the late second and third centuries, thus partially (and temporarily?) transforming Judaism into a religion, a church. What seems most important for the purposes of this section, however, is to show that through this elaboration of a *Jewish* heresiology (for instance, I rather doubt that any rabbinic circle ever had such a list of Jewish heresies as Justin cites for them; it feels just so "Christian") Justin was doing work of his own. That work could have been an early adumbration of the discursive strategy that was to become fully elaborated by the end of the fourth century: that of distinguishing from the Christian side an orthodox Judaism as the true "other" of Christianity, such that two binary pairs are put into place, Judaism/Christianity and heresy/orthodoxy, with Judaism, both supporting through semiotic opposition the notion of an autonomous Christianity, and being itself an orthodoxy, also serving to mark the semantic distinction between orthodoxy and heresy.

There is an interesting moment of inconsistency in Justin's passage concerning Jewish heretics, a moment of seeming paradox, or at any rate of incongruity,[30] that is illuminating vis-à-vis the discursive work that Justin's *Dialogue* is doing. If we read this passage closely, the implication of Justin's last sentence, especially without the added parenthetical words "(would say)," which are not in the Greek, is that Jews who do not deny the resurrection or participate in other "heresies" do, indeed, have their hearts "close to God." An unexpected binary has been set up by Justin with on the one side orthodox Jews and orthodox Christians who believe in resurrection and on the other side heretical Jews and heretical Christians who do not assert such a doctrine. In the Pseudo-Clementine texts also, there are clearly Jews, identified there as Pharisees, who are deemed close to "orthodox" Christianity, closer indeed than some Christians in their insistence on the resurrection, just as in this moment in Justin's text.[31] In at least one isogloss, belief in resurrection (which marked the difference between orthodox and heretic, for the Rabbis,[32] Justin, and the Pseudo-Clementines alike), the line is drawn between Jew and Jew and between Christian and Christian, not between Jew and Christian. Justin thus inscribes a site of overlap and ambiguity between the two "religions" that the text is at pains to construct as different. Moreover, the question of the Logos and Logos theology, which the *Dialogue* works so hard to construct as a difference between Trypho the Jew and Justin the Christian, was the source of enormous conflict among Christians in Justin's time and afterward as well.[33] The same theological issue, moreover, was a central theme of non-Christian Jewish religious contention during the same centuries.[34] On one reading, the *Dialogue* could be said to be an extended rhetorical effort to mark anti-Logos theologians (such as Callistus, slightly later than Justin) as belonging to Judaism. We see here one further and very rich example of the twinned projects of delimiting of Judaism and of heresy in the discursive production of Christianity as a religion.

Judaeo-Christianity, not now Jewish Christianity, but the entire multiform cultural system,[35] should be seen as the original cauldron of contentious, dissonant, sometimes friendly, more frequently hostile, fecund religious productivity out of which ultimately precipitated two institutions at the end of late antiquity: orthodox Christianity and rabbinic Judaism. Justin's *Dialogue* and the Mishnaic passages that will be discussed in the next part of this chapter can be read as a representation and symptom of broader discursive forces within Judaeo-Christianity, as a synecdoche of the processes of the formation of nascent orthodoxy and nascent heresiology, as well as of the vectors that would finally separate the Church from rabbinic Judaism.

Yavneh, Nicaea, and the Rabbinic Rule of Faith

Shaye Cohen has written in a now classic essay:

A year or two before the church council of Nicea Constantine wrote to Alexander and Arius, the leaders of the contending parties, and asked them to realize that they were united by their shared beliefs more than they were separated by their debate on the nature of the second person of the Trinity. Let them behave like members of a philosophical school who debate in civil fashion the doctrines of the school (Eusebius, *Life of Constantine* 2.71). The council of Nicea ignored the emperor's advice and expelled the Arians. The sages of Yavneh anticipated Constantine's suggestion. They created a society based on the doctrine that conflicting disputants may each be advancing the words of the living God.[36]

Before Cohen, most Christian and Jewish scholarship had portrayed Yavneh (Jamnia, the legendary founding council of rabbinic Judaism, following the destruction of the Temple in 70 A.C.) very differently. As Cohen himself described the "usual view" (in order to dispute it): "Sectarianism ceased when the Pharisees, gathered at Yavneh, ejected all those who were not members of their own party. Christians were excommunicated, the biblical canon was purged of works written in Greek and apocalyptic in style, and the gates were closed on the outside world, both Jewish and non-Jewish. Functioning in a 'crisis' atmosphere, the rabbis of Yavneh were motivated by an exclusivistic ethic; their goal was to define orthodoxy and to rid Judaism of all those who would not conform to it. In this interpretation, the 'synod' of Yavneh becomes a prefiguration of the church council of Nicea (325 C.E.): one party triumphs and ousts its competitors."[37]

Scholars have largely adopted Cohen's claim that Yavneh was a pluralistic council—in which there was "created a society based on the doctrine that conflicting disputants may each be advancing the words of the living God"—rather than one which established an orthodoxy and expelled heretics and Christians. Others have further unsettled the narrative of what supposedly took place at Yavneh, including the closing of the canon of the Hebrew Bible[38] and the alleged expulsion of the Jewish Christians, and by now it has become near dogma in many quarters. As one major historian writes: "[T]here is virtually unanimous agreement that in the aftermath of the destruction of the Temple, in the generations between 70 CE and the publication of the Mishnah, Jews learned how to live together without paying the price of sectarian divisiveness."[39] Cohen and his camp, therefore, seem to be denying any role to heresiology in the production of rabbinic Judaism. Indeed by explicitly drawing the contrast, as he does, between Yavneh and Nicaea, he insists on a virtually absolute ecclesiological contrast between rabbinic Judaism and orthodox (Nicene) Christianity.[40]

Martin Goodman has, however, recently reminded us that the rabbinic texts form the originating moment of Jewish heresiology.[41] He proposes that, whereas the "sects" of the Second Temple period constituted a Judaism that suffered internal differences (not, of course, entirely irenically), the Judaism of the Rabbis in the so-called post-Yavneh period was exclusivistic and allowed for no other forms of Judaism at all. It was, after all, in the texts of that time—to be specified below—that the category of *minim* and *minut* (heretics and heresy) first appeared on the Jewish scene. This suggests strongly that "defining orthodoxy" was indeed a central project of the discourse of these texts. Heresiology is, of course, the very technology of orthodoxy. Jewish sectarianism had been replaced, on Goodman's reading, by Jewish orthodoxy and Jewish heresy. In other words, the "sectarianism" of the so-called pre-Yavneh period, in Josephus's and Philo's views (and they are nearly our only contemporary witness), did not preclude inclusiveness or a sense of a "pluralistic" Israel. Cohen has surely, then, put his finger on an important issue: There was a significant shift from Second Temple Judaism to the rabbinic formation. The nature of that shift, it seems, still requires further specification.

A Note on Rabbinic Historiography

At this point I must stipulate an important assumption that I make in writing this text. I assume that rabbinic writings are necessarily evidence for the time and place in which they have come into being as texts and not necessarily for the time and place of which they tell us. That is, they *may* be evidence for earlier times but are certainly evidence that something was being thought or said at the time that the text was promulgated. I call this an assumption because it cannot be proved. The historiography of Judaism in the rabbinic period, together with its implications for the history of Christianity, had been, until quite recently, founded on the assumption that the kind of historical information that rabbinic legends could yield was somehow directly related to the narrative contents that they displayed, which were understood as more or less reliable, depending on the critical sensibility of the scholar. This scholarship was not, of course, generally naive or pious in its aims or methods, merely very old-fashioned. It asked the critical questions that Marc Bloch ascribed to an earlier generation of historians: "The documents most frequently dealt with by the early scholars either represented themselves or were traditionally represented as belonging to a given author or a given period, and deliberately narrated such and such events. Did they speak the truth?"[42] As Bloch shows, such historians did not take the narrations of such documents as the "truth," and the same goes for the historians of the rabbinic period who have followed them. More often than not, in fact, they concluded that the rabbinic narratives did not speak the truth. Despite this very critical stance, however, the assumption is that once the impossible or contradicted has been excised, the texts do, indeed, speak truth.[43]

Back to Our Story

A recurring question within the quest of the historical Yavneh had to do with the question of the credibility of a given text or passage of rabbinic literature or the recovery of its "historical kernel." Even when such recovery is successful and convincing, however, this leaves us with very slim and thin bits of historical knowledge. As long as we are engaged in the process of extracting the fact from the fiction in rabbinic legend, we shall learn precious little about the history of the rabbinic group and even less about the histories of those other Jewish groups which it is seeking to control and suppress.

Reading Gedaliah Alon's classic essay "Rabban Joḥanan B. Zakkai's Removal to Jabneh"[44] will illustrate these points. Alon begins this article by citing what is truly the remarkably naive historiography of the nineteenth century (by Jews and Christians) on this issue. These were apparently, to a man [!], prepared sim-

ply to accept the Talmud's narrative as "fact" and thus to discuss in all serious-
ness the contents of Rabban Yoḥanan's negotiations with Vespasian over the
founding of Yavneh.[45] In the end, Alon concludes that the rabbinic historiographical sources are virtually valueless and comes to the plausible conclusion
that Yavneh was a Roman internment camp and Rabban Yoḥanan a political
prisoner and not much more than that.[46]

I am prepared to grant that Alon's reconstruction is plausible in this instance, but essentially all we end up knowing from this is why the later tradition
fixed at all on Yavneh as its privileged site of origin, that is, simply because Rabban Yoḥanan was there. To adopt language of Jacob Neusner's, what I want to
know is: What do we know if we do not know anything significant about Yavneh
beyond that it was one of the places in Palestine where Jewish refugees, peace-
makers, and "deserters" were interred and that arguably (even plausibly) Rabban Yoḥanan ended up there? What sort of historical work can we do if the
kernel of truth proves so dry and fruitless?[47] If—I would suggest by way of answer—the object of research is the motives for the construction of a narrative
that is taken to attest to the political context of its telling or retelling, rather than
the "historical kernel" or truth contained in the diegesis of the narrative,[48] then
all texts are by definition equally credible (which is not to say, of course, that
they are all equally intelligible). This point—hardly "postmodern"—can also be
seconded via reference to Marc Bloch. Bloch distinguishes between two kinds of
documents that a historian may use. On the one hand there are what he calls
"intentional" texts, citing as his example the *History* of Herodotus; on the other
hand there are the texts that are not intentional and, in Bloch's view, are therefore all the more valuable for the historian: "Now, the narrative sources—to use
a rather baroque but hallowed phrase—that is, the accounts which are consciously intended to inform their readers, still continue to provide valuable as-
sistance to the scholar. . . . Nevertheless, there can be no doubt that, in the
course of its development, historical research has gradually been led to
place more and more confidence in the second category of evidence, in the evidence of witnesses in spite of themselves."[49] However, as Bloch states clearly,
even the most intentional of texts, and the rabbinic narratives of Yavneh are
nothing if not intentional in his sense, also teach us that which they did not
want us to know; they "permit us to overhear what was never intended to be
said."[50] In this sense, we can have equal "confidence" in all texts.[51] The question
of the "narrative source" versus the "witnesses in spite of themselves" can be
seen, now, as a distinction between protocols of reading texts and not as an essential difference between the texts themselves. As Bloch concludes: "Everything
that a man says or writes, everything that he makes, everything he touches can
and ought to teach us about him."[52] Whatever else rabbinic narratives might be,

they are certainly something that someone has said and written, and even when we don't know who said or wrote them "originally," we can frequently determine who, or at what historical period, someone has "touched them." I seek to learn, then, about those who have touched the stories, those who have passed on and inscribed and reformulated the anecdotes within the rabbinic documents they have produced, teaching us, perhaps, what they never intended to say: "Because history has tended to make more and more frequent use of unintentional evidence [history] can no longer confine itself to weighing the explicit assertions of the documents. It has been necessary to wring from them further confessions which they had never intended to give."[53]

All texts inscribe willy-nilly the social practices within which they originate,[54] and many also seek to locate the genealogy of those social practices in a narrative of origins, producing a reversal of cause and effect. This reversal is a mode of narration that is particularly germane to the project of replacing traditional patterns of belief and behavior ("We have always done it this way") with new ones that wish, nevertheless, to claim the authority of hoary antiquity. In short, narratives of origin are particularly useful in the invention of orthodoxies, and thus are particularly useful texts in which to study their invention.

All of the institutions of rabbinic Judaism are projected in rabbinic narrative to an origin called *Yavneh*.[55] Yavneh, seen in this way, is the effect, not the cause, of the institutions and discursive practices that it is said to "originate" in the myth: rabbinic Judaism and its primary institutions and discursive practices, "Torah," the Study House, and orthodoxy.[56] Gregory Nagy has written: "Ancient Greek institutions tend to be traditionally retrojected, by the Greeks themselves, each to a proto-creator, a culture hero who gets credited with the sum total of a given cultural institution. It was a common practice to attribute any major achievement of society, even if this achievement may have been realized only through a lengthy period of social evolution, to the episodic and personal accomplishment of a culture hero who is pictured as having made his monumental contribution in an earlier era of the given society."[57] We could imagine the Yavneh myth—with its "culture heroes" from Rabban Yoḥanan ben Zakkai to Rabbi Akiva—developing on this pattern. Demystifying the rabbinic narrative of the origins of these practices and of their hegemony allows us to inquire into their causes somewhere else, namely, in the complex interactions and negotiations that produced rabbinic Judaism itself as one of the two successfully competing forms of postbiblical religion to emerge from late antiquity, the other being, of course, orthodox Christianity. Thus, although traditional scholarly historiography refers to Yavneh—however characterized in detail—as a founding council that "restored" Judaism and established the rabbinic form as hegemonic following the disaster of the destruction of the Temple, if we want to study how people conceived of themselves as belonging to a group, it is more useful to approach Yavneh as an effect of a narrative whose purpose is to shore up—even this may be presuming too much—the attempt at predominance on the part of the Rabbis in the wake of the greater debacle following the Fall of Betar in 135.[58] That which the Rabbis wished to enshrine as authoritative, they ascribed to events and utterances that took place at Yavneh, and sometimes even to divine voices that proclaimed themselves at that hallowed site. As Seth Schwartz has recently characterized the post-Neusner historiographical project in general: "It was Neusner who first argued consistently that rabbinic documents were not simply repositories of tradition but careful selections of material, shaped by the interests, including the self-interest, of tradents and redactors. In his view the documents did not simply reflect reality but constituted attempts to construct it, that is, they are statements of ideology. Finally, they are the writings of a collectivity of would-be leaders, scholars who aspired to but never in antiquity attained widespread authority over the Jews. In sum, Neusner's work *historicized* rabbinic literature and reduced it to an artifact of a society in which it was in fact marginal."[59] It is without exaggeration that I would say that, notwithstanding important criticisms that I have at particular moments of Neusner's writings, this is the program out of which my present work is generated.

Given this assumption (or postulate), it follows that one can lay out the textual materials of the first century (Josephus, Philo, the New Testament, Qumran Documents, Apocrypha) and compare them with the rabbinic texts as representing religious currents of the second century and later. One way, then, of specifying the shift that has, according to my reading, taken place, will be looking more closely at the nature of some of the divisions from the Second Temple period, and especially in the Dead Sea Scrolls, in order to delineate the difference between that and the later rabbinic formation.

Orthodoxy in the Second Temple Period?

At Qumran, the apparent community of the Dead Sea Scrolls, we find "the first example of an underground trend of thought that would often resurface in the history of Christianity and Rabbinic Judaism. The outside world is the realm of Belial. . . . The one who does not join the community 'will not become clean by the acts of atonement, nor shall he be purified by the cleansing waters, nor shall he be made holy by the seas or rivers, nor shall he be purified by all the water of ablutions.'"[60] In two closely reasoned articles, Aharon Shemesh has argued that from a halakhic standpoint the members of the Qumran community understood themselves to be Israel and all others, including other Israelites, to be Gentiles.[61] This is consistent with other aspects of the ideology of the sectarian scrolls, which seem to imply such an identification of the community with Israel.[62] Indeed, Albert Baumgarten has proposed that this is the very definition of Jewish sectarianism: "Ancient Jewish sectarians . . . turned the means of marking separation normally applied against non-Jews against those otherwise regarded as fellow Jews, as a way of protesting against those Jews, and/or against Jewish society at large. As a result of these actions all Jews were no longer on the same footing: *sectarian Jews treated other Jews as outsiders of a new sort.*"[63] At the same time, however, Baumgarten makes clear that there were significant differences between the "introvertionist" and "greedy" Qumranite sectarianism, which allowed virtually no value at all to any other form of Judaism, and the "reformist" sects of the Pharisees and Sadducees. The latter "hold hopes of reforming the larger society, and have not given up on it or renounced it totally, still perceiving themselves as members of the whole," while the "introvertionist sort of sect, by contrast, has so finally rejected the institutions of the society as a whole as to turn in on itself completely, and to rank those outside its bounds as irredeemable."[64]

This kind of ideology seems distinct from the formation that we call orthodoxy/heresy.[65] Baumgarten describes the transition from the sectarian situation to the orthodoxy one as "the transformation of what had once been competing groups into explicit winners and losers."[66] This surely is right. I would caution, however, that we must at the same time not take at face value the claim to the position of "winner." This claim does not mean that in reality all competing groups have been vanquished but involves the self-fashioning of particular groups under particular circumstances (which *may* or *may not* comprise a certain measure of popular acceptance). It is not so much that one group has won, as that something in their own discourse and perhaps in the circumstances allows them to shift from representing themselves as the embattled group that has the truth (sect) to the always/already there possessors of the truth that others are attempting to suborn (orthodoxy/"church"). One way to think of this is that a sect describes itself as having left the larger group, owing to the corruption of that larger group, while a church, as it were, describes the others as having left (or been pushed out of) the larger group owing to their defalcation from the true way and concomitant corruption, or even as representing a contaminating force that comes from the outside. This does not necessarily represent, of course, a difference in "reality," but it does constitute an important difference in representation and self-fashioning. In terms of discourse, one distinction will be with respect to legitimation.[67] Whereas the church will frequently present itself as the heir to an apostolic succession (as we shall see in the next chapter), the sect will as frequently present itself as heir to a new revelation. As M. D. Herr has written, "Rabbinic thought projects a definite attitude regarding *continuum* and *continuity* in the chain of Torah transmission. In direct contrast to this approach the writings of the Dead Sea Sect (Damascus Document V, 2) contend that the Torah was not known at all from the era of the Judges until the end of the First Temple period. Even after the destruction, they maintain, the Torah was not really understood until the founding of the sect."[68] Another aspect, brought out recently by Adiel Schremer, is that the type of organization that I am calling an "orthodoxy" or a "church" tends to "anchor their religious praxis in the living tradition of their fathers and forefathers," as opposed to religious groups such as the Qumran one who "base their religious praxis on the halakhic rulings written in authoritative and canonized texts of Jewish law."[69] Schremer's argument leads to another very important conclusion, namely that it was precisely against the tradition of the fathers, attested by Josephus[70] and Paul,[71] inter alia, for the first century, upon which Jewish practice was at least frequently based, that the Qumran sect rebelled.[72] One consequence of this observation, that the difference between church and sect is a matter of self-representation and mode of self-legitimation and not an absolute and objective one, is that the distinctions are not essentialistic, and the same group can be at one and the same time a sect with respect to one other group and a church, or orthodoxy, with respect to a different group. I thus disagree with attempts to make an absolute and realistic difference between the Rabbis and "the Dead Sea Sect,"[73] seeing it rather as a difference in self-representation and discourse.

This does not preclude important elements of what would eventually become heresiology being prefigured in the earlier periods, such as Qumran. Note Damascus Document 12:2-3 where someone who "speaks lies?" (דיבור סרה) is indicated as having a spirit of *Beli'al* (בליעל). Especially significant is DD 5:18–6:2: "And the earth became desolate because they spoke lies about the commandments of God through Moses and the anointed ones of the Holiness, and they prophesied lies to turn Israel away from God" (ותישם הארץ כי דברו סרה על מצות אל ביד משה וגם במשיחו\ י הקודש וינבאו שקר להשיב את ישראל מאחר אל). As Shemesh argues, "speaking lies is false prophecy and indeed, this is the Torah's accusation against the prophet who lures to idol worship."[74] As we shall see below, *false prophet* is precisely the ancestor and model for *heretic* according to Justin, as well as the connection with the Devil's inspiration.[75] This suggests the particular way that a Hellenistic notion of ideological choice could be combined with a biblical notion of false (and, therefore, chosen) prophecy as one way of accounting for the genealogy of the new notion of heresy. The argument, then, that there was not yet at Qumran a structure of orthodox church and heresy should not be construed as a claim that none of the elements that would eventually constitute heresiology were already in place before their aggregation into a discourse of heresiology in the early rabbinic period.

As has frequently been pointed out, the sociological situation of the Qumran group answers to the description of a sect in the sense of a group that has broken off from the main part of a religious community in search of greater purity or stringency.[76] In a sense, the rhetoric of Qumran in this respect is similar to that of the Fourth Gospel, but just as the latter does not constitute a heresiology, neither does the former.[77] It will be seen, then, that it is all a matter of representation, that Rabbis might regard Jews who are Christians as heretics, while, they themselves, these "Jewish Christians," will regard themselves as a sect (not using the term, of course).

In this sense, both Qumran and the Johannine community are sects. Indeed, following Boccaccini and pursuing the analogy with the hypothesized Johannine community, it seems more attractive to find the roots of supersessionism (the doctrine that Christianity has supplanted Judaism as Israel) rather than the roots of heresiology in Qumran.[78] This point comes out very clearly in another discussion by Shemesh.[79] Certain members of the House of Israel, the Dead Sea community, owing to their righteousness and the therefore vouchsafed additional revelation, now constitute Israel. The structure seems analogous to Pauline thought, whereby a new revelation has taken place and, whether voluntarily or involuntarily, only some of Israel has heard it: These people constitute a New Israel. This remains a discursive structure of inclusion and exclusion, of identity formation, fundamentally different from the notion of an orthodox church. Pauline Christianity and the apparently radical Essene Qumran community[80] seem best to answer to the following definition of cult: "A small, recently created, religious organization which is often headed by a single charismatic leader and is viewed as a spiritually innovative group." On the other hand, from the point of view of other Israelites, it seems there is no evidence that the Essenes in general were considered as beyond the pale. This seems to be the case notwithstanding important theological differences between Pharisees, Sadducees, and Essenes, differences no lesser than the differences that would ultimately define Judaism and Christianity as theologically significantly different. Neither the dualism and predestination of the Essenes, nor the newfangled doctrines of resurrection and eternity of the soul of the Pharisees constituted grounds for exclusion of these sects from some version of acceptable (not normative) Judaism; differences of this order would define heresy, however, for the Rabbis. The Second Temple groups, accordingly, fit sociological definitions of sects, with the Qumran radicals perhaps constituting a cult in the sociological sense.[81]

A close and careful reading of the evidence will show, I believe, how similarly the concept of heresy developed among Christian and non-Christian Jews in the second century. Until the end of the first century, we find the notion of heresy in neither Jewish nor formative Christian texts. It is well known that the Romano-Jewish historian Flavius Josephus is our primary ancient source for Jewish sectarianism in the pre-rabbinic period. Much of the early part of Book 18 of the *Jewish Antiquities* consists in an elaborate excursus on Jewish sectarianism in the first century (as we find in *Wars* 2, as well), including the famous and controversial discussions of Jesus, James the brother of Jesus, and John the Baptist and his followers. It is remarkable, therefore, that in his *Contra Apionem*, Josephus so baldly appears to contradict himself by describing the Jews in the following terms:

To this cause above all we owe our remarkable harmony. Unity and identity of religious belief, perfect uniformity in habits and customs, produce a very beautiful concord in human character. Among us alone will be heard no contradictory statements about God, such as are common among other nations, not only on the lips of ordinary individuals under the impulse of some passing mood, but even boldly propounded by philosophers; some putting forward crushing arguments against the very existence of God, others depriving Him of His providential care for mankind. Among us alone will be seen no difference in the conduct of our lives. With us all act alike, all profess the same doctrine about God, one which is in harmony with our Law and affirms that all things are under His eye. (C. Ap. 2.179–81)

This statement stands in seemingly obvious contradiction to Josephus's careful accounts of Judaism as divided into three *philosophiai* as we find in the *Antiquities* passage (18.11),[82] as well as to his reference to them as *haireseis* (philosophical—or medical—schools of thought, the etymological origin of our term *heresies*) in other passages, such as *Antiquities* 13.171, 293 and passim. Unless we assume that in the *Contra Apionem* Josephus is simply obfuscating for the purposes of apologetic, we must conclude that he did not perceive the *haireseis* of his time as in any way disturbing the essential religious and communal unity of the Jewish people, even less than the divisions among the Greeks, which from his point of view were more extreme. As Martin Goodman has perspicaciously argued, if, indeed, Josephus were here speaking apologetically and knew that this representation contradicted the "truth," he would hardly have provided cross-references to both the *Wars* and the *Antiquities* where his extensive discussions of the Jewish *haireseis* occur.[83] Moreover, even were someone to claim that Josephus is writing here, nevertheless, in an apologetic manner, in any case the argument would hold, since he clearly understands that his audience will not read *hairesis* as "heresy" or his text would simply make no sense. *Hairesis* in the Jewish Greek of Josephus's time clearly did not yet mean "heresy." In addition, as Gabriele Boccaccini points out, while Josephus records sharp halakhic disagreement between the Essenes and the temple authorities, there was apparently no bar on either side to a John the Essene being appointed governor within the precincts of that very same temple.[84] The Essenes, for all their halakhic and theological deviance, apparently were not treated by anyone as heretics.

Historian Seth Schwartz has made a point similar to that of Goodman: "Differences should not be allowed to obscure the fact of the elite's basic, though not absolute, social cohesion to which Josephus testifies (the tensions he describes *demonstrate* rather than refute this point)."[85] It is generally accepted that, even allowing for Josephus's apologetic exaggeration of the irenic nature of the situation, for Josephus and presumably at his time, generally the term *hairesis* in Jewish Greek did not in any way conform to the meaning of *heresy* or of *minut*, its Hebrew equivalent,[86] in later Christian and rabbinic usage, respectively. Simon emphasizes that Marcus Aurelius was to found in Athens four chairs of philosophy, one for each of the great *haireseis*, Platonists, Aristotelians, Epicureans, and Stoics.[87] One could imagine Josephus founding such an academy as well, with a chair of Pharisaism, one of Sadducaism, and one of Essenism. The case of Acts is interesting. When Paul says in Acts 24:14, "I am a follower of the new way (the 'hairesis' they speak of), and it is in that manner that I worship the God of our fathers," this can be interpreted in two ways, as Simon points out. Either Paul is claiming the true way, while the Jews say it is just another school of Judaism, or Jews are already referring to Christianity as a *hairesis* in the later sense of heresy. I see no reason to adopt the second choice, and citing Justin (pace Simon) begs the question. Acts 26:5 demonstrates beyond a shadow of a doubt that for Luke, *hairesis* still means choice of belief and adherence and not heresy. Allen Brent writes too that "the Church of Rome of the mid- to late second century resembled a collection of philosophical schools."[88] Thus, with positive evidence from Josephus that *hairesis* does not yet mean heresy (even if the stronger claim about Josephus is not accepted) and evidence from silence in the total absence of any Hebrew term for heretic before the rabbinic period, it seems fair to me to conclude that the notion of heresy appears on the non-Christian Jewish scene at about the same time that it is making its appearance among Christian writers such as Justin.

The Invention of *Minut*

Only in the rabbinic literature, that is, beginning with the late second-century Mishna do we find attested in any Jewish writings a word parallel in usage with the later Christian usage of *heresy* and *heretic*, namely, *minut* and *min*. Although several conjectures have been offered as to the etymology of this Hebrew term, the best hypothesis, in my view, is to see it as derived from Hebrew "kind." Justin's usage, *genistae*, would seem clearly to reflect such an ancient understanding, as well. The Rabbis do not imagine themselves to be a sect, that is, a remnant group that alone preserves the true way and must separate from the body of Israel. Indeed, as we are about to see, they were prepared to curse such groups. Their self-appointed situation vis-à-vis the majority of Israel (the ʿ*Am Haʾareṣ*) was that of elect vanguard and leader. The Rabbis, do, however, starting with their earliest recorded texts, promulgate the category of the *minim*, the heretics. Goodman makes a significant point: "Even more striking is the coinage of the term *minut*, 'heresy,' since the creation of an abstract noun to denote a religious tendency was not otherwise common in tannaitic texts[89] (for example, there was no abstract noun in Hebrew for Pharisaism or Sadducaism),"[90] thus suggesting, at least implicitly, a Hellenic influence on the Hebrew lexical development.[91] In Josephus,[92] as we have just seen, as in Acts as well, *hairesis* still means simply "a party or sect marked by common ideas and aims," and not yet "a group that propounds false doctrine." It follows that in the latter part of the first century, the notion of heresy had not yet entered (pre)rabbinic Judaism and that the term, *min*, attested, after all, only in late second-century sources is, in fact, a later development in Jewish religious discourse.

The similarities in the development of heresiology in Christian polemical writings (Justin, Irenaeus) and in the contemporaneous Mishna allow us to understand the mutual and parallel shaping of heresy as otherness in second-century rabbinic and Christian discourse.[93] As observed by Stephen Goranson, "the taxonomies of heresy used by the rabbis and the church writers interacted in a dynamic progression."[94] In the accounts of both, a crucial element is the development of the notion of a "rule of faith," by which I mean both a rule for faith and the rules faith makes for practice that distinguishes the orthodox from the heretic,[95] and also the promulgation of a notion of apostolic succession.

I need to make clear one argument that I am *not* making. I am not suggesting à la Herford that all references to *minim* and *minut* refer to "Christianity";[96] indeed, I am not suggesting that any necessarily do. In a crucial article, Yaakov Sussmann has argued that "The term *minim* serves in general as a name for a heretic in the widest sense of the word 'heretic,' whether he is just a heretic or belongs to a sect of heretics, such as Sadducees, Baitousin, Zealots, Samaritans, and Jewish Christians."[97] I accept Sussmann's argument on this point entirely, but I am not entirely sure that these terms refer, in fact, to anyone. What I suggest is something different: that the talk of *minim* and *minut* comes to do some work that was "necessitated"—in the eyes of the Rabbis, of course—by the challenge, or identity question, raised by Justin Martyr and company.

I am not willing to accept an entity called "Gnosticism," or even "Gnostics,"[98] as real targets of rabbinic heresiological discourse, either. My reasons are threefold. First, there seems to be little, if any, evidence that when the Rabbis referred to the "Two Powers" the second power was a hostile demiurge, as the Gnostics are alleged to have believed. Indeed, for instance, when Rabbi Akiva is accused of at least nearness to Two Powers heresy, it is obvious that he has no such "gnostic" doctrine in mind.[99] Herford tellingly remarks: "But if the Minim are to be identified with such Gnostics, then we should expect that the question of the goodness of God would be frequently debated between Minim and Jews [*sic*]; and this we have not found to be the case."[100] With respect to so-called pre-Christian Jewish gnosis, noted Israeli scholar Menahem Kister has recently referred to "'Gnostic' doctrines" as "an anachronistic name for Second-Temple [apocryphal] sources."[101] Second, in spite of the arguments of Friedländer, there is almost no reason to imagine that the Jews had any knowledge of such doctrine except perhaps as the doctrine of radical, "heretical" Christians themselves.[102] Third, in the most extensive text in which Two Powers arguments are debated with *minim* (Palestinian Talmud Berakhot 12d–13a), it is obvious that these *minim* hold a Logos theology and not a "gnostic" evil-creator sort of doctrine.[103] Finally, if Kister is correct in a very attractive suggestion, there is a specific allusion to the Christian doctrine of virgin birth in this text.[104] These three considerations, which, in my opinion, cannot be emphasized enough, add up to a view that the "gnostic" myth of the evil demiurge was not the cause of rabbinic denunciations of Two Powers in Heaven heresy but rather was a warped version of the Jewish theologoumenon of Two Powers in Heaven, a.k.a. Logos theology. It was the Logos that the Rabbis sought to give over to the Christians and Christianity, thereby defining Jewish orthodoxy, not the gnostic evil demiurge. The "orthodox" Rabbis expel what the "orthodox" Christians appropriate.

In the most recent and thorough treatment of the subject, Karen King has shown beyond a shadow of a doubt that while there are, of course, significant midrashic and otherwise Jewish elements in the texts that we call "Gnostic," there is not the slightest foundation for seeing those usages as having taken place outside of a Christian context, and certainly not in a pre-Christian context. The most important of King's arguments there, in my opinion, is the claim that "the methodological fixation on origins has tended to distort the actual social and historical processes of literary production because the purpose of determining the origin of Gnosticism is less historical than rhetorical: it is aimed at delimiting the normative boundaries and definition of Christianity." Moreover, not only of modern historians does she claim this: "the core problem is the reification of a rhetorical entity (heresy) into an actual phenomenon in its own right."[105] This is, of course, precisely the claim that I am making about *minut*. It follows, then, that the search for the historical *minim* is doomed to failure since it is also a rhetorical entity, reified by modern scholarship. The *minim* are no more Gnostics than they are Christians but the rhetorical entity *minut* was, I suggest, a product of the encounter with "orthodox" Christianity, prompted a similar response from the Rabbis. This response is the production of a category of people who seem very much like Jews, but are defined as other via defects in their beliefs. Claiming that this sort of definition became necessary owing to the Christian challenge to Jewish self-definition and perhaps even in response in part to the Christian promulgation of orthodoxy, is a very different claim, I think, from that which would make out the *minim* to *be* Christians.

A relatively early textual example will prove instructive here:

The *gilyonim* and the Books of *minim* are not to be saved [on the Sabbath] from the fire. . . . Rabbi Tarfon, said: "On the life of my son, [I swear] that if they come into my hands, I will burn them together with the Divine Names that are in them. For even if someone is chasing me [to kill me], I will enter into the house of Idolatry but not into their Houses, for the idol worshipers do not know Him and deny Him, while these know Him and deny Him [or, speak falsely of Him[106]], and of them the verse says: 'And behind the door and the door post, Thou hast placed Thy Name[107] [for, deserting me, you have uncovered your bed, you have gone up to it, you have made it wide; and you have made a bargain for yourself with them, you have loved their bed, you have looked on nakedness] [Isaiah 57:8]."[108] (Tosefta Shabbat 13:5)[109]

In this text, we find, first of all, the very important, indeed crucial contrast between idol worshipers and *minim*. In other words, whomever we might think the text refers to, it certainly deals with the question of Jews who "know" Him but have been led astray into strange doctrines that now define them as so far beyond the pale that even their books of the Torah can, nay must, be burnt together with the holy names contained within them. I think, however, that we can go further here and interpret the midrash at the end as alluding to people who put mezuzot on the doorposts of their houses but still have been seduced (as the end of the verse cited argues) by false and foreign doctrines about God.[110] In other words, the analogy that Rabbi Tarfon draws is precise: Their houses with the writings of God's name on the doorposts are houses of whoredom (a frequent heresiological metaphor[111]) and their Torahs with God's name written in them are also completely profane (and thus can be destroyed). The relation between Rabbi Tarfon's statement that he would not enter their houses and that he would burn their books is clear and not arbitrary. Even though they "know Him," insists Rabbi Tarfon, they "deny Him" by maintaining heretical doctrines about Him, and therefore, their citation of "His" name is corrupt, profane, and impure. We learn from this passage that there are Jews who have the same books "we" do and even the same practices, such as placing the mezuza on the door-post, but because they have a different doctrine of God, they are heretics, *minim*, and completely beyond the pale of Judaism so far so that their Bibles are to be burnt, together with the "simulacra" of divine names within them. The *gilyonim* have been interpreted in the past as "Evan*gilyon*" not least by the talmudic Rabbis themselves, who variously distorted it into *Awen Gilyon* and *Awon Gilyon*, namely, "gilyon of wretchedness" and "gilyon of sin," which would suggest that Jewish Christians are the actual object of this passage, and thus has the passage been taken in the scholarly literature.[112] Shlomo Pines has supported this view by showing that in Syriac the term *gilyane*, exactly cognate with the Mishnaic term, also refers to the Gospels. He has shown, however, that the word is used in Syriac too in the sense of apocalypses.[113] This would be an even more attractive interpretation, and the reference would be to books like Enoch. In any case, we have clear evidence here that by the middle of the third century at the latest a full-blown notion of heresy, very similar to that of Christian orthodoxy, was extant in rabbinic circles.

Rules of Faith

Two significant texts in the Mishna help make this point. Interestingly, both of them consist in discursive efforts to ascribe to the Sadducees the status of heretic, or even non-Israel. The first Mishna of the tenth chapter of Tractate Sanhedrin reads: "These are they who have no place in the next world: One who denies the resurrection of the dead;[114] one who denies that the [Oral][115] Torah is from heaven, and [Jewish][116] Epicureans." The Epicureans are included here because they denied divine providence, as we learn from Josephus.[117] The reference would then be not to actual adherents of the Epicurean school, but to Jews who appeared to the "Pharisaic" group promulgating the eternity of the soul as a central tenet of Judaic orthodoxy, *as if* they had been contaminated and were adherents of that school.[118] Resurrection and the revealed Oral Torah are the major doctrinal points at issue between the Pharisees and the Sadducees.[119] Moreover, we can see how these issues might be directly related, since it is an enormous stretch—if not an impossibility—to find a doctrine of resurrection in the Torah, so one who does not hold with an Oral Torah might well be led to deny any such doctrine. This passage, which has been nominated the "Pharisaic Credo" by Louis Finkelstein,[120] seems to be promulgating, perhaps for the first time in a Judaism, a rule of faith to adjudicate who is orthodox and who not, one that would exclude from salvation many Jews who considered themselves both faithful and traditional.[121] The litmus test for orthodoxy, or at any rate for salvation, here names three major theological innovations vis-à-vis the traditional biblical thought maintained in the conservative religious positions of such "sects" as the Sadducees and probably in the traditional religiosity of the groups loosely and pejoratively referred to in rabbinic literature as the "People of the Land" ('Am Ha'areṣ), a term that quickly came to be synonymous with the ignorant and benighted (cf. *pagani*).[122] The passage thus excludes what previously had been taken for granted, the physical annihilation of the body and the exclusivity of the Five Books of Moses as the whole content of divine revelation at Sinai. The Rabbis insist that their body of oral interpretation and orally transmitted practice was given at Sinai and is, therefore, older and more original than the practices of the Sadducees and the country folk.[123] Such an attempt by a newly formed group to claim hegemony over traditional patterns of belief and practice by portraying themselves as ancient and originary is almost a defining characteristic of the discourse of orthodoxy, of which Nicene Christianity provides an excellent example. As has been noted, what counts as heresy in Christianity is often simply the traditional religion of a generation before.[124] This Pharisaic credo reproduces the same structure. An innovative religious discourse claims hegemony and excludes traditional religiosity, as well as the modes of authority that preceded it, thus naming them as heresy. Moreover it portrays the "heresy" as a deviation from the always already-given originary orthodoxy.[125] The Rabbis thus rabbinized Jewish religious history by portraying their religious ancestors, the Pharisees, not as a sect (and thus not as Pharisees), but as the true interpreters (or even transmitters) of universal Judaism from time immemorial.

It was the second-century tannaim who first named the "Sadducees" as "heretics"—note that this point does *not* imply (or contradict) the existence of "real" Sadducees then—in contrast to Josephus, for Josephus, though himself a Pharisee, allowed for the legitimate difference of the *haireseis* for Sadducees and Essenes. A new category, the heretic, was emerging within rabbinic discourse in the late second century.[126] This shift can be correlated with Justin and his nascent heresiology as well as with developments in Roman religion in general. As Beard, North, and Price have remarked, "In the late Republic and into the first century A.D. there seems to have been a general assumption at Rome that each foreign race had its own characteristic religious practices; even though they were no doubt thought inferior to Roman practice, the 'native' religions of the provincial populations of the Roman Empire were not systematically dismissed or derided. But from the second century at the latest—perhaps as it became more pressing for the Roman élite to define itself in relation to the provinces (and provincial élites)—that position changed."[127] I am not claiming that this shift in Roman practices of inclusion/exclusion with respect to religion was the same as the one that I detect among the Rabbis or that Le Boulluec has articulated for Justin and the Christians, but I would suggest that the same forces were at work in producing or leading to such massive and widespread epistemic developments, forces that began to wield their power in the second century and came to one sort of culmination in the fourth.

The second important text in the Mishna strongly supports this analysis, even suggesting the conclusion that "Sadducees" were not considered "Israel,"[128] albeit in this instance on grounds of ritual difference, not doctrine.[129] This text also forms the basis for a serious objection to notions that Yavneh and its rabbinical successors—including the talmudic culture of the fourth and fifth centuries—were "pluralistic" or "democratic" in their ecclesiology: the total exclusion of women from access to power/knowledge.[130] Far from being an aleatory, superficial moment in rabbinic culture, this exclusion is a cardinal and founding moment in the discourse of rabbinic authority:

> The daughters of the Sadducees, as long as they are accustomed to follow the ways of their fathers, have the same status [in matters of menstrual purity] as Samaritan women. When they have separated themselves [from the ways of their fathers] and follow the ways of Israel, they have the same status as Israel.
> Rabbi Yose says: "They always have the same status as Israel unless they separate themselves to follow the ways of their fathers." (Niddah 4:2).[131]

The implication of this text seems clear: "The ways of their [the Sadducean daughters'] fathers" are contrasted with the "ways of Israel." If that is a paradigm, then those fathers' traditional ways (very likely ancient norms), and indeed those fathers themselves, have been semantically excommunicated from Israel; the effect of this excommunication remains an open question, of course.[132] Since this text was included in the Mishna, edited at the end of the second century, it can surely be read—at least—in that historical and textual context.[133]

Lest we think, however, that the primary reason for the excommunication of the Sadducees was halakhic difference, the texts treat us to a perfect heresiological account of the very origin of the sect, as well as of the primary reason for its heresy, from the point of the Rabbis, dressed, as it were, in the garb of Pharisees. This text from the commentary on Mishna Avot, known as Avot of Rabbi Nathan, proposes a classical heresiological schema to explain the existence of the sects of Sadducees and their somewhat mysterious fellows, the Baithuseans:

> Antigonos the man of Sokho received from Shim'on the Righteous. He used to say, "Do not be as slaves who serve the Master with the intention of receiving a reward, but be as slaves who serve the Master, not with the intention of receiving a reward, and let the fear of Heaven be upon you, in order that your reward will be double in the future."

Antigonos the man of Sokho had two disciples who used to repeat his words and they would teach their disciples and their disciples, their disciples. They stood up and read the words *strictu sensu*, saying: "Why did our Fathers say this? Is it possible that a worker will work for the whole day and will not receive his pay in the evening? Rather, if our Fathers knew that there was a resurrection of the dead and another world, they would not have said thus." They arose and separated themselves from the Torah, and two schisms were created: the Sadducees and the Baithuseans. The Sadducees in the name of Sadoq, and the Baithuseans, in the name of Baithus. And they used to use vessels of gold and vessels of silver all of their days, saying the Pharisees have a tradition to make themselves suffer in this world, and in the next world they will have nothing.[134]

Unfortunately, it is impossible to date this text as contemporary with the Mishna, although it might be as old as that.[135] In any case, we can see here, at the very least, a somewhat later tradition that articulates the existence of the sects in clear and classic heresiological terms, much like those we find in Justin and Irenaeus: that is, as the descendants of a false heresiarch, by whose name they are called. Moreover, the text indicates clearly that the schism was understood, at least in some rabbinic quarters, as having been generated theologically and doctrinally, and not on grounds of halakhic difference.[136] The implication is that when halakhic traditions differ, even widely, as did those of the Houses of Shammai and Hillel, then, despite the Torah being made into two Torot (Tosefta Sotah 14:9), heresy has not been produced. When fundamental doctrinal tenets are transduced, however, then we have heresy.[137] We have here, I think, the rudiments of a full-fledged heresiology among the Rabbis.[138]

I propose a moratorium on the quest for the historical Sadducee.[139] Instead, we can learn something else from the Mishna that certainly applies *at the latest* to the late second century: that by then, at least, for rabbinic discourse there were Jews who were outside of "Israel," and that these Jews were at least sometime called Sadducees, in the same way that heretical Christians are often named "Jews" within Christian heresiological texts.[140] Whether or not the text means to refer to "genuine" Sadducees contemporary with Rabbi Yose and the Mishna, the contrast between those others and the dominant group is named by the contrast between "ways of their fathers" and "the ways of Israel." In other words, this text projects a situation in which there are historical and genealogical Israelites who are not "Israel." An institution of orthodoxy, or at any rate, a discourse of orthodoxy, is aborning, and it finally doesn't matter whether these outsiders are actual Sadducees or not. Again, this differs from the situation in Second Temple times, according to Josephus, when the various groups were all "Israel," with clear lines of demarcation between the contesting groups collectively and the true outsiders, the Gentiles.[141] In these texts, the Rabbis appropriate the name *Israel* for those who hold their creed and follow the ways that they identify as the "ways of Israel," and the "Sadducees" are heretics who are beyond the pale and outside the name *Israel*.[142] The Temple itself (or, rather, its destruction), is one of the crucial factors that explains the epistemic shift. While the Temple stood, it served as a focus of sectarian controversy but at the same time formed a unifying roof under which all the competing groups stood together, *including the earliest Christians*, and excluding, perhaps, only Qumran, who had seemingly rejected it completely. Once, however, this unifying center was gone, new modes of religious identity formation became necessary. I would suggest that the parallel legends of the "abandonment" of Jerusalem by Rabban Yoḥanan ben Zakkai, on the one hand (to Yavneh), and the Jerusalem Church, on the other (to Pella), represent these new formations of identity.[143] This, together with the challenges to "Jewish" identity provided by the growing development and importance of Gentile Christianity (that is, the Christianity of those who were neither genealogically Israel nor observers of the commandments but claimed, nevertheless, the name *Israel*), formed the background for the invention of Jewish orthodoxy by the Rabbis. A similar necessity for identifying center and borders drove, I would suggest, the parallel and virtually contemporaneous Christian invention, but more of this anon. Back, for now, to the Mishna at hand, with its Sadducean daughters and their fathers who are not Israel.

This is an illuminating instance of rabbinic heresiology for another reason, as well. The deviation in the behavior of the "Sadducee daughters," like that of the Samaritan women to whom they are compared, does not consist in laxness in the observance of menstrual purity rules, still less in a general disregard for them, but in a hyperstrictness that results, according to the Rabbis, in miscalculations. The details are instructive here. According to the practice of the Samaritan women (and by analogy, the Sadducean women) as described by the Mishna itself, any issue of blood renders the woman in the state of ritual impurity. According to the rabbinic halakha, by contrast, different "kinds" of blood are discharged by a woman. Only certain kinds render her impure, whereas others do not. Naturally, only a trained Rabbi can determine which do and which don't.[144]

In this text, women's bodies and sexuality are made an instrument in the struggle for power between the men of the rabbinic group and their rivals (the "fathers" of the Sadducean women). Other Jews, presumably behaving in accordance with ancient Jewish practice or with the ways of their fathers—a highly positively coded term when it is "our" fathers who are being invoked—are read out of Israel because they refuse the control of the rabbinic party. The ostensible justification for excluding the Samaritans and Sadducees is that, because their women would begin counting days of impurity from a spotting that, according to the Rabbis, would not render them impure, if they saw blood later on in the week, they would not begin counting from then (because they were already in the middle of the count) and accordingly would end the count "too soon." However, when the women of the Rabbis decided to declare themselves impure upon seeing any spot the size of a mustard seed (which, equally according to biblical law, would not cause impurity), this was considered praiseworthy by the Rabbis in spite of its producing precisely the same result as the Samaritan practice. In short, the issue is authority. In the early medieval Karaite "schism" in Judaism, the same pattern is repeated, with the Karaites insisting on more rigorous Sabbath observance than the Rabbis called for. This is structurally similar to such events in Christian history as the Novatian, Montanist, Meletian, and Donatist schisms, in all of which it is the rigorist party (not the lenient one) that is declared schismatic or heretical. The issue is authority.[145] Rabbi Eli'ezer, also excommunicated for his rigorist views, represents another example.

The passage from Tractate Niddah is thus completely consonant with the Sanhedrin passage cited above, which also effectively excludes from salvation and therefore from orthodoxy those who do not cleave to the Pharisaic creed.[146] What I have excavated here, then, are additional fragments attesting to a shift in culture homologous to the development of orthodoxy in Christianity, the displacement of traditional norms of belief and behavior by an organized institution which now claims for itself a pure origin in the arche of the faith and names all those traditional forms as heresy.[147]

This is not to say that the Mishna considers Sadducees to be non-Jews in general, but only that the first seeds of a heresiological discourse within rabbinic Judaism are to be located in these texts. In other words, I find in the fact that the Mishnaic text discussed above opposes "Sadducees" and "Israel" not evidence for a tolerant, nonsectarian Judaism, but rather for a Catholic Israel, a former "group" that has won the day, or at any rate, that so represents itself and defines all others as simply not in the fold at all.[148] My hypothesis is that, while not immediately directed at Christians, these boundary-making activities were, at least in part, incited by the need to inscribe border lines around Judaism, to define what is and what is not orthodox, in order to exclude Christianity from those borders. Let me make this claim clear: I am not suggesting that "Sadducee" is a cipher for Christian, not at all, but I hope by the end of this book to have convinced readers that the rabbinic heresiological effort itself is, nevertheless, "about" Christianity.

The Excommunication of Akavyah ben Mehalalel

This does not exhaust the evidence for the parallel development of rabbinic and Christian heresiology in the late second century, or for the uses of the sign of the female body, and especially control over female sexuality, in those constructions.[149] According to the Mishna Eduyyot 5:6, Rabbi Akavyah ben Mehalalel was excommunicated and his coffin was stoned after his death, simply owing to a disagreement on whether or not female freed slaves were subject to the ritual of the errant wife (Sotah) or not:

He [Akavyah] used to say: One does not give the convert and the freedwoman [the bitter waters] to drink, and the Sages say one does. They said to him: There was the case in Jerusalem of Karkemit, the freedwoman, and Shemaiah and Avtalyon gave her to drink. He said to them: They only gave her a simulacrum to drink. And they excommunicated him, and he died excommunicate, and the court stoned his coffin.

Rabbi Yehuda said: God forfend that Akavyah was excommunicated, for the Court of the Temple is not closed before an Israelite as great in wisdom and fear of sin as Akavyah ben Mehalalel. Rather, who was it that they excommunicated: Eli'ezer the son of Enoch who doubted the "purity" [a common euphemism for impurity] of the hands, and when he died the Court sent and had a stone put on his coffin, which teaches that anyone who is excommunicated and dies excommunicate, one stones his grave (Eduyyot, 5:6).

This fascinating text could do with some glossing. According to the earlier voice in the text, an important and central Pharisee (or Rabbi, according to rabbinic tradition) was excommunicated because he did not accept the view of the majority over his own tradition with regard to a halakhic matter, thus subverting the authority of the collegia of the Rabbis.

Rabbi Yehuda, a character three generations later than Akavyah in the rabbinic historiography, cannot accept this account and produces another historical tradition according to which an otherwise unknown figure was excommunicated for implicitly agreeing with Jesus on the matter of the halakhic controversy reported in Matthew 15, that is, for advocating traditional mores over rabbinic innovations. In our rabbinic story, we find, as in so many others, the recognition that what is later presented as a battle between an "us" and a "them" is as often as not the later consequence of what was once a disagreement among "us" ourselves.

The stoning of the coffin of Rabbi Akavyah ben Mehalalel, whether historically accurate or merely legendary, is surely more than a mere disciplinary measure. It is indicative of a dire exclusion from the community, precisely the parallel of the "false prophet" heresiology documented by Le Boulluec in Justin and plausibly derived by him from an older Jewish model.[150] As Justin had written: "For just as there were also false prophets in the time of the holy prophets that were among you, so there are among us also many false teachers" (*Dialogue* 82.1).[151] Indeed, as we learn from a tannaitic source in the Babylonian Talmud Sanhedrin 89b, the prescribed punishment (at least according to some authorities) for a deceiving prophet, Justin's very model of a modern major heretic, is stoning, the punishment meted out to Akavyah. This suggests that that new character, the heretic, is indeed the genealogical scion of the false prophet who must be "utterly extirpated from your midst" (Deut. 13:6).[152] Shlomo Naeh, moreover, has recently demonstrated that "in the world of the Rabbis, a charge of [false prophecy] is a charge of *minut.*"[153] The Akavyah of the Mishna, then, is seemingly a heretic, very much in the early Christian mold.

From Sectarianism to Orthodoxy and Heresy

In short, although we can accept Shaye Cohen's argument that the focal point for sectarian division over the Temple, with the concomitant production of a *particular* kind of sectarianism (separatism from the "corrupted" Jerusalem center or conflict over hegemony there), had vanished with the destruction of the Temple, nevertheless we must take seriously a broader phenomenon in which the invention of heresy played a central role. The epistemic shift marked by the emergence of rabbinic Judaism in the second century included the production of a category of Jewish "outsiders" defined by doctrinal difference. Jewish sectarianism as a form of decentralized pluralism by default had been replaced by the binary opposition of Jewish orthodox and Jewish heretics. Those who are Jews and say or do the wrong things may, therefore, no longer be called "Israel"—at least in rabbinic intention.[154] "Verus Israel," we could say, had been invented simultaneously, perhaps not coincidentally, by the Rabbis and the Gentile Christians. Sectarianism had not disappeared, but rather one group began to achieve hegemony and could now plausibly portray itself as Judaism *tout court*—or at any rate, wishfully project itself as such.[155]

Insofar as there are limits for who is in and who is out of Israel among born Judaeans,[156] and insofar as they are named in doctrinal and behavioral terms and in the use of the term *minim* for those who are excluded, early (tannaitic) rabbinic Judaism thus was similar in ecclesiology to orthodox Christianity. The first datable evidence of nascent rabbinic heresiology thus appears nearly simultaneously with what Le Boulluec has called "the intervention of Justin," and the heresiological structure of nascent rabbinic ecclesiology provides a good parallel with the discourse of the Great Church as it developed from after Justin, a universalism predicated on orthodoxy.[157]

At the same time that becoming a Christian became identified with "entering Israel" in some Christian quarters, at any rate, it likewise became necessary for the first time for a Jew to "become" or find a way to define herself as a Jew. If we don't assume that the non-Christian Jews were indifferent to the world-shaking events in the world around them, then this boundary would have to have been reconfigured from its other side as well, with Israelite and Sadducee/*min* as the rabbinic equivalent of orthodox and heretic, at least during the period within which the reconfiguration of the boundary was underway.

I don't wish to claim that the rabbinic orthodoxy acted in imitation of the Church, but rather that a structural problem had been produced for both "brothers," the problem of figuring out who was who. The anxieties about boundaries between the newly defined groups—anxieties that were evident from both sides of the boundary—were the immediate catalyst that produced the invention of the category of heresy as a means of policing borders that were hitherto not problematic because the categories that they defined did not yet exist. Christian groups also had no need to define "heresy" as long as their own self-definition did not fundamentally challenge the notion of Jewish peoplehood, that is, as long as they understood themselves as Jews and not as a "new Israel."[158]

In fine, the nascent discourse of heresiology in second-century rabbinic Judaism may very well have fulfilled precisely the same function that it did in the Christianity of Justin. It is no accident that the term *min* first appears on the rabbinic textual scene at approximately the same time that the term *heresy* shifts in meaning from philosophical choice to demonized other in the work of Justin. It seems apparent, therefore, that neither did Justin "influence" the Jews, nor did the Rabbis "influence" him. Both Justin and the Mishna were engaged in the construction of the borders of orthodoxy via the production of others who are outside them.[159] These are the heretics, the *minim*.[160] The difference between the two types of heresiological text is no more than the general difference between the modes of rabbinic and of Christian textuality, say, for instance, between the rabbinic discourse on idolatry and the *de Idolatria* of Tertullian.[161] In other words, I wish to suggest that in place of the "influence" models that even such sophisticated scholars as Le Boulluec invoke, we should be thinking in terms of intertextuality or dialogical relations between texts and traditions. Non-Jewish Christians and non-Christian Jews exercised agency in the appropriation of textual ideas, images, and representations from a shared developing pool; at the same time, these shared practices were refracted through practices specific to the particular communities, such as the writing of theologies or the production of dialectical, narrative-type texts. This process of local variation of a common tradition is known by folklorists as ecotypification. Rabbinic and orthodox Christian heresiologies are, thus, on my account, ecotypes of each other.

Justin, the Cursing of Christians, and the Placing of Partition

Insofar as the hypothesis that I have been developing is at all cogent, it bids us shift our attention from Palestine and its so-called Jewish Christians to other places, notably Asia Minor (inclusive, somewhat broadly, of Antioch) with its burgeoning Gentile Christianity (here, at least, a "native" term: the *Ekklesia ek tôn ethnôn*), as a possible point of origin for the discursive work of partitioning off a new religion, Christianity, from its Jewish other. Once again, close study of Justin Martyr's *Dialogue* will help us make sense of these historical, discursive practices. It is my contention that we miss important possibilities for a historical reading of Justin's text because of a persistent misreading (a century old) that takes it as reflecting an existing situation (an alleged "parting of the ways") rather than participating in producing it (a partitioning of religious territory). It is here that the methodological strictures offered above anent the dating of rabbinic traditions will be crucial, for another factor that has led to this misreading is an equally persistent habit among scholars before the second half of the last century (and even in some, but fewer, quarters today) to read rabbinic legends as if they reported facts of the centuries before their formulation.[162] It is important to take a closer look at a significant subtext in Justin's *Dialogue* that has been taken until now as important evidence that the apologist was reacting to Jewish hostility to and expulsion of the Christians, indeed to an allegedly already extant institution of *birkat hamminim*, the notorious (and misnamed, as we shall see) curse of the Christians. In at least three places in his *Dialogue*, Justin testifies to a curse that the Jews pronounce on Christians during their prayer.[163] In the first of these passages, Justin refers to the Jews: "cursing in your synagogues them that believe on Christ" (16:4).[164] In the second, he states: "I declare that they of the seed of Abraham who live after the Law, and believe not on this our Christ before the end of their life, will not be saved, and especially they who in the synagogues have anathematised and still anathematise, those who believe on that very Christ" (47:4).[165] The third repeats the point: "For you curse in your synagogues all who have become Christians through Him" (96:2).[166]

Until quite recently in many scholarly quarters (and to this day in most popular ones) this Justinian notice was taken as a reference to *birkat hamminim*, a curse on heretics which appears in later Jewish liturgy and which was interpreted as a project for driving the Jewish Christians out of the Synagogue and the precipitating factor of the final break between Christianity and Judaism, the so-called parting of the ways.[167] However, there is every reason to doubt that the so-called curse of the heretics was formulated under Gamaliel II at Yavneh or that it existed at all before the end of the second century. The only source we have for this "Yavnean" institution is a Babylonian talmudic story from the fourth or fifth century of Rabban Gamaliel asking Samuel the Small to formulate such a blessing—"blessing" means curse here[168]—the latter forgetting it a year later and meditating for two or three hours in order to remember it (BT Berakhot 28b–29a). This hardly constitutes reliable evidence, or indeed evidence at all.[169] The aroma of legend hovers over this entire account.[170] This supposition is strongly confirmed by a parallel passage in the Palestinian Talmud which remarks on the "forgetting" of a prayer by this Samuel but not precisely *birkat hamminim* (PT Berakhot 9c).[171] In the Palestinian Talmud Berakhot 4:3, 8a, apologetic reasons for retroactively ascribing this "blessing" to Yavneh are indicated explicitly.[172] This argument becomes particularly cogent, I believe, once we pay proper attention to the fact that Rabban Gamaliel is frequently a cipher for so-called antisectarian activity.[173] One might as well attempt to write the history of early Britain on the basis of King Lear or of colonial America using James Fenimore Cooper as one's only source.[174]

Uncoupling the discourse of rabbinic heresiology from its late legendary attributions to the first-century legendary Council of Yavneh and relocating it within the wider context of a crisis of identity formation suggested by the claim for *Verus Israel* and the beginnings of Christian heresiology forces us to abandon simple and linear accounts of the parting of the ways and to seek other modes of connecting those pieces of narrative as parts of complex relations that simultaneously connected and began to differentiate non-Christian Jews and Christians. The shift in dates from the first century to the second century is not a mere quibble but rather results in a significant decentering of the narrative of the origins of orthodox Judaism (rabbinism) and its institutions and its relations with its rivals. If we let go of the notion of a centralized and hegemonic power institution, "Yavneh" as the source of definitive boundary making gives us as well subtler, more complex ways of reading the Justinian evidence.[175] Given the state of our knowledge of diasporic Judaism in the second century, it becomes virtually impossible to assume a rabbinic institution (even if there had been one) which would have been hegemonic in western Asia or Rome at that time.[176] The talmudic evidence therefore proves a red herring for understanding the curse against the Christians in Justin's *Dialogue*. Justin's text, however, may prove less fishy as a way of accounting for the talmudic text.

Stephen G. Wilson points out that we cannot assume the Rabbis at Yavneh were in a position to dictate to the Jewish community in its entirety: "The influence of the Yavnean sages on Jewish thought and practice between 70 and 135

CE and beyond should not be overestimated. Their decisions were not imposed overnight, nor were they felt uniformly across all Jewish communities. The rabbinic account of the introduction of the *Birkat ha-minim* [curse against the heretics] is thus a retrospective, punctiliar summary of what was in reality a lengthy process. The spread of their influence was gradual and almost certainly did not encompass all Jewish communities until well beyond the second century."[177] Wilson's formulation, however, does not go far enough. Not only should we not overestimate "the influence of the Yavnean sages," we should also not overestimate our knowledge of the activity of those sages between 70 and 135. Indeed, we should query whether we know much of anything at all about them, since the earliest information we have about them is from the Mishna, redacted at the end of the second century.[178] *Birkat hamminim* is not mentioned in that document. The very first attestation of this institution is in the Tosefta, which is generally thought to have been edited some time around the middle of the third century, and thus provides a *terminus ante quem* for the development.[179] The rabbinic account of the introduction of the *birkat hamminim* is thus not only a summary at a single point in time of what had been a lengthy process, as Wilson has seen clearly, but also one for which the earliest evidence is from the mid–third century, which tells us, owing to its ambiguities, very little about Jewish practice at that time, let alone for any earlier time.

It seems hardly an accident that the first more or less datable mention of the anathema against the heretics and the first mention of the disciples of Jesus occur in the same rabbinic document, the mid-third-century Tosefta. Whereas the mention of the *birkat hamminim* there is almost certainly of somewhat earlier origin than the redacted text, it would be a real reach, in my view, to date it to the first century.[180] Moreover, the text itself indicates that the *birkat hamminim* is of recent origin: "The eighteen blessings which the Sages have said, correspond to the eighteen mentions of [God's name] in [Psalm 29]. He shall include [mention] of the *minim* [heretics] in the blessing of the Pharisees [lit. Separatists]" (Tosefta Berakhot 3:25).[181] Initially there was a blessing that mentioned פרושים (Pharisees), those who separate themselves from the community. This text has been a real *skandalon* for scholars, because it seems to imply that the Pharisees were cursed in the early synagogues. There have been many attempts to emend this text, but as Saul Lieberman points out, it cannot be emended against all witnesses. Lieberman accordingly understands "Pharisees" here to mean those in general who "separate themselves from the community," and thus as the prototypical sect (the apparent etymological meaning), thereby endangering the unity of the people. He concludes that the Tosefta is referring to an early curse on them to which a curse on the *minim* was later appended or folded in. Lieberman must, it would seem, be right. Not the historical group that we (or Josephus or the Gospels) refer to as Pharisees—and whom the Rabbis do not see as sectarians—but another group or other separatist groups are being spoken of here, perhaps even the Qumran community or a similar one.[182] I would argue then that it would be difficult to date the inclusion of "heretics" (מינים) here to earlier than the third-century context in which the Tosefta was redacted or the immediately preceding decades, in part because, as mentioned above, the very term *minim* is attested only from the Mishna at the end of the second century, but also since neither Josephus nor Philo seem to have any idea of heresy.

In any case, it is very difficult to see here a curse against the Christians in this ambiguous formulation, even for the third-century date. Origen, roughly contemporary with the Tosefta, provides indirect evidence for the point that there was no early curse against Christians or Christianity. He writes that: "up till his own days the Jews curse and slander Christ (*Hom. Jer.* X 8,2; XIX 12,31; *Hom. Ps.* 37 II 8)." "But that is not what the Birkat ha-minim is about," comments P. W. van der Horst, "and in view of the fact that no Church father was better informed about Judaism than Origen, one may reasonably assume that curses against Christianity in a synagogual [*sic*] prayer would certainly have been known to him and been mentioned by him. It is a telling fact that he fails to refer to any such prayer."[183]

The Tosefta indicates, then, that an earlier curse of the sectarians (פרושים) became the model for the curse of the heretics and did so, for all we can know, sometime in the second or third century. If this argument bears weight, then the development within rabbinic discourse would be very similar to the one in Christian writings. In the first century or so, the "curse" was directed at schismatics among the non-Christian Jews, whereas in the late second or third century it came to be directed at heretics, just as the Pauline and Ignatian discourse against schism and schismatics had become by the time of Justin and Irenaeus a heresiology. This curse became institutionalized in rabbinic discourse and rendered a "Yavnean" foundation in the narrative legend of the Babylonian Talmud, seemingly some time in the fourth century. The most inviting historical context for the talmudic narrative is, in my opinion, the anathematizing of heretics that we find attested in the legend-encrusted councils of the late third and early fourth centuries, notably the Council of Antioch (260) in which Paul of Samosata and his followers were anathematized[184] and, more famously, the Council of Nicaea (325). It is perhaps going too far to suggest that the late stories of Yavneh were, in part, a kind of reflex of stories about ecumenical councils, but it is not, I think, extravagant to imagine that something was in the air of discourse at that time. I think that formal anathematization was of importance to both nascent Christianity and Judaism at this time and for similar reasons, namely the effort on the part of certain power groups and leaders to make a difference, to construct a binary opposition where none yet existed between them.

We need another way to connect these pieces of information, the third- and fourth-century rabbinic reports of *birkat hamminim* and Justin's second-century testimony. I propose two plausible interpretations of this evidence; one that assumes that Justin is reporting what he has observed and one that assumes that this report is part of a wider but historically specific discourse of imputing Jewish hostility toward Christians for Christian apologetic purposes. In either case, I would suggest that both the talmudic legends of the institution of *birkat hamminim* and Justin's reports are instances of larger cultural processes that involved the Rabbis and Justin in a web of mutual association and coimplication in the process of the invention of orthodoxy and heresy, which is, on my reading, the very discourse of the production of "Judaism" and "Christianity" as separate and distinct religions.

I reckon that Christianity, in its own developments, struggles, and the forms of its triumphs was a vital player in the drama of the invention of Judaism, not just vice versa.[185] Once the evidence of a so-called curse of the heretics before the third century is removed from the picture, there is no warrant at all to assume an early Palestinian curse directed at any Christians.[186] I am not claiming to know that there was no such thing, but instead suggesting that we cannot know at all, and that it is certain, therefore, that we cannot build upon such a weak foundation an edifice of a Jewish-Christian parting of the ways.[187] To paraphrase Jacob Neusner, the question that animates my work is this: Once we know that we cannot know certain things, what else do we know, precisely by knowing what we cannot know?

Reversing common pictures, one possible scenario that emerges is that it was the threat of Gentile Christianity to the borders of Jewish peoplehood in Asia Minor, represented by the new second-century Christian claim to be *Verus Israel* (first attested in Justin, but surely not originated by him), that may have given rise to nonliturgically formalized or even popular curses on Gentile Christians and to the reviling of Christ in the synagogues. That development may very well have taken place first in the areas in which Jews and Gentile Christians were in intense and tense contact, that is, precisely in an area such as western Asia, that is, Asia Minor.[188] The custom might have developed in Asia and spread later to Palestine, for all we know,[189] and have been instituted as part of formal rabbinic practice only much later. This later institution would be the one reflected in the much later talmudic legend and in the roughly contemporaneous reports of Epiphanius and Jerome that the Jews curse "*minim* and *noṣrim*."[190] The version of the "blessing" that explicitly mentions Christians

(*noṣrim*) is only attested probably from this time, or later at the time of the crystallization of religious difference argued for just now.[191] Note that the collocation "*minim and noṣrim*" (heretics and [Jewish] Christians) is precisely matched
in Jerome's peroration to Augustine: "Usque hodie per totas Orientis synagogas
inter Judaeos haeresis est quae dicitur *Minaeorum,* et a Pharisaeis nunc usque
damnatur: quos vulgo *Nazraeos* nuncupant,"[192] providing a dramatic image of
the "conspiracy" between the two orthodoxies to exclude the middle. Christian
orthodoxy, I suggest, and its institutional and discursive trappings thus virtually
forced the production of a discourse of orthodoxy among the rabbinic would-
be (perhaps in both senses) Jewish leaders. This is not to claim, of course, that
the two discourses of orthodoxy are structurally or functionally exactly the same
("Judaism" could still, of course, call on literal genealogy for its legitimation).
However, in their mutual discovery of the benefits of heresiology for self-
definition in response to crises of identity and border-making, they seem very
similar indeed.

An alternative explanation would connect Justin's reports with other Asian
accusations of anti-Christian activity on the part of Jews, including the infa-
mous accounts in the martyrologies of Polycarp[193] and Pionios. As Judith Lieu
has articulated the grounding assumption: "It is in opposition that Christianity
gains its true identity, so all identity becomes articulated, perhaps for the first
time, in face of 'the other,' as well as in the face of attempts by the 'other' to deny
its existence. Conversely, the uncompromising affirmation of identity constructs the boundary against 'the other': while the manner of Polycarp's death
convinces the crowd that 'there was such a difference between the unbelievers
and the elect,' the terminology used is, of course, not theirs but that of the mar-
tyrological perspective (*Mart. Poly.* 16.1)."[194] This point helps us explain the role
of the Jews in these texts. Since the point (at least one point) of the martyrology—if not of the martyrdom—is to convince the crowd that there is such a difference between the unbelievers and the elect, and since the author wants to
include the Jews among the unbelievers, they must be presented as among the
enemies, in order to establish that the name *Christianoi* excludes the name
Ioudaioi.[195] Might not Justin's representation of the Jews as cursing Christians
have not played a similar role in his discourse, whether or not there was a regular practice of such cursing?[196]

As Lieu has emphasized, we need to understand Justin's comments in their
fullest historical context, the "*rhetorical* function of Jews and Judaism in the
early texts,"[197] and especially, it would seem, those from western Asia, such as
Melito of Sardis, and the martyrdoms of Polycarp and Pionios, both of Smyrna.
On the other hand, I am somewhat puzzled at a statement in her reading of the
Martyrdom of Polycarp: "It is, then, the more remarkable that the early martyr-

dom accounts give little support to Justin's (and others') polemical and apologetic claim that Jews are particularly implicated in the persecution of Christians (*Dialogue* 110:5; 122:2), a claim too readily believed by past scholars. Even the one apparent exception, the *Martyrdom of Polycarp*, where the Jews do play a role, does not use the martyr's confession and consequential death as a Christian to draw the boundaries which will position the Jew as the 'Other.' To our puzzlement, at this point, the Jew is not the problem, nor yet the nonproblem; the problem is not perceived."[198] On my reading, if we do not assume—as neither I nor Lieu do—that Jews were "actually" involved in the persecution of Polycarp, then the stress in the text on their involvement must mean something.[199] As Lieu remarks there, "Implicit in all I have said so far is that the martyrs as I have been speaking of them, and as they construct Christian identity, are themselves constructs, constructed by the texts which tell their story and by the survival of those texts."[200] Indeed, but then we must inquire as to what the constructive role of "the Jews" is in *Polycarp*; to my mind it is precisely the drawing of boundaries with the Jews as the other that is involved. Rather than seeing this as only a chronological issue, I would see it as a geographical one, with the insistence on Christian identity as separate from Jewish characteristic of the area from Antioch—where Christians and Christianity first got their names—through Asia. Smyrna would have been one such focus for such tensions of identity.[201]

The two explanations that I have given are, then, seemingly compatible and could both be true, that is, that on the one hand there was sufficient pressure from Gentile Christianity in Asia Minor to stimulate Jewish hostility even, perhaps, to the point of cursing, but also that there was sufficient pressure on Gentile Christian identity to produce the need for clearer articulations of separation from Judaism.[202] After the time of Justin and his promulgation of *Verus Israel*,[203] becoming a Christian (or follower of Christ) meant something different—it no longer entailed becoming a Jew—, and once becoming a Christian became identified with "entering [the true] Israel," the whole semantic/social field shifted. The boundary between Greek and Jew, the definition of Jewishness as national or ethnic identity, was breached or gravely threatened by the self-definition of Gentile Christianity as "Israel," leading to a reconfiguration of the cultural features that signal the boundary, indeed a reconfiguration of the understanding of the substance of the boundary itself from the genealogical to the religious. Hence orthodoxy/heresy came to function as a boundary marker, because the boundaries had indeed been blurred.[204]

Chapter 3
Naturalizing the Border:
Apostolic Succession in the Mishna

As has been shown in a different context by David Halperin,[1] an epistemic shift consists not in the invention of a particular form of distinction, but in the aggregation of several modes of distinction into one new categorical *dispositif.* Halperin demonstrates that all of the elements that would make up male homosexuality existed well before the nineteenth century, but their aggregation into one "name" initiated the history of sexuality. Similarly, the various elements of heresiology surely existed before Justin; the epistemic shift that this writer effected consisted in bringing together rules of faith, apostolic succession, diabolical inspiration, and false prophecy under one principle—the principle of heresy. In the last chapter, I argued that the concept of *minut*, the rabbinic equivalent to heresy and the rule of faith that defines it, could be said to have developed over the course of the second century and can be read as part of a discursive development that comprehends the beginnings of Christian heresiology. The rabbinic parallel to the second pillar of the new Christian discourse of orthodoxy, apostolic succession, was also a product of the second half of the second century, not before. For the Rabbis, some of the elements of the new heresiological discourse may have existed before the late second century, but I would suggest that the aggregate which produced rabbinic Judaism as such was first formulated in the Mishna at the very end of that century.

The new rabbinic regime of knowledge/power was epitomized—or perhaps one might better say "epistemized"—in the concept of Torah. This is the rabbinic ideology of an oral tradition communicated from Sinai, a bestowal of authority in which the Rabbis are represented as its sole heirs. Crucial to this epistemic shift in the locus of authority was the disenfranchisement of the previous holders of knowledge/power, the priests, and other traditional sources of knowledge, including perhaps women.[2] The production of a genealogy complemented this arrogation of authority by instituting a legitimating narrative of origin and succession, a story of orthodoxy perpetuated by transmission. Rabbinic Judaism thus was the end product of an extended struggle for hegemony.

It appropriated religious authority exclusively into the hands of a male elite devoted primarily to the study of Torah and genealogically normalized that elite's particular traditions and modes of interpretation. As we have seen above, the third element in the rabbinic "rule of faith" (in addition to assertion that there is resurrection and eternal life for the soul) is the assertion that the "Torah," by which is surely meant the Oral Torah, is from heaven. This article of faith constitutes, on my view, the necessity of asserting that the only source of legitimate, "orthodox" religious authority is in the institution of its House of Study. Just as, according to Le Boulluec, the notion of apostolic succession was for Justin a crucial invention for the promulgation of Christian orthodoxy, so too, I claim, it was for the development of rabbinic authority.

In his reconstruction of the earliest stages of Christian heresiology, Le Boulluec argues that the notion of apostolic succession, so crucial to the discourse of heresiology—at least in its early, Justinian and Irenaean form, to which the question of institutional authority is central[3]—is indebted to "the Jewish, i.e., rabbinic tradition of divinely inspired oral transmission."[4] As Le Boulluec writes, "Very probably through this enterprise they were able, by imitating Palestinian Rabbinism, which succeeded in securing around itself the unity of Judaism after the destruction of the Temple, to draw a list of 'succession' capable of guaranteeing the authority and validity of an ecclesiastical current."[5] Given the revisionist evaluation of rabbinic historical evidence that I adopt, I offer a friendly but pointed amendment to Le Boulluec's conclusion that "the Jewish example served once again to affirm the theme of the succession at the moment when the crucial difficulty was that of the divisions in the interior of Christianity, at the moment when Justin devised his heresiological scheme with the goal of controlling and limiting them [the divisions]. It is very likely that the effort of reconstituting and unifying Judaism accomplished by rabbinical orthodoxy was imitated by the Church, stimulated by the competitive desire to supplant once more the elder brother, a desire that the renewed vitality (of the elder brother) could not help but reinforce."[6] On the contrary, I would suggest that the heresiological techniques promulgated in the rabbinic texts are as likely to be a product of contact with Christianity as the opposite (perhaps even more so).

In both nascent rabbinism and nascent Christianity the notion of apostolic succession is a development out of the Hellenistic idea of a *diadoche*, a succession list, of recognized teachers beginning with the founding "father" of the school.[7] In both, however, this notion became transformed into a doctrine of succession of actual officeholders with the only claim to the truth of the tradition and the power to enforce that claim. The difference is parallel to that between the *École freudienne* of Paris and the "Freudian school" of psychoanalysts in the United States. The latter might very well invoke a *diadoche*,[8] but only the former would require a succession list of recognized holders of office. This progression of the idea of chain of succession is directly parallel, therefore, to the progression of the notion of *hairesis* itself discussed in the last chapter. This version of a chain of transmission in both Christianity and rabbinic Judaism thus forms an important part of the transformation of both into orthodoxies.

The rabbinic version of a *diadoche* cannot be dated before the promulgation of the Mishna at the beginning of the third century, thus well after Justin. If anything, the necessity for Judaism to constitute itself as an orthodoxy for the first time in its history came from the challenge of the younger brother. More plausibly in my view, both were equally participants in larger discursive or epistemic developments within their cultural and political context.[9] Le Boulluec can hardly be faulted for depending on what seems to have been the consensus of scholarship in rabbinic history, for most Jewish scholarship until today has assumed that, like other patterns of Jewish ecclesiology, the notion of a succession of holders of office that guarantees the authority of the dominant ecclesiastical group, the Rabbis, goes back to the first century and the Council of Yavneh, well before Justin.

Older Jewish historiography, which takes the Yavneh legends at face value, could have given Le Boulluec grounds to imagine that Justin's claim for apostolic succession as the central institution of Christian orthodoxy was significantly dependent on, in competition with, or in imitation of, an already existing rabbinic Jewish institution of orthodoxy: "à l'imitation du rabbinisme palestinien qui avait réussi à assurer autour de lui l'unité du judaïsme après la ruine du Temple."[10] Martin Goodman, like Shaye Cohen, to whose view he is otherwise so deeply opposed, yet reads the rabbinic sources that treat of Yavneh as being, indeed, about the first century. Only thus could he write: "The question I want to tackle in this paper is why some of *Josephus' contemporaries* in the nascent rabbinic schools of the land of Israel failed to take the same liberal stance as, in general, he did."[11] This stricture needs to be qualified: Both Cohen and Goodman are well aware, of course, that the evidence for Yavneh is much later and, therefore, ipso facto problematic. As Cohen writes: "All that is known of the 'synod' of Yavneh is based on the *disjecta membra* of the Mishnah and later works, all of which were redacted at least a century after the event."[12] Nevertheless, in his very next sentence, Cohen writes of the "actual contribution of Yavneh to Jewish history: the creation of a society which tolerates disputes without producing sects." The assumption underlying my work is rather different. Rather than attempting to reconstruct an obscure period out of the centuries-later legends that attest to it, I attempt to historicize the texts of a very well-attested period, namely the period(s) in which those legends about Yavneh and its consequences were produced.[13]

On my reading, at almost precisely the same time Justin was producing his notion of apostolic succession, a similar development was taking place within the institutional formation of the Rabbis. The two processes were, I would conjecture, somehow connected, and seemingly intimately so. But it is not at all obvious *how*, and certainly one cannot, on my hypothesis, simply ascribe the development within "Christianity" to influence from a putatively early "Jewish" history.

In the shift to the epistemic regime of the Rabbis, the production of a legitimating genealogy as the genealogical foundation of a heresiology began with the Mishna at the end of the second century, just as the similar process of genealogical canonization that Athanasius and his Nicaea were to bring to fruition began with Justin and Irenaeus in the second half of that century. Athanasius's *ek Pateron eis Patera* (from Fathers to Father) is strongly reminiscent of the Mishna's succession list, which represents the Oral Torah received by Moses on Sinai and codified at Yavneh by the "fathers [*avot*]" in the eponymous Mishnaic tractate called *Fathers*.

The famous introductory passage of the Tractate Avot[14] is the crucial rabbinic text for the invention of this legitimating genealogy. It has been insufficiently excavated, I think, for the history of rabbinic ecclesiology.[15] In a close reading of this text, we can see the creation of a rabbinic version of apostolic succession, a *diadoche* of the Rabbis.

The first chapter of Avot opens with the following text:[16]

Moses *received* the Torah at Sinai and *handed it down* to Joshua, and Joshua to the Elders, and the Elders to the Prophets, and the Prophets to the men of the Great Assembly. They said three things: Be deliberate in judgment, raise up many disciples, and make a fence around the Torah.

Notably lacking in this list, as Chava Boyarin has pointed out to me, are priests.[17] Since a large part of the attempted rabbinic takeover of religious power involved displacing the priests, this absence is highly telling, especially when we realize that prior succession lists of this type found in prerabbinic texts do include the priests. As Herr wrote, "The saying in Aboth I,1 is not an accurate description of what really happened. Rather, it appears that a conscious effort was made to remove the priests from the list, and insert the prophets in their stead."[18] The text can be seen, therefore, as an important political statement of sole legitimacy for the Rabbis and their Oral Torah, including its "fences," or extra stringencies. At this point, we are told that the tradition was passed on to the last of the survivors of the "Great Assembly," Rabbi Shim'on Ḥaṣṣadiq, who passed it on to his disciple Antigonos of Sokho. Each of these two is also quoted as having left behind three aphorisms. This is then followed by the description of the transmission of the "tradition" via five pairs of leaders in each generation. Each of the "pairs" "received" (קיבלו) the tradition from the ones who came before them. Each of these figures is also presented as uttering apophthegms. Various themes run through this text and its aphorisms. Moshe Kline has demonstrated compellingly that the text is tightly edited and the aphorisms are not presented randomly, nor do they have the random thematic content that we would expect to find were a simple collection of traditional materials before us. Rather they form a carefully constructed and composed "philosophical" tract— hinting at the connection between this text and the *diadoche* texts of the philosophical schools[19]—which culminates in the "pairship" of Hillel and Shammai, the disciples of Shemaiah and Avtalyon.

It is important to emphasize that already the legendary "men of the Great Assembly" are taken to have made a characteristically "Pharisaic" or even rabbinic statement: to "make a fence around the Torah," that is, to make human additions to the laws of the Torah in order that people will not inadvertently come to violate the strictures of the Law. This was one of the major issues between the Pharisees and other Jews, as is well attested in Matthew 12 and 15 and Josephus *Antiquities* 13 and 18. Just as the statements of the first pair, the "Yoses," also emphasize Pharisaic themes,[20] the words of the final pair emphasize Torah, the oral tradition, as the essential content of the transmission:

Hillel said: Be of the students of Aaron, loving peace, pursuing peace, loving one's fellow men and drawing them close to the Torah. . . .
Shammai said: Make regular your [study of the] Torah; say little and do much; and greet everyone cheerfully.

The discourses of both Hillel and Shammai are thus centered on the notion of Torah and the study of Torah. Indeed, one might easily suggest that the dominant cultural work of all of Tractate "Fathers" is the production of this theological and institutional notion. Kline concludes: "The reader has been empowered. He is no longer the student of an ancient tradition but a participant in the process of revelation. With the collapse of the institutions associated with the Temple, a new Man emerges, Rabbinic Man."[21] It is not so much a "new Man" who appears, however, nor a reader who is empowered, but a new leadership and a new form of power, which sharply excludes the ancient charismatics, the local practices of the Galilee (as manifest perhaps in the controversy texts of Matthew), the so-called People of the Land, the traditional local priesthood, and the discourse of women, as implied in the dictum not to speak with women. On reflection, in that sense, what emerges is rabbinic "Man" indeed.[22]

The chapter completes itself with three more Sages and their apophthegms. These last three Sages are ancestors of Rabbi Yehuda, the patriarch or prince,[23] editor of the Mishna, known as "Rabbi": namely, Rabban Gamaliel the Great, his son Shim'on, and *his* grandson, also Shim'on, who happens to be "Rabbi's" father. Indeed, the very next chapter of the text begins with an aphorism of this same "Rabbi" and then his son, Gamaliel III. The overall impression is, of course, of an unbroken tradition of authority from Moses at Mt. Sinai to the patriarchate and an unbroken connection between the text of the Written Torah given to Moses and the Oral Torah about to be presented in the Mishna.[24] The repeated theme of the study of Torah, the central religious innovation of the rabbinic movement, further enhances the impression of an unbroken chain of authority and authorization for this type of Judaism as the only legitimate one. Kline concludes after careful analysis: "It is clear that we are dealing with an extraordinarily complex composition. In light of the clear rules of organization . . . it is impossible to view our text as a chance collection or historical accretion. Someone put a great deal of effort into constructing this literary document."[25]

How we are to understand what was being effected in the construction of this document turns on the recognition and analysis of an insertion in the text. Scholars have long noted that the formal and literary continuation of the discourse of the Pairs is to be found in chapter 2, following the aphorism of Rabbi, when the text jumps back to Hillel[26] and then continues with Rabbi Yoḥanan ben Zakkai, who "received" from Hillel and Shammai. The list from Gamaliel I to Gamaliel III thus breaks the chronological order of the text and also does not include the formal markers, the verbs *transmitted* and *received*. It is thus apparent on purely formal grounds that two texts have been combined here, one that was marked by a chronological succession, including the verbs *receive* and *transmit*, and one, of the Gamalielite succession from Hillel, that did not include these formal markers of transmission and reception. Clearly, what we have here is a legitimating genealogy, as has been recognized, at least, since the early modern period.[27] The question—or questions—however, is what group is being legitimated, how, and why?

That it is the line of succession that leads up to Rabbi Yehuda, the editor of the text and thus consolidator of the rabbinic institution in its first phase, should come as no surprise. How and why, however, seem to allow for different interpretations than the ones currently available in the literature.

Although John Glucker grants that "it is generally agreed that the tractate in the form we have it is already a conflation of a number of earlier versions, put together and rearranged by R. Judah," he does not take seriously enough the late second-century context of the production of this text. Thus, Glucker accepts the historiographical practice of Gedaliah Alon,[28] according to which we can supposedly reconstruct actual events at Yavneh: its founding by Rabbi Yohanan ben Zakkai while the Gamalielites (true successors to Hillel) remained in Jerusalem to fight the Romans;[29] the execution of Shim'on ben Gamaliel by the Romans; the transfer to Yavneh of Gamaliel II, Shim'on's son, after the final defeat; and the ousting of Rabbi Yohanan ben Zakkai by popular acclaim.[30] As Glucker puts it: "But attempts were still made by his followers—and they included many, if not most, of the greatest sages of those generations—to oust out [*sic*] the Gamalielic Patriarch. It was only Rabbi Judah [that is, Rabbi Yehuda, the editor of the Mishna] who finally succeeded in overcoming all opposition and uniting the conflicting parties by the sheer force of his personality, which combined learning and sanctity with authority and a knowledge of the ways of the world and its rules."[31]

Alon's reconstruction, as adopted nearly entirely by Glucker,[32] swallows whole the patriarchal power play of Rabbi Yehuda by interpreting the Yohanan ben Zakkai line as the "usurper." Here is Glucker's formulation:

The original succession was, one assumes, from Moses to Hillel and Shammai—they, after all, represent the last generation of sages of Temple times proper, when the dispute with the Sadducees was still going on. To this, the name of Rabbi Yochanan was added as the *sole* successor of this pair by members of Yochanan's school, thus disputing the rival claim of Gamaliel, and the succession in this extended form—Moses to Yochanan—was incorporated in the earlier versions of the Mishna, stemming from followers of the same school. When Rabbi Judah came to edit what was to become the final (and now the only extant) version of the Mishna, he found this succession as part of that version of *Aboth* which he included, with his own additions, in his Mishna. Being a man of peace, who strove to end the controversy between the two factions, he did nothing to change this list, including Rabban Yochanan's succession to both Hillel and Shammai. This was his concession to the other party.[33]

The implication of this is, therefore, that it is the text Rabbi Yehuda found before him that represents an attempt at usurpation of the claims of an existing and legitimate Gamalielic Patriarchate[34] as the successor to Hillel, also taken to be patriarch.[35] Rabbi Yehuda, however, with almost Aaronic irenicism, chose not to challenge this usurpation and did not restore the "original" text and political situation, within which his family and only his are the legitimate successors to the paradosis and the patriarchate.

However, when we look at the text, it is clear that it is the Gamaliel-to-Yehuda line, the patriarchal succession list, that is the textual addendum in a succession list from Hillel and Shammai to Rabban Yohanan ben Zakkai.

Glucker reads this as "a very delicate and tactful compromise, which reveals Rabbi Judah at his best, quietly and peacefully—but not meekly—asserting his own authority and claims, without obliterating the tradition of the other side."[36] Rabbi Yehuda's forcible introduction of his own genealogy into someone else's is thus glossed as a quiet and peaceful compromise, rather than a near-violent preemption and appropriation. The reason for this counterintuitive interpretation is, once more, that Glucker (like Alon and most historians of rabbinic Judaism) has assumed that the patriarchate is an ancient institution going back to Yavneh itself, to the "real" Yavneh, in fact, even before, to Jerusalem under the siege. Rabban Gamaliel and his line are, therefore, the "authentic" patriarchs, perhaps even the literal descendants of Hillel,[37] and the whole meaning of the text has to be contorted in order to make sense of this putative history.

The second explanation for the insertion of the Gamaliel-to-Gamaliel lineage in the text, on this reading, is that Rabbi Yehuda succeeded, in Glucker's words, in unifying the two striving power sources, "through the force of his personality," as well as his vaunted "saintliness." However, on the conservative methodological principle that I have adopted, following my teacher Saul Lieberman, that texts are to be read in the context of their redaction, there is little reason to assume the institution of the patriarchate as such before Rabbi Yehuda himself. The purpose of much of the Yehudan literary production would be precisely to give a genealogy and legitimation to his line, over against the counter line of the Pharisaic teachers whose own succession ran from Moses to Rabban Yoḥanan.[38] The intruder or usurper here is the patriarch, almost iconically symbolized by the intrusion in the text. The reason for the highly unusual (for the Mishna) inclusion of Rabbi Yehuda's son is also now clear, for it is in the transmission of authority from the founder to the first son that the true existence of a dynasty is established.[39] On the other hand, Rabbi Yehuda could hardly expunge Rabban Yoḥanan from the *diadoche*, since virtually the whole Mishna is based on the statements of his disciples, so his "delicate compromise" alone hardly establishes him as a man of peace.

An important point that Glucker does not take into account is that the very identification of the pairs as being composed of a patriarch, a נשיא, and a president of the court, that is, as the "officeholders," so important to his reading, is also only an artifact of the latest editing of the Mishna. It does not appear in Avot at all, and in the only place where it does occur, it is tacked on as a glossing coda to a text that makes no mention of it otherwise (Ḥagiga 2:2).[40] It seems plausible to assume that it is an addition at the redactional stage of the Mishna from Rabbi Yehuda's time, toward the end of the second century or even early in the third. It cannot therefore be accounted for, as Glucker does, as providing the requisite institutional counterclaim to the Temple power base of the Sadducees.[41]

The most plausible inference would seem to be that, far from the House of Gamaliel being the legitimate successors to an institutionalized patriarchate that goes back to Hillel, if not still further, it is a relatively new power source within Jewish society—empowered, perhaps, by its connection with the principate[42]—that, joining itself, not without struggle, to the prestigious if not hegemonic Yoḥanine school tradition, was finally able to launch the ultimate establishment of rabbinic Judaism as the orthodoxy of the Jewish people, an establishment that was, nevertheless, to take centuries in the formation.[43] As Shaye Cohen has noted, "[T]he connection between the patriarchate and kingship was not made until the time of Rabbi himself."[44] Prior to that, the Gamalielites were apparently simply leaders of a school, no more, no less so than the disciples of Rabban Yoḥanan ben Zakkai.[45]

In the text, this new institution strives to legitimate itself with a double genealogy. First of all, Rabbi Yehuda provides himself with a chain of succession going back several generations in his family, including the insinuation that they are, moreover, direct descendants of Hillel. Second, this patriarchal line is grafted onto the paradosis of the Yoḥanine teachers and Rabbis. The glossing of these "pairs" as officeholders is thus a distinct anachronism, the product of a much later period when the patriarchate existed as a political entity.[46] Both the "grafting" and the glossing are precisely the sort of "fracture points" in the text that allow for historical access to the social conflicts outside of the text.[47] As Hall has remarked in quite another context, "If there existed two competing mythical variants, then there must also have existed two social groups for whom these genealogies were meaningful."[48]

Contrary to Glucker's Alon-based interpretation,[49] in which he sees the Yoḥanines as the usurpers in a legitimate political succession of officeholders, I see the Gamalielites as interlopers in the dominant school tradition of the Yoḥanines, including the leading figures of later rabbinic Judaism and especially Rabbi Akiva.[50] Both of the terms used in the Avot text, *received* (קיבל) and *transmitted* (מסר), have precise equivalents in the Greek Jewish literature of the first century, including various documents in the gospels and Paul. As Albert Baumgarten has perspicaciously noted, "the terms *paradosis* [transmission] and *paralambanein* [reception] are counterparts depicting the process of transmission from two different perspectives. The terms discussed thus far are from Greek sources, but the Semitic originals behind the Greek translations are readily recovered. *Paradosis* must reflect a form of the root *mśr* [transmit], *paralambanein* of the root *qbl* [receive],"[51] or, in other words, the precise two verb forms that we find in the Mishna in *Avot*, but not, as has been noted before, in the list running from Gamaliel I to Gamaliel III, the son of Rabbi Yehuda. Without the Gamaliel to Gamaliel pericope, we have the *diadoche* of the *paradosis* from Moses to Rabbi Yoḥanan ben Zakkai, the post-Destruction "receiver" of the tradition. Given that the text is intruded upon by a succession list beginning with Gamaliel and culminating in Rabbi's successful transmission to his son, everything points to him, the redactor of the Mishna, after all, as the composer of this text, the one who forcibly incorporated the patriarchal institution into the Yoḥanine succession of teachers and the one who sought, thereby, to "project himself as in the line of the Diadoche,"[52] the "apostolic" succession. It is in that insertion, which presumably took place at the time of the editing and promulgation of the Mishna by Rabbi Yehuda, that the *paradosis* and the *paralambanein* of the earlier tradition became combined with the political institution of the patriarchate, thus producing for the first time the notion that there is only one legitimate source of Torah for the Jews, that is, the notion that I have been documenting in the previous chapter. Thus the discourse of rabbinic Jewish orthodoxy was invented, which is not to suggest that at that time it became hegemonic, any more than Justin's discourse of orthodoxy or even Irenaeus's became hegemonic in their time.

One possible way of putting the known scraps of data together into a narrative and thus to placing these developments in a larger social context would be to imagine that it was the group known as the "Scribes"—which presumably traced its own genealogy back to Ezra, the Scribe who read the Torah, "translating it and giving the sense; so they understood the reading" (Nehemiah 8:8)— who introduced Torah study into Judaism as the central cultic practice, as Neusner has suggested. They may very speculatively be identified with the Yoḥanine group.[53] This larger perspective can perhaps illuminate the problem of the dual inscription of the origins of the Passover Haggada as recorded in the tannaitic literature. On the one hand, the Haggada itself includes a story about Rabbi Akiva and his fellows sitting in Bene Berak and telling about the Exodus from Egypt for the entire night; on the other hand, the Tosefta Pasḥa 10:12[54] tells us that Rabban Gamaliel and his fellows spent the entire night in Lydda discussing the laws of sacrifice of the Passover. The omission of any activity other than reciting the laws so amazed some medieval commentators that they emended the text and added the words "and the Exodus from Egypt" in the tradition about Rabban Gamaliel.[55] However, if we assume that the Gamalielic practice represented the Pharisaic tradition, and the one of Akiva and his associates the "Scribal" one, we can get around this problem.[56] According to Josephus himself, the Pharisees were characterized by a faithful, even slavish, devotion to tradition, without discussion or debate: "They follow the guidance of that which their doctrine has selected and transmitted as good, attaching the chief importance to the observance of those commandments which it has seen fit to dictate to them. They show respect and deference to their elders, nor do they rashly presume to contradict their proposals" (XVIII).[57] This description is congruent with the passage in Avot that describes Rabbi Eli'ezer as a "limed cistern that never loses a drop" (2:8), as well as the declaration that this Rabbi never said a word that he had not heard from his teachers. Justin Martyr still refers to the Pharisees as a Jewish sectarian, even heretical, group, a *hairesis*. According to my conjecture, the Pharisees, in Justin's time, the mid–second century, had not yet been fully amalgamated into the grand coalition of late antique rabbinic hegemony, even though seemingly their religiosity was not irreconcilable with that of the Scribes. Each group practiced the Passover according to its own custom.[58]

Counter to the view of Glucker et al.[59] then, it seems most likely that the earlier form of the text that appears in Avot was simply a list of teachers and teachings, meant to authorize a community of teachers, a school, a *hairesis*, by tracing their genealogy back to Moses and Sinai and down to Rabban Yoḥanan ben Zakkai, the putative founder of the academy at Yavneh. There is no reason to imagine, on that version of a succession list, that there could not be other equally legitimate lines of tradition, other teachers who also could trace their legitimate intellectual lineage back to Moses. There is no warrant whatever for seeing "a succession of recognized holders of office"—producing the singularity of the legitimate apostolic line—being written into this text until the time of Rabbi Yehuda and the redaction of the Mishna, when the gloss in Tractate Ḥagiga was added.[60] The institutional struggle implied by such an effort at legitimation, whether against Sadducees or within nascent "rabbinic" orthodoxy itself, is best located at the time when the Gamalielic line was inserted into the *diadoche* of the Yoḥanines. This point is supported as well by a tannaitic *baraita* in the Babylonian Talmud which records at Ketubbot 103b that when Rabbi Yehuda the Patriarch was about to die, he avowed in an oral testament: "Shim'on my son will be the Sage and Gamaliel my son will be the Patriarch." Although the Babylonian Talmud itself seems not to understand the phrase, interpreting it as if it read "Shim'on my son is a sage," it is clear from the context that two offices are being mentioned, particularly because the third clause also indicates an officeholder. In my view, this represents a memory of the same institutionalization of double leadership, scholarly and political, of the rabbinic corporation that is read backward in the Yehudan gloss that indicates that of the two "pairs," one was the patriarch and one the president of the court.[61] Since I have argued above that this transformation, this institutionalization, is one vital sign of an orthodoxy, this provides further corroboration of the thesis developed in the previous chapter that the notion of rabbinic orthodoxy came into being with the promulgation of the Mishna.

Lee Levine writes: "The sages looked favorably upon R. Judah's standing. In addition to pride in their colleague's [sic] achievement, the status of the rabbinic class within Jewish society at large was undoubtedly enhanced."[62] I certainly agree with the latter proposition. I would only, therefore, slightly modify Levine's formulation in a somewhat more skeptical direction. Not so much pride and collegiality, but pragmatic recognition of the patriarch's power was at stake. The Mishnaic "apostolic succession list" accordingly would stem, on this possible reconstruction, from the transformation of the chain of tradition of a Hellenistic philosophical school into the institution for the protection of the faith that the concurrently developed discourse within "orthodox" Christian circles originated from as well. Le Boulluec was thus correct to link the phenomena within the two "religions" as homologous, but it is impossible to substantiate the line of influence from the Rabbis to the Christians that he (and Bickerman) argued for.

The overall hypothesis suggested by these considerations is that the rabbinic movement should be essentially considered on the model of a Hellenistic philosophical school: the Rabbis, as they articulated their self-understanding in Avot, so perceived and portrayed themselves. At about the time that Christianity began to transform itself from a "collection of philosophical schools" (in Alan Brent's evocative term) into an orthodoxy, the Rabbis were making the same attempt. This political exercise is iconically symbolized in Avot via the near-violent introjection of the patriarchal line into the chain of tradition of the rabbinic *hairesis.*

The appropriation of the *paradosis* and the *diadoche* and their promotion to an apostolic succession list of officeholders, culminating in the patriarchal dynasty, at the time of the redaction of the Mishna—in short, the invention of rabbinic orthodoxy—is the Jewish parallel to the intervention of Justin, Irenaeus, and their successors at the same time. The transformation of both nascent Christianity and nascent Judaism from groups of sects—collections of philosophical schools, as Josephus had described Judaism and Brent, third-century Christianity[63]—into orthodox churches with their heretical others would be seen on this reading as part of the same sociocultural process and practice.

What I hope to have achieved in the foregoing two chapters is to show that very similar processes were taking place in the formative moments of that particular kind of Christianity that would be known as orthodoxy and that particular kind of Judaism that would be known as rabbinic. Out of structures resembling most closely the Hellenistic philosophical schools, both parties de-veloped notions of exclusive possession of the truth, guaranteed by a privileged and singular transmission from an origin, and declared any other version of Judaeo-Christianity to be heresy. Moreover, if the methodological approach that I adopt is at all compelling, there are no grounds for believing that the rabbinic developments are earlier than the Christian ones; indeed, the opposite may fre-quently have been the case. I propose to think of these two formations of nas-cent and would-be orthodoxies as produced discursively out of the system of Judaeo-Christianity in very similar ways and, moreover, very plausibly (but not ineluctably) in some kind of interaction with each other, something on the order of the development of Enlightenment or Romanticism in Europe. Whether or not the last point can be maintained, there certainly seems to be in-terpretative profit in studying these closely related developments together. In the next section of the book, the same pattern will be traced but not, this time, on the level of institutions but rather on the level of theology. Building initially on a reading of Justin already adumbrated above, I shall try to show that a theo-logical difference, acceptance or rejection of Logos theology, that was once not the marker of a difference between Judaism and Christianity was made to be so via the technologies of heresiology.

PART II

The Crucifixion of the Logos: How Logos Theology Became Christian

The Intertextual Birth of the Logos: The Prologue to John as a Jewish Midrash

As we have seen, theological discourse, the establishment of "ortho-dox" doctrine, was the major discursive vehicle for the making of a difference on both the side of nascent Christian orthodoxy and nascent rabbinic orthodoxy. There is no reason to imagine, however, that "rabbinic Judaism" ever became the popular hegemonic form of Jewish religiosity among the "People of the Land," and there is good reason to believe the opposite. Throughout the rabbinic pe-riod, there is evidence of a vital form of Judaism that was not only extrarabbinic but which the Rabbis explicitly named as a heresy, the belief in "Two Powers in Heaven," in our terms, Logos theology. This doctrine became for the Rabbis, as it had been for orthodox Christian writers from Justin on—from the exactly op-posite point of view—the touchstone of orthodoxy. Some Jews, perhaps even most Jews, resisted the efforts of Justin to appropriate the Logos exclusively for Christianity, as well as the efforts of the Rabbis to "collude" in that exclusion. For those Jews, even in Palestine, the Logos (named *memra* "word" in their spoken Aramaic) remained a pivotally important theological being. In this and the coming chapters, I shall be turning to a detailed study of the construction of rabbinic Jewish identity as orthodoxy via the instrument of the heresy of Two Powers in Heaven, understood as the rabbinic part of a virtual (not actual) "conspiracy" with the writers of Christian orthodoxy to make the difference be-tween the two.

In the earliest stages of their development—indeed I suggest until the end of the fourth century, if we consider all of their varieties and not just the nas-cent "orthodox" ones—Judaism and Christianity were phenomenologically in-distinguishable as entities, not merely in the conventionally accepted sense, that Christianity was a Judaism, but also in the sense that differences that were in the fullness of time to constitute the very basis for the distinction between the "two religions" ran through and not between the nascent groups of Jesus-following Jews and Jews who did not follow Jesus. Thus, one of the most characteristic dif-ferences between Judaism and Christianity as we know them is the belief in or denial of complexity within the godhead, but in these early centuries there were non-Christian Jews who believed in God's Word, Wisdom, or even Son as a "second God," while there were believers in Jesus who insisted that the three persons of the Trinity were only names for different manifestations of one person. The practices by which these differences *within* became reconstituted as differences *between* represent an important part of the narrative construction this book attempts. Indeed, the invention of heresy, on my reading, pivoted on the perceived necessity of making that difference, in order to make sense of the fact that there were distinct groups of *Christianoi* and *Ioudaioi* at various places, surely by the middle of the second century and almost certainly before that, as well.

In the fate of the Logos in Judaic and Christian theology, we can examine a doctrine that was originally shared but finally became central to opposing self-definitions on either side, and through it we can trace the mutual imbrication, definition, and making of a difference this involved. One of the clearest symbols of what most Christian and Jewish scholars have taken to be the early and total separation of Christianity from Judaism has been the centrality of Logos theology in Christianity from a very early date, a Logos theology that has been thought to have little to do with "authentic" or "proper" Palestinian Judaism.[1] In 1962, J. A. T. Robinson noted that much in the Gospel of John seems to indicate a close connection with first-century Palestinian realia, but that "it could still be argued that the Logos theology (for which the [Dead Sea Scrolls] provide no parallel) locates the Gospel both in place and time at a considerable remove from the Palestinian scene which it purports to describe."[2] For Robinson, Logos theology must be understood to be the product of a Christian writer far removed in place and time from Palestinian Judaism, indeed to be the product of an influx of non-Judaic and anti-Judaic thought.

The biblical scholar's sentiment is echoed by historians of dogma. Thus, Basil Studer:

From the socio-political point of view Christianity fairly soon broke away from Judaism. Already by about 130 the final break had been effected. This certainly contributed to an even greater openness towards religious and cultural influences from the Greco-Roman environment. Not without reason, then, it is exactly at that time that the rise of antijudaistic and hellenophile gnostic trends is alleged. Christian theology began gradually to draw away from Judaic tendencies. . . . In the course of separation from the Synagogue and of rapprochement with the pagan world, theology itself became more open towards the thinking of antiquity with its scientific methods. This is particularly evident in the exegesis of Holy Scripture in which the chasm separating it from rabbinic methods broadened and deepened, whereas the ancient art of interpretation as it was exercised especially in Alexandria gained the upper hand.[3]

Studer's picture is a fairly typical one. Even as sophisticated a commentator as James D. G. Dunn, who "gets it" that "the parting of the ways, if we can already so speak, was at this point also as much a parting of the ways *within* the new movement as *between* Christianity and Judaism, or better, as within Judaism,"[4] still feels moved to insist that "after the second revolt [132–35] the separation of the main bodies of Christianity and Judaism was clear-cut and final, whatever interaction there continued to be at the margins."[5] Nor is this view confined to Christian scholars. As one leading Israeli historian has put it: "With the Bar Kokhba rising, the final rift between Judaism and Christianity was complete."[6] To get some sense of the theological stakes (very ancient ones) behind this account from the Christian point of view, one can examine Eusebius, who, in his *Church History*, writes of an absolute break in the Jerusalem Church that would have occurred at that very time between the "bishops of the circumcision" before the revolt and the absolutely new episcopate from the Gentiles after it (E.H. 4.5).[7]

The legend of the Jerusalem church's flight to Pella during the revolt might even be read as part of this ideological construction of absolute breaks and partings of the ways (E.H. 3.5).[8] Frend, for instance, marks the flight to Pella of the Jerusalem church, thus absenting themselves from the heroic fight against the Romans, as a "momentous step" which damaged the Palestinian church "beyond repair."[9] However, the "flight" of Rabbi Yohanan to Yavneh at precisely the same moment as the story of the Pella flight, which in talmudic legend founds the rabbinic movement, was structurally identical to the also legendary Christian escape, and thus neither need have constituted a break with "the Jewish Nation." According to Galit Hasan-Rokem: "The story of the exit from the city [of Rabbi Yohanan] as rescue reflects . . . traditions which are common to the folk narrative of the Jews which appears in rabbinic literature and the folk literature of Jewish groups who were diverse from the culture which is canonized by the Rabbis. Also with respect to the ancient Jerusalem Christian church, it has been reported in later sources, that its remnants abandoned the city at the time of the destruction and found refuge in the city of Pella in Transjordan. *In both cases, the story of the egress from the city took on the meaning of legitimation and authorization for the founding of a religious center outside of Jerusalem after the destruction of the city.*"[10] In Hasan-Rokem's reading, therefore, the flight to Pella is not evidence for separation between the Jews and Christians, but rather the opposite. Rabbi Yohanan, after all, also explicitly opposed and ran away from the fight of the Zealots against the Romans and was hardly seen as a traitor by later "orthodox" Judaism. This event cannot, therefore, be cited as evidence for a break between Christianity and the Jewish people.[11] This tradition can be read as much as articulating an orthodox Christian break with the "heretical" Jewish

Christians as signifying a break between those and the Jews. As support for this interpretation, I would offer Epiphanius's (Pan. 30:2) notice that Ebion himself came from the Pella Church.[12]

Reexamining the historical trajectories of Logos theology has consequences for historiographic representation of the "parting of the ways." If anything, this investigation will raise the distinct possibility that Christian theology, far from "gradually draw[ing] away from Judaic tendencies," actually maintained a *more conservative* Judaic approach to the doctrine of God than did the Rabbis, and that it is they—if anyone—who drew away from earlier Jewish theology. In other words, I hope to show in the next three chapters that, on the theological level, the chimerical parting of the ways is the production of a juridical border line, the work of the heresiologists whose traces we have been following in the first section of the book.

Granted that in some areas, Asia Minor almost certainly being among them, Gentile converts began to outnumber Christian Jews at a fairly early date, and that they brought with them, almost inevitably, "hellenophile" and then "antijudaistic" tendencies,[13] however, the lion's share of the Hellenic thinking of early Christianity—and most centrally, Logos theology—was an integral part of the first-century Jewish world, including Palestine. Jewish theology had for centuries been "open to the thinking of antiquity"—whether Persian or Graeco-Roman—and the binary opposition of Judaism and Hellenism (as well as the binary opposition between Palestinian and Hellenistic Judaism) requires major rethinking. As I have pointed out above,[14] Judaism is from the very beginning a Hellenistic form of culture.[15] As remarked by Rebecca Lyman: "Justin's appeal to the ultimate authority of divine revelation in prophetic texts or to Jesus as the Logos, the original truth sought by human philosophers, is confrontational, but it is potentially powerful precisely because of its *Hellenistic, i.e. Greek and Jewish*, lineage in establishing truth through antiquity and transcendence."[16]

As I shall read the texts, Logos theology (and thence trinitarianism) emerges as a difference between Judaism and Christianity only through the activities of heresiologists on both sides of the divide. In the first and second centuries, there were Jewish non-Christians who firmly held theological doctrines of a second God, variously called Logos, Memra, Sophia, Metatron, or Yahoel; indeed, perhaps most of the Jews did so at the time.[17] There were also significant and powerful Christian voices who claimed that any distinction of persons within the godhead constituted ditheism. In short, the vertical axis—believers in Jesus versus nonbelievers in Jesus—did not form the boundary between believers in Logos theology and deniers of Logos theology. Rather, that distinction, like a horizontal axis, crossed through both categories defined by the vertical axis. Rotating this axis from the horizontal to the vertical was, as I shall try to establish, the work of the heresiologists of both communities, and by the end of our period it had become the marker of the theological difference between Judaism and Christianity. It is in this sense that heresiology is necessarily a part of the construction of Judaism and Christianity as two religions.

The Logos of Scripture

"The divinized or hypostasized Logos . . . is collaboratively invented in antiquity by writers who are (with a few minor exceptions) readers of Genesis 1 and Proverbs 8. . . . From the Gospel of John to the Gospel of Truth, from the Tripartite Tractate to Clement's Alexandrian trilogy of the Word, from Justin to Philo to Origen, Logos emerges in the dialogical play of scriptural interpretation."[18] With this observation Virginia Burrus firmly locates the beginnings of Logos theology in the complex, intertextual scriptural world of all the multiplex communities of post-Israelite religion, those that we today refer to as Jews as well as those that we today call Christians, or "Gnostics." By contrast, the dominant interpretative tradition concerning the Fourth Gospel has effectively denied any dialogical play of scriptural interpretation in that text and has sometimes read it, and its Logos, as the most "un-Jewish" in all the New Testament canon.[19] As Dunn puts it, "Only in the Fourth Gospel do we find claims on the lips of Jesus which could be understood as subversive of the unity of God." This, for Dunn, marks a subversion of Judaism and a parting of the ways. Burrus's observation challenges this topos that the Fourth Gospel is essentially and fundamentally not Jewish in its Christology and, along with it, the reigning interpretations of the Fourth Gospel and its relation to "Judaism."

On the one hand, the prevalent line of reading takes the Prologue to be simply an example and continuation of a scriptural genre, the hymn to Wisdom, and not, therefore, as either exegetical or dialogical.[20] The most extreme version of this approach, that of Bultmann, explicitly denies any genuine "Jewish" role even in the Wisdom myths that allegedly provide the Fourth Gospel with its literary models and theological antecedents.[21] The prevailing (and much less severe) consensus of this school of thought, however, is exemplified by Eldon J. Epp, who specifies an actual historical connection to explain the evident parallels between the Prologue and the Wisdom hymns: "The clear answer (developed by J. Rendell Harris in 1917) is that a model [for the Prologue] was provided by the *Wisdom hymns* of the OT and the Apocrypha. That is, the Johannine hymn to the Logos was inspired, in content, and in form, generally at least, by the hymns about or by personified Wisdom, such as those in Prov 8:1–36; Job 28:12–28; Sir 24:1–34; Bar 3:9–4:4; and Wis 7:22–10:21."[22]

On the other hand, two scholars who have explicitly related the Prologue to John, and thus its Logos doctrine, to Jewish methods of scriptural interpretation have explicitly excluded Proverbs and Wisdom from the conversation. As early as 1969, Peder Borgen provided such an understanding.[23] According to Borgen, the Prologue is a homily on the beginning of Genesis. Borgen shows how the first five verses are a "targumic" paraphrase of Genesis 1:1–5, while the rest of the Prologue is a tripartite expansion of this paraphrase, making clear that the midrash of the Logos is to be applied to the appearance of Jesus Christ.[24] More recently, Nicola Denzey has returned to this issue.[25] Denzey notes that, whereas scholars have for decades paid attention to the connection between the narrative aspect of the Prologue and "Gnostic" texts, such as the *Trimorphic Protennoia*,[26] with their "threefold salvific descent of God's co-agent into the world to redeem those who were able to recognize their divine origins," they have been puzzled about how to account for this nexus.[27] Moreover, the notion that "Gnosticism" has little to do with "Judaism" has become highly problematic in the intervening years: "Instead, scholars tend to locate early Christian heterodox thought within intellectual continuities of the ancient world, particularly within Hellenistic Jewish philosophy and exegesis."[28] Denzey emphasizes that first, we need not have recourse to "Gnosticism" in order to explain the similarities between the texts; second, we need not assume that they are both dependent on a shared body of Wisdom traditions; and third, the texts are best understood as a "soteriological myth based upon a specific, traditional way of reading and interpreting Genesis 1."[29]

I find Denzey's analysis very helpful; however, in line with the general direction of thinking in this book, I would suggest that the term "Hellenistic" in Denzey's formulation is misleading, implying as it does that there is a kind of Jewish wisdom-thinking of exegesis that is not Hellenistic. I think, moreover, that this unexamined opposition, as well as relative unfamiliarity with certain aspects of ancient Jewish homiletics, have partly misdirected her otherwise very illuminating inquiry. Thus, she essentially separates the Prologue (and the *Protennoia*) from any connection with the Wisdom texts: "The *Trimorphic Protennoia* and Johannine Prologue remain as representative examples not of a Wisdom tradition, but rather of a distinct 'Word tradition' which shared sapiental literature's dependency on Genesis yet interpreted it rather differently. This tradition attributed a creative force not to God's hypostasized forethought or Wisdom, but to his Voice or Word."[30] To be sure, as Denzey remarks, "scholars have consistently failed to consider Genesis' impact on the *Trimorphic Protennoia*";[31] they have also generally not explored in any depth the connection between Genesis 1 and John 1.[32] Denzey is right to emphasize that the Prologue is an interpretation of the first verses of Genesis and not a Wisdom Hymn, but for Denzey the "gaps" in the Genesis account are filled in the Prologue (and the *Trimorphic Protennoia*) with "philosophical ideas" and not with co-read scriptural texts.[33] This follows, I suggest, from the unhappy opposition between the Hellenistic and presumably non-Hellenistic varieties of Judaism. This allows her to reach the unnecessary conclusion that the proof of close connections between the Prologue (and the *Trimorphic Protennoia*) and Genesis adds up to a disproof of connection with Wisdom literature.[34] In a sense, however, she is reacting to and reproducing the terms of a binary opposition already set by Harris, who insists that his argument in favor of a Wisdom/Proverbs intertext for the Prologue disproves connection with Genesis.[35] I wish to argue that both are right; the Logos of the Prologue—like the theological Logos in general, in accord with the view of Burrus cited above—is the product of a scriptural reading of Genesis 1 and Proverbs 8 together. This reading will bear out my conclusion that nothing in Logos theology as a doctrine of God indicates or even implies a particularly Christian as opposed to generally Jewish, including Christian, kerygma. "The dialogical play of scriptural interpretation" to which Burrus refers is acted out on the stage of Jewish traditional hermeneutics, on which non-Jesus Jews, Jesus Jews, and those exotic Jews/Christians that we call Gnostics all had a part in the play.

In order to see this, however, we must pay attention to the formal characteristics of midrash as a mode of reading Scripture. One of the most characteristic forms of midrash is a homily on a pericope, or extract from the Pentateuch that invokes, explicitly or implicitly, texts from either the Prophets or the Hagiographa (specifically, very frequently Psalms, Song of Songs, or Wisdom literature) as the intertextual framework of ideas and language that is used to interpret and expand the Pentateuchal text being preached.[36] This hermeneutical practice is founded on a theological notion of the oneness of Scripture as a self-interpreting text, especially on the notion that the latter books are a form of interpretation of the Five Books of Moses. That is, it is a scriptural, indeed, an interscriptural practice. Gaps are not filled with philosophical ideas but with allusions to or citations of other texts. The first five verses of the Prologue to the Fourth Gospel fit this form nearly perfectly. The verses being preached are the opening verses of Genesis, and the text that lies in the background as hermeneutic intertext is Proverbs 8:22–31. The primacy of Genesis as exegeted text explains why we have here "Logos" and not "Sophia," without necessitating the assumption of a "Word" tradition of interpretation of Genesis in alleged conflict with a "Wisdom" tradition.[37] In an intertextual interpretative practice such as a midrash, imagery and language may be drawn from one intertext, but the controlling language of the discourse is naturally the text that is being exegeted and preached, not its intertextual congeners. The preacher of the Prologue to John had to speak of Logos here, because his homiletical effort is directed at the opening verses of Genesis, with their majestic utterance, "And God said: Let there be light, and there was light." It is the "saying" of God that produces the light, and indeed through this saying everything was made that was made.[38]

Philo, like others, identifies Sophia and the Logos as a single entity.[39] Consequently, nothing could be more natural than for a preacher to draw from the Wisdom hymns, especially the canonical Proverbs, the figure, epithets, and qualities of the *deuteros theos*, the companion of God and agent of God in creation, whereas for the purposes of interpreting Genesis to focus on the linguistic side of the coin, the Logos, which is alone mentioned explicitly in that text. In other words, the text being exegeted is Genesis, therefore *the Word*; the text from which the exegetical material is drawn is Proverbs, hence the characteristics of *Wisdom*:

1. In the beginning was the Word,
   And the Word was with God,
2. And the Word was God.
   He was in the beginning with God.
3. All things were made through him, and without him was not anything made that was made.
4. In him was life, and the life was the light of men.
5. The light shines in the darkness, and the darkness did not receive it.[40]

One of the most important observations that has been made about this text is that its formal structure, the envelope structure of the first two verses, is highly biblical (i.e., Hebraic) in its use of chiasm[41] and *gradatio*. This *gradatio*, "In the beginning was the *Word*, and the *Word* was God," can easily be accounted for as an expansion of the formal rhetorical pattern found in the first verse of Genesis: "In the beginning God created the heaven and the *earth*, and the *earth* was without form and void."[42] The assertion that the Word was with God is easily related to Proverbs 8:30, "Then I was beside him,"[43] and even to Wisdom in Solomon 9:9, "With thee is wisdom." As is frequently the case in rabbinic midrash, the gloss on the verse being interpreted is dependent on a later biblical text that is alluded to but not explicitly cited. The Wisdom texts, I propose, especially Proverbs 8, had become topoi in the Jewish interpretative tradition of Genesis 1. Although, paradoxically, John 1:1–5 is our earliest example of this, the form is so abundant in late antique Jewish hermeneutics that, unless we are prepared to assume evidence here for direct Johannine influence on the midrash, I think it can best be read as the product of a common tradition shared by (some) Jesus Jews and (some) non-Jesus Jews. Thus the operation of John 1:1 can be compared with the (to be sure, quite a bit later) Palestinian Targum to this very verse, which translates "In the beginning" by "With Wisdom God created,"[44] clearly also alluding to the Proverbs passage. "Beginning" is read in the Targums sometimes as Wisdom, *ḥukmǝta*, and sometimes as the Logos, *memra*: By a Beginning—Wisdom—God created.[45] To this midrash should be compared the famous Latin version of John 8:25, so beautifully read by Augustine as "Your Word, the Beginning who also speaks to us,"[46] once again reading "Beginning" twice. As Augustine paraphrases this tradition: "Wisdom is 'the Beginning': and it is in that Beginning that You made heaven and earth." For Augustine, as well, it was clear that Word and Wisdom were synonymous parallels.

We can now understand the role of the Wisdom hymns in the production of this text quite differently. They are not the formal model for the Prologue to John, but, being the intertext for the Logos midrash of these five verses, they provide access to a pre-Christian world of ideas in which Wisdom was personified and characterized in ways that are very similar to the Logos of Logos theology. They thus offer evidence that the latter is not a specifically or exclusively Christian product, but a common "Jewish" theologoumenon, or theological conception, which was later identified with the Christ.[47]

In this interpretation, the opening proem of the Prologue is a shared or Koine "Jewish" nonchristological midrashic expansion of Genesis 1:1–5 along the lines of Logos/Memra theology, followed by a christological (by which I mean only an identification of the Logos with the specific figure of Jesus, the Christ) interpretation and expansion of this inherited midrash. This suggests at least the possibility that the first part (up to verse 6 and the first appearance of the Baptist) represents a text inherited by the Evangelist. The interpretation of the text as midrashic proem and narrative expansion receives strong backing from Coptic versions, which put a break after the first five verses.[48] The introduction of the Wisdom theme as the co-text of the midrash of the first five verses, in accord with this interpretation, then allows the expansion of the narrative via an extended reading of the plot of these Wisdom "hymns." Such themes as the arrival of the Word on earth and his living among men can clearly be traced as allusions to such parts of the Wisdom aretalogy as are found in texts like Baruch 3:37: "Afterward she appeared upon earth and lived among men." The pre-existent midrash on creation is thus turned into another kind of midrash by being elaborated into an extended narrative via application as a virtual hermeneutical key to the well-attested myth of Wisdom's trimorphic frustration in her desire (and God's) that she find a home in the world, a frustration for which a new cure will be offered: God's extraordinary incarnation of his son, the Logos.

Let me now offer a reading of the Prologue based on these hermeneutical assumptions, one that does not depend on all details being equally compelling. Certainly the division of the narrative into three descents of Wisdom could be done differently; indeed, another way would have been three (failed) descents before the coming of Christ. One virtue of this reading is that it helps make eminent sense of the function of the Prologue in this Gospel. It anchors the christological story in a cosmological narrative and in the traditions of the Jews, albeit in quite a different manner from that of the Synoptics. From a literary point of view, it leads to a strong appreciation of the role of the Prologue in the Gospel as a whole.[49]

Sophia's Choice

Verse 5 ends on the following note: καὶ τὸ φῶς ἐν τῇ σκοτίᾳ φαίνει, καὶ ἡ σκοτία αὐτὸ *οὐ κατέλαβεν* (my emphasis), translated in the Revised Standard Version as "The light shines in the darkness, and the darkness has not overcome it." At first glance, this seems an appropriate translation; οὐ κατέλαβεν certainly carries the sense of "has not overcome it." This is, moreover, a plausible gloss on Genesis's "divided between the darkness and the light."[50] However, there is another sense to the verb, namely, "has not received/comprehended it."[51] This is, to my mind, almost certainly the sense that the continuation of the text reads here.[52] If verse 5 tells us that the light was continuously shining in the darkness,[53] but the darkness did not receive it, then we understand immediately the necessity for this to be followed by: "There was a man sent from God, whose name was John. He came for testimony, to bear witness to the light, that all might believe through him." No longer, as many commentators would have it, an intrusion into the text, this is a most plausible sequel to the frustration of the light's design to shine in the darkness. The near rhyme between κατέλαβεν and παρέλαβον in verse 11 lends aid to this reading as well, as does also the further repeat of this root in verse 12 and its final appearance in verse 16.[54]

Verse 6 is then a transition from the Targum of the first five verses to the narrative gloss that follows. Here, I think, another advantage of this analysis is made manifest: by reading the first five verses as a pre-existent logos that the Johannine text adopted and expanded via the next thirteen verses, we can avoid an aporia to which current literary analyses in nearly all their versions lead. One way of getting at this problem is by citing a famous controversy between Bultmann and his disciple Käsemann. According to Bultmann, since verse 5 *cannot* refer to the incarnation, then verses 6–7 must be an addition to the text from a redactor (the Evangelist) who did not understand the text before him, wherein only at verse 14 is the incarnation spoken of. (I agree with the last of these points.)[55] On the other hand, according to Käsemann, since there is no reason to strike verses 6–7 or assume that they are a later addition to the text (and here

I agree with *him*), verses 5 ff. *must* refer to the Logos Ensarkos, the Word made flesh. But they can't both be right. Brown, in fact, argues that they are both wrong,[56] and I agree, although not necessarily for his reasons.

The author of the Gospel began by proleptically indicating the role of the Baptist in the salvation history that he is about to relate, thus providing a transition from the Genesis midrash to the Wisdom-Christ aretalogy to follow. By indicting the role of the Baptist as the harbinger of the incarnation, he effectively provides an introduction and frame for the Wisdom aretalogy of verses 7–13, culminating in the Christology that follows it in verse 14, the whole recapitulated in the second framing verse mentioning the Baptist, verse 15. There is, therefore, no longer a need to assume either that verse 6 is a later interpolation into the alleged hymn or that the text comprehends the incarnation before that event is actually related in verse 14.[57] Indeed there is a perfect homology between form and content here. Just as John the Baptist represents a transition between the Jewish koine traditions and the advent of the Incarnate Logos, so his verse represents a transition in the text between the koine midrash and the advent of the specific Johannine sequel. We thus preserve both the drama of the salvation history according to John and the religio-cultural history of the relation of the Johannine community to its Jewish context.

As a further argument in favor of reading verses 6 ff. as a narrative gloss on the first five verses,[58] I offer the following consideration. Verses 10–11 read: "ἐν τῷ κόσμῳ ἦ, καὶ ὁ κόσμος δι᾽ αὐτου ἐγένετο, καὶ ὁ κόσμος αὐτὸν οὐκ ἔγνω. εἰς τὰ ἴδια ἦλθεν, καὶ οἱ ἴδιοι αὐτὸν οὐ *παρέλαβον*" [He was in the world, and the world was made through him, yet the world knew him not. He came into his own home, and his own people received him not.]. I think it is most attractive to read these verses as a Sophialogical[59] gloss on the midrash of the first five verses.[60] The common myth, the Wisdom aretalogy, the narrative of Wisdom's entry into the world and her failure to find a home there, has been applied by the Evangelist to the first five verses of Genesis as read by the Greek Targum that constitutes the first five verses of the Fourth Gospel.[61] The myth is thus rendered intertext and hermeneutical key for understanding this Targum. Accordingly, verse 10 repeats verse 3 and expands on it, whereas verse 11 repeats and expands on the idea of verse 5. The "darkness" of the Genesis midrash has now become the cosmos, which, although made by the light, does not recognize or receive it, thus explaining the need for the advent of Jesus as the Logos Incarnate and his herald.[62] The material about the Baptist has thus been tightly woven into the old Wisdom myth in a way that suggests that this was the version of the myth that this Johannine community performed, seamlessly producing a transition between the old story and their present experience (or tradition), in which the Baptist came before the Christ, witnessing the presence of the Logos in the world and preaching his coming into the world as human flesh (v. 15).[63] Verses 6 and 15 thus frame the specifically Johannine version of the myth of Wisdom's failure to be comprehended in the world and the cure for that frustration in the incarnation. Verse 6 describes the Baptist's witness before the incarnation and verse 15 his pointing to the fulfillment of his testimony after that event.

In this reading, then, these verses are anything but interruptions in the text.[64] "This was he" (v. 15), "of whom I said" (in v. 6, as it were) "He who comes." When verses 1–5 have been midrashically construed as relating the story of Wisdom's attempt to enter the world and the frustration of those attempts, we have explained the need for there to be "a man sent from God, whose name was John. He came for testimony, to bear witness to the light, that all might believe through him."[65] The narration of the events that lead up to that moment is retold in greater detail in verses 7–13, and there is no denotation of the incarnation prior to verse 14.[66]

Thus verses 10–11 narrate the first of Wisdom's (the Logos's) three attempts to enter the world.[67] This attempt was in the form of various logophanies. I reckon that they may be read following the model of Justin's argument in the *Apologies* that a certain number of people received the Logos before the incarnation.[68] In support of the suggestion that this is a Johannine idea, I would offer John 8:56, in which the Logos Incarnate claims to have revealed himself to Abraham, before the incarnation. What, after all, could be more explicit than Genesis 15:1, "And it was after these things that the Word [λόγος] of God appeared to Abraham"? In verse 6 of that chapter, which says that "Abraham believed in God and he reckoned it for him as righteousness," the Targum has, "Abraham believed the Memra of God." Abraham, then, would be one of those "who received him" and "became children of God."[69]

Indeed, this entire passage is a midrash on Genesis 15, illuminated by the Logos. Earlier in the passage, Jesus says to the "Ioudaioi," who have declared "Abraham is our father": "If you were Abraham's children, you would do what Abraham did, but now you seek to kill me, a man who has told you the truth which I heard from God; this is not what Abraham did" (8:39–40). The "Ioudaioi" answer: "We were not born of fornication; we have one Father, even God" (8:41). In other words, these Jews wish to claim that because their father Abraham received the Logos, and thereby became a child of God, they have inherited that status. To this Jesus answers that if they were indeed children of Abraham, they would behave as he had done. After much further conversation, including the notorious "You are of your father the devil" (8:44),[70] comes the passage in which, after arousing the incredulity of the people by telling them that "Your father Abraham rejoiced that he was to see my day; he saw it and was glad," to wit, "You are not yet fifty years old, and have you seen Abraham?" Jesus answers them, "Truly, truly I say to you, before Abraham was, I am" (8:56–58).

This passage seems to me full of echoes of our verses in the Prologue and supports the interpretation that I have given them. The Logos clearly claims to have appeared to Abraham, presumably in the theophany at Mamre. Abraham, of course, rejoiced, received the Logos handsomely, and was saved. His descendants make the same claim for themselves that is made for those who have accepted the Logos, namely, that "they have become children of God; who were born, not of blood nor of the will of the flesh nor of the will of man, but of God" (1:12–13),[71] and the Logos rejects their claim vigorously. This interpretation seems more compelling than current standard ones, such as, for example, Brown, who writes, "That Abraham would not kill a divine messenger may be a general inference from Abraham's character, or perhaps a specific reference to a scene like that of Gen xviii where he welcomed divine messengers."[72] Given Jesus' insistence that Abraham has seen him and he Abraham, the interpretation offered above seems to me more cogent. It should be noted that the weakness of Brown's interpretation here—if I am at all right in my judgment—is a direct consequence of his refusal to read verses 6–13 as referring to the appearance of the Logos Asarkos (without flesh) on earth prior to the incarnation.[73]

Something like my reading was current among interpreters of the Fourth Gospel until Maldonatus in the sixteenth century.[74] I am happy to be so medieval. In the next chapter, I shall adduce the targumic midrash of the Four Nights in which the Memra appeared. The first was the night of creation; on the second, the Memra appeared to Abraham. Very early Christians placed enormous importance on Mamre as the site of the appearance of the Logos to Abraham, and Constantine built an early basilica there.[75] Referring to an annual feast held at Hebron (Mamre), the church historian Sozomen writes, "Indeed this feast is diligently frequented by all nations: by the Jews, because they boast of their descent from the patriarch Abraham; by the pagans, because angels there appeared to men; and by Christians because He who has lately revealed himself through the virgin for the salvation of mankind once appeared there to the pious man" (E.H. 2,4).[76] Sozomen is either interpreting the Fourth Gospel or reflecting the same tradition. I see here a strong footing for interpreting those verses of the Prologue as referring to the time *before* the incarnation, to the prior revelations of the Logos, as in Justin, and therefore as issuing in a strong connection between the Prologue as reread here and the rest of the Gospel.

As for the much-controverted verses 1:11, 12, and 13—"He came to what was his own, and his own people did not accept him. But to all who received him, who believed in his name, he gave power to become children of God, who were born, not of blood or of the will of the flesh or of the will of man, but of God"—

these narrate the second of Wisdom's attempts to enter the world, although I take verse 13 to refer back to both of these "failed" attempts. In both the first and the second attempts, in the midst of the general failure, some few received the Logos and thus became born of God. The second attempt of Wisdom to enter the world comprised the giving of the Torah to Israel and the failure of that instrument as a means of bringing the Logos into the world, because Israel did not understand, as will be recapitulated in verse 17.[77] On this reading, these verses would provide almost a retort to the interpretation of the Wisdom myth as found in Ben Sira 24, whereby Wisdom finally finds a home in Israel in the form of the Torah.[78] Sharon Ringe has pointed out that such retorts or "parodies" were already found in non-Christian apocalyptic texts. Referring to 1 Enoch and 2 Esdras (apocalypses from the end of the Second Temple period), she writes: "In what looks like a parody on Sirach 24 and Baruch 3:9–4:4, the unrighteousness of Israel has driven Wisdom back to heaven. Jerusalem cannot contain her, nor can the Torah given to Israel provide her a toehold among humankind. Instead, what before was represented as her powerful divine presence on earth is elevated into heavenly absence and to the company of the angels. She is safely limited not in any loss of personal agency but in access by those human beings whose faith takes shape around her."[79] Here is the particularly rich exemplar from 1 Enoch:

Wisdom could not find a place in which she could dwell;
but a place was found (for her) in the heavens.
Then Wisdom went out to dwell with the children of the people,
but she found no dwelling place.
So Wisdom returned to her place
and she settled permanently among the angels. (1 Enoch 42:1–2)[80]

Furthermore, we find the following in another "perfectly Jewish" text, 4 Ezra 7:72: "Though they had understanding they committed iniquity, and though they received the commandments they did not keep them, and though they obtained the Law they dealt unfaithfully with what they received." This narrative, too, arises wholly from within "insider" Jewish narratives and theological perspectives.[81] Compare John 7:19: "Has not Moses given you the Torah? And none of you does the Torah." As Stephen Motyer has insightfully written, "Against this background the claim of the Fourth Gospel that Jesus has descended from heaven to tell 'heavenly things' (3:12) takes on new relevance. We need to read John carefully against the background of this twin concern for theodicy and revelation."[82]

According to the Evangelist, on this reading, whereas Israel, which had been given the Torah, nevertheless rejected the Logos, some others, not necessarily Israel by virtue of flesh-and-blood parentage,[83] became children of God via receiving the Logos Asarkos.[84] John's thought here would be not entirely unlike Paul's in 2 Corinthians 6:16–21, where, alluding to the Prophets, Paul says: "as God said, 'I will live in them and move among them, and I will be their God, and they shall be my people. Therefore come out from them, and be separate from them, says the Lord, and touch nothing unclean; then I will welcome you, and I will be a father to you, and you shall be my sons and daughters, says the Lord Almighty.'" It is also related to Philo's thought in the *Conf. Ling.* 145–47: "those who live in the knowledge of the One are rightly called 'sons of God.'"[85] This explains the emphasis on the Logos coming into his own home and his own people receiving him not, without necessitating an interpretation whereby the incarnation is mentioned before verse 14. Israel, which had the Torah, did not accept Wisdom; but some select Israelites such as Abraham, and even Gentiles, did. They are called "children of God."[86] The incarnation, therefore, is shown by the Evangelist to be indispensable to save the many, both of Israel and of the Nations. Wisdom had not found a home in Israel, and the revelation of the Torah was not sufficient, as will be made explicit in verse 17.[87]

This is the beginning of the specifically "Christian" kerygma.[88] According to this reading, the structure of the Prologue consists in an unexceptionably "Jewish" Logos/Memra midrash on Genesis 1:1–5, which the author of the Fourth Gospel interprets via the Sophia myth, an interpretation crying in the wilderness that beautifully prepares the way for the coming of Christ in verse 14. Reading the Prologue in this way makes the Evangelist's text much more coherent, in that we avoid the necessity of assuming a series of inchoate intimations of the incarnation before it actually is narrated in verse 14. The three sections of the Prologue are thus a general narrative of the activity of the Logos based on a midrash on Genesis 1, an expansion of that narrative via the myth of Wisdom's misfortune in the world, narrating as well the failure of Torah to bring the Logos to the People, and then the new denouement to that myth in the incarnation of the Logos as Jesus.[89] The Gospel writer has accomplished two great works through the structure of this prologue and its narrative unfolding: he anchors the story of the incarnation and the life of Christ in the whole cosmology and myth of the coming and rejection of the light, and he moors his own christological narrative in a traditional Jewish midrash on Genesis 1. This reading obviates such unsatisfactory conclusions as: "It is striking that the Fourth Gospel begins with a prologue unlike anything known to the Synoptics. For, the mention of the Baptist in the Prologue (verses 6–8, 15) stems from a later hand. It was really a hymn directed to Jesus Christ, the Logos become flesh, the highest form of heavenly being after God."[90]

We can now understand verses 16–17 in a way that I think has been underplayed, if it has been seen at all. "The law given through Moses" represents the earlier attempt of the Logos to enter the world, as adumbrated in verses 12 and 13.[91] The myth of Wisdom elaborated in verses 9–13 relates the partial failure of the Word in the world. Although the Word is the creator of all, as we have learned in verse 3, all was not capable of receiving him. Indeed, his own people did not receive him when he came in the form of the Torah. In response to this failure, however, this time Wisdom did not ascend once more into the heavens and abandon the earth and its people. Instead, God performed the extraordinary act of incarnating the Logos in flesh and blood, coming into the world as an avatar and teacher of the Word, not the words. Since the goal of the Logos was to make it possible for those who believed in his name to become, not flesh and blood, but children of God, he who was properly the only child of God, the *monogenetos*, became flesh among us. In support of this reading, two considerations may be offered. The first is the assemblage of allusions to the Sinai revelation of the Torah.[92] The second is based on very recent scholarship on the Gospel of John, which demonstrates compellingly and in detail that in the Gospel throughout, various collocations that elsewhere (including in the Fourth Gospel) refer to Scripture are in John also referred to the words of the Word on earth, indicating that for this Evangelist, at any rate, the two are equated.[93] When the incarnate Logos speaks, he speaks Torah. This point both ties the Gospel as a whole much more tightly to the Prologue and supports the interpretation of the coming of Christ as a supplement to the Torah.

For John, as for that other most "Jewish" of Gospels, Matthew—but in a very different manner—Jesus comes to fulfill the mission of Moses, not to displace it.[94] The Torah simply needed a better exegete, the Logos Ensarkos, a fitting teacher for flesh and blood. Rather than supersession in the explicitly temporal sense within which Paul inscribes it, John's typology of Torah and Logos Incarnate is more easily read within the context of what Jacques Derrida has argued is a prevailing assumption of Western thought: that oral teaching is more authentic and transparent than written texts.[95] God thus first tried the text, and then sent his voice, incarnated in the voice of Jesus.[96]After the Prologue, which truly introduces the narrative of the Word's coming into the world, its prehistory and its necessity, the Gospel moves naturally into the main Gospel narration, with a Christology informed at all points by the prehistoric, cosmic myth of the Prologue.

Seen in this way, what marks the Fourth Gospel as a new departure in the history of Judaism is not its Logos theology, since that seems to be an inheritance from pre-Christian Judaisms and to be shared with non-Christian Judaisms, but in the notion that the Logos is incarnated as Jesus, the Christ—a historical departure or, rather, advent, that is iconically symbolized in the narrative itself. That is to say: When the text announces in verse 14 that the "Word became flesh," this advent of the Logos is an iconic representation of the moment that the Christian narrative begins to diverge from the Jewish Koine and form its own nascent Christian kerygma, proclamation.

A more general way of making this point would be to suggest that the earliest Christian groups (including, or even especially, the Johannine one) distinguished themselves from non-Christian Jews not theologically, but only in their association of various Jewish theologoumena and mythologoumena with this particular Jew, Jesus of Nazareth.[97] The characteristic move that constructs what will become orthodox Christianity is, I think, the combination of Jewish messianic soteriology with equally Jewish Logos theology in the figure of Jesus.[98] I believe that this movement can be discerned in the Prologue to the Fourth Gospel, and even more in the "merging" of the Synoptics with the Fourth Gospel within the eventual Christian canon. Reading this appropriately is, therefore, key to understanding the historical relation of Christianity to Judaism. Emblematic (or, rather, a forerunner) of this "merging" would be Acts 2:36: "God made Jesus both Lord and Christ." As Dunn richly documents, it is neither the "Lord" nor "Christ" that is a novum in the new movement, it is the "Jesus."[99]

From Logos to Christology

This historiographical movement from common "Jewish" Logos theology to Christology was made by other Christian writers such as Justin, apparently independently of John.[100] A remarkable theological statement by Justin shows how vivid his notion of the Logos was, and how similar in some ways to that of the Fourth Gospel, yet how different. It thus can serve as an independent witness to the hermeneutical origins of Logos theology. Justin writes:

God has begotten as a Beginning before all His creatures a kind of Reasonable Power from Himself, which is also called by the Holy Spirit the Glory of the Lord, and sometimes Son, and sometimes Wisdom, and sometimes Angel, and sometimes God, and sometimes Lord and Word." (*Dialogue* 61:1)[101]

Clearly, presumably without reference to the Fourth Gospel, Justin also knows of a midrash that reads the word "Beginning" (ἀρχή) of Genesis 1:1 as a reference to the Logos, which, I would strongly argue, can only have been known via the sort of midrash that we find incorporated in the Targum and the Fourth Gospel. Like the midrash, these take that "Beginning" to be Sophia, Wisdom, via a detour through the verses: "God created me at the *Beginning* of his way (Proverbs 8:22) and "The *Beginning of Wisdom* is the fear of the Lord" (Psalms 111:10).[102] Thus we have in Justin precious evidence corroborating such an interpretation and such a theology among Jews, from which the traditions animating both the Evangelist and the apologist have drawn. In the beginning, God got from himself the being with the names Son, Wisdom, angel,[103] God, Lord, and Logos. As an independent witness, Justin's evocative language suggests as well the long vita of these hermeneutical associations, necessarily among Jews.

As M. J. Edwards has argued, "the womb of [Justin's] Logos-doctrine was the *Dialogue*, where the term is used to confer on Christ the powers that were already attributed in Jewish literature to the spoken and written utterance of God."[104] His final statement is even clearer: "Our conclusion, therefore, is that in the two *Apologies*, no less than in the *Dialogue with Trypho*, Christ is the Logos who personifies the Torah. In Jewish thought the Word was the source of being, the origin of Law, the written Torah and a Person next to God. Early Christianity announced the incarnation of this Person, and Justin makes the further claims that Scripture is the parent of all truth among the nations, and that the Lord who is revealed to us in the New Testament is the author and the hermeneutic canon of the Old."[105] Let me emphasize that not only Jewish thought is at work here, but Jewish hermeneutical practices as well: the association of the creative Word of *Bere'šit* with the Wisdom companion/agent of God from Proverbs, via the verse "The Beginning [*re'šit*] of Wisdom is fear of the Lord." It follows, then, that in Logos theology both John and Justin represent old, common Judaic patterns of religious thought and midrashic practice.[106] Later rabbinism, I will argue in the next chapter, retained the hermeneutical practice but deferred as heresy the Logos theology derived from it, leaving it to appear only in the pararabbinic Targums of late antiquity and among Christians.[107]

The pararabbinic targumic tradition, by which I mean contemporary with the Rabbis but distinctly different from them and which I shall discuss at some length in the next chapter, seems, then, to be a key to understanding the religious-historical situation of the Prologue to John. Recently, Gary Anderson has noted that many scholars deny any connection between the Memra and the Logos, while insisting that the only relevant background for the Logos is the Wisdom of the Bible and later Jewish literature.[108] However, as Anderson points out, once we see the close connections between the Memra and the figure of Wisdom, via analysis of the targumic materials, then we "can presume that *ḥokmâ* and *logos* are related concepts." Given this, "the understanding of *bĕrē'šît* in *Tg. Neofiti* would provide a remarkable parallel to John 1:1."[109] Anderson goes on to note that in both the "Targum" in John and in the Palestinian Targum, the term *bĕrēšît* is, in effect, translated twice, once as "in the beginning" and once as "by means of Wisdom / the Word." Moreover, in both, "preexistence and super-intendence were inextricable concepts." We must not, of course, revert to schol-arship that sees the Targum as the "background" to the Gospel of John or of Christianity, a clear anachronism, but I believe that these considerations strongly suggest a common tradition. The present interpretative perspective al-lows us to imagine an origin for the first five verses of the Prologue in the Jew-ish koine of the time of the Gospel, a koine that is then "Christianized"—avant la lettre, of course—in the succeeding verses. In other words, the advantages of this interpretation are threefold, and the three folds are homologous. On the formal or literary level (invoking the hermeneutical principle of charity), we end up with a superior text in that a history now prepares the way for the an-nouncement of the incarnation in verse 14 without, however, anticipating it and spoiling the drama. On the theological level, the Prologue now presents us with a clear account of the pre-existent Logos and the *reason* for the incarnation. On the level of the history of religions, we see that this pre-existent Logos—that is, the pre-existent Logos upon which the Fourth Gospel is founded—is a Jewish Logos, and the continuity of Johannine religion with the Judaism of its day is made plausible. In a recent essay, which appeared as this book was being com-pleted, Menahem Kister put the point thus: "It becomes clear that the Gnostics who emphasized the role of the angels in the creation of the human, as well as the latter-day followers of Marcion, who emphasized the role of matter (the earth) alongside of the creating God, as well as the Fathers of the Church who claim that from this verse can be learned the doctrine of the Father and the Son (or the Trinity), *all continue Jewish interpretations,* even when the battle between them and Judaism is at its bitterest and most uncompromising."[110] John's Pro-logue is similarly a continuation of "Jewish" interpretation, no more, no less.

The structure of the Prologue, then, according to this mode of interpreta-tion, moves from the pre-existent Wisdom/Logos that is not (yet) Christ, a notion subsisting among many first-century Jewish circles, to the incarnation of the Logos in the man Jesus of Nazareth, who is also the Messiah and thus called the Christ. Far from a supersessionist move from the particularistic Torah to the universalistic Logos (as Epp would have it), the movement of the narrative is from a universalistic Jewish Logos theology to the particularism of Johannine Christology[111]—though I put no pejorative weight on that whatsoever. Of course, for the Evangelist the incarnation supplements the Torah—that much is explicit—but only because the Logos Ensarkos is a better teacher, a better ex-egete, than the Logos Asarkos—ἐκεῖνος ἐξηγήσατο—does the incarnation take place.

Excursus: In Memory of Hymn

> *Nevertheless, in spite of his pre-eminence, every answer Bultmann gives to the really important questions he raises—is wrong.*
> —*John Ashton*[112]

Although in the nineteenth century it was fashionable to read the Johannine Logos together with the targumic Memra, in the past hundred years this line of interpretation has fallen out of favor, largely because of the theologically grounded and Jewish apologetic assertion that the Memra is not in any sense a hypostasis.[113] The two major twentieth-century interpretative strands concerning the Fourth Gospel's Prologue either implicitly or explicitly deny this nexus. One line of interpretation, which stems from J. Rendell Harris, connects the Prologue with the hymns to Wisdom in Proverbs and associated apocryphal wisdom texts.[114] Another tradition, beginning with Bultmann, denies the affiliation of John with Jewish Wisdom and asserts that the Prologue, being a hymn to the Logos, belongs to "gnostic" traditions that have little, if anything, to do with an imagined unitary "Judaism."[115]

Harris was perhaps the first scholar to note the close connections between the Prologue and certain themes in early and later Jewish Wisdom literature. He compares the Prologue to such biblical and apocryphal texts as Proverbs 8:22–31, Sirach 24, the Wisdom of Solomon, and Baruch 3:37–4:1 and argued that it belongs to the same genre. These texts do indeed provide us with impressive thematic parallels, as well as metaphorical language that is parallel to the Johannine Prologue. This line of interpretation, which connects the Prologue directly with its supposed models in Jewish Wisdom literature, severs those sapiential models (and with them the Prologue) from later Jewish traditions about the Memra.

Bultmann went much further in denying any nexus linking the Prologue to John and contemporary "Jewish thinking" by explicitly declining Harris's interpretation, preferring to locate the Gospel's models exclusively in "pagan" mythemes.[116] The evident parallels with Wisdom literature were, for Bultmann, only evidence of a demythologized and perhaps even debased appropriation by biblical writers of these pagan motifs. Bultmann's view of the Prologue and of the Fourth Gospel in general seeks to move it as far as possible from "Judaism."[117] He famously reads the Prologue to the Fourth Gospel as a hymn that originates in sources outside of Judaism, in "Mandaism" or some version of an "oriental gnostic"—that is, "pagan"—group.[118] This interpretation supports Bultmann's overall conviction that the Gospel ought be read as distant from Judaism.[119] Part of the issue is that for Bultmann "Judaism" is a reified entity, such that he can claim: "the Wisdom myth was not as such a living force in Judaism; it was only a mythological and poetic decking-out of the doctrine of the law. Everything that the myth related of Wisdom was transferred to the Torah: the Torah is pre-existent; she was God's plan of creation and instrument of creation; Wisdom, being in some sense incarnate in the law, has found in Israel a dwelling, prepared for her by God. But the Wisdom myth does not have its origin in the O.T. or in Israel at all; it can only spring from pagan mythology; the Israelite Wisdom poetry took over the myth and demythologized it."[120] The very limitations of the "history of religions" method are apparent here in its distinctions between "pagan," "Israelite," "Jewish," and "Christian." Thus, according to Bultmann, even the Book of Daniel isn't authentically "Jewish"; it is "syncretistic."[121] As James D. G. Dunn has put it, Bultmann's work led to a perception of "Christianity [that] very quickly distanced itself from its distinctively Jewish matrix and from a characteristically Jewish Jesus."[122] This is consistent, of course, with Bultmann's theological understanding of Christianity as such, particularly his reading of Paul, in which it is necessary for "Law" (a.k.a. Judaism) and "Faith" (a.k.a. Christianity) to be existential opposites. The Logos of John (in both senses) cannot, for Bultmann, be in any way a Jewish Logos. Although accoutered with a scientific justification in the "history of religions," Bultmann's argument is essentially theological.[123] For Bultmann, the absolute uniqueness of the Christ event cannot brook any unseemly dependence by the first theologian of the Church on "Judaism." It is, of course, striking how here, too, Christian apologetics and Jewish apologetics have been in concert in their mutual desire to make a difference.

Both of these versions, however, have one thing in common. They read the Prologue as a hymn.[124] An important variant of both these traditions has been the feminist branch. A group of scholars have been intrigued by the nexus between Johannine thought and a Christ who incarnates the female figure of Wisdom, whether as Sophia from a Hebrew *Ḥokmâ* or as an Isis-like figure (we might say, the Harris version and the Bultmann version, respectively). One of the most prominent of such scholars has been Elisabeth Schüssler Fiorenza, who contends that "the narrative characterization of Jesus" in the Fourth Gospel "seems to speak [for] Jesus [as] Wisdom Incarnate."[125] A recurring problem for such otherwise compelling interpretations has been the question of how Sophia became Logos in the Prologue.[126] The two alternative versions of an answer to this question for both feminists and nonfeminists have involved introducing an alien Logos figure from Greek thought into the world of Jewish Wisdom or a partriarchal Jewish Word into the feminine world of non-Jewish goddess worship. The problem with these theories is that they have "forgotten" the already deep complicity of Wisdom and Word, their very ancient equivalence, and compounded this by not analyzing the exegetical sense and technique of the Prologue with sufficient precision, thus rendering this participation even more opaque.[127]

In spite of Epp's stipulation that "this conclusion [that the Prologue is a hymn to the Logos] is widely held and, for our purpose, is in no need of further discussion,"[128] it is actually very much in need of further discussion. The arguments in favor of identifying the *Gattung* of the text as hymn are not, in and of themselves, conclusive. First, the fact that the Prologue "has in it instances of Hebrew . . . parallelism"[129] only argues for the close dependence of this text, in some way or another, on a biblical intertext. Second, the fact that hymns to Jesus Christ are mentioned in early literature from Asia Minor and that various New Testament hymnic materials (allegedly; there is circularity here) show themes similar to the Prologue hardly counts as evidence for the *form*.[130] Finally, on formal grounds, the Prologue to John is not really similar to the Wisdom Hymns to which Epp has appealed. Those hymns are mostly in the first person and represent either the speech of personified Wisdom herself or of the object of her instruction.[131] This is thematized directly at Ben Sira 24:1 in an apparent allusion to the characteristic form of the genre: "Wisdom sings her own praises, before her own people she proclaims her glory." To get some sense of why this is important, comparison with two texts to which the Prologue is most frequently compared, namely, the *Trimorphic Protennoia* and the Pronoia monologue of the Apocryphon of John is sufficient. Both of those texts represent the Sophia figure in a classical aretalogical form, telling her own story, singing, as it were, her own praises. Before undertaking to produce hypotheses regarding the relationship of the canonical Fourth Gospel to these texts, and surely before entertaining theories of the historical relationships of communities to each other, these differences of *Gattung* and thus of *Sitz im Leben* need to be attended to.[132]

The theory that the Prologue is based on a hymn has had some negative philological and interpretative consequences. For one thing, it has led to a nearly endless round of speculations about what ought and ought not to be included in the hymn, an endless round of recourse to the knife for amputations to the text.[133] As one very recent interpreter has put it: "But no hymn has emerged, at least not one on which scholars agree. Even parts of verses 1–5 are in dispute. Nor has the church ever used it as a hymn—unlike, say, Mary's canticle (Luke 1:46–55)—even though it has employed it greatly, particularly as a blessing over the sick and over newly baptized children."[134] Raymond Edward Brown affords a convenient summary of the multifarious efforts somehow to dig a hymnic text out of the text as it is, which reveal, I believe, the inevitable failure of the attempt.[135]

In assuming the recursive structures of the hymn, commentators have been free to assume that the incarnation is referred to in the text long before verse 14 with its dramatic "And the Word became flesh and dwelt among us." Thus an interpreter such as Serafin de Ausejo,[136] who strongly reads the Prologue as belonging to a *Christian* genre of hymns to Jesus, reads the entire Prologue as referring to the Logos Ensarkos, the Word made flesh, a reading that completely cuts this text off from any Jewish roots whatsoever, and Brown allows that this interpretation might be correct.[137]

Brown himself, however, prefers to read the first five verses of the Prologue in a fashion quite like the interpretation I offer. The big difference between us comes at verses 10 and following, where Brown argues, not unlike Haenchen: "The third strophe of the original hymn seems to deal with the Word incarnate in the ministry of Jesus." Brown believes that the decisive evidence for this interpretation is to be found in verse 12: "But to all who received him, who believed in his name, he gave power to become children of God, who were born, not of blood or of the will of the flesh or of the will of man, but of God." As Brown argues, "It seems incredible that in a hymn coming out of Johannine circles the ability to become a child of God would have been explained in another way than in terms of having been begotten from above by the spirit of Jesus."[138] It is this incredibility, this stone that the builders have scorned, that I make the keystone of my interpretation, for I believe, contra Brown, that until verse 14, what we have before us is a piece of perfectly unexceptional non-Christian Jewish thought that has been seamlessly woven into the christological narrative of the Johannine community.[139]

A strictly chronological narrative interpretation of the text, rather than a lyrical, hymnic one, makes for a better reading. Among the standard commentators on the Gospel, I have found this view clearly articulated only by C. H. Dodd: "The transition from the cosmical Logos to the Logos incarnate is assisted if we take the propositions in i. 9–13 to refer, as by their position they should naturally refer, to the pre-incarnate Logos."[140] It is my hope that the formal, literary analysis offered above will secure that interpretation, with all of its consequences (adumbrated as well by Dodd) for comprehending the relationship of nascent "Christianity" to "Judaism."

Chapter 5
The Jewish Life of the Logos: Logos Theology in Pre- and Pararabbinic Judaism

Erwin Goodenough has clearly articulated the problematic that gave rise to Logos theology in the first centuries of the Christian era: "The Logos then in all circles but the Stoic . . . was a link of some kind which connected a transcendent Absolute with the world and humanity. The Logos came into general popularity because of the wide-spread desire to conceive of God as transcendent and yet immanent at the same time. The term Logos in philosophy was not usually used as the title of a unique attribute of God, but rather as the most important single name among many applicable to the effulgent Power of God which reasonably had shaped and now governs the world."[1] Goodenough does not sufficiently emphasize, however, how thoroughly first-century Judaism had absorbed (and even co-produced) these central "Middle Platonic" theological notions. We have seen in the last chapter how bound up with the Bible and old traditions of its interpretation the Christian Jewish Logos is. The idea that the Logos or Sophia (Wisdom, and other variants as well) is the site of God's presence in the world—indeed, the notion of God's Word or Wisdom as a mediator figure—was a very widespread one in the world of first- and even second-century Judaic thought.[2] Rather than treating Logos theology as the specific product of "Christianity," with Philo a sort of Christian avant la lettre,[3] I wish to explore the evidence for Logos theology as a common element in Jewish, including Christian Jewish, religious imagination. As Dunn has recently written of Wisdom Christology, the close congener of Logos theology: "*the usage is Jewish through and through.*"[4] A comparative study of Philo's Logos and the Memra of the Targum will make the life of the Logos in the Judaic religious world much more vivid.

Philo's Logos, Targum's Memra: The Word in Non-Rabbinic Judaism

Historian of dogma Basil Studer has claimed that "first it has to be fully acknowledged that the beginning of trinitarian reflection was made because of the Easter experience, understood in apocalyptic terms."[5] I would suggest, in contrast, that the beginning of trinitarian reflection was in pre-Christian Jewish accounts of the second and visible God, variously, the Logos (Memra), Wisdom, or even perhaps the Son of God.[6] These linkages have been discussed before but, it seems, have been out of fashion for several decades. "*Memra* is a blind alley in the study of the biblical background of John's logos doctrines," writes C. K. Barrett[7] echoing the views of many scholars,[8] who similarly resist the idea that the Memra is indeed a hypostasis (independent divine entity, or even person), and not "but a means of speaking about God without using his name, and thus a means of avoiding the numerous anthropomorphisms of the Old Testament."[9] It is hardly beside the point, then, to rehearse the evidence for precisely that claim that contemporary scholars have found so easy to dismiss out of hand.

David Winston has argued that, although we can know very little of the philosophical context of Philo's writing, we can determine from the writings themselves that "Logos theology is the linchpin of Philo's religious thought" and "something his readers will immediately recognize without any further explanation."[10] The consequences of this point are formidable. Philo was clearly writing for an audience of Jews devoted to the Bible. If for these Logos theology was a commonplace (which is not to say that there were not enormous variations in detail), the implication is that this way of thinking about God was a vital inheritance of at least Alexandrian Jewish thought. It becomes apparent, therefore, that for one branch of pre-Christian Judaism there was nothing strange about a doctrine of a *deuteros theos*, a "second" God (although, to be sure, Philo uses this "shocking" term only once), and nothing in that doctrine that precluded monotheism.[11] Moreover, Darrell Hannah has emphasized that "neither in Platonism, Stoicism nor Aristotelian thought do we find the kind of significance that the concept has for Philo, nor the range of meanings that he gives to the term λόγος," and, therefore, that "he appears to be dependent upon a tradition in Alexandrian Judaism which was attributing a certain independence to God's word."[12] He sees the sources of that tradition as in part growing out of the Israelite Prophets themselves, at least in their Septuagint hypostasis. As he has formulated it, "The Greek OT could be read as affirming that the λόγος θεοῦ [Word of God] was an agent of both creation and revelation, roles which Philo attributes to the Logos. . . . It would appear, then, that Philo drew on a Hellenistic Jewish tradition which asserted that by means of His Word, which was the same as His Wisdom, God created the world and revealed Himself to the prophets."[13]

Philo reveals some of the crucial scriptural intertexts for his Logos doctrine:[14]

For this reason, whereas the voice of mortals is judged by hearing, the sacred oracles intimate that the words of God (τοὺς τοῦ θεοῦ λόγους) are seen as light is seen, for we are told that *all of the people saw the Voice* (Exod. 20:18), not that they heard it; for what was happening was not an impact of air made by the organs of mouth and tongue, but the radiating splendour of virtue indistinguishable from a fountain of reason. . . . But the voice of God which is not that of verbs and names yet seen by the eye of the soul, he (Moses) rightly introduces as "visible." (Philo, *Migr.* 47–48)

One of the implications of this text is the close connection that it draws between the Logos, the Word, and light. This is a nexus that will immediately arouse associations with the Prologue of the Fourth Gospel, which has been explored in the previous chapter, but that in reality has much broader early Jewish contexts.

Further, it can hardly be doubted that, for Philo, the Logos is both a part of God and a separate being, the Word that God created in the beginning in order to create everything else, the Word that both is God, therefore, and is with God. We find in Philo a passage that could just as easily fit into Justin's *Apologies*:

To His Word, His chief messenger, highest in age and honour, the Father of all has given the special prerogative, to stand on the border and separate the creature from the Creator. This same Word both pleads with the immortal as suppliant for afflicted mortality and acts as ambassador of the ruler to the subject. He glories in this prerogative and proudly describes it in these words "and I stood between the Lord and you" (Deut. v. 5), that is neither uncreated by God, nor created as you, but midway between the two extremes, a surety to both sides. (*Quis rerum divinarum heres sit*, 205–6)[15]

Philo oscillates about whether the Logos, God's Son,[16] exists separately or is totally incorporated within the godhead.[17] If Philo is not on the road to Damascus here, he is surely on a way that leads to Nicaea and the controversies over the second person of the Trinity.[18]

Given that mediation by the Logos is central to Philo's theology, it becomes less and less plausible to speak of him as having been "influenced" by Middle Platonism. Instead, that form of "Hellenistic" philosophy may simply be the Judaism of Philo and his fellows.[19] A "Hellenism" is, after all, by definition the creative synthesis of Greek and "Eastern" culture and thought, and "Philo's Logos, jointly formed by the study of Greek philosophy and of the Torah, was at once the written text, an eternal notion in the mind of the Creator and the organ of his work in time and space. Under this last aspect, it receives such epithets as

Son, King, Priest and Only-Begotten; in short it becomes a person."[20] As C. H. Dodd eloquently describes it, Philo's Logos is neither just Wisdom, the חכמה of the Bible, nor is it quite the Stoic or Platonic λόγος, nor yet the divine Word, Hebrew דבר, but some unique and new synthesis of all of these.[21] That synthesis arguably intersects with the central theological problem of Middle Platonism itself, the problem of mediation. The Logos as divine mediator is found only in Jewish (including Christian) versions of Middle Platonism, and we might, therefore, wish to say that Philo's Judaism is simply an important variety of Middle Platonism.[22] As Virginia Burrus writes: "*Historically speaking*, the figure of the Logos is more a product of scriptural interpretation than of Platonic speculation—a 'fact' that is most frequently overlooked or even deliberately obscured, swallowed by the chasm forcefully wedged open between Logos and Book. The divinized or hypostasized Logos that reappears in Derrida's texts is collaboratively invented in antiquity by writers who are (with a few minor exceptions) readers of Genesis 1 and Proverbs 8, many (but not all) of whom also happen to be readers of Plato and other philosophers. From the Gospel of John to the Gospel of Truth, from the Tripartite Tractate to Clement's Alexandrian trilogy of the Word, from Justin to Philo to Origen, Logos emerges in the dialogical play of scriptural interpretation. More intriguing still, the figure is paralleled in (if not anticipated by) the Aramaic exegesis of the Hebrew 'memra' ('word')—it is thus not only almost always a 'Jewish' but sometimes also a non-Greek invention. I might broaden the point further and say that Logos, first and foremost a product of scriptural exegesis, is also a product of a particular style of self-consciously intertextual reading that *makes* Scripture Scripture."[23] Philo, then, is as much a producer as a consumer of Middle Platonism.

Maren Niehoff emphasizes that, for this aspect of his philosophy, Philo apparently did not have previous Greek sources to draw upon. For his notion of man as an Idea, Philo could draw upon his Alexandrian predecessor, Arius Didymus, but for the concept of language itself as an Idea, indeed, perhaps, as the Idea of Ideas, Philo had no known Platonist models.[24] This is of signal importance for the present investigation, because it suggests that we look in quite other directions for the Philonic intertexts of this conceptual world: "Philo idealizes language more than man. For him, the ideal language does not at all belong to the realm of createdness. It rather seems to have preexisted with God Himself, thus entirely pertaining to the realm of the eternal, unchanging, most real and most true. In comparison to the ideal man, Divine language also plays a clearly more active and generative role. It is likely that both the enormous importance which Philo attributes to language and its active role as part of the Deity are ideas which are inspired by the natural assumption of God's speech acts throughout the biblical writings. The idea seems then to have been conceptualized in Plato's terms of ideal Forms."[25] In other words, a dual move has been made by the Middle Platonist Jew, Philo. The notion of a mediator, a personified demiurge, has been promulgated, but in addition, and perhaps even more striking, that personified mediator, as creator, is identified with the Forms of Plato, which are thus, themselves, in turn, animated or personified as the Logos. Philo's Logos seems, therefore, a close congener of the Logos theology that we find among almost all ante-Nicene Christian writers. It would appear, therefore, to have a "Jewish" genesis.

Were we to find such notions in Philo alone among non-Christian Jews, we could regard him, as he often is regarded, as a sport, a mutant, or even a voice crying in the wilderness. However, there were other Jews and not only Greek-speaking ones who manifested a version of Logos theology. Notions of the second god as the personified Word or Wisdom of God were present among Semitic-speaking Jews, as well.[26] This point is important because it further disturbs the dichotomies that have been promulgated between Hellenistic Judaism and rabbinic (by which is usually meant "authentic," "really real") Judaism.[27] There is a point that I have been hinting at until now, but which is crucial to understanding the argument in this section, namely that the Targums, as products of the synagogues, in contrast to the House of Study, were *not* rabbinic in their religious ethos. The synagogues, themselves, as has been often pointed out in recent scholarship were not under the control of the Rabbis probably until the Middle Ages.[28] The leading candidate for the Semitic Logos is, of course, the Memra of God,[29] as it appears in these synagogal, pararabbinic Aramaic translations[30] of the Bible, in textual contexts that are frequently identical to ones where the Logos hermeneutic has its home among Jews who speak Greek.[31]

"The *Memra* has a place above the angels as that agent of the Deity who sustains the course of nature and personifies the Law."[32] This position has been well established among historians of Christianity since the late nineteenth century. Alfred Edersheim saw the Memra as referring to God's self-revelation. As Robert Hayward says of Edersheim: "He also made a distinction between God and the *Memra*. Noting that Rabbinic theology has not preserved for us the doctrine of distinct persons in the Godhead, he remarks: 'And yet, if words have any meaning, the *Memra* is a hypostasis,'" that is, a divine person in its own right.[33] With this comment, Edersheim clearly implies that nonrabbinic forms of Judaism were extant and vital within the rabbinic period alongside (and even within) the rabbinic religion itself. Although, as I shall argue in the next chapter, official rabbinic theology sought to suppress all talk of the Memra or Logos by naming it the heresy of Two Powers in Heaven, before the Rabbis, contemporaneously with them, and even among them, there were a multitude of Jews, in both Palestine and the Diaspora, who held this version of monotheistic theology. If we accept Edersheim's view, the Memra is related to the Logos of Logos theology in its various Philonic and Christian manifestations.

There have been obstacles to seeing the connections between the Memra and the Logos, however. Among Jewish scholars, as Hayward has put it, "since the time of MAIMONIDES, it had been the custom to understand *Memra*, along with certain other Targumic terms like *Shekhinta'* (Presence) and *Yeqara'* (Glory),[34] as a means of avoiding anthropomorphisms in speaking of God, and thus defending a notion of his incorporeality.[35] NAHMANIDES, however, disagreed with MAIMONIDES on this issue, although he held that the words had a secret and mystical meaning which would be revealed only to those versed in the *Kabbalah.* Nonetheless, the idea that *Memra* was simply a means of speaking about God in a reverent manner befitting His omnipotence and otherness was not unknown from the time of the Middle Ages onwards."[36] The consensus of scholarship since the 1920s has agreed with Maimonides's view. Thus, "*Memrā'* (Word) as used in the targums is basically a buffer term to preserve the transcendence of God; it has no reality of its own."[37] Raymond Brown also represents the standard view: "Targum Onkelos speaks of the *Memra* of Yahweh. This is not a personification, but the use of *Memra* serves as a buffer for divine transcendence."[38]

Surely, however, this position collapses logically. If the Memra is just a name that allows one to avoid asserting that God himself has created, appeared, supported, and saved, and thus preserves his absolute transcendence, then who, after all, did the actual creating, appearing, supporting, saving? Either God himself—in which case one has hardly "protected" him from contact with the material world—or there is some other divine entity, in which case Memra is not just a name. Indeed, as Burton Mack has pointed out, Sophia/Logos developed within Judaism precisely to enable "a theology of the transcendence of God."[39] The currently accepted and dominant view ascribes to the use of the Memra only the counterfeit coinage of a linguistic simulation of a theology of the transcendence of God without the theology itself. Rather than assuming that the usage is meaningless, it seems superior on general hermeneutic grounds to assume that it means something. It follows, then, that the strongest reading of the Memra is that it is not a mere name, but an actual divine entity, or mediator.[40]

The fact that the question of connections between Logos and Memra has been posed as one concerning the interpretation of the Fourth Gospel, not as an independent issue in the study of Judaic history, has presented an additional obstacle. As Martin McNamara puts it, the question is whether or not the "targumic expression" is "a true preparation for the rich Johannine doctrine of the Logos." In that case, "the doctrine as well as the term used by John would have been prepared for in synagogue theology." The problems raised by this perspective have been clarified by Thomas Tobin: "The dating of the targums, includ-ing the recently discovered Targum Neofiti I, is very much in dispute. While Diez Macho places Targum Neofiti I in the late 1st or 2d century C.E. other schol-ars . . . place it in the 3rd century or later. . . . One should use the targums, in-cluding Targum Neofiti I, for interpreting 1st century C.E. literature such as the Prologue only with great caution and only when the parallels are clear and con-sistent. Because of this one must look elsewhere for the basic background for the Prologue of John."[41] However, if the question is not the bibliocentric search for the sources of John but rather a search for versions of Logos theology among Jews, *including* the author of the Fourth Gospel, then the targumic evidence—precisely because of its lateness and its "clear and consistent" parallelism to the Prologue—is of compelling importance, as it demonstrates that this version of Jewish theology was current among Jews for centuries after it had supposedly been stamped out.

A final obstacle has been apologetic on both sides of the Christian/Jewish divide of scholarship: The very centrality of the Gospel to Christian scholars has driven most of them away from any nexus between its Logos theology and that of contemporary and later Jews. At the same time, Jewish scholars have rebelled against any notion that Jews held a doctrine of complexity in the Godhead. Mc-Namara draws a distinction between the doctrine and the words used to express it: "His teaching on the nature of the Logos John got from the revelation of the New Testament. The source from which he drew the words that express this new doctrine is then the point at issue."[42] As an alternative to the view that John's doctrine "had been prepared in the synagogue," a view that had been rejected by all scholars, according to McNamara, Bultmann searched in "gnostic" treasure troves. "Many" other scholars, similarly unwilling to imagine any theological in-timacy between the "synagogue" and the "church," have, according to McNa-mara, "come to see the preparation for the doctrine of John in the Wisdom literature of the Old Testament, and for the term he uses in the creative word (in Hebrew *dabar*) of God."[43] Those of us who are more skeptical about revelation may be more skeptical as well about the notion of an idea without a word that then finds its word elsewhere, indeed, from the revelation of a canon that was not to come into existence for centuries. Clearly, the apologetic desire to find ab-solute uniqueness in this important moment in Christian doctrine and the con-sequent compliance with a different sort of Jewish apologetic has misdirected the inquiry.[44]

In contrast, after his discovery of the first complete manuscript of the Palestinian Targum[45] and slightly before McNamara, Alejandro Díez Macho has argued for the close connection of the Memra so widely occurring in this text and the Logos of the Fourth Gospel.[46] In all of the Palestinian Aramaic translations of the Bible, the term *Memra* as a translation of various terms that in Hebrew either simply mean "God" or are names of God is legion and theologically highly significant, because these usages parallel nearly exactly the functions of the Logos, the *deuteros theos*, in Logos theology.

We find the Memra working as the Logos works in the following ways:

Creating: Genesis 1:3, "And the *Memra* of H' said Let there be light and there was Light by his *Memra*." In all of the following verses, it is the *Memra* that performs all of the creative actions.[47]

Speaking to humans: Genesis 3:8 ff., "And they heard the voice of the *Memra* of H'. . . . And the *Memra* of H' called out to the Man."[48]

Revealing himself: Genesis 18:1, "And was revealed to him the *Memra* of H'."

Punishing the wicked: Genesis 19:24, "And the *Memra* of H' rained down on Sodom and Gomorrah."[49]

Saving: Exodus 17:21, "And the *Memra* of H' was leading them during the day in a pillar of cloud."[50]

Redeeming: Deuteronomy 32:39, "When the *Memra* of H' shall be revealed to redeem his people."

These examples lead inductively to the conclusion that the Memra performs many, if not all, of the functions of the Logos of Christian Logos theology (as well as of Wisdom),[51] and an a priori case can be made, therefore, for some kind of connection between these two, after all, etymologically cognate entities in nonrabbinic Judaism.

I therefore disagree with Larry Hurtado, who argues that the different functions "creation, redemption, revelation" are assigned to different quasi-divine figures in "Judaism," while all are assigned to one in "Christianity," thus marking the site of a significant difference.[52] Of course, one could argue that the Memra is a post-Christian development—not an impossible suggestion, and one that would make the point of continued Jewish-Christian closeness all the more eloquently. While in general I find Hurtado's argument bracing and important, his exclusive reliance on only one criterion, worship, to determine the divine nature of a given intermediary seems to me overly narrow and rigid. There may be no gainsaying his demonstration, I think, that worship of the *incarnate* Logos is a novum, a "mutation," as he styles it, introduced by Jesus people, but the *belief* in an intermediary, a *deuteros theos*, and even perhaps binitarian worship was common to them and other Jews.

On the Trail of Jewish Binitarianism

A large number of scholars have identified and discussed the various manifestations of Jewish binitarianism (and even ditheism[53]). I shall cite and discuss
here only some of the recent scholarship most relevant for the present argument. As Wolfson has put it with respect to certain early medieval Jewish mystics: "It may be said that the Jewish mystics recovered the mythical dimension of
a biblical motif regarding the appearance of God in guise of the highest of angels, called 'angel of the Lord' (*mal'akh [H']*), 'angel of God' . . . , or 'angel of the
Presence' (*mal'akh ha-panim*) which sometimes appeared in the form of a man.
Evidence for the continuity of the exegetical tradition of an exalted angel that is
in effect the manifestation of God is to be found in a wide variety of later
sources."[54] Wolfson lists Christians as only one of many such Jewish groups and
sources and cites compelling evidence for the blurring or even erasing of
boundaries between that angel and God.[55]

Moreover, there is powerful evidence that in quite early (but post-Christian)
mystical prayer, even in rabbinic circles, it was possible to pray to both "The
Lord of All" and the "Creator of Bere'shit" without this having, seemingly, any
"gnostic" meanings. Moshe Idel uses the term "binitarian" for this form of Jewish prayer in its early medieval manifestations and explicitly rejects the terminology of "gnosis" that appears in earlier scholarly writings.[56] This form of
Jewish prayer may be as early as the late second century, and at the latest is from
the fourth or fifth century.[57] It is thus at least contemporary with the later targumic texts. It becomes harder and harder to see binitarian worship as distinguishing "Judaism" from "Christianity." As Idel emphasizes, this binitarian
prayer was found in absolutely central early medieval rabbinic writers, of whom
it is almost impossible to imagine that they "invented" a binitarian worship
form that they had not received as a tradition.

There is another fascinating piece of possible evidence for Jewish binitarian prayer in the rabbinic period, albeit marked by the rabbinic text as *minut.* In
the Babylonian Talmud Sanhedrin 38b, we read:

אמר רב נחמן: האי מאן דידע לאהדורי למינים כרב אידית - ליהדר, ואי לא - לא ליהדר.
אמר ההוא מינא לרב אידית: כתיב +שמות כ"ד+ ואל משה אמר עלה אל ה', עלה אלי
מיבעי ליה! אמר ליה: זהו מטטרון, ששמו כשם רבו, דכתיב +שמות כ"ג+ כי שמי בקרבו.-
אי הכי ניפלחו ליה! - כתיב +שמות כ"ג+ אל תמר בו - אל תמירני בו. - אם כן לא ישא
לפשעכם למה לי? - אמר ליה: הימנותא בידן, דאפילו בפרוונקא נמי לא קבילניה, דכתיב
+שמות ל"ג+ ויאמר אליו אם אין פניך הלכים וגו'.

Rav Naḥman said: A person who knows how to answer the *minim* as Rav Idit, let him
answer, and if not, let him not answer. A certain *min* said to Rav Idit: "It is written, 'And

to Moses he said, come up unto the H' [Exod. 24:1].' It should have said, 'Come up to me'!"

He [Rav Idit] said to him: "This was Metatron, whose name is like the name of his master, as it is written, 'for My name is in him' [Exod. 23:21]."

"But if so, we should worship him!"

"It is written, 'Do not rebel against him' [Exod. 23:21]—Do not confuse him with me!"

"If so, then why does it say 'He will not forgive your sins'?"

"We have sworn that we would not even receive him as a guide, for it is written 'If Your face goes not [do not bring us up from here]' [Exod. 33:15]" (BT Sanhedrin 38b)[58]

This extraordinary bit of rhetoric needs some glossing and then a deeper consideration of modalities for its reading than it has received so far.[59] The *min* produces a seemingly compelling argument that there are two powers in heaven. God has been addressing the Jewish people as a whole (in chapter 23), informing them that he will send his angel before them and instructing them how to behave with respect to this angel. He then turns to Moses and tells him to come up to H' (the Tetragrammaton), implying quite strongly that H' is not the same person as the speaker of the verse.[60] Rav Idit turns back to the previous chapter and remarks that verse 21 there explicitly says that "My name is in him [that is, in the angel]." Metatron, that angel, therefore could be called by the name H', and it is to him that Moses is being instructed to ascend. At this point, the *min* responds by saying that if Metatron is indeed called by the ineffable name, then we ought to worship him as well; in other words, that Rav Idit's own answer can be turned against him. To this, Rav Idit retorts that the verse also says "Do not rebel against him," which by a typical midrashic sleight of hand can be read as "Do not substitute him," that is, even though Metatron is called by God's name, do not pray to him. The *min* says if that is what is meant, then why does it continue in the verse and say that he, Metatron, will not forgive sins? The *min* is arguing that if the people are being warned not to rebel against Metatron, because he is as powerful as God, then it makes sense to tell them that he will not forgive their sins if they do rebel, but if he is no God at all, then it is otiose to tell them that he will not forgive sins. What is his importance at all? I would suggest, moreover, that, in typical midrashic fashion, another verse lies underneath this comment of the *min*. Joshua 24:19 reads: "It will be very difficult for you to [lit. you will not be able to] worship H', for He is a holy God; He is a jealous God; He will not forgive your sins and your iniquities." In other words, the logic would run: if there it remarks of H' that he will not forgive sins and iniquities, then if the same language is being used here, ought it not indicate that the divine figure being spoken of has the same attributes as H'?[61] The comparison is rendered even stronger when we notice that exactly the same context is involved

in both the Exodus and the Joshua verse, namely the expulsion of the Canaan-
ites from the land of Israel and the warnings to the people of Israel to be worthy of this benefit and to worship H', or their sin will not be forgiven at all. It
certainly seems as if the verse in Exodus can be read as equating Metatron to H'
and therefore demanding worship for both figures. To this the answer comes
that "we" the Jews already have declared that we do not even want him, Metatron, to be our guide in the desert, as the cited verse says: "If Your face goes not."
In other words, the angelic regent was of such unimportance that, far from considering him worthy of being worshiped, Moses would not even accept him as
guide.

The rhetoric of this text is quite astounding, and analysis of it should prove
illuminating. In this, as in many other cases of such hermeneutical encounters,
the *min* certainly seems to have the upper hand to begin with, for there are
many, many scriptural texts that support the notion of an angelic vice-regent
with many of the powers of God, or even the notion of a virtual second God.
Indeed, more than anything else, this very scriptural background may have
given the greatest impetus to the various second-God theologies of Jews, including Logos, Memra, Sophia, Metatron, and others. In order to discredit the
min's quite straightforward interpretation of the verses in question—"Behold I
send before you an angel, to watch over you on the way and to bring you to the
place I have prepared. Be careful before him and obedient to him. Do not disobey him, for he will not forgive your sins, for My name is in him"—Rev Idit
needs pyrotechnics. Although, to be sure, the second of these two verses presents difficulties, at the very least it would seem that this (fairly straightforward)
translation does imply that this angel has the power to command and to remit
sins (which he will not employ), as God has delegated to him something of divine power. The *min* quite reasonably suggests that one ought to pray to such a
divine being, Metatron on Rav Idit's showing. In order to escape this seemingly
ineluctable conclusion, Rav Idit proposes to read "Be careful before him and
obedient to him. Do not confuse him with me, for he will not forgive your sins,
for my name is in him." Aside from the fact that this translation renders the
verse considerably less coherent in its logic, it also makes this angel seem absolutely insignificant, hardly worthy of mention, to which Rav Idit answers (and
this is his brilliant move) that indeed that is so. The Israelites have already reg-
istered their rejection of any interest in this insignificant angel when they insisted that God himself must go before them and no other, thus dramatizing the
rejection of the Logos theology that the Rabbis themselves perform.

For my purposes, the most important thing is that the *min* strongly argues
for worship of the angel, Metatron. There is not the slightest indication in this
text that the *min* in question means by this the worship of Jesus. Metatron may

indeed be the figure in non-Christian Jewish myth who is most closely related to Jesus, but Christians don't worship Metatron; they worship Jesus. This Jewish *min*, however, like Christians is a binitarian, who holds that the angelic vice-regent, Metatron, is to be worshiped, suggesting that the premise of Hayward's argument—even if one could accept the conclusion from it—is much weaker than he thinks. I am not suggesting that there was, necessarily, actually a *min* of the precise sort that this text projects.[62] Where Segal, in general, seeks the actual groups to which *minim* can be posited as belonging—"In order to identify the various sectarian groups, one must also identify the heretical doctrine espoused by those groups and find evidence that the doctrine can be clearly associated with an historical group at the time the rabbinic tradition arose"[63]—the method and ambitions of the present work are quite different. I seek to see how rabbinic Judaism was carving out an orthodox space for itself by naming other Jewish beliefs as heresies, thus possibly (but not always and not necessarily) producing "heresies" and even "heretical" social groups, and likewise for Christianity as well.[64] Thus, my question here will not be to what group did the *min* "really" belong but, rather, what are the Rabbis seeking to accomplish by representing a *min* who argues in this way. This suggests to me that in their project of producing an orthodoxy for Judaism, the Rabbis were disowning a Jewish practice of worship of the second God, the lesser H' [My name is in him], Metatron.

The strongest evidence for binitarian prayer among Jews comes, however, from the Mishna. The crucial text is in Mishna Megilla 4:9:

One who says, "Let the good bless you,"—behold this is the way of *minut*.[65] "May your mercy reach the nest of the bird, and your name be blessed for good; we thank Thee, we thank Thee"—we silence him. One who reads the passage in the Torah about forbidden sexual unions figuratively [Lev. 18], we silence him: One who says, "'Of your seed you should not pass to Molekh [Lev. 18:21]' [means] 'Of your seed, you must not allow to make a pagan woman pregnant'[66]"—we silence him with a rebuke.[67]

Both Talmuds identify various of the "forbidden" phrases in this Mishna as referring to those who hold Two Powers views and are therefore to be silenced when they serve as precentors in the Synagogue and utilize these "heretical" formulations in their repetition of the *Amida*, the main portion of the Synagogue prayer. The various formulations would relate in one way or another to beliefs in two divine powers in general, without any possibility of identifying particular groups who were behind one or another of these "heretical" forms.[68] The clear implication of these interdictions is, at any rate, that the performers of such prayers would have been found in the synagogues and be otherwise indistinguishable from other Jews.[69] Interestingly, however, the scholarly tradition seems to have ignored the one piece of solid information that we can glean from this Mishnaic text as to the groups who might have used these prayer forms. The last phrase of the Mishna indicates a strongly interdicted targumic reading of Leviticus 18:21 as forbidding sexual unions between Israelites and pagans. For some reason the Rabbis objected very strenuously to this reading.[70] Since this is clearly a quotation from a Targum that represents an exegesis of the verse that is well attested in extant Palestinian Targums, as well as one that was current among prerabbinic and even early rabbinic circles,[71] we can assume that this was the practice of translation of the verse in at least some Palestinian synagogues. A reasonable (but hardly ineluctable) inference in the absence of any other contravening information is that strongly related issues are being discussed in the single paragraph of the Mishna. It would follow, then, that the liturgical practices being interdicted in the first part of the Mishna also were practices of the synagogues within which the Palestinian Targums with their Memra theology were current. If we trust the interpretations of the Talmud to this Mishna, that these are anathematized because they were binitarian (Two Powers in Heaven), which again seems reasonable if by no means inevitable, then the conclusion is that binitarian prayer was known to the Rabbis as current in those same synagogues.

Given such evidence for Jewish binitarian prayer, the medieval interpretation of the late ancient prayer to the "Lord of All" and the "Creator of Bere'shit" as binitarian may be taken to be highly plausible, if not definitive.[72] It could be said, with hardly any exaggeration, that the various attempts in medieval Jewish exegesis to explain these texts theologically could be mapped onto the varieties of late ancient Christian theologies, from Marcellus of Ancyra's to Eunomius's, with an orthodox Nicene version of Judaism in there as well.[73] Indeed, the theological problem of the ontological status of Logos-like hypostases is precisely that of the possible worship of divine beings other than God. As Elliot Wolfson puts it, "The initial theoretical problem of addressing prayer to an entity that is distinct from God [the created Glory] is solved by the blurring of the ontological difference between the Creator and the image."[74] By the early medieval period, then, (at least some) Jews could pray to "second persons" in good conscience. The incarnation of the Logos in Jesus' flesh was much more of a "mutation" than was worship of the Logos or Demiurge (although the Logos personifying the Messiah seems not to have been a mutation at all[75]). It is, therefore, telling that this prayer to a binitarian God includes a moment of almost explicit anti–Jesus worship: "They pray to vanity and emptiness, and bow down to a god who cannot save [לאל לא יושיע]." The last three words, although a citation from Isaiah, are used here, in my opinion, as an ironic pun on the name of Jesus, *Soter*. This becomes more plausible when we pay attention to the whole verse of Isaiah from which the citation is drawn: "Gather and meet together, O remnant of the nations, those who carry the wood of their statue, and pray to a god who cannot save." Christians might very well be comprehended as a remnant of the nations who carry a wooden "idol." Israel Ta-Shma[76] cites a medieval Ashkenazic expanded version of the prayer that explicitly indicates that "they" worship a god who is only "flesh and blood." The insinuation is that the Logos Asarkos is kosher for Jewish worship but not the Logos Ensarkos.[77] This leads me to infer that Christianity and Judaism distinguished themselves in antiquity not via the doctrine of God, and not even via the question of worshiping a second God (although the Jewish heresiologists would make it so, as we shall see in the next chapter), but only in the specifics of the doctrine of this incarnation.[78] Not even the appearance of the Logos as human, I would suggest, but rather the ascription of actual physical death and resurrection to the Logos was the point at which non-Christian Jews would have begun to part company theologically with those Christians—not all, of course—who held such doctrines.

The Beginning of the Word

In the Targums we can see, or at any rate paint, a picture of how the Memra has also come into being in the exegesis of Genesis 1:3. Exodus 3:12–14 (the theophany of the burning bush), when read together with that verse, and its targumic expositions are key texts.[79] The Hebrew of verse 12 reads that Moses, having asked God his name so that he may say in whose name it is that he comes, receives the famous reply:

And God said to Moses: "I am that I am,"[80] and he said: "Thus shall you say unto them, 'I Am has sent me to you.'"

"I Am" is thus a name of God (the name that would be claimed by Jesus in the Fourth Gospel: *Ego Eimi*). On this verse, the Palestinian Targum[81] translates: "And the Memra of H' said to Moses: He who said [אמר], to the world from the beginning, 'Be there,' and it was there, and who is to say [יאמר] to it 'Be there,' and it will be there; and he said, Thus shall you say to the Israelites, He has sent me to you."[82] In other words, the name "I Am" has been glossed in the Targums by a reference to Genesis 1's "And God said: Let there be" and thus to the Word by which God brought the universe into being, namely, the Memra. In the verse following this one, this name for God—"He who said to the world 'Be there'— has become transformed into a divine being in its own right, the very word that was said, separate from but *homoouosios* with God: "I, My Memra, will be with you: I, My Memra will be a support for you." In verse 13, in answer to Moses' apprehension that he will not be sufficient to go to Pharaoh to bring out the Israelites, God answers: "I [Am] [אהיה] will be with you." According to the Palestinian Targum, preserved in ms. Neofiti 1, the Aramaic here reads: "I, My Memra, will be with you."[83] The other Targums maintain this interpretation, but add the element of the Memra as supporter, thus: "And he said: Because my Memra will be for your support."[84] From this we see how this Memra, Logos, is that which is revealed to Moses in the declaration I Am, provides support for him, redeems the Israelites, and so forth. In the Targum, as in Logos theology, this Word has been hypostasized, treated as an actual divine person.[85] In other words, this targumic midrash provides us with a point of origin for the term *Memra* as derived from an interpretation of Genesis 1:3. One could say that "I Am" [*Ego Eimi*] is a name for the Memra from this targumic text.

The finest evidence for the connection of the targumic Memra and the Logos of John has been adduced by Martin McNamara in the guise of the Palestinian targumic poetic homily on the "four nights." Most immediately relevant is the first night, the night of creation: "Four nights are written in the Book of Memories: The first night: when the Lord was revealed above the world to create it. The world was unformed and void and darkness was spread over the surface of the deep; AND THROUGH HIS *MEMRA* THERE WAS LIGHT AND ILLUMINATION, and he called it the first night."[86] This text appears in various witnesses to the Palestinian Targum, so it cannot be taken as a later "Christianizing" interpolation into the text. McNamara's conclusion that this text represents a cognate to the first verses of the Johannine Prologue, with their association of Logos, the Word, and light is therefore compelling: "It is legitimate, then, to presume that the author of the Fourth Gospel heard read in the synagogue that, at the very beginning of time, at the creation of the universe ('the first night'), there was an all-pervading darkness. There was also God, or 'the Word of the Lord'. This Word of the Lord was the light and it shone."[87] As McNamara shows, the midrash of the "four nights" culminates in the night of the Messiah, drawing even closer the connections between the religious tradition of the synagogues as manifested in the Targums and that of the Fourth Evangelist. Moreover, the midrash of the "four nights" is almost beyond a doubt a fragment of Paschal liturgy, which suggests even more palpably its appropriateness as intertext for a Gospel.[88]

The Gospel of John, according to this view, when taken together with the Logos of Philo and with the Targum, provides further important evidence that Logos theology, used here as a general term for various closely related binitarian theologies, was the religious koine of Jews in Palestine and the Diaspora, their theological lingua franca, which is not, of course, to claim that it was a universally held position.[89] In saying this, I am arguing, in effect, that in the doctrine of God there is no essential and crucial difference between Judaism and Christianity. Both historically and descriptively, orthodox Nicene Christianity and orthodox rabbinic Judaism represent two points—not, of course, arbitrary ones—on a graph of oscillating possibilities for approaching the theological problems of divine transcendence and the possibilities of creation, revelation, and redemption that were current in the ante-Nicene world of both.

Chapter 6

The Crucifixion of the Memra:
How the Logos Became Christian

If you come to a fork in the road, take it.
—*Lawrence Peter Berra (with gratitude to Vincent P. Bynack)*

As scholars have seen, there is an apparent and important parallel to Philo's Logos myth in the classical Palestinian midrash *Bereshith Rabba*. According to this very famous passage, Rabbi Hoshaya of Caesarea declares that God looked into the Torah as a blueprint in order to create the world. Now, on the one hand, this is obviously very close to "Philo's conception of the Logos as the instrument of God in creation," so much so that it has been virtually accepted that Rabbi Hoshaya, a contemporary of Origen, drew this idea from that disciple of Philo's disciple.[1] The passage in Philo is exquisitely evocative: "Exactly as the city which was fashioned beforehand within the mind of the architect held no place in the outer world, but had been engraved in the soul of the artificer as by a seal, in the same way the universe that consisted of ideas would have no other location than the Divine Logos, which was the author of this ordered frame. For what other place could there be for His powers sufficient to receive and contain, I say not all but any one of them whatever uncompounded and untempered?"[2] What has not been adequately noted by scholars (in my opinion) is that the shift from Logos in Philo—"what other place" indeed—to Torah in the midrash is highly significant and is consistent with the overall rabbinic insistence that the Sophia of Proverbs 8 is Torah and only Torah, in accord with their maxim that אין חכמה אלא תורה ["Wisdom" is nothing but Torah,] an exegetical remark: ὁ λόγος νόμος ἐγένετο. In other words, the "recycling," if such it is, of the Philonic idea of Sophia as the Logos is here accompanied by the precise denial of any mediator or *deuteros theos* apart from Scripture itself.[3] This is a further development from the identification of hypostasized Wisdom with the Torah that we find especially in Ben Sira 24:22 ff. We see here a pointed denial of the existence of the *angelus interpres* of apocalyptic literature,[4] and his implicit descendent, the Logos, as guide to interpretation and agent of revelation.

The finally definitive move for the Rabbis was to transfer all Logos and Sophia talk to the Torah alone,[5] thus effectively accomplishing two powerful discursive moves at once: consolidating their own power as the sole religious virtuosi and leaders of "the Jews," and protecting one version of monotheistic thinking from the problematic of division within the godhead.[6] For the Rabbis, Torah supersedes Logos, just as for John, Logos supersedes Torah. Or, to put it into more fully Johannine terms, if for John the Logos Incarnate in Jesus replaces the Logos revealed in the Book, for the Rabbis the Logos Incarnate in the Book displaces the Logos that subsists anywhere else *but* in the Book. This move on the part of the Rabbis at the end of the rabbinic period effectively displaces the structure of Western thought, embodied in the Fourth Gospel, whereby Logos is located most directly and presently in the voice of the speaker, Jesus, with the written text understood at best as a secondary reflection of the speaker's intention. It is this supersupersession of the Logos by Writing that arguably gives birth to rabbinic Judaism and its characteristic forms of textuality.

As an emblem of the parting of this long-shared way, I would advance the following juxtaposition: "θεὸν οὐδεὶς ἑώρακεν πώποτε μονογενὴς θεὸς ὁ ὢν εἰς τὸν κόλπον τοῦ πατρὸς ἐκεῖνος ἐξηγήσατο" [No one has ever seen God; the only begotten, who is in the bosom of the Father, he has made him known] (John 1:18), and "רבי אליעזר בנו של רבי יוסי הגלילי אומר תשע מאות ושבעים דורות קודם שנברא העולם היתה תורה כתובה ומונחת בחיקו של הקב״ה ואומרת שירה עם מלאכי השרת שנאמר ואהיה אצלו אמון ואהיה שעשועים יום יום משחקת לפניו" [Rabbi Eliʿezer the son of Rabbi Yose the Galilean says: Nine hundred and seventy generations before the world was created, the Torah was written and lying in the bosom of the Holy Blessed One and singing song with the serving angels, as it says: "I was his nurseling / or, and I was his little child / or, I was his betrothed,[7] and I was daily his delight, playing before him at all times"] (Prov. 8:30).[8] The verse of the Gospel seems based on an ancient midrash similar to the one found in the late rabbinic text, where the subject has been transferred from Wisdom (the Logos) to Torah.[9] For both, of course, the Logos (or anti-Logos) is generated out of the same basic concatenation of Genesis 1 and Proverbs 8, but whence the bosom? I believe that the key to explaining this midrash in both the Gospel and the late rabbinic version is, in fact, the common midrashic practice I have remarked above of building on a verse that is not cited in the text at all. In Numbers 11:12, we read: "האנכי הריתי את כל העם הזה אם אנכי ילדתיהו כי תאמר אלי שאהו בחיקך כאשר ישא האמן את היונק" [Have I conceived all of this People; did I give birth to it, that you should say to me: "Carry him in your bosom, as the nurse carries the child"?] The word that I have translated as "nurse" here—and from the context would seem to mean nursing parent—is the active participle of which the crucial vocable in the Proverbs verse is the passive, and therefore, "nurseling," "infant child." Moreover, from the verse in Numbers we learn that the nurse carries the nurseling in her/his bosom, exactly as in the verse in John and the midrashic text. In other words, the text from Numbers connects the word in the Proverbs 8 verse referring to "Wisdom" as "nurseling" to the image of being carried in the bosom of her father. For the rabbinic text, however, it is the Torah that is the beloved child that the Father carries in his bosom, the son, or daughter of God. For the earlier midrash of the Fourth Gospel, she was the Logos, the Son.

Logos as Heresy

My position is quite different from the pioneering work of Alan Segal. He writes, "a few have even suggested that there was no concept of orthodoxy in rabbinic Judaism. Part of the importance of these reports about 'two powers in heaven' is that they show us that the rabbis, in common with their brethren in the diaspora, were concerned about the theological and orthodox center of Judaism when other sectarian groups of their day seemed willing to compromise Judaism's integrity."[10] While I am in total sympathy with Segal's critique of those who see rabbinism as being a doctrine-free orthopraxy, from my point of view the orthodoxy that the Rabbis were concerned about was an orthodoxy that they were making by *constructing* Two Powers in Heaven as heresy, at just about the time when bishops were declaring belief in "One Power in Heaven," or Monarchianism, to be a leading heresy of Christianity.[11] The Rabbis, by defining elements from within their own religious heritage as not Jewish, were, in effect, producing Christianity, just as Christian heresiologists were, by defining traditional elements of their own religious heritage as being not Christian, thereby producing Judaism. The Christian heresiologists, as was their wont, were more explicit about naming the "heresy" Judaism, while the Rabbis were more circumspect. Neither was "protecting the integrity of the theological and orthodox center" of their respective religions,[12] but rather constructing them through discursive analogues of the psychic process known as splitting, wherein unwanted parts of the psyche are projected "out there," producing a sense of good self and bad other. "In so far as the objects which are presented to [the ego] are sources of pleasure, it takes them into itself, 'introjects' them . . . ; and, on the other hand, it expels whatever within itself becomes a cause of unpleasure (. . . the mechanism of projection). . . . For the pleasure-ego the external world is divided into a part that is pleasurable, which is incorporated into itself, and a remainder that is extraneous to it. It has [also] separated off a part of its own self, which it projects into the external world."[13] I find this a useful analogy for understanding how Christianity and Judaism each produced their respective others by disavowing parts of themselves.

A conceptual difficulty raised by Segal's otherwise excellent book[14] can clarify the difference and the stakes involved here. Segal summarizes his results: "It became clear that 'two powers in heaven' was a very early category of heresy, earlier than Jesus, if Philo is a trustworthy witness, and one of the basic categories by which the rabbis perceived the new phenomenon of Christianity. It was one of the central issues over which the two religions separated."[15] The conceptual problem is that, since the very category of heresy did not exist in Judaism before the rabbinic formation,[16] a point that Segal himself makes elsewhere,[17] Two Powers in Heaven could not have been an early category of heresy rather than one of the options for Jewish belief at the time. If, then, the Rabbis named this a heresy, which they did, and made it a sort of touchstone for distinguishing their "orthodox" Judaism from the *minut* of Christians (and others), their doing so cannot be formulated as one of the issues over which the two religions separated, but was, rather, the means by which a border was inscribed. That is, by naming Two Powers heresy and giving over that doctrine to Christianity (in which some Christians avidly colluded), an ancient Jewish doctrine was marked as a heresy, and the two "religions" were produced as different.[18] I would thus rewrite Segal's sentence as follows: There is significant evidence (uncovered in large part by Segal) that in the first century many—perhaps most—Jews held a binitarian doctrine of God.[19] This Jewish doctrine was named by the Rabbis as an important part of the project of constructing Jewish orthodoxy as separate from Christianity.[20]

As in Christian orthodoxy, the arch-heresy for the Rabbis involved, not surprisingly, a "flaw" in the doctrine of God:[21] Two Powers in Heaven, binitarianism, of which one major manifestation was traditional Jewish Logos theology.[22] This issue of the doctrine of God seems one archaeological site where making the distinction between the (metaphorically) excavated Synagogue and the House of Study,[23] or between rabbinic and other forms of Jewish piety in the rabbinic period, becomes crucial.[24] Alejandro Díez Macho has observed that it is no mere coincidence that the more rabbinized of the Targums (Targum Onkelos and Pseudo-Jonathan) and rabbinic literature itself noticeably suppress the term *Memra*. Indeed, in rabbinic literature it disappears entirely,[25] and in the more rabbinized Targums it appears much less frequently, suggesting a struggle between the forms of piety that were current in the synagogues and those that were centered in the Houses of Study of the Rabbis. This strongly implies that Logos theology was a living current within non-Christian Judaic circles from before the Christian era until well into late antiquity, when the Palestinian Targums were produced.[26] We must avoid the methodological error of regarding all nonrabbinic religious expression by Jews during the rabbinic period as somehow not quite legitimate or of marginalizing it by naming it "syncretistic" or "uninformed," thus simply reproducing the rabbinic ideology, rather than subjecting it to historical criticism.[27] In other words, the consensus of scholars of rabbinic Judaism referred to by Hayward simply replicates the consensus of the Rabbis themselves, whereas the current scholarly task is to read this latter consensus against its grain, in order to see what it mystified in order to construct its hegemony.[28]

Extant rabbinic texts demonstrate that the Rabbis, too, knew of Logos theology, but that they constructed their own "orthodoxy" by excommunicating the Jewish Logos from within their midst. As Robert Hayward put it, "The Logos is an intermediary, and ABELSON rightly remarks that the Rabbis repudiate all intermediaries."[29] "We must think of heresy not so much as something that attacked the church from without, as of something that grew up within it," writes C. K. Barrett, paraphrasing Bartsch,[30] and the same goes, mutatis mutandis, for the rabbinic tradition; the repudiation of all intermediaries is a repudiation of something internal, not only to "Judaism" but even to rabbinic Judaism.[31] Having shown the likelihood that Logos theology is an ancient heritage of the Jews, we can begin to imagine the complex process of splitting that ultimately gave rise to Judaism and Christianity. Christianity and Judaism became constructed in part through the rabbinic repudiation of all intermediaries, that is, its alienation of that native son, the Logos, and at the same time through the orthodox Christian nomination of this very repudiation, when enacted by Christians, as heresy and as "Judaizing." Homi Bhabha has given a perfect description of this psychocultural process:

Produced through the strategy of disavowal, the *reference* of discrimination is always to a process of splitting as the condition of subjection: a discrimination between the mother culture and its bastards, the self and its doubles, where the trace of what is disavowed is not repressed but repeated as something *different*—a mutation, a hybrid. It is such a partial and double force that . . . disturbs the visibility of the colonial presence and makes the recognition of its authority problematic. To be authoritative, its rules of recognition must reflect consensual knowledge or opinion; to be powerful, these rules of recognition must be reached in order to represent the exorbitant objects of discrimination that lie beyond its purview.[32]

One could hardly hope for a more precise description of the heresiological process in general, or of the specific instance of the production of the bastard, Two Powers in Heaven, as what is not so much repressed but disavowed, produced as a mutation, a hybrid, a "Jewish Christianity."[33]

Rabbinic discourse about Two Powers in Heaven is not a rabbinic "report" of essential differences between Christianity (or "Gnosticism") and Judaism, but rather a rabbinic production of the defining limits of what the Rabbis take to be Judaism via the abjection of one traditional element in Jewish religiosity, a production almost identical, as we shall see, to the Christian heresiological naming of One Power in Heaven (Monarchianism) as "Judaism," when, in fact, it was, of course, an internal and once-acceptable version of Christian theology.[34] I am suggesting that for the Rabbis, the discourse of heresiology, that is, the collection of laws and narratives about *minut* and especially about the "heresy" of Two Powers in Heaven, is not *about* Christianity but may be in part a response *to* Christianity. Thus when we examine particular instances of such discourse, we need not expect to find notions particular to Christianity but rather a general formation of a space between self and other, produced by marking certain differences within and differences between. "Jewish Christian" heresies function in the same way for Christian identity formation. As Jonathan Z. Smith has written: "From heresy to deviation to degeneration to syncretism, the notion of the different which claims to be the same, or, projected internally, the disguised difference within has produced a rich vocabulary of denial and estrangement. For in each case, a theory of difference, when applied to the proximate 'other,' is but another way of phrasing a theory of the 'self.'"[35] Two Powers in Heaven is such a "disguised difference within."

Karen King has observed that "the attempt at domination in naming one's opponents (as heretics, for example) has a reciprocal effect on the namer as well."[36] Taking up this observation, I hope to show how crucial elements of rabbinic Judaism—its "Modalism" (the doctrine that different persons are just different modes of appearance of the one divine person) for instance—were formed in the attempt to "other" these *minim*. Once again, to adopt a formulation of King's, "Constructing a heretical other simultaneously and reciprocally constructed an orthodox self." Another way of saying this would be to suggest that, while there were genuine differences between nascent Judaism and nascent Christianity, they were not necessarily precisely where the discourse of *minut* would place them. Rather, this discourse itself helped to shape and make the difference between the "two religions" in the place that we still, to this day, take it to be, such as, for instance, in the acceptance or rejection of the Logos and Logos theology. Put one final way, I am partially reversing Alain Le Boulluec's claim (made, to be sure, with respect to Christianity) that strategies that were initially developed in conflict with Jews and Greeks were adapted by Christians in their fight against internal differences.[37] I suggest, rather, that the tools that the Rabbis developed in their own struggles for power and identity ended up (in the same process) in marking a difference between (rabbinic) Judaism and Christianity.

Two Powers in Heaven as Jewish Theology

The notion of a second and independent divine agent can be found in the Bible itself, as has been emphasized by earlier scholars. Darrell Hannah makes the point that the Exodus angel "becomes to some extent an expression of the divine absence in that he is a substitute for Yahweh (Ex. 33.1–3). As a replacement for the divine presence, it would appear that the angel of the Exodus is beginning to have a quasi-individual existence. Significantly, unlike מלאך ה [the angel of the Lord] in the patriarchal narratives, the Exodus angel is spoken of by God in the third person (23.20–21, 32.34, and 33.2–3). So the Exodus angel seems to betray a certain development in the מלאך ה concept, away from an extension or manifestation of the divine presence and toward an individual existence."[38] Hannah makes the significant double observation that in the earlier strata of biblical writing, the patriarchal narratives and Exodus, there is frequent confusion, if not conflation, between the Angel of H' and H' himself, and that this particular hypostatization seems to disappear during the period of the monarchy, to be replaced by a host of angels who are fully separate beings and clearly subordinate to God.[39] This ambiguity in the early biblical narratives, particularly when they are read together—as one phenomenon—with the later texts and ideas, was to fuel much interpretative controversy and angst in the early years of Judaeo-Christianity, for many of these very passages served as the origin and prooftext for Logos theology, as Justin's *Dialogue* manifests on nearly every page. What is important in this context, however, is not so much the implication of the biblical passages themselves but the strenuous energy that rabbinic literature mobilized in order to *deny* these implications, an expenditure of energy that indicates the attractiveness of the *deuteros theos* idea among Jews.

An elegant example of this energy can be found in the following early rabbinic midrash:

"H' smote every first-born in the land of Egypt" [Exod. 12:29]: I might have understood by means of an angel or by means of an agent, therefore Scripture teaches: "And I have smitten all of the first-born" [Exod. 12:12]; not by means of an angel and not by means of an agent. (Mekhilta, Tractate Pisḥa, 13) [40]

Precisely the sort of ambiguity that would lead to the theological ambivalence and the production of notions of a fully divine angel is thoroughly repulsed by the rabbinic midrash. It has frequently been theorized that when the midrash writes "I might have understood," another, "sectarian," interpretation is being raised in order to discredit it. This, in any case, would be a fine example for that theory. Ancient Jews and Christian writers like Justin would certainly have seen in this combination of verses evidence for their various versions of Logos theology, and it is these findings that the Rabbis here dispute vigorously.[41] However, there is more, for there are ancient variants of the text that explicitly add to "not by means of an angel, and not by means of an agent"—"not by means of the Logos" [לא על ידי הדיבר].[42]

One very rich example for my purposes here has been treated by Robert Hayward, although I interpret the text differently. The text is from the fourth-century midrash the Mekhilta d'Rabbi Ishmael to Exodus 20:2:

I am the Lord your God [Exod. 20:2]: Why was it said? For this reason. At the sea He appeared to them as a mighty hero doing battle, as it is said: "The Lord is a man of war." At Sinai he appeared to them as an old man full of mercy. It is said: "And they saw the God of Israel" [Exod. 24:10], etc. And of the time after they had been redeemed what does it say? "And the like of the very heaven for clearness" [ibid.]. Again it says: "I beheld till thrones were placed, and one that was ancient of days did sit" [Dan. 7:9]. And it also says: "A fiery stream issued," etc. [Dan. 7:10].[43] Scripture, therefore, would not let the nations of the world[44] have an excuse for saying that there are two Powers, but declares: "The Lord is a man of war, the Lord is His name." He, it is, who was in Egypt and He who was at the sea. It is He who was in the past and He who will be in the future. It is He who is in this world and He who will be in the world to come, as it is said, "See now that I, even I, am He," etc. [Deut. 32:39]. And it also says: "Who hath wrought and done it? He that called the generations from the beginning. I, the Lord, who am the first, and with the last am the same" [Isa. 41:4].[45]

The passage from Daniel that is alluded to *but not cited* in the anti-"heretical" discourse, the "Son of Man" passage so pivotal for the development of early Christology, is the real point of contention here and the reason for the citation of Exodus 20:2. There are two descriptions of God as revealed in the Torah, one at the splitting of the Red Sea and one at the revelation of the Ten Commandments at Sinai. In the first, God is explicitly described as a warrior, that is, as a young man, as it were, while in the latter, as the Rabbis read it, God is described as an elder, full of wisdom and mercy. The problem is the doubling of descriptions of God as *senex* (judge) and *puer* (man of war) and the correlation of those two descriptions with the divine figures of Ancient of Days and Son of Man from Daniel, which together might easily lead one to think that there are Two Powers in Heaven, or indeed, that God has two persons, a Father-person and a Son-person. These were, of course, crucial loci for christological interpretations. The citation of God's Name in Exodus 20:2, at the beginning of the Ten Commandments, thus answers possible heretical implications of those verses by insisting on the unity of H' in both instances. Indeed, the verse Exodus 15:3, "The Lord is a man of war; The Lord is his name," is taken by the Rabbis to mean that the two appearances of God, as youth and elder, are two modalities of the same person—dynamic Modalism—and not two persons, thus refuting the "heretics." The text portentously *avoids* citing the Daniel verses most difficult for rabbinic Judaism, verses 13–14: "I saw in the vision of the night, and behold with the clouds of the Heaven there came one like a Son of Man and came to the Ancient of Days and stood before him and brought him close, and to him was given rulership and the glory and the kingdom, and all nations, peoples, and languages will worship him. His rulership is eternal which will not pass, and his kingship will not be destroyed."[46] The tacit contention with the Logos theology of the Targum appears especially strong when we remember that in targumic texts we can find the Son of Man identified as the Messiah.[47] Furthermore, in a talmudic passage to be discussed below (BT Ḥagiga 14a), Rabbi Akiva himself is represented as identifying the "Son of Man" with the heavenly David, and thus with the Messiah, before being "encouraged" by his fellows to abandon this "heretical" view. This would suggest the possibility that there were non-Christian Jews who would have identified the Messiah (necessarily incarnate) as the Son of Man.

Hayward believes that this midrash represents an assertion of Memra theology and concludes, therefore, that "this midrash presents Memra-Theology in Rabbinic terms, and is a means of proving nothing less than the unity of God, the *very opposite* of the use to which the Gnostics or Christians are supposed to have put it."[48] However, there is no reference whatsoever to the Memra in this or any other rabbinic text, so it seems entirely unjustified to see here a presentation of Memra theology. Indeed it is much more plausible to see here a polemic against a Memra theology that would project in rabbinic terms any doctrine of the Memra as Two Powers in Heaven and thus *minut*.

Segal has suggested independently that "in view of the importance of the name of God in this midrash it is not unlikely that the midrash is relying on the mysterious name of God which was revealed to Moses at the burning bush. 'I am that I am' is being interpreted with past and future implications of the Hebrew verb forms and is being understood to be an eternal pledge to remain with Israel."[49] We have seen, however, that this revelation and its mysterious name are indeed a central locus for deriving the Memra. The fact that our text makes no mention whatever of that hypostasis suggests that, rather than being elaborated here, Memra theology is being silently refuted, along with, perhaps, its more radical form: Logos (Son of Man) Christology. In a slightly later but still classically rabbinic parallel to these texts, which Segal also cites, we find, "And thus

Daniel says: 'I beheld till thrones were placed, and one that was ancient of days did sit.' Rabbi Ḥiyya bar Abba taught: Should a whoreson say to you, 'They are two gods,' reply to him, I am the one of the sea; I am the one of Sinai!'"[50] This seems quite plausibly an allusion to Christians, who would read the Daniel passage as referring to one like a Son of Man (the warrior at the sea; the Son) and an Ancient of Days (the judge at Sinai; the Father), not least owing to the pejorative reference to the interlocutor as "whoreson," a charge that since Celsus at least had been known to be a Jewish calumny against Jesus.[51] Jewish/Christian binitarianism is being answered, therefore, by rabbinic Modalism, or rather, Jewish/Christian Modalism is being constructed as Jewish, Jewish/Christian binitarianism as *minut*.[52]

Interestingly enough, Justin's construction of Trypho and his teachers as the opponents of Logos theology can be seen as part of the same cultural "conspiracy." That is, both the Rabbis and Justin agree that the distinction between orthodoxy and heresy or between Judaism and Christianity is marked by the signifier of the Logos. The rabbinic text could almost be the answer of a very articulate and learned Trypho to the Logos theology of Justin or the Christology of the Fourth Gospel.[53] The whole point of this text is to combat the "heresy" that there are two Gods, two powers in heaven, God and his Logos or Son (of Man), by offering what is a Modalist solution: the seeming appearance of two persons is only a manifestation of different aspects of the same person.[54] As in the Christian Modalist "heresy," the Rabbis believe in "one identical Godhead Which could be designated indifferently Father [Old Man] or Son [Mighty Hero]; the terms did not stand for real distinctions, but were mere names applicable at different times."[55]

It now becomes clear why midrashim of this period, especially in covert or overt polemic against Christianity, designate God routinely as "The One Who Spoke and the World Was." This is a name for God that resists Memra or Logos interpretations of Genesis 1, and, therefore, a designation for God that serves to displace Memra theology, naming it implicitly as the "heresy" of Two Powers.[56] Although Hayward is absolutely correct in his assertion that "the identity of those who taught that there were two *ršwywt* [powers] in heaven is uncertain: favourite candidates have included Gnostics and Judaeo-Christians,"[57] for this particular text, there really is little doubt to whom reference is made. The text tells us who its opponents are: "The Nations of the World," which in this midrash (and other works of this period, the late third century) refers to Christians, and in particular, Gentile Christians.[58] However, insofar as we have seen that Memra/Logos theology is not a Gentile product, or even a specifically Christian product, in its origins, this rabbinic text represents the movement of repudiation of which I have been speaking. A difference *within* Judaism is projected onto an external other, not only Christian, but Gentile Christian, referred to as the "Nations of the World" to distance it from Israel, to render its binary opposition to Israel even more unequivocal, a virtual given.

As in Christian heresiology, the difference within has been renominated a contamination from without. There, *disbelief* in Two Powers in Heaven (so-called Sabellianism, Modalism, or Monarchianism, that is, One Power in Heaven) is named—accurately—"Judaism,"[59] producing a binary opposition between the inside and the outside of Christianity and disavowing a threatening difference within (the Modalists "argued that the Power issuing from the God-head was distinct only verbally or in name"[60]). Here, in the rabbinic text, the *belief* in Two Powers in Heaven is excommunicated from within Judaism and named (albeit slightly, but *only* slightly, obliquely) as "Christianity." "Modalism" is, of course, rabbinic Jewish orthodoxy: all doubleness and all difference within God suggested by the Bible are to be understood, according to the Rabbis, as only aspects of the one God.

In other "Judaisms" (including some later versions of rabbinic Judaism), this was not the case. Daniel Abrams has recently named this a perennial issue in Jewish conceptions of God: "One of the central aspects of Jewish theology, and Jewish mysticism in particular, is the conception of the nature of God's being and the appearance of the divine before humanity. No one view has dominated the spectrum of Jewish interpretations, since the biblical text is the only common frame for the wide variety of speculations. At issue is whether the one God depicted in the Hebrew Bible is manifest to humans directly or through the agency of a divine, semidivine, or created power."[61] Elliot Wolfson, in a typically brilliant reconstruction, has shown that in rabbinic and extrarabbinic traditions of Jewish late antiquity (including texts of the Gnosis falsely so-called), Jacob the Father of Israel is recognized as such a second divine figure.[62] If prior to the rabbinic intervention a Jew could believe comfortably in the Logos, Wisdom, Metatron,[63] Yahoel, or the supernal Jacob as a hypostasized second God,[64] once the denial of such beliefs had been named "Judaism" by Christians in order to set themselves off theologically from Jews, the countermove for rabbinic Jews resisting Christianity was an obvious one. Two Powers in Heaven became the primary heresy for the Rabbis, and Modalism, the Christian heresy par excellence, became the only "orthodox" theology allowed to Jews. We could, moreover, almost as easily describe the developments in the opposite direction, namely, that Christianity insisted on separate persons and rejected Modalism as a response to the rabbinic insistence that binitarianism was equal to ditheism. In this context, it is important to remind ourselves that Justin and other "orthodox" theologians of the second century were constantly defending themselves against charges from other Christians that their theology was ditheistic.[65]

The same process of splitting between Christian and Christian, with one group being marked as not Christian and thus Jewish, can thus be seen at work.

Over and over again, in contexts within which the Targum has the activity of the Memra, the rabbinic midrash has the designation of God as "He who spake and the world was," thus constituting a most impressive body of evidence for the tacit, but none the less vigorous repudiation of Memra theology on the part of the Rabbis.

At Exodus 4:31, the Neofiti Targum reads[66]:

And Israel saw the mighty hand which the Lord performed on the Egyptians, and the people were afraid from before the Lord and believed in the name of the Memra of the Lord, and the prophecy of Moses his servant.

The midrash I have cited above, the Mekhilta, comments:

And they believed in the Lord and in his servant Moses. If you say that they believed in Moses, is it not implied by *Kal vaḥomer* that they believed in God? But this is to teach you that having faith in the shepherd of Israel is the same as having faith in Him who spoke and the world came into being. . . . Great indeed is faith before *Him who spoke and the world came into being.* (Bešallaḥ 6)[67]

In other words, once more, precisely in a context in which the targumic tradition refers to the Memra as a hypostasis, a person of the Godhead, the rabbinic midrash insists on referring to YHWH as the one who spoke and the world was. Do not follow those Jewish traditions that understand Genesis 1 as describing a creative Word, a Memra, a Logos separate from God, say the Rabbis implicitly, as is their wont, but rather understand that God (I was almost tempted to write "the Father") is the only creator, and his word is no more separate from him than any speech from its speaker. In an astonishing convergence, however, Nicene orthodoxy also effectively "crucifies the Logos." While not ceasing to speak of the Logos, in the move to a trinitarian theology within which the entire trinity is both self-contained and fully transcendent, Athanasius and his fellows insist that God alone, without a mediator, without an angel, without a Logos, is the creator. Logos theology is, ultimately, as thoroughly rejected within Nicene Christianity as within orthodox rabbinism.[68]

The Apostasy of Rabbi Akiva

The heresiological energy being expended within rabbinic circles to produce the heresy of Two Powers in Heaven—that is, to externalize or Christianize the internal theologoumena of a second or assistant God—helps us understand some rabbinic texts that are otherwise mysterious.[69] One of the most evocative and revealing of these texts involves the heresy of Rabbi Akiva in a discussion of the "Son of Man" passage from Daniel:

One verse reads: "His throne is sparks of fire" [Dan. 7:9] and another [part of the] verse reads, "until thrones were set up and the Ancient of Days sat" [Dan. 7:9]. This is no difficulty: One was for him and one was for David.

As we learn in a *baraita* [non-Mishnaic tannaitic tradition]: One for him and one for David; these are the words of Rabbi Akiva. Rabbi Yose the Galilean said to him: Akiva! Until when will you make the *Shekhina* profane?! Rather. One was for judging and one was for mercy.

Did he accept it from him, or did he not?

Come and hear! One for judging and one for mercy, these are the words of Rabbi Akiva. (BT Ḥagiga 14a)

As we see from this passage, the second-century Rabbi Akiva is portrayed as interpreting these verses in a way that certainly would seem consistent with Two Powers in Heaven. The crux is his identification of David, the Messiah, as the "Son of Man" who sits at God's right hand,[70] thus suggesting not only a divine figure but one who is incarnate in a human being as well.[71] "I am [the Messiah] and you shall see 'the Son of Man' sitting on the right hand of power and coming in the clouds of heaven" (Mark 14:62). Hence, his objector's taunt: "Until when will you make the Divine Presence profane"?![72] Rabbi Akiva is seemingly also projecting a divine human, Son of Man, who will be the Messiah. His contemporary Rabbi Yose the Galilean (perhaps a more assiduous reader of the Gospels) strenuously objects to Rabbi Akiva's "dangerous" interpretation and gives the verse a "Modalist" interpretation. Of course, the Talmud itself must record that Rabbi Akiva changed his mind in order for him to remain "orthodox." Two Powers in Heaven is thus not foreign even at the very heart of the rabbinic enterprise. Even a figure like Rabbi Akiva has to be educated as to the heretical nature of his position.[73]

It is not too much to suggest, I think, that the pressure against Rabbi Akiva's position was generated by the hardening of Logos theology and its variants into Christology as that was beginning to take place in the second century. "Orthodox" Jewish versions of this theological option must then be "corrected"—not incidentally, with many of the techniques which Christians in the post-Nicene era were to use in order to produce the "Fathers" as speaking with one theological voice.[74] Segal also writes, "By the third century . . . the rabbis seem to be fully aware of the kinds of claims that could be made about a 'son of man' or Metatron or any other principal angel. So they reject the idea of divine intermediaries totally."[75] I would agree with Segal but argue that there is important evidence that they did not do so entirely successfully. In the late ancient mystical text known as "The Visions of Ezekiel," a secondary divine figure, Metatron, is posited on the grounds of Daniel 7:9–10. This is the figure who in other texts of that genre is called "the Youth" [נער], that is, that figure known by other Jews (e.g., the Fourth Evangelist) as the "Son of Man."[76] Putting together the different bits and pieces that other scholars have constructed into a new mosaic, I would suggest that we have a very important clue here. From the text in Daniel it would seem that two divine figures are pictured, one who is ancient and another who is young. "Son of Man," in its paradigmatic contrast with the Ancient of Days, should be read as youth, young man (as it is even in the rabbinic texts that deny that it represents a second person). The usage is similar to "sons of doves," meaning young of the dove as in Numbers 6:10. It should be noted that the figure of the Youth appears as well (at least once) in texts accepted into the rabbinic canon itself, such as Numbers Rabbah 12:12, and is explicitly denoted there as Metatron.[77] We end up with a clear indication of a second divine person, called the Youth (Son of Man), about whom it can be discussed whether he is identical in essence, similar in essence, similar (no essence), or dissimilar entirely[78] with the first person. When he is called or calls himself the "Son of Man" this is a citation of the Daniel text.[79] He is called the "Youth," that is, the "Son of Man," in contrast to the "Ancient of Days." These traditions all understand that two divine figures are portrayed in Daniel 7, whom we might be tempted to call the Father and the Son. Evidence for this concatenation of Enoch, Metatron, and the Son of Man can be adduced from 1 Enoch 71, in which Enoch is explicitly addressed as the Son of Man—and Enoch is, of course, Metatron before his apotheosis.[80] Nonrabbinic and even antirabbinic ideas (that is, ideas that the Rabbis themselves mark as heretical) appear more than occasionally in the heart of rabbinic literature.[81]

It is not, then, as Segal would have it, that "other groups beside Christians were making 'dangerous' interpretations of that verse [Daniel 7:9]," but rather that this commonplace of theological, mystical hermeneutics had become dangerous to the Rabbis and had to be expelled from its original home. For Segal, the "enemy" is still outside, external, marginal to the rabbinic community and religious world: "Identifying the specific group about whom the rabbis were concerned in this passage can not be successful."[82] He still worries that "determining the identity of the group of heretics in question remains a serious problem,"[83] as if there *were* a real group of external heretics to whom the texts refer. From my point of view, the Rabbis are implicitly saying, "We have met the heretics and they are us," thereby expelling the Two Powers heresy from within themselves. Although he uses the point to slightly different purpose,[84] I would endorse the formulation of Nathaniel Deutsch, who writes, of the same texts Segal treats and I read here, "the reification of boundaries, therefore, rather than their crossing, is the goal of these passages."[85]

I would read the famous narrative of Elisha ben Abuya's apostasy, in the sequel to the story of Rabbi Akiva, where upon seeing a vision of the glorious being named Metatron sitting at the right hand of God, he concludes that there are Two Powers in Heaven and becomes a heretic, as a further oblique recognition and allegorical representation of the fact that this heresy was once comfortably *within* "Judaism" and has only lately become Aḥer, "Other"—*Aḥer* being, of course, the pejorative nickname for this once "kosher" Rabbi after his turn to "heresy." A brief look at this text will help make this point. According to the Talmud:

Our Rabbis have taught: Four went into the Pardes, and who are they? Ben Azzai and Ben Zoma, Aḥer, and Rabbi Akiva. . . . Aḥer chopped down the shoots. Rabbi Akiva came out safely. . . .

"Aḥer chopped down the shoots": Of him the verse says, "Do not let your mouth cause your flesh to sin" [Eccles. 5:5]. What does this mean? He saw that Metatron had been given permission to sit and write the good deeds of Israel. He said, but it is taught that on high there will be no sitting, no competition, no . . . , and no tiredness! Perhaps, G-d forbid, there are two powers! They took Metatron out and whipped him with sixty whips of fire. They said to him: "What is the reason that when you saw him, you did not get up before him?" He was given permission to erase the good deeds of Aḥer. A voice came out from heaven and said: Return O backsliding ones [Jer. 3:14, 22]—except for Aḥer.

He said, "Since that man has been driven out of that world, let him go out and enjoy himself in this world!" He went out to evil culture. He went and found a prostitute and solicited her. She said, "But aren't you Elisha ben Abuya!?" He went and uprooted a radish on the Sabbath and gave it to her. She said, "He is an other [Aḥer]. (BT Ḥagiga 15a)

This is a remarkable story, which, as can well be imagined, has excited much scholarly attention. Yehuda Liebes emphasizes correctly that it is impossible to see this as a narrative of a real Elisha who joined a heretical sect.[86] Segal nicely observes that "in its present context [the story] is an etiology of heresy. It explains how certain people, who had special Metatron traditions, risk the heretical designation of 'two powers in heaven.'"[87] This can be pushed a bit further. The structural comparison with Christian etiologies of heresy and heresiarchs suggests that, like those, Aḥer represents older theological traditions that have been anathematized as heresy by the authors of the story. Almost certainly underlying Aḥer/Elisha's vision of Metatron is the passage in Daniel that "misled" Rabbi Akiva, taking the "One like a Son of Man" to be a separate person. The latter's error was hermeneutical/theological; the former's is visionary/theological. But the error is essentially the same: the assumption that the second throne is for a second divine figure. Whether called Metatron or David, the second divine figure is the Son of Man.[88] Locating this "heretical" interpretation right at the heart of the rabbinic academy and indeed among some of its leading figures strongly suggests that these views had been current in the Jewish circles from which the Rabbis emerged and were eventually anathematized by them and driven out. Metatron is punished by being scourged with sixty *pulse* of fire. As we learn from Babylonian Talmud Baba Meṣia 47a, this practice (whatever it means in terms of realia) represents a particularly dire form of anathema or even excommunication. The dual inscription of excommunication in the narrative, that of Metatron on the one hand and of his "devotee" on the other, suggests strongly to me that the belief in this figure as second divine principle is being anathematized (although somehow the Rabbis seem unable completely to dispense with him—he was just too popular, it would seem).

A further parallel is instructive. In an amazing passage in Yoma 77a that I cannot discuss here at length, the archangel Gabriel is taken out to be scourged with the sixty *pulse* because he acted independently of the divine will, another seeming case of Two Powers in Heaven. Note that in that story, as opposed to the Aḥer one, the *possibility* of the high angel acting independently is comprehended. It is almost as if not only the heresy of Two Powers but the second power itself is being suppressed in these accounts. The statement that "Rabbi Akiva came out safely [lit. in peace]," whereas Aḥer died in infamy, would, on this possible but by no means proven interpretation, then represent a Rabbi Akiva who turned away from "heresy" to orthodoxy and an Elisha who remained adamant in the old views.

The two others who entered Pardes (the Garden, Paradise) with Rabbi Akiva and Aḥer in search of enlightenment were Ben Zoma and Ben Azzai. Of one we are told that he died and of the other that he became insane. Is it accidental that we read, then, in Genesis Rabbah the following astounding text: "Rabbi Levi said: There are among the expounders [דרושות], those who expound, for instance Ben Zoma and Ben Azzai, that the voice of the Holy, Blessed One became Metatron on the water, as it is written, 'The voice of God is on the water' [Ps. 29:3]."[89] This extraordinary passage "remembers," as it were, that such central rabbinic figures, whose halakhic opinions are authoritatively cited in the classic rabbinic literature, were, like Rabbi Akiva himself, champions of a distinct Logos theology which had to be somehow warded off via the legendary narrative of their bad end. Only Rabbi Akiva repented of his former views and therefore, we are told, only he of the four "entered in peace and left in peace" (BT Ḥagiga 14b). All four of the relevant Rabbis made statements indicating that they had believed in a *deuteros theos*. The Pardes is not, therefore, on this reading, so much the site of mystical experience or philosophical speculation as the trace of the ancient Logos theology. It seems hardly irrelevant that on this very page of the Talmud we are told that "The world was created with ten Words," which became afterward the main prooftext for the mystical doctrine of the hypostases (ספירות).[90]

Segal claims that "Rabbinic theology could withstand, and may even have encouraged, the mythic or dramatic depiction of God's attributes in various forms, including at times a *logos*-like manifestation, depicted as an angelic being such as Meṭaṭron" and, moreover, that "those who adopt a more literal view of the rabbis' view of divine unity may find any hint of plurality to be heretical. Here, however, I argue that the rabbis objected only to an opposition or competition of wills."[91] To claim this, however, is to assume that there is no opposition or competition of wills *among the Rabbis*. There are places, indeed, where *some* Rabbis' "theology could withstand, and may even have encouraged, the mythic or dramatic depiction of God's attributes in various forms, including at times a *logos*-like manifestation," but this view was vigorously disputed and finally ousted by other Rabbis, at least in its more obvious forms. This perspective obviates the need to draw a distinction between two different versions of Two Powers theology, one acceptable and one unacceptable.[92] Our story of Rabbi Akiva's "heresy" certainly does not suggest a "gnostic" version of Two Powers in opposition to each other, but rather a very "Christian"-appearing version, in which the second power is precisely the Son of Man doing his Father's will by inscribing Israel's virtues.[93] This story of Rabbi Akiva and his fellows constitutes, on this reading, a highly compressed synecdoche of the process of the repudiation of Logos theology.[94]

Remnants (almost revenants) of Logos theology within the texts constitute further evidence for the notion that it was a theologoumenon that once had been accepted but was now to be rejected within rabbinic circles. Azzan Yadin discusses a rich example.[95] The text in question can be found in the Palestinian Talmud Sukkah 1:1 [51,d] (with a parallel in the same text at Shabbat 1:2 [2,d]):[96]

Rabbi Abbahu teaches in the name of Rabbi Shim'on ben Laqish: "There I will meet you and I will speak to you from above the cover of the Ark from between the two cherubim" [Exod. 25:22]. And it is written, "You have seen that I spoke to you from the heavens" [Exod. 20:19]. Just as the verse cited there refers to a different domain [*reshut*], so the verse here refers to a different domain [*reshut*].

As Yadin points out, the term *reshut* (the term used for Two Powers), which I have translated here "domain," is ambiguous in reference. Sometimes it can mean a legal domain, in the sense of a territory controlled by a particular instance of ownership or authority. The Palestinian Talmud emphasizes this meaning in using this verse to prove that when God spoke from above the cover of the Ark, this demonstrates that the Ark constitutes a separate domain of control within the Temple precincts. However, as Yadin emphasizes, this usage of the midrash within the halakhic context of the Talmud is very forced and artificial: "the significance of this rather forced series of arguments is that the *derashah* was not generated by the previously established height of the Ark. Instead, the Palestinian Talmud is making a concerted effort to contextualize Resh Laqish's [third-century] *derashah* in a halakhic context (the height of ten *tefaḥ* marks the end of one *reshut* and the beginning of another) not provided by the *derashah* itself."[97] This argument that the present use of the *derasha* is not and cannot be its "original" meaning and, indeed, that concerted effort is being made to neutralize the original meanings suggests to Yadin that the midrash originally was making use of another sense of *reshut*, the sense in which it is used in the context of discussion of the "heresy" of Two Powers [*reshuyot*] in Heaven, reconciling the two verses, one that indicates that God spoke from Heaven and one that he came down, as it were, to speak below, by suggesting that the speaker who spoke below is not the speaker who spoke above. To represent this well-known sense of *reshut*, Yadin cites the following evocative text:

"See, then, that I, I am He" [Deut. 32:39]: This is the refutation to those who say that there is no *reshut* (i.e., atheists who claim that there is no power in heaven). He who says that there are two powers in heaven is refuted by saying it has already been written, "There is no God beside Me" [Deut. 32:39]. (Sifre Deuteronomy 329)[98]

Yadin concludes his discussion by referring to this instance in the Palestinian Talmud as "an acceptable, legal understanding camouflaging a no-longer acceptable theological position." Thus, the theology of Two Powers in Heaven, a High God and an intermediary for creation, revelation, and redemption, as we still find in the Memra theology of the Targums, was once, at least, an acceptable theological current within the circles from which the Rabbis and their theologies grew, but was offered up, as it were, in the dual production of rabbinic Judaism as Judaism and patristic Christianity as Christianity.

The Logos Conspiracy: How Difference Within Became Difference Between

By naming the traditional Logos or Memra doctrine of God a heresy, indeed, *the* heresy, Two Powers in Heaven, the rabbinic theology expels it from the midst of Judaism, hailing that heresy at least implicitly as Christianity, at the same time that, in a virtual cultural conspiracy,[99] the emerging Christian orthodoxy embraces the Logos theology and names its repudiation Judaism. We have seen this historical, sociocultural process being enacted within Justin's *Dialogue*. Without ascribing a literal value to the term *conspiracy* here, I would, nevertheless, point to the striking cooperation of the two discursive forces. The orthodox rabbinic solution to the problem of verses that seem to imply any doubleness in God is to read them Modalistically: one refers to God's aspect, or quality, of mercy and the other to God's aspect of justice. In precise symmetry, Christian orthodoxy of the second century regarded Modalism as a heresy—a heresy that could easily be named Monarchianism, One Power in Heaven—expelling the once "orthodox" Sabellius (and even Pope Callistus[100]), just as the Rabbis had done, in their stories, with Elisha.[101] J. N. D. Kelly makes the point that already in Justin's day other Christians were accusing him of ditheism because he argued that the Logos is "something numerically other" (*Dialogue* 128:3). By constructing his opponent in the *Dialogue* as a "Jew," then, Justin is also engaged in splitting off a part of his own self, so to speak, and projecting it outward as Judaism. The notion of conspiracy should be clear by now: Justin and the Rabbis, ostensibly bitter opponents, in a strong sense fondly desire the same consummation. At the same time that the Jew was being hailed by the Christian heresiologists[102] by calling Monarchianism and Modalism "Judaism,"[103] the Rabbis were constructing their own orthodoxy by naming the believer in Two Powers in Heaven the "Christian," as their heretic-in-chief, and thus in some sense calling Christianity into existence as a separate social entity. Judaism is Monarchianism; Monarchianism is Judaism. And the Rabbis, by identifying Two Powers in Heaven as the arch-heresy, thus participated in the discursive work of the making of Christian orthodoxy, while the Christian heresiologists who insisted that one *must* assert the existence of separate "persons" in order to be an orthodox Christian—in order, that is, not to be a Jew—similarly participated in the discursive work of the making of orthodox rabbinic Judaism.

The function of the denomination Two Powers in Heaven for rabbinic ecclesiology is thus formally and structurally equivalent to *Ioudaïzein* (Judaizing) within Christian writing of the time. Just as the latter is a term of opprobation and exclusion of Christians from the community because they hold ideas from within Christianity that have become anathema to certain teachers and leaders, those figures who are named as possessing the heretical notion of Two Powers in Heaven are Jews holding one traditional Jewish theological position who are now declared anathema in the new regime of the Rabbis.

The supersupersession of the Logos by writing gives birth to rabbinic Judaism and its characteristic forms of textuality. I would thus reverse Melito's famous "παλαιὸς μὲν ὁ νόμος, καινὸς δὲ ὁ λόγος " [Of old there was the Nomos, the Law, now there is the Logos], claiming for the Rabbis that formerly there was the Logos, but now God's Word can be found, literally, only in the black marks on the white parchment of the Nomos.[104] This theological stance, which only after much struggle came to characterize the rabbinic doctrine of God, carried in its wake profound shifts within rabbinic textuality, even between the earlier Palestinian and the later Babylonian Talmuds, shifts that were ultimately to serve, on my reading, as the most salient difference between orthodox Christianity and rabbinic Judaism.

PART III

Sparks of the Logos:
Historicizing Rabbinic Religion

Chapter 7

The Yavneh Legend of the Stammaim: On the Invention of the Rabbis in the Sixth Century

Of the two Talmuds and their differences, Jacob Neusner has writ-ten: "The sages of the Talmud of the Land of Israel seek certain knowledge about some few, practical things. They therefore reject—from end to beginning—the chaos of speculation, the plurality of possibilities even as to word choice; above all, the daring and confidence to address the world in the name, merely, of sagacity [that characterize the Talmud of the Babylon]. True, the [Palestinian] Talmud preserves the open-ended discourse of sages, not reduced to cut-and-dried positions. But the [Palestinian] Talmud makes decisions."[1] While this is a lucid characterization of the difference of the two Talmuds, I would reframe the point in a way that places the two Talmuds more clearly in diachronic relation. Rather than presenting the practice of the Palestinian Talmud as a deviation, a "rejection," I would prefer to imagine that it was the practice of the Babylonian Talmud that was constituted through a rejection—a rejection of the desire or hope for "certain knowledge."[2] The making of decisions, after all, is the more obvious telos of an intellectual endeavor, while the "the chaos of speculation" and "plurality of possibilities," the endless deferral of decision that characterizes the Babylonian Talmud, is more of a novellum.[3] Reframing the relation between the two Talmuds in this way follows Neusner's own documentary history ap-proach more plausibly, with the later "document" responding to the earlier one. This also correlates well with the hypothesis of David Halivni and Shamma Friedman, according to which the characteristic literary forms of the Babylo-nian Talmud take shape in the post-amoraic period, that is from 450 A.C. to 650 A.C., and "point to a shift in values that transpired in Stammaitic [the anony-mous redactors'] times. The Amoraim generally did not preserve the argumen-tation and debate, but only the final conclusions. For them, dialectical analysis was a means to an end, a process through which a sage could determine the nor-mative law or the correct explanation of a source. The Stammaim, however, val-ued analysis and argumentation as ends in and of themselves."[4] In this chapter,

I shall try to show that the realization of the crucial role of the late redactors—these anonymous "stammaim"—in forming the rhetorical structures of the Talmud, when put together with their increasingly appreciated role in shaping the talmudic legends[5] (especially about Yavneh) and the historical insight that the institutional Yeshiva is also a product of this period,[6] provides us with a powerful historical hypothesis and an attractive historical context for the formation of major structures of rabbinic Judaism in the late fifth and sixth centuries. Institution (Yeshiva), founding and instituting text (Talmud), theological innovation (indeterminacy of meaning and halakhic argument), and practice (endless study as worship in and of itself) all come together at this time to produce the rabbinic Judaism familiar to us until this day. The talmudic redactors were so successful in hiding themselves that they were able to retroject those patterns and make it seem as if they were a product of a "real" Yavneh of the first century.

The Palestinian Talmud seems to consider determination of the correctness of one of the views of paramount importance, as did apparently the earlier strata of Babylonian rabbinism (amoraic, 200–450 A.C.), whereas for the anonymous redactorial voice of the Babylonian Talmud it is most often the case that such an apparent proof of one view is considered a difficulty (*qushia*) requiring a resolution which, in fact, shows that there is no resolution, for "these and these are the words of the Living God." David Kraemer writes that "This contrast in overall compositional preferences may be the most important difference between the Bavli [Babylonian Talmud] and the Yerushalmi [Palestinian Talmud]."[7]

When seen, as it traditionally is, from the point of view of the Bavli (the hegemonic work for rabbinic Judaism) the practice of the Yerushalmi can seem strange and even defective. Thus Zecharia Frankel's classic observation that "The Yerushalmi will frequently raise questions or objections and never supply an answer to them. This phenomenon is extremely rare in the Bavli."[8] However, when looked at from a non-Bavliocentric point of view, this translates as precisely the willingness of the Yerushalmi to declare that one opinion is wrong and another right—Neusner's "making of decisions." The Bavli's practice of refusal of such closure reveals the stranger and more surprising epistemology, one that I would characterize as virtually apophatic with respect to the divine mind, its text, and intentions for practice, as well.

Whatever the true "history" of the canonization of the Babylonian Talmud, at the end of late antiquity, and ancient Judaeo-Christianity, two literary canons—the patristic corpus and the Talmud—come into existence, founding the two orthodoxies of medieval Christendom: the Catholic Church and rabbinic Judaism. It was then that the final form of rabbinic textuality and implicit ecclesiology, the so-called "pluralism" of the Rabbis, was fully instituted. However, this pluralism is pluralism only when looked at from a very particular, rabbinic insider's perspective. When viewed in terms of the dual canonization of the textual forms of Christianity and Judaism, it—like the patristic corpus from which is otherwise so different—is a highly efficient means for the securing of "consensual" orthodoxy. Richard Lim very carefully documents the political and social shifts in late Roman Christian society that transformed it from one in which controlled dissensus was not a threat but a resource to one of "simplicity," the notion that there is and always had been only one truth and the social ideal is *homonoia*, total agreement without discussion or dispute.[9] These shifts in the ideologies of discourse were central in the transformation of the classical world into the world of Byzantine culture: "An intensified advocacy for apophatic simplicity as a paradigmatic virtue was but one of many results of this confluence of competing interests. Many individuals and groups sought to domesticate the perceived threat of dissensus in public disputing, choosing from various ideological strategies and cultural values to mobilize hierarchical forms of authority against a culture that validated individualistic claims and rational argumentation."[10]

This is precisely the historical context within which rabbinic literature came into being. However, while equally transformed within this period in its ideals of discourse, rabbinic Judaism seemingly went in the opposite direction from orthodox Christianity. Since rabbinic Judaism has been interpreted by scholars more as an essence than as a historical and historically shifting cultural form, it is not surprising that it has not been much studied in the context of the histories of the developing discourses about discourse within the late Roman cultural world. While early Palestinian and Babylonian rabbinism manifests a pattern of dialectical dispute and resolution, the latest layer of Babylonian rabbinic literature, the finally redacted Talmud, not only rejected *homonoia* but promulgated instead a sensibility of the ultimate contingency of all truth claims, one that goes even beyond the skepticism of the Platonic Academy.[11]

Jeffrey L. Rubenstein has recently argued that many of the aggadot of the Babylonian Talmud and not only the redacted form of the talmudic argument represent "the Stammaitic values," especially as these are identified and described by David Halivni.[12] Rubenstein, following the best thought of modern scholarship on the Talmud and further developing it and its implications, sees these narratives as significantly reworked by the same anonymous editors who had produced the final form of the Talmudic *sugya* itself: "Bavli aggadot, and especially narrative traditions, thematize dialectical argumentation and portray it as the highest form of Torah. That this theme is absent from the parallel Palestinian versions of the traditions and from Palestinian sources in general suggests that we are dealing with a late Babylonian concern. Moreover, almost all of these

Bavli sources show evidence of Stammaitic reworking. The differences are not indicative of a distinction between the rabbinic cultures of Palestinian Amoraim and their Babylonian counterparts, but of Amoraim and Stammaim."[13] The process that Rubenstein describes is essentially the one familiar from folklorist research as "ecotypification," the modifications that oral narratives undergo as they are transferred and retold from one cultural context to another: "As the Stammaim retold the stories they received from Palestinian sources and the Babylonian amoraim, they refracted them through the prism of their experience. Many changes occurred unintentionally or subconsciously as transmitters replaced outmoded ideas with those more familiar to them."[14]

Accepting Rubenstein's strategy, I wish here to suggest both a more complex set of motivations and programs than the "values" articulated by Halivni and accepted by Rubenstein, and also to hypothesize a broader historical context for these developments. I will try to show via an analysis of several different aggadot from the Babylonian Talmud that they belong to a single redactional (stammaitic) layer and carry a similar ideologically freighted (or even driven) tendency. I am suggesting here that a corpus of narratives scattered throughout the Babylonian Talmud actually cite and refer to each other, leading to the hypothesis of a late Babylonian version of a kind of Yavneh saga. It is the nature of the inter-referentiality of these narratives that suggests strongly their redactional (post-amoraic) character, a character that is often difficult to assign with confidence. Rubenstein has not paid attention to the literary interconnections of this particular set of these stories, interconnections that would only strengthen his argument, regarding some of them, that they belong to an ideological complex formed by the Stammaim in support of their epistemological theories and rhetorical practices.[15] What I will try to show here is that this specific set of aggadot, connected to each other by a series of formal and explicit allusions, constitutes an important ideological complex, suggesting that their distribution throughout the Talmud (Berakhot, Ḥagiga, Baba Meṣia', Sanhedrin, Horayot) is not completely accidental or random but represents an important layer of both literary and ideological work that informs the Bavli as a whole. The Yavneh of the Bavli is, I will suggest, the icon of the stammaitic Yeshiva. As Charlotte Fonrobert has recently argued, these narratives "[have] to be read as talmudic mythopoesis rather than perhaps as talmudic historiography or memory of the early (tannaitic) period of the rabbinic movement. This talmudic mythopoesis centers around the utopian *beit midrash* as the institutional framework of the religion of Torah. Like Aeschylus's idealized *polis*, it is the institution that is not yet but has always already been."[16]

Rabbinic Judaism as Stammaitic Invention

The time of this mythopoeisis, I would suggest, is somewhere in the fifth and sixth centuries, the time of the redaction of the Babylonian Talmud and also when "Nicaea" was finally "taking effect."[17] What has often presented as an ahistorical definitive attribute, the pluralism of rabbinic Judaism (perhaps its most striking feature), is the product of this specific moment in history and not a transcendental essence of rabbinic Judaism. Keith Hopkins is perhaps the only scholar who has so far even adumbrated this point, arguing that "Unlike Judaism after the destruction of the Temple, Christianity was dogmatic and hierarchical; dogmatic, in the sense that Christian leaders from early on claimed that their own interpretation of Christian faith was the only true interpretation of the faith, and hierarchical in that leaders claimed legitimacy for the authority of their interpretation as priests or bishops." Hopkins describes this phenomenon historically: "Admittedly, individual leaders claimed that their own individual interpretation of the law was right, and that other interpretations were wrong. But systemically, at some unknown date, Jewish rabbis seem to have come to the conclusion, however reluctantly, that they were bound to disagree, and that disagreement was endemic."[18]

I would emend Hopkins's formulation, however, in two ways. First, I would put forth that we can locate that "unknown date" as being toward the very end of the rabbinic period, at the time of redaction of the Babylonian Talmud by the so-called Stammaim, those anonymous, post-talmudic Rabbis to whom it is becoming clearer and clearer we owe so much of what we call "Judaism." It is then, according to my conjectural reconstruction, that the significant "Yavneh" of which Shaye Cohen speaks came into being.[19] Equally importantly, while Hopkins historicizes the process through which Judaic orthodoxy came to have a certain face and a certain character, he reifies Christianity, as if it were always and everywhere (at least from "early on") "dogmatic and hierarchical." The description of Christianity also has to be similarly dynamized and historicized. The form of Christianity of which Hopkins speaks is as much the product of particular historical processes within Christianity as is the form of Judaism of which he speaks. In neither case do we have a transhistorical essence, and in both cases, I suggest that the very processes that produced the difference of which both Cohen and Hopkins speak so eloquently are complexly intertwined with each other. Another way of saying this would be that I think that both Cohen and Hopkins are right in their staging of a binary contrast between "Christianity" and "Judaism" specifically at the site of the typologies of comparative orthodoxies.

This may end up being one of the most salient differences between the two "religions" as they come out of late antiquity into the Middle Ages. Comparative heresiologies and orthodoxies seems a very productive way of interpreting the common history of late ancient Judaism and Christianity, but we need much more nuanced and historicized accounts of both, before this comparative enterprise will be anything more than a mere formula, and one, moreover, that is in ever-present danger of sounding apologetic or triumphalist.[20] At approximately the same time that rabbinic Judaism was crystallizing the characteristic discursive forms of its orthodoxy—interpretative indeterminacy and endless dispute—the orthodox Church was developing the discursive forms that were to characterize it, its nearly proverbial "dogma and hierarchy." Without ascribing any particular differentiation in social structure to the two formations on the basis of this distinction, we can nevertheless point to these shifting differences as significant moments in the epistemologies and theologies of language of the two communities.[21] These are usually taken by scholars to be unrelated developments (insofar as they are studied as developments at all), and, moreover, to represent an enormous difference at the level of sociopolitical organization. I would like to advance the notion that as opposite as these characteristics seemingly are, they can be read as sharing a common epistemic and historical context, and that so reading them will produce interesting and perhaps useful results. In this chapter I hope to make a case for regarding a fundamental discursive difference between the Palestinian (redacted fourth-century) and Babylonian (sixth-century) Talmuds as an instance of a wider epistemic shift taking place around the Mediterranean in the relevant centuries.

This shift in the dating of the significant redaction of the Babylonian Talmud (indeed, we might say of its composition) leads to an entirely new historical perspective, for it needs to be remembered that Christianity held important sway within the geocultural orbit of these Rabbis of the Persian Empire, a cultural phenomenon that arguably had impact on the development of the single most characteristic institution of rabbinic Judaism, the Yeshiva.[22] As Rubenstein has already noted, "to date the rise of the Babylonian rabbinic academy to the fifth or sixth century coheres with the broader cultural climate. Hellenistic influence increased dramatically throughout Syria and northern Mesopotamia in the fifth and sixth centuries. The Church Fathers Aphrahat (d. circa 350) and Ephrem (d. 373) wrote in Syriac and exhibit a Semitic outlook; their works are largely free of the complex Christological formulations made possible by the philosophical terminology available in Greek and Latin. In the succeeding centuries the Church Fathers within the Persian Empire express themselves in a thoroughly Hellenized idiom."[23] Rubenstein, moreover, suggests that these shifts are partly to be explained by the influx of "Nestorian" scholars from the Roman Empire to the Sassanian Empire after Chalcedon.[24] Isaiah Gafni has already identified important structural parallels between the new and very important Christian school in Nisibis and the rabbinic yeshivot, territorially very close to that city.[25] In light of these precise structural and even terminological parallels between Christian and rabbinic foundations, it becomes much more plausible to suggest common epistemic and discursive progressions, as well. Moreover, the rise of the great yeshivas as the primary institution for rabbinic learning provides a context within which a text such as the Talmud would come into being and further provides a plausible explanation for the veritable explosion of legendary material that justifies both the Yeshiva and its practices, as well as the rhetoric of the talmudic *sugya*, its halakhic (legal) discourse.

The Threat of Dissensus

In a famous *derasha* (rabbinic sermon) analyzed by David Stern, the problem of multiple contradictory views and their consequences for practice is explicitly confronted in social terms of univocity (of the community, not the text) and difference. This *derasha* is part of a large complex of Babylonian aggadot centering on Yavneh figures, which I will explore in this chapter. Let us begin, then, by reading part of this complex of legendary materials along with Stern:

> [What does the phrase] "the masters of assemblies" [mean]? These are the disciples of the wise, who sit in assemblies and study the Torah, some pronouncing unclean and others pronouncing clean, some prohibiting and others permitting, some declaring unfit and others declaring fit. Should a man say: Since some pronounce unclean and others pronounce clean, some prohibit and others permit, some declare unfit and others declare fit—how then shall I learn Torah? Therefore Scripture says: All of them "were given by one shepherd." One God gave them, one leader (i.e., Moses) proclaimed them from the mouth of the Lord of all creation, blessed be He, as it is written, "And God spoke *all* these words" [Exod. 20:1; my emphasis]. Therefore make your ear like the hopper and acquire a perceptive heart to understand the words of those who pronounce unclean and the words of those who pronounce clean, the words of those who prohibit and the words of those who permit, the words of those who declare unfit and the words of those who declare fit. [BT Ḥagiga 3a–b][26]

Here we seemingly have an explicit representation of the consequences for learning practice of the (relatively late)[27] talmudic theological principle that "these and these"—however contradictory—"are the words of the Living God." Stern, however, argues that this theology of language was not the operative ideology within the House of Study itself, but is a purely literary phenomenon. Nor does it represent the social reality of human language use but a theological representation of the divine language. It is at the level of the theology of language encoded in the redaction of the rabbinic texts themselves, in their very textuality, and not in the practice of the House of Study, that the moment of undecidability is produced: "This representation, however, is a literary artifact. . . . The phenomenon we witness in multiple interpretation, in other words, is in actuality a literary impression given by the redaction of Rabbinic literature, the result of a common choice made by its anonymous editors to preserve minority as well as majority opinions, the varieties of traditions rather than single versions."[28]

Stern introduces an important distinction here. In this homily, attributed in the legend to Rabbi Yehoshua', the reader is implicitly informed that what is in human eyes a contradiction is in God's eyes a unity: All of these contradictory words are God's words. But this "unity" does not correspond to any historical reality of rabbinic practice of disputation, according to Stern. Rabbinic literature records bitter and sometimes violent strife between the various groups that constituted Judaism after the destruction of the Temple, even if we leave out of the picture the excluded *minim*, the heretics. As he emphasizes, in the century following the founding of Yavneh, far from a "grand coalition," we find instead a scene of constant combat "to consolidate Palestinian Jewry under the form of the specific religious vision that eventually came to be known as Rabbinic Judaism. . . . The task of unification was not accomplished easily, indeed, the endemic divisiveness that was a source of tragic factionalism in Palestinian Judaism as well as a source of its individualism and creativity was never entirely eradicated."[29] I completely agree with Stern's reading. Rather than seeing this "endemic factionalism," however, as a record of the real historical situation at the time of Yavneh, I prefer to read it as a representation of Yavneh as projected in the earlier stages of rabbinic literature. That is, I suggest, the earliest strata of Yavneh legends, those from the late second to the late third centuries, project an imagined Yavneh in which the major issue was the establishment of separations between "orthodox" and "heretical" Jews. In other words, rather than presenting us with the real historical situation, these early narratives are a genealogy of the ecclesiological world within which the Mishna and its collateral literature were produced in the second and early third centuries. Emblematic of the tannaitic Yavneh, and thus of tannaitic epistemology of Torah, is the following text from the Tosefta: "Once there were many disciples to Hillel and Shammai, who did not serve [their masters, i.e., study] sufficiently, there grew many divisions within Israel, and the Torah became two Torahs" [Tosefta Ḥagiga 2:9 and Soṭa 14:9]. This is clearly not the same voice that declares that "These and these are the words of the Living God," but, as Fisch points out, it is a traditionalist and realist voice that understands the Torah that was handed down at Mt. Sinai and communicated down through the ages to the Rabbis as having been fully explicit and understood.[30] The Yavneh in which a voice from heaven declared that "these [the words of the House of Hillel] and these [the words of the House of Shammai] are the words of the Living God" represents a later version of Yavneh, the Yavneh of the Talmuds and especially of the redaction level of the Babylonian Talmud, in which the notion of a single true Torah has been abandoned.[31] The latter strata, the project of the Yavneh of the Stammaim was somewhat different from the earlier one. Rather than securing boundaries between different Jewish elites as *minim* or orthodox, it was, rather, securing hegemony over the Jewish masses.

As Shlomo Naeh shows,[32] the earlier tannaitic version of the very homily that Stern discusses takes a fairly different stance (Tosefta Soṭa 7:11–12) from the more famous talmudic version. The Babylonian Talmud represents disagreement in the halakhic discussion as normative: "[What does the phrase] 'the masters of assemblies' [mean]? These are the disciples of the wise, who sit in assemblies and study the Torah, some pronouncing unclean and others pronouncing clean, some prohibiting and others permitting, some declaring unfit and others declaring fit." In the third-century Tosefta, almost the opposite is the case: "What are the Masters of Assemblies—Those who go in and sit assembly, assembly, and say about the impure that it is impure and the pure that it is pure. 'Impure' in its appropriate place, and 'pure' in its appropriate place."[33] As Naeh remarks with regard to the Tosefta, "It would be difficult to find a clearer formulation of a description of a harmonious halakhic reality without disagreement or doubt." Naeh also shows compellingly that the problem that the Tosefta raises is the technical problem of *remembering* and understanding the text in a situation in which it is given as a series of controversies, and not the theological problem of controversy with which the Babylonian Talmud's version deals.[34] In place of the Talmud's "Therefore make your ear like the hopper and acquire a perceptive heart to understand the words of those who pronounce unclean and the words of those who pronounce clean, the words of those who prohibit and the words of those who permit, the words of those who declare unfit and the words of those who declare fit," the Tosefta reads, "Make yourself many rooms, and place in them the words of the House of Shammai and the words of the House of Hillel." This has nothing to do with a putative "pluralistic" understanding, but rather with the building of a memory palace. The continuation of the Tosefta, therefore, which looks at first glance very much like the Babylonian Talmud, can be convincingly explained (and has been by Naeh) in accordance with this interpretation. The Tosefta reads: "Lest a person say in his heart: Since 'Bet Shammai say it is impure, and Bet Hillel say it is pure,' . . . How can I learn Torah?; therefore it says, make your heart many rooms. . . ." Since "heart" means memory here (compare our "learn something by heart"), these rooms are in that memory palace. In other words, as Naeh shows, in part by citing many parallels, the problem is that there is much to learn and that it is confusing and hard to remember in its typical forms: "Bet Shammai say this; Bet Hillel say this,"[35] and not that there is an epistemological or theological problem created by the contradictions of the Sages' opinions. The best proof of this is that in the Tosefta there is no connection made between the verset "All of them were given by one shepherd" and the problem of learning.[36] For the tannaitic Tosefta, it would seem, the best that can be made of a bad situation is at least not to forget the "two Torahs" that have been produced through the careless study of the disciples of the Hillel and Shammai, not a celebration of this multiplicity as a representation of theological pluralism.[37] According to the Toseftan version, moreover, as Naeh compellingly shows, the end of the verse ("All were given by one shepherd") refers not to the differing and contradictory views expressed by the Rabbis but to the Written and the Oral Torah, which were both given by God at Sinai.[38]

As Naeh writes, "The ideology that is reflected by the final [talmudic] version of the homily is not of the original tradition of Rabbi El'azar ben Azariah and of the circle of Sages of Yavneh, but rather is the product of a change that was made in the original tradition. . . . It follows that the question of whether this ideology is a part of the system of ideas of our Rabbis is dependent on a definition of the hazy concept 'Our Rabbis.'"[39] Where, moreover, Naeh regards the development of the Talmud's version as very likely a purely technical redactorial development,[40] its consistency with the other materials that I have gathered here suggests that this rewriting is not just a formal and technical shift but represents an important epistemic change, one that takes place at the end of Jewish late antiquity. In short, the shift in meanings that Naeh has compellingly exposed corresponds perfectly to the epistemic shift for which I am arguing here.

Converging Opposites, The Genealogy of an Episteme

By the fourth century, the existence of bitter controversies within Christianity had presented a serious apologetic ("spin") problem for the leaders of the Church. One of the arguments for the truth of Christianity had been its *symphonoia*, its harmony of minds, as opposed to the constant wrangling of the philosophers. We find the following argument in Athanasius of Alexandria: "The Greeks at any rate do not acknowledge the same views, but because they argue with each other, they do not have the true teaching. But the holy fathers who are the heralds indeed of the truth both agree with each other and also are not at odds with their own people."[41] Given the topical character of this argument, the controversies of the rabbinic period must have been as disturbing to Jews as the Arian controversy was to Christians: "To many thoughtful Christians, the increasingly prominent and protracted displays of their own institutional fragmentation before nonbelievers compromised their cause incontrovertibly."[42] We find almost precisely the same problem articulated by the redactors of the Babylonian Talmud who, in our legend, imagine a student entering the yeshiva and exclaiming: "These permit, and these forbid; these render pure and these impure; why should I study Torah at all?"

With respect to the Church, Lim remarks that an increasingly common response to this crisis was to demonize—literally—the Christian sophist, "often conflated with the dialectician."[43] The response of the anonymous voice of the Babylonian Talmud to the same sort of crisis was equally effective, although almost directly opposite in strategy. It consisted of divinizing—literally—the dialectician, making God himself, as it were, into one of the disputants of a Bet ha-Midrash. One way of getting at this distinction is to look at a typical bit of paideutic advice from one of the most important thinkers of the fourth-century Church and architect of the Christian monastic habitus, Basil of Caesarea. As cited by Lim, Basil expects the Christian ascetic, that ideal Christian figure of the fourth century, to be "quiet of demeanour, not hasty in speech, nor contentious (μὴ ἐριστικός), quarrelsome (μὴ φιλόνεικος), vainglorious, nor given to interpreting of texts (μὴ ἐξηγητικός)."[44] From a talmudic perspective, this list of traits is remarkable, if not stunning. Perhaps a rabbinical mentor in Basil's position would recommend that his disciple be quiet in demeanor and not hasty in speech, but contention, quarrel, and the interpreting of texts[45] are the very habitus of the Babylonian rabbinic Study House, the House of Midrash, that very Study House which is now increasingly thought by scholars to be a product of the immediate post-amoraic period.[46]

What is striking about the talmudic text is that it denies *both* of the models that Lim has denoted. We have here neither a pattern of the discovery of truth through rational discourse, disputation, and deference to proof on the part of Sages, nor a pattern of revealed or traditional singular truth and *homonoia*. The Babylonian talmudic text elaborates a third term in the paradigm: disputation without telos. Stern notes, with respect to our homily, that though the student despairs at the possibility of studying Torah owing to the multiplicity of interpretations, there is really no cause for such despondency, for "although the sages' opinions may contradict each other, they all are part of Torah, part of a single revelation."[47] The argument of Celsus against the Christians—that their disputes discredit the truth of the Gospels and Christianity—is not different in content from the despair of the hypothesized auditor of the rabbinic disputes who is led to skepticism (How can one learn Torah?) owing to their constant disagreements. Even closer, it would seem, is the despair of the bishop at the Council of Seleucia who declared, "If to proclaim personal opinions day after day is to confess the faith, we will never express the truth with accuracy."[48] What is unique is the ultimate answer given in this narrative of the Babylonian Talmud and constitutive of a certain Jewish theology: namely, that disagreement itself, or at any rate the appearance of disagreement to humans, is exemplary of the divine mind. Instead of conducing to an ideal of *homonoia*, the Babylonian Talmud leads to an ideal of *polynoia*, the many-mindedness, as it were, of God. This difference is embodied in the famous talmudic statement that a heavenly oracle declared, with respect to the contradictory opinions of the two Houses, of Hillel and of Shammai, that "these *and* these are the words of the Living God" (BT Eruvin 13b).

I must repeat, however, that such declarations are to be found only in the latest layers of classical rabbinic literature, in the Talmuds themselves. In the earlier strata we find instead accounts of the many students of Hillel and Shammai who did not attend their masters sufficiently, with the consequence being the *first* appearance of dispute in Israel, "and the Torah became two Torot" (Tosefta Soṭa 14:9). That is, there was a declination from an originary *homonoia*, identical in structure to Justin's account of the origins of heresy or even Numenius's *On the Infidelity of the Academy Toward Plato*, in which the appearance of division in the opinions of the successors of Plato was because they "did not hold to the primitive heritage but rapidly divided."[49] In the earlier imagination, presumably sufficient investigation could discover the original truth, whether Hillel's or Shammai's; by the latter stratum, the contradictory views of the disciples of both of these Sages are being declared equally the words of the Living God in direct contravention of the original model of decline from an original situation of truth and homophony.[50] The point of the statement, as shown by Shlomo Naeh, is that neither the words of the House of Hillel nor the words of the House of Shammai should be regarded as heresy; there are not two Torahs but only one in Israel. The Talmuds thus tacitly contest the earlier tannaitic (Toseftan) formulations of the ratio of the two traditions of the two Houses to each other. Brilliantly, Naeh shows that the very phraseology used here is highly significant, because the collocation "words of the Living God" appears only once in the Bible, in Jeremiah 23:36, in connection with the "false [or lying] prophet," and, moreover, that "in the world of the Rabbis, a charge of 'falsifying the words of the Living God' is a charge of *minut*."[51] Naeh cites further supporting texts that indicate that the term "words of the Living God" is used in rabbinic texts in heresiological contexts. It follows, then, that the point of this talmudic statement is that neither the words of the House of Hillel nor those of the House of Shammai are heresy.

Naeh and I, however, evaluate these conclusions differently for historiography. Based on his assumption (an assumption that it is impossible to *disprove*, just as it is impossible to prove) that texts cited in the name of tannaim in the Talmuds are early, Naeh concludes that the statement "these and these" is a product of the crisis produced by first-century controversies between the Houses that threatened to produce schism in Israel. Following my own reading protocols (which I think cannot be disproven or proven either), I claim these statements for the talmudic layer of rabbinic thought, with the dispute of the Houses being used as a paradigm, but with a significantly different historical context. It is hard for me to see how we could harmonize the statement appearing in tannaitic texts that "the Torah became two Torot" with "these and these," which (to my mind significantly) does not appear in actual tannaitic texts at all. As Fisch has argued, since the Houses apparently no longer were in existence, even according to the myths, at the time that Yavneh was supposed to be taking place, reading "these and these" as a particular Yavnean response to an alleged crisis seems overdrawn historicism.[52] It is, rather, a structural ecclesiological and theological crisis to which, I would suppose, the Talmuds respond, not an actual historical moment of threatened schism. This suggests that even this expression, at least in its Palestinian version, does not yet encompass the final Babylonian ideology of indeterminacy.

We can, however, go even a bit further in reading than this. Here is the crucial text as it appears in the Babylonian Talmud:

R. Abba said Shmuel said: "The House of Hillel and the House of Shammai disputed for three years. These said, 'The halakah is according to us,' and those said, 'The halakha is according to us.' A heavenly voice went out and said, 'These and these are the words of the living God. But the halakha follows the House of Hillel.'"

And since "These and these are the words of the living God," why did the House of Hillel merit that the halakha would be in accord with them?

Because they were pleasant and modest, and they would teach their words and the words of the House of Shammai. Not only that, but they would mention the words of the House of Shammai before their own words. (BT Eruvin 13b)

Within the space of this text (reading it once more as a sort of potted "memory" of the shifts in rabbinic discourse), we see a transition from a time of strife and disputation for the truth to a time in which strife has been abandoned in favor of the undecidability of the true way. Note that the text explicitly remarks a period—"three years"—in which there was vigorous and exclusivistic dispute, a counterpart, I am suggesting, to the earlier period of rabbinic culture that I have constructed, the one in which the differences between the two Houses were condemned as the production of "two Torahs." However, in this latter period, the

"now" of the text, a counterpart to the developing Christian notion of simplicity, is to be found in the description of the House of Hillel as "pleasant and modest." Their simplicity, however, is not enshrined in *homonoia* but in an irenic
version of endless (literally endless) preservation of the two contradictory opinions. Indeed, in this late rabbinic tale,[53] the halakha is one and simplicity is the
touchstone of the halakha, but rabbinic disagreement—agreement to disagree—is the touchstone of that simplicity. Moreover, we are explicitly informed
that: "Where did this heavenly voice go out? It went out at Yavneh," thus inscribing, as it were, a shift in representations of Yavneh itself in the genealogy of
rabbinic modes of discourse.

What I am proposing, then, is a genealogy of a particular rabbinic episteme,[54] for the textual practice of the redactors of the Babylonian Talmud was
very effective. These anonymous Rabbis, it could be said, produced the forms of
rabbinic Judaism that were dominant throughout all of the Middle Ages and
early modernity and that even now figure most commonly (and not only by orthodox apologists) as Judaism *tout court*. Stern has already put it well: "The conclusion of such a discourse is, of course, a powerful and tendentious support for
rabbinic hegemony. . . . [T]he citation of multiple interpretations in midrash is
an attempt to represent in textual terms an idealized academy of Rabbinic tradition where all the opinions of the sages are recorded equally as part of a single divine conversation. Opinions that in human discourse may appear as
contradictory or mutually exclusive are raised to the state of paradox once
traced to their common source in the speech of the divine author."[55] My only
dissent from Stern's formulation would be to refer this not so much to "the citation of multiple interpretations in midrash" (which does not have to be understood in this theological manner—it could, after all, be just a practice of
self-effacing anthologizing of earlier views by the editors) as to the explicit theorizing of the stammaim and *their* construction of the talmudic dispute as
without end and of contradictions as all the product of the common divine
speech. In other words, the practice of the editors of the midrashic collections
with their placement of multiple interpretations side by side does not constitute
the grand theological and theoretical gesture that scholars (including me) had
claimed for it; it can be interpreted in such wise but by no means ineluctably, as
we shall, I hope, yet see.[56]

The rabbinic literary tradition itself seems to "remember" the historical
processes that generated its own construction of dissensus as constitutive of its
power and authority. We may be able to gain some further insight into this development within rabbinic discourse (if indeed my construction bears weight)
via comparison with seemingly very different shifts in the patterns of Christian
discourse and, in particular, by reading a familiar talmudic story about Yavneh

in the context of an equally powerful fifth-century and therefore contemporaneous legend about Nicaea.

The *Nachleben* of Nicaea

Lim argues that Christian theology was compelled to oppose dialectical discourse because that dialectic was so successful. He describes this situation: "In a language game that allowed for the clear articulation of nuances, people pressured each other to profess their beliefs in the middle of a controversial minefield, the features and contours of which were just beginning to be mapped."[57] This pressure led to the conclusion that the endemic dissension of the Christian church had arisen precisely because of "vain disputes and questionings,"[58] even among some who had been trained as highly skilled practitioners of this discursive modality. One solution to this "problem" was the turn to a mystical and apophatic theology, as most fully expressed in the writings of Pseudo-Dionysius. Related to this was the demand, on the part of such a centrally located theological authority as Gregory Nazianzen, to avoid dialectic and engage in Christian practice.[59] One of the responses to Christian theological argumentativeness that Gregory articulated was the catechism.

A remarkable story in the Talmud, frequently read but until now interpreted quite differently, can now be reread in this cultural context:

Rabbi Yehudah said that Rav said: In the hour that Moses ascended on high, he found the Holy Blessed One sitting and tying crowns for the letters [that is, adding the decorative serifs that appear on some letters in the written Torah scroll]. He said before him: "Master of the Universe, What [lit. who] holds you back?" He said, "There is one man who will be after several generations, and Akiva the son of Joseph is his name, who will derive from each and every stroke hills and hills of halakhot." He said before him: "Master of the Universe, show him to me." He said to him: "Turn around!" He went and sat at the back of eight rows [in the study house of Rabbi Akiva], and he didn't understand what they were saying. His strength became weak. When they reached a certain issue, the disciples said to him [to Akiva], "From whence do you know this?" He said to them: "It is a halakha given to Moses at Sinai." [Moses'] spirit became settled.

He returned and came before the Holy Blessed One. He said to him: "Master of the Universe, You have such a one and yet You give the Torah by my hand?!" He [God] said to him: "Be silent! That is what has transpired in My thought."

He said to Him: "Master of the Universe: You have shown me his Torah, show me his reward."

He said to him: "Turn around!" He turned around and saw that they were weighing the flesh of Rabbi Akiva in the market [after his martyrdom]. He said to Him: "Master of the Universe, This is the Torah and this is its reward?!" He said to him: "Be silent! That is what has transpired in My thought." (BT Menaḥot 29b)

Most interpretations take this story as being either a positive or ironic, even sarcastic, reflection on midrash. Such readings cannot be dismissed, of course, or even gainsaid, and it takes nothing away from their validity if I read the text in a wider discursive (and thus historical) context. To my mind, there is hardly a more powerful rendition of an apophatic hermeneutic, an apophatic divine will, and an apophatic theodicy, all in this one highly compressed narrative, or virtual myth, in which God will not or perhaps even, as it were, cannot explain the modalities of interpretation of his word or his activities in the universe.

It should be emphasized how thoroughly this text contradicts one way of describing rabbinic culture, articulated by Menachem Fisch as one in which "access to knowledge is not limited to members of any particular caste; in principle, anyone willing to make the effort can attain it. Second, the tools and methods for generating knowledge, and the criteria for judging knowledge claims, also all remain in the public domain."[60] In this talmudic story, knowledge is thoroughly opaque in its form; no one, not even Moses himself, could possibly know what Rabbi Akiva knows. The only way that such knowledge could be achieved is via access to the traditions of the particular community. To be sure, membership in that community is not limited to those of particular birth among male Jews, but it just as surely is not open to all and obviously not adjudicable by anyone who is not in the know.[61] Who but an Akiva could know what is meant by jots, tittles, and decorations on letters? And how could we know other than by being his disciples? The difficulty of acquiring such knowledges is, moreover, articulated precisely in multiple talmudic legends about this same Rabbi Akiva.[62]

At about the same time that Moses was being told to be quiet and recognize that there is much that human beings cannot know, Gregory Nazianzen's Cappadocian colleague and friend, Gregory of Nyssa, was elaborating his theology of language and interpretation. Nyssa's great opponent was Eunomius, the representative of a late and radical form of "Arian" insistence that the Son shared in no way the essence or substance of the Father. As Alden Mosshammer shows, according to Eunomius, humans could know God, for "God himself, as the author of language, has guaranteed the accuracy of identity between ungeneracy and the true godhead. For God would not have commanded us to seek after his knowledge if such knowledge had not been given to man. God created the usage and granted to man the knowledge of names suitable to the essences they represent. Names denote essences, and for each distinct essence there can be only one proper name. For his own essence God has granted to man the knowledge of the name 'ungeneracy.' "[63] By contrast, Nyssa insisted on the finitude of language and, therefore, its ultimate inadequacy, whether as theology or as interpretation, to encompass fully the infinitude of God, to articulate the divine nature and the divine mind, inviting an endless hermeneutical activity that can have no telos, even as there is no "end" to God.[64] As Virginia Burrus sums up her own brief but very sharp account of this aspect of the Gregorian text, "The mystagogue's foreclosure on the pursuit of God's unfolding depths and heights—rather than his assertion of divinity's mystery itself—underwrites what Richard Lim describes so compellingly as the foreclosure, through ideological mystification, of an ancient tradition of discursive reasoning and public debate."[65]

The climax of Lim's narrative is his account of the effects of the Council of Nicaea in the century immediately following the time of the great Cappadocians. The centerpiece of Lim's argument in his chapter on Nicaea and its *Nachleben* (discursive afterlife) is the analysis of a legendary encounter between a confessor and a philosopher at Nicaea as preserved in the Christian historians' writings of the late fourth and fifth centuries. Because these legends are similar in genre to the only type of "historiographical" text preserved within rabbinic literature at this precise period, they provide a particularly interesting basis for comparing discursive movements within the two formations at the time. "These legends about Nicaea are inherently interesting to the modern historian, not because accurate information can be mined from them but because they tell us much about the period in which they arose and circulated."[66]

According to the version in Rufinus of Aquileia's *Church History*, "now we may learn how much power there is in simplicity of faith from what is reported to have happened there." It seems that on a certain day at Nicaea, a great dialectician and philosopher, attracted there by the presence of so many intellects, engaged in theological debate with "our bishops, men by no means unskilled in the art of disputation." However much they tried, the bishops could not defeat the heretical philosopher through their disputations. "But that God might show that the kingdom of God is based upon power rather than speech, one of the confessors, a man of the simplest character who knew only Christ Jesus and him crucified,[67] was present with the other bishops in attendance." This man wished to debate the heretic, and overcoming the fear of the assembled dialectician bishops, he began his discourse in this way:

"In the name of Jesus Christ, O philosopher," he said, "listen to the truth. There is one God who made heaven and earth, who gave breath to man whom he had formed from the mud of the earth, and who created everything, what is seen and what is not seen, with the power of his word and established it with the sanctification of his spirit. This word and wisdom, whom we call 'Son,' took pity on the errors of humankind, was born of a virgin, by suffering death freed us from everlasting death, and by his resurrection conferred upon us eternal life. Him we await as the judge to come of all we do. Do you believe this is so, O philosopher?" But he, as though he had nothing whatever that he could say in opposition to this, so astonished was he at the power of what had been said, could only reply to it all that he thought that it was so, and that what had been said was the only truth. . . . The philosopher, turning to his disciples and to those who had gathered to listen, said, "Listen O learned men: so long as it was words with which I had to deal, I set words against words and what was said I refuted with my rhetoric. But when power rather than words came out of the mouth of the speaker, words could not withstand power, nor could man oppose God."[68]

What is stunning about this story, as well analyzed by Lim, is its staging of an opposition between the power of human reason and rhetoric and simplicity of faith, in which—of course—"nor could man oppose God." In tandem with the way I read similar rabbinic legends, I would suggest that we have here a sort of potted memory of the shift from theological disputation as the means to Christian truth to the recitations of creeds and catechisms in the context of an anti-intellectual ideology of simplicity.[69] In this context, this comment of Richard Vaggione takes on particular resonance: "the θεῖος ἀνὴρ envisaged by Eunomius was almost always also a *peritus*; the corresponding figure among Nicenes was more likely to think closeness with God was independent of intellectual expertise."[70] Moreover, the fact is surely illuminating as well that similar stories were told, at about the same time as our Nicene legend, of encounters between the "heretic" Eunomius and the Nicene champion Amphilochius, in which the former "appears in his presence as the worldly 'expert' overcome by the simplicity of a holy man."[71]

This staging can also serve as the setting for an interpretation of some of the best-known Yavneh legends from the Babylonian Talmud, which may be dealing with the very historical changes and discursive contexts that informed the developments Lim has laid bare. The most palpable comparison seems to be with the story of Rabbi Eli'ezer's controversy with the Sages, in the tale of the proverbial Stove of Akhnai, a controversy in which he was unable to convince the Sages via dialectical reasoning after arguing the entire day to support his traditions from his teachers, and even direct divine interventions on his side did not win the day. Not, of course, because his interlocutors doubted the divinity of the intervener, but because God, too, as it were, has to provide convincing argument and proof.[72] This surely is the limit case of the approbation of dialectic, in contrast to the increasing reprobation of it among orthodox Christians.

This tale, perhaps more written about than any other narrative in the Talmud, can be seen in an entirely different light when compared with Rufinus's roughly contemporaneous production:

On that day,[73] Rabbi Eli'ezer used every imaginable argument, but they did not accept it from him. He said: If the law is as I say, this carob will prove it. The carob was uprooted from its place one hundred feet. Some report four hundred feet. They said to him, One does not quote a carob as proof. He further said to them, If the law is as I say, the water pipe will prove it. The water began to flow backward. They said to him, One may not quote a water pipe as proof. Again, he said to them, If the law is as I say, the walls of the House of Study will prove it. The walls of the House of Study leaned over to fall. Rabbi Yehoshua' rebuked them, saying to them, If the disciples of the wise are striving with each other for the law, what have you to do with it? They did not fall because of the honor of Rabbi Yehoshua', and did not stand straight for the honor of Rabbi Eli'ezer. He said to them, if the law is as I say, let be proven from heaven. A voice came from heaven and announced: The law is in accordance with the view of Rabbi Eli'ezer. Rabbi Yehoshua' stood on his feet and said "it [the Torah] is not in heaven." (Baba Meşa'i 59a)

On the original halakhic question, Rabbi Eli'ezer initially tried to support his position using the "normal" rabbinic modes of rational argument, the very modes of argument (*tašuvot*) which might be said to define rabbinic rationality. When that failed, however, he didn't accept defeat, but rather turned to another source of authority: miracles and heavenly oracles, a form of authority that, in my view, it was the essence of later rabbinic Judaism to reject.[74] I would read in this story an explicit rejection of any notion of divine inspiration or prophecy in midrash. The mode of authority constituted by the House of Midrash is apostolic and institutional; the authority was constituted by Moses at Mt. Sinai—it is called Oral Torah—and passed down through a series of institutional relays (see Chapter 3, above) until it has reached the rabbinic institution, which alone has the authority to decide by its will (that is, by the will of the majority) what is correct for practice. Rabbi Eli'ezer, accordingly, by seeking divine authority for his position was totally undermining the foundations of the entire rabbinic ideology. He was, in effect, denying that the Oral Torah was from Sinai, and it is thus that he puts himself beyond the pale. Thus the walls of the House of Study threaten to fall in response to Rabbi Eli'ezer's position, and thus "If the disciples of the wise are striving with each other for the law."

This brief sequence out of the longer narrative of Rabbi Eli'ezer represents something like a close narrative parallel to and ideological inversion of Rufinus's story of the old Christian and the philosopher, for in Rufinus's text, of course, it is the miracle workers and divine voice that win the day, defeating the dialecticians, whereas in the Talmud, the dialecticians defeat the miracles and the voice of God. The talmudic story has not, to the best of my knowledge, been placed in this context before. Rufinus is "altogether reluctant to report debates" and legitimizes his account of the Council of Nicaea via the miracles performed by simple and holy confessors,[75] as expressed in his legendary narrative cited above. But for the rabbinic legend of the same moment, debate is made the crux of the religious life, and the reporting of debates becomes the very stuff of rabbinic textuality. God himself and his miracles cannot interfere with this holy dialectic, this sacred polyphony: "If the disciples of the wise are striving with each other for the law, what have you to do with it?"

Rabbi Eliʿezer, it could be said fairly, represents the modes of authority that were becoming dominant in Rufinus's Christianity—absolute reliance on allegedly unchanged tradition and on the authority of the holy man. But at *this* "Yavneh" in fourth- or fifth-century Babylonia, it is the dialecticians who win the day, in a conclusion completely opposite, of course, to those of fifth-century "Nicaea," as described by Lim. I am not suggesting that rabbinic culture was therefore more pluralistic, democratic, or open than that of Nicene orthodoxy, because it must be seen that even though the dialecticians win here, they do so not by dialectic, by proving that they are right, but by the arbitrary device of a majority vote, and a "wild" midrashic reading that supports the authority of such a vote.[76] In recent work, Evonne Levy has made the point that, already in Plato, Gorgias's "deep skepticism about the limitation of human knowledge" constituted "a threat to democracy itself."[77] Democracy, then, is predicated on the validity of arguments to command assent, which neither the Babylonian Talmud nor the post-Nicene Church seem prepared to endorse. For all their dissimilarity, the story of Rufinus and the talmudic story are also quite similar. Rabbinic "pluralism" has its strict borders and constraints. As we shall see, Rabbi Eliʿezer, possessor of the divine voice and power to do miracles, is severely punished by excommunication and exile from the House of Study for his refusal to accept the conclusions of the majority and their dialectical disputations. It is not the content of Rabbi Eliʿezer's dissent that is anathematized, but his appeal to mantic and even prophetic modes of authority, whereas the Rabbis are struggling to establish their sole control via the institution of Torah.[78] In other words, Rabbi Eliʿezer's modes of legitimation threaten the very institution of the Oral Torah, and that is something that the Rabbis themselves testify puts one beyond the pale, much more so than mere halakhic disagreement. After all, the disagreements of Bet Hillel and Bet Shammai on weighty matters having to do with purity laws were no less and even perhaps more significant than Rabbi Eliʿezer's dissent here, and the texts trouble to tell us that "even so they did not forego from accepting each other's purity." In the Yavneh myth Rabbi Eliʿezer is made to stand for an earlier understanding of Torah that the Talmud disputes. Of course, the Talmud cannot present this as a disagreement between itself and earlier authority, so it is rendered as a disagreement among the earlier authorities themselves.[79] What we find represented, then, at this latest layer of talmudic storytelling about Yavneh is a history of transformation not from a time of dissensus to a time of consensus, as the Christian orthodox tale would go (or better put a transition from originary consensus, decline into dissensus, and return to consensus after Nicaea) but rather a canonization of dissensus, unending dissensus as the very essence of the Torah as given at Sinai. The halakha must be decided, the text seems to say, in order to preserve the community, but such decision is always arbitrary, for all of the contradictory opinions were indeed given by the same God.

Rabbi Yehoshua's statement, frequently taken to be an instance of a sort of protodeconstruction,[80] in this Babylonian version represents an instance of the complete rabbinic takeover of religious life and practice via the Oral Torah.[81] Not even God, not even the angels can compete with the Rabbis and their Torah. The Torah is no longer in heaven. It is on earth in the possession of the rabbinic institution. As the fourth-century Rabbi Yirmiah glosses Rabbi Yehoshua's statement: "Since the Torah has been given on Mt. Sinai, we no longer listen to heavenly voices, for you have already written in the Torah: 'Incline after the majority' [Exod. 23:2]." Rabbinic Judaism thus represents a particular episteme of power/knowledge. In the face of the perceived failure of dialectic to produce consensus, it seeks to effect a transfer of authority and of control over discourse from heaven, reasoned and compelling argument, to earth, the allegedly God-given authority of the majority of the Rabbis.[82] Apophatic dialectic proves remarkably similar, in this sense, to apophatic simplicity.

Beyond the Spoken Word

Another historical shift is marked within the narrative of Rabbi Eli'ezer. William A. Graham has written:

Nevertheless, it is especially in traditional cultures around the world that the fundamental link between the spoken word and truth is all but indissoluble—not because oral transmission and communication are practically or technically superior to written forms, but because most traditional cultures see the loci (but not necessarily the origins) of both truth and authority primarily in persons and their utterances, not in documents and records. In such contexts, the teacher who knows the sacred text by heart and has devoted his or her life to studying and explicating it is the one and only reliable guarantor of the sacred truth. The power of the holy word is realized only through the human word of the seer, prophet or spiritual master, not through a manuscript, even where the latter is also important. However exalted its status in a particular tradition, the written text alone is typically worthless, or at least worth little, without a human teacher to transmit both it and the traditions of learning and interpretation associated with it.

To be reckoned as scripture, whether in its written or oral form, any text must be perceived in some sense as a prime locus of verbal contact with transcendental truth, or ultimate reality.[83]

This description fits the earliest stage of rabbinic tradition, understanding Rabbi Eli'ezer as a figure for the archaic (as he frequently is so understood within the literature[84]). Rabbi Eli'ezer in our Babylonian story represents that earlier stage: "a human teacher to transmit both it and the traditions of learning and interpretation associated with it," and, as such, his teaching is marked in the text "as a prime locus of verbal contact with transcendental truth, or ultimate reality." However, the narrative marks a rupture, not only with dialectic as a means of establishing truth, but also with that verbal contact as the location of truth and its guarantor. The Written Torah has become fully written, entirely inscriptional, in Rabbi Yehoshua''s voice within the story: It is no longer in heaven.[85]

This narrative both encapsulates and reverses Graham's contention that "speech always precedes writing, cosmically and anthropologically as well as historically. If there is anything that can be called protoscripture, it is surely the utterances of ecstatics, prophets, and seers, in which it is commonly held to be not they but the divinity who speaks through them as their chosen mouthpieces."[86] In the talmudic narration of rabbinic history, of "Yavneh," living oral contact, both with an authoritative tradition as represented by Rabbi Eli'ezer and directly with the divine voice itself, has been broken once and for all. Authority is transferred to another sense of Oral Torah, the endless work of human invention in front of the text,[87] the authority of which is now guaranteed by divine voices that can only confess their submission to that rabbinic power, as it were. Writing now precedes speech, and the Oral Torah is the Torah that is read, not the Torah that was spoken. It is this cultural move that constitutes the crucifixion of the Logos and the resurrection of the Oral Torah in the communal invention of the House of Midrash.

This transfer of authority and divine submission is epitomized daringly within the narrative itself. In the very next sentence we are informed that

Rabbi Natan met Elijah [the Prophet] and asked him, "What was the Holy Blessed One doing at that hour?" He said to him, "He was laughing and saying, 'My sons have defeated me; my sons have defeated me.'"

It is hard to imagine a more unambiguous and audacious account of an epistemic shift than this one. A divine voice is made the guarantor that divine voices have nothing to say in the religious lives of Jews anymore. Only the Rabbis, designed the sons of God, and their Torah serve that function. Only the majority decision of the Rabbis has power and authority, and only their knowledge is relevant.

According to the Talmud's version of this story, Rabbi Eli'ezer was then punished by an extremely harsh version of excommunication, a highly unusual practice in cases of halakhic disagreement: "On that day, all the objects that Rabbi Eli'ezer had declared clean were brought and burned in fire. Then they

took a vote and excommunicated him." The narrative here defines very sharply
what the boundaries of acceptable "pluralism" are and are not. Some "these and
these," but not all, even within the rabbinic community, are all "words of the
Living God." Rabbi Eli'ezer, in direct contrast to the House of Shammai in that
other representation, is treated as a heretic:[88]

> It has been related: On that day, they took all of the things that Rabbi Eli'ezer declared
> pure and declared them polluted. And they took a vote about him and "blessed him" [a
> euphemism for dire curse and anathema]!
> They said: "Who will go tell him?"
> Rabbi Akiva said, "I will go tell him, for if someone who is not blameless should go
> and tell him, he might destroy the entire world."

If someone less saintly than Rabbi Akiva were to inform Rabbi Eli'ezer of his
excommunication, the latter's powers of magic would be sufficient to destroy
everything:

> What did Rabbi Akiva do? He wore black clothes, and wrapped himself in a black cloak
> [signs of mourning], and went and sat before [Rabbi Eli'ezer] at a distance of four cu-
> bits [thus signaling the latter's excommunication].
> Rabbi Eli'ezer said to him: Akiva—what is different about this day?
> He said to him: My teacher, it seems as if the members of the fellowship are disso-
> ciating from you.
> He also tore his clothes and removed his shoes, and slid down and sat on the earth
> [further signs of mourning]. Tears rolled out of his eyes, and the world suffered the loss
> of a third of the olive crop, a third of the wheat crop, and a third of the rye crop.
> And there are those who say that even the dough in the hands of a woman was
> spoiled [through overrising].
> It is taught: It was so great that day that every place where Rabbi Eli'ezer's eyes fell
> was burned, and also Rabban Gamaliel was traveling in a ship. A mighty wave came to
> sink it. He said, "I believe that this is only because of Eli'ezer the son of Hyrcanus." He
> stood on his feet and said: "Master of the Universe, you know that everything I did was
> not for my own glory and not for the glory of my father's house, but for your glory, *in
> order that there would not be many controversies in Israel*." And the sea rested from its fury.

At this stage in the story we have a dramatic rendition of the conflicts of the
early stages of the formation of rabbinic Judaism, of the "bad old days" in the
Babylonian talmudic mythopoeisis. Rabban Gamaliel says that he excommunicated Rabbi Eli'ezer with the most dire form of anathema, one that renders him
as if a dead man, in order to protect Israel from controversy and division.[89] In
other words, the initial stages of the process that would lead to the alleged
"grand coalition" and antisectarianism of "Yavneh" involve the most extreme
acts of exclusion.

Shaye Cohen seems simply to accept Rabban Gamaliel's alibi when he writes that "two categories of people could not be incorporated into the Yavnean coalition: those who insisted upon a sectarian self-identification, and those who refused to heed the will of the majority." Cohen attempts to soften the implicit self-contradiction in his argument by claiming that "[t]hese sectarians were denounced, not excommunicated." However, Rabbi Eli'ezer was certainly represented as excommunicated, according to this Babylonian legend. Cohen argues: "Whatever the truth of these amoraic stories, they reflect the essential problem of the Yavnean period: the creation of the society which would tolerate, even foster, disputes and discussions but which could nonetheless maintain order. Those rabbis who could not play by the new rules were too great a danger to be punished with just a curse. They were expelled." In the end, Cohen also admits that this is only a rabbinic construction: "This rabbinic ideology is reflected in Justin's discussion of the Jewish sects: there are Jews, i.e., the 'orthodox,' and there are sects, among them the Pharisees, who scarcely deserve the name Jew."[90] Reading critically, we hardly see here the inclusiveness and tolerance that most scholars, following Cohen, now identify as the legacy of Yavneh. We find instead the production of an exclusivistic institution of orthodoxy, as in the story of Nicaea, in order, like that invention, to prevent "the proliferation of controversy."[91] To be sure, the narrative registers some ambivalence about the treatment of Rabbi Eli'ezer—the boat does almost sink—but in the end, Rabban Gamaliel's argument for authority and stability and centralized power/knowledge is affirmed "in order that there would not be many controversies in Israel." Those who will not conform to the new rabbinic program of the sole authority of the House of Study are thrown out of Israel.

Erecting the Study House Walls

At the same time as the emblem of multivocality was being produced in the late talmudic academy, the borders of the social body that was to determine the parameters of radical doubt—to erect the walls of the House of Study, as it were[92]—were being constructed through a process of "domestication" of figures who might otherwise be found outside these borders, figures such as Rabbi Eli'ezer or the early pietists. Yet frequently enough, when the texts that explicitly intimate the "pluralism" of Babylonian rabbinic ecclesiology are brushed against the grain, they indicate the sharp limits of that pluralism, in large part through their crucial and disturbing focus on gender.

The following talmudic text, from tractate Giṭṭin, dating from circa fourth-century Babylonia, exposes both the radical indeterminacy of the stammaitic theory and the sharp political limitations on pluralism. The text explores a biblical locus: "And his concubine went astray" (Judges 19:2) in the so-called concubine of Gibeah story (Judges 19–21). Two Rabbis, in interpreting this story, try to discover what had caused the concubine's husband to drive her out of his house in anger:

R. Evyatar said, He found a fly on her.
    R. Yonatan said, He found a hair on her.
    R. Evyatar met up with Elijah [the Prophet], and said to him, What is the Holy Blessed One up to?
    [Elijah] said, He is studying [the story of] the concubine of Gibeah.
    [Evyatar]: And what does He say about it?
    [Elijah] said to [Evyatar], He [God] says, Evyatar my son says thus, and Yonatan my son says thus.
    [Evyatar] said to [Elijah], God forfend—is there doubt before Heaven?
    [Elijah] said to him, These and these are the words of the Living God: [the husband] found a fly and did not get angry; [but] he found a hair and got angry.
    R. Yehudah said, The fly was in the cup, and the hair was in that place [her vulva]. The fly is disgusting, but the hair is dangerous.
    R. Ḥisda said, A man should never produce fear within his household, for behold the concubine of Gibeah; her husband produced fear in the household, and there was a massacre of tens of thousands in Israel. (Giṭṭin 6b)

This rabbinic narrative deals with one of the most horrifying of biblical stories. In this story, a wife (or concubine) leaves her husband and is eventually violated and murdered. The story is a savage narrative of the most appalling violence toward a woman. It results in civil war, but for the Rabbis it conveys the domestic moral that a husband should not display anger toward his wife, for if he does, she may run away, with devastating personal and public consequences. The Rabbis debate what fault her husband found in her that made him so angry that the concubine grew afraid and ran off, leading to the whole sorry series of events. According to one of the Rabbis, he had found an unwanted fly; according to the other, he had found unwanted hair. (An interesting bit of sexual lore is alluded to here. Women were apparently expected to shave their pudenda, and even one hair was understood to represent a danger of castration during the act of intercourse [see Rashi on this passage, referring to Deut. 23:2]).

    The remarkable thing about the rabbinic text is that it seemingly encodes radical indeterminacy in the biblical narrative itself. Let us follow this process within the text. In the first move, when Elijah, the mediator of divine knowledge, is asked what God himself has to say on the question that the rabbis are debating, the text informs us that all he does is quote his "sons," the Rabbis: "Evyatar my son says thus, and Yonatan my son says thus." According to these Rabbis, even God, the author of the Book, can only say with certainty that there

are various interpretative possibilities. He can only repeat the tradition of interpretation that is extant in the Bet Midrash. This particular and very special moment in Babylonian rabbinic discourse about interpretation does, I think, merit
the name "indeterminacy." Moreover, as Menachem Fisch makes clear, if the
Babylonian Talmud denies absolute truth to "the factual status of past oc-
curences," then such claims of absolute truth would be even further from halakhic difference, which does not involve assertions about actual states of affairs.
As if in panic at its own suggestion that the text is inhabited by such radical indeterminacy that even God can only "teach the controversy," not resolve it—"a
serious encroachment on God's omniscience"[93]—the narrative then opts for
harmonization of the two views: the husband found both fly and hair. This weak
retreat, however, can be read as only emphasizing the drastic character of what
Elijah has reported as God's knowledge or lack of knowledge about what this
text means. Yet God is still reported as being able only to report the different
views of the human readers, as it were, and not to go beyond them. At the same
time, it needs to be marked and noted well that the legitimate site of such radical undecidability, the parameters of indeterminacy, are set by Evyatar, "my son,"
and Yonatan, "my son." The male Rabbis are the only legitimate subjects of reading.[94] We see here the discursive occupation of female bodies as a means for securing rabbinic control.

   Such stories have been taken up in the contemporary writing on rabbinic
Judaism that claims it encodes either radical undecidability in the theoretical
sense or radical pluralism in the social sense. No one, scholars suggest, can exercise control over interpretation according to the rabbinic system of midrash,
for the Rabbis allegedly understood that no textual interpretation is ever definitive, not even that of the Author himself.[95] Somewhat less lyrically, but still idyl-
lically, we sometimes find this structure described as one of a radical
democratization of interpretation within the rabbinic polity.[96] Neither of these
two constructions, however, pays attention to the fact that interpretative authority is located exclusively in the rabbinic Study House. Far from representing
a utopian moment of ludic interpretative freedom,[97] the project of a hermeneutic parable like this one is to advance the rabbinic program of exclusive control
over the religious lives of Jews and to secure the interpretation of the Torah for
their institution, the House of Study, in whose controversies all truth and authority lie.[98] This recognition is, I think, one of the solid achievements of Stern's
essay.[99]

   A telling self-reflection and direct representation of these walls and boundaries can be found at least once in rabbinic literature itself. In the Palestinian
Talmud Shabbat 17b, we read the following:

Ya'aqov the man of Kefar Naburaia asked Rabbi Haggai: Is then a child who is born at twilight, circumcised at twilight? [It is considered doubtful as to whether twilight belongs to the preceding or following day, and if the child is to be circumcised on the eighth day, that doubt would be significant.] He [Haggai] said to him: If you and I were going in the same door, perhaps maybe we could discuss [decide] this point.

As pointed out by Herford in a convincing discussion,[100] this passage gives us a figure who is completely *within* the rabbinic patterns of discourse, that is, unless we understand his question as simply meant to be provocative, which we have no reason to do. This Ya'aqov seems genuinely interested in exploring a typical issue of rabbinic halakha. Rabbi Haggai is simply unwilling to engage with him on the question at all, because the two do not go in the same door, that is, in some way the questioner has disqualified himself from engaging in halakhic discourse at all. The most obvious explanation for this is that in several other places in rabbinic literature this same figure is ambiguously referred to as a *min*. Having left, presumably (or never been in), the confines of rabbinic orthodoxy in his belief, whatever his commitment to the same halakhic practices and discourses as the Rabbis, this "ghost of an ancient heretic" is no longer (or never was) a legitimate participant in Torah. As Herford perceptively remarks: "We may also perhaps infer that the distinction between Jew and Min was not regarded, from the side of the Minim, as being a very sharp one."[101] Indeed, we could go further and say that the "minim" frequently seem to have understood themselves as perfectly orthodox rabbinic Jews, even as they are represented in rabbinic literature itself.[102] It is perhaps significant, in the light of my discussions in previous chapters, that this Ya'aqov was apparently a central figure in the synagogues of his day—a maker of targums and sermons—more so, apparently, than in the rabbinic Houses of Study. It is, obviously, the door of the figurative House of Study into which he does not or may not enter.

At the same time that we recognize clearly that on a political level we are not dealing here with a relaxation of social control but rather with an elegant and powerful technique of "consensual orthodoxy"—that most telling irony of the fourth-century church—we also find before us a genuinely radical theological critique of the notion of determinate meaning of the biblical text, so radical that, as we have just seen, the last stratum of the text retreats from it in panic.[103] The notion that even God does not know (cannot know, as it were) the meaning of the text, because in a written text there is no determinate meaning to be known, is, to the best of my knowledge, never found in Palestinian rabbinism,[104] although in a sense it is dramatized (not thematized or theorized) in the final (fourth-century or later) form of Palestinian midrash, with its profusion of multiple interpretations set side by side. This results, I think, in a phenomenologically significant difference between a late ancient (post-Nicene) Christian textuality in which we find normative statements effectively of the form: St. Augustine says, *or* St. Gregory says (that is, two separate and alternative normative statements, and indeed, in "patristic orthodoxy," they say the *same* thing),[105] whereas the definitive form of the rabbinic normative statement is rather: Rabbi Evyatar says *and* Rabbi Yonatan says. For all my suspicion of triumphalist or apologetic and idealizing interpretations of this moment—including my own—I want in the end to assert that the notion that God himself suffers a fall into language, and thus into linguistic indeterminacy, may be the most powerful and creative, perhaps even unique, theological notion of rabbinic Judaism. And this is a distinction that made a difference.[106]

Rabbi Eliʿezer's End

I suggest that the Talmud itself "remembers" and relates the story of a shift in rabbinic episteme. On one reading, at least, we can observe the Talmud dramatizing the answer to my question in the form of a diachronic shift by rendering it as a sequence in the "biography" of Rabbi Eliʿezer. I wish to claim the narrative of the excommunication of Rabbi Eliʿezer to be a moment of rabbinic mythopoetic historiography, a narrative within which the Babylonian Talmud remembers its own history, producing a diachronic myth of origins, one that not only describes the structure of the present sociocultural system but that narrates its development as well. Like "synchronic" founding legends, texts like this do not represent the "actual" past, but they do represent a mythic memory of change within the cultural system, a cultural memory that is interesting in its own right for presenting the structure of cultural practice. In this case the narrative records a historical shift from a regime of orthodoxy, heresy to a regime in which control is secured by defanging controversy of any power to subvert. This needs more clarification.

In the continuation of the Babylonian talmudic narrative found in Tractate Sanhedrin, in contrast to the unfortunate Akavyah ben Mehalalel of the third-century Mishna, Rabbi Eliʿezer of the fifth/sixth-century Talmud is fully rehabilitated at the end of his life. This story can be read as a virtual historical allegory[107] of the retrospective construction of catholic Israel on the part of the later Rabbis, especially, but not exclusively, by the Babylonian Talmud:

It is taught: When Rabbi Eliʿezer was sick, Rabbi Akiva and his colleagues went in to visit him. He was sitting in his canopied bed, and they were sitting in his anteroom. . . .

When the sages saw that his mind was clear,[108] they went and sat down four cubits from him [thus indicating that according to this text, Rabbi Eliʿezer is still excommunicate].

He said to them: "Why have you come?"

They said to him: "To learn Torah we have come."

He said to them: "And until now, why have you not come?"

They said: "We didn't have time."

He said to them: "I will be amazed if they die a natural death."

Rabbi Akiva then said to him: "What about me?"

He said: "Yours is more severe than all of them."

He [Eli'ezer] took his two arms and placed them on his heart and said: "Aiih to these two arms that are like two Scrolls of the Torah rolled up. I have learned much Torah, and I have taught much Torah. I have learned much Torah and I didn't diminish from the teaching of my masters even as much as a dog licks from the sea. I have taught much Torah, and my disciples have not diminished from my teaching so much as the brush in its case.[109]

"And not only that but I teach three hundred laws in the matter of leprosy, and no one ever asked me a question about them, and in the planting of cucumbers, and no one ever asked me about them, except for Akiva ben Yosef. Once he and I were walking on the way. He said to me: 'Teach me their planting.' I said a word and the field was full of cucumbers. He said to me: 'Rabbi, you have taught me their planting; now teach me their uprooting.' I said another word, and they were all gathered into one place."

The [Sages then] said to him: A ball, a slipper, and a cameo [that are made of leather and filled with wool].

He said to them: "They are pure."

And his soul left him in purity.

Rabbi Yehoshua' stood on his feet and said: "The vow is released. The vow is released!"

On the going out of the Sabbath, he met Rabbi Akiva on the way [in the funeral procession] from Caesarea to Lydda. He was smiting his flesh until the blood flowed to the ground. [Rabbi Akiva] opened his eulogy and said: "'My father, my father, the chariot of Israel and its cavalry' (2 Kings 2:12). I have many coins and no banker to change them." (BT Sanhedrin 68a)

Rabbi Eli'ezer is reincorporated into the rabbinic community just before his death "in purity." It is not his views on halakha that have changed, but the manner of discourse. He has been rabbinized, and real dissent has been neutralized. He is no longer a "heretic"—his mind has become clear—and whether he is correct or not on the matter of halakha is not important. What is important is that the dispute, the endless dispute, take place within the confines of the Bet ha-Midrash and its discursive rules. The dialectic can go on forever without resolution. We can read this shift within the narrative at the moment when Rabbi Eli'ezer turns from magic planting and harvesting of cucumbers to answering the Rabbis' purity question. He moves, as it were, from one episteme to another, accepting the terms of the new regime. Thus the story becomes a mini–historical allegory of the shift in the social status of ongoing dialectic from the second- and third-century to the fifth- and sixth-century context.

As Jacob Neusner has pointed out,[110] older traditions of Rabbi Eli'ezer hardly mention his commitment to the study of Torah as the central act of Jewish piety,[111] while here, the disciples come to "learn Torah," and the "much Torah" that Eli'ezer has learned and taught are now central to his self-image.[112] According to the Tosefta (Yevamot 3:1; ed. c. 250 A.C.), Rabbi Eli'ezer never said a word that he had not heard from his teachers, fitting perfectly Josephus's description of the Pharisees who follow their traditions and do not argue with their elders.[113] As Alon Goshen-Gottstein has emphasized, the passage in Avot 2:8 in which the characteristics and evaluation of the five disciples of Rabban Yoḥanan ben Zakkai is given also marks this situation of Rabbi Eli'ezer as the "limed cistern that never loses a drop," while Rabbi El'azar ben 'Arakh is the "overflowing fountain," the creative student of Torah that the new "Akivan" episteme favors.[114] Moreover, we see a shift in the very nature of Rabbi Eli'ezer's personality. From a mantic who relies on absolutely unchanging tradition, prophetic signs, oracles, and magic, Rabbi Eli'ezer is transformed within the space of the story into a proper talmudic sage,[115] converted into a Rabbi, a reader.[116] Rabbi Eli'ezer, historically perhaps a problematic and dissident Pharisee, has been thoroughly domesticated. What is narrated in the text as a story of transgression and repentance can be reread historically as the story of appropriation into rabbinic orthodoxy of a "heterodox" strand of Pharisaic Judaism.

It is vital to emphasize, however, that Rabbi Eli'ezer is finally reappropriated, not via a change in the position that originally led to his excommunication, but via his symbolic acceptance of the rules of rabbinic dialectic, even while maintaining his dissident halakhic position. It is not so much, then, that the Rabbi has changed. Instead, the rules of the game have changed in such a way that he can be accommodated. The House of Study, we might say, has become a more capacious institution, though one that maintains the precise contours of its walls. Had Rabbi Eli'ezer continued in his refusal to accept the normal modes of how rabbinic authority is made, and had he insisted on the absolute truth claims of his combination of hoary tradition and divine semiotics—the two touchstones of Christian orthodox authority in the post-Nicene period—he would have indeed collapsed the walls of the House of Study. We can then perhaps return to Shaye Cohen's point that "two categories of people could not be incorporated into the Yavnean coalition: those who insisted upon a sectarian self-identification, and those who refused to heed the will of the majority," more sharply recognizing the will to power embodied in this move of the sixth-century Rabbis instead of seeing "Yavneh" as a move toward democratization. The possibility of pluralism, we might say, was won precisely by excluding any possibility of real dissent, and in that sense was perhaps even more "successful" than the exclusionary practices of Christian orthodoxy. We have here an instance of what Lim referred to: "Many individuals and groups sought to domesticate the perceived threat of dissensus in public disputing, choosing from various ideological strategies and cultural values to mobilize hierarchical forms of authority against a culture that validated individualistic claims and rational argumentation."[117] The fascinating thing about the rabbinic practice was the very use of rational pseudo-argumentation precisely and surprisingly as a means of mobilizing hierarchical forms of authority.

Astonishingly, the Talmud seems to sense the depth of these paradoxes within the narrative itself. In the continuation of the story in Baba Meṣia' itself, rather than the death of Rabbi Eli'ezer in purity, another death is narrated, namely the death of Rabban Gamaliel:

Mother Peace, the wife of Rabbi Eli'ezer, was the sister of Rabban Gamaliel. From the day of the above events and on, she would not let Rabbi Eli'ezer prostrate himself [in supplication]. A certain day was the New Moon and she became confused between a full month [of 29 days] and a lacking month [of 28].[118] And there are those who say that, rather, a poor man came and stood at the door, and she took bread out to him [and thus relaxed her guard]. She found him [Eli'ezer] fallen on his face. She said to him: Get up, for you have killed my brother! At that very moment, a trumpet was sounded in the house of Rabban Gamaliel, for he had died. He said to her: How did you know? She said to him: Thus I have a tradition from the House of father: All of the gates are closed except for the gate of affront.

Rabbi Eli'ezer's wife knows that the depth of his affront is so profound that if he supplicates and pours out tears, the "gates will not be closed," and heaven will seek redress for his shame by killing her brother, Gamaliel. And indeed, she was correct. Once, when she dropped her guard and her husband prostrated himself in supplication, immediately her brother died. In a powerful reading of this part of the story, Charlotte Fonrobert argues that the text here indicates its deep sympathy for Eli'ezer, even God's sympathy for him: "God, depicted as being in charge of the emotional fabric of human life, thus remains on Rabbi Eli'ezer's side in this last staging of the story. Ultimately, Rabban Gamaliel's death seriously calls into question the earlier rabbinic victory over Rabbi Eli'ezer."[119] Fonrobert is surely right. I would, however, extend the analysis in a slightly different direction. Rather than seeing the issue here as only or even primarily "the emotional fabric of human life"—although I would not deny the salience of this dimension—I would prefer to read here the exploration of a paradox, the very paradox of the "pluralism" of the Babylonian House of Study. Instead of seeing the text as manifesting its sympathy on one side or another, I would read its seemingly contradictory moves as a thematizing of the "historical moment." On the one hand, as Cohen opines, Rabbi Eli'ezer has been excommunicated because he was unwilling to accept the "democratic" norms of the new episteme, but on the other, his exclusion marks the exclusionary politics of the politics of inclusion themselves. In producing the myth of a tolerant rabbinic regime that supersedes the sectarianism that came before, the talmudic narrative reveals to what an extent "tolerance" within constitutes a deadly intolerance for those who would remain without, the *minim* in all of their varieties, including an unreconstructed Rabbi Eli'ezer. Pluralism is power: "Each pole of the antagonism is inherent to its opposite, so that we stumble upon it at the very moment when we endeavour to grasp the opposite pole for itself, to posit it 'as such.'"[120] As a final argument in favor of this reading, I would offer the seeming non sequitur of the death being that of Rabban Gamaliel and not Rabbi Yehoshua' with whom the conflict was joined.[121] It is not only that Rabban Gamaliel was the "Patriarch," which made him the target of these deadly supplications, but also, I would suggest, the fact that he represents within the mythopoetic world of these talmudic stories the bad old regime of excommunication and exclusion. And yet, in the story, Eli'ezer's antagonist seemingly represents the good new days, the days of democratic votes in the House of Study and God's pleasurable hand-clapping at the audacity of midrash. At every level of the narrative, the story and its meanings are replicated: inclusion is exclusion.[122] "These and these are the words of the Living God" is a powerful technique for the maintenance of absolute control, and the Talmud seems to know this. All the levels and wrinkles, paradoxes and aporias of the rabbinic narrative of Yavneh, and hence of our own, are thus encompassed within the profound narrative art of this talmudic legend cycle.

A Genealogy for Indeterminacy

Stern notes the tension between many individual incidents of bitter controversy recorded in the Talmud and a narrative framework of open-ended dialogism. The redactors of the later rabbinic texts chose to enshrine multiple views as being of equal validity: "In making this choice, the Rabbinic editors did not act without precedent; indeed, they followed in a venerable tradition of early Jewish literature that included such other sacred 'compromise texts' as the Pentateuch, in which separate documentary sources are combined into a single composition as though their agenda and ideologies were compatible (which eventually they are made out to be). . . . The difference between these earlier texts and the Rabbinic midrashim is simply that in the latter, editorial policy was elevated to the order of exegetical ideology, to the conception of polysemy as a trait of sacred Scripture. Here, for the first time, editorial pluralism has become a condition of meaning."[123] Stern thus draws a distinction between earlier Palestinian texts and the "editorial policy" of rabbinic literature by indicating that it is only within the latter that we find "scriptural polysemy" not only enacted, but thematized, lifted up as a theological principle in the form of aggadic narratives. What Stern fails to look at, however, is how the work of these redactors themselves is part of the history of rabbinic Judaism and thus of the Rabbis. In his privileging of the individual voices and traditions as the reality of rabbinic practice, versus the redactors, whose work is taken to be as merely a "literary artifact," an idealization, Stern both implies a positivist position[124] (to which I don't think he really subscribes) and misses an opportunity to do some real historical work on the development of the features of rabbinic textuality that have come (at least in our time) to be the defining features of rabbinic Judaism per se—its vaunted (if haunted) "pluralism" and "undecidability" or "indeterminacy," the lack of resolution of debates in the Babylonian Talmud, and the multiple, contradictory interpretations of the midrashim.

I envision a somewhat more complex historical process than Stern: I think that we have to distinguish between two parallel processes, one having to do with midrash and one with halakhic discussion. As noted by Stern, we find a venerable literary practice in which contradictory versions were placed together in canonical texts without any attempt to discern between them as separate voices: The Pentateuch, Kings/Chronicles, and perhaps even the Four Gospels. The midrash collections are essentially a more self-aware version of this pattern. In these texts, contradictory biblical interpretations were placed side by side without any attempt to decide which is the correct one, but this does not yet constitute, pace Stern, a theorization or theologization of indeterminacy (or even "scriptural polysemy") but only a reluctance to decide between opposing views and traditions. At this stage, moreover, in the halakhic discourse, the goal is still to determine and prove the correct practice. Chronologically, the redaction of the Palestinian Talmud and the great midrash collections are coeval (fourth century). It needs to be emphasized that had things remained at that stage, we would not be seriously tempted, I think, to argue for indeterminacy of meaning as a rabbinic theological/theoretical principle, any more than the Mishna or the Four Gospels lead to such an assertion of indeterminacy.[125] The great midrashic collections are thus still only a variety of "Sacred Compromise Texts." It is only in the final stage, represented by the redactorial level of the Babylonian Talmud (the stammaim—approximately in the sixth century) that we find the multiplicity of interpretations as well as the multiplicity of halakhic views thematized as the very essence of Torah, as its very quintessence as representative of the divine mind on earth. It is only from this perspective, moreover, that we now go back and read the literary practice of the midrash editors as if they too embodied a theology of indeterminacy of meaning. It may very well be that the textual practice of the redactors of the midrash played a major role in the inspiration of the stammaitic theological invention. One way to articulate the difference between the final, Babylonian stage of this development and the earlier stages would be to say that if for the earlier Talmudic authorities, undecidability seems to be the product of the limitations of human knowing, for the redactors of the Babylonian Talmud (the stammaim) it would seem to be a condition of language itself, so that the idea that even God cannot know the truth of the text can at least be entertained. This explicit and thematized theologoumenon truly deserves the name of indeterminacy.

I would propose, therefore, that Stern's synchronic literary terms—"traditions" and "redactions"—correspond instead to diachronic developments within rabbinic literature and thus in rabbinic culture. Rather than employing a hermeneutic that contrasts one type of information as being about the real speech situation of the rabbinic academies (historical reality) and the other an ideological idealization, I would read both as representations of ideological positions regarding both human and divine speech. Read thus, the texts record a change in the status of multiple meaning within rabbinic ideology, practice, and memory. In other words, the thematized representation of the multiplicity of meaning that we find at the redactional level of the rabbinic texts is itself historical in that it discloses the ideology of that late stage in the development of rabbinism, one that has had a decisive effect on the later development of Judaism *tout court*, forming indeed its very habitus. The remarkable conclusion to which this hypothesis leads is that the most decisive theological characteristics of rabbinic Judaism, those that we frequently take to be its very defining features, are the production of Jewish thinkers whose names we will never know, as they hid them so successfully behind the pseudepigraphic mask: the Talmud.

As Stern points out, there is tension between the framing discourses of the Talmud and the sources of which it is composed. Thus Rabbi Yehoshua''s very homily of irenic multiplicity of views, all a part of Torah and all a part of the divine mind, is framed by the following narrative:

Our Sages have taught: There was an incident in which Rabbi Yoḥanan ben Beroqa and Rabbi El'azar Ḥasma went to visit Rabbi Yehoshua' in Peqi'in. He said to them: "What was the innovation in the House of Study today?" They said to him: "We are your students, and we drink your water." He said to them: "Even so, there cannot be a [session of] the House of Study without an innovation. Whose Shabbat was it?"—"It was the Shabbat of Rabbi El'azar the son of 'Azaria"—"And what was the Haggada today?"

The disciples go on to detail the teaching of the day in the House of Study and then Rabbi Yehoshua' himself provides them with the *derasha* on the "disciples of the wise, who sit in assemblies and study the Torah, some pronouncing unclean and others pronouncing clean, some prohibiting and others permitting, some declaring unfit and others declaring fit," of which it is said that all of these contradictory views are the words of the same God given by the same shepherd Moses. Stern notes the extreme tension between the narrative situation in which Rabbi Yehoshua' is in exile for his dissent from Rabban Gamaliel's halakhic position and the *derasha* which implies a perfect irenicism of rabbinic dissensus: "Make your ear like a hopper and take in the words of those who permit and those who forbid, for they were all given by one God; one shepherd said them all." The question which gives rise to this "pluralistic" answer in the *derasha* is strikingly like, moreover, the question raised for Christians by their theological controversies, namely: If some permit and some forbid, some render pure and some impure, why should I learn Torah? Why should I consider this as truth? The context and the question make palpably clear the crisis to which Rabbi Yehoshua' is responding, an epistemological crisis very much akin to the Christian one.

The question "Whose Shabbat was it?" is an explicit allusion to another talmudic legend, in which, as we shall see immediately below, anything but an irenic pluralism is comprehended. The narrative context, therefore, ironizes the irenicism implied by the *derasha*, which can thus be read as if it were a plea on the part of Rabbi Yehoshua' for such a pluralistic approach and indicates that it was, at best, a utopian ideal, an ideal, moreover, that is only promulgated in the latest layers of the talmudic redaction but one which had profound effects on the later formation of rabbinic Judaism. On the narrative level it is a plea, but on the rhetorical level of the Talmud, it is an apparatus for the production of a certain type of institution, the rabbinic Yeshiva with its culture of endless study and argumentation.

The very specific allusion to another talmudic narrative, "Whose Shabbat?" can be taken as yet another piece in the aggadic structuring, thematization, and justification for the stammaitic practices of rhetorical invention and the linguistic practices of the Yeshiva. Referring to this narrative from Babylonian Talmud Berakhot 27b–28a will further support the evincing of a shift within rabbinic ecclesiology, a shift that the rabbinic narrators themselves seem to remember as such. This legend represents the time of Yavneh as a time of exclusivity, centralized authority and monovocality in halakhic discourse, in direct opposition to the later talmudic representation that "these and these are the words of the Living God." The narrative, however, also encodes a transformation of the power/knowledge nexus of the rabbinic academy. This passage and its seeming contradiction of the dominant self-representation of the culture have been much discussed in the literature.

According to this story, Rabban Gamaliel forces Rabbi Yehoshua' to submit to his position on a particular matter of practice, indeed "to appear before him with his stick and rucksack on the day [that Rabbi Yehoshua' held to be] The Day of Atonement."[126] Rabbi Yehoshua' has had the temerity to disagree with Rabban Gamaliel and for this act has been forced to humiliate himself and publicly violate the halakhic principles for which he stood—hardly an instantiation of "pluralism." Moreover, in revolt against Rabban Gamaliel's act against the popular Rabbi, the Rabbis deposed him from the patriarchate and installed Rabbi El'azar ben 'Azaria in his place. In the end of the story, Rabban Gamaliel apologizes to Rabbi Yehoshua' and is restored to his position, but the latter, it seems, at least according to this narrative, remained injured and adamant and did not return to Yavneh.

This understanding is supported strongly by a doubling within the Ḥagiga text. Immediately following Rabbi Yehoshua''s homily, we find a story in which Rabbi Eli'ezer is visited by his disciple Rabbi Yose ben Dormaskit while the former is absent (in exile) from the House of Study in the wake of the Akhnai narrative, which as we have just seen, left him excommunicated. Rabbi Yehoshua''s homily in which all the contradictions and controversies are contained within Torah and within the divine mind is thus framed perfectly with two narratives that refer to extreme, almost violent controversies and exclusions over questions of what is permitted and what is forbidden, what is pure and what is impure. In this doublet-tale, the master asks the pupil to tell what has transpired in the House of Study at Yavneh, to which the latter replies that a majority had decided a certain point of halakha having to do with the sabbatical year. Rabbi Eli'ezer responds furiously (to the point of blinding the pupil, a miraculous affliction later cured by equally miraculous means when he has calmed himself), not because he disagrees with the ruling, but because it is a tradition "received from Rabban Yoḥanan ben Zakkai, who heard it from his teacher, and he from his teacher—a halakha [given] to Moses from Sinai" [Babylonian Talmud Ḥagiga 3b]. Rabbi Eli'ezer becomes so angry because the Rabbis seem to be deriving from logic and interpretation that which is already known from the only type of authority that he recognizes: direct divine revelation.

His question, "Whose Shabbat?" thus links the Ḥagiga text to the story in Berakhot, while the placement of Rabbi Eli'ezer in exile links up with the story of the Stove of Akhnai from Baba Meṣia', and thence, to the story of Rabbi Eli'ezer's end and the death of Rabban Gamaliel from Sanhedrin, producing the verisimilar effect of one continuous narrative, rendered all the more compelling for its having been distributed this way.

In this narrative of conflict and hierarchy, we have the precise opposite of the ideological position enshrined in the sentence "These and these are the words of the Living God." The question that needs to be raised is: Why would the Talmud represent a reality so at variance with its own ideological position on the role of halakhic diversity? As Haim Shapira has put it, "The behavior of Rabban Gamaliel towards Rabbi Yehoshua requires explanation, for it does not sit well with the approach that lends legitimacy to controversy in the world of the Sages."[127]

An answer to this question can be found in the sequence of the narrative that follows this. First, as we have seen, the Sages in the academy rise up and rebel against Rabban Gamaliel for his high-handed treatment of the popular Rabbi Yehoshua', and Rabban Gamaliel is deposed from his position, according to the legend. The text continues, however, with a vitally important narrative sequence, one that once more is found only in the Babylonian talmudic version:

It is taught: On that day they removed the guard at the door [of the Study House] and gave permission for the students to enter.

For Rabban Gamaliel used to announce and say: "Any student whose inner self is not identical to his outer self shall not enter the Study House."

On that day they added many benches.

Some authorities claim, in fact, that four hundred benches were added and some that seven hundred were added. As shown by Haim Shapira, there is virtual unanimity among talmudic philologists that this narrative is a Babylonian talmudic production.[128] The phrase "on that day" is explicitly referred in the text to this foundational shift in the politics of the House of Study, remembered, memorialized, and narrated exclusively in the tradition of the Babylonian Talmud. "That day" is the day on which a shift took place to a "democratic" and "pluralistic" form of rabbinism from Rabban Gamaliel's version of a Judaism in which there was a central authority who decided whose "inner self was identical to his outer self"—a hermeneutics of the person corresponding to a monistic hermeneutics of the text as well.[129] The text even takes the trouble to inform us that everywhere in the Talmud that it says that something happened "on that day," this is the fateful day that is meant. The exclusion practiced by Rabban Gamaliel cannot be interpreted as only some form of moral exhortation, for if that were the case, there would have been no need for guards to enforce it, or any possibility that guards could enforce it, so it must have referred to some sort of test of orthodoxy and submission to the authority of Rabban Gamaliel. Those whose "inner selves were not identical to their outer selves" are thus plausibly interpreted as those who look and walk like rabbinic Jews but hold theological views deemed heretical by the rabbinic institution. Rabban Gamaliel's dictum would on this reading represent an earlier exclusionary stage in the development of rabbinism, one that gave way eventually to the ostensibly inclusionist form that became hegemonic.

This shift in the system explains the otherwise nearly unprecedented treatment of Rabbi Yehoshua‘ in our story. In this legendary form, the Talmud itself is preserving/constructing a memory of when things were not quite as they are now, but also not quite as the Talmud ordinarily memorializes Yavneh, in order to deal with or dispense with that alternative memory. We find in this narrative a structure not unlike that found in Athenian mythmaking, including even the drama,[130] for instance, in the *Oresteia*. A currently dominant institution (whether the Law Courts of Athens or the rabbinic House of Study) establishes its authority via a myth of foundation that represents the bad old days that it displaced and replaced.[131] This aggada narrates this as a conflict between Rabban Gamaliel and Rabbi Yehoshua‘, whom we have already met as dominant dramatis personae in the Yavneh narrative.

The Talmud makes its values entirely transparent here by informing us that Rabban Gamaliel was upset when he saw the change, thinking that he had withheld the Torah from Israel. In a dream, he sees, however, pitchers full of ashes, implying that all the newly admitted scholars are unworthy, and Rabban Gamaliel is comforted, thinking that his former behavior has been divinely approved. The talmudic narrator, however, from that latest stage of redactorial activity, takes the trouble to inform us that it wasn't so, that the only reason that Rabban Gamaliel was afforded this dream was to calm him down. The new regime of open access to Torah is thus firmly and definitively approbated by the authoritative voice of the talmudic narrator, matching up well with the literary practices of the talmudic and midrashic redactors.

The stammaitic aggada thus narrates a diachronic change in the ecclesiological pattern, the end of "the bad old days" associated with Rabban Gamaliel, the Babylonian mythic representation of the Palestinian Patriarch. The comparison to the *Oresteia* is, I think, particularly apt, for just as that narrative marks a shift in power structure within the Athenian polity to one of "democracy" and "rationality," so does the talmudic epic before us. And just as that narrative appalls at least some of us for its violent imposition of order together with its representation of the respective worth of men and women, so also the talmudic story appalls for its severe exclusionary practices in the name of pluralism. The vanquishing of real religious dissent in Israel and the safe haven of power and privilege which the Rabbis had achieved by the fifth century enabled a portrayal of themselves as the ultimate democrats and meritocrats. All who would once have produced real dissension were now firmly out of the community, so within: Let pluralism ring! According to the Talmud, in the beginning, there was a "Monarchian bishop" in Judaism,[132] symbolized by the figure of Rabban Gamaliel, and, in the end, a kind of democratic meritocracy. The Babylonian Talmud itself "remembers" that there has been a change in the pattern of rabbinic truth, a redeployment of the terms of orthodoxy and heresy, so that where once borders were being thrown up with insistence on only one true Torah, now the notion of many indeterminate truths can safely be promulgated. The Talmud thus thematizes in aggada the diachronic difference which the redaction of the Babylonian Talmud itself signifies.

Shattering the Word

The theological principle of the undecidability of the divine language came into being in the Babylonian moment, the moment when real dissent was banished from Israel. To pay attention only to the negative or critical aspect of that moment, however, is to misread rabbinic culture, for it was in that moment that the characteristic forms of rabbinic literary and religious creativity became crystallized, as well. On the social level, the legendary decision to allow all to enter the House of Midrash may demand of us a very suspicious hermeneutic, but it very compellingly parallels the development of hermeneutical theory as well. The notion of only allowing to enter him whose "inner self was identical to his outer self" is predicated on a kind of hermeneutical certainty that is the very opposite of the *hermeneutical*—again not social—free play that characterizes the later midrash and constitutes its very mark of cultural and literary creativity.[133]

Isaak Heinemann describes midrash, long before Derrida, as the "shattering of the Logos."[134] I will read here the locus classicus for this image and thus for the notion of midrashic indeterminacy. As we shall see, this locus is a Babylonian site (of the stammaim), in spite of its being cited in the name of Palestinian Rabbis:[135]

Rav Asi asked Rabbi Yoḥanan, "If two have said the same law from two verses, what is the law?" He said, "They are not counted as more than one." From where is this principle? Abayye said, "For the verse says, *One spoke God, these two have I heard.*[136] One verse gives rise to several laws [meanings], but one law does not come out of several verses." He of the house of R. Ishmael teaches it, "*Like a hammer which shatters a rock;*[137] just as the hammer is divided into several sparks, so a single verse gives rise to several laws." (BT Sanhedrin 34a)

The talmudic text begins by articulating a rather surprising principle in rabbinic legal hermeneutics: on the one hand, it is excluded that the Torah ever repeats the same law in two places; on the other, any given verse can have multiple meanings. Here, indeed, we find thematized and theorized for the first time the theological principle that will motivate so much of rabbinic thinking thereafter, that the divine language produces manifold and different meanings. Now we go back and read the midrashic practice, not merely as one of editorial tact but as a textual representation of this special theology of the divine Word. This principle that any verse can have multiple meanings demonstrates how thoroughly different this rabbinic conception of language is from that which for "us" is so commonplace that we can hardly think our way out of it long enough to understand another culture. In the end, however, the shattering of the Logos reflected in such a conception of language provides the most significant clue for understanding how rabbinic Judaism and orthodox Christianity formed distinct religiocultural systems—at least for a time at the end of late antiquity—and not just distinct social groups.

I would suggest, then, that the Sanhedrin text provides, indeed, evidence for a special understanding of semiology among some Rabbis: The question is: Which Rabbis? There is an important parallel to the Sanhedrin passage which may direct us to an answer. In Shabbat 88b we read:

Rabbi Yoḥanan said: What is written, "H' gives a word; great is the company of those who announce it [Psalm 68:12]"? Each and every word that came out of the mouth of the Power was divided into seventy languages. The one of the House of Rabbi Ishmael teaches: "And like a hammer smashes a rock," just as this hammer gives rise to many sparks, so each and every word that went out from the mouth of the Holy Blessed One was divided into seventy languages.

As Azzan Yadin has recently pointed out, the Shabbat text, seemingly an almost exact parallel to the Sanhedrin passage, has, in fact, nothing whatever to do with "polysemy."[138] Yadin compellingly argues, by citing well-known (but previously misunderstood) and recently discovered texts, that the "seventy languages" of the Shabbat text has to be interpreted as seventy different human tongues, and not seventy different meanings, as one would perhaps predict from the Sanhedrin text. This point is of some importance, for as Yadin has demonstrated, within the tannaitic corpora, Rabbi Ishmael and his school stand for anything but midrashic indeterminacy. Not for the school of Rabbi Ishmael does one text give rise to many and contradictory meanings. Moreover, in the relative logocentrism of the Ishmaelic school, the translatability of the text into other languages would be both plausible and expected. The point can perhaps be made more widely of Palestinian thought, since Rabbi Yoḥanan—also, of course, an early Palestinian—seems to be making it in the Shabbat passage. Moreover, the idea of the Torah being given in many languages is to be found in other tannaitic texts, as well, such as Mishna Soṭa 7:5, where it is a gloss on "fully explicated" (Deut. 27:8). If, indeed, as Yadin compellingly argues, the Shabbat version represents an earlier iteration of this text, then we would have some tentative further evidence for the point that the notion of the polysemy of the biblical language (as directly opposed to its translatability) is a late Babylonian notion, with the Sanhedrin text a stammaitic revision of the Palestinian topos still quoted more or less in its original form in Shabbat. We have here a precious example of precisely how the earlier meaning is revised. It would seem most plausible that the Stamma who rephrased the crucial clause in the Sanhedrin text already understood the Shabbat parallel to mean that which he himself thought. The transformation of the text was unconscious. Evidence for this possibility is surely to be found in the fact that until Yadin, even critical scholars detected no difference between the versions.

In the stammaitic final form of the topos, the image of God's word as a hammer striking sparks off an anvil made of rock is made to be a striking representation of the inherent multiplicity of meaning in the language of the Torah, the always already status of inscriptionality that comes with a necessary dissemination of meaning. It is, therefore, precisely what it claims to be, a powerful metaphor for multivalence. There is testimony here for a late Babylonian talmudic understanding of hermeneutics which denies completely the concept of a Logos lying behind and outside of the text, limiting and controlling meaning, an understanding that produces commentary that is very different equally from the hermeneutics of the so-called simple meaning, from a Philonic allegorical interpretation,[139] from the "incarnational" interpretations of Origen,[140] and from the hermeneutics of the hierarchic fourfold meaning.[141] This understanding of hermeneutics correlates elegantly with the ideology of noncontradiction that we have seen embodied in the aggada of this layer of the talmudic redaction, and thus of this period in rabbinic religious history, as well as with the practice of the stammaim in representing rabbinic dialectic as dialectic without resolution, without telos, and in itself a representation of the *polynoia* of the divine Word and the divine mind.

Comparing our stammaitic version of the passage with its Palestinian talmudic parallel will prove suggestive for this point. In that Talmud we can read:

"Remember" and "Keep" were said in one utterance, something which is impossible for the mouth to say and for the ears to hear. . . . And so also it says "One spoke God" in speech, "these two I have heard," and it is written, "And as a hammer smashes a rock." (PT Nedarim 3:2, 37d)

In this text, the topos "as a hammer shatters a rock," at first seemingly the same as in the Babylonian Talmud, performs an entirely different function. It explains away obvious contradictions within the biblical text. In one version of the Ten Commandments, the Jews are enjoined to "remember the Sabbath Day" (Exod. 20:7), while in the other, they are enjoined to "keep the sabbath day" (Deut. 5:11).

But the two versions of the Ten Commandments refer, of course, to only one speech event on the part of God. The Palestinian Talmud and its midrashic parallels cite in this context several laws whose versions in Deuteronomy and in the earlier parts of the Pentateuch seem to be contradictory, and in every case they conclude that God made only one statement, which was heard as two, that is, that God said the two things at the same time, and it is up to humans to reconcile the apparent contradiction. The hammer striking the rock here thus refers to the mysterious nature of the divine speech: it can make two statements at the same moment, which are then heard as if they were two statements but need to be reconciled hermeneutically, as the midrash does here, articulating a way in which the Sabbath is both remembered and kept.

A parallel from the Palestinian midrash texts demonstrates that the verses "God has spoken one; two we have heard" and the hammer striking the rock are used here in a sense almost exactly opposite to the one that the midrash of the verse and the hermeneutical theory it implies would develop in the latest strata of the Babylonian Talmud. In the Mekhilta of Rabbi Shim'on to Exodus, we read:

The words said here are identical to the words said there. They both mean the same thing, which is impossible for the mouth to say and for the ears to hear. Here it says, "And God spoke all of these words," and further on it says, "One spake God, these two have I heard." And it also says, "Behold my word is like fire, the utterance of God etc." Just as that fire is divided into several sparks, so one matter is brought out in several verses.

Whereas the Sanhedrin passage of the Babylonian Talmud insists that one utterance of the Torah has several meanings, here it is claimed that one proposition, one meaning, may appear in more than one place in the written text of the Torah and in synonymous but different language—precisely the concept that the final version of the passage in the Babylonian Talmud vigorously denies. This parallel again supports both Yadin's argument and my larger argument that the notion of scriptural polysemy, "indeterminacy" a fortiori, belongs to a relatively late layer in the formation of rabbinic textuality, one that can be found in narrative and theoretical formulations virtually exclusively in the very latest stratum of the Babylonian Talmud.

Going Back to Yavneh (and Nicaea): Theology, Ecclesiology, Books

The strategies of the Church are represented in the scholarly literature as directly opposite to those of the Rabbis. Nicene Christianity comes, at least in theory, to reject dialectic entirely and insist on a "simple," traditionalist, and miraculously authorized monovocal truth, while the Talmud raises ever-unresolved dialectic to the level of a divine principle. Once more, in order to forestall any misunderstanding, the point is *not* that debate ceased with the canonization of Nicaea—quite the opposite seems to have been the case—but rather that on the ideological level, debate was no longer considered appropriate for the determination of Christian truth.[142] Moreover, it must be emphasized (as Lim does not sufficiently, perhaps) that calls for such monovocality of truth and "simplicity" without dialectic go back in Christian writing as far as Paul and are well represented in such Christian writers as Tertullian.[143] Nevertheless, we can perceive a shift taking place around the beginning of the fifth century. The final decision on the crucial question of trinitarian theology was decided by the Emperor Theodosius after a night of prayer;[144] whereas final decisions for the Rabbis are deferred forever with the theological statement that "these and these are the words of the living God." Owing to the overwhelming effect of the Babylonian Talmud, this pattern of truth became the intellectual legacy of medieval rabbinic Judaism everywhere. The nexus between textual habits of Palestinian Jews and the canonized, theologically sanctioned undecidability of the Babylonian Talmud, as symbolized by the legends of Yavneh, is analogous to the hypothesized causal connection between the textual habitus and the textual practices of the "consensual" orthodoxy of the late fourth- and fifth-century Church, as symbolized by the legends of Nicaea. If Nicaea was a belated legendary invention that helped produce a Christianity "in which dissent and debate were literally swept aside,"[145] Yavneh as a "grand coalition" in which everybody in Jewish antiquity who wasn't an outright "heretic" was a Rabbi and all opinions were equally "Torah" was an equally belated talmudic invention. This late moment of literary crystallization was the juncture at which the "agreement to disagree" was raised to a theological and hermeneutical principle of the highest order, indeed, to a divine institution.

The successful production of the *homonoia* of post-Nicene orthodoxy entailed or was enabled by a set of textual practices (not only legends). In order for the *polynoia* of the writings of pre-Nicene theologians (those accepted into the canon of the orthodox) to be converted into a single-voiced corpus of the Fathers, discursive work had to be done, providing the canonical literary objective correlative of the legendary work that Lim has described. Lim adumbrated this issue when he described the transposition of Theodosius's call for "fair and open examination of the disputed matters" to a call to submission "to the views of 'those teachers who lived previous to the dissension in the church.'"[146] As Lim points out, this shift within Theodosius's own sense of how Christian truth is found and maintained "may be regarded as part of the germinating ideological justification for the patristic florilegia that would play a large role in Christian councils."[147] Examining yet another vector in the development of Christian textual practices, Éric Rebillard has cited a well-known Western author, Vincent of Lerins, on the justification behind the florilegia: "If no council decision has dealt with the question debated, Vincent recommends that 'one collect and examine the opinions of the ancients who, although they come from different places and times, remained however in the communion and faith of the one Catholic Church, and appeared as commendable teachers. One must understand that he too can believe without doubt what has been openly, frequently, and constantly taught, written and defended not by one or two, but by all in the same way, according to one and the same consensus."[148] For Augustine, as Rebillard shows, it is the agreement, the consensus, of all Catholic authorities that is the measure of orthodox truth.[149] The ecclesiastical writers speak "with one heart, one voice, one faith."[150] It is riveting that Augustine actually imagines this corpus of the writings of the Fathers as both an imaginary council and as a book: "If a synod of bishops were summoned from all over the world, I wonder whether that many men of their caliber could easily be assembled. After all, these men did not live at the same time; rather, at different periods of time and in distant places, God sends, as he pleases and as he judges helpful, a few of his faithful ministers who are excellent beyond the many others. And so, you see these men gathered from different times and regions, from the East and from the West, not to a place to which human beings are forced to travel, *but in a book which can travel to them.*"[151]

This citation, I think, is sufficient to evoke the fascinating similarity of cultural worlds that produced the Talmud, also a collection of the sayings of many "excellent" Rabbis over centuries and in different places made into a book that travels in space and time to the faithful. And this powerful similarity also points up the enormous difference in the mode of discourse of the two new books: one voice versus many voices but both, I warrant, in support of the "same" kind of project, the production of a bounded, concerted orthodox "religion."

Other scholars, however, have located at least the planting of the seed of these florilegia in the textual practices of the century before Theodosius and Augustine. In a brief essay published in *Studia Patristica*, as well as in a couple of unpublished works, Patrick Gray has examined the processes through which the single-voiced institution called Fathers of the Church was produced in the fourth century.[152] Mark Vessey has also shown the significance of the formation of a patristic canon of citation in the fourth century and its contribution to the "forging of orthodoxy."[153]

Virginia Burrus's examination of the formative influence of Athanasius's literary corpus in producing the textual practices of fourth-century and later Christian orthodoxy, the modes of its discourse, its habitus, is particularly evocative. Positioning her mediation in relation to Lim's claim that it is with the death of the last "eyewitness," Athanasius, that the "legends about Nicaea began to emerge,"[154] Burrus writes: "Athanasius' death marked the *end* of a crucial phase in the *literary* invention of Nicaea; and, furthermore, the layered inscription of his 'historical' or 'apologetic' texts—resulting in his retroactive construction of a virtual archive for the council—contributed heavily to the creation of a documentary habit that was, as Lim and others have demonstrated, crucial to the success of the late antique council in producing 'consensual' orthodoxy."[155] By substituting "end" for "beginning" and "literary" for "legendary," Burrus both supports Lim's argument and adds another dimension to it. "In Athanasius's texts—in his sensitivity to 'textuality' itself—we sense something of what Richard Lim describes as a late-antique trend toward a 'growing reliance on textual authority.'"[156]

Lim had emphasized that Nicaea, in contrast to other synods and councils, left no written record of its acts. Agreeing with him, Burrus shows through close readings of the Athanasian dossier on Nicaea that Athanasius, through the arrangement and redacting of materials, documentary and otherwise, produced ex post facto virtual *acta* for "his" council. Burrus's reading allows us to perceive that Athanasius may have made a contribution through this activity to the practice of the production of such archives and *acta* for other conciliar formations, as well as to the system of textual practices, in general, that constituted late ancient "patristic" orthodoxy, including especially that great late ancient Christian book of books, The Fathers of the Church. Nicaea, the Council—and not only or primarily Nicene doctrine—was "invented" through the writings of Athanasius. Athanasius's literary exertions thus produced retrospectively a certain account of Nicaea,[157] an account that, as Burrus argues, was generative for the future history of Christian textual practices. Burrus focuses our attention on the particular form of textuality and the textual form of particular types of orthodoxy and their habitus, and on the correlation between those textual practices and habitus and the habitus that Lim has uncovered in his work. These literary practices (arguably, at least, centered around Athanasius—whether an Athanasius self-fashioned or fashioned by others) and their collation with the legends of Nicaea provide the richest backdrop for investigating the cognate but different relations between talmudic legends of Yavneh and the textual practices that constitute the great late ancient Jewish non-book of books, the Babylonian Talmud itself.

Burrus writes, "Sorting through the complicatedly intercalated writings either authored or ghostauthored or edited and published by the bishop of Alexandria [Athanasius], we observe Nicaea and its frozen Logos being produced as the cumulative effect of a series of very deliberate textual acts of self-defense, by which the armoured body of the bishop was also conceived."[158] In the even more complicatedly intercalated pseudospeech of the Rabbis as edited and published in the Babylonian Talmud,[159] a similar body, that of the Rabbi, was being conceived, and an institution, the Yeshiva, was being brought on line and legitimated. If, in Burrus's words, "the Alexandrian Father conceives Nicaea as the 'ecumenical' council of the Fathers who begat the immortal body of the written word," then the Talmud conceives Yavneh as the ecumenical council of Fathers who transmitted the immortal (but ever-growing and shifting) body of the Oral Torah. Just as Athanasius promulgated "the strikingly close identification of the divinely begotten Word with the written texts that now incarnate 'Nicaea,'"[160] so, too, did the Rabbis of the Talmud closely identify their own founding text, the Mishna, and their own commentaries on it with the divinely given Oral Torah. The redactors of the Talmud are the collective rabbinic Athanasius, insofar as it is he who invented The Fathers of the Church as a nameable literary entity. Where the ideal of the orthodox Christian "Word" was its monovocality, its many-authored texts speaking with one voice, the ideal of the classical orthodox rabbinic Oral Torah as finally formulated in the Babylonian Talmud was of one many-voiced text with no author. At a time when, as related by Lim, dialectic was being increasingly demonized by Christian orthodox writers, talmudic narrators, using the same tropes and topoi—for instance, of dialecticians as "shield-bearers"[161]—were raising forever unresolved dialectic to the highest level of religious discourse.

In sum, just as the story of Nicaea "gives rise to the 318 conciliar 'fathers,' and also to their only begotten credal Word,"[162] the story of Yavneh gives rise to the father Rabbis[163] and their only begotten Oral Torah. Yavneh was projected back into the first century, Nicaea only into the beginning of the fourth.[164] Both legendary councils claim, moreover, to have the divine truth, Yavneh its Oral Torah, and Nicaea its apostolic teaching. Moreover, as I have shown above in Chapter 3, both authorize their claim to such truth in the same way, via a myth of apostolic succession. Both are myths of foundation of an orthodoxy.[165] The Talmud itself, as the unauthored and frequently seemingly chaotic record of constant *polynoia*, is a different kind of text from both the Athanasian corpus and the monovocal Church Fathers that late ancient Christian orthodoxy produced. The difference in those forms of textuality is prefigured in the distinction between the exclusive orthodoxy of the end point of the Nicaea myth and the equally exclusive, divinely sanctioned heterodoxy of the end point of the Yavneh myth embodied in the late talmudic saying: "These and these are the words of the living God," which, according to legend, "went out" at Yavneh. For all of their similarities in terms of the exercise of power, these two theologies of language were distinctly different in the kinds of textuality to which they led and in the forms of biblical interpretation which they produced.

In an insightful and very sympathetic (if somewhat too exculpatory, I think[166]) essay on rabbinic Judaism, Rosemary Radford Ruether has described the Talmud in the following terms:

Classical Judaism, by contrast, produced a literature which looks at first sight like someone's grandmother's attic in which endless quantities of curious things which "might some day come in handy" have been passed down like so many balls of string lovingly collected over the years and piled on top of each other without apparent concern for distinctions between weighty and trivial matters. It is only with the greatest difficulty that those accustomed to systematic modes of thought, logical progression, and hierarchical ordering can adjust themselves to the discursive and unsystematic style of the rabbis and begin to discern the thread of thought that underlies what appears to be random discussion and linking of themes. But gradually one comes to see that this apparent jumble of piety and trivia is the medium of the rabbinic message which is the effort to penetrate every corner of ordinary life with God's presence. This expressed itself in an innocence of most of the Christian hierarchies of being, order, and value, and in an ability to see theological meaning in details of ordinary life. The rabbis think nothing of making their most profound comments on the nature of God in the midst of discussing the uses of cheese![167]

An example of such discussion, characterized by R. Travers Herford as "dry and tedious"[168] will exemplify Ruether's point. This text exemplifies in both its theme and its discursive method the differentiating and distinctive workings of late Babylonian rabbinic orthodoxy:

Rabbi Abbahu taught before Rabbi Yoḥanan: Gentiles and shepherds, one does not help them out nor throw them in, but the *minim* [Jewish heretics] and the *delatores* [informers] and apostates [to paganism],[169] they would throw them in and not help them out.

He said to him, but I teach: "*all* of the losses of your brother" [Deut. 22:3] to add the apostate, and you have said: they would throw them in.

Remove from here "the apostates."

The text begins with Rabbi Abbahu citing a tannaitic teaching to the effect that if idol worshipers and shepherds (considered thieves) fall into a hole, one does not rescue them, but one does not push them in either, while the second category of *minim*, *delatores* (Judas Iscariots), and apostates are to be pushed into a hole and not rescued from there. To this, Rabbi Yoḥanan objects that he has a tradition that the verse that enjoins saving the lost objects of one's brother includes even brothers who are apostates,[170] so how is it possible that Jews are enjoined to endanger the apostates' lives? The answer is that apostates are to be entirely removed from the list of those to be thrown into pits. Notice that at this point in the talmudic text—the point at which the Palestinian Talmud (and the amoraic level of the Babylonian Talmud) would have stopped[171]—we have a sharp point of disagreement. Are the apostates included in the category of the worst deviants who are to be put to death, or are they in the category of "brothers," to whom one returns a lost object? Effectively, moreover, by citing the authoritative Rabbi Yohanan and emending Rabbi Abbahu's tradition, the hypothetical earlier Talmud has decided the question in favor of the latter option: Apostates are indeed "brothers."

We see here, accordingly, the clear difference of the layers of the talmudic text and of talmudic textual practice, for the redactors of the Talmud, the anonymous voice known as the Stam, cannot leave this conclusion alone. The stammaim cannot, it seems, tolerate such a situation of rational resolution of a question. The text continues:

But he could have said to him: This is talking about an apostate who eats nonkosher meats out of appetite, and that refers to an apostate who eats nonkosher meats out of spite.

For it is said: the apostate: Rav Aha and Ravina disagree about him. One said, an apostate out of appetite is an apostate, and for spite is a *min*, while the other said, even for spite is still an apostate, and what is a *min*?; someone who worships an idol [i.e., a Jew who worships an idol]. He thought that one who eats nonkosher meats out of spite is a *min*. (BT Avoda Zara 26b)

Here we are back in the world of clean and unclean meats, as Origen had put it. The Talmud asks: Why did Rabbi Abbahu so readily accede to the emendation of his text in response to Rabbi Yohanan's objection? He had a better way out. He could have said that there are two kinds of apostates. In the case of the one who eats nonkosher meats out of appetite, we still consider him a "brother" and we rescue his lost object, and a fortiori his person, but an apostate who eats nonkosher meats demonstratively, to "spite," to make a religious point, that is the one whom we not only do not redeem but indeed endanger. To this the answer is that Rabbi Yohanan was of the opinion that such a one who eats nonkosher meats in order to spite the Jewish Torah is not an apostate but a *min*. The Talmud, that is, the Stam, backs this point up by citing an amoraic (later rabbinic, in this case very late Babylonian) argument as to the definition of the apostate and the *min*.

The tannaitic (early rabbinic) text projects a clear hierarchy of "evil-doers." Gentiles and shepherds are obviously of a higher status than the *minim*, the apostates, and the *delatores*. In the course of Rabbi Yohanan's intervention, apostates, whatever they are, are not only raised into a higher category than the *minim* and the informers but even into a higher category than the Gentiles, for the latter are neither rescued nor endangered, while the former are rescued as well. However, the most important aspect of the talmudic discussion (the *sugya*) is the new distinction it produces between the two types of apostates, a new and seemingly important category distinction not known from the earlier amoraic text. This distinction is between apostates for appetite, the typical case being one who is desirous and sees nonkosher meat and eats it, and apostates "for spite," those who choose to disobey the laws of the Torah out of religious conviction (someone like Saul of Tarsus, for instance). At this point, the Talmud says these latter are to be considered *minim*. In other words, *minim* are a category that is constructed ideologically, even when that ideological difference manifests itself behaviorally; it is the ideological difference that constitutes the *min*. Finally, according to one of the views of the two amoraim, it is an even stronger ideological difference that constitutes *minut*, namely an improper belief in God. According to the other view, such a Christian would be considered a *min* even if she had no defects in her theological doctrine, *except for the very fact of her ideological refusal to keep the commandments, which is, itself, a theological statement*, and the case remains undecided.

At first glance, it would seem that the lack of resolution of such a significant question does indeed project an agreement to disagree, a form of epistemological pluralism. We note, however, that in either view, a person who refuses to keep the commandments for ideological reasons (such as Paul), whether called an apostate or a *min*, fits into the category of the worst deviants, who are subject to righteous murder. The "pluralism" of the Talmud encompasses just as harsh exclusionary practices against deviants as does any earlier form of Judaism, including Christianity. We are told that Rabbi Yoḥanan, who places apostates in a very high category indeed, means only the apostates for appetite, so we take them out of the category of those to be executed, because apostates for ideology have been transferred into the category of *minim*, anyway. The other position leaves the apostates, meaning the apostates for ideology, in the category of those to be executed; it just does not call them *minim*. Surely to the potentially (or rather theoretically) to-be-executed ones the precise rubric under which they are being executed hardly makes a difference. Thus, while our reconstructed early (hypothetically Palestinian) *sugya* resolves the question of the status of the apostate, it does so while keeping the actual original controversy alive as a distinction that would make a difference. The Babylonian Talmud keeps a simulacrum of distinction alive, while defanging it of any power to make a difference. It is hard to see then how Hopkins's "dogmatic and hierarchical" marks a difference between orthodox Christianity and rabbinic Judaism. It is in the end, I think, rather the form of textuality, the types of books that are made, that marks the phenomenological differences between the Christian and Jewish orthodoxies of late antiquity. No small differences, to be sure, but of a very different sort, I think, than the differences that are usually claimed for the two "religions."

The End

In his final pages, Lim describes eloquently the late fifth-century situation of orthodox textual practice:

Indeed, shedding their complexities and messiness, entire councils were reduced to icons encapsulating simple lessons. The Council of Nicaea, for example, endured as the triumph of orthodoxy and Arius' Waterloo. The number 318[172] became the canonical number of the saintly fathers who formulated the Nicene creed, the touchstone of orthodoxy, though that tally surely does not correspond exactly to the number of bishops who attended Nicaea. The power of patristic consensus exhibited in various florilegia can only be fully appreciated in light of their visual representations in early Byzantine frescoes and illuminated manuscripts, in which solid phalanxes of saintly bishops in serried ranks embody the principle of *homonoia*. Against this overwhelming consensus, dissent and debate were literally swept aside.[173]

Talmudic Judaism seemingly could not be more different in its posture toward debate and disagreement than this. What must be emphasized, however, is that at one level these seeming opposites actually lead to the same point: the rejection of rational decision-making processes through dialectical investigation, the habitus of both earlier Christian and Jewish groups. The dual displacements of the Logos—the Rabbis' by anathematizing it and the Fathers' via its resurrection in the Trinity—are played out as well in the dual and parallel, but similarly different, strategies for defanging Logos in human discourse. If post-Nicene orthodox Christianity bound the Logos to heaven (the full transcendentalizing of the Son), the late ancient Rabbis broke it (the tablets have been smashed, and the Torah is not in heaven). In both cases, there results what might be called a certain apophatic theology of the Divine Voice. Humans, paradoxically, have lost the power to discover truth through *ratio* and dialectic. The distinction between binding and breaking, however, seems to be a distinction that makes a difference.[174] At the same time, then, that I remain thoroughly skeptical of accounts that seek to find and celebrate in rabbinic Judaism, even in its latest Babylonian avatar, a model of democratic pluralism and interpretative freedom, I do continue to take deep intellectual and spiritual pleasure in, and wish to celebrate the creativity and originality of, its talmudic textuality. If not a model for political or social practice, the texts of rabbinic Judaism remain an alternative way of understanding both interpretation and the search for knowledge. The volubility of human voices that issued from the very different Babylonian rabbinic and (neo-)Nicene strategies of defanging disputation of its power to produce truth is conducive to significant contrasts in the modes of textuality within the two religious cultures and the two orthodoxies that emerged triumphant, each in its own (unequal) sphere, at the end of late antiquity.

"When the Kingdom Turned to Minut": The Christian Empire and the Rabbinic Refusal of Religion

At the end of the fourth century and in the first quarter of the fifth century, we can find several texts attesting how Christianity's new notion of self-definition via "religious" alliance was gradually replacing self-definition via kinship and land.[1] These texts, belonging to very different genres, indeed to entirely different spheres of discourse—heresiology, historiography, and law—can nevertheless be read as symptoms of an epistemic shift of great importance. As Andrew Jacobs describes the discourse of the late fourth and early fifth centuries, "Certainly this universe of discourses engendered different means of establishing normativity: the disciplinary practices of Roman law, for instance, operated in a manner quite distinct from the intellectual inculcation of historiography or the ritualized enactment of orthodoxy. Nevertheless, the common goal of this discursive universe was the reorganization of significant aspects of life under a single, totalized, imperial Christian rubric."[2] Jacobs specifies: "As the Christian holy land rose in prominence it was construed in the manner of [David] Chidester's 'frontier zone,' a complex site within which we find Christian authors producing knowledge about Jews in order to construct a comprehensive vision of 'Christianness.'"[3]

This construction of "Christianness" primarily involved the invention of Christianity as a religion, disembedded, in Seth Schwartz's words, from other cultural practices and identifying markers. Susanna Elm shows that fourth-century Christians were already committed to the idea of religions and even understood quite well the difference between religious definition and other modes of identity formation. Elm argues that the first usage of *Hellenism* as a denotation for a "religion" can be found in Julian.[4] He insists that only one who believes in Hellenism can understand it and teach it, as justification for his denial of the right to teach philosophy to Christian teachers.[5] Vasiliki Limberis emphasizes how, for all Julian's hatred of Christianity, his religiosity has been deeply structured by the model of Christianity.[6] As Limberis puts it: "Christians had never been barred from letters. Not only was this an effective political tool to stymie Christians, it had the remarkable effect of inventing a new religion and religious identity for people in the Roman empire. For the first time, *paideia* became a prized commodity, one that Julian sought to control in order both to exclude Christians and to insure a kind of orthodoxy."[7] I would slightly modify Limberis's formulation by noting that Julian did not so much invent a new religion as participate in the invention of a new notion of religion as a category and as a regime of power/knowledge. She writes: "In particular, Julian echoes Christianity's *modus operandi* by turning pagan practices into a formal institution that one must join."[8] The great fourth-century Cappadocian theologian Gregory Nazianzen retorted to Julian: "But I am obliged to speak again about the word . . . Hellenism[:] to what does the word apply, what does one mean by it? . . . Do you want to pretend that Hellenism means a religion, or, and the evidence seems to point that way, does it mean a people, and the language invented by this nation. . . . If Hellenism is a religion, show us from which place and what priests it has received its rules. . . . Because the fact that the same people use the Greek language who also profess Greek religion does not mean that the words belong therefore to the religion, and that we therefore are naturally excluded from using them. This is not a logical conclusion, and does not agree with your own logicians. Simply because two realities encounter each other does not mean that they are confluent, i.e. identical."[9] Gregory clearly has some sort of definition of the object "religion" in mind here, distinct from and in binary semiotic opposition to *ethnos*, contra the commonplace that such definitions are an early modern product.[10] I thus agree with Talal Asad that "religion" is not a "transhistorical and transcultural phenomenon," and that it does not have "an autonomous essence."[11] "Religion" is, I concur, a Christian cultural product (then appropriated by others, such as Jews and pagans). Where we part company is in Asad's insistence that the notion of religion as such is "the product of a unique post-Reformation history." Once more I agree with him that "what appears to anthropologists today to be self-evident, namely that religion is essentially a matter of symbolic meanings linked to ideas of general order (expressed through either rite or doctrine), that it has generic functions/features, and that it must not be confused with any of its particular historical or cultural forms, is in fact a view that has a specific Christian history."[12] I would locate this "specific Christian history" much further back than he does.

Gregory knew precisely "what kinds of affirmation, of meaning, must be identified with practice in order for it to qualify as religion":[13] it must have received its rules from some place (some book? Gregory surely doesn't mean geographical locations, for then he would be playing into Julian's hands) and some priests. While Gregory's definition of *religion,* is, of course, quite different from the Enlightenment one (a difference oddly homologous to the difference be-tween Catholicism and Protestantism), he nevertheless clearly has a notion of religion as an idea that can be abstracted from any particular manifestation of it; for Gregory, different peoples have different religions (some right and some wrong), and some folks have none. I therefore disagree with Asad's declaration that "When the fifth-century bishop of Javols spread Christianity into the Au-vergne, he found the peasants 'celebrating a three-day festival with offerings on the edge of a marsh. . . . 'Nulla est religio in stagno,' he said: 'There can be no re-ligion in a swamp.' For medieval Christians, religion was not a universal phe-nomenon."[14] It may be that there can be no religion in a swamp, just as, for Gregory, there can be no religion without priests handing down rules, but this does imply that there can be religions other than Christianity, whether true or false. Even the Enlightenment concept of religion is not dependent, as is some-times claimed, on the assumption that religion is simply a natural faculty of all human groups, that all humans have religion. As Chidester has amply demon-strated, Christians who explicitly did recognize the existence of other reli-gions—Judaism, Islam, and paganism—nevertheless were quite capable, as late as the beginning of the nineteenth century, of denying that the indigenes of southern Africa had any religion at all, even an idolatrous one.[15] As he shows there, these early "ethnographers" would observe various ceremonies but insist that they were not religion, and by this they did *not* mean that they were not Christian. This point contradicts one observation frequently made of the sup-posed Enlightenment notion of "religion," to wit, that it assumes religion to be a universal.[16] Furthermore, it must be emphasized that Julian himself already maintained exactly that notion of religion as a universal that is claimed for the Enlightenment: "The universal yearning for the divine that is in all men whether private persons or communities, whether considered as individuals or as races. For all of us, without being taught, have attained to a belief in some sort of di-vinity"[17] Julian clearly did regard religion as an essential human characteristic, but apartheid ethnographers of the Enlightenment did not necessarily do so. I would take their position as exactly analogous to Javols's comments on his swamp folk. They don't have any religion, but this does not mean that only Christianity is religion, nor that he lacks a concept of religion as a "substance" common to both "right" and "wrong" religion.

Whichever way the evidence pointed for Nazianzen, it is clear, as Elm demonstrates, that for Julian, "Hellenism" was indeed *a* religion. Gregory af-fords a definition of religion as clear as that of later comparatists (although quite different from them). A religion is something that has priests, rites, rules, and sacrifices. It is absolutely clear, moreover, from Gregory's discourse that, for this Christian, "the emergence of religion as a discrete category of human experience—religion's *disembedding*," in Schwartz's terms,[18] has taken place fully and finally as he explicitly separates religion from ethnicity and language. As Schwartz explicitly writes, "religion" is not a dependent variable of *ethnos*; indeed, almost the opposite is the case.[19] A corollary of this is that language itself shifted its function as identity marker. As Claudine Dauphin has argued, in the fifth century, linguistic identity was tied to religious affiliation and identity, and not to geographic or genealogical identification.[20]

Gregory, in the course of arguing that Hellenism is not a religion, at the same time exposes the conditions that would enable some entity other than Christianity to lay claim to that name. Other fourth-century Christian writers, especially ones less threatened than Gregory by the innovations of Julian (or prior to him) readily accepted the notion that "Hellenism" was a religion. Eusebius of Caesarea, the first church historian and an important theologian in his own right,[21] could write "I have already said before in the *Preparation*[[22]] how Christianity is something that is neither Hellenism nor Judaism, but which has its own particular characteristic piety" [ὁ Χριστιανισμὸς οὔτε Ἑλληνισμός τις ἐστιν οὔτε Ἰουδαϊσμός, οἰκεῖον δέ τινα φέρων χαρακτῆρα θεοσεβείας],"[23] the implication being that both Hellenism and Judaism have, as well, their own characteristic forms of piety (however, to be sure, wrong-headed ones). He also writes: "This compels us to conceive some other ideal of religion, by which they [the ancient Patriarchs] must have guided their lives. Would not this be exactly that third form of religion midway between Judaism and Hellenism, which I have already deduced as the most ancient and venerable of all religions, and which has been preached of late to all nations through our Saviour. . . . The convert from Hellenism to Christianity does not land in Judaism, nor does one who rejects the Jewish worship become ipso facto a Greek.[24]

Here we find in Eusebius a clear articulation of Judaism, Hellenism, and Christianity as religions. There is something called "religion," which takes different "forms." This represents a significant conceptual shift from the earlier uses of the term *religion* in antique sources, in which a *religio* is an appropriate single act of worship, not a conceptual or even practical system separate from culture and politics, and in which there is, therefore, not something called "religion" at all, no substance that we could discover and look at in its different forms. Elizabeth Castelli has well phrased what has become the generally scholarly consensus: "From the vantage point of a post-Enlightenment society that understands the separation of the political and the religious as an ideal to be protected, the Roman imperial situation requires careful attention to the myriad ways in which 'Roman religion' might, it could be defensibly argued, not quite exist. That is, insofar as practices that could conventionally be called 'religious' intersected so thoroughly with political institutions, social structures, familial commitments, and recognition of the self-in-society, there is very little in ancient Roman society that would not as a consequence qualify as 'religious.'[25] Although Castelli specifically refers to ancient Roman society, the description could be extended to virtually all ancient societies, except for pieces of nascent Christendom (and in some ways to other early partial formations such as the Isiac cult). It was the project of some early Christians precisely to invent their identity as a "religion"; to perform this, religion itself had to be invented as well. This is where, I suggest, heresiology came into the picture.

The fullest expression of this conceptual shift may be located in the heresiology of Epiphanius, although his terminology is not entirely clear. For him, not only "Hellenism" and "Judaism" but also "Scythianism" and even "Barbarianism" are no longer the names of ethnic entities[26] but of "heresies," that is, religions other than orthodox Christianity.[27] Although Epiphanius's use of the term is confusing and perhaps confused,[28] apparently what he means by "heresies" is often what other writers of his time call "religions": "Hellenism originated with Egyptians, Babylonians and Phrygians, and it now confused men's ways."[29] It is important to see that Epiphanius's comment is a transformation of a verse from the Pauline literature, as he himself informs us.[30] In Colossians 3:11 we find "Here there cannot be Greek and Jew, circumcised and uncircumcised, barbarian, Scythian, slave, free man, but Christ is all, and in all."[31] This is a lovely index of the semantic shift. For Pseudo-Paul, these designations are obviously not the names of religious formations but of various ethnic and cultural groupings,[32] whereas for Epiphanius they are the names of "heresies," by which he means groups divided and constituted by religious differences fully disembedded from ethnicities: How, otherwise could the religion called "Hellenism" have originated with the Egyptians?[33] Astonishingly, Epiphanius's "Hellenism" seems to have nothing to do with the Greeks; it is Epiphanius's name for what other writers would call "paganism." Epiphanius, not surprisingly, defines "the topic of the Jews' religion" as "the subject of their beliefs."[34] For an Epiphanius, as for Gregory, a major category (if not the only one) for dividing human beings into groups is "the subject of their beliefs," hence the power/knowledge regime of "religion." The system of identities had been completely transformed during the period extending from the first to the fifth centuries. The systemic change resulting in religious difference as a modality of identity that began, I would suggest, with the heresiological work of Christians such as Justin Martyr works itself out through the fourth century and is closely intertwined with the triumph of orthodoxy. Orthodoxy is thus not only a discourse for the production of difference within, but functions as a category to make and mark the border between Christianity and its proximate other religions, particularly a Judaism that it is, in part, inventing.

There is a new moment in fifth-century Christian heresiological discourse. Where in previous times the general move was to name Christian heretics "Jews" (a motif that continues alongside the "new" one), only at this time (notably in Epiphanius and Jerome) is distinguishing Judaizing heretics from orthodox Jews central to the Christian discursive project.[35] As one piece of evidence for this claim, I would adduce an explosion of heresiological interest in the "Jewish-Christian heresies" of the Nazoreans and the Ebionites at this time. At the beginning of the nineteenth century, J. K. L. Gieseler already recognized that "the brightest moment in the history of these two groups doubtless falls about the year 400 A.D., at which time we have the best accounts concerning them."[36] Given that, in fact, it seems unlikely that these sects truly flourished at this particular time,[37] we need to discover other ways of understanding this striking literary flowering. The Ebionites and Nazoreans, in my reading, function much as the mythical "trickster" figures of many religions, in that precisely by transgressing borders that the culture establishes, they reify those boundaries.[38] As Rachel Havrelock has written, "For Levi-Strauss and his adherents, myth does not comprise a genre, but rather a system of thought in which the binary oppositions are bridged. Myth's bridging of conceptual poles, however, functions to reinforce rather than dissolve such binaries. In myth, polarities are mediated by a trickster figure whose liminality generates ambiguity. The trickster is not the hero to be emulated, but the mediator who points to the uncertainties inherent within interstitial zones. The implication of the trickster's ambiguity for the audience is that instability results from mediation while individual and communal stability is insured by maintenance of binary opposition."[39] The discourse of the "Judaizing heretics" thus performs this very function of reinforcing the binaries.

The purpose of Epiphanius's discourse on the Ebionites and Nazoreans is to participate in the imperial project of control of (in this case) Palestine by "identifying and reifying the . . . religions." Epiphanius explicitly indicates that this is his purpose by writing of Ebion, the heresiarch and founder of the sect: "But since he is practically midway between all the sects, he is nothing. The words of scripture, 'I was almost in all evil, in the midst of the church and synagogue' [Proverbs 5:14], are fulfilled in him. For he is Samaritan, but rejects the name with disgust. And while professing to be a Jew, he is the opposite of Jews—though he does agree with them in part."[40] Epiphanius's declaration that the Ebionites "are nothing," especially when put next to Jerome's famous declaration that the Nazoreans think that they are Christians and Jews but in reality are neither, strongly recalls for me the insistence in the modern period that the people of southern Africa have no religion, not because they are not Christians but because they are not pagans.[41] Suddenly it seems important to these two writers to assert a difference between Judaizing heretics and Jews. The ascription of existence to the "hybrids" assumes (and thus assures) the existence of nonhybrid, "pure" religions. Heresiology is not only, as it is usually figured, the insistence on some (or another) right doctrine but on a discourse of the pure as opposed to the hybrid, a discourse that then requires the hybrid as its opposite term. Once again, the discourse of race as analyzed by Bhabha proves helpful: "The exertions of the 'official knowledges of colonialism—pseudo-scientific, typological, legal-administrative, eugenicist—are imbricated at the point of their production of meaning and power with the fantasy that dramatizes the impossible desire for a pure, undifferentiated origin."[42] We need only substitute "heresiological" for "eugenicist" in this sentence to arrive at a major thesis of this book. Thus if on one level, as I have tried to express, orthodox Judaism is produced as the abject of Christian heresiology, and orthodox Christianity as the abject of Jewish heresiology, on yet another level, the "heretics" and the *minim* are the same folks, perhaps literally so, but certainly discursively so: they constitute the impossible desire of which Bhabha speaks.

Jerome, Epiphanius's younger contemporary, is the other most prolific writer about "Jewish-Christians" in antiquity.[43] Jacobs reads Jerome's Hebrew knowledge as an important part of the "colonialist" project of the Theodosian age.[44] I want to focus here on only one aspect of Jerome's discourse about Jews, his discussions of the "Jewish-Christians." Hillel Newman has recently argued that Jerome's discourse about the Judaizers and Nazoreans is more or less constructed out of whole cloth.[45] It thus sharply raises the question of motivation, for, as historian Marc Bloch notes, "[T]o establish the fact of forgery is not enough. It is further necessary to discover its motivations. . . . Above all, a fraud is, in its way, a piece of evidence."[46] I would suggest that Jerome, in general a much clearer thinker than Epiphanius, moves in the same direction but with greater lucidity. For him, it is absolutely unambiguous that rabbinic Judaism is *not* a Christian heresy but a separate religion. The *Mischlinge* thus explicitly mark out the space of illegitimacy, of no religion:

Usque hodie per totas orientis synagogas inter Iudaeos haeresis est, quae dicitur Minaeorum, et a pharisaeis huc usque damnatur, quos uulgo Nazaraeos nuncupant, qui credunt in Christum, filim dei natum de Maria uirgine, et eum dicunt esse, qui sub Pontio Pilato et passus est et resurrexit, in quem et nos credimus, sed, cum uolunt et Iudaei esse et Christiani, nec Iudaei sunt nec Christiani.[47]

[In our own day there exists a sect among the Jews throughout all the synagogues of the East, which is called the sect of the Minei, and is even now condemned by the Pharisees. The adherents to this sect are known commonly as Nazarenes; they believe in Christ the Son of God, born of the Virgin Mary; and they say that He who suffered under Pontius

Pilate and rose again, is the same as the one in whom we believe. But while they desire to be both Jews and Christians, they are neither the one nor the other.]

This proclamation of Jerome's comes in the context of his discussion with Augustine about Galatians 2, in which Augustine, disallowing the notion that the apostles dissimulated when they kept Jewish practices, suggests that their "Jewish Christianity" was legitimate. Jerome responds vigorously, understanding the "danger" of such notions to totalizing imperial orthodoxy.[48] What is new here is not, obviously, the condemnation of the "Jewish Christian" heretics but that the Christian author condemns them, in addition, for not being Jews, thus at least implicitly marking the existence and legitimacy of a "true" Jewish religion alongside Christianity, as opposed to the falsities of the *Mischlinge*. This move parallels, then, Epiphanius's insistence that the Ebionites are "nothing." Pushing Jacobs's interpretation a bit further, I would suggest that Jerome's insistence on translating from the Hebrew is both an instance of control of the Jew (Jacobs's point) and also the very marking out of the Jews as "absolute other" to Christianity. I think that it is not going too far to see here a reflection of a social and political process like that Chidester remarks in an entirely different historical moment: "The discovery of an indigenous religious system on southern African frontiers depended upon colonial conquest and domination. Once contained under colonial control, an indigenous population was found to have its own religious system."[49] Following out the logic of this statement suggests that there may have been a similar nexus between the containment of the Jews under the colonial eye of the Christian empire that enabled the discovery/invention of Judaism as a religion. Looked at from the other direction, the assertion of the existence of a fully separate-from-Christianity "orthodox" Judaism functioned for Christian orthodoxy as a guarantee of the Christian's own bounded and coherent identity and thus furthered the project of imperial control, as marked out by Jacobs. The discursive processes in the situation of Christian empire are very different from the projects of mutual self-definition that I have been pursuing in the earlier chapters.

Hegemonic Christian discourse also produced Judaism (and paganism, for example, that of Julian) as other religions precisely in order to cordon off Christianity, in a purification and crystallization of its essence as a bounded entity. Julian cleverly reverses this procedure and turns it against Christianity. In at least one reading of Julian's "Against the Galileans," the point of that work is to *reinstate* a binary opposition between Greek and Jew, Hellenism and Judaism, by inscribing Christianity as a hybrid. Eusebius's claim that the one who leaves Hellenism does not land in Judaism and the reverse now constitutes an argument that Christianity is a monstrous hybrid, a mooncalf: "For if any man should wish to examine into the truth concerning you, he will find that your impiety is compounded of the rashness of the Jews and the indifference and vulgarity of the Gentiles, for from both sides you have drawn what is by no means their best but their inferior teaching, and so have made for yourselves a border of wickedness."[50] Julian further writes: "It is worth while . . . to compare what is said about the divine among the Hellenes and Hebrews; and finally to enquire of those who are neither Hellenes nor Jews, but belong to the sect of the Galileans."[51] Julian, as dedicated as any Christian orthodox writer to policing border lines, bitterly reproaches the "Galileans" for contending that they are Israelites and argues that they are no such thing, neither Jews nor Greeks but impure hybrids.[52] Here Julian sounds very much like Jerome when the latter declares that those who think they are both Jews and Christians are neither, or Epiphanius when he refers to the Ebionites as "nothing." This would make Julian's project structurally identical to the projects of the Christian heresiologists who, at about the same time, were rendering Christianity and Judaism in their "orthodox" forms the pure terms of a binary opposition, with the "Judaizing" Christians—the hybrids who must be excluded from the semiotic system—being "monsters." I suggest, then, a deeper explanation of Julian's insistence that you cannot mix Hellenism with Christianity. It is not only that Hellenism and Christianity are separate religions that, by definition, cannot be mixed with each other, but even more that Christianity is always already (if you will) an admixture, a syncretism. Julian wants to reinstate the binary of Jew and Greek. He provides, therefore, another instance of the discursive form that I am arguing for in the Christian texts of his time, a horror of supposed hybrids. To recapitulate, in Julian's very formation of Hellenism (or should I say "Hellenicity"?[53]), as a religious difference, he mirrors the efforts of the orthodox churchmen. This is another instantiation of the point made above by Limberis.[54] While he was protecting the borders between Hellenism and Judaism by excluding Christianity as a hybrid, Julian, it seems, was, unbeknownst to himself, smuggling some wheelbarrows of his own.

This interpretation adds something to that of Jacobs, who writes that "among the deviant figures of Christian discourse we often find the Jew, the 'proximate other' used to produce the hierarchical space between the Christian and the non-Christian."[55] I am suggesting that the heretic can also be read as a proximate other, producing a hierarchical space between the Christian and the Jew. This point is at least partially anticipated by Jacobs himself when he writes that "Jews exist as the paradigmatic 'to-be-known' in the overwhelming project of conceptualizing the 'all in all' of orthodoxy. This comes out most clearly in the [Epiphanian] accounts of 'Jewish-Christian' heresies."[56] One way of spinning this would be to see heresiology as central to the production of Judaism as the "pure other" of Christian orthodoxy, while the other way of interpreting it would be to see Judaism as essential to the production of orthodoxy over against heresy. My point is that both of these moments in an oscillating analysis are equally important and valid. Seen in this light, orthodoxy itself, orthodoxy as an idea or as a regime (as opposed to any particular orthodox position) is crucial in the formation of Christianity as the universal and imperial religion of the late Roman Empire and, later on, of European Christendom as well.

In a not inconsiderable sense, Epiphanius's *Panarion* (Medicine Chest),[57] a classification of all the many varieties of heresy, can be seen as performing a function for the disciplining of religion that Krafft-Ebing's similar work on the perversions played in the disciplining of sexuality at the end of the nineteenth century.[58]

The Conversion of Count Joseph

A puzzling moment in Epiphanius's text, the narrative of the conversion of Count Joseph of Tiberias, supports the suggestion that the exporting of hybridity from within to without in the form of heresiology is complicit in the production of Christianity and Judaism as separate, unequal orthodoxies.[59] Count Joseph was a Jew and a high official in the court of the Patriarch—and thus, certifiably orthodox—who at some time, as reported by Epiphanius, became converted to orthodox Christianity.

After citing the heretical christological doctrines of the Ebionites and related heresies, Epiphanius remarks that they use only the Gospel of Matthew, called "According to the Hebrews."[60] There follows a strange remark that some will object that the Jews secretly hold in their "treasuries" copies of the Gospel of John and the Acts of the Apostles translated into Hebrew. "So the Jews who have been converted to Christ by reading it have told me." The text already inscribes, therefore, two differing spaces, a "heretical" one in which the Gospel according to the Hebrews is the Gospel, and an "orthodox" Jewish space in which other texts are kept, enabling (inadvertently?) Jews to convert to orthodox Christianity. In other words, the relevant opposition being inscribed is that between orthodoxy and heresy and not between Judaism and Christianity. Orthodox Judaism and orthodox Christianity, surprisingly, are lined up on one side of a semantic opposition, with the heretics, who do not respect properly the difference between being Jew or being Christian and think to combine them, positioned on the other side. The Joseph story follows immediately upon these declarations, and, in my reading, is powerfully contextualized by them. From the beginning to the end of the narrative, Epiphanius emphasizes over and over

the "orthodoxy" of Joseph's Christianity. He has as a houseguest Bishop Eusebius of Vercelli, "since Constantius had banished him for his orthodox faith,"
and, at the very beginning and as a sort of headline to the conversion narrative
itself, "Josephus was not only privileged to become a faithful Christian, but a de-
spiser of Arians as well. In that city, Scythopolis, he was the only orthodox
Christian—they were all Arian. . . . But there was another, younger man in town
too, an orthodox believer of Jewish parentage."[61] The intimate connection between Jewishness and orthodoxy within the Epiphanian discourse is thus
doubled in this conversion narrative.

The first step toward Joseph's conversion is his observation (through a key-
hole) of the deathbed baptism of no lesser a person than the Patriarch, "Ellel."
Thus at the very heart and head of the orthodox Jewish power structure they
understand that salvation is only through conversion to Christianity. Joseph is
understandably "troubled over the subject of baptism."[62] Upon the death of this
Ellel, Joseph and another one of the Patriarch's "apostles" are made regents over
his minor son, the infante Patriarch, one "Judas" by name. This is indeed a name
common in the patriarchal family, but Epiphanius twice marks that he does not
know that that is his name—"I suppose that he was called that,"[63] suggesting to
this reader, at any rate, that the name is being marked as emblematic. This
young man is a libertine. While Joseph watches, a beautiful young Christian
woman is saved from his magical charms by the cross that she carries, once
more raising thoughts in Joseph's mind, "but at this point he was by no means
convinced that he should become a Christian."[64] During this time, as well,
Joseph reads the Gospels, an Ebionite Matthew (originally in Hebrew), canonical John (translated into Hebrew) and canonical Acts (also translated), which
are kept in the secret treasury of the patriarchs. Upon becoming deathly ill,
Joseph is informed by the elders, who whisper in his ear, that if he believes in the
Christian creed, he will be healed; Epiphanius has, moreover, heard such a story
from another Jew as well. Still Joseph's heart is hard, but after the young Patriarch, Judas, grows up, he makes our Joseph tax gatherer for the province of Cili-
cia, where Joseph lodges next to the church, befriends the bishop, borrows the
Gospels, and reads them again. The Jews, full of resentment for his offensive
against their corruption, upon discovering that he is reading the Gospels, fall
upon Joseph, take him to the synagogue, "and whip . . . him as the Law pre-
scribes."[65] At this point, Joseph accepts baptism, goes to Constantine's court,
and is offered very high rank in the imperial realm by the "good emperor—a
true servant of Christ, and after David, Hezekiah and Josiah, the king with the
most godly zeal."[66] After being permitted to build churches in the Jewish towns
of the Galilee, Joseph sets up furnaces to burn the lime for them. The "natural-
born Jews" perform sorcery to make these fires deviate from their own nature

and be ineffective. When Joseph hears of this, he cries out in the name of Jesus and sprinkles water on the furnaces. The spell is thereby broken, the fire blazes up, "and the crowds of [all Jewish] spectators cried, 'there is (only) one God, the help of the Christians.'" All of the formerly orthodox Jews have now become orthodox Christians, a conversion portrayed as without remainder. The Ebionites, with their heretical gospel "According to the Hebrews," are safely marked as the true locus of hybridity. The discursive entities, orthodox Judaism and orthodox Christianity, work very similarly to the discourse of race as Young puts it: "The idea of racial purity [orthodoxy] here shows itself to be profoundly dialectical: it only works when defined against potential intermixture, which also threatens to undo its calculations altogether."[67]

After relating the tale, Epiphanius returns to his main point. He argues, "So much for my account and description of these events, which I recalled here because of the translation of the books, the rendering from Greek to Hebrew of the Gospel of John and the Acts of the Apostles. But I resume—because of the Gospel according to Matthew the progress of the discussion obliged me to give the sequel of the knowledge which had come my way. Now in what they call a Gospel according to Matthew, though it is not entirely complete, but is corrupt and mutilated—and they call this thing 'Hebrew'!—the following passage occurs."[68] I would argue that this true Gospel and Acts, found in the hands of the true Jews, are being dramatized in opposition to that fake gospel, neither Christian nor Jewish: "And they [the Ebionites] call this thing Hebrew!"

Most scholars believe that this story has been interpolated into the midst of Epiphanius's account of the Ebionites because of the metonymical link between the books that Joseph found and the Ebionite "Jewish Christians."[69] I think that it plays a more central role in Epiphanius's text. Stephen Goranson sends us in the right direction: "The story of Joseph of Tiberias is of a conversion from one orthodoxy to another, skipping over middle groups, more numerous at the time in Galilee."[70] I submit that the story of Joseph further underlines Epiphanius's distinction between those who are "something"—Jews or Christians or pagans—and those who are nothing, the *Mischlinge*. The function of the story is hardly to use the somethingness of the "religions" in order to establish the "nothingness" of the Ebionites and their associates, but can more plausibly read in the opposite manner, namely using their nothingness to establish the somethingness of the absolutely distinguished "real" religions.

Thus a narrative that inscribes the binary opposition between a "pure," orthodox Judaism and a "pure," orthodox Christianity, as well as the ambiguous tricksters, the Jewish-Christian hybrids, can be seen to be participating in the same process of the production of absolute boundaries, of "individual and communal stability." I thus read a narrative interposed by Epiphanius, seemingly almost by accident,[71] as a hermeneutic key for understanding at least one of the crucial motives of his text. It is not just, as Goranson puts it, "that the church has in the interim, from the first to the fourth centuries, decided that Ebionites and Nazarenes are heretical," but rather that the discursive project of imperial Christian self-definition requires an absolute separation from Judaism. In order to help produce that, Epiphanius (a.k.a. the church) needs to make space for an orthodox Judaism that is completely other to Christianity. Now we can see the fifth-century explicit notices of curses of "Nazoreans" in synagogues as participating in the same project.[72] The Jews who curse the middle groups are discursively necessary for the orthodox project, performing the same function as orthodox Jews, like Count Joseph, who absolutely convert to orthodox Christianity, thus guaranteeing the latter's legitimacy. Joseph was the only "orthodox Christian" in all of Scythopolis. It was his initial complete separation from Christianity as an "orthodox" Jew that enabled his transformation into a purely orthodox Christian. In other words, a Jewish orthodoxy is produced by the Christian legend, in order to help guarantee a Christian orthodoxy, over and against hybrids. The hybrids, however, also produce the no-man's-land, the mestizo territory, that guarantees the purity of the orthodox formations.

Orthodox Judaism as State-Sanctioned (but False) Religion in the Theodosian Code

In support of this interpretation of Epiphanius and Jerome, I would adduce a further bit of contemporaneous evidence of a very different sort, the law code. In turning to the law codes, I am not turning from the ideal or even the ideological to the real. The point has been made often enough that law codes themselves are ideological state apparatuses as often as they are repressive state apparatuses (to invoke Althusser's famous distinction),[73] at least de facto if not de jure. The payoff from study of the law codes is, instead, how they render certain investments of a power structure more transparent (and, perhaps, less effective, as Foucault has taught us). The relevant code for this particular investigation is the empire-wide Code of Theodosius of 438.[74]

In order to more fully appreciate the import of that code, we must focus on the semantic shift in the terms *religio* and *superstitio*.[75] In Latin, as has been well documented, in its earliest appearances *superstitio* was not in binary opposition to *religio*. Indeed, too much *religio* could be *superstitio*. It was not the index of worship of the right gods, but of the right or wrong worship of the gods.[76] Maurice Sachot concurs that in the Latin of the early empire, *superstitio* was not so much the opposite of *religio* as a type of *religio*, a dangerous and illegitimate ex-

cess of *religio* itself.[77] As Peter Brown puts it, "Outside Epicurean circles, superstition was not treated as a cognitive aberration—an 'irrational' belief in non-
existent or misperceived beings. Superstition was a social *gaffe* committed in the
presence of the gods. It betrayed a lack of the ease and candour that were supposed to characterise a free man's relations with any persons, human or divine.
Excessive observance was strictly analogous to flattery and ostentation; and
magic was a form of graft and manipulation."[78] Beard, North, and Price write,
"[*Superstitio*] was ambiguous between two meanings: excessive forms of behaviour, that is 'irregular' religious practices ('not following the custom of the
state') and excessive commitment, an excessive commitment to the gods." The
same authors have further pointed out that "the term *superstitio* was used initially to categorize the improper behaviour of individuals rather than groups,
and was focussed on internal irregularities in Rome itself rather than Italy and
the provinces."[79] Even when, somewhat later, as these authors document, *superstitio* is more often used to characterize "the religious practices of particular foreign peoples, . . . it was not, of course, the case that all 'non-Roman' cults were
branded in this way."[80] There was no way, therefore, that it could have simply
been an index of the difference between Roman and others' religions. Improper
Roman worship of Roman gods might be marked as *superstitio*, whereas the
worship by others of their own God or gods could be *religio*. When a foreign cult
is marked as *superstitio tout court*, as Judaism occasionally is in early writings,[81]
this represents the writer's judgment that that cult's observances—for example,
the Sabbath, circumcision, and kashruth—are in and of themselves excessive
and dangerous. "A Roman author such as Seneca does not condemn Judaism as
a *superstitio* but refers to certain Jewish practices (as well as some practices of
the Roman State and 'a variety of popular forms of worship') as *superstitiones*."[82]
Caroline Humfress writes, "From the early Republic illicit *superstitiones* (meaning 'excessive' religious practices, that were usually seen as a threat to the Roman
public order) had been contrasted with licit *religiones*. Individuals accused of *superstitio* were undesirables, excluded from the pagan commonwealth."[83] *Superstitio* is thus virtually an index of what tradition had determined to be licit and
illicit or appropriate and excessive practices, and not the signifier of the truth or
falsity of different belief systems.

   This meaning shifts under Christianity.[84] When Christians displaced the
referent of *superstitio* to paganism (CTh XVI.10.2–3), they were not only changing its object, but introducing a significant turnabout in the semantics of the
term. It no longer referred primarily to the practices of the worshiper, but solely
to the object of belief and worship. In the Theodosian Code we read that
"Should [one] attempt to honor vain images with the offering of a gift, which
even though it is humble, still is a complete outrage against religion, such per-

son, as one guilty of the violation of religion, shall be punished by the forfeiture of that house or landholding in which it is proved that he served a pagan superstition" (CTh XVI.10.12).[85] The key phrase here is "even though it is humble," that is, not excessive and, therefore, not *superstitio* in the earlier acceptation. *Superstitio*, therefore, has transformed in meaning from particular "excessive" and politically destabilizing rituals to the delineation of "wrong belief and worship"—not improper or illicit worship of the right gods, but any worship of the wrong gods. Necessarily, with the shift in the meaning of its fellow traveler in the semantic field, *superstitio*, *religio* must have shifted in meaning as well.

In later Christian Latin, *religio* is not defined as the practices that are useful and appropriate for maintaining Roman solidarity and social order, but as the belief in that which is true, that is, as sanctioned by an authoritatively and ultimately legally produced ecumenical orthodoxy. Beard, North, and Price support this point:

"*Religio* is worship of the true god, *superstitio* of a false,"[86] as the Christian Lactantius remarked in the early fourth century A.D.—so asserting that alien practices and gods were not merely inferior to his own, but actually bogus. The traditional Roman distinction seems to have made no such assumption about truth and falsehood: when Romans in the early empire debated the nature of *religio* and *superstitio* they were discussing instead different *forms* of human relations with the gods. This is captured in Seneca's formulation that "*religio* honours the gods, *superstitio* wrongs them."[87]

A somewhat different way of naming this shift is to point out that, in the earlier usage, *religiones* and *superstitiones* are the names of acts—including speech acts—and the results of such acts. If Judaism (sometimes) and Christianity (always) are referred to as *superstitiones* in non-Christian literature, that is a judgment on all of the acts that members of those communities perform, but not a name for the community itself. After the shift, *religio* and *superstitio* are the names of institutions and communities. Before, one performs a *religio* or a *superstitio*; now one belongs to one.

This helps explain why the Epiphanian narrative of conversion is so crucial in establishing the new sense of *religio*, for the possibility of conversion itself converts Christianity into an institution, rather than only a set of practices, an institution that we might name "the Church."[88] Now it becomes possible for Christianity to be a true *religio*, whereas Judaism and paganism are false *religiones*, another name for which is *superstitiones* in its new sense. This will be clearest if we remember that in earlier antiquity the term *religiones* in the plural never names institutions (much less mutually exclusive ones). After the invention of sexuality in the nineteenth century, everyone has a sexuality; after the invention of religion, in the fourth, the same thing happens. Greek, we might say, also rises to the occasion of this semantic and social shift, with the once very rare word θρησκεια stepping into the new semantic slot now occupied by *religio* in its post-Christian sense in Latin. This semantic development is paralleled in Hebrew דת which in biblical and early rabbinic usage means something like *religio* in the old Latin sense and comes to mean "religion" only in the Middle Ages.

A paradox in the representation of Judaism within the Theodosian Code illustrates these points. Throughout the code, Judaism is sometimes nominated *religio* and sometimes *superstitio*, but, as legal historian Amnon Linder observes, after 416 only *superstitio* is used. In the older Roman usage this shift to exclusive designation as *superstitio* ought to mark an absolute delegitimation of Judaism, entirely unlike its prior status as *religio licita*, in Tertullian's famous—if pleonastic—phrase. However, Linder also describes a complex and increasing legislative *legitimation* of Judaism through the fourth and fifth centuries. As Günter Stemberger has written, "If it were the case that the emperor Theodosius I was the first to honour the Jewish patriarchs with the highest rank, this would flatly contradict the widespread assumption of a constant deterioration in the Jews' position since the Christianization of the Roman empire."[89] So also Lee Levine in the most exhaustive study of the patriarchate writes: "With the backing of Christian emperors, extensive leverage was once again added to [Jewish] religious authority. From all indications the last century of the Patriarchate, which coincided with the advent of Byzantine rule, was one of the most flourishing in the history of the office."[90] On Levine's evidence I would go further and suggest that the fourth century was probably the zenith of patriarchal authority. That is, a Jewish religious institution first attested with certainty in the mid–third century achieved its heyday in the fourth and early fifth centuries.[91]

How can it be, then, that Judaism definitively became a *superstitio* precisely when "the Christian Empire—to a far greater extent than the pagan Empire—accepted Judaism as a religion rather than as a nation or a people?"[92] The answer I will develop is that *superstitio* itself has shifted in meaning; indeed, the whole semantic field has shifted. First, however, let me sharpen the apparent paradox. The legitimation of Judaism went so far as to comprehend recognition of the Jewish Sabbath and festivals, including Purim (CTh XVI.8.18)[93] (provided the Jews didn't mock the crucifixion on that occasion[94]—an exemplary instance, perhaps, of mimicry turned mockery), the Jewish priesthood,[95] and the synagogue. The following has a particularly "modern" ring: "[Buildings] which are known to be used by Jews for their meetings, and which are described as synagogues, let no-one dare to desecrate or occupy; for all shall keep their own with rights undisturbed, without attacks on religion or worship" (CTh XVI.8.20 of 26 July 412 [Honorius]).[96] Particularly dramatic is the continued, even enhanced, right of the *primates* of the Jews (including probably Rabbis) to excommunicate (CTh XVI.8.8).[97] This power continued well after 416, and during that time Jewish religious autonomy was enhanced by other laws as well.[98] Indeed, "in a law of Justinian from 553 (No. 66), the lawful observance of the Jewish religion and its cult was taken for granted."[99] Furthermore, through the fourth century the Jewish religion received greater and greater legitimacy in the recognition of the Jewish Patriarch as the virtual Metropolitan of the Jews.[100] As Seth Schwartz writes: "In the late fourth century the patriarchs reached the peak of their power. The Palestinian church father Epiphanius and the Codex Theodosianius both indicate that the *apostole*, or *aurum coronarium* [the Jewish head tax, exacted by the patriarchs from the Diaspora], was now collected as if it were a conventional tax."[101] In 397, Arcadius and Honorius affirm that "We shall imitate the ancients by whose sanctions it was determined that those privileges which are conferred upon the first clerics of the venerable Christian religion shall continue, by the consent of Our Imperial Divinity, for those persons who are subject to the power of the Illustrious Patriarchs, for the rulers of the synagogues, the patriarchs, and the priests, and for all the rest who are occupied in the ceremonial of that religion" (CTh XVI.8.13).[102] This law was reaffirmed in 404.[103] Despite the explicit rhetoric of the law of 397, Schwartz makes the important point that "the laws about the Jews in the Theodosian Code are not at all conservative. By their very existence they constitute a significant innovation, because they imply that by the late fourth century the Roman state consistently regarded the Jews as a discrete category of humanity. I would suggest that the state had not done so, at least not consistently, between the first and the fourth centuries."[104] In my reading of the archives, more even than providing evidence of the growing importance of the Patriarch (which I am not, to be sure, denying), these materials suggest the high importance of the *representation*, perhaps a sort of colonial trompe l'oeil, in Bhabha's terms,[105] of a powerful and prestigious Jewish Patriarch in the discourse of the orthodox Christian empire.[106]

With the shift in designation Linder dates to 416, Judaism, paradoxically, became in effect a *superstitio licita* (an oxymoron, of course),[107] a genuine, though wrong religion from which conversion was possible, leaving a remainder that guaranteed the existence of the Christian herself.[108] In a law variously dated to 412, 418, and 420,[109] we read, "Let no one, as long as he is innocent, be disparaged and subject to attacks because he is a Jew, *by whatever religion* [CTh XVI.8.21, emphasis added]."[110] "By whatever religion" must comprehend more than just Christianity, or this sentence would make no sense whatsoever. The licit status of the *superstitio*, Judaism, as opposed to "heresy"—and consequently the crucial conversion of Judaism from heresy to *superstitio*, or alternative but wrong religion—is beautifully indicated in the following edict of Honorius and Theodosius:

> We punish with proscription of their goods and exile, Manichaeans and those persons who are called Pepyzites [Montanists]. Likewise those persons who are worse than all other heretics in this one belief, namely, that they disagree with all others as to the venerable day of Easter, shall be punished with the same penalty if they persist in the aforesaid madness.
>
>   But we especially command those persons who are truly Christians . . . that they shall not abuse the authority of religion and dare to lay violent hands on Jews and pagans who are living quietly and attempting nothing disorderly or contrary to law. (CTh XVI.10.24)[111]

If they do do so, continues the edict, "they shall also be compelled to restore triple or quadruple that amount which they robbed." As Humfress remarks on this law of 423, "This vision of peaceful, law-abiding, fifth-century 'pagans' and Jews legally pursuing hard-line Christians through the courts of the Roman empire, for the fourfold restitution of their robbed property, is diametrically opposed to the more usual fifth century rhetoric of Christian triumphalism. And it provides stimulus and justification for an account of the *evolution* of late paganism as an alternative to a repetition of the traditional historiographical story of its demise."[112] Hal Drake has commented on explicit fourth-century discourse that indicates the coexistence of Christians and pagans, with heretics marked off as the genuine enemy.[113] If that is so for "late paganism," then it is even more so for "early Judaism." Judaism was evolving within the context of the world that Christianity, Christendom, and the Christian empire had made for it. As Neusner has perspicaciously noted, the success of rabbinic Judaism and its final triumph as Judaism *tout court* was at least in large part a product of its effectiveness in providing an answer to Christian challenges, challenges to the relevance of Jewish peoplehood, genealogy, and the physical practice of the Torah. As Neusner writes, "in context Christianity (and later on, Islam) made rabbinic Judaism permanently relevant to the situation in which Jews found themselves. That Judaism had successfully responded to the urgent issues raised by the Christian challenge from the fourth century onward." Although I would dissent in some measure from the specific time frame of this argument, its major notional base appeals to me. Rabbinic Judaism was successful as Judaism for two reasons: (1) Christianity "needed" a Jewish orthodoxy with which to think itself, and (2) rabbinic Judaism provided a winning set of responses to the Christian questions: "The rabbinic Sages produced responses to the Christian challenge in their enduring doctrines of the meaning of history, of the conditions in which the Messiah will come to Israel, and of the definition of Israel. Rabbinic Judaism's symbolic system, with its stress on Torah, the eschatological teleology of that system, with stress on the messiah-sage coming to obedient Israel, the insistence on the equivalence of Israel and Rome, Jacob and Esau, with Esau penultimate and Israel at the end of time, these constituted in Israel powerful responses to the Christian question."[114]

Christianity needed a Jewish orthodoxy. Everything about Title 8 of Book XVI suggests that Judaism is to be legitimated, while vigorously protecting Christians and Christianity from any temptations to cross the border. The indictment of the Quartodecimans as worse than Manichaeans in the passage just read makes this point eloquently.[115] The trenchant condemnation of the "Caelicolists," by all signs a combination of Christianity and Judaism, in this Title (8. 19) immediately preceding a law (8.20) enjoining the absolute protection of synagogue and Sabbath for Jews also argues for this interpretation.[116] It is hybridity that is at once the threat and the guarantor of the "purity" of Christianity and Judaism, the whole system necessary for the discursive production of an orthodoxy which was "one of the primary discursive formations around which ancient Christian strategies of self-definition coalesced."[117]

The Kingdom Turns to *Minut*

There is a small but suggestive body of evidence that Christianity takes on a different role in the self-understanding of rabbinic Judaism in this period, as well. As I have noted above in Chapter 6, already in later Palestinian texts—the midrashim—we frequently find the expression "nations of the world" as a reference to Christianity. In a precise mirror of the contemporary Christian move in which ethnic difference is made religious, for the latter Rabbis religious difference has been ethnicized; Christians are no longer seen as a threatening other within but as an entity fully other, as separate as the Gentiles had been for the Jews of Temple times. It is not that the *referent* of the term *minut* has shifted from "Jewish Christianity" to Gentile Christianity, but that with the historical developments of the centuries, its significance has changed. Since Christianity itself is no longer a threatening blurring within but a clearly defined without, *minut* comes now simply to mean the religious practices of the Gentiles, the Christian Romans. For the Jews of the fourth century, the Gentiles are now the Christians. Whatever the Mishna [Sotah 9:15] meant in predicting that when the Messiah comes, "The Kingdom will turn to *minut*," for the Talmuds [PT Sotah 23b, BT Sotah 49b], I would warrant: "The Kingdom has turned to *minut*" refers to the Christianization of the empire, but it also means, of course, that *minut* has turned (in)to the empire. The Christians are now the Gentiles.

In the Talmud, *minut* clearly no longer means what it had meant in the Mishna and the Tosefta. As Richard Kalmin observes: "Th[e] notion of the powerful attraction that *minut* ('heresy') and Christianity exerted on rabbis and their families is found almost exclusively in tannaitic collections such as the Tosefta, but also in tannaitic sources in the Babylonian Talmud that have toseftan parallels. Statements attributed to later Palestinian and Babylonian amoraim in both Talmuds, in contrast, reveal no hint of this notion."[118] This argument can be further substantiated by observing that the Babylonian Talmud almost systematically "forgets" what the meaning of the term *min* is. Indeed, according to that Talmud, *minut* becomes simply a name for the "other" religion, Christianity to the Jews, Judaism to the Christians. As I have said, it is no longer the name for a Jewish heresy but simply refers to false religious practices, functionally equivalent to *idolatry* in biblical usage and consequently of no particular attraction to Jews, any more than idolatry had been in Second Temple times.[119] And they imagine that this is the term under which they might, in turn, be persecuted by the Christian empire. We see, therefore, a real asymmetry; whereas the Christian discourse in this time develops a three-term paradigm—Christians, Jews, and heretics—rabbinic discourse only imagines two terms: we and the Gentiles. Religious difference has been, it seems, fully re-ethnicized.

Two moments in the Babylonian Talmud support this proposition. The first comes from the continuation of the Talmud's version of the narrative about the arrest of Rabbi Eli'ezer that I have discussed at length in previous work.[120] In one early (mid-third-century) Palestinian story, Rabbi Eli'ezer is arrested by the Romans on suspicion of being a Christian, referred to as *minut* in the story. This is the excerpt:

It happened to Rabbi Eli'ezer that he was arrested for sectarianism (*minut*=Christianity),[121] and they took him up to the platform to be judged.
　　The ruler said to him: "A sage such as you having truck with these matters!?"
　　He said to him: "I have trust in the judge."
　　The ruler thought that he was speaking of him, but he meant his Father in Heaven. He said to him: "Since you trust me, I also have said: Is it possible that these gray hairs would err in such matters? *Dimus [=Dimissus]!* Behold, you are dismissed." (Tosefta Ḥullin, 2:24)[122]

Having tricked the Roman, he then confesses to his fellows that he has, indeed, had improper friendly religious conversation with a disciple of Jesus; indeed, on my reading, that he had been "arrested by *minut*," that is, found heresy arresting, and not only arrested for *minut*—the Hebrew phrase allows for both meanings. The fact that this alleged James, the disciple of Jesus, cites midrashic interpretations of his Master makes even more palpable both the Jewishness of *minut* and, as well, that the issue of this story is the attraction of the Christian *minut* for even the most prominent of Rabbis. So far, in this text, which has its origins in Palestine, *minut* means what we would expect it to mean, a Jewish heresy, which we might call Christianity.

In the earlier Tosefta and the Palestinian midrash, this text appears without a sequel, but in the Babylonian Talmud we find the following continuation:

Our Rabbis have taught: When Rabbi El'azar the son of Perata and Rabbi Ḥanina the son of Teradyon were arrested for sectarianism [*minut*], Rabbi El'azar the son of Perata said to Rabbi Ḥanina the son of Teradyon: "Happy art thou, who have been arrested for only one thing. Woe unto me, who have been arrested for five things." Rabbi Ḥanina the son of Teradyon said to him: "Happy art thou, who have been arrested for five things and will be rescued. Woe unto me, who have been arrested for one thing and will not be saved, for you busied yourself with Torah and with good deeds, while I only busied myself with Torah."—This is in accord with the view of Rav Huna, who said that anyone who busies himself with Torah alone is as if he had no God. . . .

In contrast to Rabbi Eli'ezer, where the "*minut*" involved is explicitly Christianity, these two Rabbis clearly are under no suspicion whatever of Christianity. Their fictive arrest clearly happens during the Hadrianic persecutions of the early second century (not under Trajan in the second half of the first) and has to do with the public teaching of Torah, forbidden by Hadrian for political reasons. In other words, they are arrested for practicing Judaism, not as Christians. And yet the Talmud refers to it as an arrest for *minut*. The term *minut* has clearly shifted meaning for the Babylonian Talmud. It no longer refers to Jewish heresy, but to the binary opposition between Jewish and Gentile religion. Judaism is *minut* for the Romans; Roman religion and Christianity are *minut* for Jews. This semantic shift changes the interpretation of Rabbi Eli'ezer's arrest in the talmudic context via what is in effect a misreading.[123] It is unthinkable to this Talmud that Rabbi Eli'ezer had been under suspicion—much less justifiable suspicion—for association with *minim*. Therefore the text has to make it a code name for arrest for being Jewish, for teaching Torah—that is, *minut*, heresy, as seen from the viewpoint of the Roman order, not from the viewpoint of Judaism. In my view, we have evidence, then, that by the time of the editing of the Babylonian Talmud, and perhaps at that geographical distance from the center of contact, Palestine, Jewish Christianity (not in its heresiological sense but in the sense of the Christianity of Jews who remained Jews) had receded into the distance for rabbinic Judaism; Christianity was sufficiently definable as a separate "religion" that it no longer posed a threat to the borders of the Jewish community.

We now have an explanation for the well-known fact that in the Babylonian Talmud, the term *min* no longer refers to a difference within Judaism, an excluded heretical other, but has come to mean Gentiles and especially Gentile Christians. Once more, as in the period of the Second Temple (up until 70 A.C.) and before, the excluded other of Judaism is the Gentile and not the heretic within.

The second piece of evidence comes from another story, which historians have read quite differently:

Rabbi Abbahu used to praise Rav Safra [a Babylonian immigrant to Caesarea Maritima] to the *minim* that he was a great man [i.e., a great scholar]. They released him from excise taxes for thirteen years.

One day they met him. They said to him: "It is written: Only you have I known from all of the families of the earth; therefore I will tax you with all of your sins" [Amos 3:2]. One who is enraged,[124] does he punish his lover?

He was silent, and didn't say anything to them. They threw a scarf on him and were mocking him.

Rabbi Abbahu came and found them.

He said to them: "Why are you mocking him?"

They said to him: "Didn't you say that he is a great man, and he could not even tell us the interpretation of this verse!"

He said to them: "That which I said to you has to do with Mishnah, but with respect to the Scripture, I didn't say anything."

They said to him: "What is it different with respect to you that you know [Scripture also]?"

He said to them: "We who are located in your midst, take it upon ourselves and we study, but they do not study." (BT Avoda Zara 4a)

Following the principle set out by Saul Lieberman—that talmudic legend may be read as useful information for the history of the time and place of its production and not the time and place of which it speaks[125]—there is no way that this story, only attested in the Babylonian Talmud, should be taken to represent Palestinian reality. Its mere existence only there demonstrates that it does not, because the genre of encounters between Rabbis and *minim* is very rare in Palestinian sources, but very common in Babylonian texts, as Kalmin has recently shown.[126] Almost always these Babylonian narratives relate the confrontation between a Palestinian sage and a *min* of whatever variety. A story such as this may tell us something, therefore, about Babylonian reality in the fourth and fifth centuries.[127] In that time and space, this text explicitly testifies, Christians were no longer an internal threat to the integrity of the religious life-world of the Rabbis: "They [the Babylonians] do not study Bible, because you [the *minim*] are not found in their midst." Although this text is frequently read as indicating that there weren't Christians or Christianity in the Sassanian environs of the Babylonian Rabbis, this is not, I think, the only—or even the right—way to read it. Christianity may not have been the state religion, but it was certainly present, active, and in open dispute with the Jews there.[128] I would suggest, rather, seeing here an indication of separation of the two "religions." This is not to be taken as a sign that Christianity did not have powerful effects on the historical development of Judaism in Babylonia (and the reverse),[129] but only that, with the borders clearly established, Christianity was no longer considered a subversive danger for believing Jews. It is thus perhaps not surprising that, as we have seen in the previous chapters, it is in the Babylonian Talmud that early Palestinian Judaism comes to be re-presented as a "a society based on the doctrine that conflicting disputants may each be advancing the words of the living God." With the borders of unanimity secured, there are no more internal others (at least in theory).

In the imagination of the Rabbis, Judaism has been reconfigured as a grand coalition of differing theological and even halakhic views *within the clear and now uncontested borders of rabbinic Judaism*. It is this reconfigured *imaginaire* of a Jewish polity with no heresies and no heresiologies that Gerald Bruns has described: "From a transcendental standpoint, this [rabbinic] theory of authority is paradoxical because it is seen to hang on the heteroglossia of dialogue, on speaking with many voices, rather than on the logical principle of univocity, or speaking with one mind. Instead, the idea of speaking with one mind . . . is explicitly rejected; single-mindedness produces factionalism."[130] The Rabbis, in the end, reject and refuse the Christian definition of a religion, understood as a system of beliefs and practices to which one adheres voluntarily and defalcation from which results in one's becoming a heretic. At this moment, then, we first find the principle that has been ever since the touchstone of Jewish ecclesiology: "an Israelite, even though he sin, remains an Israelite," which we find only once in all of classical rabbinic literature, in the Babylonian Talmud and then in the name of a late amora (Sanhedrin 44a). This same watchword becomes nearly ubiquitous and foundational for later forms of rabbinic Judaism. There is now virtually no way that a Jew can stop being a Jew, since the very notion of heresy was finally rejected and Judaism (even the word is anachronistic) refused to be, in the end, a *religion*. For the Church, Judaism is a religion, but for the Jews, as I have stated in the introduction to this book, only occasionally, ambivalently, and strategically is it so. To add one more piquant bit to the material already adduced above, let me just mention that, when Jews teach Judaism in a department of religious studies, they are as likely to be teaching Yiddish literature or the history of the Nazi genocide as anything that might be said (in Christian terms) to be part of a Jewish religion!

Jonathan Boyarin writes, "The question of the imbalance between a totalizing categorical usage of the term 'diaspora' and the discourses within various diasporic formations that may not recognize that category leads us to the necessary recognition that whatever the criterion for judging our own discourse may be, it cannot rest on a simplistic notion of pluralist (different but in the same ways) tolerance."[131] Empowered by the Christian interpellation of Judaism as a religion, the Jews, nevertheless, significantly resisted the (ambiguous) tolerance enacted by the Theodosian Empire's emplacement of "a frontier all the more mysterious . . . because it is abstract, legal, ideal."[132] Refusing to be different in quite the same ways, not a religion, not quite, Judaism (including the bizarrely named Jewish orthodoxy of modernity) remained something else, neither quite here nor quite there. Among the various emblems of this different difference remains the fact that there are Christians who are Jews, or perhaps better put, Jews who are Christians, even up to this very day.

Concluding Political Postscript: A Fragment

"The role of the intellectual is not to tell others what they have to do. By what right would he do so? . . . The work of an intellectual is not to shape others' political will; it is, through the analysis that he carries out in his field, to question over and over again what is postulated as self-evident, to disturb people's mental habits, the way they do and think things, to dissipate what is familiar and accepted, to reexamine rules and institutions and on the basis of this re-problematization (in which he carries out his specific task as an intellectual) to participate in the formation of a political will (in which he has his role as citizen to play)."[1]

And Walter Benjamin has famously declared:

Whoever has emerged victorious participates to this day in the triumphal procession in which the present rulers step over those who are lying prostrate. According to traditional practice, the spoils are carried along in the procession. They are called cultural treasures, and a historical materialist views them with cautious detachment. For without exception the cultural treasures he surveys have an origin which he cannot contemplate without horror. They owe their existence not only to the efforts of the great minds and talents who have created them, but also to the anonymous toil of their contemporaries. There is no document of civilization which is not at the same time a document of barbarism. And just as such a document is not free of barbarism, barbarism taints also the manner in which it was transmitted from one owner to another. A historical materialist therefore dissociates himself from it as far as possible. He regards it as his task to brush history against the grain.[2]

Brushing history against the grain, however, does not mean losing sight of the tapestry when viewed along the grain. That is the practice of this book (successfully or not I cannot say: the baker cannot testify to his dough, say the Rabbis). Our religious cultural treasures of late antiquity are indeed monuments of barbarism, barbaric exclusion and repression of women and sexual minorities, exclusion and repression of those designated "heretics," perhaps some "Jewish" violence toward Christians, and, for sure, much Christian violence toward Jews. In exposing these, in reading the texts against the grain, I propose, however, that the goal is not to discard these products of "great minds and talents" but rather to perform the doubled operation that the Rabbis themselves recommend in another context: honor them and suspect them! There is beauty (and maybe even something like truth) in these textual practices and their products, something that offers us not only the possibility of "the triumphal procession in which the present rulers step over those who are lying prostrate," but something else as well, or even better—one hopes, instead, a way of appropriating these treasures for other practices and other forms of life.

Ah, voglio che questo sogno
sia la santa poesia
e l'ultimo bisogno
dell'esistenza mia.
Ecco . . . la nuova turba
al guardo mio si svela!

Arrigo Boito

Notes

Preface

1. If I am at all plausible in my reading, this category of "some Jews" may go historically very far back indeed; Daniel Boyarin. *Dying for God: Martyrdom and the Making of Christianity and Judaism*, The Lancaster/Yarnton Lectures in Judaism and Other Religions for 1998 (Stanford: Stanford University Press, 1999), 26–41. My own, perhaps dangerous, identification with Rabbi Eli'ezer is presumably clear by now.

2. Daniel Boyarin. *Unheroic Conduct: The Rise of Heterosexuality and the Invention of the Jewish Man*, Contraversions: Studies in Jewish Literature, Culture, and Society (Berkeley and Los Angeles: University of California Press, 1997), xiii–xxiv.

3. My colleague Prof. Ibrahim Muhawi writes to me in a personal communication: "Eastern Christianity has always had a bad time with the Western variety, beginning perhaps with the Crusades. But there is also something which is more than merely Eastern Christianity; there is also a Semitic Christianity (the same Semitic Christianity with which you deal in your book)—Arab (Eastern Orthodox, Greek Catholic, Coptic, Maronite), Chaldean, and a number of other offshoots. The alliance of certain brands of American Christianity with Zionism is at the same time an alliance against Arab Christians like me." I wish to thank him for this very important intervention. I was in danger of a very significant occlusion.

4. By writing "my Judaism," I hope to be evading the very essentialist trap that my book sets out to counter. I do not wish to be understood, however, as claiming that even "my" Judaism is a wholly politically correct thing; it is rabbinic Judaism warts and all, but no version of that ever incorporated the total disdain for any but Jewish lives and bodies that seems—I hope I am wrong—to characterize the lion's share of self-identifying Jews in the world today.

Chapter 1. Introduction

1. Jacques Derrida, *Glas*, trans. John P. Leavey Jr. and Richard Rand (Lincoln: University of Nebraska Press, 1990), 189b.

2. See Daniel Boyarin, *Dying for God: Martyrdom and the Making of Christianity and Judaism*, The Lancaster/Yarnton Lectures in Judaism and Other Religions for 1998 (Stanford: Stanford University Press, 1999), 93–130, in which an argument is made for people attending both synagogue and church in third-century Caesarea as the "smugglers" who transported discourses of martyrology in both directions across the "abstract, legal, and ideal" frontier between Judaism and Christianity. I would add here "Jewish Christian" communities, such as that of the Pseudo-Clementine productions.

3. I do not of course claim that terms such as *ethnicity* and *class* are unhistorical givens; I just use these terms as convenient shorthand for various modes of group identity-making.

4. Karen King has made the point that for early Christian writers "heresy" was always defined with respect to Judaism; too much Judaism, and you were a Judaizer, too little, a "gnostic" (*What Is Gnosticism?* [Cambridge, Mass.: Harvard University Press, 2003]).

5. Walter Bauer, Gerhard Krodel, and Robert A. Kraft, *Orthodoxy and Heresy in Earliest Christianity*, ed. Gerhard Krodel (Philadelphia: Fortress Press, 1971). For a concise, accurate, and illuminating account of the background and reception of Bauer, see Michel Desjardin, "Bauer and Beyond: On Recent Scholarly Discussions of Αἵρεσις in the Early Christian Era," *The Second Century* 8 (1991): 65–82.

6. Alain Le Boulluec, *La notion d'hérésie dans la littérature grecque IIᵉ–IIIᵉ siècles* (Paris: études Augustiniennes, 1985). See especially, building on Le Boulluec, Virginia Burrus, *The Making of a Heretic: Gender, Authority, and the Priscillianist Controversy*, Transformations of the Ancient World (Berkeley and Los Angeles: University of California Press, 1995); and J. Rebecca Lyman, "The Making of a Heretic: The Life of Origen in Epiphanius *Panarion* 64," *Studia Patristica* 31 (1997): 445–51.

7. Pace Thomas A. Robinson (*The Bauer Thesis Examined: The Geography of Heresy in the Early Christian Church*, Studies in the Bible and Early Christianity [Lewiston, N.Y.: Edwin Mellen Press, 1988], 4, n. 4), it is not the province of historians to inquire into theological truth. To the extent that such inquiry is an academic pursuit at all, it belongs to the theologians and not the historians.

8. This lucid summary of Le Boulluec's thesis is given by David T. Runia, "Philo of Alexandria and the Greek *Hairesis*-Model," *Vigiliae Christianae* 53, no. 2 (May 1999): 118.

9. Le Boulluec, *La notion*, 110. Runia, "Philo and *Hairesis*," 126, thinks he has unsettled Le Boulluec's claim via evidence that in Philo the term *hairesis* "implies condemnation." I do not see his argument at all, however. Philo writes in the text cited by Runia: "All the philosophies that have flourished in Greece and in other lands sought to discover the principles of nature, but were unable to gain a clear perception of even the slightest one. Here is the clear proof, namely the disagreements and discords and doctrinal differences of the practitioners of each *hairesis* who refute each other and are refuted in turn." This extract does not, in my opinion, show that the term *hairesis* had undergone the semantic transformation to "heresy." What Philo is saying here is that all of Greek philosophy is invalid, as evidenced by the *dissensio philosophorum*. All *hairesis* means here is "philosophical school"; it is Greek philosophy itself that is being condemned, not "heresy." Interestingly enough, Runia's own argument throughout the paper militates against seeing already in Philo the shift to "a heretical group that propounds false doctrine."

10. For the issue with "Judaism," see Chapters 2 and 3 below. With respect to "Gnosticism," falsely so-called, see Elaine Pagels, "Irenaeus, the 'Canon of Truth,' and the *Gospel of John*: 'Making a Difference' Through Hermeneutics and Ritual," *Vigiliae Christianae* 56, no. 4 (2002): 339–71; and especially J. Rebecca Lyman, "The Politics of Passing: Justin Martyr's Conversion as a Problem of 'Hellenization,'" in *Conversion in Late Antiquity and the Early Middle Ages*, ed. Anthony Grafton and Kenneth Mills (Rochester, N.Y.: University of Rochester Press, forthcoming), who interprets "Gnosticism" itself as a "polemical invention" of Justin and friends. See also Christoph Markschies, *Valentinus Gnosticus?*

Untersuchungen zur valentinianischen Gnosis mit einem Kommentar zu den Fragmenten Valentins, Wissenschaftliche Untersuchungen zum Neuen Testament (Tübingen: J. C. B. Mohr, 1992).

11. This suggestion is compatible with the work of Denise Kimber Buell, "Race and Universalism in Early Christianity," *Journal of Early Christian Studies* 10, no. 4 (Winter 2002): 429–68, as we are speaking of different centuries.

12. Timothy J. Horner, *Listening to Trypho: Justin Martyr's Dialogue Reconsidered*, Contributions to Biblical Exegesis and Theology (Leuven: Peeters, 2001), 8.

13. See also, partially anticipating Le Boulluec, H.-D. Altendorf, "Zum Stichwort: Rechtgläubigkeit und Ketzerei in ältesten Christentum," *Zeitschrift für Kirchengeschichte* 80, no. 1 (1969): 61–74.

14. Israel Jacob Yuval, *Two Nations in Your Womb: Perceptions of Jews and Christians* (in Hebrew) (Tel-Aviv: Alma/Am Oved, 2000), to appear also as *"Two Nations in Your Womb": Perceptions of Jews and Christians in the Middle Ages* (Berkeley and Los Angeles: University of California Press, 2003).

15. Yuval, *Nations*, 35–36.

16. So do Hermann Strack and Paul Billerbeck, *Kommentar zum Neuen Testament aus Talmud und Midrasch* (Munich: C. H. Beck, 1924), and a host of scholars in their wake (Yuval, *Nations*, 37, n. 33).

17. Yuval, *Nations*, 41.

18. Ibid., 50–52.

19. Naomi Koltun-Fromm, "Psalm 22's Christological Interpretive Tradition in Light of Christian Anti-Jewish Polemic," *Journal of Early Christian Studies* 6, no. 1 (Spring 1998): 37–57. And see Boyarin, *Dying for God*, 176–77, nn. 14–16.

20. For a similar view on the commonalities of the midrashic themes of the birth of the Messiah, see Galit Hasan-Rokem, *The Web of Life—Folklore in Rabbinic Literature: The Palestinian Aggadic Midrash Eikha Rabba*, trans. Batya Stein, Contraversions: Jews and Other Differences (Stanford, Calif.: Stanford University Press, 2000), 165 (Hebrew version). For a general theoretical perspective closer to the one that I adopt, see Galit Hasan-Rokem, "Narratives in Dialogue: A Folk Literary Perspective on Interreligious Contacts in the Holy Land in Rabbinic Literature of Late Antiquity," in *Sharing the Sacred: Religious Contacts and Conflicts in the Holy Land, First–Fifteenth Centuries CE*, ed. Guy Stroumsa and Arieh Kofsky (Jerusalem: Yad Ben Zvi, 1998), esp. 127; and Elchanan Reiner, "From Joshua to Jesus: The Transformation of a Biblical Story to a Local Myth: A Chapter in the Religious Life of the Galilean Jew," in *Sharing the Sacred: Religious Contacts and Conflicts in the Holy Land, First–Fifteenth Centuries CE*, ed. Guy Stroumsa and Arieh Kofsky (Jerusalem: Yad Ben Zvi, 1998), esp. 248–69; and my discussion in *Dying for God*, 10–12 and 17. That said, I would add, nevertheless, that I find in Yuval's work a number of compelling instances in which the rabbinic text seems to be responding to particular Christian interpretations, theologoumena, and practices.

21. Jacob Neusner, *Judaism and Christianity in the Age of Constantine: History, Messiah, Israel, and the Initial Confrontation*, Chicago Studies in the History of Judaism (Chicago: The University of Chicago Press, 1987).

22. Shaye J. D. Cohen, "A Virgin Defiled: Some Rabbinic and Christian Views on the Origins of Heresy," *Union Seminary Quarterly Review* 36, no. 1 (Fall 1980): 4; Desjardin, "Bauer and Beyond," 82.

23. Judith Lieu, "'I Am a Christian': Martyrdom and the Beginning of 'Christian'

Identity," in *Neither Jew Nor Greek? Constructing Christian Identity* (Edinburgh: T & T Clark, 2003).

24. Rosemary Radford Ruether, "Judaism and Christianity: Two Fourth-Century Religions," *Sciences Religieuses/Studies in Religion* 2 (1972): 1–10.

25. Ania Loomba, *Colonialism/postcolonialism*, New Critical Idiom (London: Routledge, 1998), 38–39.

26. Ibid., 54.

27. John J. Collins, "Cult and Culture: The Limits of Hellenization in Judea," in *Hellenism in the Land of Israel*, ed. John J. Collins and Gregory Sterling, Christianity and Judaism in Antiquity (Notre Dame, Ind.: University of Notre Dame, 2000), 39.

28. For this, if for no other reason, referring to the history of modern Hinduism as its Semiticization is both inaccurate and disturbing (Daniel Boyarin, "Jewish Cricket," *PMLA* 113, no. 1 [January 1998]: 40–45).

29. Judith P. Butler, *Excitable Speech: A Politics of the Performative* (New York: Routledge, 1997), 2.

30. Edward Schiappa, *The Beginnings of Rhetorical Theory in Classical Greece* (New Haven, Conn.: Yale University Press, 1999), 28–29.

31. Virginia Burrus, "Hailing Zenobia: Anti-Judaism, Trinitarianism, and John Henry Newman," *Culture and Religion* 3 (2002): 163–77.

32. Butler, *Excitable Speech*, 2.

33. Robert A. Markus, *The End of Ancient Christianity* (Cambridge: Cambridge University Press, 1990), 28.

34. Rowan Williams, "Does It Make Sense to Speak of Pre-Nicene Orthodoxy?" in *The Making of Orthodoxy: Essays in Honour of Henry Chadwick*, ed. Rowan Williams (Cambridge: Cambridge University Press, 1989), 3.

35. See also Amram Tropper, "*Tractate Avot* and Early Christian Succession Lists," in *The Ways That Never Parted*, ed. Peter Schaeffer (Berlin: Mohr Siebeck, 2003), for a convincing articulation of difference in the roles of heresiology within Christian proto-orthodox and rabbinic circles from nearly the very beginning.

36. We sometimes attempt in our language to naturalize this ambiguity, to reduce the shape-shifting quality of Judaism by drawing a distinction between Judaism and Jewishness, exploited to good effect in Shaye J. D. Cohen, *The Beginnings of Jewishness: Boundaries, Varieties, Uncertainties*, Hellenistic Culture and Society 31 (Berkeley and Los Angeles: University of California Press, 1998), but it needs to be emphasized that this parallels no distinction made from within any traditional Jewish discourse, to the best of my knowledge, at least until the nineteenth century.

37. Wilfred Cantwell Smith, *The Meaning and End of Religion* (London: SPCK, 1978); Talal Asad, *Genealogies of Religion: Discipline and Reasons of Power in Christianity and Islam* (Baltimore: Johns Hopkins University Press, 1993).

38. See too Vasiliki Limberis, "'Religion' as the Cipher for Identity: The Cases of Emperor Julian, Libanius, and Gregory Nazianzus," *Harvard Theological Review* 93, no. 4 (2000): 374–77.

39. Maurice Sachot, "Comment le Christianisme est-il devenu *religio*," *Revue des sciences religiuses* 59 (1985): 95–118; Maurice Sachot, "«*Religio/Superstitio*»," Historique d'une subversion et d'un retournement," *Revue d'histoire des religions* 208, no. 4 (1991): 355–94. See also Eric Laupot, "Tacitus' Fragment 2: The Anti-Roman Movement of the *Christiani* and the Nazoreans," *Vigiliae Christianae* 54, no. 3 (2000): 233–47, who argues that the

word *religio* has been susbstituted for an original *superstitio* in a Tacitean fragment re-produced in Sulpicius Severus's Chronicle. See also the interesting formulation of Frend: "After circa A.D. 100 there was less of a tendency for Christians to claim to be Israel and more of a tendency to contrast Christianity and Judaism as separate religions. Christian-ity claimed to be heir to the universalist claims of Judaism. 'Catholic' or 'universal' was applied to the church for the first time. One can recognize the transition in Ignatius's let-ters," W. H. C. Frend, *The Rise of Christianity* (Philadelphia: Fortress Press, 1984), 124.

40. Seth Schwartz, *Imperialism and Jewish Society from 200 B.C.E. to 640 C.E.* (Prince-ton, N.J.: Princeton University Press, 2001), 179.

41. For a similar argument with respect to the emergence of sexuality as such a dis-crete category, see David M. Halperin, "How to Do the History of Male Homosexuality," *GLQ: A Journal of Lesbian and Gay Studies* 6, no. 1 (2000): 87–123. This must be distin-guished, however, from the concept of precursor.

42. Denis Guénoun, *Hypothèses sur l'Europe: Un essai de philosophie* (Belfort: Circé, 2000), 117.

43. David Runia shows this explicitly in the work of Isidore of Pelusium who uses Judaism and polytheism in a topos similar to that of Gregory of Nyssa, who describes or-thodoxy as the perfect midpoint between Sabellianism and Arianism ("'Where, Tell Me, Is the Jew . . . ?': Basil, Philo and Isidore of Pelusium," *Vigiliae Christianae* 46, no. 2 [June 1992]: 172–89). See too on this question Le Boulluec, *La notion*, 193–208. In this passage, Le Boulluec explicitly writes that the hermeneutical effort being exerted by Justin is to protect the Bible from the assaults of the gnostics (for difficulties with this precise de-nomination, see Pagels, "Irenaeus," 340–45). This would support the very hypothetical suggestion that we may have some of Justin's lost *Syntagma* preserved in certain passages of the *Dialogue* (Pierre Prigent, *Justin et l'Ancien Testament: L'argumentation Scripturaire du traité de Justin contre toutes les hérésies comme source principale du Dialogue avec Tryphon et de la première Apologie* [Paris: J. Gabalda, 1964]).

44. Schwartz, *Jewish Society*, 179.

45. My quotation marks here indicate simply my awareness that, while analogous to later colonialism, the situation of the Christian empire vis-à-vis the Jews was not, of course, the same.

46. Homi K. Bhabha, *The Location of Culture* (London: Routledge, 1994), 110–11.

47. David Berger, *The Rebbe, the Messiah, and the Scandal of Orthodox Indifference* (Portland, Ore.: Littman Library of Jewish Civilization, 2001).

48. David Chidester, *Savage Systems: Colonialism and Comparative Religion in Southern Africa* (Charlottesville: University Press of Virginia, 1996), 4.

49. Ibid., 22–23.

50. R. P. C. Hanson, *The Search for the Christian Doctrine of God: The Arian Con-troversy, 318–381 A.D.* (Edinburgh: T & T Clark, 1988).

51. Rudolf Lorenz, *Arius judaizans? Untersuchungen zur dogmengeshichtlichen Einordnung des Arius* (Göttingen: Vandenhoek and Ruprecht, 1979). For a notable exam-ple of this discursive phenomenon, see Gregory of Nyssa's life of Moses (Gregory, *The Life of Moses*, trans. Abraham J. Malherbe and Everett Ferguson, preface by John Meyen-dorff [New York: Paulist Press, 1978], 184 and n. 294).

52. I think that this point is important for understanding the virulence of the Quar-todeciman controversy at this time, as it is also, I think, largely about establishing a Christianity that is completely separate from Judaism.

53. In the Middle Ages, as shall be discussed below in Chapters 4–6, there was as rich and technical a theological controversy on the nature of godhead among Jews as there had been in late antiquity among Christians, yet it did not issue in a structure of orthodoxy and heresy.

54. As elegant an exemplification of the hybridity of hybridity itself as one could want can be found in the fact that Rebecca Lyman reads Justin under the sign of post-colonial hybridity ("Politics"). Note especially her remark: "Ironically, due to Justin's and later Irenaeus' successful polemics about 'deviant' teachers, we hesitate to give him as a 'teacher' a central place in the construction of orthodox Christian identity."

55. Arieh Kofsky, "Mamre: A Case of a Regional Cult?" in *Sharing the Sacred: Religious Contacts and Conflicts in the Holy Land, First–Fifteenth Centuries* CE, ed. Guy Stroumsa and Arieh Kofsky (Jerusalem: Yad Ben Zvi, 1998), 19–30.

56. Which is not to assert, of course, that it is unknown in or even atypical of other times.

57. For the persistence of the "monster" as a modern trope for human hybrids, see Kipling and Carlyle as quoted in Robert Young, *Colonial Desire: Hybridity in Theory, Culture, and Race* (London: Routledge, 1995), 3, 5 respectively.

58. Bhabha, *Location*, 38–39, and see Chidester, *Savage*, xv.

59. Bhabha, *Location*, 33.

60. Young, *Desire*, 161.

61. Language adopted from the otherwise nearly scurrilous Marjorie Perloff, "Cultural Liminality/aesthetic Closure?: The 'Interstitial Perspective' of Homi Bhabha," http://wings.buffalo.edu/epc/authors/perloff/bhabha/html.

62. Bhabha, *Location*, 13.

63. Asad, *Genealogies*, 17.

64. Young, *Desire*, 19.

65. For other versions of problematization of "pure precolonial" selves as projected by certain versions of postcolonial analyses, see Loomba, *Colonialism/postcolonialism*, 181–82. Richard King argues that "Bhabha's notion of 'hybridity' implies that the colonial space involves the interaction of two originally 'pure' cultures (the British/European and the native) that are only rendered ambivalent once they are brought into direct contact with each other" (*Orientalism and Religion Postcolonial Theory, India and the Mystic East* [London: Routledge, 1999], 204). While I am somewhat doubtful as to whether this critique is properly applied to Bhabha, it does seem relevant to me in considering the post-colonial model for reading Judaism and Christianity in antiquity, as they are surely always/already hybridized with respect to each other.

66. Schwartz, *Jewish Society*, 184.

67. This is a point that will be further developed below. I do not enter here into the question as to whether *Christiani* was a derogatory epithet taken by the Christians themselves as an instance of reverse discourse (the view of Harold Mattingly, "The Origin of the Name Christiani," *Journal of Theological Studies* n.s. 9 [1958]: 26–37, to which view I am inclined) or a name that they named themselves originally (the view of Elias Bickerman, "The Name of the Christians," *Harvard Theological Review* 42 [1949]: 109–24). Most recently, supporting Mattingly's position, see Lieu, "I Am." See also Judith Lieu, *Image & Reality: The Jews in the World of the Christians in the Second Century* (Edinburgh: T & T Clark, 1996), 23–24.

68. Buell, "Race."

69. For a parallel continuum between Jews who "were to all intents and purposes standard Greco-Roman pagans," and "hard core representatives of Judaism, mainly the rabbis," see Schwartz, *Jewish Society*, 176. Moreover, "most Jews were caught in between."

70. It should be emphasized that wave theory is the historical or diachronic complement of dialect geography. For discussion of the latter and the fuzzy boundaries that it indicates between dialects, see William Labov, "The Boundaries of Words and Their Meanings," in *New Ways of Analyzing Variation in English*, ed. Charles-James N. Bailey and Roger W. Shuy (Washington, D.C.: Georgetown University Press, 1973), 344–47.

71. Mary Louise Pratt, *Imperial Eyes: Travel Writing and Transculturation* (London: Routledge, 1992).

72. See however above at n. 65.

73. "Hellenistic ways of life, thought and expression were integral to Jewish Palestinian culture from at least the mid third century [B.C.] on, and these tendencies affected Pharisaism and later Rabbinic writings. Hellenistic schools were especially influential on Jewish modes of organization and expression. The emergence of definable sects, Pharisees, Sadducees, etc. and more importantly the attention given to them fits most comfortably into the Greco-Roman world with its recognized philosophical schools, religious societies and craft assocations" (Anthony Saldarini, *Scholastic Rabbinism: A Literary Study of the Fathers According to Rabbi Nathan* [Chico, Calif.: Scholars Press, 1982], 19). My only emendation to this important statement would be to abandon language of "influence" and simply understand that "Judaism" is itself a species of Hellenism. See the formulation in Saldarini, *Scholastic*, 21, which comes closer, I think, to this perspective. Cf. most recently Lee I. Levine, *Judaism & Hellenism in Antiquity: Conflict or Confluence*, The Samuel & Althea Stroum Lectures in Jewish Studies (Seattle: University of Washington Press, 1998). In this vein, see Erich S. Gruen, *Heritage and Hellenism: The Reinvention of Jewish Tradition*, Hellenistic Culture and Society 30 (Berkeley and Los Angeles: University of California Press, 1998), esp. 292: "The [Palestinian] Jews were not so much permeated by the culture of the Greeks as they were a part of it." Also most recently Schwartz, *Jewish Society*.

74. Such is the compelling argument of Schwartz, *Jewish Society*, from which I have learned much. I am grateful to Prof. Schwartz for providing me a copy of his book prior to publication.

75. Young, *Desire*, 65.

76. Jonathan M. Hall, *Ethnic Identity in Greek Antiquity* (Cambridge: Cambridge University Press, 1997).

77. To be sure, he is careful to ascribe this version of wave theory to a single scholar, W. F. Wyatt (Hall, *Ethnic Identity*, 166).

78. Labov, "Boundaries," 347.

79. Hall, *Ethnic Identity*, 172.

80. Ibid., 135.

81. For this distinction, see Louis Althusser, "Ideology and Ideological State Apparatuses (Notes Toward an Investigation)," in *Mapping Ideology*, Mapping (London: Verso, 1994), 100–140.

82. Mary Beard, John A. North, and S. R. F. Price, *Religions of Rome* (Cambridge: Cambridge University Press, 1998), 249.

83. For this connection, see George Lakoff, *Women, Fire, and Dangerous Things: What Categories Reveal About the Mind* (Chicago: University of Chicago Press, 1987), 15.

84. My application of this theory to these issues has been partially anticipated by Beard et al., who cite R. Needham, "Polythetic Classification: Convergence and Consequences," *Man* n.s. 10 (1975): 349–69.

85. Chana Kronfeld, *On the Margins of Modernism: Decentering Literary Dynamics*, Contraversions (Berkeley and Los Angeles: University of California Press, 1996), 28. I wish specifically to thank Prof. Kronfeld for suggesting this direction, which has proved very fruitful for me, and for much else.

86. Just in case my formulation has not done so already, I wish to make absolutely clear that the distinction that I am drawing here is not between "folk" and "scientific" modes of classification but between the classifications of groups of people and things that people do and the classifications of nonhuman objects. These are related cognitive tasks, of course, but also significantly different. See also Robert D. Baird, *Category Formation and the History of Religions* (The Hague: Mouton, 1971).

87. Kronfeld, *Margins*, 27.

88. Albert I. Baumgarten, "Literary Evidence for Jewish Christianity in the Galilee," in *The Galilee in Late Antiquity*, ed. Lee I. Levine (New York: Jewish Theological Seminary of America, 1992), 39–50.

89. For the general perspective see Alan F. Segal, *The Other Judaisms of Late Antiquity*, Brown Judaic Studies 127 (Atlanta, Ga.: Scholars Press, 1987).

90. Kronfeld, *Margins*, 29.

91. For a good general introduction to this theory, see Lakoff, *Women, Fire*, 12–58.

92. Eleanor Rosch, *Basic Objects in Natural Categories* (Berkeley: University of California, Language Behavior Research Laboratory, 1975).

93. Kronfeld, *Margins*, 29.

94. Lakoff, *Women, Fire*, 44–45.

95. The situation of law-observing "Jewish Christians" in Justin's *Dialogue* would be a case in point. "People of the Land" in rabbinic parlance is another.

96. As Kronfeld remarks, "turkey" is the best example of bird on Thanksgiving.

97. Kronfeld, *Margins*, 30.

98. Lakoff, *Women, Fire*, 45.

99. Another riveting analogy comes to the fore: Kronfeld writes, "My investigations of Hebrew and Yiddish modernist poetry have consistently presented a fascinating paradox: that although many modernists defined very clearly their poetic principles (typically formulated in rather strong terms by group manifestoes or individual aesthetic credos), the best examples—or prototypes—that came to represent these trends (individual poets or even individual works) are often quite atypical of or only marginally consistent with the principles of the group" (Kronfeld, *Margins*, 31). One might revealingly compare to this, I think, a paradox uncovered by Shaye Cohen, who shows that the prototypical converts to Judaism (from "paganism") in the Talmuds do not follow the explicit rules laid down for conversion (Shaye J. D. Cohen, "The Conversion of Antoninus," in *The Talmud Yerushalmi and Graeco-Roman Culture*, ed. Peter Schäfer, Texte und Studien zum Antiken Judentum 71 [Tübingen: Mohr Siebeck, 1998], 167 and passim). Cohen could have made, I think, further progress on analyzing this paradox (to which he merely points) by considering comments such as the following: "Focusing on these modernist prototypes tends to foreground one or two highly salient poetic features which fulfill or match some particular (artistic, linguistic, ideological, or social) need. In each case, there are specific reasons, which need to be reconstructed and analyzed, why a particular fea-

ture came to be perceived as exemplary within the particular conditions for the creation and reception of a particular brand of modernism at a particular historical and cultural juncture. This contextually motivated salience raising creates, among other things, a series of 'deviant prototypes,' artistic paragons and exemplary texts that do not centrally belong to any trend but have nevertheless come to represent it" (Kronfeld, *Margins*, 31–32).

100. Jerome, *Correspondence*, ed. Isidorus Hilberg, Corpus Scriptorum Ecclesiasticorum Latinorum (Vienna: Verlag der Österreichischen Akademie der Wissenschaften, 1996), vol. 55, 381–82. For discussion, see below, Chapter 7.

101. One of the interesting phenomena about religious categories is the ways that subgroups will mutually deny each other's salience or centrality as member of the group. We might think that "Pharisee" is a Jew if anyone is a Jew (just as integer is a number if anything is a number), but it seems that (on the Talmud's account itself), there were others who would have denied that claim, because by believing the resurrection of the dead, Pharisees were rendering themselves less Jewish than others! Interestingly, this feature, believing in resurrection of the dead, is taken as absolutely necessary for being a Jew by some non-Christian Jews and for being a Christian by some Christians and denied by some of both. In other words, we have a doubly complicated system here, for while a group such as the Fox Indians (example from Lakoff, *Women, Fire*, 23–24) may have complicated rules for determining who is an "uncle," with graded salience of prototypicality in the category, in our case there are, in effect, competing groups claiming the right to be called "uncle" or not or to be "better" uncles than others. The semantic situation remains, nevertheless, the same. It is fascinating that one of the characteristic claims of heresiologists is that they are "Christians" while others are hyphenated in some way, e.g., Valentinian Christians; in other words that the claim is that "we" are the prototype itself. Similarly, the Rabbis' name for their "heretics," "kinds" (מינים) can be read as serving to imply that "we" are the prototype of Jew, while they, by being "kinds" of Jews are less salient, less centrally members of the category. This kind of semantics gives us tools for understanding the complexity of the discourses of religious categorization.

102. J. L. Austin, *Philosophical Papers.* (Oxford: Clarendon Press, 1961), 72.

103. This gives us a way of making sense of the fact that it was precisely the discourse of orthodoxy that proved dominant in the history of the Church without assuming in any way the inevitability of such a telos owing to the content of orthodox doctrines, which anyway, as has been noted, contradict each other. Case in point: Justin's "heretical" chiliasm.

104. Lakoff, *Women, Fire*, 118.

105. For something like this claim, working however, out of a somewhat different theoretical model, see Hasan-Rokem, "Narratives in Dialogue."

106. Louis Althusser, "Ideology and Ideological State Apparatuses (Notes Towards an Investigation)," in *Lenin and Philosophy, and Other Essays* ([London]: New Left Books, 1971), 166.

107. Loomba, *Colonialism/postcolonialism*, 37.

108. The scare quotes on "ethnicity" are simply to remind myself that I do not mean by this anything quite like the modern sense of this term but something closely related to the ancient senses of both *ethnos* and *genos*.

109. Allen Brent, "Diogenes Laertius and the Apostolic Succession," *Journal of Ecclesiastical History* 44, no. 3 (July 1993): 367–89.

110. For this process, see, e.g., Charles Kannengiesser, "Alexander and Arius of Alexandria: The Last Ante-Nicene Theologians," *Compostellanum* 35, no. 1–2 (1990): 391–403.

111. Jeffrey L. Rubenstein, *The Culture of the Babylonian Talmud* (forthcoming).

112. This notion of differentiation via different responses to the same problem which I have developed since *Carnal Israel: Reading Sex in Talmudic Culture*, The New Historicism: Studies in Cultural Poetics 25 (Berkeley and Los Angeles: University of California Press, 1993) turns out to be an important part of the work of Niklas Luhmann, *Love as Passion: The Codification of Intimacy*, Cultural Memory in the Present (Stanford, Calif.: Stanford University Press, 1998), 10, which came to my attention far too late to be incorporated into this book. I won't make that mistake again (with Luhmann).

Chapter 2. Justin's Dialogue with the Jews

1. Timothy J. Horner, *Listening to Trypho: Justin Martyr's Dialogue Reconsidered*, Contributions to Biblical Exegesis and Theology (Leuven: Peeters, 2001).

2. This point of view provides, perhaps, a way of accommodating what might otherwise seem an extreme and implausible view expressed by Pierre Prigent, *Justin et l'Ancien Testament: L'argumentation Scripturaire du traité de Justin contre toutes les hérésies comme source principale du Dialogue avec Tryphon et de la première Apologie* (Paris: J. Gabalda, 1964), that the whole issue of Trypho and Judaism is just a sideshow in the *Dialogue*, and that it is, in fact, a text based entirely on Justin's otherwise lost (except in Irenaeus, according to Le Boulluec) *Syntagma Against the Heresies*. Once we see, however, that the heresiological project and the project of construction of a Christianity separate from Judaism are deeply imbricated with each other, we can capture Prigent's insights without making the counterintuitive step of ignoring Trypho and his Judaism. Note that the argument holds even if we accept Horner's recent, provocative, and highly attractive hypothesis (in *Trypho*) that the *Dialogue* as we have it is a composite produced by Justin out of an earlier Trypho text of his and a later rewriting. Indeed, since much of the "heresiological" matter does not appear in the Trypho sections, we might combine Horner's and Prigent's insights, seeing the text as a hybrid between the original Tryphonic dialogue and a rewritten or, at any rate, cannibalized *Syntagma*, thus dramatizing the argument of the integral and essential joining of the two discourses, precisely by Justin's production of such a hybrid text out of his earlier works.

3. This is not unlike strategies analyzed in Judith Lieu, "'I Am a Christian': Martyrdom and the Beginning of 'Christian' Identity," in *Neither Jew nor Greek? Constructing Christian Identity* (Edinburgh: T & T Clark, 2003). As Lieu points out, early Greek Jewish martyrology has such markers as adherence to kashruth (dietary rules) as its fulcrum of identity. See Tessa Rajak, "Dying for the Law: The Martyr's Portrait in Jewish-Greek Literature," in *Portraits: Biographical Representation in the Greek and Latin Literature of the Roman Empire*, ed. M. J. Edwards and Simon Swain (Oxford: Clarendon Press, 1997), 39–67. It is doubly fascinating, therefore, to observe that in later rabbinic Jewish literature the crux of the martyrology is precisely a declaration of identity through faith, the recitation of the "Hear O Israel," and not an attempt to force Rabbi Akiva, for instance, to eat something not kosher. I have discussed this point extensively in *Dying for God:*

Martyrdom and the Making of Christianity and Judaism, The Lancaster/Yarnton Lectures in Judaism and Other Religions for 1998 (Stanford, Calif.: Stanford University Press, 1999), chapter 4.

4. I have slightly modified the translation for clarity.

5. A. Lukyn Williams, ed. and trans., *Justin Martyr: The Dialogue with Trypho*, Translations of Christian Literature (London: SPCK, 1930), 265–66. Justin, *Dialogus cum Tryphone*, ed. Miroslav Marcovich, Patristische Texte und Studien 47 (Berlin: Walter de Gruyter, 1997), 292–93. I am grateful to Elliot Wolfson, who reminded me of the importance of this passage.

6. This would eventually develop into the theology associated with Marcellus of Ancyra in the fourth century.

7. Contra Shlomo Pines, "God, the Glory and the Angels According to a Theological System of the Second Century," in Hebrew, *Jerusalem Studies in Jewish Thought* 6, no. 3–4 (1987): 4–5, who claims that Justin is arguing against Jews here as well. Had Justin intended Jews here, he would have said so. On the other hand, it was a virtual topos (to be sure, a slightly later one) of Christian heresiologists to connect Christian dynamic modalism with Judaism, as Justin is implicitly doing here according to my reading.

8. Cf. Judith Lieu, *Image & Reality: The Jews in the World of the Christians in the Second Century* (Edinburgh: T & T Clark, 1996), 147, on Justin's use of the same terminology to attack Jews and heretics. I mostly agree with Lieu's interpretation of this phenomenon, but I dissent at some points. For Justin's successor Irenaeus and his own double articulation of orthodoxy twixt Judaism and heresy, see now the very important Elaine Pagels, "Irenaeus, the 'Canon of Truth,' and the *Gospel of John*: 'Making a Difference' Through Hermeneutics and Ritual," *Vigiliae Christianae* 56, no. 4 (2002): 368. I shall not be treating Irenaeus in this book but think that there is nothing in his work that would contradict the thesis presented here.

9. Οὐ γὰρ ὅπερ ἡ παρ' ὑμῖν λεγομενη αἱρεσι δογματιζει φαιην ἀν εγω αληθες ειναι, η οι εκεινης διδασκαλοι δύνανται.

10. Williams, *Dialogue*, 129; Justin, *Dialogus cum Tryphone*, 176–77, emphasis added.

11. I am grateful for the help of Erich Gruen and Chava Boyarin in construing this passage, although neither is responsible for my interpretation. Cf. the old translation in the AN Fathers edition: "For I would not say that the dogma of that heresy which is said to be among you is true, or that the teachers of it can prove that [God] spoke to angels, or that the human frame was the workmanship of angels" (Justin Martyr, *Dialogue with Trypho*, vol. 1: The apostolic fathers—Justin Martyr—Irenaeus, of *The Ante-Nicene Fathers: Translations of the Writings of the Fathers Down to A.D. 325*, ed. Alexander Roberts and James Donaldson [Grand Rapids, Mich.: William B. Eerdmans, 1989], 228). David Runia translates: "For personally I do not think the explanation is true which the so-called sect among you declares, nor are the teachers of that sect able to prove that he spoke to angels or that the human body is the creation of angels" (David T. Runia, "'Where, Tell Me, Is the Jew . . . ?': Basil, Philo and Isidore of Pelusium," *Vigiliae Christianae* 46, no. 2 [June 1992]: 178).

12. For Luke, see Hubert Cancik, "The History of Culture, Religion, and Institutions in Ancient Historiography: Philological Observations Concerning Luke's History," *Journal of Biblical Literature* 116, no. 4 (1997): 677, 688.

13. Marcel Simon, "From Greek Hairesis to Christian Heresy," in *Mélanges R. M. Grant, Early Christian Literature and the Classical Intellectual Tradition*, ed. W. R.

Schoedel and R. L. Wilken, Théologie Historique 53 (Paris: Éditions Beauchesne, 1979), 106.

14. It is overlooked in Jarl Fossum, "Gen 1,26 and 2,7 in Judaism, Samaritanism, and Gnosticism," *Journal for the Study of Judaism* 16, no. 2 (1989): 202–39, and recently in the excellent Menahem Kister, "'Let Us Make a Man'—Observations on the Dynamics of Monotheism," in Hebrew, in *Issues in Talmudic Research: Conference Commemorating the Fifth Anniversary of the Passing of Ephraim E. Urbach, 2 December 1996* (Jerusalem: Israel Academy of Sciences, 2001), 28–65.

15. Cf. Simon, "Hairesis," 106 and Alain Le Boulluec, *La Notion d'hérésie dans la littérature grecque IIe–IIIe siècles* (Paris: études Augustiniennes, 1985), 1:78. Both consider Justin's *hairesis* here as unidentifiable. Furthermore, David Runia writes, "If Justin's evidence is taken seriously, at least one branch [of *minim*] represents a Gnosticizing group within Judaism, whose negative attitude to material creation encourages them to introduce angels into the interpretation of the creation account" (Runia, "Where is the Jew," 179). Given the interpretation of this verse in Bereshit Rabbah, cited by Runia himself, this conclusion is hard to maintain. I detect no phantom gnostics here. See also Ephraim E. Urbach, *The Sages: Their Concepts and Beliefs*, trans. Israel Abrahams (Jerusalem: Magnes Press, 1975), 203–8, who cites the Justin passage but seems not to have seen the relevance of the Mekhilta to it.

16. J. Z. Lauterbach, ed. and trans., *Mekilta DeRabbi Ishmael* (1934; reprint, Philadelphia: Jewish Publication Society, 1961), 1:248.

17. See Menahem Kahana, "The Critical Editions of *Mekhilta De-Rabbi Ishmael* in the Light of the Genizah Fragments," in Hebrew, *Tarbiz* 55, no. 4 (Fall 1985): 499–515. He shows that ancient mss. preserve traditions from which it might appear that Papos/Papias maintained "gnosticizing" views, a not irrelevant point for our comparison here with Justin. (See, however, Kister, "'Let Us,'" 34.) Note that it is precisely with reference to Gen. 3:22 that the "heretical" view is attributed in both Justin and the Mekhilta, while the interpretation that Gen. 1:26, "Let us make man," is addressed to angels can be found in the "orthodox" rabbinic voice of Bereshit Rabbah 8, as pointed out in the important Runia, "Where is the Jew." On the Justin passage, see Kister, "'Let Us,'" 42–43, as well. Kister observes that the rabbinic formulation "God took counsel with the angels" constitutes a mitigation of the Logos-theological view (expressed by Justin) that God actually had a partner in the creation of Adam. Note that this "solution" was unavailable for 3:22, which explains, perhaps, why Papos's view was considered heresy, even though it seems closely related to the "orthodox" Bereshit Rabbah statement. Particularly impressive is Kister's brilliant suggestion that the speaker in Bereshit Rabbah who says that "God spoke to his heart" intends God's hypostasized Wisdom, or Logos (Kister, "'Let Us,'" 45–46). For reasons that should be obvious, I would not agree, however, to Kister's strong nexus between Justin and the *Timaeus*. Kister himself supplies a better explanation on "'Let Us,'" 53, namely, that the Jewish Logos/Sophia doctrine grew up in Second Temple theology as a way of deflecting polytheistic understandings, out of reading Genesis with Proverbs 8. See also M. J. Edwards, "Justin's Logos and the Word of God," *Journal of Early Christian Studies* 3, no. 3 (Fall 1995): 261–80; and Virginia Burrus, "Creatio Ex Libidine: Reading Ancient Logos Differantly," *Other Testaments: Derrida in Religion* (London: Routledge, 2004), on this point. Cf. BT Sanhedrin 38b, where "heretical" interpretation of Gen. 1:26 as implying two creators is "refuted." See too the following: Hans-Martin Schenke, *Der Gott "Mensch" in der Gnosis ein religionsgeschichtlicher Beitrag zur*

Diskussion über die paulinische Anschauung von der Kirche als Leib Christi. (Göttingen: Vandenhoeck and Ruprecht, 1962), 120–43; McL. R. Wilson, "The Early History of the Exegesis of Gen. 1:26," *Studia Patristica* 1 (1957): 420–37; Leslie W. Barnard, *Justin Martyr: His Life and Thought* (London: Cambridge University Press, 1967).

18. In other words, I am saying that this text can certainly not be dated before Rabbi Akiva and possibly could be later. Assuming a dating, then, sometime between the mid–second century (or a bit earlier) and the late third is reasonable. Looking for discursive developments from about the middle of that period, we would land somewhere in the late second century, roughly the time of Justin. For another similar parallel between Justin and the Mekhilta, see discussion in Horner, *Trypho*, 143–44, and earlier Marc Hirshman, *A Rivalry of Genius: Jewish and Christian Biblical Interpretation in Late Antiquity*, trans. Batya Stein, SUNY Series in Judaica: Hermeneutics, Mysticism, and Religion (Albany: State University of New York Press, 1996), 55–59; and see too David Rokeah, *Justin Martyr and the Jews*, Jewish and Christian Perspectives Series (Leiden: Brill, 2002), 35–42, the argument of which I find less than compelling. Once again, it is Justin who provides suggestive evidence for the antiquity of Mekhiltan traditions and not the opposite. Horner makes the lovely point that Trypho's knowledge of rabbinic traditions seems less than that of Justin, and "in fact, if he [Trypho] were to display an insider's knowledge alongside his other characteristics, this might compromise our belief in his authenticity because it would be possible to assume that Justin imposed this knowledge on the character" (Horner, *Trypho*, 145).

19. Even in his *Jewish Sects at the Time of Jesus* (Minneapolis, Minn.: Fortress Press, 1967), 85–107, where he discusses the entire Justinian catalogue of Jewish heresies, Simon ignores Justin's mention of the Pharisees, so set is he on his notion that orthodox Judaism at this time is consubstantial with Pharisaism.

20. Who also deny the resurrection of the dead and are, therefore, singled out. See Le Boulluec, *La notion*, 71–72.

21. Following the conjecture Ἑλληλιανῶν (accepted in Justin, *Dialogus cum Tryphone*, 209) which gives "Hellelians" and not "Hellenians" as Williams has it. To this, compare the text from the Tosefta which refers to the Shammaites and the Hillelites as having divided the Torah into two Torahs, which will be discussed below in Chapter 7. See also for discussion Daniel Gershonson and Giles Quispel, "'Meristae,'" *Vigiliae Christianae* 12 (1958): 19–26; Matthew Black, "The Patristic Accounts of Jewish Sectarianism," *Bulletin of the John Rylands Library* 41, no. 2 (March 1959): 285–303; Simon, *Sects*, 74–85; Barnard, *Justin*, 49–52.

22. I would take "Genistae and Meristae" to be a Greek calque on the Tosefta's *minim weparošim*, i.e., as those who separate themselves (this passage of the Tosefta will be discussed below in the next chapter). For μερισμός as a term of art in (proto)heresiology, see Ignatius's Philadelphians 2:1 (William R. Schoedel, *Ignatius of Antioch: A Commentary on the Letters of Ignatius of Antioch*, ed. Helmut Koester, trans. and ed. William R. Schoedel, Hermeneia—a Critical and Historical Commentary on the Bible [Philadelphia: Fortress Press, 1985], 197). Cp. Gershonson and Quispel, "'Meristae.'" The Galileans can plausibly be identified with the *minim gliliim* (Galilean heretics) of the Mishna Yadayim, a reading found only in manuscripts of the Mishna, as observed by Yaakov Sussmann, "The history of halakha and the Dead Sea Scrolls: Preliminary observations on *Miqsat Ma'ase Ha-torah* (4QMMT)," *Tarbiz* 59, no. 1–2 (Spring 1990): 51. Sussman does not connect them with Justin's notice here. These Baptists are almost surely the "morn-

ing baptizers" mentioned as heretics in the Tosefta Yadayim 2:20 (M. S. Zuckermandel, ed., *Tosephta: Based on the Erfurt and Vienna Codices, with Lieberman, Saul, "Supplement" to the Tosephta*, in Hebrew [Jerusalem: Bamberger and Wahrmann, 1937], 684). The net result is that Justin seems to have had very good knowledge of Jewish heresiology, indeed, even of some of its obscure corners. This increases my confidence in his knowledge of matters Jewish and even rabbinic in his time.

23. Williams, *Dialogue*, 169–71; Justin, *Dialogus cum Tryphone*, 208–9. For the crucial (Platonic) distinction between being called a Jew and being one, see Shaye J. D. Cohen, *The Beginnings of Jewishness: Boundaries, Varieties, Uncertainties*, Hellenistic Culture and Society 31 (Berkeley and Los Angeles: University of California Press, 1998), 60–61. See, on this passage, Le Boulluec, *La notion*, 71, who considers that "La représentation hérésiologique a cependant besoin de déformer la conception juive des divers courants religieux pour attendre son efficacité entière." In my view, this is less of a deformation than Le Boulluec would have it.

24. Shaye J. D. Cohen, "The Significance of Yavneh: Pharisees, Rabbis, and the End of Jewish Sectarianism," *Hebrew Union College Annual* 55 (1984): 29.

25. Ibid., 49.

26. Black, "Patristic"; Barnard, *Justin*, 50–52. See also Le Boulluec, *La notion*, 72: "La suggestion de M. Black . . . est tout à fair fantaisiste."

27. Earlier, Justin's explanation of the origins of the philosophers' *haireseis* bears some relation to this topos: "But the reason why [philosophy] has become a hydra of many heads I should like to explain. It happened that they who first handled philosophy, and for this reason became famous, were followed by men who made no investigation after truth, but were only amazed at their patience and self-restraint and their unfamiliar diction, and supposed that whatever each learned from his own teacher was true. And then they, when they had handed on to their successors all such things, and other like them, were themselves called by the name borne by the originator of the teaching" (*Dialogue* 2.2, Williams, *Dialogue*, 4). The implication of this statement is, of course, that there is "philosophy" and there are the *haireseis* (although the term is not used here), named after the divergent originators of each school. Of course, from the point of view of the Rabbis, the name *Christian* would be just such an "other name." See also CTh 16.5.6: "the contamination of the Photinian pestilence, the poison of the Arian sacrilege, the crime of the Eunomian perfidy, and the sectarian monstrosities, *abominable because of the ill-omened names of their authors*, shall be abolished even from the hearing of men." Clyde Pharr, *The Theodosian Code and Novels, and the Sirmondian Constitutions: A Translation with Commentary, Glossary, and Bibliography*, in collaboration with Theresa Sherrer Davidson and Mary Brown Pharr, introd. by C. Dickerman Williams ([Princeton, N.J.]: Princeton University Press, 1952), 451 (emphasis added).

28. See 1 Corinthians 1:10–17 for a somewhat related but by no means identical idea.

29. Cf. also Stephen Goranson, "The Joseph of Tiberias Episode in Epiphanius: Studies in Jewish and Christian Relations" (Ph.D. diss., Duke University, 1990), 80, speaking to these points.

30. Pointed out to me by Shamma Boyarin.

31. See Albert I. Baumgarten, "Literary Evidence for Jewish Christianity in the Galilee," in *The Galilee in Late Antiquity*, ed. Lee I. Levine (New York: Jewish Theological Seminary of America, 1992), 39–50; and, more generally, F. Stanley Jones, *An Ancient Jewish Christian Source on the History of Christianity: Pseudo-Clementine Recognitions*

1.27–71, Texts and Translations: Christian Apocrypha Series (Atlanta, Ga.: Scholars Press, 1995).

32. Christine E. Hayes, "Displaced Self-Perceptions: The Deployment of *Mînîm* and Romans in *B. Sanhedrin* 90b–91a," in *Religious and Ethnic Communities in Later Roman Palestine*, ed. Hayim Lapin (Lanham: University Press of Maryland, 1999), 249–89.

33. The richest picture of this conflict that I have found is Allen Brent, *Hippolytus and the Roman Church in the Third Century: Communities in Tension Before the Emergence of a Monarch-Bishop*, Supplements to Vigiliae Christianae (Leiden: E. J. Brill, 1995).

34. See Chapter 5 for extensive documentation of this point.

35. Boyarin, *Dying for God.*

36. Cohen, "Yavneh," 51. For a less idealized account of the intentions of Constantine in convening the council, see Athanasius, *Athanasius Werke*, ed. H. G. Opitz (Berlin: Walter de Gruyter, 1934), 3: 41–42, as well as discussion and literature cited in Richard Lim, *Public Disputation, Power, and Social Order in Late Antiquity*, Transformations of the Classical Heritage (Berkeley and Los Angeles: University of California Press, 1994), 184. The role of Constantine seems to have been as much to prevent free discussion as much as to promote it (Lim, Disputation, 215). See also Hal A. Drake, "Constantine and Consensus," *Church History* 44 (1995): 1–15; and especially Hal A. Drake, "Lambs Into Lions: Explaining Early Christian Intolerance," *Past and Present* no. 153 (1996): 30, n. 51. Constantine was, according to Drake and his sources, irenic with respect to pagans and eristic toward "heretics," precisely the pattern that my researches would predict. The actual Constantinian document can now conveniently be consulted in Eusebius, *Life of Constantine*, trans. and with commentary by Averil Cameron and Stuart G. Hall, Clarendon Ancient History Series (Oxford: Clarendon Press and Oxford University Press, 1999), 116–20.

37. Cohen, "Yavneh," 28. Helen Tartar has contributed the interesting remark that on that standard account Yavneh is a virtual typology with a "Jewish" event that prefigures a "Christian" one, and perhaps Cohen himself meant us to understand this ironic critique.

38. It is not clear to me on what basis Gabriele Boccaccini, *Beyond the Essene Hypothesis: The Parting of the Ways Between Qumran and Enochic Judaism* (Grand Rapids, Mich.: William B. Eerdmans, 1998), 84, determines that the biblical canon has been set by "Rabbinic Judaism."

39. Albert I. Baumgarten, *The Flourishing of Jewish Sects in the Maccabean Era: An Interpretation*, Supplements to the Journal for the Study of Judaism 55 (Leiden: E. J. Brill, 1997), 134.

40. Baumgarten, *Jewish Sects*, 195, makes eminently clear how dependent this view is on the assumption that after 70 A.C., rabbinism is virtually synonymous with Judaism. Only thus could one write that "authorities held different views, but those who held one position did not reach the point of boundary marking against those who reached other conclusions." I doubt the precision of this commonly held view even for the Rabbis before the fourth century, a fortiori for those "others," the *minim*, or even the *'am ha'areṣ*, excluded in various ways and to various degrees from their vaunted "agreement to disagree." I do agree with Baumgarten that sects did not flourish in the rabbinic period but would characterize the shift as being into an orthodoxy/heresy structure, not one of irenic consensus, as I shall try to make clear below in this chapter.

41. Martin Goodman, "The Function of Minim in Early Rabbinic Judaism," in

Geschichte—Tradition—Reflexion: Festschrift für Martin Hengel zum 70. Geburtstag, ed. H. Cancik, H. Lichtenberger, and P. Schäfer (Tübingen: Mohr Siebeck, 1996), 1:501–10. Cohen's statement that "at no point in antiquity did the rabbis develop heresiology and ecclesiology, creeds and dogmas. At no point did they expel anyone from the rabbinic order or from rabbinic synagogues, because of doctrinal error or because of membership in some heretical group" ("Yavneh," 41) is simply stunning for its apologetic refusal to confront the evidence that so clearly renders it false. Contra Cohen I would cite Shaye J. D. Cohen, "A Virgin Defiled: Some Rabbinic and Christian Views on the Origins of Heresy," *Union Seminary Quarterly Review* 36, no. 1 (Fall 1980): 1–11.

42. Marc Bloch, *The Historian's Craft: Reflections on the Nature and Uses of History and the Techniques and Methods of Those Who Write It*, trans. Peter Putnam (New York: Vintage Books, 1953), 89.

43. The work of Gedaliah Alon discussed immediately below is an excellent example of this. After decisively showing that nearly nothing of the legend of Rabban Yoḥanan ben Zakkai's removal to Yavneh can be sustained, he, nevertheless, continues to believe that the event itself took place and even busies himself with the question of whether Vespasian or Titus was the real emperor who met and negotiated with Rabban Yoḥanan.

44. Gedaliah Alon, "Rabban Joḥanan B. Zakkai's Removal to Jabneh," in *Jews, Judaism and the Classical World: Studies in Jewish History in the Times of the Second Temple and Talmud*, trans. Israel Abrahams (Jerusalem: Magnes Press, 1977), 269–313.

45. "Removal," 269. In spite of his overall critical stance to the material, it must be said that Alon is, by our standards, remarkably credulous as well. Thus he can deliver himself of a statement such as the following: "Thus the fact, recorded in Avot de-R. Nathan, that they signalled with arrows that Rabban Joḥanan was 'a friend of Caesar', testifies that the Romans were at this juncture close to the gates" ("Removal," 276), a simply astonishing statement given that the rabbinic text cited is one of the latest of all classical rabbinic texts and that there is no reason whatsoever to imagine that it preserves anything like eyewitness accounts from hundreds of years earlier (nor that it wished to!). Truly oddly, from my (and I think more than my) perspective is Alon's treatment of the late midrash and Josephus as roughly equivalently valuable historical sources for the first century. (Truth to tell, he is sometimes more critical with respect to Josephus, "Removal," 279.) My point here is not to attack Alon, who was a great scholar and whose work necessarily informs our own at every turn, but to point out the enormous epistemic differences between his time and ours.

46. Alon, "Removal," 294.

47. Neusner's original formulation for a slightly different instance was: "What do we know if we do not know that Rabbi X really said what is attributed to him? What sort of historical work can we do if we cannot do what Frankel, Graetz, and Krochmal thought we could do?" Jacob Neusner, *Reading and Believing: Ancient Judaism and Contemporary Gullibility*, Brown Judaic Studies (Atlanta, Ga.: Scholars Press, 1986), 33.

48. Cf. also Alon Goshen-Gottstein, *The Sinner and the Amnesiac: The Rabbinic Invention of Elisha Ben Abuya and Eleazar Ben Arach* (Stanford, Calif.: Stanford University Press, 2000), 9.

49. Bloch, *Historian's Craft*, 60–61.

50. Ibid., 63.

51. I heard this point made thirty years ago by my teacher, Prof. Saul Lieberman, OBM.

52. Bloch, *Historian's Craft*, 66.

53. Ibid., 89.

54. This is the fundamental insight of the "new historicism." See most recently Catherine Gallagher and Stephen Greenblatt, *Practicing New Historicism* (Chicago: University of Chicago Press, 2000).

55. See Günter Stemberger, *Jews and Christians in the Holy Land: Palestine in the Fourth Century* (Edinburgh: T & T Clark, 1999), 275.

56. Cf. Neusner, *Reading and Believing*, 37.

57. Gregory Nagy, *Poetry as Performance: Homer and Beyond* (Cambridge: Cambridge University Press, 1996), 76.

58. See, making a closely related point, Jacob Neusner, "Judaism After the Destruction of the Temple: An Overview," in *Formative Judaism: Religious, Historical, and Literary Studies, Third Series: Torah, Pharisees, and Rabbis*, vol. 46, Brown Judaica Series (Chico, Calif.: Scholars Press, 1983), 83–98. For the impact that this revisionist work has already had on New Testament studies, see, e.g., Stephen Motyer, *Your Father the Devil? A New Approach to John and "the Jews,"* Paternoster Biblical and Theological Studies (Carlisle, Eng.: Paternoster Press, 1997), 75. Motyer, however, seems too readily to assume that Neusner's conclusions have been generally accepted, not noticing that the very example he gives of work done under the "old paradigm" was published quite a bit after Neusner's. Moreover, at least in his "The Formation of Rabbinic Judaism: Yavneh (Jamnia) from A.D. 70 to 100," in *Principat: Religion (Judentum: Pälastinisches Judentum [Forts.])*, ed. Wolfgang Haase, Aufstieg und Niedergang der Römischen Welt (Berlin: Walter de Gruyter, 1979), 3–42, Neusner seemed prepared to ascribe a much greater role to a real, historical Yavneh than I would. See on this point, discussion in Isaiah M. Gafni, *Land, Center and Diaspora Jewish Constructs in Late Antiquity*, Journal for the Study of the Pseudepigrapha, Supplement series (Sheffield, Eng.: Sheffield Academic Press, 1997), 64.

59. Seth Schwartz, *Imperialism and Jewish Society from 200 B.C.E. to 640 C.E.* (Princeton, N.J.: Princeton University Press, 2001), 8.

60. Boccaccini, *Beyond the Essene Hypothesis*, 67. But why "underground"?

61. Aharon Shemesh, "The Origins of the Laws of Separatism: Qumran Literature and Rabbinic Halacha," *Revue de Qumran* 18, no. 2 (December 1997): 223–41; Aharon Shemesh, "'The One Who Divides Between the Children of Light and the Children of Darkness, Between Israel and the Nations,'" in Hebrew in *Atara l'Haim: Studies in the Talmud and Medieval Rabbinic Literature in Honor of Professor Haim Zalman Dimitrovsky*, ed. Daniel Boyarin et al. (Jerusalem: Magnes Press, 2000), 209–20.

62. Boccaccini, *Beyond the Essene Hypothesis*, 66. As far as I can tell, the terminology of the community distinguished between themselves as "The House of Judah" and those who were outside of that in-group, that is, a distinction among Israelites, not between Israelites and non-Israelites. See, e.g., James H. Charlesworth, *The Dead Sea Scrolls: Hebrew, Aramaic, and Greek Texts with English Translations: Volume 2, Damascus Document, War Scroll, and Related Documents*, ed. James H. Charlesworth, Princeton Theological Seminary Dead Sea Scrolls Project (Louisville, Ky.: Westminster/John Knox Press, 1994), 19.

63. Baumgarten, *Jewish Sects*, 9, emphasis original.

64. Ibid., 12–13.

65. Baumgarten writes: "I would not want my description of the rise and fall of sec-

tarianism among Jews to cause me to be classified among the native believers in a primitive orthodoxy, from which sectarianism was a deviance. Such primitive orthodoxies are usually little more than illusions promoted by successful religious movements as a means of denouncing dissidents" (*Jewish Sects*, 16).

66. Ibid., 26.

67. See also Sussmann, "Preliminary Observations," 36–37.

68. Moshe David Herr, "Continuum in the Chain of Torah Transmission," *Zion* 44 (1979): x, in Hebrew with English summary.

69. Adiel Schremer, "'[T]He[y] Did Not Read in the Sealed Book': Qumran Halakhic Revolution and the Emergence of Torah Study in Second Temple Judaism," in *Historical Perspectives: From the Hasmoneans to Bar Kochba in the Light of the Dead Sea Scrolls*, ed. David Goodblatt, Avital Pinnick, and Daniel R. Schwartz (Leiden: E. J. Brill, 2001), 105.

70. Steve Mason, *Flavius Josephus on the Pharisees: A Composition-Critical Study*, Studia Post-Biblica 39 (Leiden: E. J. Brill, 1991), 230–40.

71. Albert I. Baumgarten, "The Pharisaic *Paradosis*," *Harvard Theological Review* 80 (1987): 63–77.

72. Schremer, "They Did Not Read," 111. It does not, of course, follow from this (pace Schremer) that this paradosis was Pharisaic, per se, or that its content approximates to rabbinic halakha. Finally, I would register slight dissent from one more conclusion of Schremer's, namely that what characterized Pharisaic/rabbinic religion was a similar "return to the text." Far from it, insofar as the central mode of legitimation within rabbinic Judaism was the "Oral Torah," what we have is rather the appropriation of the legitimation by Scripture for the purposes of an essentially traditionalistic (not necessarily traditional but traditionalistic) community. For traditionalism as the mode of justification native to the church, or to "orthodoxy," see the next chapter as well.

73. Herr, "Continuum," xi.

74. Aharon Shemesh, *Punishment and Sins from the Bible to Rabbinic Literature*, in Hebrew (Jerusalem: Magnes Press, 2003).

75. "Le Boulluec carefully analyzes the way that Justin changes the connotation of the terms hairesis and diadoche from their more general philosophic usage in order to characterize those he regards as false Christians as "liars and apostates" inspired by—and descended from—Satan" (Pagels, "Irenaeus," 340).

76. I am accordingly reserving the name *sect* precisely for those communities which Baumgarten calls "introvertionist" and "greedy." See, however, Baumgarten's elegant argument for using the term *sect* for all of the Second Temple groups, including Qumran (*Jewish Sects*, 14). My line of writing here does not constitute a disagreement in substance with Baumgarten, but rather a slightly different usage of terminology in order to make the distinctions that I need to emphasize for this analysis. Note that my own usage of the term *sect* answers to some, but not all, of the criteria established in Ernst Troeltsch, *The Social Teaching of the Christian Churches*, trans. Olive Wyon (New York: Harper and Row, 1960).

77. Connections between the Fourth Gospel and Qumran have, of course, been explored extensively. See James H. Charlesworth, ed., *John and the Dead Sea Scrolls*, Christian Origins Library (New York: Crossroad, 1990).

78. See Boccaccini, *Beyond the Essene Hypothesis*, 123, on the Damascus Document and 155 on Qumran in general.

79. Aharon Shemesh, "Expulsion and Exclusion in the *Community Rule* and the *Damascus Document*," *Dead Sea Discoveries* 9, no. 1 (2002): 44–74.

80. This is a controversial point of identification but still seems to be the most widely held opinion among specialists.

81. See also Lorne Dawson, "Church/Sect Theory: Getting It Straight," *North American Religion* 1 (1992): 5–28.

82. Flavius Josephus, *Books XVIII–XX*, vol. IX of *Jewish Antiquities*, trans. L. H. Feldman, Loeb Classical Library (Cambridge: Harvard University Press, 1965), 9 and passim.

83. Goodman, "Minim," 502. See also Simon, "Hairesis."

84. Boccaccini, *Beyond the Essene Hypothesis*, 183–84.

85. Schwartz, *Jewish Society*, 11.

86. Note that in both Christian and rabbinic usage from late antiquity, heresy is figured as a snakebite. For the rabbinic usage, see Boyarin, *Dying for God*, 35. For Christian usage of this image, see J. Rebecca Lyman, "Origen as Ascetic Theologian: Orthodoxy and Heresy in the Fourth-Century Church," in *Origeniana Septima: Origenes in Den Auseinandersetzungen Des 4. Jahrhunderts*, ed. W. A. Bienert and U. Kühneweg, Bibliotheca Ephemeridum Theologicarum Lovaniensium 137 (Leuven: Peeters, 1999), 187–94.

87. Simon, "Hairesis," 104–5.

88. Allen Brent, "Diogenes Laertius and the Apostolic Succession," *Journal of Ecclesiastical History* 44, no. 3 (July 1993): 368.

89. Tannaitic texts are the rabbinic literature that cites the opinions of the Rabbis who lived before the promulgation of the Mishna in the beginning of the third century. Amoraic literature, the literature following them through the third, fourth, and fifth centuries and into the sixth. The tannaitic texts were edited earlier than the amoraic ones, but only—paradoxically—after the Mishna, which is represented as their culmination. Thus, based on either the date of the materials projected by the texts themselves or the dates of redaction projected by scholars, the tannaitic is earlier than the amoraic.

90. Goodman, "Minim," 503–4.

91. Stephen Goranson, "Others and Intra-Jewish Polemic as Reflected in Qumran Texts," in *The Dead Sea Scrolls: A Comprehensive Account*, ed. P. Flint and J. Vanderkam (Leiden: E. J. Brill, 1999), 2: 534–51.

92. Mason, *Flavius Josephus on the Pharisees*, 202.

93. See Boccaccini, *Beyond the Essene Hypothesis*, 189. He writes of how "the Christian claim to be the 'new Israel' against the parallel claim of Rabbinic Judaism to be the 'one eternal Israel' outshone even the memory of the pluralistic environment from which both the Church and the Synagogue [*sic*] emerged."

94. Goranson, "Joesph of Tiberius Episode," 97.

95. Pagels, "Irenaeus." One of the many virtues of Talal Asad's work is the clarity with which it interrupts any binary opposition between faith and practice in the formation of Christian heresiology, Talal Asad, *Genealogies of Religion: Discipline and Reasons of Power in Christianity and Islam* (Baltimore: Johns Hopkins University Press, 1993), 39. This is important, inter alia, because it is frequently claimed that Jewish orthodoxy is a matter of deed; Christian, of creed.

96. R. Travers Herford, *Christianity in Talmud and Midrash* (1903; reprint, New York: Ktav, 1978), 380 and passim. Herford even claims to know precisely what kind of Christianity, namely the Christianity represented by the Epistle to the Hebrews.

97. Sussmann, "Preliminary Observations," 54, n. 176. I have skipped in the citation Sussmann's references to particular texts. Sussmann, it needs to be said, is the first scholar in over a century who has attempted an independent, more or less comprehensive, and philologically rigorous gathering of texts about *minim*. Importantly, Sussmann also shows that the term does not refer (at least in the early period and in Palestine) to Gentiles.

98. Michael Allen Williams, Rethinking "Gnosticism": *An Argument for Dismantling a Dubious Category* (Princeton, N.J.: Princeton University Press, 1996).

99. As we shall see below in Chapter 6.

100. Herford, *Christianity*, 322.

101. Kister, "'Let Us,'" 52.

102. Moriz Friedländer, *Der Vorchristliche jüdische Gnosticismus* (Göttingen: Vandenhoeck and Ruprecht, 1898). Herford (*Christianity*, 368–76) has demolished Friedländer's arguments and shown them to be more than once special pleading. See also the heroic but unconvincing attempt to revive Friedländer's hypothesis in Birger Pearson, "Friedländer Revisited," *Studia Philonica* 2 (1973): 23–39.

103. For extensive and compelling argumentation to this effect with respect to this crucial text, see Herford, *Christianity*, 255–66, 298–99. This text will be treated extensively by my student Ron Reissberg in his forthcoming dissertation.

104. Kister, "'Let Us,'" 55–57. That is, when Rabbi Simlai argues that the first man was made from earth and the first woman from the man, he adds, seemingly gratuitously, "And since then, 'in our image and in our likeness,' no man [can give birth] without woman, and no woman without man, nor the two of them without the Shekhina." By showing that Christian polemic for the virgin birth did cite the "birth" of Eve as evidence, Kister compellingly demonstrates that this represents a further argument against the *minim* on the part of Rabbi Simlai, and that the *minim* (at least here) are obviously a representation of Christian, and not so-called gnostic, doctrine ("'Let Us,'" 54–55). The text cited by Kister is worth quoting here, since it represents a beautifully constructed *qol weḥomer* (a fortiori) argument that would have done any Rabbi proud (not surprisingly, in the case of a Syrian Father): "If Eve the birth-giver was born of the man who never gives birth, how much must you believe that the daughter of Eve, gave birth to a boy without a man." The citation is from Ephrem's hymns on the nativity, Ephraem, *Des Heiligen Ephraem des Syrers Hymnen de Nativitate [Epiphania]*, ed. E. Beck, SR, CSCO (Louvain: Peeters, 1959), 3. In yet another example, in which Rabbi Simlai interprets as synonyms three divine names in a verse describing creation, Kister plausibly suggests that he does this it to counter trinitarian claims about creation.

105. Karen L. King, *What Is Gnosticism?* (Cambridge: Harvard University Press, 2003).

106. Herford, *Christianity*, 155–56, translates, "speak falsely concerning Him," an attractive translation that I am not sure can be justified philologically. It may be that "deny" in this context means virtually the same thing, however. These people with holy books with God's Holy Name in them are obviously not atheists, so "denying Him" must be equivalent to holding false doctrine with respect to God.

107. The word זכרון, like the word אזכרות, from the same root, translated as "Names" in Rabbi Tarfon's utterance, originally come from a root meaning "to mention, to name," which later on takes on the meaning of "to remember."

108. The bracketed words are a translation of the continuation of the verse, uncited in the Tosefta but, in my interpretation, a necessary part of the context of the allusion.

109. Saul Lieberman, *Order Mo'ed*, vol. 2 of *The Tosefta According to Codex Vienna, with Variants from Codices Erfurt, London, Genizah Mss. and Editio Princeps (Venice, 1521)* (New York: Jewish Theological Seminary of America, 1962), 58.

110. Cf. the fantastic interpretation of this text given by Friedländer, *Vorchristliche jüdische Gnosticismus*, 80, and Herford's animadversions to him, *Christianity*, 372–73.

111. Virginia Burrus, "The Heretical Woman as Symbol in Alexander, Athanasius, Epiphanius, and Jerome," *Harvard Theological Review* 84 (1991): 229–48.

112. Saul Lieberman, *Order Mo'ed*, vol. 3 of *Tosefta Ki-Fshuta: A Comprehensive Commentary on the Tosefta* (New York: Jewish Theological Seminary of America, 1962), 206.

113. Shlomo Pines, "Notes on the Parallelism Between Syriac Terminology and Mishnaic Hebrew," in Hebrew, in *Yaakov Friedman Memorial Volume* (Jerusalem: Institute for Jewish Studies, 1974), 206–9. The term, which can be translated from the Syriac as "revelations" was also used, according to Pines, as a name for apocalypses and in particular the canonical Apocalypse. I am grateful to my friend Shlomo Naeh for pointing out this very important publication to me.

114. The words which follow here in the editions, "is a dogma of the Torah," are missing in most manuscripts.

115. My interpretation. For an alternative view, namely, that the reference originally was to a definition of the Epicurean, who believes neither in life after death nor the intervention of God in human affairs in the here and now (glossed as "Revelation"), see Chaim Milikovsky, "Gehenna and 'Sinners of Israel' in the Light of Seder 'Olam," in Hebrew, *Tarbiz* 55, no. 3 (April–June 1986): 335. While possible, this interpretation seems to me less plausible than my own, if only because it would assume that the editors of the phrase in the Mishna already did not understand it. Milikovsky, it must be said, explicitly defends this option, which is not by any means excluded. For the view adopted here, see Lawrence H. Schiffman, *Who Was a Jew? Rabbinic and Halakhic Perspectives on the Jewish Christian Schism* (Hoboken, N.J.: Ktav, 1985), 46, although not precisely for the reasons adopted here.

116. For the clear distinction between Gentile and Jewish Epicureans (with the latter considered much more severely, of course), see Tosefta Sanhedrin 13:4–5 (Zuckermandel, *Tosephta*, 434) and BT Sanhedrin 38b.

117. Milikovsky, "Gehenna," 335, n. 102 and literature cited there. See also the interesting passage in the PT Sanhedrin 27d, in which the "Epicurean" is interpreted by one Rabbi as one who says "that Scribe," and by another as one who says, "those Rabbis," i.e., uses expressions of contempt for Scribes and Rabbis, that is, clearly a Jew who adheres to non-rabbinic forms of Judaism.

118. For that reason, Epicureans are the archetypical heretics within much of rabbinic literature. This interpretation is similar to that of Elias Bickerman [Élie Bikerman], "La chaîne de la tradition pharisienne," *Revue biblique* 59, no. 1 (January 1952): 47, n. 4; contra Hanoch Albeck, *Mishna* (Jerusalem: Mossad Bialik, 1953), ad loc., who writes, "One who follows the system of the Greek philosopher Epicurus, who taught the people to seek pleasure, and this is a designation for anyone who despises the Torah and the Sages, who command the person to take upon himself the yoke of the Kingdom of Heaven" (my translation); and contra Herbert Danby, ed. and trans., *The Mishnah* (London: Oxford University Press, 1974), 397, n. 4. In support of my reading, see too "Aristotle is blamed because his cosmology endangered the idea of divine providence and his

theory of the fifth element the immortality of the soul. These are however fundamental dogmas of *Schulplatonismus* which regarded Aristotle and Epicurus as the representatives of 'godlessness' *par excellence.* Cf. Origen, c. Cels. I. 21; VIII. 45" (Barnard, *Justin*, 9). Interestingly enough, one of the primary categories of heresy for Justin is also those who negate resurrection and are called by him "godless, impious heretics" (*Dialogue* 80). See also with reference to Philo, "the Epicureans were regularly attacked for destroying divine providence" (Pheme Perkins, "Ordering the Cosmos: Irenaeus and the Gnostics," in *Nag Hammadi, Gnosticism, and Early Christianity*, ed. Charles W. Hedrick and Robert Hodgson Jr. [Peabody, Mass.: Hendrickson, 1986], 224). This usage would be, on my view, similar to the accusation by Christians of other Christians that they were "Jews." For such Jewish "Epicureans," see Alan F. Segal, *Two Powers in Heaven: Early Rabbinic Reports About Christianity and Gnosticism*, Studies in Judaism in Late Antiquity 25 (Leiden: E. J. Brill, 1977), 85, n. 4, and literature cited there. See too Henry A. Fischel, *Rabbinic Literature and Greco-Roman Philosophy. A Study of Epicurea and Rhetorica in Early Midrashic Writings*, Studia Post-Biblica (Leiden: E. J. Brill, 1973), 35–50.

119. For the afterlife as a major issue between Sadducees and Pharisees, see Josephus, *Antiquities* 18 and *Wars* 2, and passim, Acts 23:6–10, and the evidence of the Pseudo-Clementines as discussed in Baumgarten, "Literary Evidence." For the paradosis, which I take to be the meaning of "Torah" in this Mishnaic passage, see: Josephus, *Antiquities* 13.298; Matthew 15:1–2. Pace Saldarini, I would be inclined to connect Paul's report of having been a Pharisee in Philippians 3:5 with his statement in Galatians 1:14 that he was advanced in the paradosis of the fathers. Cf. Anthony Saldarini, *Pharisees, Scribes, and Sadducees in Palestinian Society* (Edinburgh: T & T Clark, 1989), 135–41, who does not seem to make this connection. One wonders, then, how the Christians would fit in to this typology. Interestingly enough, nothing in this creed would exclude Christians per se from orthodoxy in "Israel." This is a vitally important point, particularly when we remember that as late, at least, as the third century there were Christians who identified themselves as Pharisees and considered Sadducees (and certainly Epicureans) to be heretics (Baumgarten, "Literary Evidence"). See also William David Davies, *The Setting of the Sermon on the Mount* (Cambridge: Cambridge University Press, 1976), 259, and, for an earlier adherent of the view that the Mishna produces a heresiology, Ben Zion Bokser, *Pharisaic Judaism in Transition* (New York: Jewish Theological Seminary of America, 1935), 1–6.

120. Louis Finkelstein, *Introduction to Tractates Fathers and The Fathers of Rabbi Nathan*, in Hebrew (New York: Jewish Theological Seminary of America, 1950), 206. This is a slightly disguised allusion to the Apostles' Creed.

121. Treating a parallel rabbinic or proto-rabbinic text, at least—seemingly—as old as the Mishna and perhaps even older (Seder Olam Rabbah), Chaim Milikovsky has noted that the entire list of sinners who suffer eternal punishment in Gehinnom are theological (he calls it "ideological") deviants ("Gehenna," 331–32). It is interesting, however, to note that these grave sinners are anathematized in that text as schismatics "who have separated from the ways of the public," which matches the earlier form of the liturgy as presumed by the Tosefta, "the curse of the Separatists," as well, perhaps, as the Ignatian stage of heresiology in formation, wherein it is primarily schism that is excoriated. This, incidentally, or perhaps not so incidentally, might provide a partial answer to Albert Baumgarten's desideratum: "If only we could know what Jewish opponents thought of the Essenes or of Qumran!" (*Jewish Sects*, 61). I can offer some confirmation for Baum-

garten's speculation that nonsectarian Jews would have responded to the sects by saying "that sectarian ideas were new-fangled inventions of the minds of their devotees" and "that if traditional practice had been good enough for generations past there was no need to change it" (*Jewish Sects*, 62) by offering the exemplum of Matthew 12, in which this is precisely the argument of Jesus, the "nonsectarian" Jew, against the sectarian Pharisees! From the point of view of the protorabbinic authors of this list, then, those who do not accept these theological principles are excluded from "Israel." In the list in the Seder Olam, there are additional members, *minim, meshumadim* (those who refuse to keep the commandments—presumably in their protorabbinic interpretation) for theological reasons, and *masorot*, which are, as Milikovsky shows, Jews who slander for religious reasons what the text defines as "the Jews" to foreign, oppressive, authorities ("Gehenna," 333–34).

122. These groups are arguably descended from the people who had not gone into exile in Babylonia: "Those who had been permitted by the Babylonians to remain in the land in essence did not change their life style, economic structure, and religious-cultic customs, notwithstanding the loss of political sovereignty and cultic institutions and the incurrence of economic hardship. They were the conservatives who clung to their established system of values, despite the changed circumstances" (Shemaryahu Talmon, "The Emergence of Jewish Sectarianism in the Early Second Temple Period," in *Ancient Israelite Religion: Essays in Honor of Frank Moore Cross*, ed. Patrick D. Miller, Paul D. Hanson, and S. Dean McBride [Philadelphia: Fortress Press, 1987], 596). See furthermore Daniel Boyarin, "The *Ioudaioi* in John and the Prehistory of 'Judaism,'" in *Pauline Conversations in Context: Essays in Honour of Calvin J. Roetzel* (Sheffield, Eng.: Continuum, 2002), 224–50.

123. For an astute characterization of Sadducees and their Pharisaic portrayal, see Sussmann, "Preliminary Observations," 47–48.

124. See, e.g., Charles Kannengiesser, "Alexander and Arius of Alexandria: The Last Ante-Nicene Theologians," *Compostellanum* 35, no. 1–2 (1990): 391–92. See too J. Rendell Harris, who already opines in 1917: "We now begin to see that the controversy between Arius and Athanasius is not a mere struggle of an orthodox Church with an aggressive and cancerous heresy: the heretic is the orthodox conservative, and the supposed orthodox champion is the real progressive" (*The Origin of the Prologue to St. John's Gospel* [Cambridge: Cambridge University Press, 1917], 49).

125. Goranson, "Intra-Jewish Polemic," 542. Also: "[W]here there is heresy, orthodoxy must have preceded. For example, Origen puts it like this: 'All heretics at first are believers; then later they swerve from the rule of faith.'" Origen, *The Song of Songs: Commentary and Homilies*, trans. R. P. Lawson, Ancient Christian Writers 26 (Westminster, Md.: Newman Press, 1957), 3; Walter Bauer, Gerhard Krodel, and Robert A. Kraft, *Orthodoxy and Heresy in Earliest Christianity.*, ed. Gerhard Krodel (Philadelphia: Fortress Press, 1971), 13–14. A neat bit of illustration of this with respect to the Pharisees is to be found in Matthew 15, where the *halakhot* of the Pharisees are taken to be innovations, i.e., the Christians are the traditionalists and the Pharisees the deviators. The Pharisees, of course, object that the Christians are "transgressing the traditions of the elders" (v. 2) by not washing their hands ritually before eating. When Jesus says there that it is not "what goes into the mouth that defiles a man, but what comes out of the mouth, this defiles a man" (11), he is not deprecating the laws of kashruth and abrogating them but resisting the halakhic innovations of the Pharisees, which these wish to impose as

traditions of the elders. With respect to the hand-washing ritual before eating, the Evangelist surely has the upper hand historically. Rabbinic literature is still at some pains hundreds of years later to justify this relatively new (and apparently sectarian) practice (see BT Berakhot 62b; for the fraughtness of this issue even late in rabbinic times see BT Sotah 4b; and, most strikingly: "Washing of the hands is a commandment. What is the commandment? Said Abbaye [fourth century], the commandment to obey the Sages!" [BT Ḥullin 106a]). The battle of Jesus with the Pharisees over this issue was apparently still being fought *within "Jewish" circles* nearly half a millennium later. The Pharisees with their *halakha*, which goes back to the oral (and thus esoteric) communication of God with Moses at Sinai, are the object of the contemptuous Qumran term *dorshe ḥalaqot* "promulgators of unctuous things," almost surely a cacophemism of *dorshe halakhot* "the promulgators of laws," which the Pharisees would have used as their own self-designation (Goranson, "Intra-Jewish Polemic," 542).

126. Naomi Janowitz, "Rabbis and Their Opponents: The Construction of the 'Min' in Rabbinic Anecdotes," *Journal of Early Christian Studies* 6, no. 3 (Fall 1998): 460, accurately perceives that the category of the "min" is about the construction of an orthodox, rabbinic Judaism, at the time of Rabbi Judah the Prince, analogous to the production of Christian orthodoxy. See also Hayes, "Minim and Romans."

127. Mary Beard, John A. North, and S. R. F. Price, *Religions of Rome* (Cambridge: Cambridge University Press, 1998), 221.

128. According to the versions preserved in the *textus receptus* of the Sanhedrin Mishna, it would be the case that there too the deviants are excluded from the name "Israel." In the talmudic version and in the prints we read: "All Israel have a place in the next world, and these are they who have no place etc." The most straightforward interpretation of the Mishnaic passage, on this reading, seems to be that the three who are denied a place in the next world are indeed not Israel. Otherwise the text logically contradicts itself. Traditional interpretations involve complex and forced interpretations to maintain both halves of what seems like a self-contradiction, such as adding the word "potentially" in the first stich, which completely denudes the text of meaning. For a similar reading to mine, see Hayes, "Minim and Romans," 276: "After all, the mishnah's formulation makes it clear that those who doubt resurrection are those outside the community of Israel, and they are by definition *mînîm* of various types." I am grateful to Prof. Hayes for sharing her work with me prior to its publication. However, this exegetical point is only strictly valid with respect to the later reworking of the Mishna as we find it in the Talmuds and the prints of the Mishna. The seventeenth-century rabbinic scholar Rabbi Shelomo Luria already recognized that this sentence is indeed a very late addition to the Mishna, so it is very difficult to build anything upon it.

129. If, however, the interpretation of the previous text is acceptable, then I could suggest a different conclusion here. The Sadducees are not Israel owing to their theological deviance; it is this that makes them heretics, and, therefore, their practices are not the practices of Israel either. This would be consistent, I believe, with the arguments of both Milikovsky, "Gehenna," and Baumgarten, *Jewish Sects*, 76–80, which is not to say, of course, that either scholar would necessarily agree with the interpretation.

130. Daniel Boyarin, "Women's Bodies and the Rise of the Rabbis: The Case of Soṭah," *Studies in Contemporary Jewry: Jews and Gender, the Challenge to Hierarchy* 16 (2001): 88–100.

131. See Charlotte Fonrobert, "When Women Walk in the Ways of Their Fathers:

On Gendering the Rabbinic Claim for Authority," *Journal of the History of Sexuality: Special Issue: Sexuality in Late Antiquity* 10, no. 3/4 (July/October 2001): 398–415. I had originally translated here "ancestors" and "Sadducean women," but am persuaded by Fonrobert that the father/daughter relation is very important to the text. Fonrobert's work suggests (very carefully) that we might even discover these "daughters of the Sadducees" among Jewish-Christian women. In support of the general notion that the time of Rabbi Yehuda Hannassi, the editor of the Mishna, was pivotal for the development of rabbinic heresiology, including the "excommunication" of the Samaritans, see Lawrence H. Schiffman, "The Samaritans in Tannaitic Halakhah," *Jewish Quarterly Review* 75 (1985): 336–37; and Alan D. Crown, "Redating the Schism Between the Judaeans and the Samaritans," *Jewish Quarterly Review* 82, nos. 1–2 (1991): 17–50. On the question of gender in the production of rabbinic authority and orthodoxy, see too Boyarin, "Women's Bodies."

132. This argument would seem to challenge Sussmann's claim that Sadducees were only "excommunicated," as it were, in later rabbinic literature and not in tannaitic texts (Sussmann, "Preliminary Observations," 50, n. 168). Indeed, the Babylonian Talmud's bald statement (in the name of a *baraita*) that "The Sadducee is equal to a gentile" [Eruvin 68b] could be tacitly based on this very Mishna.

133. By which I simply mean that this argument does not preclude an earlier instantiation of this text and its ideology but only that, I would claim, it was surely still relevant, in some cultural sense, at the time that the Mishna was edited. This is not an uncontroversial position. See Daniel Boyarin, "Archives in the Fiction: Rabbinic Historiography and Church History," in *Festschrift for Elizabeth Clark*, ed. Dale Martin and Patricia Miller (forthcoming, 2004).

134. Solomon Shechter, ed., *Aboth de Rabbi Nathan* (1887; reprint, New York: Philipp Feldheim, Publisher, 1967).

135. On this passage, see too Albert Baumgarten, "Rabbinic Literature as a Source for the History of Jewish Sectarianism in the Second Temple Period," *Dead Sea Discoveries* 2 (1995): 14–57.

136. Note as well the technical term for apostolic succession in rabbinic heresiology, *received*, to be discussed at length in the next chapter of this book.

137. Sussmann, "Preliminary Observations," 37, n. 119. It seems to me that we must, on the one hand, take into account the observation of Sussmann, "Preliminary Observations," 36, that what differentiated the Qumran community in their own eyes were halakhic differences and, on the other hand, pay close attention to the fact that according to this text (as noted by Sussmann, "Preliminary Observations," 53), the critical differences were theological. Sussmann remarks that this text is of problematic dating and may be later. One way of sorting this out would be to see it as a testimony to the shift from the earlier, prerabbinic period to the later rabbinic period, with only the latter manifesting a Jewish heresiology; in other words, precisely the argument that I am here advancing. We must consider, as well, the evident fact that among the differences between Bet Hillel and Bet Shammai are such that ought to render each other unsuitable as marriage partners for each other, just as much as the alleged difference between Jews who permit female-initiated divorce and those who don't. Something else keeps the "Houses" together and drives Qumran and the Pharisees apart. Compare, on this matter, Adiel Schremer, "Papyrus Zeelim 13 and the Question of the Right of Women to Divorce Their Husbands in the Early Jewish Halakha," *Zion* 63 (1998): 380 (in Hebrew), who is not suf-

ficiently attentive, in my view, to this issue. The difference, I suggest, must be ideological, something on the order of what we call theological, and not halakhic. It follows, then, that his argument that it is impossible to imagine nonrabbinic norms for divorce, because of "the danger of a social rift between those of the Jews who accepted the rabbinic halakha (whatever their number and social importance), and those who followed a different halakhic norm" (Schremer, "Papyrus Zeelim," 381) cannot be sustained. This argument would seem invalidated, on the face of it, by the rabbinic willingness to imagine—at least—that the two Houses married between themselves, notwithstanding halakhic difference as significant and incommensurable (and, moreover, matters of actual occurrence) as those between the alleged normative rabbinic halakha and the reconstructed alternative halakha within which women could initiate divorce. This is not to say that I am unconvincd by Schremer's overall argument but only that this line of reasoning must be disqualified. It is, after all, Schremer himself who has compellingly shown that the question of the halakhic difference between Bet Shammai and Bet Hillel with respect to the "co-wife of the daughter" was an actual matter of law and practice and one with no less potential to cause a "rift in the People," which, according to tradition, it did not (Adiel Schremer, "Qumran Polemic on Marital Law: CD 4:20–5:11 and Its Social Background," in *The Damascus Document: A Centennial of Discovery*, ed. Joseph M. Baumgarten, Esther G. Chazon, and Avital Pinnick [Leiden: E. J. Brill, 2000], 147–60)!

138. Martin Goodman, "Sadducees and Essenes After 70 CE," in *Crossing the Boundaries: Essays in Biblical Interpretation in Honour of Michael D. Goulder*, ed. Stanley E. Porter, Paul Joyce, and David E. Orton, Biblical Interpretation Series (Leiden: E. J. Brill, 1994), 347–56.

139. See on this point Cohen, "Yavneh," 32–33, and Neusner, *Reading and Believing*, 84–85. However, Goodman, "Sadducees and Essenes," also needs to be taken seriously.

140. Contra Cohen, "Yavneh," 39, n. 30. To be sure, I agree with Cohen (ad loc.) that the usage becomes more prominent in later rabbinic texts.

141. For this interpretation of Josephus, see Schwartz, *Jewish Society*, 91–98. Schwartz makes the telling point that according to Josephus (Ant. 18.6–9) it was the founding of an additional sect by Judas the Galilean that "constituted a dangerous and illegitimate innovation," thus implying strongly that the other three sects were considered legitimate aspects of "Israel."

142. I thus partly accept and partly dissent from Sussmann's description of Sadducees as those who disagree with the Rabbis in halakha, and the *minim* "as a general name for those [who dissent] with respect to belief, and [hold] heretical opinions" (Sussmann, "Preliminary Observations," 53). I would argue that what rendered the Sadducees not Israel were their heretical beliefs, and from this it follows that their practice is not acceptable, either. One proof of this observation is the famous discussion between Rabbi Eli'ezer and the *min*, discussed inter alia in Boyarin, *Dying for God*, 26–30, in which it is clear that it is the very "Christianness" of the interlocutor and *not* his halakhic opinions that renders the latter invalid.

143. Boyarin, *Dying for God*, 136, n. 19.

144. For "sectarian" halakha as being more stringent than Pharisaic/rabbinic halakha, see Sussmann, "Preliminary Observations," 64–65. On this particular issue, see Charlotte Fonrobert, *Menstrual Purity: The Reconstruction of Biblical Gender in Chris-*

tianity and Rabbinic Judaism, Contraversions: Jews and Other Differences (Stanford, Calif.: Stanford University Press, 2000).

145. Christine Trevett, "Gender, Authority and Church History: A Case Study of Montanism," *Feminist Theology* 17 (January 1998): 9–24.

146. Interestingly, in an earlier paper Shaye Cohen had captured this nuance quite precisely: Cohen, "Virgin," 4. In his later "Yavneh," Cohen retreats from this insight. Saldarini also misses the point here, in my opinion. He writes: "The Sadducean women who do not follow mishnaic custom are contrasted with Israelite women and thus are treated as less than good Jews, like Samaritans" (Saldarini, *Pharisees*, 232). But those who are contrasted with Israelites are not "less than good Jews"; they are not Jews are all—precisely like Samaritans. At another point, Saldarini writes: "The later sources, especially the Babylonian Talmud, paint the Sadducees in even more lurid colors and suggest in places that they were not really Jews, but heretics. Such is certainly not historically true, but the result of a later defense of rabbinic authority and its way of life" (Saldarini, *Pharisees*, 302). I must admit that the last sentence gives me pause. What is Saldarini denying here? What could the opposite—namely that it *is* historically true "they were not really Jews, but heretics" possibly mean?

147. Once again, the Epicureans here are very likely simply Jews who deny, in traditional fashion, the eternity of the soul.

148. Cf. Schwartz, *Jewish Society*, 12, n. 17. Indeed, "by the third century [the Rabbis] were probably far more cohesive than the scribes and priests of the first century had been, and it is certain that the literature they produced was far less diverse," as Schwartz writes, but this cannot in any way be taken as support for Cohen's description of the significance of Yavneh, except by dint of an optical illusion on the order of holding up one's thumb and thereby obscuring the sun.

149. For differently inflected but structurally parallel phenomena in Christian heresiology, see Virginia Burrus, "The Heretical Woman," and Kate Cooper, "Insinuations of Womanly Influence: An Aspect of the Christianization of the Roman Aristocracy," *Journal of Roman Studies* 82 (1992): 150–64. Note also the topos invoked in the title of Cohen, "Virgin."

150. Le Boulluec, *La notion*, 65 and 33–34. Compare the death of James the Just, clearly marked as the execution of a false prophet by stoning in Eusebius II.23. Hugh Jackson Lawlor and John Ernest Leonard Oulton, trans. and eds., *Eusebius, Bishop of Caesarea, the Ecclesiastical History and the Martyrs of Palestine* (London: Society for Promoting Christian Knowledge, 1927), 58.

151. A. L. Williams, *Dialogue*, 174. See also the explicit association of *hairesis* and false prophets at 51.1 (A. L. Williams, *Dialogue*, 102).

152. Aharon Shemesh has, however, argued compellingly that the model under which Akavyah was condemned was the "rebellious elder" and not the "false prophet." Indeed, his argument suggests that the two had come to be more or less equated among the Rabbis, for whom prophecy was, in any event, largely a dead letter (Aharon Shemesh, "Law and Prophecy: False Prophet and Rebellious Elder," in Hebrew, in *Renewing Jewish Commitment: The Work and Thought of David Hartman*, ed. Avi Sagi and Zvi Zohar [Jerusalem: Shalom Hartman Institute and Hakkibutz Hameuchad, 2001], 923–41). The "false prophet" model is vital for the development of early Christian heresiology, for otherwise the name *hairesis* and even the *diadoche* suggest one legitimate grouping among others, as in the case of the philosophical schools, and not the one true way from which

all others deviate. Athanasius is still struggling with this issue at the beginning of his *Orations Against the Arians*: "For though we have a succession of teachers and become their disciples, yet, because we are taught by them things of Christ, we both are, and are called, Christians all the same" (c. Ar. 1.3), as opposed, of course, to the Arians, who are called "Arians." See also Virginia Burrus, "Fathering the Word: Athanasius of Alexandria," in *"Begotten Not Made": Conceiving Manhood in Late Antiquity*, Figurae (Stanford, Calif.: Stanford University Press, 2000), 36–79. Christine Hayes points out, appropriately, that there is a difference between Christian and rabbinic heresiology in that the anathematizing of Akavyah (and of Rabbi Eli'ezer) was occasioned more by differences in halakha than credo. We agree, however, that this does not invalidate the underlying comparison. According to Guy Stroumsa, the term "false prophet" first appears in Hebrew at Qumran and then "reappears later, in the midrashic literature of late antiquity," which supports my general point (Guy Stroumsa, "False Prophets in Early Christianity: Montanus, Mani, Muhammad," [conference presentation, Hartford, Conn., 1999], photocopy). See too Johannes Reiling, "The Use of Pseudoprophètes in the Septuagint, Philo and Josephus," *Novum Testamentum* 13 (1971): 147–56.

153. Shlomo Naeh, "'Make Yourself Many Rooms': Another Look at the Utterances of the Sages About Controversy" (in Hebrew), in *Renewing Jewish Commitment: The Work and Thought of David Hartman*, ed. Avi Sagi and Zvi Zohar (Jerusalem: Shalom Hartman Institute and Hakkibutz Hameuchad, 2001), 857. It should be noted, moreover, that the case that on which Naeh focuses in that article involves halakhic disagreements. He demonstrates that the insistence that "These [the words of the House of Shammai] and these [the words of the House of Hillel] are the words of the Living God" is a declaration that neither are heretics, while showing that one who perverts the words of the Living God is a false prophet and a heretic, in rabbinic parlance, following Jeremiah 23:26, 36.

154. I am, of course, playing on the title of another essay of Cohen's here (Shaye J. D. Cohen, "'Those Who Say They Are Jews and Are Not': How Do You Know a Jew in Antiquity When You See One?" in *Diasporas in Antiquity*, ed. Shaye J. D. Cohen and Ernest S. Frerichs, Brown Judaic Studies 288 [Atlanta, Ga.: Scholars Press, 1993], 1–45), alluding, of course, in turn to the Apocalypse.

155. To be sure, the category of the *'am ha'areṣ*, those Jews who are neither in the rabbinic fold nor out as *minim*, Sadducees, or Epicureans (note that at least according to the Babylonian Talmud, the *'am ha'areṣ* is explicitly awarded a place in the next world, in contradistinction to the *minim* and the excluded figures of the Sanhedrin Mishna, BT Ketubbot 111b) represent for a significant time yet to come a living challenge to the rabbinic claim for religious hegemony and orthodoxy. Aharon Oppenheimer, *The Am Ha'areṣ: A Study in the Social History of the Jewish People*, Arbeiten zur Literatur und Geschichte des Hellenistischen Judentums (Leiden: E. J. Brill, 1977); Lee I. Levine, "The Sages and the Synagogue in Late Antiquity: The Evidence of the Galilee," in *The Galilee in Late Antiquity*, ed. Lee I. Levine (New York: Jewish Theological Seminary of America, 1992), 201–24; Lee I. Levine, *The Rabbinic Class of Roman Palestine in Late Antiquity* (New York: Jewish Theological Seminary of America, 1989), 40–42. And see especially Levine, *Rabbinic Class*, 112–13, for highly cogent arguments that these were not or could not have been a sectarian group but represent rather the masses of nonrabbinic population. On my hypothesis, then, they are a continuation of the non-*Ioudaioi* of the time of John's Gospel, including, as it were, the non-Christian descendants of the founders of Johan-

nine community (Boyarin, "Ioudaioi"). On the other hand, it is impossible to imagine that these rural Galilean masses did not have their own religious leadership and religious customs and traditions, i.e., we cannot simply go along with the rabbinic view that dubs them as simple ignoramuses. Thus when the baraita informs us that "one who engages in the study of Torah in front of an *'am ha'areṣ* is like one who has intercourse with his bride in front of one," this cannot simply refer to ignorant masses, for the very cure for their ignorance would be engaging in the study of Torah in their presence. This is a group that had, somehow, to be kept out, because of their different practices or attitudes, deviant from the rabbinic perspective, including perhaps greater closeness to or toler- ance of Jewish Christianity. Galit Hasan-Rokem, "Narratives in Dialogue: A Folk Liter- ary Perspective on Interreligious Contacts in the Holy Land in Rabbinic Literature of Late Antiquity," in *Sharing the Sacred: Religious Contacts and Conflicts in the Holy Land, First–Fifteenth Centuries CE*, ed. Guy Stroumsa and Arieh Kofsky (Jerusalem: Yad Ben Zvi, 1998), 109–29. In this, Cynthia Baker must surely be right ("Neighbor at the Door or Enemy at the Gate? Notes Toward a Rabbinic Topography of Self and Other" [paper pre- sented at American Academy of Religion, New Orleans, 1996]). According to the nicely made point of Martin Goodman, rabbinic law for the Sabbath was followed precisely be- cause it was derived from "local custom sanctioned by local elders." Martin Goodman, *State and Society in Roman Galilee, A.D. 132–212* (Totowa, N.J.: Rowman and Allanheld, 1983), 98. Another way to think of this would be that Israelite religion in the first century consisted of a number of related cults with the rabbinic religion standing in relation to them much as Frankfurter describes the relation of Roman "paganism" and then Chris- tianity to the local cults of Egypt. David Frankfurter, *Religion in Roman Egypt: Assimila- tion and Resistance* (Princeton, N.J.: Princeton University Press, 1998), 45.

156. Cohen, *Beginnings of Jewishness*, 69–106.

157. As argued by Cohen himself in another context ("Virgin"). It should be remembered that Christian heresiology included a component that had to do with dif- ferent practice as well as different creed too, for instance, the Quartodeciman contro- versy, or the question of Eucharist on Saturdays. See also the related insight of Caroline Humfress: "The churches of the Christians, unlike the temples of the pagans, made pro- visions for lecture rooms where the Sacred Scripture which lay behind the beliefs and liturgical practices of Christianity could be expounded. Christians were expected to un- derstand their creeds and not just memorize them. In fact the late antique church de- manded a long period of theological instruction for its catechumens, as a necessary qualification for baptism. A comparison can be made with the equally important shift in late antique Judaism towards the imposition of rabbinical interpretative methods on Jewish communities in Mesopotamia, Palestine and elsewhere. For the average late Roman citizen the practice of religion increasingly went hand-in-hand with theological dogma" (Caroline Humfress, "Religion," in *The Evolution of the Late Antique World*, by Peter Garnsey and Caroline Humfress [Oxford: Orchard Academic Press, 2001], 135–70). It will be finally one of the works of this book, however, to distinguish between the "im- position of rabbinical interpretative methods" and "theological dogma" as modes of tex- tuality and technologies of "consensual orthodoxy." Both share, in a sense, as Carlin Barton has commented to me, in their replacement of "schools" for face-to-face tradi- tion in the production of community.

158. The unproblematic heterogeneity of Syrian Christianity in the early period as discussed by Han Drijvers would be an elegant example for this point. He describes early

Christianity in Syria as: "die Gesamtheit aller Interpretationen Jesu von Nazareth durch Personen und Gruppen." H. J. W. Drijvers, "Rechtgläubigkeit und Ketzerei im ältesten Syrischen Christentum," *Oriens Christianus Analecta* 197 (1974): 291.

159. For the analysis of a rabbinic text which provides an exact match for one of Justin's arguments, see Segal, *Two Powers*, 119.

160. The argument here is thus in direct contradiction to Goodman's earlier held opinion that "precisely [in] the period in which Christian self-definition was achieved through the exclusion of theological concepts defined by patristic writers as heretical[, t]he rabbis were not interested in doing the same thing" (Goodman, *State and Society*, 105). I imagine that Goodman would change this view now in light of Goodman, "Minim." In Chapter 6, I will return to the "Two Powers in Heaven" heresy that so exercises the Rabbis, arguing that far from a deviation from "Judaism," it represented a common Jewish theological view, prior to the rabbinic intervention.

161. Segal (*Two Powers*, x) has also made the point that the forms of rabbinic textuality have misled many into thinking that they had no doctrine, no sense of "orthodoxy," even in the broadest acceptation of the term.

162. I don't routinely assume that such texts do not preserve more ancient information sometimes, but only that we can almost never know when they do, and, in any case, in the details of formulation which surely develop over time, very important, ideological shifts are encoded and masked. For demonstration of this last point, see Chapter 7 below.

163. See William Horbury, *Jews and Christians in Contact and Controversy* (Edinburgh: T & T Clark, 1998), 67. That is prayer in the general sense. Although it is highly significant that Justin does *not* mention that this curse took place during the central liturgy of the Synagogue, the "eighteen blessings," it is nevertheless the case that he emphasizes that the cursing took place in synagogue, most plausibly at some point in a prayer service, in the broadest sense. It is highly significant, moreover, that at yet another place, Justin explicitly remarks the cursing of Christ, at any rate, as occurring "after the prayer" (137.2), positively excluding *birkat hamminim*, on which see below in the text. See already to this effect (Gedaliah Alon, "Jewish Christians: The Parting of the Ways," in *The Jews in Their Land in the Talmudic Age [70–640 C.E.]*, ed. and trans. Gershon Levi [Jerusalem: Magnes Press, 1984], 289). On the other hand, Alon's suggestion that the fact that a Genizah fragment of liturgy includes a curse of *minim* and *noṣrim* is evidence for "the original formulation as laid down in the days of Rabban Gamaliel" seems nothing short of fantastic to me ("Jewish Christians," 290; see already Emil Schürer, *Geschichte des jüdischen Volkes im Zeitalter Jesu Christi*, 4, reprint, 1901 [Hildesheim: Olms, 1964], ii, 543, whose argument seems unassailable). Alon's conflation of this evidence as supposedly belonging to the first century and that of Jerome from the fifth is symptomatic.

164. A. L. Williams, *Dialogue*, 33; Justin, *Dialogus cum Tryphone*, 97. See A. H. Goldfahn, "Justinus Martyr und die Agada," *Monatsschrift für Geschichte und Wissenschaft des Judentums* 22 (1873): 56; Oskar Skarsaune, *The Proof from Prophecy—a Study in Justin Martyr's Proof-Text Tradition: Text-Type, Provenance, Theological Profile* (Leiden: E. J. Brill, 1987), 290; and Hermann Strack and Paul Billerbeck, *Kommentar zum Neuen Testament aus Talmud und Midrasch* (Munich: C. H. Beck, 1924), iv, 212.

165. A. L. Williams, *Dialogue*, 94; Justin, *Dialogus cum Tryphone*, 147–48.

166. A. L. Williams, *Dialogue*, 202; Justin, *Dialogus cum Tryphone*, 235.

167. For the literature see Horbury, *Contact*, 68–70. See too the recent Rokeah, *Justin*

[English], 16–17, who seems content still to simply "believe" the rabbinic legend as to the early promulgation of the "curse of the heretics."

168. Not a euphemism, the "blessings" are that which Jews pray for; the curse is a curse on our enemies and thus a blessing to us, so to speak.

169. Pace Günther Stemberger, "Die sogennante 'Synode von Jabne' und das frühe Christentum," *Kairos* 19 (1977): 16. For a concise discussion (in Hebrew) of the compelling reasons for doubting the high antiquity of tannaitic texts (*baraitot*) found in the Babylonian Talmud, see Milikovsky, "Gehenna," 319, n. 35.

170. It has no more probative value than legends that ascribe the same prayers to the legendary "Men of the Great Assembly," for which legends see Horbury, *Contact*, 80–81; Horbury, nevertheless, does not see the analogy and its consequences. And yet, on the basis of these data, Skarsaune is prepared to conclude that "The prayer was introduced between 70 and 100 A.D., and had for its purpose to prevent Jewish Christians and other heretics from staying within the synagogue community" (Skarsaune, *Proof from Prophecy*, 290). Skarsaune insists that "the patristic evidence cannot easily be dismissed," but, as I shall argue immediately, there simply is no patristic witness that counts as evidence for the proposition that a formal liturgical curse against Christians existed before the fourth century. On this basis as well, I cannot accept the arguments of Horbury (*Contact*, 10, and 82–96), which are entirely dependent on accepting the talmudic report as gospel. As Horbury himself sums up his position, "the datum for comparison with second-century Christian evidence is not the Twelfth Benediction as we have it, but the formula 'of the *minim*' approved at Jamnia" (Horbury, *Contact*, 96). Compare the naively astonished but finally wise comment of Herford (*Christianity*, 313–14) that "it is remarkable that the Mishnah passes over in silence the famous change in the liturgy made by Gamliel II at Javneh when the 'formula concerning the Minim' was drawn up."

171. To be sure, the prayer that Samuel forgot was the blessing that includes the *minim* in its later versions, but there is no evidence there that it included *minim* in the version of that Palestinian talmudic text. Indeed, the fact that the blessing ends with "He subdues the brazen" (מכניע זדים) and not something about *minim* rather suggests, once more, that the *minim* were added later. According to Flusser, in fact, two entirely different blessings were combined, rendering this argument even stronger, "Some of the Precepts of the Torah from Qumran (4QMMT) and the Benediction Against the Heretics," in Hebrew, with English summary, *Tarbiz* 61, no. 3–4 (April–September 1992): 351–53. Flusser, however, considers that the joining of the two original blessings, one about *minim* and one about the brazen, was accomplished at Yavneh by our Samuel, a view that I find hard to support especially in the light of the Tosefta. One can only derive such a result by combining the two parallel narratives, one in the Palestinian and one in the Babylonian Talmud, while the narratives are, in fact, almost certainly simply doublets of each other. See, too, David Flusser, *Judaism and the Sources of Christianity* (Jerusalem: Magnes Press, 1988), 637–43, for an earlier version of Flusser's argument, substantially the same as the latter, Hebrew version but without the addition of significant material from the Dead Sea Scrolls in the latter.

172. Another reason for this particular identification would be to counter persistent Christian assertions that Gamaliel II was, himself, a crypto-Christian (Goranson, "Episode," 58). However, most importantly, as Gedaliah Alon already pointed out more than fifty years ago, many rabbinic ordinances were precisely "to provide authoritative support for certain ancient *halachot*, which were not firmly established . . . and to

refute those who challenge their validity." That being the case, it is quite obvious why such ordinances, including the famous "eighteen matters that were ordained *on that day*"—the mythical day on which rabbinic Judaism was founded at Yavneh—and liturgical forms, would be ascribed to Yavnean foundations. *Birkat hamminim* would fit easily into the same category, not necessarily "ancient" but coming from some other source than the Rabbis themselves. I am not saying that this is the way it happened, but it certainly could have been thus. For the meaning of "on that day," see further below.

173. Below, Chapter 7. Note how interestingly this matches with the persistent Christian representations of this figure (or his putative descendants) as having become crypto-Christians, as mentioned in the previous note.

174. Cf. Rokeah, *Justin* [English], 16 and especially 117–18. For Rokeah, moreover, even late talmudic narratives have the status of historical witnesses.

175. Cf. "That the specific included the Birkath ha-minim discussed above can be neither proven nor excluded, for Justin's language is too inexact to make a clear contribution to the disputed history of that prayer" (Lieu, *Image*, 134). Lieu's own discussion of Justin on the curse (132–35) is both rich and nuanced, as we have come to expect.

176. Note that Justin himself ascribes the curse not to the "teachers" but to the "archisynagogoi," a distinctly diasporic leadership group [137.2], in a context where he explicitly refers to the "Pharisaic teachers" as well. This is a highly significant piece of evidence, till now ignored, against the theory that Justin refers to *birkat hamminim*. See too Horner, *Trypho*, 134 and n. 185 there.

177. Stephen G. Wilson, *Related Strangers: Jews and Christians 70–170 C.E.* (Minneapolis, Minn.: Fortress Press, 1995), 181.

178. For a defense of my position on rabbinic historiography, see Boyarin, "Archives."

179. It is at least interesting to note that, as Jonathan Klawans has shown, it is only in this document that the notion of ritual Gentile impurity is first clearly articulated, Jonathan Klawans, "Notions of Gentile Impurity in Ancient Judaism," *AJS Review* 20, no. 2 (1995): 308–9. Could these two phenomena be connected? This is particularly salient when we emphasize (as Klawans does not) that ritual impurity was entirely a theoretical matter at the time of this document, and indeed at the time of the Mishna which also, according to Klawans's demonstration, adumbrates the notion. In other words, ascribing levitical impurity to Gentiles would have had no implications for behavior at all by this time (since after the Temple's destruction, levitical impurity had no force) and was purely a rhetorical construct.

180. Most of the liturgical innovations of the postdestruction period which the Rabbis accept as normative are ascribed by them to Yavneh and Yavnean Sages. This does not constitute positive evidence. It is entirely plausible that such innovations were developed at various times and in various centers (both cultural centers and geographical centers), and those which the Rabbis adopted were then ascribed by them to their own legendary proto-institution, the "Council of Yavneh."

181. Saul Lieberman, *Order Zeraim*, vol. 1 of *The Tosefta According to Codex Vienna, with Variants from Codices Erfurt, London, Genizah Mss. and Editio Princeps (Venice, 1521)* (New York: Jewish Theological Seminary of America, 1955), 17–18.

182. I would relate this to the famous rabbinic injunction not to separate from the public (Mishna Avot 2:4), which would mean, on this interpretation, not to remove oneself to a desert community. Note that the Qumran community refers to itself as having

"separated" from the majority of the people: פרשנו מרוב העם ש[ואתם יודעים]; see Elisha Qimron and John Strugnell, eds. and trans., *Qumran Cave 4.5: Miqṣat Ma'e Ha-Torah*, in collaboration with Y. Sussmann, contribution by A. Yardeni, Discoveries in the Judaean Desert (Oxford: Oxford University Press, at the Clarendon Press, 1994), 58. See also discussion of Sussmann, "Preliminary Observations," 38. The consideration offered above would support Sussmann's point there, that it was, indeed, the separatism of the Qumran community that marked them as a sect and not their halakhic or theological differences. But see there also 36, n. 115, for Sussmann's own qualification of this point. Note that Flusser, "Some Precepts," also considers the Essenes the original bearers of the curse in this blessing; however, he would regard them as the original referent of *minim*, whereas, in my view, it is the original form of the blessing in which *paroshim* were mentioned and not *minim* that intended the Essenes, or rather the Qumran sect, while the later version added the *minim*, as the Tosefta explicitly witnesses. These latter cannot, therefore, be the same as the former. In any case, Flusser ("Some Precepts," 350) certainly supports the view that the earliest levels of the "blessing" did not include Christians at all.

183. Pieter W. van der Horst, "The Birkat Ha-Minim in Recent Research," in *Hellenism-Judaism-Christianity: Essays on Their Interaction*, Contributions to Biblical Exegesis and Theology (Leuven: Peeters, 1998), 116.

184. See Virginia Burrus, "Rhetorical Stereotypes in the Portrait of Paul of Samosata," *Vigiliae Christianae* 43 (1989): 215–25, with earlier literature.

185. In other words, I am not simply reversing here the traditional narrative of Christianity's emergence from Judaism by substituting an opposing and equally simple-minded narrative of Judaism's emergence from Christianity. Rather, the narrative that I will be developing here is of mutual co-emergence of the two religious formations in the development of the episteme of religion.

186. See also Goodman, *State and Society*, 86, implying as well such a denial.

187. Reuven Kimelman has suggested that the assumption that the so-called curse of the *minim* automatically denotes Christians "is behind the oft-repeated assertion that about the year 100 the breach between Judaism and Christianity became irreparable" (Reuven Kimelman, "Birkat Ha-Minim and the Lack of Evidence for an Anti-Christian Jewish Prayer in Late Antiquity," in *Aspects of Judaism in the Greco-Roman Period*, ed. E. P. Sanders, A. I. Baumgarten, and Alan Mendelson, Jewish and Christian Self-Definition, 2 [Philadelphia: Fortress Press, 1981], 226–44; 391–403).

188. Although Justin himself has a Palestinian (Samaritan) background, the *Dialogue* is located in Ephesus, and I'm assuming that that is where he lived at some time before he wrote it, and that it may, therefore, be responsive to local conditions there. In addition to Justin, such texts as Melito's *Peri Pascha* and the martyrdoms of Polycarp and Pionios attest to both the closeness and the tenseness of the contact between Jews and Gentile Christians early on in that area. See Judith Lieu, "Accusations of Jewish Persecution in Early Christian Sources, with Particular Reference to Justin Martyr and the *Martyrdom of Polycarp*," in *Tolerance and Intolerance in Early Judaism and Christianity*, ed. Graham N. Stanton and Guy G. Stroumsa (Cambridge: Cambridge University Press, 1998), 279–95. And see especially Lieu, *Image*, 132, on the plausibility that Justin is referring to *local* practice and not to the *birkat hamminim*.

189. As suggested as well in Lieu, *Image*, 134.

190. Note that my position is somewhat different from Kimelman's in that I am

denying that there is any evidence for this "blessing" at all before the mid–third century, while he accepts its existence from the first century but argues that it was only against the Jewish Christian minority and not all Christians. Van der Horst essentially accepts Kimelman's argument, claiming as well that the alleged early *birkat hamminim* was not directed against Gentile Christians, but "in all probability it was only in the course of the fourth century (probably the second half) that the rapidly deteriorating relation between Christianity and the government on the one hand, and Judaism on the other, eventually led to the insertion of the curse against Christians *in general* into the Eighteen Benedictions. This curse is not the cause but the effect of the ever growing separation between the two religions. The original Birkat ha-minim, whatever its text may have been, was never intended to throw Christians out of the synagogues—that door always remained open, even in Jerome's time—but it was a berakhah that served to strengthen the bonds of unity within the nation in a time of catastrophe by deterring all those who threatened it" (van der Horst, "Birkat-Haminim," 124, emphasis added). Although van der Horst's hypothetical reconstruction is somewhat different from my conjecture, it is compatible as well with the revision of Judaeo-Christian history that I am proposing herein.

191. Kimelman, "Birkat Ha-Minim," 6. Compare Aline Pourkier, *L'Hérésiologie chez épiphane de Salamine*, Christianisme Antique 4 (Paris: Éditions Beauchesne, 1992), 470, who believes that the only difference between Justin and Origen's reports and those of Epiphanius and Jerome is that the latter had better Jewish informants, an interpretation of the evidence that seems highly unlikely to me. Pourkier's analysis of this whole question is marred by anachronism. Whether or not, in Acts, *Nazoréens* is a name for all Christians is not at all material to understanding what it might have meant in a fourth- or fifth-century setting, whether rabbinic or Christian.

192. Jerome, *Correspondence*, ed. Isidorus Hilberg, Corpus Scriptorum Ecclesiasticorum Latinorum (Vienna: Verlag der Österreichischen Akademie der Wissenschaften, 1996), 381–82.

193. For the latest treatment of this text, see Leonard L. Thompson, "The Martyrdom of Polycarp: Death in the Roman Games," *The Journal of Religion* 82, no. 1 (2002): 27–52.

194. Lieu, "I Am."

195. For a further (compatible) explanation, see Thompson, "Polycarp," 50.

196. Judith Lieu has made this point with respect to Justin's insistence that Jews were particularly involved in the persecution of Christians ("Accusations").

197. Lieu, *Image*, ix, emphasis original.

198. Lieu, "I Am."

199. It seems to me likely that I have simply mistaken Lieu's thrust here, since elsewhere she clearly writes: "The presence of the Jews alongside the pagans at 12.2, therefore, must be quite deliberate" (*Image*, 61). My interpretation of this "deliberateness" remains, however, quite distinct from hers. On the other hand, her developed interpretation is much richer than my schematic statement and possibly, at the end of the day, simply compatible with it. See especially pp. 78–79.

200. Lieu, "I Am."

201. Stephen Gero, "Jewish Polemic in the Martyrium Pionii and a 'Jesus' Passage from the Talmud," *Journal of Jewish Studies* 29 (1978): 164–68. Similar but even stronger arguments can be advanced with respect to the martyrdom of Pionius, which seems clearly to be a writing that models itself closely on the allegedly century-older Polycarp.

As Elizabeth Castelli has recently written: "Indeed, commentators have long recognized Pionius' strategy for articulating Christian identity succeeds only at the expense of his Jewish neighbors. Although he also attacks the 'pagan' community of Smyrna, Pionius reserves his starker and most venomous rhetoric for the Jews of the city." And again, "Moreover, Pionius places the onus on the Jews for construing the Christians as their enemies, leaving his Christian community innocent of such declarations" (Elizabeth A. Castelli, *Martyrdom and Memory: Early Christian Culture-Making* [Columbia University Press, 2003], chapter 3). "Many readers of Pionius' speeches have sought to situate them quite concretely in the precise historical situation of relations between Christians and Jews in third-century Smyrna. Such reconstructions tend to accept more or less at face value Pionius' rhetoric and accusations, rather than reading his speech as a contributor to the relations in question. Insofar as Pionius seeks to change his community's relationship with Jews in Smyrna, he provides no straightforward description of either community, but rather make a polemical intervention into their interactions. The identity, 'Christian,' that Pionius seeks to consolidate in his self-portrait in this text is a rhetorical and interpretive construction, not a simple historical datum," for "Pionius is also the guardian of the church's borders and arbiter of what counts as legitimate religion. The problem he diagnoses in this speech concerns the fact that Jews have been inviting Christians into the synagogues." The discourse of martyrdom in these West Asian texts is ostensibly against the pagans, but the centrality of the Jews in these Asian martyrdoms, as in chronotopical cotexts, such as Melito of Sardis's *Peri Pascha*, suggests strongly the discursive work of partitioning that was being carried out in this time and place.

202. This formulation seems to me compatible with the slightly different emphasis of Rebecca Lyman, who writes, "I am suggesting therefore that the creation of orthodoxy was a philosophical project of the marginalized, not the intellectual expression of an inevitable 'dogmatism' of Christianity" (J. Rebecca Lyman, "The Politics of Passing: Justin Martyr's Conversion as a Problem of 'Hellenization,'" in *Conversion in Late Antiquity and the Early Middle Ages*, ed. Anthony Grafton and Kenneth Mills [Rochester, N.Y.: University of Rochester Press]).

203. In other words, after the relative ecclesiastical triumph of Paulinism over Petrine or early Jacobite Christianity. While I do not subscribe to the older form of the Tübingen theory that held that there were two distinct strands of Christianity as institutions, Jewish and Gentile Christianity, with separate theologies, etc., it seems to me that Joan Taylor far underestimates the radical innovation within Christianity that Paul represents with his sharp move against and away from the Law, how much opposition such a move occasioned within earliest Christianity, and the significance of his eventual triumph, as it were. Joan E. Taylor, *Christians and the Holy Places: The Myth of Jewish-Christian Origins* (Oxford: Clarendon Press and Oxford University Press, 1993), 20. Adherence to the Law meant rather more than maintaining "a Jewish life-style" (pace Taylor, *Christians*, 21); it is a fundamental theological difference. It is, perhaps, Taylor's failure to appreciate this that leads her to underestimate the significance of this split within the early Christian movements.

204. For Paul's attack as being on the traditional "boundary markers" of Jewishness, see James D. G. Dunn, *Jesus, Paul and the Law: Studies in Mark and Galatians* (Louisville, Ky.: Westminster/John Knox Press, 1990), 183–214. I do not mean to be ascribing only one cause to this breach. Cohen (*Beginnings of Jewishness*, 70) argues that "all occurrences of the term *Ioudaios* before the middle or end of the second century B.C.E. should be trans-

lated not as 'Jew,' a religious term, but as 'Judaean,' an ethnic-geographic term. In the second half of the second century B.C.E. the term *Ioudaios* for the first time is applied even to people who are not ethnic or geographic Judaeans but who either have come to believe in the God of the Judaeans (i.e., they have become 'Jews') or have joined the Judaean state as allies or citizens (i.e., they have become 'Judaeans' in a political sense). Behind this semantic shift lies a significant development in the history of Judaism," and see ibid., 92–93, for an impressive bit of evidence for this claim. I am suggesting that this shift— huge to be sure—in the history of Judaism was necessary, but not sufficient, for precipitating the shift from a locative to a fully religious definition of "Jew" which was to take place only four centuries later in the second century A.C. Converts can be understood as adopted members of a family or naturalized citizens, and there is no indication yet that Jews could ever cease to be Jews by believing or practicing in the wrong way. The ways that one leaves a collective (voluntary or not) are as significant for defining the nature of that collective as the ways that one joins it. As Cohen himself points out, in the Hasmonean period, Jews could become "apostates," but they did not, thereby, cease to be Jews (Cohen, *Jewishness*, 105). It seems telling that in his consideration of crossing the boundary between Jew and non-Jew, Cohen never considers the question of crossing out—transgressing, yes (via intermarriage)—but not actual crossing out of the community. This is because he is apparently accepting as a phenomenological given the theological principle articulated by the Rabbis that "an Israelite, even one who has sinned, remains an Israelite." But I suggest that this principle, only found in late fourth-century Babylonian rabbinic sources, is itself a contingent piece of rabbinic ecclesiology (and even contingent within rabbinic ecclesiology) and not an essential principle of "Jewishness." This interpretation of Cohen here is supported by his position, explicitly held elsewhere, that dissidents from the rabbinic community were not excommunicated but merely denounced (Cohen, "Yavneh," 49). Indeed, Cohen explicitly claims that the Rabbis never considered the status of the apostate at all, leaving it for the rabbinic authorities of the Middle Ages to confront (Cohen, *Jewishness*, 333–34). It is my hypothesis—hypothesis, not assertion—that the status of one kind of dissident or deviant, the "heretic," was an explicit concern of early rabbinic Judaism, just as it was of Christianity at that time—indeed, because of it.

Chapter 3. Naturalizing the Border

1. David M. Halperin, "How to Do the History of Male Homosexuality," *GLQ: A Journal of Lesbian and Gay Studies* 6, no. 1 (2000): 87–123.

2. Daniel Boyarin, "Women's Bodies and the Rise of the Rabbis: The Case of Soṭah," *Studies in Contemporary Jewry: Jews and Gender, the Challenge to Hierarchy* 16 (2001): 88–100.

3. In his second volume, Le Boulluec argues for a somewhat different notion of heresy among the Christian platonists of Alexandria, Clement and Origen, namely not that which violates scriptural or apostolic authority, or which stands outside the institutional ecclesia, but that which is illogical or philosophically contradictory to the "pattern of Christian truth."

4. David T. Runia, "Review of Le Boulluec," *Vigiliae Christianae* 42 (1988): 189.

5. "C'est dans cette entreprise, très probablement, qu'il pouvait, à l'imitation du rabbinisme palestinien qui avait réussi à assurer autour de lui l'unité du judaïsme après la ruine du Temple, dresser une liste de «succession» capable de garantir l'autorité et la validité d'un courant ecclésiastique" (Alain Le Boulluec, *La notion d'hérésie dans la littérature grecque IIe–IIIe siècles* [Paris: études Augustiniennes, 1985], 90); and see also: "Dans le mesure même où le *Dialogue* exploite un thème juif pour le détourner au bénéfice du christianisme, on est en droit de considérer que c'est à travers l'emprunt au judaïsme qu'un tel motif a chez Justin des traits grecs. Ce n'est pas le modèle des écoles philosophiques qui gouverne sa conception de la validité de la tradition. Son influence n'est qu'indirecte et passe par l'adaptation antériure en milieu juif" [To the extent that the *Dialogue* indeed utilizes a Jewish theme in order to turn it to the advantage of Christianity, one has the right to think that it is through a loan from Judaism that such a motif in Justin has Greek characteristics. It is not the model of the philosophical schools which rule his conception of the validity of the tradition. The influence of this model is but indirect and passes through the earlier adaptation via the Jewish milieu] (Le Boulluec, *La notion*, 86). Moreover: "L'existence de cette *diadochè* de l'erreur dans l'hérésiologie de Justin conduit á penser qu'il devait lui opposer une *diadochè* de vérité. Nous avons vu que cell-ci dérivait comme une conséquence logique du modèle d'origine juive que Justin retournait contre le judaïsme pour garantir l'authenticité de la tradition chrétienne" [The existence of this *diadoche* of error in the heresiology of Justin leads us to think that we ought to oppose to it a *diadoche* of truth. We saw that this one was derived as a logical consequence from the model of the Jewish origin which Justin turned against Judaism in order to guarantee the authenticity of the Christian tradition] (Le Boulluec, *La notion*, 89).

6. "Il convient cependant de préciser que l'exemple juif a dû affirmer encore le thème de la succession véritable au moment où la difficulté cruciale a été celle des divisions à l'intérieur du christianisme et où Justin a mis en place le schéma hérésiologique ayant pour fin de les contrôler et de les réduire. Il est très vraisemblable en effet que l'effort de reconstitution et d'unification du judaïsme accompli par l'orthodoxie rabbinique ait été imité par l'église, à la faveur de l'émulation stimulante que ce regain de vitalité du frère aîné, à supplanter de nouveau, n'a pu manquer de renforcer" (Le Boulluec, *La notion*, 111).

7. Elias Bickerman [Élie Bikerman], "La Chaîne de la tradition pharisienne," *Revue biblique* 59, no. 1 (January 1952): 44–54.

8. As noted by David T. Runia, "Philo of Alexandria and the Greek *Hairesis*-Model," *Vigiliae Christianae* 53, no. 2 (May 1999): 123.

9. Of course, the paradoxes of younger (Jacob) and elder (Esau) here have been inspiring interpretation since antiquity. See Geoffrey D. Dunn, "Tertullian and Rebekah: A Re-Reading of an 'Anti-Jewish' Argument in Early Christian Literature," *Vigiliae Christianae* 52, no. 2 (May 1998): 119–45. Also the vital Israel Jacob Yuval, *Two Nations in Your Womb: Perceptions of Jews and Christians*, in Hebrew (Tel-Aviv: Alma/Am Oved, 2000), 16–44, or Israel Jacob Yuval, *Two Nations in Your Womb: Perceptions of Jews and Christians in the Middle Ages* (Berkeley and Los Angeles: University of California Press, 2003), Chapter 1.

10. Cf. "Tout cela fut une innovation à Jérusalem, et serait une révolution ailleurs. Lois et traditions non écrites, *opiniones quas a maioribus accepimus de diis immortalibus*, étaient partout le fondement de la foi" [All of this was an innovation from Jerusalem. It

was a revolution there. Law and unwritten traditions, *opiniones quas a maioribus accepimus de diis immortalibus* were everywhere the basis of the religion] (Bickerman, "La Chaîne," 52). If I understand Bickerman's somewhat cryptic comment correctly, he, like Le Boulluec, locates the Christian revolution in a "Jewish" innovation, not surprisingly, since even this otherwise highly critical scholar simply "believes" the historical reports of the rabbinic literature and accordingly locates aspects of the tradition in high antiquity (Bickerman, "La Chaîne," 53).

11. Martin Goodman, "The Function of Minim in Early Rabbinic Judaism," in *Geschichte—Tradition—Reflexion: Festschrift für Martin Hengel zum 70. Geburtstag*, ed. H. Cancik, H. Lichtenberger, and P. Schäfer (Tübingen: Mohr Siebeck, 1996), 502, emphasis added. Oddly, Goodman here contradicts his own explicit methodological stricture in a much earlier work in which he wrote: "I shall follow the lead of Neusner in confining my use of the rabbinic texts to those that are contemporary. The Jerusalem Talmud . . . and the Babylonian Talmud . . . may well contain trustworthy traditions about the tannaitic period, but it has been shown that even those stories and laws that appear most reliable—because they are ascribed in the texts to tannaim and are couched in tannaitic Hebrew and Mishnaic formulas—are likely to be either misremembered in the light of subsequent changes in rabbinic thought or even deliberately falsified to aid such changes." Martin Goodman, *State and Society in Roman Galilee*, A.D. 132–212 (Totowa, N.J.: Rowman and Allanheld, 1983), 8, and see also p. 11 there where Goodman explicitly allows that "Yavnean" legal rulings very likely represent the assumptions of the Galilee of the late second century, and stories a fortiori, so how, then can we know anything of Josephus's contemporaries from rabbinic texts?

12. Shaye J. D. Cohen, "The Significance of Yavneh: Pharisees, Rabbis, and the End of Jewish Sectarianism," *Hebrew Union College Annual* 55 (1984): 29.

13. This is more in the spirit of Cohen's own indication that what he learns from the Mishnaic texts on Yavneh is that the tannaim (i.e., the Rabbis of the *second* century) refused to see themselves as Pharisees (although I draw different conclusions from this refusal).

14. Frequently called in English the "Ethics of the Fathers," a highly misleading designation.

15. The one exception seems to be Shaye J. D. Cohen, "A Virgin Defiled: Some Rabbinic and Christian Views on the Origins of Heresy," *Union Seminary Quarterly Review* 36, no. 1 (Fall 1980): 1–11 who, while arguing a position similar to the one in his later "Yavneh" seems to sense the difficulty that the Avot passage presents for his approach. See there especially, "Thus this chain of tradition clearly asserts that rabbis and Rabbinic Judaism stand in a direct line with Moses 'our Rabbi,' i.e., that rabbinic authority is of Mosaic origin and character. . . . This is unfortunate for our purposes, since the idea that Moses received at Sinai an eternal *regula fidei* or set of principles but otherwise left no binding legacy on future generations is very close to the Christian theory analyzed above" (Cohen, "Virgin," 3). See also Günther Stemberger, "Die sogenannte 'Synode von Jabne' und das frühe Christentum," *Kairos* 19 (1977): 21. Most recently (as this book was in its final stages of preparation) Amram Tropper, "*Tractate Avot* and Early Christian Succession Lists," in *The Ways That Never Parted*, ed. Peter Schaeffer (Berlin: Mohr Siebeck, 2002) appeared, coinciding with several points made here, while suggesting a different approach to some of the issues. I have been able to incorporate several references to his discussion, mostly in the notes.

16. I am using the translation here of Moshe Kline, "The Art of Writing the Oral Tradition: Leo Strauss, the Maharal of Prague, and Rabbi Judah the Prince" (Jerusalem, 1998), www.chaver.com/Torah/Articles/The Art-H.HTM. I have found his formalist analysis of this pericope illuminating as well, as the following discussion should demonstrate. For a fascinating account of the *contents* of this chapter with attention to the particular historical-social circumstances of its production, see Albert I. Baumgarten, *The Flourishing of Jewish Sects in the Maccabean Era: An Interpretation*, Supplements to the Journal for the Study of Judaism 55 (Leiden: E. J. Brill, 1997), 147–49.

17. See also Moshe David Herr, "Continuum in the Chain of Torah Transmission," *Zion* 44 (1979): 43–56, x–xi, in Hebrew with English summary; Steven D. Fraade, "Shifting from Priestly to Non-Priestly Legal Authority: A Comparison of the Damascus Document and the Midrash Sifra," *Dead Sea Discoveries* 6 (1999): 109–25.

18. Herr, "Continuum," x. Israel Yuval has noted a parallel erasure of the priests within rabbinic literature. Second Temple texts know of a priestly messiah, a messiah of the lineage of Aaron or of Levi (Yuval, *Nations*, 50 and literature cited there), while such a figure is unknown from rabbinic texts, which have substituted a messiah the son of Joseph for the earlier priestly messiah. This seems definitely to follow the same pattern of priestly displacement by the Rabbis. See also Fraade, "Shifting."

19. Bickerman, "La Chaîne."

20. Judah Goldin, "The First Pair (Yose Ben Yoezer and Yose Ben Yohanan) or the Home of a Pharisee," *AJS Review* 5 (1980): 41–62.

21. Kline, "Art of Writing," 12.

22. In other words, I am suggesting that rather than mere misogyny, the statement of Yose ben Yohanan has to do with a power struggle in which rabbinic authority—that is whatever rabbinic authority was actually won—is won at the expense of traditional sources of religious knowledge, including that of women. Galit Hasan-Rokem has contributed the insight that the insistence of the Rabbis on resurrection of the dead was not disconnected from the production of the particular "utopian thinking" embodied in the *diadoche* of the Rabbis (Galit Hasan-Rokem, *The Web of Life—Folklore in Rabbinic Literature: The Palestinian Aggadic Midrash Eikha Rabba*, trans. Batya Stein, Contraversions: Jews and Other Differences [Stanford, Calif.: Stanford University Press, 2000], 180–81).

23. It is, interestingly enough, Rufinus of Aquileia who first uses the term *Princeps* to translate Origen's *Patriarchos* (Lee I. Levine, "The Status of the Patriarch in the Third and Fourth Centuries," *Journal of Jewish Studies* 47, no. 1 [Spring 1996]: 22).

24. Following the reasonable conjecture that this text originally stood at the beginning of the Mishna as its "introduction."

25. Kline, "Art of Writing," 6.

26. For the distinct possibility that this is not a return to Hillel but a continuation of the line of the patriarchs with a Rabbi Hillel in that line, see Menahem Kister, *Iyunim be-Avot de-R. Natan Nosah, Arikhah u-Farshanut* (Jerusalem: Ha-Universitah ha-Ivrit, ha-Hug la-Talmud Yad Yitshak Ben Tsevi, ha-Makhon le-Heker Erets-Yi sra el ve-Yishuvah, 1998), 117–21. The argument from *lectio dificilior*, however, cuts both ways here, since a wise scribe was as likely to write Rabbi Hillel in order to continue the patriarchal line and "straighten out" the chronology of the text as to substitute the much more familiar Hillel for the less well-known Rabbi Hillel. In any case, my argument for interpolation (which, itself, is as old as some early modern scholars) is not damaged either way. I thank

Ishay Rosen-Zvi, who called my attention to the relevance here of this important scholarly work.

27. Rabbi Shimʻon ben Tsemaḥ Duran (1381–1444) noted it.

28. David N. Myers, *Re-Inventing the Jewish Past: European Jewish Intellectuals and the Zionist Return to History*, Studies in Jewish History (New York: Oxford University Press, 1995). The most important of the scholars of the "Jerusalem School" about which Myers writes is, arguably, Gedaliah Alon, upon whom Glucker relies. See Gedaliah Alon, "The Patriarchate of Rabban Joḥanan B. Zakkai," in *Jews, Judaism and the Classical World: Studies in Jewish History in the Times of the Second Temple and Talmud*, trans. Israel Abrahams (Jerusalem: Magnes Press, 1977), 314–43. See recently, Seth Schwartz, *Imperialism and Jewish Society from 200 B.C.E. to 640 C.E.* (Princeton, N.J.: Princeton University Press, 2001), 111–12: "G. Alon, who always ascribed to the rabbis absolutely as much power and popularity as the most romantically sentimental reading of rabbinic literature would allow." The point is not that Alon was a naive scholar; he wasn't that, but he certainly had a very different set of assumptions about the relationship of rabbinic legends to historical realities than most scholars would now subscribe to.

29. But it should be carefully noted that Alon himself was not condemnatory of Rabban Yoḥanan ben Zakkai ("Patriarchate," 324–25).

30. Alon, "Patriarchate," 334–43.

31. John Glucker, *Antiochus and the Late Academy*, Hypomnemata Heft 56 (Göttingen: Vandenhoeck and Ruprecht, 1978), 361. However brilliant, Alon's positivism and naive reliance on the texts as reflections of reality have been long superseded within the field. See, e.g., Stemberger, "Synode," and literature cited there. For work that is still being written in this mold, see, e.g., Ephrat (Rubin) Habas, "Rabban Gamaliel of Yavneh and His Sons: The Patriarchate Before and After the Bar Kokhva Revolt," *Journal of Jewish Studies* 50, no. 1 (1999): 21–37.

32. Although, it should be noted, Alon himself was capable of much more critical formulations as well: "We have no real proof that the Nasi had any official constitutional status in the Sanhedrin during the Second Commonwealth. On the contrary, it is much more likely that he was simply the de facto leader of his party, occupying no legally recognized office. Consequently, Rabban Gamaliel can be described in Acts of the Apostles (5.34) simply as one highly respected member of the Sanhedrin, much as Josephus describes Shemaya (or Shammai)" (Gedaliah Alon, *The Jews in Their Land in the Talmudic Age [70–640 C.E.]*, ed. and trans. Gershon Levi [Jerusalem: Magnes Press, 1984], 194). See also Ephraim E. Urbach, *The Sages: Their Concepts and Beliefs*, trans. Israel Abrahams (Jerusalem: Magnes Press, 1975), 580, 593.

33. Glucker, *Antiochus*, 361.

34. Explicitly so according to Gedaliah Alon, "The Patriarchate of Rabbi Yoḥanan Ben Zakkai," in Hebrew, in *Studies in Jewish History in the Times of the Second Temple, the Mishna and the Talmud* (Tel Aviv: Hakibbutz Hameuchad, 1967), 273: "And even here the mainstay of the usurpers of the family of the Patriarchs was Rabban Yoḥanan ben Zakkai."

35. Alon, "Patriarchate," 265 and for the Gamalielites as his descendants, Alon, "Patriarchate," 271.

36. Glucker, *Antiochus*, 362.

37. On this question, see David Goodblatt, *The Monarchic Principle: Studies in Jewish Self-Government in Antiquity*, Texte und Studien zum Antiken Judentum 38 (Tübin-

gen: Mohr Siebeck, 1994), 144; and now Haim Shapira, "The Deposition of Rabban Gamaliel: Between History and Legend," in Hebrew with English summary, *Zion* 64, no. 1 (1999): 17–19 whose own conclusions corroborate from another angle the suggestions offered here.

38. Avot could then be seen as an instance of the genre of literature Περι διαδοχων, on which see W. von Kienle, "Die Berichte über die Sukzessionen der Philosophen in der hellenistischen und spätantiken Literatur" (Berlin: Freiuniversität, 1961), cited in Runia, "Philo and *Hairesis*," 123 [but unexamined by me], and R. G. Andria, *I frammenti delle successioni dei filosofi* (Naples: Università degli studi di Salerno, 1989). This is essentially the point of Bickerman, "La Chaîne," except that I would hesitatingly suggest that it characterizes the whole tractate, not merely its introductory section.

39. See, too, Tropper, "Succession," who makes a similar point and compares the succession list of Sextus Empiricus in which the latter added his own philosophical genealogy onto someone else's list and ended it up with himself and with his disciple.

40. It is simply not the case, then, contra Glucker, that "By the time the successionlist was formulated, it was already conceived as a succession to two *offices*" (Glucker, *Antiochus*, 359, n. 84). Alon had already noted that this is an anachronism (Alon, "Patriarchate," 254, n. 4). See also Lee I. Levine, *The Rabbinic Class of Roman Palestine in Late Antiquity* (New York: Jewish Theological Seminary of America, 1989), 75. See also Mishna Ta'anit 2:1. All other sources are even later than this.

41. Glucker, *Antiochus*, 358, n. 83.

42. Although this is probably only a much later development read back in legend onto Rabbi Yehuda. For compelling argument to this effect, see Schwartz, *Jewish Society*, 111. Cf.: "In all probability, many of the privileges and the extensive authority of the Patriarchate reflected in later, non-Jewish sources (especially *Codex Theodosianus*, Libanius and several of the Church fathers) were first granted to R. Judah" (Levine, *Rabbinic Class*, 34). Moreover, Levine grants that while Rabbi Yehuda's grandfather, Rabban Gamaliel II, may have had contacts with Roman authorities, "it is difficult to assess his official position and the extent of his authority within the Jewish community," so on what grounds, I ask, does one speak of a "decline" in the status of the office of the patriarch in the days of Rabbi Yehuda's father, Rabbi Shim'on? (Pace Levine, *Rabbinic Class*, 34.) Jean Juster, *Les Juifs dans l'Empire Romain: Leur condition juridique, economique et sociale* (Paris: P. Geuthner, 1914), 1:393, followed by Michael Avi-Yonah, *The Jews of Palestine: A Political History from the Bar Kokhba War to the Arab Conquest* (New York: Schocken Books, 1976), 56 ff., also hold that the patriarch was a typical Roman client-king, established as such after the Bar Kokhba rebellion by Antoninus Pius in order to have a puppet government to control the Jews, and that Rabbi Yehuda was, therefore, the first. See now, however, Schwartz, *Jewish Society*, 111–13, who argues compellingly that this reconstruction is implausible and sees Rabbi Yehuda's patriarchate in quite a different light. Schwartz's arguments would not materially affect the present line of reasoning. This puts, of course, something of a different spin on the legends of the great friendship between Antoninus and Rabbi Yehuda in the Talmuds. See meanwhile Shmuel Krauss, *Antoninus und Rabbi* (Frankfurt am Main: Sanger and Friedberg, 1910); Luitpold Wallach, "The Colloquy of Marcus Aurelius with the Patriarch Judah 1," *Jewish Quarterly Review* 31 (1940): 259–86. Indeed, given the paucity of references to even Rabbi Yehuda I as "patriarch" in even the rabbinic texts, as well as the fact that the earliest external references to the office are from the mid–third century (Origen), it seems not impossible that it was

only his son or grandson who was fully established in this office. The reference in Origen is fascinating, for it indicates that the Jews called the patriarch a king as part of a propaganda effort against Christians, who cited Gen. 39:10 which says that the Messiah will come after "rulers shall fail from Judah and the leaders from his thighs, when he shall come for whom it [the kingdom] is reserved," as indicating that the Christ had come. As Origen writes, "For it is abundantly clear from history and from what we see at the present day that after the times of Christ kings have not existed among the Jews" (Origen, *On First Principles*, trans. and introd. by G. W. Butterworth, introd. by Henri de Lubac [Gloucester, Mass.: Peter Smith, 1973], 259). To this charge, Jews apparently rebutted that "what is said by Jacob in Genesis is said of Judah, and who declare that there remains to this day a ruler who comes from the tribe of Judah, that is to say, that person who is the ruler of the Jewish nation and whom they call the Patriarch, and, they add, men of his seed cannot fail to continue until the advent of that Christ whom they picture to themselves" (Origen, *On First Principles*, 260. Cf. also the passage in Origen's *Ep. ad Africanum* 14 [P.G. 11, 82 ff.]). Justin Martyr, tellingly, cites the same Christian argument against the Jews and knows of some Jewish answers to the charge, referring to High Priests and prophets, but none referring to the patriarch as ruler and king of the Jews (A. Lukyn Williams, ed. and trans., *Justin Martyr: The Dialogue with Trypho*, Translations of Christian Literature [London: SPCK, 1930], 103–4). It is also possible that the patriarch did not, in fact, have any real power until the fourth century, with some prestige, however, accruing to the office by the mid–third century, given that we cannot ignore the evidence of Origen.

43. This position is, of course, consistent with the most current views on the patriarchate, which see it as growing in power through the fourth century, as summed up by Levine, "Status." Seth Schwartz has proposed an elegant hypothesis to account for the beginnings of patriarchal power in the early third century, arguing that since Jewish communities both in Palestine and the Diaspora had lost much of their power after the various revolts (115, Diaspora; 135, Palestine), they needed some form of semi-official representation if any petitions of theirs were to be heard in the imperial court: "If the patriarchs now assumed the role of Herodian-style advocates for diaspora communities, they would have acquired political leverage—and enhanced fund-raising potential—there, not to mention visibility in the Imperial court (is this the reality behind the fictional tales of the meetings of 'Antoninus and Rabbi'?), and renown at home" (Schwartz, *Jewish Society*, 114).

44. Shaye J. D. Cohen, "Patriarchs and Scholarchs," *Proceedings of the American Academy of Jewish Research* 48 (1981): 74. This is a very important paper, which I am sure Cohen would today modify so that his talmudic texts about Yavneh and the patriarchate would be read as parallels to the fourth-century neoplatonic and neoperipatetic texts that he cites and not be referred to the second or the first century, but there is vision, yet, for another day!

45. Israel Lévy, "L'Origine davidique de Hillel," *Revue des études Juives* 31 (1895): 202–11.

46. See also, on this point, Tropper, "Succession."

47. Cf. "In fact, the Pelopid stemma bears all the hallmarks of having been 'grafted on' to the Argive genealogies" (Jonathan M. Hall, *Ethnic Identity in Greek Antiquity* [Cambridge: Cambridge University Press, 1997], 90).

48. Hall, *Ethnic Identity*, 99.

49. Alon argues that Rabban Yoḥanan ben Zakkai was a patriarch because he is called *Rabban* as the patriarchs are, rather than *Rabbi*. The texts, however, are all hundreds of years later and could easily reflect this grafting and not some historical "reality." From my perspective, the latter explanation is almost certainly preferable. *Rabban*, moreover, itself, may have simply been the name of the leader of a school and only later taken as the title of the patriarch. It is important to note that Rabbi Yehuda himself is never referred to as *Rabban*. The references to Gamaliel in Acts hardly seem to be representing him as other than the dominant Pharisaic teacher and head of a Pharisaic school.

50. Cf. Albert I. Baumgarten, "The Akivan Opposition," *Hebrew Union College Annual* 50 (1979): 179–97.

51. Albert I. Baumgarten, "The Pharisaic *Paradosis*," *Harvard Theological Review* 80 (1987): 67.

52. Language adopted from Erich S. Gruen, *Heritage and Hellenism: The Reinvention of Jewish Tradition*, Hellenistic Culture and Society 30 (Berkeley and Los Angeles: University of California Press, 1998), 263, with reference to a different text and a different figure but a similar discursive and political move. Interestingly, Kline's analysis, building on that of the sixteenth-century Rabbi Loewe of Prague, demonstrates as well that thematically, the discourse of the pairs begins with aphorisms about home life and proceeds through ever-expanding rungs of authority—student, judge, teacher—until Hillel and Shammai are effectively giving rules for leaders of the entire people. This could be taken as a covert recognition that the leadership of the rabbinic movement is, indeed, a recent acquisition, or even (most likely) just wishful thinking. See also Baumgarten, who writes: "Note that the core of *m. 'Avot* is Pharisaic, but literary analysis has shown that the core underwent substantial revision before becoming the text of *m. 'Avot* as we know it now" (Baumgarten, "Pharisaic *Paradosis*," 67). This reconstruction can be supported by reference to the A version of Avot d'Rabbi Natan (a later commentary on Avot, based, however, on an earlier rescension), in which indeed Yoḥanan ben Zakkai comes immediately after Hillel and Shammai, as remarked by Anthony Saldarini, *Scholastic Rabbinism: A Literary Study of the Fathers According to Rabbi Nathan* (Chico, Calif.: Scholars Press, 1982), 11. Saldarini comes closest to the position articulated here (Saldarini, *Scholastic Rabbinism*, 16) without, however, I think taking into consideration the full implications of the point. As conveniently summarized by Saldarini (*Scholastic Rabbinism*, 15), it is easy to see how the present hypothesis differs from previous ones, in which the chain of tradition ends with Hillel and Shammai and the Rabbi Yoḥanan ben Zakkai pericope is an entirely separate literary source (held by such major authorities as J. N. Epstein, *Introductions to the Literature of the Tannaim*, in Hebrew [Jerusalem: Magnes/Dvir, 1957], 232; Louis Finkelstein, *Introduction to Tractates Fathers and The Fathers of Rabbi Nathan*, in Hebrew [New York: Jewish Theological Seminary of America, 1950], and in another realm Dieter Georgi, "The Records of Jesus in the Light of Ancient Accounts of Revered Men," in *Proceedings of the Society of Biblical Literature* [Chico, Calif.: Scholars Press, 1972], 538–39). What all these analysts have missed, in my opinion, is that the literary form of the Yoḥanan sayings themselves indicate that it was the original continuation and conclusion of the chain of tradition. Moreover, since, as Saldarini has seen, "The introduction [of the traditions] of Johanan's disciples resembles that given the saying of the Men of the Great Assembly in ch. 1" and, therefore, "suggests that Johanan's disciples are part of the chain of tradition." I would opine, against all the authorities cited above, that we have *one* original source into which Rabbi Yehuda the Pa-

triarch has forcibly interpolated the patriarchal chain. That original source consisted in the *diadoche* of the Rabbis up to the founding of the school by Rabbi Yoḥanan and then continued with "the listing and characterization of his disciples," which is "common in the lives of Hellenistic philosophers" (Saldarini, *Scholastic Rabbinism*, 12).

53. Jacob Neusner, "The Formation of Rabbinic Judaism: Yavneh (Jamnia) from A.D. 70 to 100," in *Principat: Religion (Judentum: Pälastinisches Judentum [Forts.])*, ed. Wolfgang Haase, Aufstieg und Niedergang der Römischen Welt (Berlin: Walter de Gruyter, 1979), 39–40. I find Neusner's hypothesis somewhat overdrawn but it moves us in a compelling direction.

54. Saul Lieberman, *Order Mo'ed*, vol. 2 of *The Tosefta According to Codex Vienna, with Variants from Codices Erfurt, London, Genizah Mss. and Editio Princeps (Venice, 1521)* (New York: Jewish Theological Seminary of America, 1962), 198.

55. Saul Lieberman, *Order Mo'ed*, vol. 3 of *Tosefta Ki-Fshuta: A Comprehensive Commentary on the Tosefta* (New York: Jewish Theological Seminary of America, 1962), 655.

56. For a different historical explanation of this doubling of the story, see Yuval, *Nations*, 77–78, and esp. 82.

57. Flavius Josephus, *Books XVIII–XX*, vol. IX of *Jewish Antiquities*, trans. L. H. Feldman, Loeb Classical Library (Cambridge: Harvard University Press, 1965), 11. Feldman's comment *apud* Josephus's description of the Sadducees: "they reckon it a virtue to dispute with the teachers of the path of wisdom that they pursue" (Josephus, *Antiquities*, 15), that this means the Sadducees are argumentative and boorish, because "even a cursory examination of the Talmud will reveal that the Pharisees were no whit inferior to the Sadducees in skill of disputation" (Josephus, *Antiquities*, 14), is dependent on a pietistic conflation of Pharisees and later Rabbis.

58. See too Israel Jacob Yuval, "The Haggadah of Passover and Easter," in Hebrew, *Tarbiz* 65, no. 1 (October–December 1995): 10, Israel Jacob Yuval, "Easter and Passover as Early Jewish-Christian Dialogue," in *Passover and Easter: Origin and History to Modern Times*, ed. Paul F. Bradshaw and Lawrence A. Hoffman, Two Liturgical Traditions 5 (Notre Dame, Ind.: University of Notre Dame Press, 1999), 127–60.

59. Glucker, *Antiochus*, 359, n. 83.

60. Note that, on other grounds, Lee I. Levine has denied the existence of permanent schools with *diadochoi* before the third century in Palestine. See Levine, *Rabbinic Class*, 29 and passim. Note as well that this interpretation supports Glucker's general argument that a *hairesis* was not a school in the sense of an organized institution but only in the import of a school of thought. Tropper makes very similar distinctions within the Christian traditions between traditions of succession that were the *diadochoi* of teachers and those that provided a list of "rulers" of the Church, arguing that "Robert Grant has noted that 'as a schoolman Eusebius was aware of the importance of legitimate succession, especially in the teaching of philosophy' and Grant accordingly suggests 'that along with Eusebius' primary emphasis on episcopal succession there is a clearly identifiable emphasis on school succession, which actually existed, in his view, at Alexandria and Caesarea.' Now even if Alexandria was not home to an established Christian school, Eusebius lent the aura of an academy to what may have been an informal educational setting by employing the Hellenistic successions genre. In addition, the institutional and scholastic successions in Eusebius's history intersect in Dionysius of Alexandria who was both a bishop and the head of the Christian school in Alexandria. For Eusebius, the institutional succession of church leaders reflected the history of Christian leadership

while the scholastic succession of the school reflected the Christian intellectual tradition and these two streams united where the successions merged, in the person of Dionysius of Alexandria." Tropper notes, moreover, that Dionysius was contemporary with Rabbi Yehuda; in fact, the parallels with the history of the rabbinic schools are stunning (Tropper, "Succession"). This, then, would provide an elegant parallel to the uniting of two streams conjectured above in the formation of the rabbinic movement *at the same time* as this Dionysius. A fascinating collection of texts from rabbinic literature gathered by Ofra Meir (but woefully underread) suggests that the derivation of Yehuda's line from King David was a myth meant to establish the political succession, while the putative derivation from Hillel was equally a myth to establish the legitimacy of the scholastic succession. The transformation of the pairs into officeholders at a very late date in the production of the Mishna would be an attempt to produce that same synthesis. Meir herself reads as if the first is an ideological legend, while the second is "fact" (Ofra Meir, *Rabbi Judah the Patriarch: Palestinian and Babylonian Portrait of a Leader*, in Hebrew, Sifriyat "Helal Ben-Hayim" [Tel-Aviv: Hakibbutz Hameuhad, 1999], 27–33).

61. As Yehoram Biton has remarked to me, another clause in "Rabbi's Testament," his command to Gamaliel III to "conduct your Patriarchate with severity, and strike fear into the hearts of the sages," points in this direction as well (oral communication, July 13, 1999).

62. Levine, *Rabbinic Class*, 36.

63. Allen Brent, "Diogenes Laertius and the Apostolic Succession," *Journal of Ecclesiastical History* 44, no. 3 (July 1993): 367–89.

Chapter 4. The Intertextual Birth of the Logos

1. This view was less current, interestingly enough, in the nineteenth century. See for instance, Samuel Hirsch, *Die Religionsphilosophie der Juden*, Jewish Philosophy, Mysticism, and the History of Ideas (New York: Arno Press, 1980), 706. I thank Dr. Dirk Westerkamp for this reference. Hirsch is only the tip of the iceberg. In research that she is pursuing now, Almut Bruckstein will show that this was one of the major scholarly issues in the study of early Judaism/Christianity in that century.

2. James A. T. Robinson, "The Relationship of the Prologue to the Gospel of St. John," *New Testament Studies* 9 (March 1962): 128. In fairness, I wish to point out that the judicious Robinson appropriately qualifies his statement.

3. Basil Studer, *Trinity and Incarnation: The Faith of the Early Church*, ed. Andrew Louth, trans. Matthias Westerhoff (Collegeville, Minn.: Liturgical Press, 1993), 14.

4. James D. G. Dunn, *The Partings of the Ways Between Christianity and Judaism and Their Significance for the Character of Christianity* (London: SCM Press and Trinity Press International, 1991), 135. Since for Dunn—and, I think, quite compellingly so—the major departure from anything like the Jewish koine of any first-century "Christian" is Paul's rejection of the Law (for my defense of this interpretation of Paul, see Daniel Boyarin, *A Radical Jew: Paul and the Politics of Identity*, Contraversions: Critical Studies in Jewish Literature, Culture, and Society [Berkeley and Los Angeles: University of California Press, 1994]), the primary gap would be between "Christian" and "Christian," not be-

tween "Christian" and "Jew." Not surprisingly, in Paul's own works his conflicts with other Jewish Christians are much more marked than his conflicts with "Jews."

5. Dunn, *Partings*, 238.

6. Yitzhaq Baer, "Israel, the Christian Church, and the Roman Empire from the Time of Septimius Severus to the Edict of Toleration of A.D. 313," in *Studies in History*, ed. Alexander Fuks and Israel Halpern, Scripta Hierosolymitana 7 (Jerusalem: Magnes Press, 1961), 82. For a more recent expression of this view, see David Rokeah, *Jews, Pagans, and Christians in Conflict*, Studia Post-Biblica (Jerusalem and Leiden: Magnes Press, Hebrew University and E. J. Brill, 1982), 78. It should be emphasized that a new generation of Israeli scholars are changing this picture dramatically, including as a representative sample Galit Hasan-Rokem, "Narratives in Dialogue: A Folk Literary Perspective on Interreligious Contacts in the Holy Land in Rabbinic Literature of Late Antiquity," in *Sharing the Sacred: Religious Contacts and Conflicts in the Holy Land, First-Fifteenth Centuries C.E.*, ed. Guy Stroumsa and Arieh Kofsky (Jerusalem: Yad Ben Zvi, 1998), 109–29; and Israel Jacob Yuval, "Jews and Christians in the Middle Ages: Shared Myths, Common Language: Donatio Constantini and Donatio Vespasiani," in *Demonizing the Other: Antisemitism, Racism, and Xenophobia*, ed. Robert S. Wistrich, Studies in Antisemitism, vol. 4 (Chur: Harwood Academic Publishers, 1999), 88–107, among others.

7. Hugh Jackson Lawlor and John Ernest Leonard Oulton, trans. and eds., *Eusebius, Bishop of Caesarea, the Ecclesiastical History and the Martyrs of Palestine* (London: Society for Promoting Christian Knowledge, 1927), 106–7. See also Yohanan Lederman, "Les évêques juifs de Jérusalem," *Revue biblique* 104 (1997): 211–22, and discussion in Andrew S. Jacobs, "The Imperial Construction of the Jew in the Early Christian Holy Land" (Ph.D. diss., Duke University, 2001), 41, n. 47.

8. Lawlor and Oulton, *Eusebius*, 68; Gerd Lüdemann, "The Successors of Pre-70 Jerusalem Christianity: A Critical Evaluation of the Pella-Tradition," in *Jewish and Christian Self-Definition*, ed. E. P. Sanders (Philadelphia: Fortress Press, 1980), 161–73.

9. W. H. C. Frend, *The Early Church* (Minneapolis, Minn.: Fortress Press, 1965), 33–34.

10. Galit Hasan-Rokem, *The Web of Life—Folklore in Rabbinic Literature: The Palestinian Aggadic Midrash Eikha Rabba*, in Hebrew (Tel Aviv: Am Oved, 1996), 201 (emphasis added).

11. See also Daniel Boyarin, "Masada or Yavneh? Gender and the Arts of Jewish Resistance," in *Jews and Other Differences: The New Jewish Cultural Studies*, ed. Daniel Boyarin and Jonathan Boyarin (Minneapolis: University of Minnesota Press, 1997), 306–29.

12. See also Craig Koester, "The Origin and Significance of the Flight to Pella Tradition," Catholic Biblical Quarterly 51 (1989): 90–106; Jacobs, "Construction of the Jew," 58.

13. The impact of the early Pauline congregations in this area would have been, ex hypothesi, one of the leading factors in the production of this kind of Christianity, in opposition perhaps to the Petrine Christianity that typified Palestine and Syria. Justin, one of the earliest manifestations of this form of Christianity, may have been significantly influenced by the Pauline letters, as argued recently by David Rokeaḥ, *Justin Martyr and the Jews*, in Hebrew, "Kuntresim": Texts and Studies 84 (Jerusalem: Hebrew University, Dinur Center for Research in Jewish History, 1998). Although this position is contrary to the consensus of Justin scholarship today, my own researches on Galatians and Justin suggest to me that it is, at least, arguably the case. It is in Justin's writing that we find for

the first time several topoi of a distinct anti-Judaic Christian identity, among them the notion of an Israel replaced for its sins by a new Israel and that the "Jews" are responsible for pagan hostility to Christians *(Dialogue* 17.1, A. Lukyn Williams, ed. and trans., *Justin Martyr: The Dialogue with Trypho,* Translations of Christian Literature [London: SPCK, 1930], 34–35). This topos would later appear frequently in west Asian texts; Judith Lieu, "Accusations of Jewish Persecution in Early Christian Sources, with Particular Reference to Justin Martyr and the *Martyrdom of Polycarp,*" in *Tolerance and Intolerance in Early Judaism and Christianity,* ed. Graham N. Stanton and Guy G. Stroumsa (Cambridge: Cambridge University Press, 1998), 279–95. For a reconstruction similar to mine, without marking its specifically west Asian nature, however, see Birger Pearson, "The Emergence of the Christian Religion," in The *Emergence of the Christian Religion: Essays on Early Christianity* (Harrisburg, Pa.: Trinity Press International, 1997), 17.

14. Introduction, n. 73.

15. This perspective entails a revision of such formulations as "It has often seemed plausible that a Hellenistic Judaism, like Philo's but less sophisticated, was the background for Justin's and Theophilus' writing" (Alan F. Segal, *Two Powers in Heaven: Early Rabbinic Reports About Christianity and Gnosticism,* Studies in Judaism in Late Antiquity, vol. 25 [Leiden: E. J. Brill, 1977], 167). See now also M. J. Edwards, "Justin's Logos and the Word of God," *Journal of Early Christian Studies* 3, no. 3 (Fall 1995): 261–80. Raymond E. Brown already understood this point well in his introduction to his commentary on John (Raymond Edward Brown, *The Gospel According to John,* with an introduction by Raymond Edward Brown [Garden City, N.Y.: Doubleday, 1966], 56.) See also Larry W. Hurtado, *One God, One Lord: Early Christian Devotion and Ancient Jewish Monotheism,* 2d ed. (Edinburgh: T & T Clark, 1998), 7–9, especially "So, if we use the term 'Palestinian Judaism' to mean the religion and culture of the Jews living in Palestine at that time, it designates a bilingual phenomenon which included within it significant variation."

16. J. Rebecca Lyman, "The Politics of Passing: Justin Martyr's Conversion as a Problem of 'Hellenization,'" in *Conversion in Late Antiquity and the Early Middle Ages,* ed. Anthony Grafton and Kenneth Mills (Rochester, N.Y.: University of Rochester Press, forthcoming), emphasis added.

17. I am conflating all of these under the sign of Logos theology. As Hindy Najman has pointed out to me (personal communication), this is not, strictly speaking, appropriate as there is important variation between these doctrines (gender for one!), but for the purposes of the present argument this conflation is not only helpful but, I think, appropriate, as these doctrines are all, I believe, genetically, as well as typologically, related.

18. Virginia Burrus, "Creatio Ex Libidine: Reading Ancient Logos Differantly." In addition to my general expressions of thanks to Prof. Burrus, I need to add here a very specific acknowledgment. Much of what I have said and will say about Logos theology in these chapters was generated in the course of conversations with her over several years. It is hard for me to say, then, what is mine, what is hers, what is ours— but much of this is hers indeed, and there would be none of it without these conversations.

19. See the excursus to this chapter for further discussion of the tradition.

20. J. Rendell Harris, *The Origin of the Prologue to St. John's Gospel* (Cambridge: Cambridge University Press, 1917).

21. Again, see discussion in the excursus to this chapter.

22. Eldon Jay Epp, "Wisdom, Torah, Word: The Johannine Prologue and the Pur-

pose of the Fourth Gospel," in *Current Issues in Biblical and Patristic Interpretation. Studies in Honor of Merrill C. Tenney Presented by His Former Students*, ed. Gerald F. Hawthorne (Grand Rapids, Mich.: William B. Eerdmans, 1974), 130.

23. Peder Borgen, "Observations on the Targumic Character of the Prologue of John," *New Testament Studies* 16 (1969/1970): 288–95; Peder Borgen, "Logos Was the True Light: Contributions to the Interpretation of the Prologue of John," *Novum Testamentum* 14 (1972): 115–30. For discussions of other midrashic aspects of the Fourth Gospel, see Peder Borgen, "Observations on the Midrashic Character of John 6," *Zeitschrift für Neutestamentliche Wissenschaft* 54 (1963): 232–40; also Hartwig Thyen, "Das Heil kommt von den Juden," in *Kirche. Festschrift für Günther Bornkamm zum 75. Geburtstag*, ed. D. Lührmann and G. Strecker (Tübingen: Mohr Siebeck, 1980), 163–83.

24. The resistance of the community of New Testament scholars to this insight—it has simply been ignored—and their persistence in maintaining the view that the Prologue is a hymn in spite of Borgen's compelling arguments are themselves a striking comment. This resistance has consequences that ripple through scholarship. For instance, in a very recent paper John Turner writes: "Although present evidence is inconclusive, the parallels in imagery and structure between the Pronoia monologue and the Johannine prologue suggest that they may be nearly contemporaneous compositions. If so, the notion of a redeemer's threefold or three-stage descent to rescue those few who recognize him or her from the realm of darkness or chaos to the realm of light was celebrated in the form of various liturgical hymns sometime in the late first century" (John D. Turner, "Sethian Gnosticism and Johannine Christianity," conference presentation, Society of Biblical Literature [Denver, 2001]). If the proposals suggested in this chapter are accepted, however, hypotheses such as this one would be very difficult to sustain and nearly impossible to demonstrate. Certain elements of the hypothesis entertained in Turner's paper are dependent upon the assumption that the Prologue was originally a "hymnic prologue honoring the Baptist," a hypothesis that falls on the assumption that the *Gattung* of the Prologue is not hymn at all but homily.

25. Nicola Frances Denzey, "Genesis Traditions in Conflict? The Use of Some Exegetical Traditions in the *Trimorphic Protennoia* and the Johannine Prologue," *Vigiliae Christianae: A Review of Early Christian Life and Language* 55, no. 1 (2001): 20–44.

26. John Turner, "The Trimorphic Protennoia," in *Nag Hammadi Codices XI, XII, XIII*, ed. Charles W. Hedrick, Nag Hammadi Studies (Leiden: E. J. Brill, 1990).

27. Denzey, "Genesis Traditions," 20–22.

28. "Genesis Traditions," 22. Note that in this quote Denzey is careful not to use the term *gnostic*. This is because she has fully assimilated the lessons of Michael Allen Williams, *Rethinking "Gnosticism": An Argument for Dismantling a Dubious Category* (Princeton, N.J.: Princeton University Press, 1996). In one sense, I could call the present project *Rethinking Judaism* with no less justice, but I don't dare.

29. Denzey, "Genesis Traditions."

30. "Genesis Traditions," 28. Note the assumption of Genesis's historical, textual priority over Wisdom literature upon which her formulation is based, an assumption that can hardly be relied upon. There is no reason to assume that Proverbs 1–8 is later than and dependent in any way on Genesis.

31. I must admit that I find her argument for the impact of Genesis 1 on the *Trimorphic Protennoia* less than compelling. Compared with the explicit verbal parallels in the Prologue to John, the associations in the Nag Hammadi text are considerably looser

and only generally thematic. See also on this point, Elaine Pagels, "Exegesis of Genesis 1 in the Gospels of Thomas and John," *Journal of Biblical Literature* 118, no. 3 (1999): 493.

32. Denzey, "Genesis Traditions," 31. See, however, Yvonne Janssens, "Un source gnostique du prologue?" in *L'Évangile de Jean: Sources, rédaction, théologie*, ed. Marinus de Jonge, Bibliotheca Ephemeridum theologicarum Lovaniensium (Gembloux: Duculot, 1977), 355: "It is easy enough to establish a parallel between the first five verses of the prologue of John and those of Genesis," cited in Denzey, "Genesis Traditions," 36. And see most recently Pagels, "Exegesis."

33. Denzey, "Genesis Traditions," 34.

34. "Both the *Trimorphic Protennoia* and the Prologue closely follow the sequence of events in Genesis' creation account; . . . this alone makes Genesis a more convincing source for the texts than the disparate Wisdom accounts which scholars have cobbled together in an attempt to provide for them a cohesive structural framework" ("Genesis Traditions," 33).

35. Harris, *Origin*, 48.

36. Jacob Mann, *The Bible as Read and Preached in the Old Synagogue: A Study in the Cycles of the Readings from Torah and Prophets, as Well as from Psalms, and in the Structure of the Midrashic Homilies* (New York: Ktav, 1971); Joseph Heinemann, "The Proem in the Aggadic Midrashim: A Form-Critical Study," *Scripta Hierosolymita* 22 (1971): 100–122.

37. Cf. also the *Teachings of Sylvanus* in which it is written: "For the Tree of Life is Christ. He is Wisdom. For he is Wisdom; he is also the Word." Jan Zandee, ed. and trans., *The Teachings of Sylvanus (Nag Hammadi Codex VII, 4): Text, Translation, Commentary*, Egyptologische Uitgaven (Leiden: Nederlands Instituut voor het Nabije Oosten, 1991), 390. (See discussion in Elliot R. Wolfson, "The Tree That Is All: Jewish-Christian Roots of a Kabbalistic Symbol in Sefer Ha-Bahir," in *Along the Path: Studies in Kabbalistic Myth, Symbolism, and Hermeneutics* [Albany: State University of New York Press, 1995], 79.) This text demonstrates that there is nothing bizarre at all at having a masculine Jesus be the incarnation of a feminine Wisdom!

38. Contrast Rudolf Karl Bultmann, "The History of Religions Background of the Prologue to the Gospel of John," in *The Interpretation of John*, ed. John Ashton, Studies in New Testament Interpretation (1923; reprint, Edinburgh: T & T Clark, 1997), 37. Compare to the Fourth Gospel the following from Philo: "Akin to these two is the creative power called God because through this the Father, who is its begetter and contriver, made the universe; so that 'I am thy God' is equivalent to 'I am thy maker and artificer'" (Mut. 29) (Philo, "The Changing of Names," in *Philo*, vol. 5, trans. F. H. Colson and G. A. Whitaker, Loeb Classical Library [London: Heinemann, 1934], 159).

39. See Denzey, "Genesis Traditions," 27 and n. 32, for this point, as well as citation of relevant earlier literature. Fascinatingly, the third-century author and important Logos theologian Hippolytus clearly identified the Logos with Sophia (Allen Brent, *Hippolytus and the Roman Church in the Third Century: Communities in Tension Before the Emergence of a Monarch-Bishop*, Supplements to Vigiliae Christianae [Leiden: E. J. Brill, 1995], 71).

40. For this translation—*receive*, as opposed to *overcome*—see commentaries. For my reasons for adopting it, see below.

41. For a convenient summary of previous chiastic structural analyses, see Alan Culpepper, "The Pivot of John's Prologue," *New Testament Studies* 27 (1980): 6–9; and

also Ernst Haenchen, *John: A Commentary on the Gospel of John*, ed. Robert Walter Funk, trans. Robert Walter Funk, Hermeneia—a Critical and Historical Commentary on the Bible (Philadelphia: Fortress Press, 1984), 110, 125.

42. The first of these points suggests that the excision of the second verse from the alleged hymn is impossible—it is an essential aspect of the style—whereas the second indicates strong connection with Hebrew style, as well. Together they raise significant problems for the hymnic reading.

43. Harris, *Origin*, 5. Cf. Bultmann, "History of Religions," 36.

44. Michael L. Klein, ed., *The Fragment-Targums of the Pentateuch According to Their Extant Sources*, trans. Michael L. Klein, Analecta Biblica (Rome: Biblical Institute Press, 1980), 43.

45. One consequence of this observation is that we need not hypothesize "a previously existing [Sophia] composition" that has been adopted and adapted by the Evangelist, pace Harris, *Origin*, 6.

46. Confessions XI, 8. Augustine, *Confessions Books I–XIII*, trans. F. J. Sheed, with an introduction by Peter Brown (Indianapolis, Ind.: Hackett, 1993), 217, 254. I am less persuaded than Raymond Brown that "The Latin translations give prominence to a mistaken reading which cannot be justified by the Greek. They take 'the beginning' as a nominative instead of an accusative and render: '[I am] the beginning who also speaks to you' or '[I am] the beginning because I speak to you'" (R. E. Brown, *John*, i, 348).

47. Pace Rudolf Schnackenburg, *The Gospel According to St. John* (London: Burns & Oates; New York: Herder & Herder, 1968), 233: "The prologue (or the Logos-hymn) is orientated from the start to the incarnate Logos. . . . Vv. 1–2 are not a cosmological meditation put forward for its own sake, but the first strophe of a Christian hymn of praise for the Redeemer. . . . The personal character of the Logos forms a definite contrast to the Wisdom speculation of Hellenistic Judaism, to the doctrine of the Logos in Philo." I fail to see this "complete contrast" and think that it is only perceived with eyes of faith. Of course, the Evangelist, in telling the story of creation via the Logos, its attempts to reveal itself in the world, and the ultimate Oekonomia, has the end in mind from the beginning, but he is too good a narrator to anticipate the end in the beginning. More to the point, his Logos theology, until the incarnation, is, I warrant, not substantially different from that of other Jews. The same apologetic point, I think, leads Schnackenburg to assert that "Wisdom (Sophia, *hokhmah*) is pictured as God's companion and partner in the creation of all things, but the Logos is really there before creation, in personal fellowship with God, living in God and from God" (Schnackenburg, *John*, 234). Reading Proverbs 8 will reveal no difference between the existence of Wisdom and that of the Logos here. She too was "with him at the Beginning." Could she not too have been "in the bosom of the Father" (pace Schnackenburg)? This author seems absolutely determined at all cost to maintain the supersession of the Old Testament Wisdom and Jewish Logos in the Logos of John.

48. As I am informed by Karen King. For the transition between midrashic and liturgical forms, such as the Piyyut (the synagogue poetry of the Byzantine period, which has much affinity with Christian hymnody), see Aaron Mirsky, *The Origin of Forms of Early Hebrew Poetry* (Jerusalem: Magnes Press, 1985).

49. Below I shall note the increasing tendency of scholars to see the Prologue as much more tightly woven into the Gospel than they had previously done.

50. For other related glosses to this verse, see F. Stanley Jones, *An Ancient Jewish*

Christian Source on the History of Christianity: Pseudo-Clementine Recognitions 1.27–71, Texts and Translations: Christian Apocrypha Series (Atlanta, Ga.: Scholars Press, 1995), 52.

51. As translated in the King James version. Interestingly, the same two meanings can be found in the Hebrew השיגו, which is how Delitzsch renders the Greek in Hebrew.

52. So Haenchen, *John*, 114: "The darkness has not comprehended it." Similarly Schnackenburg, *John*, 246–47: "If the evangelist is thinking in v. 5 of the encounter of the Logos, the light, with the world of men—as can hardly be doubted after v. 4—then of the two possible meanings of καταλαμβανειν, "master" (= overwhelm) and "grasp" (= embrace with mind and will), only the second can be considered." See also R. E. Brown, *John*, 8.

53. Cf. Rudolf Karl Bultmann, *The Gospel of John: A Commentary*, trans. G. R. Beasley-Murray (Oxford: Basil Blackwell, 1971), 45–46.

54. I happily follow here Bultmann, *John*, 48, n. 1.

55. Bultmann, "History of Religions," 42.

56. R. E. Brown, *John*, 26.

57. Almost all interpreters since Maldonatus, according to Schnackenburg, *John*, 258—including Büchsel, Bauer, Harnack, and Käsemann (R. E. Brown, *John*, 30)—have claimed that the Logos Incarnate is referred to well before v. 14. But see R. E. Brown, *John*, 28–29, who, while accepting this interpretation himself, refers to Westcott, Bernard, and Boismard as holding "that the reference to the Word's presence in the world in vss. 10–12 is to be interpreted in terms of the activity of the divine word in the OT period." According to my construal of the structure of the Prologue, one can hold such a view without assuming that "this view means that the editor of the Prologue misunderstood the hymn in inserting the reference to John the Baptist before vs. 10" (pace R. E. Brown, *John*, 29).

58. For an earlier exposition of this reading strategy, see Borgen, "Targumic Character," 291. I part company with Borgen on two issues: his occlusion of Proverbs 8 and the Wisdom aretalogies in interpreting the Prologue and his assumption that the Logos Ensarkos is referred to in vv. 9 and 11, as well as 14.

59. For Sophialogy, especially as relevant to the Fourth Gospel, see Michael E. Willett, *Wisdom Christology in the Fourth Gospel* (San Francisco: Mellen Research University Press, 1992); Martin Scott, *Sophia and the Johannine Jesus*, Journal for the Study of the New Testament. (Sheffield, Eng.: JSOT Press, 1992); Elisabeth Schüssler Fiorenza, *Jesus, Miriam's Child, Sophia's Prophet: Critical Issues in Feminist Christology* (New York: Continuum, 1994); Sharon H. Ringe, *Wisdom's Friends: Community and Christology in the Fourth Gospel* (Louisville, Ky.: Westminster/John Knox Press, 1999); and Burton L. Mack, *Logos und Sophia: Untersuchungen zur Weisheitstheologie im hellenistischen Judentum*, Studien zur Umwelt des Neuen Testaments (Göttingen: Vandenhoeck and Ruprecht, 1973).

60. Note that this interpretation removes the concern that vv. 9–11 are a tautological repetition of 4–5; rather, they are an interpretative gloss on them. Cf. R. E. Brown, *John*, 26. See also Bultmann, *John*, 53–58, for a somewhat similar approach.

61. Pace Haenchen, *John*, 102. I would suggest that if in 1 Corinthians 1:21 ff. Paul is referring to this myth, it is a very sour version of it indeed, consistently varying, I would add, with the difference between his version of the role of the Torah and that of the Fourth Evangelist.

62. "'Darkness' in John means primarily the world estranged from God, the place of man's existence not yet (or no longer, if the dawn of creation is considered) illuminated by divine light" (Schnackenburg, *John*, 245). This provides an excellent example of the confluence of apocalyptic mythopoeisis and Wisdom traditions, so common in the "Judaism" of the period, as described by Seth Schwartz, *Imperialism and Jewish Society from 200 B.C.E. to 640 C.E.* (Princeton, N.J.: Princeton University Press, 2001), 74–87.

63. Thus, in my opinion, it is quite unnecessary to claim that "v. 16 does not represent a continuation of the words of the Baptist. Rather v. 16 continues the confession of the community in v. 14" (Culpepper, "Pivot," 11), because the words of the Baptist are being cited in the confession of the community. On the other hand, I do not believe that the present position of vv. 6–8 indicates that the following verses are about the Logos Ensarkos, for reasons that will become clear below, contra, e.g., Emanuel Hirsch, *Studien zum Vierten Evangelium (Text/Literarkritik/Entstehungsgeschichte)*, Beiträge zur Historischen Theologie (Tübingen: Mohr Siebeck, 1936), 45.

64. Cf. also Morna D. Hooker, "John the Baptist and the Johannine Prologue," *New Testament Studies* 16 (1969): 354–58.

65. Cf. Haenchen, *John*, 114–17, for a good summary of the current views.

66. For an eloquent defense of this position, see Charles Harold Dodd, *The Interpretation of the Fourth Gospel* (Cambridge: Cambridge University Press, 1960), 282–83. In the following pages, Dodd considers the other possible interpretation, namely that vv. 12–13 describe the activity of the Logos Ensarkos, in my opinion a much weaker approach. See also Bultmann, "History of Religions," 29–30, who sees two levels within the text: an original one in which the Logos Asarkos was intended and a "Christian" one in which the "tragedy of Jesus' life" is comprehended. See also Bultmann, *John*, 46–47.

67. I take Pagels, "Exegesis," 481, to be the equivalent of the threefold descent myth.

68. For a similar interpretation, see Schnackenburg, *John*, 256–57. This was, according to Schnackenburg, the almost unanimous interpretation, as well, of the Fathers of the Church. As the Rabbis say: When the elders say "spend," and the juveniles say "save"—then spend!

69. Contra R. E. Brown, *John*, 29, who thinks that "children of God" can only be after the incarnation. Cf., however, Dodd, *Interpretation*, 270–71, for an interpretation very close to the one given here. See the similar idea in the apparently independent Justin Martyr in Ap. 1.46.2–3.

70. This passage needs to be re-evaluated in the light of the fact that early rabbinic Jews referred to other rabbinic Jews who disagreed with them as "the first-born of Satan"! (BT Yebamot 16a, PT Yebamot 3a). The text is instructive: "There was a case in which the Elders went to R. Dosa the son of Hyrcanus to ask him about the daughter's co-wife [a complicated issue in the law of forbidden unions]. They said to him: 'You are the one who permits co-wives.' He said to them, 'What did you hear—Dosa or the son of Hyrcanus.' They said, 'The son of Hyrcanus.' He said to them, 'Jonathan my brother was the first-born of Satan, one of the disciples of the House of Shammai.'" This usage is a hapax in rabbinic literature, to the best of my knowledge, but it nevertheless reveals the possibilities of Jewish rhetoric against Jews, even within the "rabbinic/Pharisaic" community, and a fortiori beyond it. Such rhetoric in the mouth of the Johannine Jesus does not, then, imply that the Johannine community did not see themselves as Jews. Segal quite appropriately concludes, "Such common terminology between Jewish and Christian communities [referring to Polycarp's anathematization of Marcion as "the first born

of Satan"] is important to us because it points to a relationship between them [—wheel-barrows]" (Segal, *Two Powers*, 235).

71. Brown ad loc. completely overlooks this possibility of interpretation, in spite of the clear verbal echoes between the language of chapter 8 and that of the Prologue.

72. R. E. Brown, *John*, 357.

73. Cf. also the not atypical interpretation of Macgregor: "Late Jewish thought [*sic!*] depicted the patriarchs as rising from Sheol to greet the Messiah on his appearance. . . . The meaning is not that Abraham had any such vision while still on earth, . . . but that he is *not* dead, as the Jews wrongly hold" (G. H. C. Macgregor, *The Gospel of John*, The Moffatt New Testament Commentary [London: Hodder and Stoughton, 1936], 223; Bultmann, *John*, 326–27). Bultmann (*John*, 326–27) also understands that it is the eschatalogical day that is being spoken of. Similarly, Lightfoot: "There is other evidence of a Jewish belief that Abraham rejoiced in a foresight of the messianic age" (R. H. Lightfoot, *St. John's Gospel: A Commentary*, ed. C. F. Evans [Oxford: Oxford University Press, 1956], 197).

74. R. E. Brown, *John*, 359.

75. Aryeh Kofsky, "Mamre: A Case of a Regional Cult?" in *Sharing the Sacred: Religious Contacts and Conflicts in the Holy Land, First–Fifteenth Centuries CE*, ed. Guy Stroumsa and Arieh Kofsky (Jerusalem: Yad Ben Zvi, 1998), 22–23. See also the discussion in Jacobs, "Construction of the Jew," 179–80.

76. Translated in Kofsky, "Mamre," 24.

77. Dodd, *Interpretation*, 271, 295; C. K. Barrett, *The Gospel According to St. John: An Introduction with Commentary and Notes on the Greek Text* (London: SPCK, 1978), 136; both hold a version of this view. This would be a direct challenge to Bultmann's statement that the Prologue contains no "history of revelation" (Bultmann, *John*, 21).

78. Note that the Torah (Wisdom) spreads out branches of χαρις in Ben Sira, suggesting again the possibility of Johannine allusion to that passage.

79. Ringe, *Wisdom's Friends*, 42. See, in general, pp. 37–45 for a succinct and clear account of the role of personified Wisdom in the biblical and postbiblical literature. I dissent from her, as above, only in her account of why Sophia has become the Logos in the Fourth Gospel. Epp's statement that "both the Wisdom hymns and the Judaism of the time recognized the *equation of Wisdom and Torah*" (Epp, "Wisdom," 133) must, therefore, be modified: *Some* of the Wisdom hymns recognized this equation, and others denied it. In any case, what can be meant by positing the "Wisdom hymns" and "Judaism" as two separate entities in the same category?

80. James H. Charlesworth, *The Old Testament Pseudepigrapha* (Garden City, N.Y.: Doubleday and Company, 1985), 1:33 On this text, see also Gabriele Boccaccini, "The Preexistence of the Torah: A Commonplace in Second Temple Judaism or a Later Rabbinic Development?" *Henoch* 17 (1995): 329–50. See also Harris, *Origin*, 39.

81. The significance of this reading for the question of the "antisemitism" of the Fourth Gospel should be obvious.

82. Stephen Motyer, *Your Father the Devil? A New Approach to John and "the Jews,"* Paternoster Biblical and Theological Studies (Carlisle, Eng.: Paternoster Press, 1997), 85.

83. Dodd, *Interpretation*, 271.

84. I see no need, therefore, to multiply entities by assuming that the original hymnologist "probably still means the time before the Incarnation. The evangelist, however, has the eschatological revelation of the incarnate Logos constantly before his mind" (Schnackenburg, *John*, 245).

85. Culpepper, "Pivot," 21.

86. Culpepper cites several rabbinic passages insisting that Israel according to the flesh is the Children of God. He argues that these can best be understood as an answer to the Christian claim. One text—albeit a relatively late, fourth-century one—makes this explicit (Culpepper, "Pivot," 22). In a text like John 2:29, on the other hand, "everyone who does right [δικαιοσύνην] is born of him."

87. Allusions to Sinai, as heard by Boismard here, are by no means out of place (M. E. Boismard, *St. John's Prologue* [London: Blackfriars Publications, 1957], 136–40). My interpretation is related to that of Pagels, "Exegesis," 489, although by no means identical to it.

88. Pagels, "Exegesis," 491, citing Dodd, *Interpretation*, 97–114, 250–85.

89. Cf. "The cultic hymn thus reconstructed consists of four strophes. The first proclaims the primordial and divine being of the Logos and his role in creation, the second describes his significance for the world of men (life and light), the third laments the rejection of his work in humanity before the Incarnation, and the fourth finally praises the joyful event of the Incarnation which brings salvation to those who believe" (Schnackenburg, *John*, 226–27). Why, therefore, assume a Logos hymn at all? To be sure, the Logos exists before the incarnation, but why assume a pre-existent hymn? We end up with statements such as "It is quite possible that the original hymn envisaged in strophes 2 and 3 the activity of the λόγος ἄσαρκος and that it was only the evangelist who saw everything in the perspective of the λόγος ἐνσαρκος, because in his Gospel all the interest is centered on the acceptance or rejection of the incarnate Son of God" (Schnackenburg, *John*, 228). This doubleness, certainly a blunting of Ockham's razor if nothing else, seems unnecessary to me. Assuming that up to v. 14 we have the Logos Asarkos makes better work of John's narrative.

90. Haenchen, *John*, 122.

91. Cf. Epp, "Wisdom," 136, who reads this connection differently. There are, nevertheless, some strong affinities between his interpretation and the one offered here. The biggest difference is methodological. Epp assumes that rabbinic theologoumena, attested in texts centuries later, are contemporary with the Gospel, thus positing that the Gospel reacts to the "Jewish" ideas, reproducing inadvertently the supersessionist narrative. I, by contrast, prefer to read the rabbinic texts in their own chronological context as very possibly a reaction to Christian developments.

92. Boismard, *St. John's Prologue*, 136–40.

93. Jaime Clark-Soles, "The Word(s) of the Word in the Fourth Gospel," conference presentation, Society of Biblical Literature (Denver, Colo., 2001).

94. "From other references in the [fourth] gospel the reader can then be led to see that what the Torah was intended to, but could not, effect has been effected in Jesus" (John Suggit, "John XVII. 17. ΛΟΓΟΣ Ο ΣΟΣ ΑΛΗΘΕΙΑ ΕΣΤΙΝ," *Journal of Theological Studies* 35 [1984]: 107).

95. Jacques Derrida, *Of Grammatology* (Baltimore, Md.: Johns Hopkins University Press, 1976). Contrast here the reading of Epp, "Wisdom," 140–41, who would inscribe a much more stringent contrast between Matthew's and John's views of the Torah than I would.

96. "The letter, says Lacan, cannot be divided: 'But if it is first of all on the materiality of the signifier that we have insisted, that materiality is *odd* [singulière] in many ways, the first of which is not to admit partition.' This indivisibility, says Derrida, is odd

indeed, but becomes comprehensible if it is seen as an *idealization* of the phallus, whose integrity is necessary for the edification of the entire psychoanalytical system. With the phallus safely idealized and located in the voice, the so-called signifier acquires the 'unique, living, *non-mutilable integrity*' of the self-present spoken word, unequivocally pinned down to and by the *signified.*' Had the phallus been per(mal)-chance divisible or reduced to the status of a partial object, the whole edification would have crumbled down, and this is what has to be avoided at all cost" (Barbara Johnson, "The Frame of Reference: Poe, Lacan, Derrida," in *The Purloined Poe,* ed. John P. Muller and William J. Richards [Baltimore, Md.: Johns Hopkins University Press, 1987], 225; my emphasis). See also L. Alexander, "The Living Voice: Scepticism Towards the Written Word in Early Christian and Graeco-Roman Texts," in *The Bible in Three Dimensions,* vol. 87, ed. David J. A. Clines, Stephen E. Fowl, and Stanley E.Porter, Journal for the Study of the Old Testament Supplement Series (Sheffield, Eng.: Sheffield University Press, 1990), 221–47.

97. My point of view is, therefore, somewhat different from that of Hurtado (*One God,* 11), who considers binitarian devotion to be the novum of Christian Jews, albeit growing out of "Jewish" rootstock. I believe that the binitarianism is not specifically Christian; only its association with Jesus is. Here is perhaps the sharpest way to demonstrate the difference between and similarity of our approaches. Hurtado writes: "given the cultic veneration of Jesus, the development of the concept of his preexistence is not such a big step" (*One God,* 13). Hurtado, of course, is well aware of Jewish notions of preexistent Wisdom, but prefers to locate the association of these with Jesus as a secondary development growing out of the worship of Jesus, whereas I would argue that the opposite development is much more intuitive, to wit, that Jesus was identified with the Word or with Sophia and then worshiped accordingly.

98. Cf. "The Christ myth develops out of two subsidiary myths or narrative patterns of Judaism: the descent of the feminine divine hypostasis 'Wisdom' (Greek *Sophia,* Hebrew *Ḥokhmah*) and the narrative pattern featuring the paradigmatic righteous man, who suffers and is vindicated by God" (Pearson, "Emergence," 14). Compare the somewhat different but related formulation in Jack Miles, *Christ: A Crisis in the Life of God* (New York: Alfred A. Knopf, 2001), 27: "The improbable and appalling conjunction of expiatory lamb and messianic warlord receives its first statement here, and the disturbing power of Jesus as a character has everything to do with such combinations. No set of foreign ideas could surpass, in its ability either to attract or offend a Jewish audience, these native Jewish ideas made daring and new by unforeseen combination." And see too *Christ,* 47: "Transformative expansion is what occurs when the 'son of man' of Daniel 7 is made to refer not just to the period following Alexander the Great but also to an actual human being, Jesus of Nazareth, who was born during this period."

99. Dunn, *Partings,* 165–69, 188–94.

100. Haenchen, *John,* 13; Helmut Koester, "Ancient Christian Gospels: Their History and Development" (Harrisburg: Trinity Press International, 1990), 246.

101. A. L. Williams, *Dialogue,* 126; Justin, *Dialogus cum Tryphone,* ed. Miroslav Marcovich, Patristische Texte und Studien 47 (Berlin: Walter de Gruyter, 1997), 174–75.

102. Interpretation by association is very common in midrash. Cf. Harris, *Origin,* 20.

103. For discussion of this appellation, see Darrell D. Hannah, *Michael and Christ: Michael Traditions and Angel Christology in Early Christianity,* Wissenschaftliche Untersuchungen zum Neuen Testament (Tübingen: Mohr Siebeck, 1999), 1 and throughout.

104. Edwards, "Justin's Logos," 262.

105. Edwards, "Justin's Logos," 279.

106. See also Burrus, "Creatio."

107. In his insistence that there is nothing "Jewish" about John, Bultmann also spurns the connection between the Logos of the Fourth Gospel and the Memra: "[Bultmann] has spoken out against the earlier popular supposition that the Johannine Logos is the 'he said' (εἶπεν, ויאמר), become a person, in the creation narrative of the LXX. In the first place, there is no mention of the creation in John 1:1 f. In the second place, Judaism never took that 'and God said' (εἶπεν) as a person standing alongside God. The designation in the Talmud מימרא (=Word) always appears as the *Memra* of Yahweh or of Adonai." These arguments of Haenchen/Bultmann's are very problematic indeed. A perusal of Bultmann, *John*, 20–21, suggests that the opinions cited are only partly Bultmann's, although they convey the general tenor of his position. Thus Bultmann certainly does not deny the presence of the creation in John 1.1. Rather, he writes: "It would be hard for the Evangelist to begin his work with ἐν ἀρχῇ, without thinking of the בראשית of Gen. 1.1." Nor does he make the mistake of discussing the Memra in the Talmud— where it never appears. Nevertheless, the entire thrust of Bultmann's discourse in those pages (through p. 37 and passim) is to deny any connection between John and something that Bultmann calls "Judaism," since John's Prologue derives from something that Bultmann calls "Gnosticism."

Haenchen is simply wrong. In the first place, having seen that the Prologue is a midrash on Genesis, one cannot say that creation is not mentioned here. In the second place, statements about what "Judaism" did or did not do have to be disqualified as a prioristic invocations of a reified hypostasis that we should, in fact, be interrogating throughout our research. Third, invoking the Talmud here is irrelevant, since the Talmud never mentions the Memra at all. Finally, the fact that the Memra is the "Memra H'"— the Word of God—does not in the slightest discredit it as a hypostasis. "The Wisdom of God" in Paul is obviously such an hypostasis (Harris, *Origin*, 3) as, indeed, is the "Son of God" in other Christian texts. Picking up on these points and expanding them, the current reading of the Prologue suggests an entirely different understanding of the task of a "history of religions" with respect to these issues.

108. See, e.g., Martin McNamara, "Logos of the Fourth Gospel and *Memra* of the Palestinian Targum," *Expository Times* 79 (1968): 115.

109. Gary Anderson, "The Interpretation of Genesis 1:1 in the Targums," *Catholic Biblical Quarterly* 52, no. 1 (1990): 28.

110. Menahem Kister, "'Let Us Make a Man'—Observations on the Dynamics of Monotheism," in Hebrew, in *Issues in Talmudic Research: Conference Commemorating the Fifth Anniversary of the Passing of Ephraim E. Urbach, 2 December 1996* (Jerusalem: Israel Academy of Sciences, 2001), 54.

111. See, on this point of Johannine particularism by comparison with the *Trimorphic Protennoia*, Denzey, "Genesis Traditions," 37.

112. John Ashton, *Understanding the Fourth Gospel* (Oxford: Clarendon Press and Oxford University Press, 1993), 45.

113. I will dispute this at length in the next chapter.

114. Harris, *Origin*.

115. Bultmann, "History of Religions." Note Segal's excellent account of why Christology can best be explained without any connection whatsoever with a "gnostic savior hypothesis" (*Two Powers*, 208).

116. Bultmann, *John*, 23, n. 1; Rudolf Karl Bultmann, *Theology of the New Testament* (New York: Scribner, 1955), 2:3–14. It is somewhat disconcerting to find Bultmann listed as the author of "groundbreaking work [that] first alerted the academic community to the Prologue's dependence on Wisdom imagery," and as following Harris's hypothesis, in Denzey, "Genesis Traditions," 27, n. 28.

117. Bultmann, *John*, 21.

118. For an especially clear, concise, and convenient version of Bultmann's approach, see Bultmann, "History of Religions." See esp.: "If my supposition is correct, then in the Gospel of John we have fresh proof of the extraordinarily early impact of eastern gnostic speculations upon early Christianity," Bultmann, "History of Religions," 43. As Bultmann remarks, in a passage cited below, these "eastern gnostic speculations" come from anywhere but "Judaism." See also, much later and more definitively: "The Logos concept of the Prologue does not have its origin in the philosophical tradition of Hellenism, but in mythology" (Bultmann, *John*, 13, n. 1), by which Bultmann surely means something "oriental" and "gnostic." This can be seen explicitly on pp. 24–31 of the commentary, esp. p. 29, to wit: "It [the Prologue to John] belongs to the sphere of early oriental Gnosticism." Contrast to this Moshe Idel ("Meṭaṭron: Notes Towards the Development of Myth in Judaism," in Hebrew, in *Eshel Beer-Sheva: Occasional Publications in Jewish Studies* [Beer-sheva, Israel: Ben-Gurion University of the Negev Press, 1996], 41), who traces direct continuity from biblical angel speculation down to the Kabbalah, "so much so that it is difficult to see the necessity for gnostic influences that stimulated the development of Jewish thought."

119. Bultmann, *John*, 21.

120. Bultmann, *John*, 23.

121. Bultmann, *John*, 27.

122. Dunn, *Partings*, 9.

123. As Ashton remarks, this "refusal to dissociate theology and exegesis" makes Bultmann's John such a colossus (Ashton, *Understanding*, 45).

124. Haenchen, *John*, 136. There are, of course, some important dissenters from the interpretation of the Prologue as a hymn. C. K. Barrett writes: "The Prologue, then, stands before us as a prose introduction which has not been submitted to interpolation and was specially written (it must be supposed) to introduce the gospel" (*John*, 126–27). In a similar vein, see F. F. Bruce, *The Gospel of John* (Grand Rapids, Mich.: William B. Eerdmans, 1983), 28; and Dodd, *Interpretation*, 272. See also C. H. Giblin, "Two Complementary Literary Structures in John 1:1–18," *Journal of Biblical Literature* 104 (1985): 87–103, for the main formal literary argument against reading the Prologue as a hymn. I throw my lot in with this minority. (See also the discussion in Hooker, "John the Baptist.").

125. Schüssler Fiorenza, *Miriam's Child*, 152. See also: "Rather than just being *influenced* by Sophia speculation, the Christology of the Fourth Gospel is nothing less than a *thoroughgoing* Sophia Christology" (Scott, *Sophia and the Johannine Jesus*, 29); and Alison E. Jasper, *The Shining Garment of the Text: Gendered Readings of John's Prologue*, Journal for the Study of the New Testament (Sheffield, Eng.: Sheffield Academic Press, 1998).

126. This has been an issue for nonfeminist versions of the "Wisdom hymn" theory as well, e.g., Haenchen, *John*, 126. Pace Denzey, "Genesis Traditions," 29, this problem is much older than Jarl Fossum's article of 1995.

127. I want at least to gesture toward the deeper historical connections between these and ancient Egyptian wisdom, refracted through both biblical and archaic Greek texts. Those ancient myths of Moses and Plato as deeply related are not as anachronistic as one might suppose, I think. Jan Assmann, *Moses the Egyptian: The Memory of Egypt in Western Monotheism* (Cambridge, Mass.: Harvard University Press, 1997), has much to teach us in this regard. See also, however, Harris, *Origin*, 11.

128. Epp, "Wisdom," 130.

129. Epp, "Wisdom," 129.

130. Pace R. E. Brown, *John*, 20–21, and arguing against Serafin de Ausejo, "¿Es un himno a Cristo el prólogo de San Juan?" *EstBib* 15 (1956): 223–77; 381–427. In W. D. Davies, *Paul and Rabbinic Judaism: Some Rabbinic Elements in Pauline Theology*, 2d ed. (1955; reprint, London: Society for the Promotion of Christian Knowledge, 1965), 151–52, we find a magnificent interpretation of Col. 1:15–20 (another alleged "hymn"), which demonstrates that this text is also a homily on Genesis cum Proverbs 8, very much in the mold of the one I am arguing for in the Fourth Gospel. Whether or not this passage is "Pauline" I shall leave to my betters in New Testament scholarship to decide, but I am certain that it is *formally* akin, almost identical in form and structure (as well as thought) to the first five verses of John's Prologue. If, therefore, as Davies demonstrates, that text is midrash, then ours is as well.

131. Proverbs 8 claims "H' created me at the beginning of his ways," and Ben Sira 24 reads "I came forth from the mouth of the Most High." Epp clearly senses the formal differences between the Prologue to John and the "OT and Apocrypha Wisdom hymns," which "do not match the former in conciseness" (Epp, "Wisdom," 130)!

132. Cf. Turner, "Sethian Gnosticism."

133. Cf. the epigraph to this section, from Davies, *Paul and Rabbinic Judaism*, 151.

134. Thomas L. Brodie, *The Gospel According to John: A Literary and Theological Commentary* (New York: Oxford University Press, 1993), 134.

135. R. E. Brown, *John*, 21–23.

136. De Ausejo, "Himno."

137. R. E. Brown, *John*, 23.

138. R. E. Brown, *John*, 28–29.

139. Cf. "I conclude that the substance of a Logos-doctrine similar to that of Philo is present all through the gospel, and that the use of the actual term λόγος in the Prologue, in a sense corresponding to that doctrine, though it is unparalleled in the rest of the gospel, falls readily in place" (Dodd, *Interpretation*, 279).

140. Dodd, *Interpretation*, 281.

Chapter 5. The Jewish Life of the Logos

1. Erwin Ramsdell Goodenough, *The Theology of Justin Martyr: An Investigation into the Conceptions of Early Christian Literature and Its Hellenistic and Judaistic Influences* (Amsterdam: Philo Press, 1968), 140–41.

2. See the discussion of 3 Enoch and *The Apocalypse of Abraham* in John Ashton, *Understanding the Fourth Gospel* (Oxford: Clarendon Press and Oxford University Press, 1993), 142–47. And see also his continuing discussion of related matters, Ashton, *Under-*

standing, 143–50. The problem with Ashton's excellent analysis is that it leads him to conclude that "The Qumran fragments and the Gospel testify to a boldly speculative alternative theology that orthodox Judaism could not absorb—or even acknowledge" (150), a statement that is certainly true except that he understands "orthodox Judaism" to be extant already at the time of the composition of the Fourth Gospel, an assumption for which there is no warrant whatever. "Orthodox Judaism," by which we *must* mean rabbinism, was to gradually expel such "alternative theologies" over a period of centuries, following the time of the Fourth Gospel, and drive them underground, whence they would reappear in the form of the Kabbalah in the early Byzantine period.

3. J. E. Bruns, "Philo Christianus: The Debris of a Legend," *Harvard Theological Review* 66 (1973): 141–45. See also David T. Runia, *Philo in Early Christian Literature: A Survey*, Compendia Rerum Iudaicarum Ad Novum Testamentum (Minneapolis, Minn.: Fortress Press, 1993), 3–33.

4. James D. G. Dunn, *The Partings of the Ways Between Christianity and Judaism and Their Significance for the Character of Christianity* (London Philadelphia: SCM Press and Trinity Press International, 1991), 195 (emphasis original).

5. Basil Studer, *Trinity and Incarnation: The Faith of the Early Church*, ed. Andrew Louth, trans. Matthias Westerhoff (Collegeville, Minn.: Liturgical Press, 1993), 39.

6. As well as other designations. See Jarl Fossum, "Jewish-Christian Christology and Jewish Mysticism," *Vigiliae Christianae* 37 (1983): 260–87; Jarl Fossum, *The Name of God and the Angel of the Lord: Samaritan and Jewish Conceptions of Intermediation and the Origin of Gnosticism*, Wissenschaftliche Untersuchungen zum Neuen Testament (Tübingen: Mohr Siebeck, 1985), 333. For the Logos as the "first-begotten son of the Uncreated Father" in Philo, see David Winston, *Logos and Mystical Theology in Philo of Alexandria* (Cincinnati, Ohio: Hebrew Union College Press, 1985), 16. Cf. Dunn, *Partings*, 202–3. Cf. also: "If Philo remains within the spectrum of recognizable and acceptable first-century Judaism, would the same not be true for Hebrews also? It would be hard to answer anything other than Yes" (Dunn, *Partings*, 211), with which "yes" I heartily concur.

7. C. K. Barrett, *The Gospel According to St. John: An Introduction with Commentary and Notes on the Greek Text* (London: SPCK, 1978), 128.

8. Rudolf Schnackenburg, *The Gospel According to St. John* (London: Burns & Oates; New York: Herder & Herder, 1968), 484–87.

9. Barrett, *John*, 128.

10. Winston, *Logos*, 11. So also Alan F. Segal, *Two Powers in Heaven: Early Rabbinic Reports About Christianity and Gnosticism*, Studies in Judaism in Late Antiquity, vol. 25 (Leiden: E. J. Brill, 1977), 163: "There were others in Philo's day who spoke of a 'second god,' but who were not as careful as Philo in defining the limits of that term."

11. For a fine discussion of this moment in Philo's writing, see Segal, *Two Powers*, 159–81.

12. Darrell D. Hannah, *Michael and Christ: Michael Traditions and Angel Christology in Early Christianity*, Wissenschaftliche Untersuchungen zum Neuen Testament (Tübingen: Mohr Siebeck, 1999), 80.

13. Ibid., 80–81.

14. As pointed out by Maren R. Niehoff, "What is in a Name? Philo's Mystical Philosophy of Language," *Jewish Studies Quarterly* 2 (1995): 223.

15. See also the discussion in Hannah, *Michael*, 82–83.

16. E.g., at *De Agricultura* 51.

17. This ambiguity has been concisely articulated in Thomas H. Tobin, "Logos," in *The Anchor Bible Dictionary 4* (New York: Doubleday, 1992), 351.

18. See also J. Rendell Harris, *The Origin of the Prologue to St. John's Gospel* (Cambridge: Cambridge University Press, 1917), 52: "Here we see Philo wrestling with a similar problem to that of the early Christian thinkers," exactly in the context of the problems that would lead to Nicaea.

19. "Within Platonism a lively, if conservative, scholasticism originated in Asia Minor, claiming to recover and restore the pure teachings of Plato; Numenius of Apamea in the second century offered a universal and polemical philosophy which integrated not only Plato and Pythagoras, but Egyptian, Persian, and Hebrew wisdom." J. Rebecca Lyman, "The Politics of Passing: Justin Martyr's Conversion as a Problem of 'Hellenization,'" in *Conversion in Late Antiquity and the Early Middle Ages*, ed. Anthony Grafton and Kenneth Mills (Rochester, N.Y.: University of Rochester Press, forthcoming). Lyman's project of disrupting binary oppositions of "Christianity" and "Hellenism" can be seen as parallel to mine of disrupting such oppositions between "Judaism" and "Hellenism" or "Hellenistic Judaism" and "proper [Palestinian, rabbinic] Judaism." On Numenius, see the interesting remarks of Segal, *Two Powers*, 246.

20. M. J. Edwards, "Justin's Logos and the Word of God," *Journal of Early Christian Studies* 3, no. 3 (Fall 1995): 263.

21. Charles Harold Dodd, *The Interpretation of the Fourth Gospel* (Cambridge: Cambridge University Press, 1960), 269–79.

22. This idea was originally suggested to me in conversations with Virginia Burrus, but I take full responsibility for the formulation. Moreover, as Rebecca Lyman points out (personal communication), the parade example of a "pagan" Middle Platonist turns out to be Numenius, a philosopher who, while nominally neither Jewish nor Christian, quotes quite a bit of Scripture for his purpose, not to mention his famous: "Who is Plato, if not Moses speaking Greek." See also David Dawson, *Allegorical Readers and Cultural Revision in Ancient Alexandria* (Berkeley and Los Angeles: University of California Press, 1992), 190–91; John Dillon, *The Middle Platonists: 80 B.C. to A.D. 220* (Ithaca, N.Y.: Cornell University Press, 1977), 378–79.

23. Virginia Burrus, "Creatio Ex Libidine: Reading Ancient Logos Differantly." Burrus also refers to John Dillon's apparent discomfiture in not being able to locate a Logos outside of scriptural interpretation except, and only very peripherally and controversially in one place in Plutarch (Plutarch, "De Iside et Osiride," in *Moralia V*, trans. Frank Cole Babbitt [Cambridge, Mass.: Harvard University Press, 1936]). Thus, for instance, in Plutarch's own "Ad Principem Ineruditem," in *Moralia X*, trans. Harold North Fowler (Cambridge, Mass.: Harvard University Press, 1936), 57, "logos" is being used in the sense of reason and not as a hypostasized divine principle, contra Glenn F. Chesnut, "The Ruler and the Logos in Neopythagorean, Middle Platonic, and Late Stoic Political Philosophy," in *Principate: Religion*, ed. Wolfgang Haase, Aufstieg und Niedergang der Römischen Welt (Berlin: Walter de Gruyter, 1978), 1323. (See too Hindy Najman, *Seconding Sinai: Mosaic Discourse in Second-Temple Judaism* [Leiden: E. J. Brill, 2003], 87.) In further support of Burrus, I would offer Plutarch, "Ad Principem Ineruditem," 65, a passage wherein a Philo or an Origen would surely be asserting the Logos as the mediator between a fully transcendent deity and matter. Plutarch, by contrast, apparently knows of no such mediating entity.

24. Niehoff, "What Is in a Name?" 226. This is not to say, of course, that there are

no anticipations of this development within Platonism, or even Plato himself. Azzan Yadin (personal communication) writes, "The issue is not so much Language as God as Language as intermediary, and here Philo has, arguably, Platonic precedent. I am thinking of the relationship between the aporia that ends the Cratylus and the way language is used in the Sophist, the Statesman, and the Parmenides. One needs different intertexts for language as God but it is not clear that this is the more important of the two for the issue at hand" (letter of November 2000). See now too Mark Julian Edwards, *Origen Against Plato*, The Ashgate Studies in Philosophy and Theology in Late Antiquity (Burlington, VT: Ashgate, 2002), 16, making just this point. It is unfortunate that this book arrived on these shores just a bit too late for me to take full cognizance of it in the body of this text, but a careful reading suggests that it would not materially affect the hypothesis of this chapter or its sequel. On the question of the Idea of man in Plato himself, see now Edwards, *Origen Against Plato*, 49.

25. Niehoff, "What Is in a Name?" 226.

26. Leslie W. Barnard, *Justin Martyr: His Life and Thought* (London: Cambridge University Press, 1967). To the evidence that I shall offer below, we might add the figure Yahoel, in the probably second-century Apocalypse of Abraham 10.3 and passim (G. H. Box, ed. and trans., *Apocalypse of Abraham* [London: SPCK, 1918]). See also the important discussion in Hannah, *Michael*, 52–54. Moreover: "Apparently, Justin Martyr also knew of Jews who allowed one name of God to refer to something like a *Logos*, but refused to identify the *Logos* with Jesus as he had done" (Segal, *Two Powers*, 13). See also W. D. Davies, *Paul and Rabbinic Judaism: Some Rabbinic Elements in Pauline Theology*, 2d ed. (1955, reprint, London: Society for the Promotion of Christian Knowledge, 1965), 147–76; and Siegfried Schulz, *Untersuchungen zur Menschensohn-Christologie im Johannesevangelium zugleich ein Beitrag zur Methodengeschichte der Auslegung des 4. Evangeliums* (Göttingen: Vandenhoeck and Ruprecht, 1957). I wish to thank Prof. François Bovon for directing my attention to this last source.

27. For Goodenough, writing in 1923, there are "Judaism proper" and "Hellenistic Judaism," and he claims that the latter provides Justin's theology with its theoretical base (*Justin*, 33). Goodenough explicitly indicates that the Logos theology was an explicitly Hellenistic Jewish tradition (*Justin*, 147). Although in the intervening decades such notions have loosened up considerably, they are by no means gone from the world.

28. On this point, see the vitally important remarks of Günter Stemberger, *Jews and Christians in the Holy Land: Palestine in the Fourth Century* (Edinburgh: T & T Clark, 1999), 277–79, who refers to the "powerlessness of the rabbis in synagogues" and even points to specific points of disagreement between the Rabbis and the Targums, where the Rabbis were powerless to prevent the people from practicing in accord with the Targums' view. See also: "In late antiquity, though the rabbis were not totally insignificant, the real religious leaders probably were the heads of the synagogues" (Seth Schwartz, *Imperialism and Jewish Society from 200 B.C.E. to 640 C.E.* [Princeton, N.J.: Princeton University Press, 2001], 13).

29. For a fairly early explicit rabbinic Jewish understanding that Memra is the Logos, see the early tenth-century David al-Muqammis, as cited in Elliot R. Wolfson, *Through a Speculum That Shines: Vision and Imagination in Medieval Jewish Literature* (Princeton, N.J.: Princeton University Press, 1994), 150. He writes, "This is the mistake of the Christians who say that God lives according to life, which is the Holy Spirit, and He lives according to Wisdom, which is the Logos (*ma'amar* [=*memra*]), which they call the

Son." The only reason for al-Muqammis to use the term *ma'amar* and not, for instance, *dibbur* would be that he connects the Aramaic cognate *memra* of the Targums with the Logos of the Christians. See also the illuminating discussion of Wolfson as well.

30. That is, in the ancient Palestinian and Babylonian synagogues. They are pararabbinic in that, being synagogue products, they frequently represent religious ideas and practices parallel in time and space but not by any means identical to those of the "official" rabbinic Judaism represented in the rabbinic literature, the product of the Study House. Some of the Targums, notably Targum Onkelos and the Targum known as Pseudo-Jonathan, have been modified somewhat to make them better fit rabbinic ideologies and interpretations. The principle that whatever disagrees with the Mishna must be pre-Mishnaic can no longer be maintained, given what we now think about Jewish religious diversity within the rabbinic period and the difficulties of the Rabbis in gaining hegemony over the Synagogue and its liturgy. See, inter alia, Richard S. Sarason, "On the Use of Method in the Modern Study of Jewish Liturgy," in *Approaches to Ancient Judaism: Theory and Practice,* ed. W. S. Green (Missoula, Mont.: Scholars Press, 1978), 146; Joseph Heinemann, *Prayer in the Talmud Forms and Patterns,* Studia Judaica (Berlin: Walter de Gruyter, 1977), 7. Heinemann's form criticism seems to me rather confusing in that he blurs the distinction between the distinct topoi of Study House and Synagogue, together with their associated *Gattungen.* Thus, for him, Targum, a Synagogue *Gattung* par excellence, belongs to the Study House (Heinemann, *Prayer,* 265)! I find his reasoning and argument, therefore, very difficult to follow. Much clearer and more convincing are Lee I. Levine, "The Sages and the Synagogue in Late Antiquity: The Evidence of the Galilee," in *The Galilee in Late Antiquity,* ed. Lee I. Levine (New York: Jewish Theological Seminary of America, 1992), 201–24; Cynthia Baker, "Neighbor at the Door or Enemy at the Gate? Notes Toward a Rabbinic Topography of Self and Other," paper presented at American Academy of Religion (New Orleans, 1996). There is increasing evidence that the religion of the late ancient Palestinian countryside, even well into the Byzantine period, was by no means identical with that projected by the Rabbis. On this point, see also Elchanan Reiner, "From Joshua to Jesus: The Transformation of a Biblical Story to a Local Myth: A Chapter in the Religious Life of the Galilean Jew," in *Sharing the Sacred: Religious Contacts and Conflicts in the Holy Land, First–Fifteenth Centuries* CE, ed. Guy Stroumsa and Arieh Kofsky (Jerusalem: Yad Ben Zvi, 1998), 224–25, who argues that "It will be necessary to distinguish between the normative religious world, as formulated in talmudic literature, and the religious world represented by those lists [of Jewish holy places] and the associated literature. We may possibly have to acknowledge the existence of a Galilean community whose religious milieu differs from that presently known." Surprisingly (or not so, by now), the life of this "religious world" represented a set of identity formations (narrative traditions) in which "Judaism" and "Christianity" were not nearly so clearly distinct as they are in the normative texts. See, finally, Galit Hasan-Rokem, "Narratives in Dialogue: A Folk Literary Perspective on Interreligious Contacts in the Holy Land in Rabbinic Literature of Late Antiquity," in *Sharing the Sacred: Religious Contacts and Conflicts in the Holy Land, First–Fifteenth Centuries* CE, ed. Guy Stroumsa and Arieh Kofsky (Jerusalem: Yad Ben Zvi, 1998), 109–29.

31. The Hebrew behind the Aramaic *memra* is apparently *'imra*, its etymological equivalent, as found, in parallelism with *davar* and Torah, in Ps. 119. In that Psalm, the LXX translates λóγος and sometimes νóμος.

32. Edwards, "Justin's Logos," 263.

33. Robert Hayward, *Divine Name and Presence: The Memra*, Oxford Centre for Postgraduate Hebrew Studies (Totowa, N.J.: Allanheld, Osmun, 1981), 3.

34. Sic transit gloria mundi. There is no hamza at the end of these words, and they ought to be spelled without the '. I only trouble to point this out, because it is an egregious error made increasingly frequently.

35. Nathaniel Deutsch, *Guardians of the Gate: Angelic Vice Regency in Late Antiquity*, Brill's Series in Jewish Studies (Leiden: E. J. Brill, 1999), 5–7.

36. Hayward, *Memra*, See Vinzenz Hamp, *Der Begriff "Wort" in den aramäischen Bibelübersetzungen ein exegetischer Beitrag zur hypostasen-frage und zur Geschichte der Logos-spekulationen* (Munich: Neuer Filser-verlag, 1938). For a good and judicious discussion of the three Aramaic terms in question, see Arnold Maria Goldberg, *Untersuchungen über die Vorstellung von der Schekhinah in der frühen rabbinischen Literatur: Talmud und Midrash* (Berlin: Walter de Gruyter, 1969), 1–12. See also Deutsch, *Guardians*, 5–7.

37. Tobin, "Logos," 352.

38. Raymond Edward Brown, *The Gospel According to John*, with an introduction by Raymond Edward Brown (Garden City, N.Y.: Doubleday, 1966), 524.

39. Burton L. Mack, *Logos und Sophia: Untersuchungen zur Weisheitstheologie im hellenistischen Judentum*, Studien zur Umwelt des Neuen Testaments (Göttingen: Vandenhoeck and Ruprecht, 1973), 6. Similarly, J. D. G. Dunn argues that the purpose of Sophia is to impart "God's active concern in creation, revelation and redemption, while at the same time protecting his holy transcendence and wholly otherness" (James D. G. Dunn, *Christology in the Making: A New Testament Inquiry into the Origins of the Doctrine of the Incarnation* [Philadelphia: Westminster Press, 1980], 176).

40. The argument that the Targums have sometimes "God" and sometimes the "Memra" in the same contexts is hardly decisive, since the ambiguity between God and the Logos is to be found wherever Logos theology is to be found, pace Martin McNamara, "Logos of the Fourth Gospel and *Memra* of the Palestinian Targum," *Expository Times* 79 (1968): 115. In later Jewish usage, one says "The Name" instead of actually citing any divine name. Although this usage has been compared to the use of the *Memra* in the Targums, they are not at all comparable. The later practice is a simple linguistic substitution to avoid profaning the Holy Name by pronouncing it, which the phrase *Memra H'* obviously does not accomplish. (I am using *H'* to represent the Hebrew *nominum sacrum*.)

41. Tobin, "Logos," 352–53.

42. McNamara, "Logos," 115.

43. Ibid.

44. On this point in general, see Jonathan Z. Smith, *Drudgery Divine: On the Comparison of Early Christianities and the Religions of Late Antiquity*, Chicago Studies in the History of Judaism (Chicago: University of Chicago Press, 1990).

45. Alejandro Díez Macho, *Neophyti 1, Targum Palestinense Ms. de la Biblioteca Vaticana* (Madrid: Consejo Superior de Investigaciones Científicas, 1968).

46. Alejandro Díez Macho, "El Logos y el Espíritu Santo," *Atlántida* 1 (1963): 381–96.

47. Michael L. Klein, ed., *The Fragment-Targums of the Pentateuch According to Their Extant Sources*, trans. Michael L. Klein, Analecta Biblica (Rome: Biblical Institute Press, 1980), 43.

48. Klein, *Fragment-Targums*, 45–46.

49. Klein, *Fragment-Targums*, 53.

50. Klein, *Fragment-Targums*, 74. Cf. Philo, *Her.* 205, in which the Logos is identified as this very angel.

51. Davies, *Paul and Rabbinic Judaism*, 152, pace Tobin, "Logos," 352.

52. Larry W. Hurtado, *One God, One Lord: Early Christian Devotion and Ancient Jewish Monotheism*, 2d ed. (Edinburgh: T & T Clark, 1998), 21.

53. Deutsch, *Guardians*, 11, points to a significant group of scholars who derive the demiurge of the "gnostic" texts entirely from Jewish traditions transformed and "radicalized." This fits my intuitions about these texts as well.

54. Wolfson, *Speculum*, 255. See also Elliot R. Wolfson, *Along the Path: Studies in Kabbalistic Myth, Symbolism, and Hermeneutics* (Albany: State University of New York Press, 1995); Gedaliahu Stroumsa, "Form(s) of God: Some Notes on Metatron and Christ," *Harvard Theological Review* 76 (1983): 269–88. Elliot R. Wolfson, "God, the Demiurge, and the Intellect: On the Usage of the Word *Kol* in Abraham Ibn Ezra," *Revue des études Juives* 149 (1990): 77–111.

55. See the rather stunning evidence in Wolfson, *Speculum*, 256–60. See too the work of Wolfson's student Daniel Abrams, "The Boundaries of Divine Ontology: The Inclusion and Exclusion of Meṭaṭron in the Godhead," *Harvard Theological Review* 87, no. 3 (July 1994): 291–321. In other words, much of the later rabbinic tradition rejected the rejection of binitarian theology that the Rabbis attempted to enforce (*Speculum*, 261, n. 310). Finally, see Elliot R. Wolfson, "Judaism and Incarnation: The Imaginal Body of God," in *Christianity in Jewish Terms*, ed. Tikva Simone Frymer-Kensky, Radical Traditions (Boulder, Colo.: Westview Press, 2000), 244.

56. Moshe Idel, "Prayer in Provençal Kabbalah," in Hebrew, *Tarbiz* 62, no. 2 (1993): 269.

57. For a discussion of dating as well as references to earlier literature, see Michael D. Swartz, "*Alay Le-Shabbeaḥ*: A Liturgical Prayer in Maʿaśeh Merkabah," *Jewish Quarterly Review* 87, no. 2–3 (October–January 1986): 186, n. 21. Scholem dated the prayer very early (Gershom Scholem, *Jewish Gnosticism, Merkabah Mysticism and Talmudic Tradition*, 2d ed. [New York: Jewish Theological Seminary of America, 1965], 27). This prayer survived in "orthodox" rabbinic circles, presumably because it lent itself to a monotarian interpretation, reading the two clauses as simultaneous parallels, as it is interpreted even today within orthodox Jewish prayer.

58. I have included the Hebrew here, since the text depends on a pun that Hebrew readers will best understand in the original.

59. For previous readings, see Segal, *Two Powers*, 68–69, and Deutsch, *Guardians*, 49. For a much older reading, see R. Travers Herford, *Christianity in Talmud and Midrash* (1903; reprint, New York: Ktav, 1978), 285–90.

60. The medieval Bible commentary of Ibn Ezra solves this problem by referring to other verses in which a speaker refers to himself by his own name.

61. Segal, *Two Powers*, 131–32, shows that this verse was a site of controversy between Rabbis and others independently of this locus.

62. But see Justin's *Dialogue* at 75. Even though for our rabbinic *min*, this angelic vice-regent is Metatron, for Justin he is clearly the Christ.

63. Segal, *Two Powers*, 7. Segal goes so far as to propose that, by dating various shifts within the rabbinic representation of *minim*, we can suggest "a progression and relative chronology of apocalypticism, mysticism, Christianity and gnosticism as historical movements" (Segal, *Two Powers*, 18–19).

64. As I have pointed out above, Segal is inconsistent in this and sometimes seems to be reaching for a formulation of the issue not unlike mine. Thus: "At any rate, these reports seem to reflect the actual beliefs of various Jewish groups, which are evidenced in extra-rabbinic reports long before we can ascertain their presence from rabbinic literature" (Segal, *Two Powers*, 114), ergo, not rabbinically constructed but actual identifiable heresies. At many places, Segal assumes actual heresies that depart from or corrupt authentic Jewish belief and that the Rabbis combat. Thus: "The increasing number of biblical passages regarded as dangerous testifies to the expansion rather than diminution of the heretical challenge" (Segal, *Two Powers*, 121).

65. For some possible background to this statement, see the material analyzed in Yehuda Liebes, "God and His Qualities," in Hebrew, *Tarbiz* 70, no. 1 (October–December 2000): 51–73.

66. Following the reading of the Mishna in all of the most important manuscripts.

67. I.e., excommunicate him.

68. Segal, *Two Powers*, 106.

69. I find Segal's conjecture that the Christian Eucharist is being referred to rather far-fetched (*Two Powers*, 101).

70. For an explanation of this severe objection, see Aharon Shemesh, "The Dispute Between the Pharisees and the Sadducees on the Death Penalty," in Hebrew, *Tarbiz* 70, no. 1 (October–December 2000): 26–29.

71. Geza Vermes, "Leviticus 18:21 in Ancient Jewish Bible Exegesis," in *Studies in Aggadah, Targum, and Jewish Liturgy in Memory of Joseph Heinemann*, ed. Jakob Josef Petuchowski, E. Fleischer, and Joseph Heinemann (Jerusalem: Magnes Press and Hebrew Union College Press, 1981), 113–17, well documents this line of interpretation of the verse from the Book of Jubilees through the Palestinian Targums. This Targum is found in the margin of Codex Neofiti and in the "Jerusalem Targum." Incidentally, the principle advocated by Vermes (as well as by many other Targum scholars) that "as it is anti-Mishnaic, it is no doubt pre-Mishnaic" (Vermes, "Leviticus 18:21," 118) simply cannot be maintained any longer, once it is recognized that there were active Jewish groups that did not accept the sovereignty of the Rabbis well into late antiquity and particularly as attested in the Palestinian Targums. Here, moreover, this is simply meaningless. Insofar as the Mishna condemns the practice, it *must* be "pre-Mishnaic," but insofar as it is found in the Targums of late antiquity, it is obviously not only pre-Mishnaic.

72. For another remnant of late ancient Jewish prayer directed to a secondary divine being of one sort or another, see Daniel Abrams, "From Divine Shape to Angelic Being: The Career of Akatriel in Jewish Literature," *Journal of Religion* (1996): 43–63; and Daniel Abrams, "The Dimensions of the Creator—Contradiction or Paradox?: Corruptions and Accretions to the Manuscript Witnesses," *Kabbalah: Journal for the Study of Jewish Mystical Texts* 5 (2000): 35–53.

73. Note that in the Byzantine Jewish theologian Shabbatei Donnolo the relation of the Sefirot to God is described as the relation of the flame to a coal (Wolfson, *Speculum*, 138), an image found in trinitarian theology as well.

74. Wolfson, *Speculum*, 198.

75. Although Segal correctly points to the Fourth Gospel as the earliest Jewish text that explicitly makes this connection, its presence in other Jewish texts not directly in-

fluenced in any way by the Gospel suggests a wider Jewish circulation, perhaps even a pre-Christian one. Wolfson's use of the terms *incarnation* and *docetic* will be confusing to scholars of Christianity familiar with these terms from that sphere. For Wolfson, "incarnation means the notion that God assumes the form of a human being" (Wolfson, *Speculum*, 217), whereas by "docetism" he indicates a doctrine that there is no vision of anything at all, but only inner psychological experience. Wolfson's "incarnation," then, is precisely what is meant by "docetism" in Christian writings, namely, a doctrine that God only *appeared* in human form, but appear He did. Wolfson's "docetism," on the other hand, does not correspond to any Christian doctrine known to me. In other words, incarnation in Christian doctrine means that God has assumed the *body* of a human being, not its form, while docetism is the doctrine that God only assumed the form of a human being.

76. Israel M. Ta-Shma, "The Origin and Place of *ʿaleinu le-Shabbeaḥ* in the Daily Prayerbook: *Seder Ha-Maʿamadot* and Its Relation to the Conclusion of the Daily Service," in Hebrew, in *The Frank Talmage Memorial Volume*, vol. 1, ed. Barry Walfish (Haifa: University of Haifa Press, 1993), 90.

77. The question of "Meṭaṭron and Jesus" is also treated by Abrams, "Meṭaṭron," 316–21. See also Stroumsa, "Form(s) of God."

78. It is not beside the point to note that, in traditional Jewish prayer from the Byzantine period to now, prayer to the "attributes" of God is known as well as prayer to the Ministering Angels (Yehuda Liebes, "The Angels of the Shofar and the Yeshua Sar-Hapanim," *Jerusalem Studies in Jewish Thought* 6, no. 1–2 [1987]: 171–95, in Hebrew). These prayers were rectified by nineteenth-century Jewish authorities, who saw in them (suddenly?) a threat to monotheism.

79. I am in agreement with the argument of Hayward, *Memra*, 16–20, that this a key targumic textual nexus for understanding the Memra, although I disagree with various points in his interpretation. Hayward, needless to say, is not concerned there with the Johannine parallel.

80. For reasons of his own, Hayward translates here "I am there," which does not seem warranted or necessary to me.

81. Both in the manuscript known as the Fragment Targum and in the Genizah Fragments.

82. Klein, *Fragment-Targums*, i, 175.

83. Díez Macho, *Neophyti 1, Targum Palestinense Ms. de la Biblioteca Vaticana.*, ad loc.

84. The association of Memra with supporting, as well as redeeming, and revealing is almost commonplace in the Targums, as we have seen above.

85. It is fascinating that in the binitarian theology of later medieval Kabbalism, the first "I am" is taken to refer to the Demiurge and the second to Wisdom (Idel, "Prayer in Provençal Kabbalah," 274–75).

86. Klein, *Fragment-Targums*, ii, 47.

87. McNamara, "Logos," 116.

88. See now Roger Le Déaut, *La Nuit Pascale: Essai sur la signification de la Pâque juive a partir du Targum d'Exode XII 42* (Rome: Biblical Institute Press, 1980). Note that R. E. Brown, *John*, 523, has shown that some of the citations of Torah in the Fourth Gospel are neither from the Hebrew nor from the Septuagint but from the targumic tradition.

89. Hurtado, *One God*, 17. I would disagree with Hurtado's assumption that "Although we do not actually have first-century Jewish documents that tell us directly what Jewish leaders thought of Christian devotion, there seems to be every reason to assume that the attitude was very much like the one reflected in slightly later Jewish sources, which apparently rejected cultic devotion to Jesus as constituting an example of the worship of 'two powers in heaven,' that is, the worship of two gods" (Hurtado, *One God*, 2). This statement reveals the following assumptions, none of which I share: (1) that there were Jewish leaders in the first century who are necessarily not Christian; (2) that the notion of a heresy of "Two Powers in Heaven" can already be assumed from that time; and (3) that it was worship of two gods (rather than binitarianism in general) that was identified with this so-called heresy. The primary gap between us seems to be in what each of us is willing to call "Jewish" or "Christian" or, indeed, the applicability of that distinction at all in the first or even second centuries. Hurtado, moreover, seems inclined to see the major development between the first and subsequent centuries as being a change in the nature of "heresy" rather than a change in the nature of Jewish heresiology. Cf. p. 19, where he writes that "in the surviving literature of the pre-Christian period, however, it is not clear that any of the chief figures were seen as sharing the unique veneration due to God alone or that Jewish monotheism was fundamentally modified by the interest shown in these figures." But, once again, we find here a reification of "Jewish monotheism" as a real entity, which is either modified or not, but not as a construction that might very well have come into being through the exclusion of certain traditional beliefs, namely the elaboration of "two powers" heresiology—not the invention of two powers heresy. For a succinct indication of the ways that Hurtado's and my positions are direct contradictories, see Hurtado, *One God*, 37. Hurtado's exclusive use of liturgy, of worship, as a taxon for distinguishing binitarianism seems to me overdrawn. Belief in intermediaries in the performance of God's functions can also be binitarian in its ethos. It is important to remember that *binitarian* is not the opposite of *monotheistic*, unless one makes it so, as the Rabbis seem to have done. Thus any evidence for Jewish binitarianism does not constitute a "weakening" of pure monotheism, any more than Christian trinitarianism does, except from the point of view of Modalists such as rabbinic Jews (i.e., the Rabbis), who regard it as heresy, of course. See also Robert M. Grant, "Les Êtres intermédiaires dans le judaïsme tardif," in *Le Origini Dello Gnosticismo, Colloquio di Messina 13–18 Aprile 1966*, vol. 12, ed. Ugo Bianchi, Studies in the History of Religions (supplements to *Numen*) (Leiden: E. J. Brill, 1967), 141–54.

Chapter 6. The Crucifixion of the Memra

1. David Winston, *Logos and Mystical Theology in Philo of Alexandria* (Cincinnati, Ohio: Hebrew Union College Press, 1985), 25.

2. Opif. 20, see Maren Niehoff, *Philo on Jewish Identity and Culture in Roman Egypt* (Tübingen: Mohr Siebeck, 2002), 205. On the one hand, Niehoff marks the difference between the Philonic Logos and the rabbinic Torah, but without emphasizing the theological significance of this shift. On the other, she offers us yet another comparison between a Philonic parable and a parable of Rabbi Hoshaya, within an explicitly polemical encounter with Christianity (Bereshit Rabbah 8:10).

3. This puts a somewhat different spin on Dodd's remark that "many of the propositions referring to the Logos in the Prologue are the counterparts of rabbinic statements referring to the Torah" (Charles Harold Dodd, *The Interpretation of the Fourth Gospel* [Cambridge: Cambridge University Press, 1960], 85). These were the traditional epithets of the Logos, which the Rabbis tenaciously transferred without exception to the Torah, by which they mean the written physical Torah in the world (as well as the activity of its study, of course). This is a rabbinic interpretation of the old Wisdom myth that resolutely rejects any interpretation that involves a hypostasis alongside God. God looks into the Torah, a text, in order to create the world. He doesn't delegate the creation to Wisdom. We've got to get our timings and sequences right here; as long as scholars and interpreters think that rabbinic literature is older than the Gospels, matters will always be confused. Cf., e.g., Kittel in *TDNT* 4:136. See also Menahem Kister, "'Let Us Make a Man'—Observations on the Dynamics of Monotheism," in Hebrew, in *Issues in Talmudic Research: Conference Commemorating the Fifth Anniversary of the Passing of Ephraim E. Urbach, 2 December 1996* (Jerusalem: Israel Academy of Sciences, 2001), 47–48, on the distance between Philo and the rabbinic parable, and "'Let Us,'" 51–52, on the possibility of a myth of the Torah as a hypostasis of God, as reflected in Qur'anic theology, as well. However, even if the Muslim theologoumenon had "Jewish" antecedents, they need not, of course, have been rabbinic (and probably were not).

4. Darrell D. Hannah, *Michael and Christ: Michael Traditions and Angel Christology in Early Christianity*, Wissenschaftliche Untersuchungen zum Neuen Testament (Tübingen: Mohr Siebeck, 1999), 30–31.

5. W. D. Davies, *Paul and Rabbinic Judaism: Some Rabbinic Elements in Pauline Theology*, 2d ed., (1955; reprint, London: Society for the Promotion of Christian Knowledge, 1965), 170–72, gives an excellent account of the attribution to Torah of all of the former attributes of Wisdom. He, however, considers this a development which *precedes* Paul (and thus a fortiori the Fourth Gospel). I am reversing the narrative whereby the Fourth Gospel, and by implication Christian theology in general, "transfers to the Logos the functions ascribed in Jewish literature to Wisdom or the Torah, which took on later in Jewish thought [meaning the pre-Christian era] the role of giver of light which Wisdom had played since creation" (Rudolf Schnackenburg, *The Gospel According to St. John* [London: Burns & Oates; New York: Herder & Herder, 1968], 253). This is simply a reproduction in scholarly-historical terms of the Evangelist's own narrative of the relation of the Torah to the incarnation and does not bear the weight of historical scrutiny.

6. My hypothesis is thus the direct contrary of the fairly widespread view that "in part, the Johannine doctrine of the Word was formulated as a Christian answer to Jewish speculation on the Law" (Raymond Edward Brown, *The Gospel According to John*, introd. by Raymond Edward Brown [Garden City, N.Y.: Doubleday, 1966], 523). This conventional view ascribes a strongly supersessionist theology to John, which I think cannot be maintained in the face of the evidence that the Evangelist is working from a traditional Jewish story of the Torah coming down to bring Wisdom to the world. According to my story, it was the Rabbis who needed to thoroughly displace this story and reassert the Ben Sira happy ending version of the myth, in order to define themselves over and against a Logos theology become Christology. The contemporary supersessionist motivations of the accepted scholarly version are thematized only too directly by Brown: "Not the Torah but Jesus Christ is the creator and source of light and life. He is

the *Memra*, God's presence among men. And yet, even though all these strands are woven into the Johannine concept of the Word, this concept remains a unique contribution of Christianity. It is beyond all that has gone before, even as Jesus is beyond all who have gone before" (*John*, 524).

7. Suggested by one possible meaning for the Septuagint translation of the verse: ἤμην παρ᾽ αὐτῷ ἁρμόζουσα. See 2 Corinthians 11:2.

8. Solomon Shechter, ed., *Aboth de Rabbi Nathan* (1887; reprint, New York: Philipp Feldheim, 1967), 91. Judah Goldin, trans., *The Fathers According to Rabbi Nathan*, Yale Judaica Series (New Haven, Conn.: Yale University Press, 1955), 126–27.

9. Cf. also Burton L. Mack, "Wisdom Makes a Difference: Alternatives to 'Messianic' Configurations," in *Judaisms and Their Messiahs at the Turn of the Christian Era*, ed. Jacob Neusner, William Scott Green, and Ernest S. Frerichs (Cambridge: Cambridge University Press, 1987), 44–47, for a somewhat different and very stimulating approach to this question.

10. Alan F. Segal, *Two Powers in Heaven: Early Rabbinic Reports About Christianity and Gnosticism*, Studies in Judaism in Late Antiquity, vol. 25 (Leiden: E. J. Brill, 1977), x.

11. Thus the question posed by Segal ("A most significant question is whether or not such ideas were ever current within rabbinic Judaism," *Two Powers*, 69) in fact begs the question. Rabbinic Judaism, in my view, is precisely the religion that is made by expelling "such ideas" by crossing them and their traditionalist believers with a border of orthodoxy. On Monarchianism, see R. Heine, "The Christology of Callistus," *Journal of Theological Studies* 49 (1998): 56–91.

12. Segal is capable, of course, of also seeing the matter in a much more critical and nuanced light: "Preliminary indications are, therefore, that many parts of the Jewish community in various places and periods used the traditions which the rabbis claim is an heretical conception of the deity" (Segal, *Two Powers*, 43), yet he is still willing to speak of a "theological and orthodox center of Judaism," which these "many parts of the Jewish community" seem "willing to compromise."

13. Sigmund Freud, "Instincts and Their Vicissitudes," in *The Standard Edition of the Complete Psychological Works of Sigmund Freud*, vol. 14, ed. and trans. James Strachey and Anna Freud, trans. Alix Strachey and James Strachey (1915; reprint, London: Hogarth Press, 1955), 136.

14. Segal, *Two Powers*.

15. Ibid., ix.

16. As I have argued in Daniel Boyarin, "A Tale of Two Synods: Nicaea, Yavneh and the Making of Orthodox Judaism," *Exemplaria* 12, no. 1 (Spring 2000): 21–62. Cf. also the complications that Segal makes for himself in *Two Powers*, 215, because he has not completely clarified these two issues (the existence of "two powers" theology and the appearance of the notion of heresy).

17. Segal, *Two Powers*, 5–6.

18. This position is comparable to the general view of Lawrence H. Schiffman, "At the Crossroads: Tannaitic Perspectives on the Jewish-Christian Schism," in *Aspects of Judaism in the Greco-Roman Period*, ed. E. P. Sanders, A. I. Baumgarten, and Alan Mendelson, Jewish and Christian Self-Definition 2 (Philadelphia: Fortress Press, 1981), 115–56, 338–52. Schiffman sees a transition from "sectarianism" to "consensus" in the rabbinic period and even remarks that certain views that had been accepted among Jews were now defined as *minut* and thus left to the Christians. He considers the rise of Christian-

ity to be a main cause for this development within Judaism. My disagreements with Schiffman would be two: First, he would locate this development a century earlier than I would, and second, for his "consensus" I would substitute "orthodoxy."

19. Segal, *Two Powers*, 43.

20. At the same time that I am (gratefully) building on the vital work that Segal performs in his book, I must comment that Segal consistently confounds his own project and mislays, as it were, his own best insights. He writes: "It is not possible to decide exactly when rabbinic opposition to such doctrines started. For one thing, it is nearly impossible to be sure of the wording of rabbinic traditions before 200 C.E. much less before 70 C.E., when the rabbis became the leaders of the Jewish community [*sic*]. Most rabbinic traditions, at least as we have them, were written subsequently. So we cannot blithely assume that the rabbinic reports date from the Second Commonwealth" (Segal, *Two Powers*, 43). So far so good, but then he continues, "However, with Philo's evidence, we have reason to suppose their antiquity." Segal has begun asking about the dating of the rabbinic opposition to the doctrine, and seems to have tried to supply an answer by citing Philo, but Philo, of course, is only evidence for the *existence* of the doctrine and not for rabbinic opposition to it; in fact Philo himself holds a version of the "heresy," as Segal states explicitly in Segal, *Two Powers*, 50. This ambiguity concerning the question at hand pervades Segal's discussion and frequently weakens his answers. A clearer distinction between the search for the doctrine and the search for its expulsion as "heretical" would have served his inquiry well. There is, I submit, no pre-Christian (or even first-century) evidence for the latter. This distinction should also serve (negatively) the enterprise of the search for the so-called Jewish origins of Gnosticism. See the otherwise compelling Kister, "'Let Us,'" at p. 53, who also seems to hold that there is some essentialist entity called "Jewish Monotheism," which various doctrines can threaten or endanger, rather than seeing that very entity as being a constructed and contested field. An indication of how misleading Segal's formulation could be can be seen in the following: "In his *Two Powers in Heaven*, [Segal] notes how the Jewish category of heresy (belief in two powers in heaven) antedates the New Testament" (Michel Desjardins, "Bauer and Beyond: On Recent Scholarly Discussions of Αἵρεσις in the Early Christian Era," *The Second Century* 8 [1991]: 76).

21. See the near-classic R. P. C. Hanson, *The Search for the Christian Doctrine of God: The Arian Controversy, 318–381 A.D.* (Edinburgh: T & T Clark, 1988).

22. Daniel Boyarin, "The Gospel of the Memra: Jewish Binitarianism and the Crucifixion of the Logos," *Harvard Theological Review* 94, no. 3 (2001): 243–84.

23. Thus, e.g., it has often been remarked that nearly all of the late ancient synagogues excavated in Palestine significantly contradict rabbinic prescriptions for the building of such edifices.

24. Cf. Galit Hasan-Rokem, "Narratives in Dialogue: A Folk Literary Perspective on Interreligious Contacts in the Holy Land in Rabbinic Literature of Late Antiquity," in *Sharing the Sacred: Religious Contacts and Conflicts in the Holy Land, First–Fifteenth Centuries C.E.*, ed. Guy Stroumsa and Arieh Kofsky (Jerusalem: Yad Ben Zvi, 1998), 128, who somewhat underplays this dimension, in my opinion. For other instances of disparity between the "Judaism" of the Rabbis and that of the Synagogue in late ancient Palestine, see William Horbury, "Suffering and Messianism in Yose Ben Yose," in *Suffering and Martyrdom in the New Testament Studies Presented to G. M. Styler*, ed. William Horbury and Brian McNeil (Cambridge: Cambridge University Press, 1980), 143–82.

25. See, however, Hans Bietenhard, "Logos Theologie im Rabbinat," ANRW 2 (Berlin: Walter de Gruyter, 1979), 580–617.

26. Note how different this formulation is from the traditional scholarly one, whereby John's Logos was influenced by the Targum's Memra. See, e.g., Martin McNamara, "Logos of the Fourth Gospel and *Memra* of the Palestinian Targum," *Expository Times* 79 (1968): 115–17.

27. An error that the otherwise very astute Hannah commits as well, Hannah, *Michael*, 109–10.

28. See also Naomi Janowitz, "Rabbis and Their Opponents: The Construction of the 'Min' in Rabbinic Anecdotes," *Journal of Early Christian Studies* 6, no. 3 (Fall 1998): 449–62; Christine E. Hayes, "Displaced Self-Perceptions: The Deployment of *Mînîm* and Romans in *B. Sanhedrin* 90b-91a," in *Religious and Ethnic Communities in Later Roman Palestine*, ed. Hayim Lapin (Lanham, Md.: University Press of Maryland, 1999), 249–89.

29. Robert Hayward, *Divine Name and Presence: The Memra*, Oxford Centre for Postgraduate Hebrew Studies (Totowa, N.J.: Allanheld, Osmun, 1981), 4.

30. C. K. Barrett, "Jews and Judaizers in the Epistles of Ignatius," in *Jews, Greeks and Christians: Religious Cultures in Late Antiquity. Essays in Honor of W. D. Davies* (Leiden: E. J. Brill, 1976), 223.

31. Compare Rebecca Lyman's very helpful discussion of Christian heresiology: "I am suggesting that problems of assimilation and authority were already present in the form of universal Christianity taught by Justin, which could lead to the polemical invention of 'Gnosticism' as philosophical and superstitious at once, whatever may have actually been taught by Valentinus or Ptolemy. Irenaeus' concern with identifying valid sacraments, lasting conversions, and legitimate successions reveals the instability of the inherited discourse of Justin, and the necessity of establishing the correct *diadoche* and belief within the baptized community itself. If we restore a primary teaching identity to Irenaeus as a leader, the controversial rhetoric of his text reflects a continuing debate over identity and authority by competitive intellectuals within the community rather than a defensive protection against outsiders," J. Rebecca Lyman, "The Politics of Passing: Justin Martyr's Conversion as a Problem of 'Hellenization,'" in *Conversion in Late Antiquity and the Early Middle Ages*, ed. Anthony Grafton and Kenneth Mills (Rochester, N.Y.: University of Rochester Press, forthcoming).

32. Homi K. Bhabha, *The Location of Culture* (London: Routledge, 1994), 111.

33. Even to the point of helping us understand the insistence on "consensual orthodoxy."

34. Bhabha, *Location*, 44–45, provides an elegant theoretical analysis of the mechanics of such specular differentiating and identification, without, however, being able to see such processes as mutual (quite). See also the discussion in Virginia Burrus, *The Sex Lives of Saints*, Divinations: Reading Late Ancient Religions (Philadelphia: University of Pennsylvania Press, 2003), chap. 3, and esp. Willis Johnson, "Henry III's Circumcised Pennies," *British Numismatic Journal* 65 (1995).

35. Jonathan Z. Smith, "Differential Equations: On Constructing the 'Other'" (lecture, Tempe, Arizona, 1992, pamphlet), 14.

36. Karen L. King, *What Is Gnosticism?* (Cambridge, Mass.: Harvard University Press, 2003).

37. Alain Le Boulluec, *La notion d'hérésie dans la littérature grecque IIe–IIIe siècles* (Paris: études Augustiniennes, 1985), 1:16; King, *Making Heresy*, chap. 2.

38. Hannah, *Michael*, 21.

39. Ibid., 22.

40. S. Horovitz and Israel Abraham Rabin, eds., *Mechilta d'Rabbi Ismael* (Jerusalem: Wahrmann Books, 1970), 43, cf. p. 33.

41. Judah Goldin, "Not by Means of an Angel and Not by Means of a Messenger," in *Religions in Antiquity: Essays in Memory of Erwin Ramsdell Goodenough*, ed. Jacob Neusner (Leiden: E. J. Brill, 1968), 412–24.

42. See Arthur Marmorstein, *The Old Rabbinic Doctrine of God* (London: Oxford University Press, 1937), 57, "Israel was delivered neither by the Logos, nor angels, but by God Himself." This version of the text was originally published from more than one Genizah fragment by Israel Abrahams, "Some Egyptian Fragments of the Passover Haggada," *Jewish Quarterly Review, old series* 10 (1898): 41, who understood these readings as "repeated references to the Memra or Logos." The Targum reads here, "And I will pass in my *Memra* [var. I will be revealed in my Memra] through the land of Egypt this night *of the Passover*, and I will kill all the first-born in the land of Egypt" (Martin McNamara, trans., with notes by Robert Hayward, *Targum Neofiti 1: Exodus*, The Aramaic Bible [Edinburgh: T & T Clark, 1994], 47–48). In my opinion, it is difficult to see this as a mere *façon de parler*. According to the Wisdom of Solomon, 18, this plague was carried out by the Logos. See David Winston, trans. and commentary, *The Wisdom of Solomon*, Anchor Bible (Garden City, N.Y.: Doubleday, 1979), 313, and his fascinating notes (with which I partially disagree, for reasons that will be obvious), 317–19; Joseph Reider, *The Book of Wisdom: An English Translation with Introduction and Commentary*, Dropsie College Edition: Jewish Apocryphal Literature (New York: Harper and Brothers, 1957), 210–11, with whom my disagreement is even sharper. Similarly, for Melito, Christ executed the Plague (Melito of Sardis, *On Pascha and Fragments*, ed. S. G. Hall, Oxford Early Christian Texts [Oxford: Oxford University Press, 1979], line 657). For the view I maintain, see Shlomo Pines, "'From Darkness to Light': Parallels to *Haggada* Texts in Hellenistic Literature," in Studies in Literature Presented to Simon Halkin, in Hebrew, ed. Ezra Fleischer (Jerusalem: Magnes Press, 1973), 176–79. Apart from every other argument, if the memra of the Targum was "purely a phenomenon of translation, not a figment of speculation," as George Foote Moore maintains (George Foot Moore, *Judaism in the First Centuries of the Christian Era*, vol. 1 [New York: Schocken, 1971], 419), and if the Logos of Wisdom "is in reality God himself in one of his aspects," and, therefore, "our author's position is almost identical with that of the rabbis" (Winston, *Wisdom*, 319), then why was so much rabbinic textual energy expended in denying that God had any agent in the execution of the plague (even if we grant, with Winston, that "not by means of the Logos" is a Byzantine innovation in the text)? Pines, it should be emphasized, was also one of the first to see that "influences" could run from Christian texts such as Melito to rabbinic texts, an important line of research continued in Israel Jacob Yuval, "Easter and Passover as Early Jewish-Christian Dialogue," in *Passover and Easter: Origin and History to Modern Times*, ed. Paul F. Bradshaw and Lawrence A. Hoffman, Two Liturgical Traditions, 5 (Notre Dame, Ind.: University of Notre Dame Press, 1999), 127–60. See also Menahem Kasher, *Hagadah Shel Pesaḥ Lel Shimurim* (Jerusalem: Bet Torah Shelemah, 1982), 42, and Israel Jacob Yuval, *Two Nations in Your Womb: Perceptions of Jews and Christians*, in Hebrew (Tel-Aviv: Alma/Am Oved, 2000), 95–97. Yuval quite brilliantly argues that certain features of the Haggada for Passover, namely, the total absence of Moses, can be best explained as a tacit polemic against "Christian" notions of mediation.

43. Segal, *Two Powers*, 40, understands the citation of v. 10 to be an attempt to answer the claim of the heretics, because it says that "A fiery stream issued from *Him*," implying only one divine figure, and writes that "the argument of the rabbis is not completely convincing for the text may only be referring to one of the two figures at this point" (Segal, *Two Powers*, 40, n. 9). Segal misconstrues the text, however. According to midrashic form the citation "and it also says" must be a continuation of the problem and not the answer. The "etc." refers, then, to the following verses, in which it seems clear that two divine figures are envisioned. This citation is, then, indeed part of the problem (and not an unconvincing solution, pace Segal). The solution comes with the citation of Exodus 20:2, which is precisely what the midrashic form would lead us to expect.

44. Segal remarks that the text has "identified the people who believe in 'two powers in heaven' as gentiles" (Segal, *Two Powers*, 41) and then later is somewhat nonplussed, remarking, "they must have been gentiles well-versed in Jewish tradition to have offered such a dangerous and sophisticated interpretation of Dan. 7:9f" (Segal, *Two Powers*, 55). Well, Gentiles who are so well versed and who would make such a dangerous and sophisticated interpretation, precisely of Daniel 7, are called Christians! What he misses is that "nations of the world" in the Mekhilta usually refers to Christians, "the Church from the *ethne*," to be sure, although he does allow for this as a possibility (56–57). Precisely with reference to that group, the Mekhilta frequently insists on referring to God as "He who spoke and the world was," which I have interpreted as an attack on the Memra, as an insistence that there is none—only the "Father" who spoke and the world was.

45. Horovitz and Rabin, *Mechilta*, 220–21. Cf. the following parallel text:

H' is a man of war; H' is his name [Exod. 15:3]: Why was it said? For this reason. At the sea He appeared to them as a mighty hero doing battle, as it is said: "The Lord is a man of war." At Sinai he appeared to them as an old man full of mercy. It is said: "And they saw the God of Israel" [Exod. 24:10], etc. And of the time after they had been redeemed what does it say? "And the like of the very heaven for clearness" [ibid.]. Again it says: "I beheld till thrones were placed, and one that was ancient of days did sit" [Dan. 7:9]. And it also says: "A fiery stream issued," etc. [Dan. 7:10]. Scripture, therefore, would not let the nations of the world have an excuse for saying that there are two Powers, but declares: "The Lord is a man of war, the Lord is His name." He, it is, who was in Egypt and He who was at the sea. It is He who was in the past and He who will be in the future. It is He who is in this world and He who will be in the world to come, as it is said, "See now that I, even I, am He," etc. [Deut. 32:39]. And it also says: "Who hath wrought and done it? He that called the generations from the beginning. I, the Lord, who am the first, and with the last am the same" [Isa. 41:4]. (J. Z. Lauterbach, ed. and trans., *Mekilta DeRabbi Ishmael* [1934; reprint, Philadelphia: Jewish Publication Society, 1961], 2: 31–32; Horovitz and Rabin, *Mechilta*, 129–30).

For extensive discussion of this and parallel passages, see Segal, *Two Powers*, 33–57. I will refer to this analysis as relevant for my particular focus on the text and the questions involved.

Reading this parallel text, Hayward argues that its purpose is to say that "the fact that the divine Name YHWH is found twice in one verse of Scripture is not to be taken as a point of departure for the heretical proposition that there are two Lords." Hayward, however, misunderstands how midrash "works." The verse that is cited at the opening of the midrash is not the verse that causes the problem, but the verse that will provide a solution to the problem. The point of the midrash is to demonstrate the *necessity* for the verse cited in the lemma by showing that without it, there would be some error or difficulty. The text cited in my main text demonstrates in any case that the "repetition" of the name is not the difficulty here. Hayward is in good company here, namely, Segal, *Two Powers*, 36. I believe that the same false interpretation is proferred by Segal to Sifre Deuteronomy 379, where the text cites the verse "So now that I, even I, am He" as a *refutation* to heretics, whereas Segal sees it as the heretical provocation (Segal, *Two Powers*, 86). The verse asserts that God is identical with himself, making it an effective refutation of binitarianism rather than a support for it. Even less plausible is Segal's remark with regard to another passage that it, too, "uses the repetition in scripture as an occasion to discuss 'two powers in heaven'" (Segal, *Two Powers*, 90). The alleged "repetition" here is simply the use of the conjunctive "and," which Rabbi Akiva used for all sorts of *derashot* on many themes and has absolutely nothing to do with "two powers." Cf. also Elliot R. Wolfson, *Through a Speculum That Shines: Vision and Imagination in Medieval Jewish Literature* (Princeton, N.J.: Princeton University Press, 1994), 32–35.

46. For another instance in which, also in a polemical context, the Rabbis avoid citing the really difficult part of Daniel 7, see Segal, *Two Powers*, 132.

47. Sigmund Olaf Plytt Mowinckel, *He That Cometh: The Messiah Concept in the Old Testament and Later Judaism*, trans. G. W. Anderson (Oxford: B. Blackwell, 1956), 357. See also Moshe Idel, *Messianic Mystics* (New Haven, Conn.: Yale University Press, 1998), 89.

48. Hayward, *Memra*, 31.

49. Segal, *Two Powers*, 37. Segal prefers to analyze the shorter version of the Mekhilta DeRashbi. However, it is almost certain that this text is dependent on the earlier Mekhilta of Rabbi Ishmael and frequently misunderstands his sources, as held with respect to this passage by J. Z. Lauterbach, "Some Clarifications on the Mekhilta," in Hebrew, in *Sefer Klausner Maasaf le-Mada Ule-Sifrut Yafah Mugash le-Prof. Josef Klausner le-Yobel Ha-Shishim*, N. H. Torczyner et al. (Tel-Aviv: Hozaat Va ad-Hayobel, 1937), 181–88; and strongly demonstrated recently by Menahem Kahana, *Two Mekhiltot on the Amalek Portion: The Originality of the Version of the Mekhilta De'Rabbi Ishma'el with Respect to the Mekhilta of Rabbi Shim on Ben Yohay*, in Hebrew (Jerusalem: Magnes Press, 1999).

50. Pesikta Rabbati 21 100b.

51. As argued, correctly in my view, by R. Travers Herford, *Christianity in Talmud and Midrash* (1903; reprint, New York: Ktav, 1978), 304, as well as by Jacob Zallel Lauterbach, *Rabbinic Essays* (New York: Ktav, 1973), 549. Oddly, Segal claims both that a "gnostic impulse" was the cause of the redaction of this text (Segal, *Two Powers*, 54) and then later that "'two powers' refers to Christians and not extreme gnostics" (Segal, *Two Powers*, 58) on the basis of the same passage. I obviously agree with the latter point and not the former. See too Wolfson, *Speculum*, 39–40.

52. For at least a hint that Modalism is the dominant rabbinic doctrine of God, see Elliot R. Wolfson, "Judaism and Incarnation: The Imaginal Body of God," in *Christianity in Jewish Terms*, ed. Tikva Simone Frymer-Kensky, Radical Traditions (Boulder, Colo.: Westview Press, 2000), 241.

53. I am accordingly in great sympathy with the line of argument taken by Díez Macho in general and particularly in his "El Logos y el Espíritu Santo," *Atlántida* 1 (1963): 392.

54. What Hayward took to be the problem of the Midrash, the dual appearance of the name H' in the verse, is in fact the solution: both appearances are the same God, the same hypostasis. See above n. 45.

55. J. N. D. Kelly, *Early Christian Doctrines*, rev. ed. (New York: Harper and Row, 1978), 120.

56. This was surely not the most common or general designation for the deity in rabbinic texts. Thus, for instance, the slightly earlier Mishna usually refers to God as "Heaven." This shift in the midrashic literature of the latter half of the third century seems to me significant, therefore, particularly as it appears in texts that can be otherwise arguably read as anti-Christian propaganda.

57. Hayward, *Memra*, 31.

58. Daniel Boyarin, *Dying for God: Martyrdom and the Making of Christianity and Judaism*, The Lancaster/Yarnton Lectures in Judaism and Other Religions for 1998 (Stanford, Calif.: Stanford University Press, 1999), 113. For this identification, see too Yuval, *Nations*, 91, n. 111.

59. Note that according to Hippolytus, Noetus, the most important of the early Modalists, used the same verses to argue against the Second Person that the Rabbis used against Two Powers heretics (Segal, *Two Powers*, 229).

60. Kelly, *Doctrines*, 119–20. For a fine, succinct discussion of Modalism, see Kelly, *Doctrines*, 119–23.

61. Daniel Abrams, "The Boundaries of Divine Ontology: The Inclusion and Exclusion of Meṭaṭron in the Godhead," *Harvard Theological Review* 87, no. 3 (July 1994): 291.

62. Elliot R. Wolfson, "The Image of Jacob Engraved upon the Throne: Further Reflection on the Esoteric Doctrine of the German Pietists," in *Along the Path: Studies in Kabbalistic Myth, Symbolism, and Hermeneutics* (Albany: State University of New York Press, 1995), 4–7 and throughout. See also esp.: "In the earliest sources the motif of the icon of Jacob engraved on the throne may have been related to the hypostatization of the Logos" ("Image," 18).

63. Into this context Enoch traditions also fit. Again, Abrams has phrased the point well: "Moshe Idel has drawn our attention to texts that understand Enoch to be the angelic figure of Meṭaṭron and yet others where Meṭaṭron is identified with God, bridging all the gaps between humanity and God" (Abrams, "Meṭaṭron," 292–93, citing Moshe Idel, "Enoch is Meṭaṭron," *Immanuel* 24/25 [1990]: 220–40. See also Gedaliahu Stroumsa, "Form(s) of God: Some Notes on Metatron and Christ," *Harvard Theological Review* 76 [1983]: 269–88).

64. Idel, Messianic Mystics, 85–94. Almost unbelievably, we learn there (Idel, *Messianic Mystics*, 85) of a medieval Jewish mystic who writes, "'Enoch is Metatron' . . . and the first name out of the seventy names of Metatron is Yaho'el whose secret is Ben [Son!]." As Idel remarks compellingly, it is impossible to imagine that in the Christian Middle Ages an orthodox Jewish thinker would have produced such a "dangerously" Christian-sounding text; therefore, we must be dealing with a mythologoumenon from the time when Judaism and Christianity were not yet distinct theological entities, when it was still possible for the second God to be referred to as the "Son" by "Jewish" writers. It is not the Logos that distinguishes Judaism from Christianity. See also Nathaniel Deutsch, *The Gnostic Imagination: Gnosticism, Mandaeism, and Merkabah Mysticism*, Brill's Series in Jewish Studies (Leiden: E. J. Brill, 1995), 98, and Gedaliahu Stroumsa, *Savoir et salut* (Paris: éditions du Cerf, 1992), 58–59. As Idel perspicaciously puts the possibilities: "How early such a text was is difficult to calculate. Whether this text reflects a pre-Christian Jewish concept of the angelic son who possesses or constitutes the divine name is also hard to ascertain. If late, the Christian, or Jewish-Christian, nature of such a Hebrew text cannot be doubted" (Idel, *Messianic Mystics*, 87). In any event, stunningly, it cannot be doubted that it remained, in the end, part and parcel of a non-Christian

"Jewish" traditional mythologoumenon/theologoumenon. The reader interested in early Christology who reads these pages of Idel's work will be, I think, illuminated. Another important example of the same phenomenon, of distinctly christological motifs preserved in early medieval Kabbalistic texts, is exposed in Elliot R. Wolfson, "The Tree That Is All: Jewish-Christian Roots of a Kabbalistic Symbol in Sefer Ha-Bahir," in *Along the Path: Studies in Kabbalistic Myth, Symbolism, and Hermeneutics* (Albany: State University of New York Press, 1995), 63–88. Wolfson, "Imaginal," 244–46, is also very important.

65. See Hippolytus, *Refutation of All Heresies*, 9.7:

And having even venom embedded in his heart, and forming no correct opinion on any subject, and yet withal being ashamed to speak the truth, this Callistus, not only on account of his publicly saying in the way of reproach to us, "Ye are Ditheists," but also on account of his being frequently accused by Sabellius, as one that had transgressed his first faith, devised some such heresy as the following. Callistus alleges that the Logos Himself is Son, and that Himself is Father; and that though denominated by a different title, yet that in reality He is one indivisible spirit. And he maintains that the Father is not one person and the Son another, but that they are one and the same; and that all things are full of the Divine Spirit, both those above and those below. And he affirms that the Spirit, which became incarnate in the virgin, is not different from the Father, but one and the same. And he adds, that this is what has been declared by the Saviour: "Believest thou not that I am in the Father, and the Father in me?" For that which is seen, which is man, he considers to be the Son; whereas the Spirit, which was contained in the Son, to be the Father. "For," says (Callistus), "I will not profess belief in two Gods, Father and Son, but in one. For the Father, who subsisted in the Son Himself, after He had taken unto Himself our flesh, raised it to the nature of Deity, by bringing it into union with Himself, and made it one; so that Father and Son must be styled one God, and that this Person being one, cannot be two."

66. Hayward, *Memra*, 82. Hayward himself wishes to take from this a point directly opposite to mine. For Hayward (*Memra*, 87), the designation of God as "He who spake and the world was" is "intimately bound up with the Targumic Memra," a point with which I certainly agree, seeing it, however—in direct contrast to Hayward—as the denial of the Memra, not as its assertion. It is not the Memra, the Logos, the Word that does these activities, say the Rabbis, but God himself, the God who spake and the world was, without any intermediary, hypostasized Word.

67. Lauterbach, *Mekilta DeRabbi Ishmael*, 1:252.

68. Virginia Burrus, *"Begotten, Not Made": Conceiving Manhood in Late Antiquity*, Figurae (Stanford, Calif.: Stanford University Press, 2000).

69. Segal, *Two Powers*, 47–49.

70. It is almost impossible not to hear echoes of Psalms 110:1 here, or of the story of Aḥer, who sees Metatron sitting at God's right hand and writing the merits of Israel. But if this seems over-reading, the point still stands, if a bit less elegantly.

71. Segal, *Two Powers*, 47.

72. Segal writes that "both apocalyptic Jews and Christians can be shown to combine the angelic or divine interpretations of the passage with their messianic candidate" (Segal, *Two Powers*, 49). Pace Segal, the doctrine of God's two attributes is not used here as a remedy to messianism per se but as a remedy to binitarianism.

73. Moreover, as pointed out by Segal (*Two Powers*, 48), "nor was R. Akiva alone in the rabbinic movement in identifying the figure in heaven as the messiah."

74. E.g., "the coercive inscription of consensuality by which an authoritative patris-

tic body of literature is continually reconstituted as such—not least via lengthy catenae of citations meant to demonstrate widespread ancient unanimity on a given point" (Burrus, *Begotten*, 16). See also Patrick T. R. Gray, "'The Select Fathers': Canonizing the Patristic Past," *Studia Patristica* 23 (1989): 21–36; Mark Vessey, "The Forging of Orthodoxy in Latin Christian Literature: A Case Study," *Journal of Early Christian Studies* 4, no. 4 (Winter 1996): 495–513; Éric Rebillard, "A New Style of Argument in Christian Polemic: Augustine and the Use of Patristic Citations," *Journal of Early Christian Studies* 8, no. 4 (2000): 559–78.

75. Segal, *Two Powers*, 71.

76. Segal, *Two Powers*, 67. See Nathaniel Deutsch, *Guardians of the Gate: Angelic Vice Regency in Late Antiquity*, Brill's Series in Jewish Studies (Leiden: E. J. Brill, 1999), 45–46, from whose discussion it would seem that Metatron is paradoxically the Ancient of Days here (and not the Son of Man), a development that I am at a loss to understand, nor am I convinced that it is a necessary one in the context. The rabbinic texts that Deutsch adduces to indicate identification of the Youth (Son of Man) and the Ancient of Days seem to me less than relevant, since they are primarily evidence, in my view, for rabbinic Modalism, in contrast and opposition to the distinction of persons in the other texts. I thus disagree with Deutsch's conflation of the rabbinic polemic against binitarianism with binitarianism itself. Somewhat polemically myself, I daresay that more sustained reading of these texts together with early Christian traditions would reveal much that is left obscure in most scholarly treatments of them (as well, perhaps, as obscuring some matters that are revealed in contemporary scholarship).

77. Contra Segal (*Two Powers*, 67), who claims that the name נער is never used in this sense in rabbinic literature (unless I have misread him).

78. *Homoousious, homoiousious, homoian,* or *anomoian.*

79. Although Scholem famously interpreted "youth" in these contexts as "servant," there is little warrant for this interpretation. David J. Halperin, "A Sexual Image in Hekhalot Rabbati and Its Implications," *Jerusalem Studies in Jewish Thought* 6, no. 1–2 (1987): 125.

80. See on this also Deutsch, *Guardians*, 32. For Metatron as Enoch, see Idel, "Enoch."

81. Cf. "The line between rabbinic and Hekhalot literature is sometimes difficult to discern" (Deutsch, *Guardians*, 49).

82. Segal, *Two Powers*, 71.

83. Ibid., 55.

84. Deutsch is referring to the ontological boundaries between divine and human that the texts reify; I, to the social boundaries between orthodox and heretical. The two references are homologous.

85. Deutsch, *Guardians*, 48.

86. Yehuda Liebes, *The Sin of Elisha: Four Who Entered* Pardes *and the Nature of Talmudic Mysticism*, in Hebrew (Jerusalem: Academon, 1990), 12, emphasis added.

87. Segal, *Two Powers*, 62.

88. According to this reading, the "sitting" is the crux of the matter, as it invokes the Daniel 7 passage as interpreted, e.g., in Mark with the "Son of Man" sitting at the right hand of God. This is the source of Rabbi Akiva's "error" as well, for which see "The Apostasy of Rabbi Akiva" above. This passage deserves a longer treatment than I can give it here, particularly in the light of questionable interpretations of the textual evidence that

have been offered recently (Deutsch, *Guardians*, 48–77). Since these interpretations rely on variant readings within the Ashkenazi ms. tradition as relating to different stages of redaction within the rabbinic period, they rest on a very weak reed, but fuller demonstration of this point as well as reinterpretation will have to wait for another context.

89. Genesis Rabbah 5.

90. Daniel Abrams, "'The Book of Illumination' of R. Jacob Ben Jacob HaKohen: A Synoptic Edition from Various Manuscripts," in Hebrew (New York: New York University, 1993), 70. For another recent discussion of the "Aḥer" material, see Abrams, "Meṭaṭron," 293–98. Dunn, in contrast, still speaks of "the emergence of the 'two powers heresy'" (James D. G. Dunn, *The Partings of the Ways Between Christianity and Judaism and Their Significance for the Character of Christianity* [London: SCM Press and Trinity Press International, 1991], 219), which, of course, I would regard rather as the rabbinic projection and abjection of the two powers heresy. This is doubly surprising in that Dunn's view of the history of Judaism is nuanced enough to contain a statement like "the period between 70 and 100 saw the first proponents of rabbinic Judaism taking a deliberate step to mark themselves off from other claimants to the broad heritage of pre-70 Judaism" (Dunn, *Partings*, 221). I would completely agree with this formulation in spite of dating this development quite a bit later than Dunn does, given the methodology—which Dunn himself insists on elsewhere—of dating material in rabbinic texts as roughly pertaining to the time of attestation and not the time of which the text speaks. This difference in dating is, of course, highly significant, because insofar as Dunn allows himself to credit certain developments, such as the introduction of the "curse of the heretics," to the "historical Yavneh" and to see these as representing a growing early consensus in Judaism, he will date "partings of the ways" far earlier than I would.

91. Abrams, "Meṭaṭron," 298.

92. Cf. Segal, *Two Powers*, 5–6.

93. Cf. Dunn, *Partings*, 218–19, and a small library of prior literature.

94. Compare the similar conclusion, expressed in different theoretical terms, of Segal himself: "Since the tradition comes to us only in a later text, we must be prepared to accept the probability that the alternate interpretation of Dan. 7:9f.—namely, that the two thrones were for mercy and justice—was a later addition, ascribing the 'orthodox' interpretation to a great rabbinic leader, whom time had proven wrong. Thus, the messianic controversy over Dan. 7:13 is probably from R. Akiba's time; the mercy-justice revision is probably from his students" (Segal, *Two Powers*, 49). Once again, I would shift "time had proven wrong" to the idea that the rabbinic production of orthodoxy is being enacted through this story of Rabbi Akiva's error and his reproof and repentance.

95. Azzan Yadin, "*Shenei Ketuvim* and Rabbinic Intermediation," *Journal for the Study of Judaism in the Persian, Hellenistic, and Roman Periods* 33, no. 4 (2002): 386–410.

96. I have used Yadin's translation but modified it here and there.

97. Yadin, "*Shenei Ketuvim* and Rabbinic Intermediation."

98. Louis Finkelstein, ed., *Sifre on Deuteronomy* (1939; reprint, New York: Jewish Theological Seminary of America, 1969), 379.

99. This metaphor of conspiracy, as used by linguists in particular, refers to forces that converge in producing the same result even if they cannot be understood as being causally connected to each other. It is particularly apposite as metaphor here, where the converging result actually serves the interests of the two social groups involved.

100. Heine, "Callistus."

101. Kelly, *Doctrines*, 83–132.

102. Virginia Burrus, "Hailing Zenobia: Anti-Judaism, Trinitarianism, Athanasius," *Culture and Religion* 3, no. 2 (2002): 163–77.

103. As they would later so nominate "Arianism," Rudolf Lorenz, *Arius judaizans? Untersuchungen zur dogmengeshichtlichen Einordnung des Arius* (Göttingen: Vandenhoek and Ruprecht, 1979).

104. In a fascinating study, Glenn Chesnut has shown that the Logos and the Nomos were, in some important Hellenistic philosophies, alternate names for the *same* principle of divine order present in the soul of the ruler-savior. Glenn F. Chesnut, "The Ruler and the Logos in Neopythagorean, Middle Platonic, and Late Stoic Political Philosophy," in *Principate: Religion*, ed. Wolfgang Haase, Aufstieg und Niedergang der Römischen Welt (Berlin: Walter de Gruyter, 1978), 1312–13. For the king as "Living Nomos," see "Ruler and Logos," 1317, and Frances Dvornik, *Early Christian and Byzantine Political Philosophy* (Washington, D.C.: Dumbarton Oaks, 1966), 1:245–48. And for the king as "Living Logos," in parallel with Nomos, see Chesnut, "Ruler and Logos," 1323, referring to Plutarch, *To an Uneducated Ruler*, 780c. I disagree, somewhat, however, with Chesnut's interpretation of this passage. The text reads:

Τίς οὖν ἄρξει τοῦ ἄρχοντος; ὁ
νόμος ὁ πάντων βασιλεὺς
θανατῶν τε καὶ ἀθανάτων,
ὡς ἔφη Πίνδαρος. οὐκ ἐν βιβλίοις ἔξω γεγραμμένος οὐδέ τισι ξύλοις, ἀλλ'
ἔμψυχος ὢν ἐν αὐτῷ λόγος.

[Who, then, shall rule the ruler? The
Law, the king of all,
Both mortals and immortals,
as Pindar says—not law written outside him in books or on wooden tablets or the like,
but reason endowed with life within him.]

It is clear from this passage that Plutarch is *not* speaking of the King as a Living Nomos or as a Living Logos but rather as the lifeless Logos being endowed with life by dwelling within a human being. The comparison with Paul's comments in 1 Corinthians about the Law written on tablets and the Law written on the heart seems more apposite here than notions of incarnation or other christological intimations.

Chapter 7. The Yavneh Legend of the Stammaim

1. Jacob Neusner, *Judaism in Society: The Evidence of the Yerushalmi: Toward the Natural History of a Religion* (Atlanta, Ga.: Scholars Press, 1991), 110–11. The last two sentences could do, perhaps, with a bit of glossing. Neusner means that the Palestinian Talmud does not just give the final decision as a law code would; it does give the opposing views, but then it decides between them.

2. For an extensive epistemological treatment of the Babylonian Talmud partly in concert and partly disconcerting for my analysis, see Menachem Fisch, *Rational Rabbis: Science and Talmudic Culture*, Jewish Literature and Culture (Bloomington: Indiana University Press, 1997).

3. For an exhaustive discussion of these characteristics of the Babylonian Talmud, also dating them to the redactional level of the text but presented in a somewhat different explanatory framework, see David Charles Kraemer, *The Mind of the Talmud: An Intellectual History of the Bavli* (New York: Oxford University Press, 1990). Christine Hayes, *Between the Babylonian and Palestinian Talmuds* (Oxford: Oxford University Press, 1997) is also very instructive in this regard.

4. Jeffrey L. Rubenstein, "The Thematization of Dialectics in Bavli Aggada," *Journal of Jewish Studies* 53, no. 2 (2002): 1, summarizing the argument of David Halivni, *Midrash, Mishnah, and Gemara: The Jewish Predilection for Justified Law* (Cambridge, Mass.: Harvard University Press, 1986), 76–104. See also Shamma Friedman, "Chapter 'Ha'isha Rabba' in the Babylonian Talmud," in *Researches and Sources*, ed. H. Z. Dimitrovsky (New York: Jewish Theological Seminary of America, 1977), 227–441.

5. Jeffrey L. Rubenstein, *Talmudic Stories: Narrative Art, Composition, and Culture* (Baltimore, Md.: Johns Hopkins University Press, 1999); Rubenstein, "Thematization."

6. David M. Goodblatt, *Rabbinic Instruction in Sasanian Babylonia*, Studies in Judaism in Late Antiquity, vol. 9 (Leiden: E. J. Brill, 1975).

7. Kraemer, *Mind*, 95.

8. As paraphrased in Kraemer, *Mind*, 96.

9. I think, however, that like any grand recit of cultural change (including my own, of course), there will always be residue, for Origen is already capable of writing:

Just as providence is not abolished because of our ignorance . . . so neither is the divine character of scripture, which extends through all of it, abolished because our weakness cannot discern in every sentence the hidden splendour of its teachings, concealed under a poor and humble style. For "we have a treasure in earthen vessels, that the exceeding greatness of the power of God may shine forth" and may not be reckoned as coming from us who are but men. For if it had been the hackneyed methods of demonstration used among men and preserved in books that had convinced mankind, our faith might reasonably have been supposed to rest in the wisdom of men and not in the power of God. But now it is clear that "the word and the preaching" have prevailed among the multitude "not in persuasive words of wisdom, but in demonstration of the Spirit and of power." (First Principles 4.1.7)

10. Richard Lim, *Public Disputation, Power, and Social Order in Late Antiquity*, Transformations of the Classical Heritage (Berkeley and Los Angeles: University of California Press, 1994), 20.

11. On this point, see the illuminating discussion in John Glucker, *Antiochus and the Late Academy*, Hypomnemata Heft 56 (Göttingen: Vandenhoeck & Ruprecht, 1978), 31–97.

12. Rubenstein, "Thematization," 2.

13. Rubenstein, "Thematization."

14. Jeffrey L. Rubenstein, *The Culture of the Babylonian Talmud* (forthcoming).

15. Rubenstein, *Talmudic Stories*.

16. Charlotte Fonrobert, "When the Rabbi Weeps: On Reading Gender in Talmudic Aggada," *Nashim: A Journal of Jewish Women's Studies and Gender Issues* 4 (2001): 58.

17. For a very rich account of this "taking effect," see Richard Paul Vaggione, *Eunomius of Cyzicus and the Nicene Revolution*, Oxford Early Christian Studies (Oxford: Oxford University Press, 2000), throughout and esp. 151–57.

18. Keith Hopkins, "Christian Number and Its Implications," *Journal of Early Christian Studies* 6, no. 2 (1998): 217.

19. Shaye J. D. Cohen, "The Significance of Yavneh: Pharisees, Rabbis, and the End of Jewish Sectarianism," *Hebrew Union College Annual* 55 (1984): 27–53.

20. Compare my own writing as recently as Boyarin, *Dying for God*, chapter 2, a fortiori my earlier assays at such comparisons.

21. It should be probably emphasized that I do not necessarily endorse the precise terms (particularly insofar as they have a pejorative cast) of Hopkins's categorization. They do, however, point to something significant in the difference of self-presentation of ideal orthodox Christian discourse versus the self-presentation of ideal orthodox rabbinic discourse.

22. Goodblatt, *Rabbinic Instruction*, argued that this institution only arose in Babylonia in post-amoraic times. His argument has been recently upheld by Rubenstein, who shows that seeming counterevidence from the Talmud must (or at any rate very plausibly may) be dated to a post-amoraic layer in that text.

23. Rubenstein, *Culture of the Babylonian Talmud.*

24. Note that the seat of the Nestorian *catholikos* was in very close proximity to Maḥoza, one of the major centers of Babylonian rabbinic learning.

25. Isaiah Gafni, "Nestorian Literature as a Source for the History of the Babylonian *Yeshivot*," *Tarbiz* 51 (1981): 571.

26. As translated in David Stern, *Midrash and Theory: Ancient Jewish Exegesis and Contemporary Literary Studies*, Rethinking Theory (Evanston, Ill.: Northwestern University Press, 1996), 19.

27. That is, unattested in tannaitic literature (the rabbinic literature redacted in the third and early fourth centuries, and only known from the late fourth-century [Palestinian] and sixth-century [Babylonian] Talmuds).

28. Stern, *Midrash and Theory*, 33. This practice is, accordingly, quite different from the patristic practices discussed by Elizabeth A. Clark, *Reading Renunciation: Asceticism and Scripture in Early Christianity* (Princeton, N.J.: Princeton University Press, 1999), 128–32. In rabbinic literature, this practice is more closely analogous to the controversies between Rabbis and "heretics" (*minim*) than they are to the inner-rabbinic hermeneutical controversies that the midrash so lovingly reproduces (or makes up).

29. Stern, *Midrash and Theory*, 34.

30. Fisch, *Rational Rabbis*, 62. Fisch should be corrected, however, on two points. First, the expression "and the Torah became two Torot" is original to the Tosefta and not an innovation of the Babylonian Talmud. Second, the Palestinian Talmud's statement that "they became two sects" (Ḥagiga ii, 77d, which reference I owe to Fisch, *Rational Rabbis*, 211, n. 18) is not more forceful than the Tosefta, since the word in the Tosefta, "divisions" [מחלוקות], which is usually translated "controversies" following later usage, should, in tannaitic literature, be rendered "divisions," i.e., sects. The Palestinian Talmud's gloss is thus included in the original tannaitic language itself. In other words, the "traditionalist" and "realist" view of Torah, which corresponds both epistemologically and institutionally to Christian orthodoxy, is fully comprehended within the tannaitic texts.

31. Thus, while I endorse Fisch's distinction of two different voices within rabbinic literature, I am unconvinced by his arguments that the Mishna already reflects the "antitraditionalist" position, pace Fisch (*Rational Rabbis*, 66–78). It is beyond the scope of the present work to make the argument in detail, but it seems to me that the distinctions Fisch makes there between the Mishna and the Tosefta are not conclusive, and in each

case the Mishna can be read as showing the same set of views as the Tosefta. Much of Fisch's argumentation is based on attractive but not finally compelling arguments *e silentio*. Finally, however, I repeat: overall, my points are compatible with those made by Fisch, whatever the historical disagreements between us (a history to which Fisch is not committed, in any case). I find much more compelling his demonstration of a difference among the Tosefta, the Yerushalmi, and the Bavli with respect to another story here, a difference which sets these texts in a series from—using Fisch's terminology—most traditionalist to most antitraditionalist (Fisch, *Rational Rabbis*, 96–110).

32. Shlomo Naeh, "'Make Yourself Many Rooms': Another Look at the Utterances of the Sages About Controversy," in Hebrew, in *Renewing Jewish Commitment: The Work and Thought of David Hartman*, ed. Avi Sagi and Zvi Zohar (Jerusalem: Shalom Hartman Institute and Hakkibutz Hameuchad, 2001), 862.

33. Saul Lieberman, *Order Nashim*, vol. 8 of *Tosefta Ki-Fshuta: A Comprehensive Commentary on the Tosefta* (New York: Jewish Theological Seminary of America, 1973), 194–95 (translation added).

34. Naeh, "Rooms," 865–67.

35. These are, in this version of the *derasha*, citations of the typical forms of tannaitic transmission, as Naeh points out. It is not, therefore, the propositional contents of the transmission that cause the difficulty, but the forms and the predicament of remembering them.

36. Thus in the Tosefta the *derasha* on "lest a man say in his heart" ends with דברים, הדברים, אלה הדברים, כל הדברים ["words," "the words," "these are the words," "all of the words"]. As shown by Naeh, these refer to Moses' own organization of the Written Torah in "many rooms," i.e., organized to aid memory and understanding. The *derasha* on "they were all given by one shepherd" is the beginning of an entirely new thought, namely, that the Written and Oral Torahs were both given by God through Moses. Only the combination of these two, originally independent *derashot* produced the interpretation that the Babylonian Talmud gives to the source. See Shlomo Naeh, "On Structures of Memory (and the Forms of Text) in Rabbinic Literature," in Hebrew (forthcoming), n. 131. Here is another example, if we needed one, of how difficult it would be to reconstruct early Palestinian rabbinic Judaism from Babylonian talmudic sources. What might have seemed, therefore, a difficulty for my thesis that the notion of irresolvable controversy as a good is a talmudic and not tannaitic idea turns out to be an elegant proof of that very thesis.

37. As Fisch point out, such splits occur in the context of a traditionalism and realism and are permanently irresolvable, as is the history of Christian orthodoxy (Fisch, *Rational Rabbis*, 67).

38. Naeh, "Structures of Memory."

39. Naeh, "Rooms," 874. This provides, moreover, another example of how misleading it can be to read tannaitic quotations in the Talmuds as actual tannaitic thought. Note, once more, however, the perspicacious definition of "our Rabbis" given by Fisch: "the epistemological and methodological positions it attributes to the 'rabbis' or the 'sages' are, therefore, for the most part those of the latter-day framers, compilers, and editors of the texts as we find them" (Fisch, *Rational Rabbis*, xxi). As long as this principle is explicit, the problem implied by Naeh does not arise.

40. Naeh, "Rooms," 873. Naeh's position is, therefore, not unlike Stern's. See now, however, the more nuanced formulations of Naeh, "Structures of Memory."

41. Athanasius, *Athanasius Werke*, ed. H. G. Opitz (Berlin: Walter de Gruyter, 1934), 2:4, cited in Lim, *Disputation*, 109.

42. Lim, *Disputation*, 110.

43. Lim, *Disputation*, 111, and see the fine discussion in Alain Le Boulluec, *La notion d'hérésie dans la littérature grecque IIᵉ–IIIᵉ siècles* (Paris: études Augustiniennes, 1985), 2:281–88.

44. Cited in Lim, *Disputation*, 144, n. 190. Of course, ideas such as this circulated in Christian hands before Basil, notably in Tertullian, who also advises his charges to avoid interpreting texts (*Prescriptions Against Heretics* 17–19), to seek "simplicity of heart," and avoiding speculation and dialectic (*Prescriptions Against Heretics* 7), and see discussion in Karen L. King, *What Is Gnosticism?* (Cambridge, Mass.: Harvard University Press, 2003), chap. 2.

45. As Origen had already put it: "Moreover, there was in Judaism a factor which caused sects to begin, which was the variety of the interpretations of the writings of Moses and the sayings of the prophets." Henry Chadwick, trans. and ed., *Origen: Contra Celsum* (Cambridge: Cambridge University Press, 1965), 135.

46. Goodblatt, *Rabbinic Instruction*.

47. Stern, *Midrash and Theory*, 20. That this fear was not an idle one can be shown from the following quotation from the antirabbinite Karaite text: "I have set the six divisions of the Mishna before me. And I looked at them carefully with mine eyes. And I saw that they are very contradictory in content. This one Mishnaic scholar declares a thing to be forbidden to the people of Israel, while that one declares it to be permitted. My thoughts therefore answer me, and most of my reflections declare unto me, that there is in it no Law of logic nor the Law of Moses the Wise" (Leon Nemoy, *Karaite Anthology, Excerpts from the Early Literature*, Yale Judaica Series vol. 7 [New Haven, Conn.: Yale University Press, 1969], 71; and see Moshe Halbertal, *People of the Book: Canon, Meaning, and Authority* [Cambridge, Mass.: Harvard University Press, 1997], 46). Although this early medieval tradition is surely later than our talmudic text, it eloquently indicates the sort of polemic (and not merely psychomachia) that our text might be responding to. As pointed out by Chadwick (*Origen: Contra Celsum* 135, n. 4), the background of these discussions is "probably the Sceptic contention that because on all serious questions philosophers disagree one can only suspend judgment; Sextus Emp. *P.H.* I, 165; Philo *de Ebriatate* 198 ff."

48. Socrates, E.H. 2. 40. 20, cited in Vaggione, *Eunomius*, 222.

49. Frag. 24; see also David Dawson, *Allegorical Readers and Cultural Revision in Ancient Alexandria* (Berkeley and Los Angeles: University of California Press, 1992), 198–99.

50. It might be objected at this point that there is really no comparability between the Christian and rabbinic situations, since the former is engaged with questions of theology, the latter with questions of practice. This difference is, to be sure, significant in itself but not at the level of analysis which I adopt here, the level of the analysis of the history of systems of thought per se. Foucault already remarked that the systematicity characteristic of discursive practices and the shifts in such systematicity transcend particular disciplines: "Each discursive practice thus implies a play of prescriptions that governs the exclusions and choices. Now these sets of regularities do not coincide with individual works; even if they are manifested through time, even if it happens that they stand out, for the first time, in one of them, these regularities go largely beyond them,

while often regrouping a considerable number of them. But neither do they necessarily coincide with what we usually call sciences or disciplines, although their boundaries may be sometimes provisionally the same; it happens more frequently that a discursive practice brings together diverse disciplines or sciences, or, again, that it traverses a certain number of them and regroups into a sometimes unapparent unity several of their regions" (Michel Foucault, *The Will to Knowledge,* as translated and cited in Arnold I. Davidson, *The Emergence of Sexuality: Historical Epistemology and the Formation of Concepts* [Cambridge, Mass.: Harvard University Press, 2002], 197). In fact, as Davidson makes crystal clear, precisely this transdisciplinarity of a discursive practice is significant epistemologically: "If there is a knowledge (*savoir*) common to more than one science, if there is an order of knowledge uniting different sciences, then this system of knowledge constitutes what Foucault called an *épistémè*. Isolating the discursive regularities of given sciences may allow one to discover that there is a set of relations that unites these discursive practices; this set of relations provides the "epistemological space" for these sciences, their *épistémè*" (Davidson, *Emergence,* 201). This book, and especially the essay "On Epistemology and Archeology: From Canguilhem to Foucault" (pp. 192–206), from which the quotation was drawn, represent, to my mind, the best concise introduction to Foucault that we have in English.

51. Naeh, "Rooms," 857.

52. Fisch, *Rational Rabbis,* 69.

53. See Rubenstein, *Talmudic Stories,* 1–3 and passim. Significantly, the presumably older version in the Palestinian Talmud does not include the voice that inscribes modesty as the virtue that led to the primacy of Hillel's halakha, but merely says that: "Since the heavenly voice went out, anyone who violates the words of Bet Hillel is subject to the death penalty: We are taught that a heavenly voice went out and said, 'These and these are the words of the Living God, but the *halakha* is like Bet Hillel.' And where did the heavenly voice go out? Rabbi Bibi said in the name of Rabbi Yoḥanan, 'In Yavneh the heavenly voice went out'" (PT Sotah 19a).

54. "An 'episteme' is the ensemble of factors—historical, social, institutional, intellectual, and so on—that render a certain form of thought possible; it is not the 'essence' of that thought" (Philipp W. Roseman, *Understanding Scholastic Thought with Foucault,* The New Middle Ages [New York: St. Martin's Press, 1999], x). Roseman is referring to "what Foucault might have called the 'Scholastic episteme.'"

55. Stern, *Midrash and Theory,* 37.

56. This is, in part, not entirely different from Stern's argument in "Midrash and Indeterminacy," *Critical Inquiry* 15, no. 1 (Autumn 1988): 132–62. My distinction, however, between the Palestinian midrash and the Babylonian Talmud, however, will recast the argument considerably.

57. Lim, *Disputation,* 153–54. See the related point in Vaggione, *Eunomius,* 83. We could say, perhaps, that Nicaea represents the failure of the dialectical tradition precisely because, as Vaggione puts it there, "they were all too bitterly aware that they could cite no passage of scripture which would of itself convince their opponents." The Rufinian story that we are about to read could be read as a representation of this very frustration. In other words, I am very carefully suggesting that something like the "breakdown of effective dialogue in 341" (Vaggione, *Eunomius,* 97–104) might have led, in part, to the breakdown of the idea of effective dialogue, with similar analogues in the rabbinic world, as exemplified by the "How shall I learn Torah" of the narrative discussed above.

58. The *Vita Dianielis* 90, cited in Lim, *Disputation*, 156, n. 35. See also Neil McLynn, "Christian Controversy and Violence in the Fourth Century," *Kodai* 3 (1992): 15–44. Particularly striking and amusing in our present sociocultural context is the description by Gregory Nazianzen of dialecticians as being analogous to professional wrestlers and not even genuine athletes, apud Lim, *Disputation*, 162.

59. For the Cappadocians on Eunomius's "logic chopping," see Vaggione, *Eunomius*, 93.

60. Fisch, *Rational Rabbis*, xv, referring as well to the work of Steinsalz and Funkenstein.

61. It is not, I suggest, that Fisch is wrong, but his characterization of rabbinic culture is not, in my opinion, sufficiently responsive to historical differentiations within that culture.

62. See Daniel Boyarin, *Carnal Israel: Reading Sex in Talmudic Culture*, The New Historicism: Studies in Cultural Poetics, vol. 25 (Berkeley and Los Angeles: University of California Press, 1993), 136–56. Several details of that reading will have to be corrected in the light of recent research by Shamma Friedman (unpublished), but its major contours still stand, in my opinion.

63. A. Mosshammer, "Disclosing but Not Disclosed: Gregory of Nyssa as Deconstructionist," in *Studien zu Gregor von Nyssa und der Christliche Spätantike: Supplements to Vigiliae Christianae* (Leiden: E. J. Brill, 1990), 100.

64. On this point, see as well Vaggione, *Eunomius*, 169–71 and especially 237–65, whose interpretation of this controversy seems to me slightly different from (but perhaps compatible with) Mosshammer's. See, however: "What they claimed [Eunomius and Aetius] was that their knowledge of God was *exactly* like his: that is not κατ᾽ ἐπίνοιαν, not discursive. Thus, . . . the best way to honour the reality communicated by ἀγέννητος is silence" (Vaggione, *Eunomius*, 257–58).

65. Virginia Burrus, *"Begotten, not Made": Conceiving Manhood in Late Antiquity*, Figurae (Stanford, Calif.: Stanford University Press, 2000), 109.

66. Lim, *Disputation*, 187.

67. I take this narrative as, in effect, a midrash on 1 Corinthians 1:20–24: "Where is the wise? where is the scribe? where is the disputer of this world? hath not God made foolish the wisdom of this world? for after that in the wisdom of God the world by wisdom knew not God, it pleased God by the foolishness of preaching to save them that believe. For the Jews require a sign and the Greeks seek after wisdom: but we preach Christ crucified, unto the Jews a stumbling block, and unto the Greeks foolishness; but unto them which are called, both Jews and Greeks, Christ the power of God, and the wisdom of God."

68. Rufinus, *The Church History of Rufinus of Aquileia, Books 10 and 11*, trans. Philip R. Amidon (New York: Oxford University Press, 1997), 10–11. Compare the somewhat different version of Lim, *Disputation*, 192.

69. See, too, how Frances Young articulates this shift within Christianity: "a dispassionate look at the gospel records hardly suggests a figure with episcopal authority propounding dogma and excluding debaters or doubters" (Frances M. Young, *The Making of the Creeds* [London and Philadelphia: SCM Press and Trinity Press International, 1991], 2).

70. Vaggione, *Eunomius*, 365.

71. Vaggione, *Eunomius*, 369.

72. For recent readings of this much read story, see Rubenstein, *Talmudic Stories*, 34–64, and Fonrobert, "When the Rabbi Weeps."

73. As noted above, according to the Babylonian Talmud itself, "on that day" always refers to the crucial day of decision at Yavneh when the characteristic forms of Babylonian talmudic rabbinism were set in stone.

74. See also Stern, *Midrash and Theory*, 30. To forestall any misunderstanding, I am *not* claiming that the Rabbis were more rational than their opponents among the Jewish leaders. Their own modes of authorizing themselves, notably divination through the reading of Torah, as in some forms of midrash, are hardly, from our perspective, less magical than divination via carob trees, but this is for another day. The point is that their own divination was thematized as Oral Torah, but not the divinatory methods of opponents or dissenters. Compare: "Here Rabbinic Judaism and Christianity part company, because the former took the view that prophecy ceased with Malachi and the other latter-day prophets, while Christianity began with the advent of the greatest personality of all: God Incarnate, authorizing a new age of prophecy. But in practice both Rabbinic Judaism and Christianity recognized supernatural events and personalities in the here and now of ordinary life—and appealed to them to impose the authority of the Torah or of the Church upon the community of the faithful" (Bruce Chilton and Jacob Neusner, *Types of Authority in Formative Christianity and Judaism* [London: Routledge, 1999], 7). Arguably the Qumran Community did explicitly claim prophetic authority for their hermeneutics. See Aharon Shemesh and Cana Werman, "Halakhah at Qumran: Genre and Authority," *Dead Sea Discoveries* (2002). See also Elliot R. Wolfson, *Through a Speculum That Shines: Vision and Imagination in Medieval Jewish Literature* (Princeton, N.J.: Princeton University Press, 1994), 328.

75. Lim, *Disputation*, 196.

76. For a very different take on this material, see Fisch, *Rational Rabbis*, 82. A major difference between our approaches turns on my interpretation that Rabbi Eli'ezer first attempted to prove his view and only turned to signs and wonders when he failed to convince the others, whereas for Fisch such a reading is impossible, since he wishes to see in Rabbi Eli'ezer an older and purely "traditionalist" view, within which debate and critical decision-making are simply anathema. I believe that my interpretation is the philologically stronger one, but Fisch's is certainly defensible.

77. Evonne Levy, *Propaganda and the Jesuit Baroque* (Berkeley and Los Angeles: University of California Press, 2003), chapter 2.

78. Contrast a late fourth-century contest between a Manichaean sage and a Christian in Egypt: "The easy shift from public debate to ordeal . . . reminds us of the limitations of the cultural realm within which formal public disputations were appreciated. Illiterate and unlearned audiences found demonstrations of power by deeds more convincing than the ability to spin arguments. In encounters between religious rivals, deeds of wonder were commonly, though not necessarily, interpreted as signs of divine favor, whereas skill in argument was viewed as being of human, or even diabolical origin" (Lim, *Disputation*, 81).

79. Cf. the similar but somewhat different treatment of this issue in Fisch, *Rational Rabbis*, 63–64. Fisch's considered, nonhistoricist approach will lead us to certain differences of interpretation within a broad framework that is otherwise similar in many ways, likewise with respect to the story about Rabban Gamaliel that I treat below and that Fisch treats in the continuation of the cited context. Let me cite one concrete example:

Where Fisch would write that "the existence of conflicting traditions is simply not a problem for the antitraditionalist" (Fisch, *Rational Rabbis*, 68), I would write that the "antitraditionalist" position was developed as a response to the problem of multiplicity of views.

80. Including by the present writer in a former scholarly life.

81. See, too, the discussion in Albert I. Baumgarten, *The Flourishing of Jewish Sects in the Maccabean Era: An Interpretation*, Supplements to the Journal for the Study of Judaism 55 (Leiden: E. J. Brill, 1997), 135, who presents a version of the view articulated here in the name of a "cynic," but still leaves open the question as to whether he adopts said cynical view or not.

82. It is interesting to note the different authority base for Qumran halakha, as discerned by Shemesh and Werman, "Genre," where the correct halakhic interpretation, understood as esoteric, was revealed directly to the Teacher of Righteousness.

83. William A. Graham, *Beyond the Written Word: Oral Aspects of Scripture in the History of Religion* (Cambridge: Cambridge University Press, 1987), 68.

84. Yitzhak D. Gilat, *R. Eliezer Ben Hyrcanus: A Scholar Outcast*, Bar-Ilan Studies in Near Eastern Languages and Culture (Ramat Gan: Bar-Ilan University Press, 1984), and see below n. 110.

85. I find very telling Graham's remark that "So tied are we to the written or printed page that we have lost any awareness of the essential orality of language, let alone of reading" (Graham, *Beyond the Written Word*, 9). Graham's insistence on an essentiality to the orality of language crosses his own historicizing project: "In historical perspective, our own current conception of the book (and therefore of the reading process and literacy as well) proves to be quite limited and limiting" (Graham, *Beyond the Written Word*, 10). I would suggest that Graham's rhetoric of essentiality and loss is equally as limited and limiting from a historical perspective. On the other hand, I would quite agree with him that forgetting the very different and "oral" moments of written language in many (if not most) "other" cultures is pernicious. For argument to this effect, cf. Daniel Boyarin, "Placing Reading: Ancient Israel and Medieval Europe," in *The Ethnography of Reading*, ed. Jonathan Boyarin (Berkeley and Los Angeles: University of California Press, 1993), 10–37.

86. Graham, *Beyond the Written Word*, 65. This example represents a significant challenge to Graham's "always," if not to the general applicability of his observation.

87. Similar, in this respect, to Gregory of Nyssa (Mosshammer, "Disclosing") but also to Origen as well (Patricia Cox Miller, *The Poetry of Thought in Late Antiquity: Essays in Imagination and Religion* [Burlington, Vt.: Ashgate, 2001]). This is a point that will need further elaboration in future work.

88. Dina Stein, "Folklore Elements in Late Midrash: A Folkloristic Perspective on Pirkei de Rabbi Eliezer, in Hebrew with English abstract (diss., Hebrew University, 1998), 173–81, photocopy. Stein makes the point that Rabbi Eliʿezer is precisely the type of the internal other, the heretic, as opposed to the apostate who leaves the community entirely.

89. See Naeh, "Rooms," 855, for the important observation that מחלוקת [division] here does not mean merely controversy but actual potential political schism, and that this is the original meaning of the Hebrew מחלוקת, paralleling the Greek *stasis* in semantic development. This observation enables me to make another. When the Mishna says, "Any division that is not for the sake of heaven will not perdure, whereas any division that is for the sake of heaven will perdure. Which is the division that is not for the

sake of heaven? that of Korah and his congregation. And which is the division that is for the sake of heaven? that of the Houses of Hillel and Shammai" (Avot 5:16), this is not equivalent to the later talmudic declaration that the words of the House of Hillel and the words of the House of Shammai are equally the words of the Living God. It is entirely possible that the later pronouncement may be a virtually organic development from the former (especially once the sense of the Hebrew term shifts from a group of people to a controversy). Rather, the point is that, since the Houses of Hillel and of Shammai are both deemed to have acted for the sake of heaven, neither of them is excised from Israel, as Korah and his congregation (the Christians?) have been. Note the parallel to the preceding statement, "Any assembly that is for the sake of heaven will perdure." Once more, we see how precision in attending to nuances of language and meaning that have been conflated is crucial to perceiving the history of rabbinic thought.

90. Cohen, "Yavneh," 49.

91. Cf. Lim, *Disputation.* Cf. also the important observation by Fisch that "Jabne was unwilling to extend its pluralism to the second-order, metahalakhic, procedural level of halakhic decision making. . . . And this point presumably marked the extent of their toleration. For the reformed Jabne the principle of tolerance applied widely, but only to to those who accepted it" (Fisch, *Rational Rabbis,* 82).

92. Fonrobert, "When the Rabbi Weeps."

93. Fisch, *Rational Rabbis,* all 209, n. 12.

94. I would disagree somewhat with Stern's statement that "there is little evidence to support the existence of explicit mechanisms for internal censorship in Rabbinic society" (David Stern, "Forms of Midrash II: Homily and the Language of Exegesis," in *Midrash and Theory* [Evanston, Ill.: Northwestern University Press, 1996], 26). The condemnation of interpretations as leading to the view that there are Two Powers in Heaven, as explored in Chapter 6, certainly seems to constitute such evidence.

95. See Susan Handelman, "Fragments of the Rock: Contemporary Literary Theory and the Study of Rabbinic Texts—a Response to David Stern," *Prooftexts* 5 (1985): 73–95.

96. See Halbertal, *People,* 7. In fact, this is no more a democratization than is the "medicalization of childbirth," on the assumption that "everyone" can become a gynecologist. Halbertal explicitly refers to the fact that all men (!) had theoretical access to the Bet Midrash as proof of its democratic nature, not noticing that the stringent controls that the institution placed on interpretation, legitimate and illegitimate, represented an even more general set of exclusions (that is, of all those who did not accept the rabbinic program) rather than simply the exclusion of women, which Halbertal duly and fully remarks.

97. Cf. Susan Handelman, *The Slayers of Moses: The Emergence of Rabbinic Interpretation in Modern Literary Theory* (Albany: State University of New York Press, 1982), and David Stern, "Moses-Cide: Midrash and Contemporary Literary Criticism," *Prooftexts* 4 (1984): 193–204.

98. I mean by this to ascribe nothing sinister to the Rabbis, although the effects on some Jews (especially women) might well have been very deleterious, as the subject matter chosen for this hermeneutic parable might hint. It is not inapposite for me to mention that I am one of the scholars whose (former) opinions I am here revising—cf. Daniel Boyarin, *Intertextuality and the Reading of Midrash* (Bloomington: Indiana University Press, 1990), esp. 33–37.

99. This point alone does not, however, serve to dismiss the claim for a theoretical

"indeterminacy" akin to deconstruction alive in these Babylonian texts. We should not forget the will to power wielded by theory either, something of which Derrida, at least, is ever mindful, as opposed, perhaps, to some of his American epigones.

100. R. Travers Herford, *Christianity in Talmud and Midrash* (1903; reprint, New York: Ktav, 1978), 336–37.

101. Herford, *Christianity*, 337. I must add, however, two caveats. First, I do not see evidence here that this Ya'aqov was necessarily a real historical figure, and, second, I find weak the comparison with the story of Rav Safra (treated in the previous chapter), to which Herford compares it, because I believe that Herford has mistaken the import of that story. The fact, however, that this very Ya'aqov is cited as a halakhic authority in the Babylonian Talmud is very telling, as Herford does not fail to remark.

102. See Virginia Burrus, *The Making of a Heretic: Gender, Authority, and the Priscillianist Controversy*, Transformations of the Ancient World (Berkeley and Los Angeles: University of California Press, 1995); J. Rebecca Lyman, "The Making of a Heretic: The Life of Origen in Epiphanius *Panarion* 64," *Studia Patristica* 31 (1997): 445–51, for Christian examples of "reluctant" heretics.

103. See, for a quite similar point, Stern, *Midrash and Theory*, 34–35.

104. To be sure, there is a version of the "Stove of Akhnai" in the Palestinian Talmud 81 c–d that approaches this idea. Since Rabbi Yirmiah, the fourth-century Babylonian, is cited centrally within that text, however, we have a *terminus post quem* for it after his time. See also David Charles Kraemer, *The Mind of the Talmud: An Intellectual History of the Bavli* (New York: Oxford University Press, 1990), 122–23, for discussion of crucial differences between the two versions. For the distinction itself, as between "realist" and "conventionalist" accounts of meaning, see Fisch, *Rational Rabbis*, 57: "The conventionalist's claim is ontological, however, rather than epistemic: it is not merely the claim that we have no way of *knowing* God's intentions—to which many realists would readily agree—but that there is *in reality* no such thing as an a priori, God-intended, true reading of the Written Torah" (emphasis original).

105. For a modern, "radical orthodox" statement of this dogma, see Michel René Barnes, "The Fourth Century as Trinitarian Canon," in *Christian Origins: Theology, Rhetoric, and Community*, ed. Lewis Ayres and Gareth Jones (London: Routledge, 1998), 47–67.

106. Cf. Mosshammer, "Disclosing," 103–20. But Gregory, I think, would not assert or hint that even God cannot finally know God's own language, as the Babylonian Rabbis seem to do.

107. My method of reading the rabbinic narrative has much in common with that of James Louis Martyn, *History and Theology in the Fourth Gospel* (Nashville, Tenn.: Abingdon, 1979), in his studies of the Fourth Gospel. I have learned much from Martyn and his method of reading. I am less persuaded by the critique of Martyn's method in Stephen Motyer, *Your Father the Devil?: A New Approach to John and "the Jews,"* Paternoster Biblical and Theological Studies (Carlisle, Eng.: Paternoster Press, 1997), 28–30, than by his critique of Martyn's "partial use of [Jewish] evidence" in the pages just prior to the cited ones. If my own way of reading rabbinic narratives as representations in legends about individuals of broad social, cultural, and political developments proves compelling on its own grounds, then one will no longer be able to claim against such works as Martyn and Raymond E. Brown, *The Community of the Beloved Disciple: The Life, Loves and Hates of an Individual Church in New Testament Times* (New York: Paulist

Press, 1979) that, "there seems to be no literary precedent for this kind of allegorical narrative" (pace Motyer, *Your Father*, 29). Indeed, are not the biblical narratives of the "patriarchs" in some sense plausibly read as "allegories" of the origins, connections, and fates of communities?

108. I.e., that he was no longer heretical. For the idiom, see Justin Martyr *Dial.* 39.3: παραφρονεῖς ταῦτα λέγων, ἐπίστασθαί σε βούλομαι (Justin, *Dialogus cum Tryphone*, ed. Miroslav Marcovich, Patristische Texte und Studien 47 [Berlin: Walter de Gruyter, 1997], 135).

109. On this passage, see discussion in Jacob Neusner, *Why No Gospels in Talmudic Judaism?* Brown Judaic Studies, 135 (Atlanta, Ga., 1988), 52; Stein, *Folklore*, 166–67.

110. Neusner makes the excellent point that in the earlier documents, Eliʿezer is never rabbinized, never depicted as making the study of Torah central to his piety. He is, moreover, never depicted in the earlier stages of the tradition as a disciple of Rabbi Yoḥanan ben Zakkai, but rather as a representative of the old Pharisaic cultic practices. These, too, have been displaced in the production of rabbinic authority, of the House of Study as the sole locus of power, as our story represents it. Jacob Neusner. *Eliezer Ben Hyrcanus: The Tradition and the Man*, 2 vols., Studies in Judaism in Late Antiquity, vol. 3–4 (Leiden: E. J. Brill, 1973), 2: 301.

111. Jacob Neusner, "The formation of rabbinic Judaism: Yavneh (Jamnia) from A.D. 70 to 100," in *Principat: Religion (Judentum: Pälastinisches Judentum [Forts.])*, ed. Wolfgang Haase, Aufstieg und Niedergang der Römischen Welt (Berlin: Walter de Gruyter, 1979), 36. See also Shaye J. D. Cohen, "Epigraphical Rabbis," *Jewish Quarterly Review* 72 (1981): 1–17; Catherine Hezser, *The Social Structure of the Rabbinic Movement in Roman Palestine*, Texte und Studien zum Antiken Judentum (Tübingen: Mohr Siebeck, 1997), 119–23, for the relative insignificance of the study of Torah in the earliest periods and even among some groups that called themselves "Rabbis."

112. My student Gerald Roth has pointed out a similar development with respect to Pinḥas ben Yaʿir, another early charismatic, who in the early sources produces an ascetic rule in which "diligence leads to cleanliness, cleanliness to purity, purity to sexual abstinence," and finally via resurrection to "Elijah"—prophetic vision (Mishna Sotah 9:15). In the Babylonian Talmud's version of this, the list begins with Torah (absent entirely from the early version) and ends with the resurrection—no prophecy (BT Avoda Zara 20b).

113. Flavius Josephus, *Books XVIII–XX*, vol. IX of *Jewish Antiquities*, trans. L. H. Feldman, Loeb Classical Library (Cambridge, Mass.: Harvard University Press, 1965), 10–11. On this see as well the important Eliezer Shimshon Rosenthal, "Tradition and Innovation in the *Halakha* of the Sages," in Hebrew with English summary, *Tarbiz* 63, no. 3 (April–June 1994): 321–74, xix–xx, which would put that description of the "real" Rabbi Eliʿezer into question. Our interest here is not, however, in the actual historical figure and his practices but in his representation at different stages of the rabbinic tradition, on which see also Neusner, *Eliezer Ben Hyrcanus*.

114. Alon Goshen-Gottstein, "A Lonely Sage on His Death-Bed: The Story of the Death of Rabbi Eliʿezer (Sanhedrin 68a), an Ideological Analysis," in Hebrew, in *Memorial Volume for Tirzah Lifshitz* (forthcoming). I find, however, Goshen-Gottstein's reading strange in that, although he cannot ignore the fact that Rabbi Eliʿezer's "excommunication" is thematized in the story, he minimizes it and its implications to an extent that almost decontextualizes the narrative. If the sages only physically approach the Rabbi upon deciding that his "mind is clear," that, in my view, indicates that here

clarity of mind is a cipher for "orthodoxy," as it very frequently is in the discourse of the period (in Greek and Latin, at least). It was Prof. Lieberman who originally compared this to the usage of *mania* as a name for heresy or heterodoxy; see now Ferdinando Zuccotti, "*Furor haereticorum*" *studi sul trattamento giuridico della follia e sulla persecuzione della eterodossia religiosa nella legislazione del tardo Impero Romano* (Milano: Giuffrè, 1992). It should be also pointed out that Goshen-Gottstein's interpretation departs even from the classical tradition of interpretation of the story, which reads it as the final act in the drama of his excommunication; indeed any reading that denies this seems to me bordering on the perverse. Not that this, of course, disqualifies Goshen-Gottstein's interpretation, but it makes it a bit harder, I think, to render my reading simply an "exaggeration."

115. It is perhaps not inapposite to mention that at approximately the same time there was a struggle against the "New Prophecy" of the Montanists or Kataphrygians as well. It is fascinating that the leadership of this group was always referred to by its enemies as "Montanus and the women," e.g., Eusebius E.H. V. xvi 20–22, Hugh Jackson Lawlor and John Ernest Leonard Oulton, trans. and eds., *Eusebius, Bishop of Caesarea, the Ecclesiastical History and the Martyrs of Palestine* (London: Society for Promoting Christian Knowledge, 1927), 161. I am not, however, claiming a strong connection between these events, just a certain suggestiveness to the coincidence.

116. This interpretation is consistent as well with the argument made by Kalmin that the Babylonian Talmud so thoroughly "rabbinizes" such figures as the charismatic, antic, wonder-working holy men Honi Hame'agel and Ḥanina ben Dosa that it actually has them studying Torah and thus "forgetting" that they were in their Palestinian origin an antithetical force and factional opposition party to nascent rabbinic Judaism. Richard Kalmin, *Sages, Stories, Authors, and Editors in Rabbinic Babylonia*, Brown Judaic Studies 300 (Atlanta, Ga.: Scholars Press, 1994), 158; William Scott Green, "Palestinian Holy Men: Charismatic Leadership and Roman Tradition," in *Aufstieg und Niedergang der Römischen Welt II, Principat 19,2*, ed. Wolfgang Haase (Berlin: Walter de Gruyter, 1979), 619–47; Sean Freyne, "The Charismatic," in *Ideal Figures in Ancient Judaism: Profiles and Paradigms*, ed. George Nickelsburg and John Collins, Septuagint and Cognate Studies Series, no. 12. (Chico, Calif.: Scholars Press, 1980).

117. Lim, *Disputation*, 20.

118. At the New Moon prostration is forbidden, so she assumed that it was "safe" to relax her guard on her husband, but she has mistaken the date.

119. Fonrobert, "When the Rabbi Weeps," 63. Fonrobert's reading delves deeply into the gendering of the story, especially with respect to tears and emotionality. This, however, is beyond the scope of the present analysis.

120. Slavoj Žižek, "Introduction," in *Mapping Ideology*, Mapping (London: Verso, 1994), 3.

121. Rubenstein, *Talmudic Stories*, 44.

122. I have already argued this point with respect to Pauline universalism in *A Radical Jew: Paul and the Politics of Identity*, Contraversions: Critical Studies in Jewish Literature, Culture, and Society (Berkeley and Los Angeles: University of California Press, 1994).

123. Stern, *Midrash and Theory*, 34.

124. "In reality," writes Stern (*Midrash and Theory*, 34). Stern goes on, after this "in reality," to represent rabbinic legend as historical fact.

125. This is a major point of Stern, "Midrash and Indeterminacy."

126. It is interesting to compare the activity of "the Wicked Priest" in *Pesher Habakkuk* col. 11 (ll. 4–8) on Habakkuk 2:15: "Its interpretation concerns the Wicked Priest who 5 pursued the Teacher of Righteousness to consume him with the ferocity 6 of his anger in the place of his banishment, in festival time, during the rest 7 of the day of Atonement. He paraded in front of them, to consume them 8 and make them fall on the day of fasting, the sabbath of their rest" (trans. in Florentino García Martínez, *The Dead Sea Scrolls Translated: The Qumran Texts in English*, trans. Wilfred G. E. Watson [Leiden: E. J. Brill, 1994]), clearly an earlier example of a narrative of an authority forcing a dissident group to violate their appointed Day of Atonement. I would go so far as to suspect that the rabbinic story is a late reflex of the same topos. Even though by the time of the Rabbis (at least among them) it would seem certain that the solar calendar was no longer an issue, calendrical conflict still remained a major bone of contention.

127. Haim Shapira, "The Deposition of Rabban Gamaliel: Between History and Legend," in Hebrew with English summary, *Zion* 64, no. 1 (1999): 25–26. See also citation and discussion of earlier scholarship there. As Shapira shows, the Palestinian talmudic and Babylonian talmudic versions of these stories about Yavneh in no wise represent first-century realities but the particular political situations of the relatively late Palestinian and Babylonian rabbinic polities in which they were told, and only the Babylonian version raises the issue of legitimate controversy and who may enter the House of Study. It must be emphasized, moreover, that it will not do to argue that the Rabbis held a view in which disagreement on matters of theory or "mere" interpretation was legitimate but Rabban Gamaliel had to enforce singularity in practice here, *because the narrative itself does not allow such an interpretation.* It represents Rabban Gamaliel's action as well as his general stance as having been highly improper and requiring virtual *metanoia* on his part, or as I suggest, on the part of the rabbinic institution, for which this is a sort of autobiographical narrative.

128. Shapira, "Deposition," 35–36. It needs to be emphasized, however, that Shapira (and I, as well, only too recently) were content, then, to "date" such narratives to the fourth century when the bulk of Babylonian talmudic (amoraic) traditions were formulated. Rubenstein, however, correctly castigates Shapira (and, by implication, Boyarin): "Shapira's dating of the story to the 4th century shows no awareness of the process of redaction of the Bavli. The fact that Rava's statement is attributed to Rabban Gamaliel in the story suggests that the redactors borrowed from Rava, not that Rava or Rava's students created the story" (Rubenstein, "Thematization," 11).

129. As pointed out to me by Dina Stein. David Goodblatt, "The Story of the Plot Against R. Simeon b. Gamaliel II," in Hebrew, *Zion* 49, no. 4 (1984): 362–69, has shown that the motif of a guard at the doors of the House of Study is itself an exclusively Babylonian element.

130. Froma Zeitlin, *Playing the Other; Gender and Society in Classical Greek Literature*, Women in Culture and Society (Chicago: University of Chicago Press, 1996); Nicole Loraux, *The Children of Athena: Athenian Ideas About Citizenship and the Division Between the Sexes* (Princeton, N.J.: Princeton University Press, 1983).

131. See, on the *Oresteia*, Froma Zeitlin, "The Dynamics of Misogyny: Myth and Mythmaking in Aeschylus's *Oresteia*," in *Playing the Other; Gender and Society in Classical Greek Literature*, Women in Culture and Society (Chicago: University of Chicago Press, 1996), 87–119. Charlotte Fonrobert independently articulates a similar comparison of these texts with the *Oresteia*, especially Zeitlin's reading of it (Fonrobert, "When the

Rabbi Weeps," 58). Interestingly, Fonrobert fastens on different aspects of this text in making the comparison, only strengthening its cogency.

132. David Goodblatt, *The Monarchic Principle: Studies in Jewish Self-Government in Antiquity*, Texte und Studien zum Antiken Judentum 38 (Tübingen: Mohr Siebeck, 1994).

133. I am grateful to Dina Stein for helping me see this point.

134. Isaak Heinemann, *Darxei Ha'agada*, in Hebrew (1954; reprint, Jerusalem: Magnes Press, 1970), 101–2 and passim.

135. For earlier discussions, see Stern, "Moses-Cide"; Handelman, "Fragments"; David Stern, "Literary Criticism or Literary Homilies? Susan Handelman and the Contemporary Study of Midrash," *Prooftexts* 5 (1985): 96–103; and Stern, *Midrash and Theory*, 15–38.

136. Psalm 62:12.

137. Jeremiah 23:29.

138. Azzan Yadin, "The Hammer and the Rock: Polysemy and the School of Rabbi Ishma'el," *Jewish Studies Quarterly* 9 (2002): 1–17.

139. It certainly seems telling to me that while Thomas H. Tobin, S.J. (*The Creation of Man: Philo and the History of Interpretation*, The Catholic Biblical Quarterly Monograph Series, vol. 14 [Washington, D.C.: The Catholic Biblical Association of America, 1983], 166) understands that Philo could consider mutually contradictory interpretations all "divinely inspired" and worthy of recording side by side, Winston considers this a "desperate solution" (David Winston, *Logos and Mystical Theology in Philo of Alexandria* [Cincinnati, Ohio: Hebrew Union College Press, 1985], 23), a position that Winston would hardly maintain if it were late midrash of which we spoke.

140. Karen Jo Torjesen, *Hermeneutical Procedure and Theological Method in Origen's Exegesis*, Patristische Texte und Studien (Berlin: Walter de Gruyter, 1986).

141. Henri de Lubac, *Medieval Exegesis: The Four Senses of Scripture*, trans. Mark Sebanc (Grand Rapids, Mich.: William B. Eerdmans, 1998).

142. See too Vaggione, *Eunomius*, 71.

143. As Karen King has reminded me.

144. Lim, *Disputation*, 203.

145. Lim, *Disputation*, 227.

146. Lim, *Disputation*, 201–2, citing Socrates Scholasticus, E.H. 5.10.

147. Lim, *Disputation*, 202–3. See M. Richard, "Les florilèges diphysites du Ve et VIe siècle," in *Das Konzil von Chalkedon Geschichte und Gegenwart*, ed. Alois Grillmeier and Heinrich Bacht (Würzburg: Echter-Verlag, 1951), 1:721–48. See also: "*Akribeia's* intolerance of ambiguity made it impossible for Eunomius or his community to take any part in the controversies of the rising generation: he was now definitively a 'heretic.' He [Eunomius] and his followers were obliged to observe the theological world of the next century from the sidelines, their proper voice audible only in (heavily doctored) *florilegia*" (Vaggione, *Eunomius*, 368). The point is not, of course, that controversy stopped in the Nicene Church but that the modes by which it was carried out were different. See immediately below on the Pelagian Controversy. The same is true, mutatis mutandis, of the Nestorian Controversy.

148. Éric Rebillard, "A New Style of Argument in Christian Polemic: Augustine and the Use of Patristic Citations," *Journal of Early Christian Studies* 8, no. 4 (2000): 560.

149. Rebillard, "New Style," 575.

150. Augustine, *Against Julian* 1.3.5, cited in Rebillard, "New Style," 576.

151. *Against Julian* 2.10.37, cited in Rebillard, "New Style," 577, emphasis added. See

too Mark Vessey, "*Opus Imperfectum*: Augustine and His Readers, 426–435 A.D.," *Vigiliae Christianae* 52, no. 3 (August 1998): 271.

152. Patrick T. R. Gray, "'The Select Fathers': Canonizing the Patristic Past," *Studia Patristica* 23 (1989): 21–36.

153. Mark Vessey, "The Forging of Orthodoxy in Latin Christian Literature: A Case Study," *Journal of Early Christian Studies* 4, no. 4 (Winter 1996): 495–513.

154. Lim, *Disputation*, 186.

155. Burrus, *Begotten*, 59 (emphasis added).

156. Burrus, *Begotten*, 56–57.

157. See also Barnes, "Trinitarian Canon."

158. Burrus, *Begotten*, 59.

159. In the same Mesopotamian environment, the formal public debates of Manichaeans were also being recorded in writing at about the same time (Lim, *Disputation*, 71).

160. Burrus, *Begotten*, 67.

161. See Lim, *Disputation*, 119, citing Philostorgius, and cf. BT Berakhot 27b, discussed above.

162. Burrus, *Begotten*, 60.

163. Referred to frequently in the literature, indeed, as "Father of the World" (Burton L. Visotzky, *Fathers of the World: Essays in Rabbinic and Patristic Literatures*, Wissenschaftliche Untersuchungen zum Neuen Testament 80 [Tübingen: J. C. B. Mohr (Paul Siebeck), 1995]).

164. If, as scholars agree, it is virtually impossible to determine what "actually" happened at the very well documented Nicaea (Vaggione, *Eunomius*, 52), how much more so the virtually mythic Yavneh!

165. Barnes, "Trinitarian Canon."

166. As I am sure Ruether does now, as well.

167. Rosemary Radford Ruether, "Judaism and Christianity: Two Fourth-Century Religions," *Sciences Religieuses/Studies in Religion* 2 (1972): 7–8.

168. Herford, *Christianity*, 176. Herford's understanding of the talmudic passage is inaccurate in several details.

169. משומד (*mešummad*) following the mss. According to the brilliant interpretation of Shlomo Pines, "Notes on the Parallelism Between Syriac Terminology and Mishnaic Hebrew," in Hebrew in *Yaakov Friedman Memorial Volume* (Jerusalem: Institute for Jewish Studies, 1974), 209–11, to the effect that a משומד is one who has become a "pagan," it follows that *minim*, Jewish Christians, are in a much worse category than Jews who have become "pagans." This is an excellent example of how muddying the categories is the greatest threat of all.

170. By virtue of the addition of the word "all."

171. That is, we don't actually have here a Palestinian parallel, but, given the general style of the Palestinian Talmud, the pericope would have ended here. There is a chronological and geographical break, moreover, between this part of the pericope which is early and Palestinian and the continuation which is later and Babylonian, so my conjecture is not without further foundation.

172. Significantly, the number equals the number of Abraham's retainers in Genesis 14.

173. Lim, *Disputation*, 227.

174. This point of view helps us make sense of the full emergence of representations of multivocality at the same time that midrash as exegesis is becoming less and less employed and hardly relied on in the actual discursive work of the Rabbis, which is one of the main arguments of David Halivni, *Peshat and Derash: Plain and Applied Meaning in Rabbinic Exegesis* (New York: Oxford University Press, 1991), and see too Halivni, *Midrash, Mishnah, and Gemara: The Jewish Predilection for Justified Law* (Cambridge, Mass.: Harvard University Press, 1986).

Chapter 8. *"When the Kingdom Turned to* Minut*"*

1. Hal A. Drake, "Lambs Into Lions: Explaining Early Christian Intolerance," *Past and Present* 153 (1996): 25. Drake's theory is germane to the hypothesis of this chapter. Limberis argues that for second-generation Christians this process was reversed (Vasiliki Limberis, "'Religion' as the Cipher for Identity: The Cases of Emperor Julian, Libanius, and Gregory Nazianzus," *Harvard Theological Review* 93, no. 4 [2000]: 377). I am not entirely persuaded by her argument on this point but do not wish to entirely disallow it, either. One way of thinking about it would be to see who is left out of "us." In both the earlier rabbinic and orthodox Christian formations, exemplified by Nazianzen below, there are those tied to us by tradition, kinship, and land who are, nevertheless, not us; they are heretics. See also Rosemary Radford Ruether, "Judaism and Christianity: Two Fourth-Century Religions," *Sciences Religieuses/Studies in Religion* 2 (1972): 1–10; and Jacob Neusner, *Judaism and Christianity in the Age of Constantine: History, Messiah, Israel, and the Initial Confrontation*, Chicago Studies in the History of Judaism (Chicago: University of Chicago Press, 1987), who take related positions.

2. Andrew S. Jacobs, "The Imperial Construction of the Jew in the Early Christian Holy Land" (Ph.D. diss., Duke University, 2001), 28–29.

3. Jacobs, "Construction," 31.

4. Susanna Elm, "Orthodoxy and the True Philosophical Life: Julian and Gregory of Nazianzus" (unpublished manuscript, Berkeley, 2000). I am grateful to Prof. Elm for sharing her work with me prior to publication. See also Limberis, "Cipher," 383.

5. Although Gideon Foerster and Yoram Tsafrir, "Nysa-Scythopolis—a New Inscription and the Titles of the City on Its Coins," *Israel Numismatic Journal* 9 (1986): 53–58, has been cited as relevant in this context, it seems to me not so. Even accepting the interpretation of the publishers of this inscription that the unique designation of Scythopolis as "one of Coele Syria's Greek cities" was to insist on the "Hellenic-Pagan" character of the city owing to a threat posed by its mixed population of Jews and Samaritans, we still need not conclude that "Hellenic" here means the religion.

6. Limberis, "Cipher," 378, 382, and throughout.

7. Limberis, "Cipher," 386.

8. Limberis, "Cipher," 399. I accept Limberis's assent to Asad's critique of Geertz, but nevertheless see much more continuity and a shift toward something that could be called "religion" in the modern sense taking place precisely in these fourth-century echoes of Christianity.

9. *Oration* 4.5 and 96–109, cited in Elm. See also Limberis, "Cipher," 395, on this passage.

10. Cf., e.g., Talal Asad, *Genealogies of Religion: Discipline and Reasons of Power in Christianity and Islam* (Baltimore, Md.: Johns Hopkins University Press, 1993), 40–41.

11. Asad, *Genealogies*, 28.

12. Ibid., 42.

13. Ibid., 45.

14. Ibid.

15. David Chidester, *Savage Systems: Colonialism and Comparative Religion in Southern Africa* (Charlottesville: University Press of Virginia, 1996), 11–16.

16. Cf. also: "It was in the seventeenth century, following the fragmentation of the unity and authority of the Roman church and the consequent wars of religion, which tore European principalities apart, that the earliest systematic attempts at producing a universal definition of religion were made" (Asad, *Genealogies*, 40).

17. Julian and Wilmer Cave France Wright, "Against the Galileans," in *The Works of the Emperor Julian*, trans. Wilmer Cave France Wright, Loeb Classical Library (London: Heinemann Macmillan, 1913), 321.

18. Seth Schwartz, *Imperialism and Jewish Society from 200 B.C.E.. to 640 C.E.* (Princeton, N.J.: Princeton University Press, 2001), 179.

19. This point is not contradicted in any way by Denise Kimber Buell, "Race and Universalism in Early Christianity," *Journal of Early Christian Studies* 10, no. 4 (Winter 2002): 429–68, which was published as I was putting the final touches on this book. Buell's compelling analysis of second- and third-century texts indicates early Christianity's struggle to find a mode of identity, with notions of Christianness as a new *ethnos/genos* being very prevalent indeed. However, Buell herself marks a shift that takes place in the fourth century: "Beginning in the fourth century, ethnic reasoning serves to naturalize the equation of Christianness with gentileness, or Romanness, in part through the oppositional construction of non-Jewish non-Christians as 'pagans'" (Buell, "Race," 465). I would argue, however, that such a classification marks the undoing of an ethno/racial definition of Christianness, insofar as in general throughout the fourth century "pagans" were understood to be just as Roman as Christians. "Pagan" surely did not constitute an ethnic or racial designation but a religious one. Even in the earlier writings considered by Buell, where Christianity is defined as an *ethnos* or a *genos*, these terms are the dependent variables of "faith." This is decidedly not the case for Jews much before the Christian era nor for Judaism since the early Middle Ages. Buell argues elegantly that Christian universalism should not be seen in opposition to or against the background of a putative Jewish particularism: "Seeing that early Christians defined themselves in and through race requires us to dismantle an oppositional definition of Christianness and Jewishness on the basis of race or ethnicity. Doing so may also contribute to resisting periodizations that mark an early and decisive split between Christianities and Judaisms. Not only do many early Christians define themselves as a people, even competing for the same name—Israel—but early Christians adapt and appropriate existing forms of Jewish universalism in formulating their own universalizing strategies in the Roman period. . . . Since ethnic reasoning also resonates with non-Jewish cultural practices of self-definition, it offers an analytic point of entry that treats both Jewish and non-Jewish frames of reference as integrally part of Christian self-definition, not as its 'background'" (Buell, "Race," 467). At the same time, notwithstanding Buell's reference to Isaiah as "emphasizing attachment to Yahweh as defining membership in Israel," I would suggest that the notion of "orthodoxy" as defining membership in the Christian com-

munity and the feints in that direction in rabbinic literature that define orthodoxy as the criterion for membership in Israel represent a "new thing." That new thing would ultimately be called "religion."

20. Claudine Dauphin, *La Palestine byzantine: Peuplement et populations*, 3 vols., BAR International Series (Oxford: Archaeopress, 1998), 1:133–55. See also the discussion in Jacobs, "Construction," 75–100.

21. J. Rebecca Lyman, *Christology and Cosmology: Models of Divine Activity in Origen, Eusebius, and Athanasius*, Oxford Theological Monographs (Oxford: Oxford University Press, Clarendon Press, 1993).

22. Eusebius, *Preparation for the Gospel*, trans. Edwin Hamilton Gifford, 2 vols. (Grand Rapids, Mich.: Baker Book House, 1981).

23. Eusebius, *The Proof of the Gospel*, ed. and trans. W. J. Ferrar, Translations of Christian Literature (London: SPCK, 1920), 1:7. The translation here follows Jacobs, "Construction," 33.

24. Eusebius, *Proof*, 1:9. I am grateful to my student Ron Reissberg for this reference.

25. Elizabeth A. Castelli, *Martyrdom and Memory: Early Christian Culture-Making* (New York: Columbia University Press, 2003), chapter 2. I am grateful to Prof. Castelli for allowing me to see her work prior to publication. A seeming exception to this claim would be the Isiac cult, already known in Rome before Christianity and apparently defining a form of religious identity, or the Eleusinian Mysteries. However, as pointed out in Mary Beard, John A. North, and S. R. F. Price, *Religions of Rome* (Cambridge: Cambridge University Press, 1998), 309, these cults did not in any way command or demand exclusivity, and so religion could hardly have been, by then, a mode of primary identity formation. Although in some sense Isiacism was decoupled from *Romanitas*, per se, it did not yet form a separate mode of identity.

26. I use this term in the broadest sense.

27. *The Panarion of Epiphanius of Salamis, Book I, Sections 1–46*, trans. Frank Williams (Leiden: E. J. Brill, 1987), 16–50. Cf., however, Eusebius's *Demonstratio evangelica* 1.2.1 (Eusebius, *Proof*, 9).

28. Frances Young, "Did Epiphanius Know What He Meant by 'Heresy'?" *Studia Patristica* 17, no. 1 (1982): 199–205.

29. *Panarion*, 17–18. In another part of the Christian world, Frankfurter points out, for the fifth-century Coptic abbot Shenoute, "*Hellene* did not carry the sense of ethnically 'Greek' and therefore different from 'Egyptian,' but simply 'pagan'—'not Christian'" (David Frankfurter, *Religion in Roman Egypt: Assimilation and Resistance* [Princeton, N.J.: Princeton University Press, 1998], 79).

30. *Panarion*, 9.

31. Cf. Jacobs, "Construction," 55–56.

32. For a highly salient and crystal clear delineation of these terms *ethnic* and *cultural*, see Jonathan M. Hall, *Hellenicity Between Ethnicity and Culture* (Chicago: The University of Chicago Press, 2002), esp. 9–19.

33. As has been noted by previous scholars, for Epiphanius "heresy" is a much more capacious and even baggy-monster category than for most writers (Aline Pourkier, *L'Hérésiologie chez Épiphane de Salamine*, Christianisme Antique 4 [Paris: Éditions Beauchesne, 1992], 85–87; Young, "Epiphanius"). See the discussion in Jacobs, "Construction," 56.

34. *Panarion*, 24.

35. Justin's discussion of Jewish heresies is a different move from this, as analyzed in Chapter 2 above.

36. Johann Karl Ludwig Gieseler, "Über die Nazaräer und Ebioniten," *Archive für alte und neue Kirchengeschichte* 4, no. 2 (1819): 279, as cited in Glenn Alan Koch, "A Critical Investigation of Epiphanius' Knowledge of the Ebionites: A Translation and Critical Discussion of *Panarion* 30" (Ph.D. diss., University of Pennsylvania, 1976), 10.

37. Günter Stemberger, *Jews and Christians in the Holy Land: Palestine in the Fourth Century* (Edinburgh: T & T Clark, 1999), 80, writes: "It seems that there were no significant Jewish-Christian communities left in Palestine itself, and the primary problem for the wider church was the attraction of Judaism for the members of Gentile Christianity."

38. Nathaniel Deutsch, *Guardians of the Gate: Angelic Vice Regency in Late Antiquity*, Brill's Series in Jewish Studies (Leiden: E. J. Brill, 1999), 19.

39. Rachel Havrelock (unpublished essay, Berkeley, 2002).

40. *Panarion*, 120.

41. Chidester, *Savage*, 11–16.

42. Homi K. Bhabha, *The Location of Culture* (London: Routledge, 1994), 71.

43. For a useful (if methodologically uncritical) summary of the material, see Ray A. Pritz, *Nazarene Jewish Christianity: From the End of the New Testament Period Until Its Disappearance in the Fourth Century* (Jerusalem: Magnes Press, 1992), 48–70.

44. Jacobs, "Construction," 76–77.

45. Hillel Newman, "Jerome's Judaizers," *Journal of Early Christian Studies* 9, no. 4 (December 2001): 421–52.

46. Marc Bloch, *The Historian's Craft: Reflections on the Nature and Uses of History and the Techniques and Methods of Those Who Write It*, trans. Peter Putnam (New York: Vintage Books, 1953), 93.

47. Jerome, *Correspondence*, ed. Isidorus Hilberg, Corpus Scriptorum Ecclesiasticorum Latinorum (Vienna: Verlag der Österreichischen Akademie der Wissenschaften, 1996), vol. 55, 381–82.

48. See the discussion in Jacobs, "Construction," 114.

49. Chidester, *Savage*, 19.

50. Julian and Wright, "Against the Galileans," 389.

51. Ibid., 319–21.

52. Julian and Wright, "Against the Galileans," 393–95. Fascinatingly, this perspective gives us another way of understanding Julian's intention to allow the temple in Jerusalem to be rebuilt. A large part of his polemic consists, as we have seen, of charges that Christians are nothing, since they have abandoned Hellenism but not become Jews, given that they do not follow the Torah. He imagines a Christian answering him that the Jews, too, do not sacrifice as they are enjoined (Julian and Wright, "Against the Galileans," 405–7). What better way to refute this Christian counterclaim and demonstrate that the only reason that Jews do not sacrifice is that they have no temple, than to help them rebuild their temple and reinstitute the sacrifices?

53. Hall, *Hellenicity Between Ethnicity and Culture*, xix. Hall's book was published too late for its results to be incorporated into the discussion in my book.

54. Wright points out that Julian has Christlike figures in his own theology (Julian and Wright, "Against the Galileans," 315).

55. Jacobs, "Construction," 30.

56. Ibid., 57.

57. *Panarion*, treated by Jacobs, "Construction," 54–64. My treatment is somewhat different in emphasis from that of Jacobs but, once again, not antithetical.

58. R. von Krafft-Ebing, *Psychopathia Sexualis: A Medico-Forensic Study* (New York: Putnam, 1965). For the almost literal connection between histories of sexuality and histories of heresiology, see now Arnold I. Davidson, *The Emergence of Sexuality: Historical Epistemology and the Formation of Concepts* (Cambridge, Mass.: Harvard University Press, 2002), 118.

59. *Panarion*, 122–29. On this text, see Stephen Goranson, "The Joseph of Tiberias Episode in Epiphanius: Studies in Jewish and Christian Relations" (Ph.D. diss., Duke University, 1990); Stephen Goranson, "Joseph of Tiberias Revisited: Orthodoxies and Heresies in Fourth-Century Galilee," in *Galilee Through the Centuries: Confluence of Cultures*, ed. Eric M. Meyers, Duke Judaic Studies Series (Winona Lake, Ind.: Eisenbrauns, 1999), 335–43; Stemberger, *Jews and Christians*, 75–77.

60. Epiphanius of Salamis, *Panarion*, 122.

61. *Panarion*, 123 both quotes.

62. Epiphanius of Salamis, *Panarion*, 124.

63. Ibid., 127.

64. Ibid., 126.

65. Ibid., 128.

66. Ibid.

67. Robert Young, *Colonial Desire: Hybridity in Theory, Culture, and Race* (London: Routledge, 1995), 19.

68. *Panarion*, 129 both quotations.

69. For the previous scholarship of this sort, see (citing it to oppose it) Goranson, "Revisited," 337.

70. Goranson, "Revisited," 338. I am not entirely sure on what basis Goranson can make the positivist claim in the final clause, but I assume he has good basis for it. In any case, my argument is not dependent on such propositions about the actual situation. See the discussion immediately below concerning Jerome's notices of "Jewish Christians." Note, in any case, that in Goranson's reading, as accepted and extended here, Frédéric Manns is wrong ("Joseph de Tibériade, un judéo-chrétien du quatrième siècle," in *Christian Archaeology in the Holy Land, New Discoveries: Essays in Honour of Virgilio C. Corbo, OFM*, ed. Giovanni Claudio Bottini [Jerusalem: Franciscan Printing Press, 1990], 553–60). The whole point of the story is that Joseph does not become a "Jewish Christian" but a Christian who is not Jewish. See, making a similar point with respect to another scholar's work (Goranson, "Episode," 8).

71. Thus one scholar has recently argued that the only function of this story in Epiphanius's text is to provide some entertaining relief for the reader (T. C. G. Thornton, "The Stories of Joseph of Tiberias," *Vigiliae Christianae* 44 [1990]: 54–63). My interpretation is both similar to and subtly different from that of Jacobs, "Construction," 62–63, to which it should be compared. The two readings are probably compatible. I somewhat disagree, however, with Jacobs's last point: "The entire fabric of Joseph's story in the *Panarion* prepares us to understand how the imperial Christian is to overcome the onslaught of the unorthodox 'other': Jews then, Arians now, a bewildering multitude of gnostics, Jewish-Christians, encratites, Origenists, or any other theological deviant who might cross the Christian's future path. If they can be as thoroughly comprehended as the Jew, their threat will be as easily squashed as an annoying insect" (Jacobs, "Con-

328 Notes to Pages 214–216

struction," 63–64). My way of phrasing this point would be that Epiphanius produced the orthodox Jew as the absolute other of the Christian in order to draw the lines clearly and thus have a space for the absolute delegitimation of other Christians, especially the "Arians," who are shown to have no religion at all by this move (a motive that appears over and over within the narrative).

72. *Panarion*, 119. Compare my reading with that of Pourkier, *Épiphane*.

73. Louis Althusser, "Ideology and Ideological State Apparatuses (Notes Towards an Investigation)," in *Lenin and Philosophy, and Other Essays* ([London]: New Left Books, 1971), 127–86, now Louis Althusser, "Ideology and Ideological State Apparatuses (Notes Toward an Investigation)," in *Mapping Ideology* (London: Verso, 1994), 100–140.

74. On the promulgation of the codex, see now John Matthews, *Laying Down the Law: A Study of the Theodosian Code* (New Haven, Conn.: Yale University Press, 2000); earlier the essays in Jill Harries and I. N. Wood, *The Theodosian Code*, ed. Jill Harries (Ithaca, N.Y.: Cornell University Press, 1993); Tony Honoré, *Law in the Crisis of Empire, 379–455 A.D.: The Theodosian Dynasty and Its Quaestors; with a Palingenesia of Laws of the Dynasty* (Oxford: Clarendon Press, 1998).

75. For an analogous and similarly ramified shift in the meanings of terms within an imperial situation, see Young, *Desire*, 50, on the vicissitudes of *civilization* and *culture*.

76. Maurice Sachot, "'Religio/Superstitio': Historique d'une subversion et d'un retournement," *Revue d'histoire des religions* 208, no. 4 (1991): 355–94.

77. Sachot, "Superstitio," 375. As Michele R. Salzman makes clear ("'Superstitio' in the Codex Theodosianus and the Persecution of Pagans," *Vigiliae Christianae* 41 [1987]: 174), this meaning is already a development from even earlier meanings.

78. Peter Brown, *Authority and the Sacred: Aspects of the Christianization of the Roman World* (Cambridge: Cambridge University Press, 1995), 35.

79. Beard, North, and Price, *Religions of Rome*, 217.

80. Beard, North, and Price, *Religions of Rome*, 221–22.

81. Thus in Tacitus. See Beard, North, and Price, *Religions of Rome*, 222–23.

82. Beard, North, and Price, *Religions of Rome*, 218, citing *On Superstition*. See, however, Plutarch, *On Superstition* 8, and Strabo 16.2.37.

83. Caroline Humfress, "Religion," in *The Evolution of the Late Antique World*, by Peter Garnsey and Caroline Humfress (Oxford: Orchard Academic Press, 2001), 135–70. For *superstitio* as "excessive commitment to the gods," see Beard, North, and Price, *Religions of Rome*, 217.

84. Interestingly enough, according to Beard, North, and Price the beginnings of the semantic shift, within Roman, i.e., "pagan" usage, are to be found in the second century. This is not surprising, and it indicates that Christianity itself was a product of the forces that we come to understand as "Christianization," as well as an agent in them.

85. Clyde Pharr, *The Theodosian Code and Novels, and the Sirmondian Constitutions: A Translation with Commentary, Glossary, and Bibliography*, in collaboration with Theresa Sherrer Davidson and Mary Brown Pharr, introd. by C. Dickerman Williams ([Princeton, N.J.]: Princeton University Press, 1952), 474.

86. *Religio ver dei cultus est, superstitio falsi*, 4.28.11.

87. Beard, North, and Price, *Religions of Rome*, 216. See earlier Maurice Sachot: "Dans la bouche de chrétien *religio* renvoie désormais non plus seulement à pratiques et à des institutions individuelles, familiales ou civiles, mais aussi et avant tout à un rapport

absolu à la vérité" (Maurice Sachot, "Comment le Christianisme est-il devenu *religio*," *Revue des sciences religiuses* 59 [1985]: 97). This should almost surely be connected up with other semantic shifts in Latin as well, notably the shift in the meaning of verus itself (Carlin A. Barton, "The 'Moment of Truth' in Ancient Rome: Honor and Embodiment in a Contest Culture," *Stanford Humanities Review* [1998]: 16–30).

88. In an expanded version of this argument, to appear as a separate paper, I shall discuss another late ancient narrative of conversion, The Conversion of the Jews of Minorca.

89. Stemberger, *Jews and Christians*. See, however, my discussion below, which would militate against the ineluctability of this conclusion.

90. Lee I. Levine, "The Jewish Patriarch (Nasi) in Third Century Palestine," in *Aufstieg und Niedergang der Römischen Welt II, Principat 19,2* (Berlin: Walter de Gruyter, 1979), 685.

91. And see the quotation from Seth Schwartz in the next paragraph.

92. Amnon Linder, *The Jews in Roman Imperial Legislation*, ed. and trans. Amnon Linder (Detroit, Mich., and Jerusalem: Wayne State University Press and Israel Academy of Sciences and Humanities, 1987), 68.

93. Pharr, *Theodosian Code*, 469.

94. For this issue, see Elliott S. Horowitz, "The Rite to Be Reckless: On the Perpetration and Interpretation of Purim Violence," *Poetics Today* 15, no. 1 (1994): 9–54.

95. Stemberger, *Jews and Christians*, 29.

96. See the discussion in Stemberger, *Jews and Christians*, 155.

97. Pharr, *Theodosian Code*, 468. "It does remain likely that there were rabbis among the *primates* mentioned in the law codes" (Schwartz, *Jewish Society*, 118). See also J. H. W. G. Liebeschuetz, *Antioch: City and Imperial Administration in the Later Roman Empire* (Oxford: Clarendon Press, 1972), 12, 16; Limberis, "Cipher," 382.

98. Stemberger, Jews and Christians, 308.

99. Linder, *Legislation*, 69.

100. Compare the roughly analogous insistence in the code that the high priest of Egypt must *not* be a Christian (XII.1.112) and see the discussion in Frankfurter, *Religion*, 24. According to Stemberger, even this, however, is an understatement with respect to the patriarch. He shows that in the fourth century the patriarch was higher in authority than the governor (Stemberger, *Jews and Christians*, 242–43). Levine writes that in the fourth century the patriarch was more powerful than the Herodian kings (Levine, "Patriarch," 651).

101. Schwartz, *Jewish Society*, 116. For the patriarch as a perceived threat to Christianity, see Cyril, Wilhelm Karl Reischl, and Joseph Rupp, *Cyrilli Hierosolymarum Archiepiscopi Opera Quae Supersunt Omnia.*, ed. Wilhelm Karl Reischl (Hildesheim: Olms, 1967), 2:24, and discussion by Jacobs, "Construction," 51.

102. Pharr, *Theodosian Code*, 468. See also Schwartz, *Jewish Society*, 103–4, although "the patriarch, or *nasi*, by the middle of the fourth [century] had become a very estimable figure indeed, the rabbis did not have any officially recognized legal authority until the end of the fourth century and even then it was severly restricted and in any case not limited to rabbis." Moreover, and very importantly, "As for the patriarchs, they acquired much of their influence precisely by relaxing their ties to the rabbis and allying themselves instead with Palestinian city councillors, wealthy diaspora Jews, and prominent gentiles." See also Stemberger, *Jews and Christians*, 34.

103. Pharr, *Theodosian Code*, 469.

104. Schwartz, *Jewish Society*, 187.

105. Bhabha, *Location*, 85.

106. This would suggest a possible qualification to claims such as those made by Shaye Cohen, "Pagan and Christian Evidence on the Ancient Synagogue," in *The Synagogue in Late Antiquity*, ed. Lee I. Levine (Philadelphia: American Schools of Oriental Research, 1987), 170–75.

107. Although this term does not, to the best of my knowledge, exist, Beard, North, and Price (*Religions of Rome*, 237) strongly imply that its virtual synonym, *religio illicita*, does, but only in Christian texts, a fact that, if it could be verified, would strengthen my case.

108. Stemberger, *Jews and Christians*, 35, even seems to suggest that, when the Theodosian Code (XII.1.158) writes "irrespective of what religion (*superstitio*) they profess," this might even include Christianity as one of the religions.

109. Linder, *Legislation*, 428.

110. Idem aa. philippo praefecto praetorio per illyricum. nullus tamquam iudaeus, cum sit innocens, obteratur nec expositus eum ad contumeliam religio qualiscumque perficiat.

111. Pharr, *Theodosian Code*, 476.

112. Humfress, "Religion."

113. Drake, "Lambs," 27–29.

114. Jacob Neusner, *Frequently Asked Questions About Rabbinic Judaism* (Peabody, Mass.: Hendrickson, 2003). I appreciate Prof. Neusner's willingness to let me see this material prior to publication.

115. Note that since belief is the crucial modus for determining of Christian legitimacy, the Quartodeciman heresy is described as a belief and not a practice. Orthodox Judaism would tend to do the opposite, describing wrong beliefs as bad practice.

116. Pharr, *Theodosian Code*, 469.

117. Virginia Burrus, "'In the Theater of This Life': The Performance of Orthodoxy in Late Antiquity," in *The Limits of Ancient Christianity: Essays on Late Antique Thought and Culture in Honor of R. A. Markus*, ed. William E. Klingshirn and Mark Vessey, Recentiores: Late Latin Texts and Contexts (Ann Arbor: University of Michigan Press, 1999), 81.

118. Richard Kalmin, "Christians and Heretics in Rabbinic Literature of Late Antiquity," *Harvard Theological Review* 87, no. 2 (April 1994): 160.

119. Moshe Halbertal and Avishai Margalit, *Idolatry* (Cambridge, Mass.: Harvard University Press, 1992).

120. For much longer and more detailed discussion, see Daniel Boyarin, *Dying for God: Martyrdom and the Making of Christianity and Judaism*, The Lancaster/Yarnton Lectures in Judaism and Other Religions for 1998 (Stanford, Calif.: Stanford University Press, 1999), chap. 1.

121. This identification is explicit in the continuation (not cited here), in which Rabbi Eli'ezer refers to his intercourse with a certain James, the disciple of Jesus. Jerome knows that the term *min* (sectarian) is a name for Jewish Christians, as we see from his famous letter to Augustine (Jerome, *Correspondence*, vol. 55, 381–82). This letter was written about 404 (Pritz, *Nazarene Jewish Christianity*, 53).

122. M. S. Zuckermandel, ed., *Tosephta: Based on the Erfurt and Vienna Codices, with*

Lieberman, Saul, "Supplement" to the Tosephta, in Hebrew (Jerusalem: Bamberger and Wahrmann, 1937), 503.

123. In the early Palestinian version of the narrative, there is not a hint of the term *minut* with respect to the arrest and martydom of these Rabbis. Louis Finkelstein, ed., *Sifre on Deuteronomy* (1939; reprint, New York: Jewish Theological Seminary of America, 1969), 346. For a discussion, see Daniel Boyarin, "A Contribution to the History of Martyrdom in Israel," in *Festschrift for Prof. H. Z. Dimitrovsky,* ed. Menahem Hirschman et al., in Hebrew (Jerusalem: Magnes Press, 1999).

124. Translation following Rashi ad loc.

125. Saul Lieberman, "The Martyrs of Caesarea," *Annuaire de l'institut de philologie et d'histoire orientales et slaves* 7 (1939): 395.

126. Kalmin, "Christians and Heretics."

127. Cf., e.g., Lee I. Levine, *The Rabbinic Class of Roman Palestine in Late Antiquity* (New York: Jewish Theological Seminary of America, 1989), 87, and also Lieberman, "Martyrs of Caesarea," 398.

128. Jacob Neusner, *Aphrahat and Judaism: The Christian-Jewish Argument in Fourth-Century Iran,* Studia Post-Biblica (Leiden: E. J. Brill, 1971).

129. Daniel Boyarin, "Martyrdom and the Making of Christianity and Judaism," *Journal of Early Christian Studies* 6, no. 4 (December 1998): 577–627.

130. Gerald Bruns, "The Hermeneutics of Midrash," in *The Book and the Text: The Bible and Literary Theory,* ed. Regina Schwartz (Oxford: Basil Blackwell, 1990), 199.

131. Jonathan Boyarin, "Introduction," in *Powers of Diaspora: Two Essays on the Relevance of Jewish Culture,* by Jonathan Boyarin and Daniel Boyarin (Minneapolis: University of Minnesota Press, 2002), 23.

132. Jacques Derrida, *Glas,* trans. John P. Leavey Jr. and Richard Rand (Lincoln: University of Nebraska Press, 1990), 189b.

Concluding Political Postscript

1. Michel Foucault and Lawrence D. Kritzman, *Politics, Philosophy, Culture: Interviews and Other Writings, 1977–1984,* ed. and trans. Lawrence D. Kritzman (New York: Routledge, 1988), 265.

2. Walter Benjamin, "Theses on the Philosophy of History," in *Illuminations,* ed. Hannah Arendt, trans. Harry Zohn (New York: Schocken, 1969), 253–64.

Bibliography

Abrahams, Israel. "Some Egyptian Fragments of the Passover Haggada." *Jewish Quarterly Review*, old series 10 (1898): 41–51.

Abrams, Daniel. "'The Book of Illumination' of R. Jacob Ben Jacob HaKohen: A Synoptic Edition from Various Manuscripts." In Hebrew. New York: New York University, 1993.

———. "The Boundaries of Divine Ontology: The Inclusion and Exclusion of Meṭaṭron in the Godhead." *Harvard Theological Review* 87, no. 3 (July 1994): 291–321.

———. "The Dimensions of the Creator—Contradiction or Paradox? Corruptions and Accretions to the Manuscript Witnesses." *Kabbalah: Journal for the Study of Jewish Mystical Texts* 5 (2000): 35–53.

———. "From Divine Shape to Angelic Being: The Career of Akatriel in Jewish Literature." *Journal of Religion* (1996), 43–63.

Albeck, Hanoch. *Mishna*. Jerusalem: Mossad Bialik, 1953.

Alexander, L. "The Living Voice: Scepticism Towards the Written Word in Early Christian and Graeco-Roman Texts." In *The Bible in Three Dimensions*, vol. 87, edited by David J. A. Clines, Stephen E. Fowl, and Stanley E. Porter. Journal for the Study of the Old Testament Supplement Series, 221–47. Sheffield: Sheffield University Press, 1990.

Alon, Gedaliah. "Jewish Christians: The Parting of the Ways." In *The Jews in Their Land in the Talmudic Age (70–640 C.E.)*. 2 vols. Edited and translated by Gershon Levi, 288–307. Jerusalem: Magnes Press, 1984.

———. *The Jews in Their Land in the Talmudic Age (70–640 C.E.)*. 2 vols. Edited and translated by Gershon Levi. Jerusalem: Magnes Press, 1984.

Alon, Gedaliahu. "The Patriarchate of Rabbi Joḥanan Ben Zakkai." In Hebrew. In *Studies in Jewish History in the Times of the Second Temple, the Mishna and the Talmud*, 253–73. Tel Aviv: Hakibbutz Hameuchad, 1967.

Alon, Gedalyahu. "The Patriarchate of Rabban Joḥanan B. Zakkai." In *Jews, Judaism and the Classical World: Studies in Jewish History in the Times of the Second Temple and Talmud*, translated by Israel Abrahams, 314–43. Jerusalem: Magnes Press, 1977.

———. "Rabban Joḥanan B. Zakkai's Removal to Jabneh." In *Jews, Judaism and the Classical World: Studies in Jewish History in the Times of the Second Temple and Talmud*, translated by Israel Abrahams, 269–313. Jerusalem: Magnes Press, 1977.

Altendorf, H.-D. "Zum Stichwort: Rechtgläubigkeit und Ketzerei in ältesten Christentum." *Zeitschrift für Kirchengeschichte* 80, no. 1 (1969): 61–74.

Althusser, Louis. "Ideology and Ideological State Apparatuses (Notes Toward an Investigation)." In *Mapping Ideology*, 100–140. London: Verso, 1994.

———. "Ideology and Ideological State Apparatuses (Notes Towards an Investigation)." In *Lenin and Philosophy, and Other Essays*, 127–86. [London]: New Left Books, 1971.

Anderson, Gary. "The Interpretation of Genesis 1:1 in the Targums." *Catholic Biblical Quarterly* 52, no. 1 (1990): 21–29.

Andria, R. G. *I frammenti delle successioni dei filosofi*. Naples: Arte tipografica, 1989.

Arac, Jonathan, Wlad Godzich, and Wallace Martin, eds. *The Yale Critics: Deconstruction in America*. Theory and History of Literature. Minneapolis: University of Minnesota Press, 1983.

Asad, Talal. *Genealogies of Religion: Discipline and Reasons of Power in Christianity and Islam*. Baltimore, Md.: Johns Hopkins University Press, 1993.

Ashton, John. *Understanding the Fourth Gospel*. Oxford: Clarendon Press and Oxford University Press, 1993.

Assmann, Jan. *Moses the Egyptian: The Memory of Egypt in Western Monotheism*. Cambridge, Mass.: Harvard University Press, 1997.

Athanasius. *Athanasius Werke*. Edited by H. G. Opitz. Berlin: Walter de Gruyter, 1934.

Augustine. *Confessions Books I–XIII*. Translated by F. J. Sheed, with an introduction by Peter Brown. Indianapolis, Ind.: Hackett, 1993.

Austin, J. L. *Philosophical Papers*. Oxford: Clarendon Press, 1961.

Avi-Yonah, Michael. *The Jews of Palestine: A Political History from the Bar Kokhba War to the Arab Conquest*. New York: Schocken Books, 1976.

Baer, Yitzhaq. "Israel, the Christian Church, and the Roman Empire from the Time of Septimius Severus to the Edict of Toleration of A.D. 313." In *Studies in History*, edited by Alexander Fuks and Israel Halpern. Scripta Hierosolymitana 7, 79–147. Jerusalem: Magnes Press, 1961.

Baird, Robert D. *Category Formation and the History of Religions*. The Hague: Mouton, 1971.

Baker, Cynthia. "Neighbor at the Door or Enemy at the Gate? Notes Toward a Rabbinic Topography of Self and Other." Paper presented at American Academy of Religion, New Orleans, 1996.

Barnard, Leslie W. *Justin Martyr: His Life and Thought*. London: Cambridge University Press, 1967.

Barnes, Michel René. "The Fourth Century as Trinitarian Canon." In *Christian Origins: Theology, Rhetoric, and Community*, edited by Lewis Ayres and Gareth Jones, 47–67. London: Routledge, 1998.

Barrett, C. K. *The Gospel According to St. John: An Introduction with Commentary and Notes on the Greek Text*. London: SPCK, 1978.

———. "Jews and Judaizers in the Epistles of Ignatius." In *Jews, Greeks and Christians: Religious Cultures in Late Antiquity. Essays in Honor of W. D. Davies*, 220–44. Leiden: E. J. Brill, 1976.

Barton, Carlin A. "The 'Moment of Truth' in Ancient Rome: Honor and Embodiment in a Contest Culture." *Stanford Humanities Review* (1998), 16–30.

———. *Roman Honor: The Fire in the Bones*. Berkeley and Los Angeles: University of California Press, 2001.

Bauer, Walter, Gerhard Krodel, and Robert A. Kraft. *Orthodoxy and Heresy in Earliest Christianity*. Edited by Gerhard Krodel. Philadelphia: Fortress Press, 1971.

Baumgarten, Albert I. "The Akivan Opposition." *Hebrew Union College Annual* 50 (1979): 179–97.

———. *The Flourishing of Jewish Sects in the Maccabean Era: An Interpretation*. Supplements to the Journal for the Study of Judaism 55. Leiden: E. J. Brill, 1997.

———. "Literary Evidence for Jewish Christianity in the Galilee." In *The Galilee in Late Antiquity*, edited by Lee I. Levine, 39–50. New York: Jewish Theological Seminary of America, 1992.

———. "The Pharisaic *Paradosis*." *Harvard Theological Review* 80 (1987): 63–77.

———. "Rabbinic Literature as a Source for the History of Jewish Sectarianism in the Second Temple Period." *Dead Sea Discoveries* 2 (1995): 14–57.

Beard, Mary, John A. North, and S. R. F. Price. *Religions of Rome*. Cambridge: Cambridge University Press, 1998.

Benjamin, Walter. "Theses on the Philosophy of History." In *Illuminations*, edited by Hannah Arendt, translated by Harry Zohn, 253–64. New York: Schocken, 1969.

Berger, David. *The Rebbe, the Messiah, and the Scandal of Orthodox Indifference*. Portland, Ore.: Littman Library of Jewish Civilization, 2001.

Bhabha, Homi K. *The Location of Culture*. London: Routledge, 1994.

Bickerman, Elias [Bikerman, Élie]. "La chaîne de la tradition pharisienne." *Revue biblique* 59, no. 1 (January 1952): 44–54.

———. "The Name of the Christians." *Harvard Theological Review* 42 (1949): 109–24.

Bietenhard, Hans. "Logos Theologie im Rabbinat." ANRW II, 580–617. Berlin: Walter de Gruyter, 1979.

Black, Matthew. "The Patristic Accounts of Jewish Sectarianism." *Bulletin of the John Rylands Library* 41, no. 2 (March 1959): 285–303.

Bloch, Marc. *The Historian's Craft: Reflections on the Nature and Uses of History and the Techniques and Methods of Those Who Write It*. Translated by Peter Putnam. New York: Vintage Books, 1953.

Bloom, Harold. *Deconstruction and Criticism*. New York: Seabury Press, 1979.

Boccaccini, Gabriele. *Beyond the Essene Hypothesis: The Parting of the Ways Between Qumran and Enochic Judaism*. Grand Rapids, Mich.: William B. Eerdmans, 1998.

———. "The Preexistence of the Torah: A Commonplace in Second Temple Judaism or a Later Rabbinic Development?" *Henoch* 17 (1995): 329–50.

Boismard, M. E. *St. John's Prologue*. London: Blackfriars Publications, 1957.

Bokser, Ben Zion. *Pharisaic Judaism in Transition*. New York: Jewish Theological Seminary of America, 1935.

Borgen, Peder. "Logos Was the True Light: Contributions to the Interpretation of the Prologue of John." *Novum Testamentum* 14 (1972): 115–30.

———. "Observations on the Midrashic Character of John 6." *Zeitschrift für Neutestamentliche Wissenschaft* 54 (1963): 232–40.

———. "Observations on the Targumic Character of the Prologue of John." *New Testament Studies* 16 (1969/1970): 288–95.

Le Boulluec, Alain. *La notion d'hérésie dans la littérature grecque IIe–IIIe siècles*. 2 vols. Paris: Études Augustiniennes, 1985.

Box, G. H., ed. and trans. *Apocalypse of Abraham*. London: SPCK, 1918.

Boyarin, Daniel. "Archives in the Fiction: Rabbinic Historiography and Church History." In *Festschrift for Elizabeth Clark*, edited by Dale Martin and Patricia Miller. Forthcoming, 2004.

———. *Carnal Israel: Reading Sex in Talmudic Culture*. The New Historicism: Studies in Cultural Poetics 25. Berkeley and Los Angeles: University of California Press, 1993.

———. "A Contribution to the History of Martyrdom in Israel." In *Festschrift for Prof. H. Z. Dimitrovsky*, edited by Menahem Hirschman, Daniel Boyarin, Shamma

Friedman, Menahem Schmelzer, and Israel Ta-Shma. In Hebrew. Jerusalem: Magnes Press, 1999.

———. *Dying for God: Martyrdom and the Making of Christianity and Judaism.* The Lancaster/Yarnton Lectures in Judaism and Other Religions for 1998. Stanford, Calif.: Stanford University Press, 1999.

———. "The Gospel of the Memra: Jewish Binitarianism and the Crucifixion of the Logos." *Harvard Theological Review* 94, no. 3 (2001): 243–84.

———. *Intertextuality and the Reading of Midrash.* Bloomington: Indiana University Press, 1990.

———. "The *Ioudaioi* in John and the Prehistory of 'Judaism.'" In *Pauline Conversations in Context: Essays in Honour of Calvin J. Roetzel,* 224–50. Sheffield: Continuum, 2002.

———. "Jewish Cricket." *PMLA* 113, no. 1 (January 1998): 40–45.

———. "Martyrdom and the Making of Christianity and Judaism." *Journal of Early Christian Studies* 6, no. 4 (December 1998): 577–627.

———. "Masada or Yavneh? Gender and the Arts of Jewish Resistance." In *Jews and Other Differences: The New Jewish Cultural Studies,* edited by Daniel Boyarin and Jonathan Boyarin, 306–29. Minneapolis: University of Minnesota Press, 1997.

———. "Placing Reading: Ancient Israel and Medieval Europe." In *The Ethnography of Reading,* edited by Jonathan Boyarin, 10–37. Berkeley and Los Angeles: University of California Press, 1993.

———. *A Radical Jew: Paul and the Politics of Identity.* Contraversions: Critical Studies in Jewish Literature, Culture, and Society. Berkeley and Los Angeles: University of California Press, 1994.

———. "A Tale of Two Synods: Nicaea, Yavneh and the Making of Orthodox Judaism." *Exemplaria* 12, no. 1 (Spring 2000): 21–62.

———. *Unheroic Conduct: The Rise of Heterosexuality and the Invention of the Jewish Man.* Contraversions: Critical Studies in Jewish Literature, Culture, and Society. Berkeley and Los Angeles: University of California Press, 1997.

———. "Women's Bodies and the Rise of the Rabbis: The Case of Soṭah." *Studies in Contemporary Jewry: Jews and Gender, the Challenge to Hierarchy* 16 (2001): 88–100.

Boyarin, Jonathan. "Introduction." In *Powers of Diaspora: Two Essays on the Relevance of Jewish Culture,* by Jonathan Boyarin, and Daniel Boyarin, 1–33. Minneapolis: University of Minnesota Press, 2002.

Brent, Allen. "Diogenes Laertius and the Apostolic Succession." *Journal of Ecclesiastical History* 44, no. 3 (July 1993): 367–89.

———. *Hippolytus and the Roman Church in the Third Century: Communities in Tension Before the Emergence of a Monarch-Bishop.* Supplements to Vigiliae Christianae. Leiden: E. J. Brill, 1995.

Brodie, Thomas L. *The Gospel According to John: A Literary and Theological Commentary.* New York: Oxford University Press, 1993.

Brown, Peter. *Authority and the Sacred: Aspects of the Christianization of the Roman World.* Cambridge: Cambridge University Press, 1995.

Brown, Raymond E. *The Community of the Beloved Disciple: The Life, Loves and Hates of an Individual Church in New Testament Times.* New York: Paulist Press, 1979.

———. *The Gospel According to John.* 2 vols. Garden City, N.Y.: Doubleday, 1966

Bruce, F. F. *The Gospel of John.* Grand Rapids, Mich.: William B. Eerdmans, 1983.

Bruns, Gerald. "The Hermeneutics of Midrash." In *The Book and the Text: The Bible and Literary Theory*, edited by Regina Schwartz, 189–213. Oxford: Basil Blackwell, 1990.

Bruns, J. E. "Philo Christianus: The Debris of a Legend." *Harvard Theological Review* 66 (1973): 141–45.

Buell, Denise Kimber. "Race and Universalism in Early Christianity." *Journal of Early Christian Studies* 10, no. 4 (Winter 2002): 429–68.

Bultmann, Rudolf Karl. *The Gospel of John: A Commentary*. Translated by G. R. Beasley-Murray. Oxford: Basil Blackwell, 1971.

———. "The History of Religions: Background of the Prologue to the Gospel of John." In *The Interpretation of John*, edited by John Ashton. Studies in New Testament Interpretation, 27–46. 1923. Reprint, Edinburgh: T & T Clark, 1997.

———. *Theology of the New Testament*. 2 vols. New York: Scribner, 1955.

Burrus, Virginia. *"Begotten, not Made": Conceiving Manhood in Late Antiquity*. Figurae. Stanford, Calif.: Stanford University Press, 2000.

———. "Creatio Ex Libidine: Reading Ancient Logos Differantly." In *Other Testaments: Derrida and Religion*, edited by Keven Hart and Yvonne Sherwood. London: Routledge, 2004.

———. "Fathering the Word: Athanasius of Alexandria." In *"Begotten Not Made": Conceiving Manhood in Late Antiquity*. Figurae. Stanford, Calif.: Stanford University Press, 2000.

———. "Hailing Zenobia: Anti-Judaism, Trinitarianism, and John Henry Newman." *Culture and Religion* 3, no. 2 (2002): 163–77.

———. "The Heretical Woman as Symbol in Alexander, Athanasius, Epiphanius, and Jerome." *Harvard Theological Review* 84 (1991): 229–48.

———. "'In the Theater of This Life': The Performance of Orthodoxy in Late Antiquity." In *The Limits of Ancient Christianity: Essays on Late Antique Thought and Culture in Honor of R. A. Markus*, edited by William E. Klingshirn and Mark Vessey. Recentiores: Late Latin Texts and Contexts, 80–96. Ann Arbor: University of Michigan Press, 1999.

———. *The Making of a Heretic: Gender, Authority, and the Priscillianist Controversy*. Transformations of the Ancient World. Berkeley and Los Angeles: University of California Press, 1995.

———. "Rhetorical Stereotypes in the Portrait of Paul of Samosata." *Vigiliae Christianae* 43 (1989): 215–25.

———. *The Sex Lives of Saints*. Divinations: Reading Late Ancient Religions. Philadelphia: University of Pennsylvania Press, 2003.

Butler, Judith P. *Excitable Speech: A Politics of the Performative*. New York: Routledge, 1997.

Cancik, Hubert. "The History of Culture, Religion, and Institutions in Ancient Historiography: Philological Observations Concerning Luke's History." *Journal of Biblical Literature* 116, no. 4 (1997): 673–95.

Castelli, Elizabeth A. *Martyrdom and Memory: Early Christian Culture-Making*. New York: Columbia University Press, 2003.

Chadwick, Henry, trans. and ed. *Origen: Contra Celsum*. Cambridge: Cambridge University Press, 1965.

Charlesworth, James H. *The Dead Sea Scrolls: Hebrew, Aramaic, and Greek Texts with English Translations: Volume 2, Damascus Document, War Scroll, and Related Docu-*

ments. Edited by James H. Charlesworth. Princeton Theological Seminary Dead Sea Scrolls Project. Louisville, Ky.: Westminster/John Knox Press, 1994.

—. *The Old Testament Pseudepigrapha.* 2 vols. Garden City, N.Y.: Doubleday and Company, 1985.

—, ed. *John and the Dead Sea Scrolls.* Christian Origins Library. New York: Crossroad, 1990.

Chesnut, Glenn F. "The Ruler and the Logos in Neopythagorean, Middle Platonic, and Late Stoic Political Philosophy." In *Principate: Religion,* edited by Wolfgang Haase. Aufstieg und Niedergang der Römischen Welt, 1310–32. Berlin: Walter de Gruyter, 1978.

Chidester, David. *Savage Systems: Colonialism and Comparative Religion in Southern Africa.* Charlottesville: University Press of Virginia, 1996.

Chilton, Bruce, and Jacob Neusner. *Types of Authority in Formative Christianity and Judaism.* London: Routledge, 1999.

Clark, Elizabeth A. *Reading Renunciation: Asceticism and Scripture in Early Christianity.* Princeton, N.J.: Princeton University Press, 1999.

Clark-Soles, Jaime. "The Word(s) of the Word in the Fourth Gospel." Conference presentation. Society of Biblical Literature. Denver, Colo., 2001.

Cohen, Aryeh. *Rereading Talmud: Gender, Law and the Poetics of Sugyot.* Brown Judaic Studies 318. Atlanta, Ga.: Scholars Press, 1998.

Cohen, Shaye J. D. *The Beginnings of Jewishness: Boundaries, Varieties, Uncertainties.* Hellenistic Culture and Society 31. Berkeley and Los Angeles: University of California Press, 1998.

—. "The Conversion of Antoninus." In *The Talmud Yerushalmi and Graeco-Roman Culture,* edited by Peter Schäfer. Texte und Studien zum Antiken Judentum 71, 141–71. Tübingen: Mohr Siebeck, 1998.

—. "Epigraphical Rabbis." *Jewish Quarterly Review* 72 (1981): 1–17.

—. "Pagan and Christian Evidence on the Ancient Synagogue." In *The Synagogue in Late Antiquity,* edited by Lee I. Levine, 159–81. Philadelphia: American Schools of Oriental Research, 1987.

—. "Patriarchs and Scholarchs." *Proceedings of the American Academy of Jewish Research* 48 (1981): 57–83.

—. "The Significance of Yavneh: Pharisees, Rabbis, and the End of Jewish Sectarianism." *Hebrew Union College Annual* 55 (1984): 27–53.

—. "'Those Who Say They Are Jews and Are Not': How Do You Know a Jew in Antiquity When You See One?" In *Diasporas in Antiquity,* edited by Shaye J. D. Cohen and Ernest S. Frerichs. Brown Judaic Studies 288, 1–45. Atlanta, Ga.: Scholars Press, 1993.

—. "A Virgin Defiled: Some Rabbinic and Christian Views on the Origins of Heresy." *Union Seminary Quarterly Review* 36, no. 1 (Fall 1980): 1–11.

Collins, John J. "Cult and Culture: The Limits of Hellenization in Judea." In *Hellenism in the Land of Israel,* edited by John J. Collins and Gregory Sterling. Christianity and Judaism in Antiquity, 38–61. Notre Dame, Ind.: University of Notre Dame, 2000.

Cooper, Kate. "Insinuations of Womanly Influence: An Aspect of the Christianization of the Roman Aristocracy." *Journal of Roman Studies* 82 (1992): 150–64.

Crouzel, Henri. *Origen: The Life and Thought of the First Great Theologian.* Translated by A. S. Worrall. San Francisco: Harper and Row, 1989.

Crown, Alan D. "Redating the Schism Between the Judaeans and the Samaritans." *Jewish Quarterly Review* 82, no. 1–2 (1991): 17–50.

Culpepper, Alan. "The Pivot of John's Prologue." *New Testament Studies* 27 (1980): 1–31.

Cyril, Wilhelm Karl Reischl, and Joseph Rupp. *Cyrilli Hierosolymarum Archiepiscopi Opera Quae Supersunt Omnia*. 2 vols. Edited by Wilhelm Karl Reischl. Hildesheim: Olms, 1967.

Danby, Herbert, ed. and trans. *The Mishnah*. London: Oxford University Press, 1974.

Dauphin, Claudine. *La Palestine byzantine: Peuplement et populations*. 3 vols. BAR International Series. Oxford: Archaeopress, 1998.

Davidson, Arnold I. *The Emergence of Sexuality: Historical Epistemology and the Formation of Concepts*. Cambridge, Mass.: Harvard University Press, 2002.

Davies, William David. *Paul and Rabbinic Judaism: Some Rabbinic Elements in Pauline Theology*. 2d ed. 1955. Reprint, London: Society for the Promotion of Christian Knowledge, 1965.

———. *The Setting of the Sermon on the Mount*. Cambridge: Cambridge University Press, 1976.

Dawson, David. *Allegorical Readers and Cultural Revision in Ancient Alexandria*. Berkeley and Los Angeles: University of California Press, 1992.

Dawson, Lorne. "Church/Sect Theory: Getting It Straight." *North American Religion* 1 (1992): 5–28.

de Ausejo, Serafin. "¿Es un himno a Cristo el prólogo de San Juan?" *EstBib* 15 (1956): 223–77, 381–427.

de Lubac, Henri. *Medieval Exegesis: The Four Senses of Scripture*. Translated by Mark Sebanc. Grand Rapids, Mich.: William B. Eerdmans, 1998.

Denzey, Nicola Frances. "Genesis Traditions in Conflict? The Use of Some Exegetical Traditions in the *Trimorphic Protennoia* and the Johannine Prologue." *Vigiliae Christianae: A Review of Early Christian Life and Language* 55, no. 1 (2001): 20–44.

Derrida, Jacques. *Glas*. Translated by John P. Leavey Jr. and Richard Rand. Lincoln: University of Nebraska Press, 1990.

———. *Of Grammatology*. Baltimore, Md.: Johns Hopkins University Press, 1976.

Desjardins, Michel. "Bauer and Beyond: On Recent Scholarly Discussions of Αἵρεσις in the Early Christian Era." *The Second Century* 8 (1991): 65–82.

Deutsch, Nathaniel. *The Gnostic Imagination: Gnosticism, Mandaeism, and Merkabah Mysticism*. Brill's Series in Jewish Studies. Leiden: E. J. Brill, 1995.

———. *Guardians of the Gate: Angelic Vice Regency in Late Antiquity*. Brill's Series in Jewish Studies. Leiden: E. J. Brill, 1999.

Le Déaut, Roger. *La Nuit Pascale: Essai sur la signification de la Pâque juive a partir du Targum d'Exode XII 42*. Rome: Biblical Institute Press, 1980.

Dillon, John. The Middle Platonists: 80 B.C. to A.D. 220. Ithaca, N.Y.: Cornell University Press, 1977.

Díez Macho, Alejandro. "El Logos y el Espíritu Santo." *Atlántida* 1 (1963): 381–96.

———. *Neophyti 1, Targum Palestinense Ms. de la Biblioteca Vaticana*. Madrid: Consejo Superior de Investigaciones Científicas, 1968.

Dodd, Charles Harold. *The Interpretation of the Fourth Gospel*. Cambridge: Cambridge University Press, 1960.

Drake, Hal A. "Constantine and Consensus." *Church History* 44 (1995): 1–15.

————. "Lambs Into Lions: Explaining Early Christian Intolerance." *Past and Present* no. 153 (1996): 3–36.

Drijvers, H. J. W. "Rechtgläubigkeit und Ketzerei im ältesten Syrischen Christentum." *Oriens Christianus Analecta* 197 (1974): 291–308.

Dunn, Geoffrey D. "Tertullian and Rebekah: A Re-Reading of an 'Anti-Jewish' Argument in Early Christian Literature." *Vigiliae Christianae* 52, no. 2 (May 1998): 119–45.

Dunn, James D. G. *Christology in the Making: A New Testament Inquiry into the Origins of the Doctrine of the Incarnation.* Philadelphia: Westminster Press, 1980.

————. *Jesus, Paul and the Law: Studies in Mark and Galatians.* Louisville, Ky.: Westminster/John Knox Press, 1990.

————. *The Partings of the Ways Between Christianity and Judaism and Their Significance for the Character of Christianity.* London: SCM Press and Trinity Press International, 1991.

Dvornik, Frances. *Early Christian and Byzantine Political Philosophy.* 2 vols. Washington, D.C.: Dumbarton Oaks, 1966.

Edwards, M. J. "Justin's Logos and the Word of God." *Journal of Early Christian Studies* 3, no. 3 (Fall 1995): 261–80.

Elm, Susanna. "Orthodoxy and the True Philosophical Life: Julian and Gregory of Nazianzus." Unpublished manuscript. Berkeley, 2000.

Ephraem. *Des Heiligen Ephraem des Syrers Hymnen de Nativitate [Epiphania].* Edited by E. Beck. SR. CSCO. Louvain: Peeters, 1959.

Epiphanius of Salamis. *The Panarion of Epiphanius of Salamis, Book I, Sections 1–46.* Translated by Frank Williams. Leiden: E. J. Brill, 1987.

Epp, Eldon Jay. "Wisdom, Torah, Word: The Johannine Prologue and the Purpose of the Fourth Gospel." In *Current Issues in Biblical and Patristic Interpretation. Studies in Honor of Merrill C. Tenney Presented by His Former Students*, edited by Gerald F. Hawthorne, 128–46. Grand Rapids, Mich.: William B. Eerdmans, 1974.

Epstein, J. N. *Introductions to the Literature of the Tannaim.* In Hebrew. Jerusalem: Magnes/Dvir, 1957.

Eusebius. *Life of Constantine.* Translated and with commentary by Averil Cameron and Stuart G. Hall. Clarendon Ancient History Series. Oxford: Clarendon Press and Oxford University Press, 1999.

————. *Preparation for the Gospel.* Translated by Edwin Hamilton Gifford. 2 vols. Grand Rapids, Mich.: Baker Book House, 1981.

————. *The Proof of the Gospel.* Edited and translated by W. J. Ferrar. 2 vols. Translations of Christian Literature. London: SPCK, 1920.

Finkelstein, Louis, *Introduction to Tractates Fathers and The Fathers of Rabbi Nathan.* In Hebrew. New York: Jewish Theological Seminary of America, 1950.

————, ed. *Sifre on Deuteronomy.* 1939. Reprint, New York: Jewish Theological Seminary of America, 1969.

Fisch, Menachem. *Rational Rabbis: Science and Talmudic Culture.* Jewish Literature and Culture. Bloomington: Indiana University Press, 1997.

Fischel, Henry A. *Rabbinic Literature and Greco-Roman Philosophy. A Study of Epicurea and Rhetorica in Early Midrashic Writings.* Studia Post-Biblica. Leiden: E. J. Brill, 1973.

Flusser, David. *Judaism and the Sources of Christianity.* Jerusalem: Magnes Press, 1988.

————. "Some of the Precepts of the Torah from Qumran (4QMMT) and the Benediction Against the Heretics." In Hebrew, with English summary. *Tarbiz* 61, no. 3–4 (April–September 1992): 333–74, ii.

Foerster, Gideon, and Yoram Tsafrir. "Nysa-Scythopolis—a New Inscription and the Titles of the City on Its Coins." *Israel Numismatic Journal* 9 (1986): 53–58.

Fonrobert, Charlotte. *Menstrual Purity: The Reconstruction of Biblical Gender in Christianity and Rabbinic Judaism.* Contraversions: Jews and Other Differences. Stanford, Calif.: Stanford University Press, 2000.

———. "When the Rabbi Weeps: On Reading Gender in Talmudic Aggada." *Nashim: A Journal of Jewish Women's Studies and Gender Issues* 4 (2001): 56–83.

———. "When Women Walk in the Ways of Their Fathers: On Gendering the Rabbinic Claim for Authority." *Journal of the History of Sexuality: Special Issue: Sexuality in Late Antiquity* 10, no. 3/4 (July/October 2001): 398–415.

Fossum, Jarl. "Gen 1,26 and 2,7 in Judaism, Samaritanism, and Gnosticism." *Journal for the Study of Judaism* 16, no. 2 (1989): 202–39.

———. "Jewish-Christian Christology and Jewish Mysticism." *Vigiliae Christianae* 37 (1983): 260–87.

———. *The Name of God and the Angel of the Lord: Samaritan and Jewish Conceptions of Intermediation and the Origin of Gnosticism.* Wissenschaftliche Untersuchungen zum Neuen Testament. Tübingen: Mohr Siebeck, 1985.

Foucault, Michel, and Lawrence D. Kritzman. *Politics, Philosophy, Culture: Interviews and Other Writings, 1977–1984.* Edited and translated by Lawrence D. Kritzman. New York: Routledge, 1988.

Fraade, Steven D. *From Tradition to Commentary: Torah and Its Interpretation in the Midrash Sifre to Deuteronomy.* Judaica: Hermeneutics, Mysticism, and Religion. Albany, N.Y.: State University of New York Press, 1991.

———. "Shifting from Priestly to Non-Priestly Legal Authority: A Comparison of the Damascus Document and the Midrash Sifra." *Dead Sea Discoveries* 6 (1999): 109–25.

Frankfurter, David. *Religion in Roman Egypt: Assimilation and Resistance.* Princeton, N.J.: Princeton University Press, 1998.

Freeman, Charles. *The Closing of the Western Mind: The Rise of Faith and the Fall of Reason.* London: Heinemann, 2002.

Frend, W. H. C. *The Early Church.* Minneapolis, Minn.: Fortress Press, 1965.

———. *The Rise of Christianity.* Philadelphia: Fortress Press, 1984.

Freud, Sigmund. "Instincts and Their Vicissitudes." In *The Standard Edition of the Complete Psychological Works of Sigmund Freud*, vol. 14, edited and translated by James Strachey and Anna Freud, translated by Alix Strachey and James Strachey. 1915. Reprint, London: Hogarth Press, 1955.

Freyne, Sean. "The Charismatic." In *Ideal Figures in Ancient Judaism: Profiles and Paradigms*, edited by George Nickelsburg and John Collins. Septuagint and Cognate Studies Series, no. 12. Chico, Calif.: Scholars Press, 1980.

Friedländer, Moriz. *Der Vorchristliche jüdische Gnosticismus.* Göttingen: Vandenhoeck and Ruprecht, 1898.

Friedman, Shamma. "Chapter 'Ha'isha Rabba' in the Babylonian Talmud." In *Researches and Sources*, edited by H. Z. Dimitrovsky, 227–441. New York: Jewish Theological Seminary of America, 1977.

———. *Talmud Arukh Perek Ha- Sokher et Ha-Umanin: Bavli Bava Metsi'a Perek Shishi:*

Mahadurah al Derekh Ha-Mehkar Im Perush Ha-Sugyot. 2 vols. Jerusalem: Bet ha-midrash le-rabanim ba-Amerikah, 1990.

Gafni, Isaiah M. *Land, Center and Diaspora: Jewish Constructs in Late Antiquity.* Journal for the Study of the Pseudepigrapha. Supplement series. Sheffield, Eng.: Sheffield Academic Press, 1997.

———. "Nestorian Literature as a Source for the History of the Babylonian *Yeshivot.*" *Tarbiz* 51 (1981).

Gallagher, Catherine, and Stephen Greenblatt. *Practicing New Historicism.* Chicago: University of Chicago Press, 2000.

García Martínez, Florentino. *The Dead Sea Scrolls Translated: The Qumran Texts in English.* Translated by Wilfred G. E. Watson. Leiden: E. J. Brill, 1994.

Georgi, Dieter. "The Records of Jesus in the Light of Ancient Accounts of Revered Men." In *Proceedings of the Society of Biblical Literature,* 527–42. Chico, Calif.: Scholars Press, 1972.

Gero, Stephen. "Jewish Polemic in the Martyrium Pionii and a 'Jesus' Passage from the Talmud." *Journal of Jewish Studies* 29 (1978): 164–68.

Gershonson, Daniel, and Giles Quispel. "'Meristae.'" *Vigiliae Christianae* 12 (1958): 19–26.

Giblin, C. H. "Two Complementary Literary Structures in John 1:1–18." *Journal of Biblical Literature* 104 (1985): 87–103.

Gieseler, Johann Karl Ludwig. "Über die Nazaräer und Ebioniten." *Archive für alte und neue Kirchengeschichte* 4, no. 2 (1819): 279–330.

Gilat, Yitzhak D. *R. Eliezer Ben Hyrcanus: A Scholar Outcast.* Bar-Ilan Studies in Near Eastern Languages and Culture. Ramat Gan: Bar-Ilan University Press, 1984.

Glucker, John. *Antiochus and the Late Academy.* Hypomnemata Heft 56. Göttingen: Vandenhoeck and Ruprecht, 1978.

Goldberg, Arnold Maria. *Untersuchungen über die Vorstellung von der Schekhinah in der frühen rabbinischen Literatur: Talmud und Midrash.* Berlin: Walter de Gruyter, 1969.

Goldfahn, A. H. "Justinus Martyr und die Agada." *Monatschrift für Geschichte und Wissenschaft des Judentums* 22 (1873): 49–60, 104–15, 145–53, 193–202, 257–69.

Goldin, Judah. "The First Pair (Yose Ben Yoezer and Yose Ben Yohanan) or the Home of a Pharisee." *AJS Review* 5 (1980): 41–62.

———. "Not by Means of an Angel and Not by Means of a Messenger." In *Religions in Antiquity: Essays in Memory of Erwin Ramsdell Goodenough,* edited by Jacob Neusner, 412–24. Leiden: E. J. Brill, 1968.

———, trans. *The Fathers According to Rabbi Nathan.* Yale Judaica Series. New Haven, Conn.: Yale University Press, 1955.

Goodblatt, David. *The Monarchic Principle: Studies in Jewish Self-Government in Antiquity.* Texte und Studien zum Antiken Judentum 38. Tübingen: Mohr Siebeck, 1994.

———. *Rabbinic Instruction in Sasanian Babylonia.* Studies in Judaism in Late Antiquity, vol. 9. Leiden: E. J. Brill, 1975.

———. "The Story of the Plot Against R. Simeon b. Gamaliel II." In Hebrew. *Zion* 49, no. 4 (1984): 350–74.

Goodenough, Erwin Ramsdell. *The Theology of Justin Martyr: An Investigation into the Conceptions of Early Christian Literature and Its Hellenistic and Judaistic Influences.* Amsterdam: Philo Press, 1968.

Goodman, Martin. "The Function of Minim in Early Rabbinic Judaism." In *Geschichte—*

Tradition—Reflexion: Festschrift für Martin Hengel zum 70. Geburtstag, edited by H. Cancik, H. Lichtenberger, and P. Schäfer, 1.501–10. Tübingen: Mohr Siebeck, 1996.

———. "Sadducees and Essenes After 70 C.E." In *Crossing the Boundaries: Essays in Biblical Interpretation in Honour of Michael D. Goulder*, edited by Stanley E. Porter, Paul Joyce, and David E. Orton. Biblical Interpretation Series. Leiden: E. J. Brill, 1994.

———. *State and Society in Roman Galilee*, A.D. *132–212*. Totowa, N.J.: Rowman and Allanheld, 1983.

Goranson, Stephen. "The Joseph of Tiberias Episode in Epiphanius: Studies in Jewish and Christian Relations." Ph.D. diss., Duke University, 1990.

———. "Joseph of Tiberias Revisited: Orthodoxies and Heresies in Fourth-Century Galilee." In *Galilee Through the Centuries: Confluence of Cultures*, edited by Eric M. Meyers. Duke Judaic Studies Series, 335–43. Winona Lake, Ind.: Eisenbrauns, 1999.

———. "Others and Intra-Jewish Polemic as Reflected in Qumran Texts." In *The Dead Sea Scrolls: A Comprehensive Account*, edited by P. Flint and J. Vanderkam, 2: 534–51. Leiden: E. J. Brill, 1999.

Goshen-Gottstein, Alon. "A Lonely Sage on His Death-Bed: The Story of the Death of Rabbi Eli'ezer (Sanhedrin 68a), an Ideological Analysis." In Hebrew. In *Memorial Volume for Tirzah Lifshitz* (forthcoming).

———. *The Sinner and the Amnesiac: The Rabbinic Invention of Elisha Ben Abuya and Eleazar Ben Arach*. Stanford, Calif.: Stanford University Press, 2000.

Graham, William A. *Beyond the Written Word: Oral Aspects of Scripture in the History of Religion*. Cambridge: Cambridge University Press, 1987.

Grant, Robert M. "Les Êtres intermédiares dans le judaïsme tardif." In *Le Origini Dello Gnosticismo, Colloquio di Messina 13–18 Aprile 1966*, vol. 12, edited by Ugo Bianchi, 141–54. Studies in the History of Religions (supplements to *Numen*). Leiden: E. J. Brill, 1967.

Gray, Patrick T. R. "'The Select Fathers': Canonizing the Patristic Past." *Studia Patristica* 23 (1989): 21–36.

Green, William Scott. "Palestinian Holy Men: Charismatic Leadership and Roman Tradition." In *Aufstieg und Niedergang der Römischen Welt II, Principat 19,2*, edited by Wolfgang Haase, 619–47. Berlin: Walter de Gruyter, 1979.

Gregory. *The Life of Moses*. Translated by Abraham J. Malherbe and Everett Ferguson, with a preface by John Meyendorff. New York: Paulist Press, 1978.

Gruen, Erich S. *Heritage and Hellenism: The Reinvention of Jewish Tradition*. Hellenistic Culture and Society 30. Berkeley and Los Angeles: University of California Press, 1998.

Guénoun, Denis. *Hypothèses sur l'Europe: Un essai de philosophie*. Belfort: Circé, 2000.

Habas, Ephrat (Rubin). "Rabban Gamaliel of Yavneh and His Sons: The Patriarchate Before and After the Bar Kokhva Revolt." *Journal of Jewish Studies* 50, no. 1 (1999): 21–37.

Haenchen, Ernst. *John: A Commentary on the Gospel of John*. Edited and translated by Robert Walter Funk. Hermeneia—a Critical and Historical Commentary on the Bible. Philadelphia: Fortress Press, 1984.

Halbertal, Moshe. *People of the Book: Canon, Meaning, and Authority*. Cambridge, Mass.: Harvard University Press, 1997.

Halbertal, Moshe, and Avishai Margalit. *Idolatry*. Cambridge, Mass.: Harvard University Press, 1992.

344   Bibliography

Halivni, David. *Mekorot u-Masorot Be'urim Ba-Talmud: Masekhet Bava Kama.* Jerusalem: Magnes Press, 1993.
———. *Midrash, Mishnah, and Gemara: The Jewish Predilection for Justified Law.* Cambridge, Mass.: Harvard University Press, 1986.
———. *Peshat and Derash: Plain and Applied Meaning in Rabbinic Exegesis.* New York: Oxford University Press, 1991.
Hall, Jonathan M. *Ethnic Identity in Greek Antiquity.* Cambridge: Cambridge University Press, 1997.
———. *Hellenicity Between Ethnicity and Culture.* Chicago: The University of Chicago Press, 2002.
Halperin, David J. "A Sexual Image in Hekhalot Rabbati and Its Implications." *Jerusalem Studies in Jewish Thought* 6, nos. 1–2 (1987): 117–32.
Halperin, David M. "How to Do the History of Male Homosexuality." *GLQ: A Journal of Lesbian and Gay Studies* 6, no. 1 (2000): 87–123.
Hamp, Vinzenz. *Der Begriff "Wort" in den aramäischen Bibelübersetzungen ein exegetischer Beitrag zur hypostasen-frage und zur Geschichte der Logos-spekulationen.* Munich: Neuer Filser-verlag, 1938.
Handelman, Susan. "Fragments of the Rock: Contemporary Literary Theory and the Study of Rabbinic Texts—a Response to David Stern." *Prooftexts* 5 (1985): 73–95.
———. *The Slayers of Moses: The Emergence of Rabbinic Interpretation in Modern Literary Theory.* Albany: State University of New York Press, 1982.
Hannah, Darrell D. *Michael and Christ: Michael Traditions and Angel Christology in Early Christianity.* Wissenschaftliche Untersuchungen zum Neuen Testament. Tübingen: Mohr Siebeck, 1999.
Hanson, R. P. C. *The Search for the Christian Doctrine of God: The Arian Controversy, 318–381 A.D.* Edinburgh: T & T Clark, 1988.
Harries, Jill, and I. N. Wood. *The Theodosian Code.* Edited by Jill Harries. Ithaca, N.Y.: Cornell University Press, 1993.
Harris, J. Rendell. *The Origin of the Prologue to St. John's Gospel.* Cambridge: Cambridge University Press, 1917.
Hartman, Geoffrey H. *Criticism in the Wilderness: The Study of Literature Today.* New Haven, Conn.: Yale University Press, 1980.
Hasan-Rokem, Galit. "Narratives in Dialogue: A Folk Literary Perspective on Interreligious Contacts in the Holy Land in Rabbinic Literature of Late Antiquity." In *Sharing the Sacred: Religious Contacts and Conflicts in the Holy Land, First–Fifteenth Centuries C.E.* Edited by Guy Stroumsa and Arieh Kofsky, 109–29. Jerusalem: Yad Ben Zvi, 1998.
———. *The Web of Life—Folklore in Rabbinic Literature: The Palestinian Aggadic Midrash Eikha Rabba.* In Hebrew. Tel Aviv: Am Oved, 1996.
———. *The Web of Life—Folklore in Rabbinic Literature: The Palestinian Aggadic Midrash Eikha Rabba.* Translated by Batya Stein. Contraversions: Jews and Other Differences. Stanford, Calif.: Stanford University Press, 2000.
Havrelock, Rachel. Unpublished essay. Berkeley, 2002.
Hayes, Christine. *Between the Babylonian and Palestinian Talmuds.* Oxford: Oxford University Press, 1997.
———. "Displaced Self-Perceptions: The Deployment of *Mînîm* and Romans in B. San-

hedrin 90b-91a." In *Religious and Ethnic Communities in Later Roman Palestine*, edited by Hayim Lapin, 249–89. Lanham, Md.: University Press of Maryland, 1999.

Hayward, Robert. *Divine Name and Presence: The Memra*. Oxford Centre for Postgraduate Hebrew Studies. Totowa, N.J.: Allanheld, Osmun, 1981.

Heine, R. "The Christology of Callistus." *Journal of Theological Studies* 49 (1998): 56–91.

Heinemann, Isaak. *Darxei Ha'agada*. In Hebrew. 1954. Reprint, Jerusalem: Magnes Press, 1970.

Heinemann, Joseph. *Prayer in the Talmud Forms and Patterns*. Studia Judaica. Berlin: Walter de Gruyter, 1977.

———. "The Proem in the Aggadic Midrashim: A Form-Critical Study." Scripta Hierosolymita 22 (1971): 100–22.

Herford, R. Travers. *Christianity in Talmud and Midrash*. 1903. Reprint, New York: Ktav, 1978.

Herr, Moshe David. "Continuum in the Chain of Torah Transmission." In Hebrew with English summary. *Zion* 44 (1979): 43–56, x–xi.

Hezser, Catherine. *The Social Structure of the Rabbinic Movement in Roman Palestine*. Texte und Studien zum Antiken Judentum. Tübingen: Mohr Siebeck, 1997.

Hirsch, Emanuel. *Studien zum Vierten Evangelium (Text/Literarkritik/Entstehungsgeschichte)*. Beiträge zur Historischen Theologie. Tübingen: Mohr Siebeck, 1936.

Hirsch, Samuel. *Die Religionsphilosophie der Juden*. Jewish Philosophy, Mysticism, and the History of Ideas. New York: Arno Press, 1980.

Hirshman, Marc. *A Rivalry of Genius: Jewish and Christian Biblical Interpretation in Late Antiquity*. Translated by Batya Stein. SUNY Series in Judaica: Hermeneutics, Mysticism, and Religion. Albany: State University of New York Press, 1996.

Honoré, Tony. *Law in the Crisis of Empire, 379–455 A.D.: The Theodosian Dynasty and Its Quaestors; with a Palingenesia of Laws of the Dynasty*. Oxford: Clarendon Press, 1998.

Hooker, Morna D. "John the Baptist and the Johannine Prologue." New Testament Studies 16 (1969): 354–58.

Hopkins, Keith. "Christian Number and Its Implications." *Journal of Early Christian Studies* 6, no. 2 (1998): 185-226.

Horbury, William. *Jews and Christians in Contact and Controversy*. Edinburgh: T & T Clark, 1998.

———. "Suffering and Messianism in Yose Ben Yose." In *Suffering and Martyrdom in the New Testament Studies Presented to G. M. Styler*, edited by William Horbury and Brian McNeil, 143–82. Cambridge: Cambridge University Press, 1980.

Horner, Timothy J. *Listening to Trypho: Justin Martyr's Dialogue Reconsidered*. Contributions to Biblical Exegesis and Theology. Leuven: Peeters, 2001.

Horovitz, S., and Israel Abraham Rabin, eds. *Mechilta d'Rabbi Ismael*. Edited by S. Horovitz. Jerusalem: Wahrmann Books, 1970.

Horowitz, Elliott S. "The Rite to Be Reckless: On the Perpetration and Interpretation of Purim Violence." *Poetics Today* 15, no. 1 (1994): 9–54.

Humfress, Caroline. "Religion." In *The Evolution of the Late Antique World*, by Peter Garnsey and Caroline Humfress, 135–70. Oxford: Orchard Academic Press, 2001.

Hurtado, Larry W. *One God, One Lord: Early Christian Devotion and Ancient Jewish Monotheism*. 2d ed. Edinburgh: T & T Clark, 1998.

Idel, Moshe. "Enoch is Meṭaṭron." *Immanuel* 24/25 (1990): 220–40.

————. *Messianic Mystics.* New Haven, Conn.: Yale University Press, 1998.

————. "Meṭaṭron: Notes Towards the Development of Myth in Judaism." In Hebrew. In *Eshel Beer-Sheva: Occasional Publications in Jewish Studies,* 29–44. Beer-sheva, Israel: Ben-Gurion University of the Negev Press, 1996.

————. "Prayer in Provençal Kabbalah." In Hebrew. *Tarbiz* 62, no. 2 (1993): 266–86.

Jacobs, Andrew S. "The Imperial Construction of the Jew in the Early Christian Holy Land." Ph.D. diss., Duke University, 2001.

Janowitz, Naomi. "Rabbis and Their Opponents: The Construction of the 'Min' in Rabbinic Anecdotes." *Journal of Early Christian Studies* 6, no. 3 (Fall 1998): 449–62.

Janssens, Yvonne. "Un source gnostique du prologue?" In *L'Évangile de Jean: Sources, rédaction, théologie,* edited by Marinus de Jonge. Bibliotheca Ephemeridum theologicarum Lovaniensium, 355–58. Leuven: Leuven University Press Uitgeverij Peeters, 1987.

Jasper, Alison E. *The Shining Garment of the Text: Gendered Readings of John's Prologue.* Journal for the Study of the New Testament. Sheffield, Eng.: Sheffield Academic Press, 1998.

Jerome. *Correspondence.* Edited by Isidorus Hilberg. Corpus Scriptorum Ecclesiasticorum Latinorum. Vienna: Verlag der Österreichischen Akademie der Wissenschaften, 1996.

Johnson, Barbara. "The Frame of Reference: Poe, Lacan, Derrida." In *The Purloined Poe,* edited by John P. Muller and William J. Richards, 213–51. Baltimore, Md.: Johns Hopkins University Press, 1987.

Johnson, Willis. "Textual Sources for the Study of Jewish Currency Crimes in 13th-Century England." *British Numismatic Journal* 66 (1996): 21–32.

Jones, F. Stanley. *An Ancient Jewish Christian Source on the History of Christianity: Pseudo-Clementine Recognitions 1.27–71.* Texts and Translations: Christian Apocrypha Series. Atlanta, Ga.: Scholars Press, 1995.

Josephus, Flavius. *Books XVIII–XX.* Vol. IX of *Jewish Antiquities.* Translated by L. H. Feldman. Loeb Classical Library. Cambridge, Mass.: Harvard University Press, 1965.

Julian, and Wilmer Cave France Wright. "Against the Galileans." In *The Works of the Emperor Julian,* translated by Wilmer Cave France Wright. 3 vols. Loeb Classical Library, 313–433. London: Heinemann Macmillan, 1913.

Juster, Jean. *Les Juifs dans l'Empire Romain: Leur condition juridique, economique et sociale.* Paris: P. Geuthner, 1914.

Justin Martyr. *Dialogue with Trypho.* Vol. 1: The apostolic fathers—Justin Martyr—Irenaeus, of *The Ante-Nicene Fathers: Translations of the Writings of the Fathers Down to A.D. 325.* Edited by Alexander Roberts and James Donaldson. Grand Rapids, Mich.: William B. Eerdmans, 1989.

Justin. *Dialogus cum Tryphone.* Edited by Miroslav Marcovich. Patristische Texte und Studien 47. Berlin: Walter de Gruyter, 1997.

Kahana, Menahem. "The Critical Editions of *Mekhilta De-Rabbi Ishmael* in the Light of the Genizah Fragments." In Hebrew. *Tarbiz* 55, no. 4 (Fall 1985): 489–524.

————. *Two Mekhiltot on the Amalek Portion: The Originality of the Version of the Mekhilta De'Rabbi Ishma'el with Respect to the Mekhilta of Rabbi Shim on Ben Yohay.* In Hebrew. Jerusalem: Magnes Press, 1999.

Kalmin, Richard. "Christians and Heretics in Rabbinic Literature of Late Antiquity." *Harvard Theological Review* 87, no. 2 (April 1994): 155–69.

————. *Sages, Stories, Authors, and Editors in Rabbinic Babylonia*. Brown Judaica Studies 300. Atlanta, Ga.: Scholars Press, 1994.

Kannengiesser, Charles. "Alexander and Arius of Alexandria: The Last Ante-Nicene Theologians." *Compostellanum* 35, no. 1–2 (1990): 391–403.

Kasher, Menahem. *Hagadah Shel Pesaḥ Lel Shimurim*. Jerusalem: Bet Torah shelemah, 1982.

Kelly, J. N. D. *Early Christian Doctrines*. Rev. ed. New York: Harper and Row, 1978.

Kienle, W. von. "Die Berichte über die Sukzessionen der Philosophen in der hellenistischen und spätantiken Literatur." Berlin: Freiuniversität, 1961.

Kimelman, Reuven. "Birkat Ha-Minim and the Lack of Evidence for an Anti-Christian Jewish Prayer in Late Antiquity." In *Aspects of Judaism in the Greco-Roman Period*, edited by E. P. Sanders, A. I. Baumgarten, and Alan Mendelson. Jewish and Christian Self-Definition 2: 226–44, 391–403. Philadelphia: Fortress Press, 1981.

King, Karen L. *What Is Gnosticism?* Cambridge, Mass.: Harvard University Press, 2003.

King, Richard. *Orientalism and Religion: Postcolonial Theory, India and the Mystic East*. London: Routledge, 1999.

Kister, Menahem. *Iyunim be-Avot de-R. Natan Nosaḥ, Arikhah u-Farshanut*. Jerusalem: Ha-Universitah ha-Ivrit, ha-Hug la-Talmud Yad Yitshak Ben Tsevi, ha-Makhon le-Heker Erets-Yisrael ve-Yishuvah, 1998.

————. " 'Let Us Make a Man'—Observations on the Dynamics of Monotheism." In Hebrew. In *Issues in Talmudic Research: Conference Commemorating the Fifth Anniversary of the Passing of Ephraim E. Urbach, 2 December 1996*, 28–65. Jerusalem: Israel Academy of Sciences, 2001.

Klawans, Jonathan. "Notions of Gentile Impurity in Ancient Judaism." *AJS Review* 20, no. 2 (1995): 285–312.

Klein, Michael L., ed. *The Fragment-Targums of the Pentateuch According to Their Extant Sources*. Translated by Michael L. Klein. Analecta Biblica. Rome: Biblical Institute Press, 1980.

Kline, Moshe. "The Art of Writing the Oral Tradition: Leo Strauss, the Maharal of Prague, and Rabbi Judah the Prince." Jerusalem, 1998. www.chaver.com/Torah/Articles/The Art-H.HTM.

Koch, Glenn Alan. "A Critical Investigation of Epiphanius' Knowledge of the Ebionites: A Translation and Critical Discussion of *Panarion* 30." Ph.D. diss., University of Pennsylvania, 1976.

Koester, Craig. "The Origin and Significance of the Flight to Pella Tradition." *Catholic Biblical Quarterly* 51 (1989): 90–106.

Koester, Helmut. "Ancient Christian Gospels: Their History and Development." Harrisburg, Pa.: Trinity Press International, 1990.

Kofsky, Arieh. "Mamre: A Case of a Regional Cult?" In *Sharing the Sacred: Religious Contacts and Conflicts in the Holy Land, First–Fifteenth Centuries CE*, edited by Guy Stroumsa and Arieh Kofsky, 19–30. Jerusalem: Yad Ben Zvi, 1998.

Koltun-Fromm, Naomi. "Psalm 22's Christological Interpretive Tradition in Light of Christian Anti-Jewish Polemic." *Journal of Early Christian Studies* 6, no. 1 (Spring 1998): 37–57.

Kraemer, David Charles. *The Mind of the Talmud: An Intellectual History of the Bavli*. New York: Oxford University Press, 1990.

Krafft-Ebing, R. von. *Psychopathia Sexualis: a Medico-Forensic Study*. New York: Putnam, 1965.

Krauss, Shmuel. *Antoninus und Rabbi*. Frankfurt am Main: Sanger and Friedberg, 1910.

Kronfeld, Chana. *On the Margins of Modernism: Decentering Literary Dynamics*. Contraversions. Berkeley and Los Angeles: University of California Press, 1996.

Kugel, James. *The Idea of Biblical Poetry*. New Haven, Conn.: Yale University Press, 1981.

Labov, William. "The Boundaries of Words and Their Meanings." In *New Ways of Analyzing Variation in English*, edited by Charles-James N. Bailey and Roger. W. Shuy, 340–73. Washington, D.C.: Georgetown University Press, 1973.

Lakoff, George. *Women, Fire, and Dangerous Things: What Categories Reveal About the Mind*. Chicago: University of Chicago Press, 1987.

Laupot, Eric. "Tacitus' Fragment 2: The Anti-Roman Movement of the *Christiani* and the Nazoreans." *Vigiliae Christianae* 54, no. 3 (2000): 233–47.

Lauterbach, Jacob Zallel. *Rabbinic Essays*. New York: Ktav, 1973.

———. "Some Clarifications on the Mekhilta." In Hebrew. In *Sefer Klausner Maasaf le-Mada Ule-Sifrut Yafah Mugash le-Prof. Josef Klausner le-Yobel Ha-Shishim*, edited by N. H. Torczyner, A. Tcherikover, A. A. Kubed, and B. Shortman, 181–88. Tel-Aviv: Hozaat Va'ad-Hayobel, 1937.

———, ed. and trans. *Mekilta DeRabbi Ishmael*. 1934. Reprint, Philadelphia: Jewish Publishing Society, 1961.

Lawlor, Hugh Jackson, and John Ernest Leonard Oulton, trans. and eds. *Eusebius, Bishop of Caesarea, the Ecclesiastical History and the Martyrs of Palestine*. 2 vols. London: Society for Promoting Christian Knowledge, 1927.

Lederman, Yohanan. "Les évêques juifs de Jérusalem." *Revue biblique* 104 (1997): 211–22.

Levine, Lee I. "The Jewish Patriarch (Nasi) in Third Century Palestine." In *Aufstieg und Niedergang der Römischen Welt II, Principat 19,2*, 649–88. Berlin: Walter de Gruyter, 1979.

———. *Judaism and Hellenism in Antiquity: Conflict or Confluence*. The Samuel and Althea Stroum Lectures in Jewish Studies. Seattle: University of Washington Press, 1998.

———. *The Rabbinic Class of Roman Palestine in Late Antiquity*. New York: Jewish Theological Seminary of America, 1989.

———. "The Sages and the Synagogue in Late Antiquity: The Evidence of the Galilee." In *The Galilee in Late Antiquity*, edited by Lee I. Levine, 201–24. New York: Jewish Theological Seminary of America, 1992.

———. "The Status of the Patriarch in the Third and Fourth Centuries." *Journal of Jewish Studies* 47, no. 1 (Spring 1996): 1–32.

Levy, Evonne. *Propaganda and the Jesuit Baroque*. Berkeley and Los Angeles: University of California Press, 2003.

Lévy, Israel. "L'origine davidique de Hillel." *Revue des études Juives* 31 (1895): 202–11.

Lieberman, Saul. "The Martyrs of Caesarea." *Annuaire de l'institut de philologie et d'histoire orientales et slaves* 7 (1939): 395–446.

———. *Order Mo'ed*. Vol. 2 of *The Tosefta According to Codex Vienna, with Variants from Codices Erfurt, London, Genizah Mss. and Editio Princeps (Venice, 1521)*. New York: Jewish Theological Seminary of America, 1962.

———. *Order Mo'ed*. Vol. 3 of *Tosefta Ki-Fshuta: A Comprehensive Commentary on the Tosefta*. New York: Jewish Theological Seminary of America, 1962.

———. *Order Nashim.* Vol. 8 of *Tosefta Ki-Fshuta: A Comprehensive Commentary on the Tosefta.* New York: Jewish Theological Seminary of America, 1973.

———. *Order Zeraim.* Vol. 1 of *The Tosefta According to Codex Vienna, with Variants from Codices Erfurt, London, Genizah Mss. and Editio Princeps (Venice, 1521).* New York: Jewish Theological Seminary of America, 1955.

Liebes, Yehuda. "The Angels of the Shofar and the Yeshua Sar-Hapanim." In Hebrew. *Jerusalem Studies in Jewish Thought* 6, no. 1–2 (1987): 171–95.

———. "God and His Qualities." In Hebrew. *Tarbiz* 70, no. 1 (October–December 2000): 51–73.

———. *The Sin of Elisha: Four Who Entered Pardes and the Nature of Talmudic Mysticism.* In Hebrew. Jerusalem: Academon, 1990.

Liebeschuetz, J. H. W. G. *Antioch: City and Imperial Administration in the Later Roman Empire.* Oxford: Clarendon Press, 1972.

Lieu, Judith. "Accusations of Jewish Persecution in Early Christian Sources, with Particular Reference to Justin Martyr and the *Martyrdom of Polycarp.*" In *Tolerance and Intolerance in Early Judaism and Christianity,* edited by Graham N. Stanton and Guy G. Stroumsa, 279–95. Cambridge: Cambridge University Press, 1998.

———. "'I Am a Christian': Martyrdom and the Beginning of 'Christian' Identity." In *Neither Jew nor Greek? Constructing Christian Identity.* Edinburgh: T & T Clark, 2003.

———. *Image & Reality: The Jews in the World of the Christians in the Second Century.* Edinburgh: T & T Clark, 1996.

Lightfoot, R. H. *St. John's Gospel: A Commentary.* Edited by C. F. Evans. Oxford: Oxford University Press, 1956.

Lim, Richard. *Public Disputation, Power, and Social Order in Late Antiquity.* Transformations of the Classical Heritage. Berkeley and Los Angeles: University of California Press, 1994.

Limberis, Vasiliki. "'Religion' as the Cipher for Identity: The Cases of Emperor Julian, Libanius, and Gregory Nazianzus." *Harvard Theological Review* 93, no. 4 (2000): 373–400.

Linder, Amnon. *The Jews in Roman Imperial Legislation.* Edited and translated by Amnon Linder. Detroit, Mich. and Jerusalem: Wayne State University Press and Israel Academy of Sciences and Humanities, 1987.

Loomba, Ania. *Colonialism/postcolonialism.* New Critical Idiom. London: Routledge, 1998.

Loraux, Nicole. *The Children of Athena: Athenian Ideas About Citizenship and the Division Between the Sexes.* Princeton, N.J.: Princeton University Press, 1983.

Lorenz, Rudolf. *Arius judaizans? Untersuchungen zur dogmengeshichtlichen Einordnung des Arius.* Göttingen: Vandenhoek and Ruprecht, 1979.

Luhmann, Niklas. *Love as Passion: The Codification of Intimacy.* Cultural Memory in the Present. Stanford, Calif.: Stanford University Press, 1998.

Lüdemann, Gerd. "The Successors of Pre-70 Jerusalem Christianity: A Critical Evaluation of the Pella-Tradition." In *Jewish and Christian Self-Definition,* edited by E. P. Sanders, 161–73. Philadelphia: Fortress Press, 1980.

Lyman, J. Rebecca. *Christology and Cosmology: Models of Divine Activity in Origen, Eusebius, and Athanasius.* Oxford Theological Monographs. Oxford: Oxford University Press and Clarendon Press, 1993.

————. "The Making of a Heretic: The Life of Origen in Epiphanius *Panarion* 64." *Studia Patristica* 31 (1997): 445–51.

————. "Origen as Ascetic Theologian: Orthodoxy and Heresy in the Fourth-Century Church." In *Origeniana Septima: Origenes in den Auseinandersetzungen des 4. Jahrhunderts*, edited by W. A. Bienert and U. Kühneweg. Bibliotheca Ephemeridum Theologicarum Lovaniensium 137, 187–94. Leuven: Peeters, 1999.

————. "The Politics of Passing: Justin Martyr's Conversion as a Problem of 'Hellenization.'" In *Conversion in Late Antiquity and the Early Middle Ages*, edited by Anthony Grafton and Kenneth Mills. Rochester, N.Y.: University of Rochester Press, forthcoming.

Macgregor, G. H. C. *The Gospel of John.* The Moffatt New Testament Commentary. London: Hodder and Stoughton, 1936.

Mack, Burton L. *Logos und Sophia: Untersuchungen zur Weisheitstheologie im hellenistischen Judentum.* Studien zur Umwelt des Neuen Testaments. Göttingen: Vandenhoeck and Ruprecht, 1973.

————. "Wisdom Makes a Difference: Alternatives to 'Messianic' Configurations." In *Judaisms and Their Messiahs at the Turn of the Christian Era*, edited by Jacob Neusner, William Scott Green, and Ernest S. Frerichs, 15–48. Cambridge: Cambridge University Press, 1987.

Mann, Jacob. *The Bible as Read and Preached in the Old Synagogue: A Study in the Cycles of the Readings from Torah and Prophets, as Well as from Psalms, and in the Structure of the Midrashic Homilies.* New York: Ktav, 1971.

Manns, Frédéric. "Joseph de Tibériade, un judéo-chrétien du quatrième siècle." In *Christian archaeology in the Holy Land, New Discoveries: Essays in Honour of Virgilio C. Corbo, OFM*, edited by Giovanni Claudio Bottini, 553–60. Jerusalem: Franciscan Printing Press, 1990.

Markschies, Christoph. *Valentinus Gnosticus? Untersuchungen zur valentinianischen Gnosis mit einem Kommentar zu den Fragmenten Valentins.* Wissenschaftliche Untersuchungen zum Neuen Testament. Tübingen: J. C. B. Mohr, 1992.

Markus, Robert A. *The End of Ancient Christianity.* Cambridge: Cambridge University Press, 1990.

Marmorstein, Arthur. *The Old Rabbinic Doctrine of God.* London: Oxford University Press, 1937.

Martin, Dale. *The Corinthian Body.* New Haven, Conn.: Yale University Press.

Martyn, James Louis. *History and Theology in the Fourth Gospel.* Nashville, Tenn.: Abingdon, 1979.

Mason, Steve. *Flavius Josephus on the Pharisees: A Composition-Critical Study.* Studia Post-Biblica 39. Leiden: E. J. Brill, 1991.

Matthews, John. *Laying Down the Law: A Study of the Theodosian Code.* New Haven, Conn.: Yale University Press, 2000.

Mattingly, Harold. "The Origin of the Name Christiani." *Journal of Theological Studies* n.s. 9 (1958): 26–37.

McLynn, Neil. "Christian Controversy and Violence in the Fourth Century." *Kodai* 3 (1992): 15–44.

McNamara, Martin. "Logos of the Fourth Gospel and *Memra* of the Palestinian Targum." *Expository Times* 79 (1968): 115–17.

McNamara, Martin, trans. *Targum Neofiti 1: Exodus*. Notes by Robert Hayward. The Aramaic Bible. Edinburgh: T & T Clark, 1994.

Meir, Ofra. *Rabbi Judah the Patriarch: Palestinian and Babylonian Portrait of a Leader*. In Hebrew. Sifriyat "Helal Ben-Hayim." Tel-Aviv: Hakibbutz Hameuchad, 1999.

Melito of Sardis. *On Pascha and Fragments*. Edited by S. G. Hall. Oxford Early Christian Texts. Oxford: Oxford University Press, 1979.

Miles, Jack. *Christ: A Crisis in the Life of God*. New York: Alfred A. Knopf, 2001.

Milikovsky, Chaim. "Gehenna and 'Sinners of Israel' in the Light of Seder 'Olam." In Hebrew. *Tarbiz* 55, no. 3 (April–June 1986): 311–43.

Miller, Patricia Cox. *The Poetry of Thought in Late Antiquity: Essays in Imagination and Religion*. Burlington, Vt.: Ashgate, 2001.

Mirsky, Aaron. *Yesode Ṣurot Ha-Piyuṭ Ṣemiḥatan we-Hitpatḥutan Šel Ṣurot Ha-Širah Ha-Ereṣ-Yisre'elit Ha-Qeduma*. Jerusalem: Magnes Press, 1985.

Moore, George Foot. *Judaism in the First Centuries of the Christian Era*. Vol. 1. New York: Schocken, 1971.

Mosshammer, A. "Disclosing but Not Disclosed: Gregory of Nyssa as Deconstructionist." In *Studien zu Gregor von Nyssa und der Christliche Spätantike: Supplements to Vigiliae Christianae*, edited by Hubertus R. Drobner and Christoph Klock, 103–20. Leiden: E. J. Brill, 1990.

Motyer, Stephen. *Your Father the Devil? A New Approach to John and "the Jews."* Paternoster Biblical and Theological Studies. Carlisle, England: Paternoster Press, 1997.

Mowinckel, Sigmund Olaf Plytt. *He That Cometh: The Messiah Concept in the Old Testament and Later Judaism*. Translated by G. W. Anderson. Oxford: B. Blackwell, 1956.

Myers, David N. *Re-Inventing the Jewish Past: European Jewish Intellectuals and the Zionist Return to History*. Studies in Jewish History. New York: Oxford University Press, 1995.

Naeh, Shlomo. "'Make Yourself Many Rooms': Another Look at the Utterances of the Sages About Controversy." In Hebrew. In *Renewing Jewish Commitment: The Work and Thought of David Hartman*, edited by Avi Sagi and Zvi Zohar, 851–75. Jerusalem: Shalom Hartman Institute and Hakkibutz Hameuchad, 2001.

———. "On Structures of Memory (and the Forms of Text) in Rabbinic Literature." In Hebrew. Forthcoming.

Nagy, Gregory. *Poetry as Performance: Homer and Beyond*. Cambridge: Cambridge University Press, 1996.

Najman, Hindy. *Seconding Sinai: Mosaic Discourse in Second-Temple Judaism*. Leiden: E. J. Brill, 2003.

Needham, R. "Polythetic Classification: Convergence and Consequences." *Man* n.s. 10 (1975): 349–69.

Nemoy, Leon. *Karaite Anthology, Excerpts from the Early Literature*. Yale Judaica Series, vol. 7. New Haven, Conn.: Yale University Press, 1969.

Neusner, Jacob. *Aphrahat and Judaism: The Christian-Jewish Argument in Fourth-Century Iran*. Studia Post-Biblica. Leiden: E. J. Brill, 1971.

———. *The Documentary Foundation of Rabbinic Culture: Mopping up After Debates with Gerald L. Bruns, S. J. D. Cohen, Arnold Maria Goldberg, Susan Handelman, Christine Hayes, James Kugel, Peter Schaefer, Eliezer Segal, E. P. Sanders, and Lawrence H. Schiffman*. Atlanta, Ga.: Scholars Press, 1995.

———. *Eliezer Ben Hyrcanus: The Tradition and the Man.* 2 vols. Studies in Judaism in Late Antiquity, vol. 3–4. Leiden: E. J. Brill, 1973.

———. "The Formation of Rabbinic Judaism: Yavneh (Jamnia) from A.D. 70 to 100." In *Principat: Religion (Judentum: Pälastinisches Judentum [Forts.]),* edited by Wolfgang Haase. Aufstieg und Niedergang der Römischen Welt, 3–42. Berlin: Walter de Gruyter, 1979.

———. *Frequently Asked Questions About Rabbinic Judaism.* Peabody, Mass.: Hendrickson, 2003.

———. "Judaism After the Destruction of the Temple: An Overview." In *Formative Judaism: Religious, Historical, and Literary Studies, Third Series: Torah, Pharisees, and Rabbis,* vol. 46. Brown Judaica Series, 83–98. Chico, Ca.: Scholars Press, 1983.

———. *Judaism and Christianity in the Age of Constantine: History, Messiah, Israel, and the Initial Confrontation.* Chicago Studies in the History of Judaism. Chicago: The University of Chicago Press, 1987.

———. *Judaism in Society: The Evidence of the Yerushalmi: Toward the Natural History of a Religion.* Atlanta, Ga.: Scholars Press, 1991.

———. *Reading and Believing: Ancient Judaism and Contemporary Gullibility.* Brown Judaic Studies. Atlanta, Ga.: Scholars Press, 1986.

———. *Why No Gospels in Talmudic Judaism?* Brown Judaic Studies, no. 135. Atlanta, Ga.: Scholars Press, 1988.

Newman, Hillel. "Jerome's Judaizers." *Journal of Early Christian Studies* 9, no. 4 (December 2001): 421–52.

Niehoff, Maren. *Philo on Jewish Identity and Culture in Roman Egypt.* Tübingen: Mohr Siebeck, 2002.

———. "What Is in a Name? Philo's Mystical Philosophy of Language." *Jewish Studies Quarterly* 2 (1995): 220–52.

Oppenheimer, Aharon. *The Am Ha'areṣ: A Study in the Social History of the Jewish People.* Arbeiten zur Literatur und Geschichte des Hellenistischen Judentums. Leiden: E. J. Brill, 1977.

Origen. *On First Principles.* Translated and introduced by G. W. Butterworth, with an introduction by Henri de Lubac. Gloucester, Mass.: Peter Smith, 1973.

———. *The Song of Songs: Commentary and Homilies.* Translated by R. P. Lawson. Ancient Christian Writers 26. Westminster, Md.: Newman Press, 1957.

Pagels, Elaine. "Exegesis of Genesis 1 in the Gospels of Thomas and John." *Journal of Biblical Literature* 118, no. 3 (1999).

———. "Irenaeus, the 'Canon of Truth,' and the *Gospel of John*: 'Making a Difference' Through Hermeneutics and Ritual." *Vigiliae Christianae* 56, no. 4 (2002): 339–71.

Pearson, Birger. "The Emergence of the Christian Religion." In *The Emergence of the Christian Religion: Essays on Early Christianity,* 7–22. Harrisburg, Pa.: Trinity Press International, 1997.

———. "Friedländer Revisited." *Studia Philonica* 2 (1973): 23–39.

Perkins, Pheme. "Ordering the Cosmos: Irenaeus and the Gnostics." In *Nag Hammadi, Gnosticism, and Early Christianity,* edited by Charles W. Hedrick and Robert Hodgson Jr., 221–38. Peabody, Mass.: Hendrickson, 1986.

Perloff, Marjorie. "Cultural Liminality/aesthetic Closure? The 'Interstitial Perspective' of Homi Bhabha." http://wings.buffalo.edu/epc/authors/perloff/bhabha/html.

Pharr, Clyde. *The Theodosian Code and Novels, and the Sirmondian Constitutions: A*

Translation with Commentary, Glossary, and Bibliography. In collaboration with Theresa Sherrer Davidson and Mary Brown Pharr, with an introduction by C. Dickerman Williams. Princeton, N.J.: Princeton University Press, 1952.

Philo. "The Changing of Names." In *Philo*, vol. 5, translated by F. H. Colson and G. A. Whitaker, 128–281. Loeb Classical Library. London: Heinemann, 1934.

Pines, Shlomo. "'From Darkness to Light': Parallels to *Haggada* Texts in Hellenistic Literature." In Hebrew. In *Studies in Literature Presented to Simon Halkin*, edited by Ezra Fleischer, 173–79. Jerusalem: Magnes Press, 1973.

———. "God, the Glory and the Angels According to a Theological System of the Second Century." In Hebrew. *Jerusalem Studies in Jewish Thought* 6, no. 3–4 (1987): 1–14.

———. "Notes on the Parallelism Between Syriac Terminology and Mishnaic Hebrew." In Hebrew. In *Yaakov Friedman Memorial Volume*, 205–13. Jerusalem: Institute for Jewish Studies, 1974.

Plutarch. "Ad Principem Ineruditem." In *Moralia X*, translated by Harold North Fowler, 52–71. Cambridge, Mass.: Harvard University Press, 1936.

———. "De Iside et Osiride." In *Moralia V*, translated by Frank Cole Babbitt. Cambridge, Mass.: Harvard University Press, 1936.

Pourkier, Aline. *L'Hérésiologie chez Épiphane de Salamine.* Christianisme Antique 4. Paris: Éditions Beauchesne, 1992.

Pratt, Mary Louise. *Imperial Eyes: Travel Writing and Transculturation.* London: Routledge, 1992.

Prigent, Pierre. *Justin et l'Ancien Testament: L'argumentation Scripturaire du traité de Justin contre toutes les hérésies comme source principale du dialogue avec Tryphon et de la première Apologie.* Paris: J. Gabalda, 1964.

Pritz, Ray A. *Nazarene Jewish Christianity: From the End of the New Testament Period Until Its Disappearance in the Fourth Century.* Jerusalem: Magnes Press, 1992.

Qimron, Elisha, and John Strugnell, eds. and trans. *Qumran Cave 4.5: Miqṣat Maʿśe Ha-Torah.* In collaboration with Y. Sussmann, contribution by A. Yardeni. Discoveries in the Judaean Desert. Oxford: Oxford University Press, at the Clarendon Press, 1994.

Rajak, Tessa. "Dying for the Law: The Martyr's Portrait in Jewish-Greek Literature." In *Portraits: Biographical Representation in the Greek and Latin Literature of the Roman Empire*, edited by M. J. Edwards and Simon Swain, 39–67. Oxford: Clarendon Press, 1997.

Rebillard, Éric. "A New Style of Argument in Christian Polemic: Augustine and the Use of Patristic Citations." *Journal of Early Christian Studies* 8, no. 4 (2000): 559–78.

Reider, Joseph. *The Book of Wisdom: An English Translation with Introduction and Commentary.* Dropsie College Edition: Jewish Apocryphal Literature. New York: Harper and Brothers, 1957.

Reiling, Johannes. "The Use of Pseudoprophètes in the Septuagint, Philo and Josephus." *Novum Testamentum* 13 (1971): 147–56.

Reiner, Elchanan. "From Joshua to Jesus: The Transformation of a Biblical Story to a Local Myth: A Chapter in the Religious Life of the Galilean Jew." In *Sharing the Sacred: Religious Contacts and Conflicts in the Holy Land, First–Fifteenth Centuries* CE, edited by Guy Stroumsa and Arieh Kofsky, 223–71. Jerusalem: Yad Ben Zvi, 1998.

Richard, M. "Les florilèges diphysites du Ve et VIe siècle." In *Das Konzil von Chalkedon,*

Geschichte und Gegenwart, edited by Alois Grillmeier and Heinrich Bacht, 1:721–48. Würzburg: Echter-Verlag, 1951.

Ringe, Sharon H. *Wisdom's Friends: Community and Christology in the Fourth Gospel.* Louisville, Ky.: Westminster/John Knox Press, 1999.

Robinson, James A. T. "The Relationship of the Prologue to the Gospel of St. John." *New Testament Studies* 9 (March 1962): 120–29.

Robinson, Thomas A. *The Bauer Thesis Examined: The Geography of Heresy in the Early Christian Church.* Studies in the Bible and Early Christianity. Lewiston, N.Y.: Edwin Mellen Press, 1988.

Rokeah, David. *Jews, Pagans, and Christians in Conflict.* Studia Post-Biblica. Jerusalem and Leiden: Magnes Press, Hebrew University and E. J. Brill, 1982.

———. *Justin Martyr and the Jews.* In Hebrew. "Kuntresim": Texts and Studies 84. Jerusalem: Hebrew University, Dinur Center for Research in Jewish History, 1998.

———. *Justin Martyr and the Jews.* Jewish and Christian Perspectives Series. Leiden: E. J. Brill, 2002.

Rosch, Eleanor. *Basic Objects in Natural Categories.* Berkeley: University of California, Language Behavior Research Laboratory, 1975.

Roseman, Philipp W. *Understanding Scholastic Thought with Foucault.* The New Middle Ages. New York: St. Martin's Press, 1999.

Rosenthal, Eliezer Shimshon. "Tradition and Innovation in the *Halakha* of the Sages." In Hebrew with English summary. *Tarbiz* 63, no. 3 (April–June 1994): 321–74, xix–xx.

Rubenstein, Jeffrey L. *The Culture of the Babylonian Talmud.* Baltimore, Md.: Johns Hopkins University Press, 2003.

———. *Talmudic Stories: Narrative Art, Composition, and Culture.* Baltimore, Md.: Johns Hopkins University Press, 1999.

———. "The Thematization of Dialectics in Bavli Aggada." *Journal of Jewish Studies* 53, no. 2 (2002): 1–14.

Ruether, Rosemary Radford. "Judaism and Christianity: Two Fourth-Century Religions." *Sciences Religieuses/Studies in Religion* 2 (1972): 1–10.

Rufinus. *The Church History of Rufinus of Aquileia, Books 10 and 11.* Translated by Philip R. Amidon. New York: Oxford University Press, 1997.

Runia, David T. *Philo in Early Christian Literature: A Survey.* Compendia rerum Iudaicarum ad Novum Testamentum. Minneapolis, Minn.: Fortress Press, 1993.

———. "Philo of Alexandria and the Greek *Hairesis*-Model." *Vigiliae Christianae* 53, no. 2 (May 1999): 117–47.

———. "Review of Le Boulluec." *Vigiliae Christianae* 42 (1988): 188–207.

———. "'Where, Tell Me, is the Jew . . . ?' Basil, Philo and Isidore of Pelusium." *Vigiliae Christianae* 46, no. 2 (June 1992): 172–89.

Sachot, Maurice. "Comment le Christianisme est-il devenu *religio.*" *Revue des sciences religiuses* 59 (1985): 95–118.

———. "*«Religio/Superstitio»*. Historique d'une subversion et d'un retournement." *Revue d'histoire des religions* 208, no. 4 (1991): 355–94.

Saldarini, Anthony. *Pharisees, Scribes, and Sadducees in Palestinian Society.* Edinburgh: T & T Clark, 1989.

———. *Scholastic Rabbinism: A Literary Study of the Fathers According to Rabbi Nathan.* Chico, Calif.: Scholars Press, 1982.

Salzman, Michele R. "'Superstitio' in the Codex Theodosianus and the Persecution of Pagans." *Vigiliae Christianae* 41 (1987): 172–88.

Sarason, Richard S. "On the Use of Method in the Modern Study of Jewish Liturgy." In *Approaches to Ancient Judaism: Theory and Practice*, edited by W. S. Green, 97–172. Missoula, Mont.: Scholars Press, 1978.

Schenke, Hans-Martin. *Der Gott "Mensch" in der Gnosis ein religionsgeschichtlicher Beitrag zur Diskussion über die paulinische Anschauung von der Kirche als Leib Christi.* Göttingen: Vandenhoeck and Ruprecht, 1962.

Schiappa, Edward. *The Beginnings of Rhetorical Theory in Classical Greece.* New Haven, Conn.: Yale University Press, 1999.

Schiffman, Lawrence H. "At the Crossroads: Tannaitic Perspectives on the Jewish-Christian Schism." In *Aspects of Judaism in the Greco-Roman Period*, edited by E. P. Sanders, A. I. Baumgarten, and Alan Mendelson. Jewish and Christian Self-Definition, Volume 2, 115–56; 338–52. Philadelphia: Fortress Press, 1981.

———. "The Samaritans in Tannaitic Halakhah." *Jewish Quarterly Review* 75 (1985): 323–50.

———. *Who Was a Jew? Rabbinic and Halakhic Perspectives on the Jewish Christian Schism.* Hoboken, N.J.: Ktav, 1985.

Schnackenburg, Rudolf. *The Gospel According to St. John.* London: Burns & Oates; New York: Herder & Herder, 1968.

Schoedel, William R. *Ignatius of Antioch: A Commentary on the Letters of Ignatius of Antioch.* Edited by Helmut Koester, translated and edited by William R. Schoedel. Hermeneia—a Critical and Historical Commentary on the Bible. Philadelphia: Fortress Press, 1985.

Scholem, Gershom. *Jewish Gnosticism, Merkabah Mysticism and Talmudic Tradition.* 2d ed. New York: Jewish Theological Seminary of America, 1965.

Schremer, Adiel. "Papyrus Zeelim 13 and the Question of the Right of Women to Divorce Their Husbands in the Early Jewish Halakha." In Hebrew. *Zion* 63 (1998): 377–91.

———. "Qumran Polemic on Marital Law: CD 4:20–5:11 and Its Social Background." In *The Damascus Document: A Centennial of Discovery*, edited by Joseph M. Baumgarten, Esther G. Chazon, and Avital Pinnick, 147–60. Leiden: E. J. Brill, 2000.

———. "'[T]He[y] Did Not Read in the Sealed Book': Qumran Halakhic Revolution and the Emergence of Torah Study in Second Temple Judaism." In *Historical Perspectives: From the Hasmoneans to Bar Kochba in the Light of the Dead Sea Scrolls.* Edited by David Goodblatt, Avital Pinnick, and Daniel R. Schwartz, 105–26. Leiden: E. J. Brill, 2001.

Schulz, Siegfried. *Untersuchungen zur Menschensohn-Christologie im Johannesevangelium zugleich ein Beitrag zur Methodengeschichte der Auslegung des 4. Evangeliums.* Göttingen: Vandenhoeck and Ruprecht, 1957.

Schürer, Emil. *Geschichtedes jüdischen Volkes im Zeitalter Jesu Christi.* 4. 1901. Reprint, Hildesheim: Olms, 1964.

Schüssler Fiorenza, Elisabeth. *Jesus, Miriam's Child, Sophia's Prophet: Critical Issues in Feminist Christology.* New York: Continuum, 1994.

Schwartz, Seth. *Imperialism and Jewish Society from 200 B.C.E. to 640 C.E.* Princeton, N.J.: Princeton University Press, 2001.

Scott, Martin. *Sophia and the Johannine Jesus.* Journal for the Study of the New Testament. Sheffield: JSOT Press, 1992.

Segal, Alan F. *The Other Judaisms of Late Antiquity*. Brown Judaic Studies 127. Atlanta: Scholars Press, 1987.

———. *Two Powers in Heaven: Early Rabbinic Reports About Christianity and Gnosticism*. Studies in Judaism in Late Antiquity 25. Leiden: E. J. Brill, 1977.

Shapira, Haim. "The Deposition of Rabban Gamaliel: Between History and Legend." In Hebrew with English summary. *Zion* 64, no. 1 (1999): 5–38.

Shechter, Solomon, ed. *Aboth de Rabbi Nathan*. 1887. Reprint, New York: Philipp Feldheim, 1967.

Shemesh, Aharon. "The Dispute Between the Pharisees and the Sadducees on the Death Penalty." In Hebrew. *Tarbiz* 70, no. 1 (October–December 2000): 17–33.

———. "Expulsion and Exclusion in the *Community Rule* and the *Damascus Document*." *Dead Sea Discoveries* 9, no. 1 (2002): 44–74.

———. "Law and Prophecy: False Prophet and Rebellious Elder." In Hebrew. In *Renewing Jewish Commitment: The Work and Thought of David Hartman*, edited by Avi Sagi and Zvi Zohar, 923–41. Jerusalem: Shalom Hartman Institute and Hakkibutz Hameuchad, 2001.

———. "'The One Who Divides Between the Children of Light and the Children of Darkness, Between Israel and the Nations.'" In Hebrew. In *Atara l'Haim: Studies in the Talmud and Medieval Rabbinic Literature in Honor of Professor Haim Zalman Dimitrovsky*, edited by Daniel Boyarin, Shamma Friedman, Marc Hirshman, Menahem Schmelzer, and Israel M. Ta-Shma, 209–20. Jerusalem: Magnes Press, 2000.

———. "The Origins of the Laws of Separatism: Qumran Literature and Rabbinic Halacha." *Revue de Qumran* 18, no. 2 (December 1997): 223–41.

———. *Punishment and Sins from the Bible to Rabbinic Literature*. In Hebrew. Jerusalem: Magnes Press, 2003.

Shemesh, Aharon, and Cana Werman. "Halakhah at Qumran: Genre and Authority." *Dead Sea Discoveries* (2002). Forthcoming.

Simon, Marcel. "From Greek Hairesis to Christian Heresy." In *Mélanges R. M. Grant, Early Christian Literature and the Classical Intellectual Tradition*, edited by W. R. Schoedel and R. L. Wilken. Théologie Historique 53, 101–16. Paris: Éditions Beauchesne, 1979.

———. *Jewish Sects at the Time of Jesus*. Minneapolis, Minn.: Fortress Press, 1967.

Skarsaune, Oskar. *The Proof from Prophecy—a Study in Justin Martyr's Proof-Text Tradition: Text-Type, Provenance, Theological Profile*. Leiden: E. J. Brill, 1987.

Smith, Jonathan Z. "Differential Equations: On Constructing the 'Other.'" Lecture, Tempe, Arizona, 1992. Pamphlet.

———. *Drudgery Divine: On the Comparison of Early Christianities and the Religions of Late Antiquity*. Chicago Studies in the History of Judaism. Chicago: University of Chicago Press, 1990.

Smith, Wilfred Cantwell. *The Meaning and End of Religion*. London: SPCK, 1978.

Stein, Dina. *Folklore Elements in Late Midrash: A Folkloristic Perspective on Pirkei de Rabbi Eliezer*. In Hebrew with English abstract. Dissertation, Hebrew University, 1998.

Stemberger, Günter. *Jews and Christians in the Holy Land: Palestine in the Fourth Century*. Edinburgh: T & T Clark, 1999.

———. "Die sogennante 'Synode von Jabne' und das frühe Christentum." *Kairos* 19 (1977): 14–21.

Stern, David. "Forms of Midrash II: Homily and the Language of Exegesis." In *Midrash and Theory*, 55–71. Evanston, Ill.: Northwestern University Press, 1996.

———. "Literary Criticism or Literary Homilies? Susan Handelman and the Contemporary Study of Midrash." *Prooftexts* 5 (1985): 96–103.

———. "Midrash and Indeterminacy." *Critical Inquiry* 15, no. 1 (Autumn 1988): 132–62.

———. *Midrash and Theory: Ancient Jewish Exegesis and Contemporary Literary Studies.* Rethinking Theory. Evanston, Ill.: Northwestern University Press, 1996.

———. "Moses-Cide: Midrash and Contemporary Literary Criticism." *Prooftexts* 4 (1984): 193–204.

Strack, Hermann, and Paul Billerbeck. *Kommentar zum Neuen Testament aus Talmud und Midrasch.* Munich: C. H. Beck, 1924.

Stroumsa, Gedaliahu. "Form(s) of God: Some Notes on Metatron and Christ." *Harvard Theological Review* 76 (1983): 269–88.

———. *Savoir et salut.* Paris: Éditions du Cerf, 1992.

Stroumsa, Guy. "False Prophets in Early Christianity: Montanus, Mani, Muhammad." Conference presentation. Trinity University, Hartford, Conn., 1999.

Studer, Basil. *Trinity and Incarnation: The Faith of the Early Church.* Edited by Andrew Louth. Translated by Matthias Westerhoff. Collegeville, Minn.: Liturgical Press, 1993.

Suggit, John. "John XVII. 17. Ο ΛΟΓΟΣ Ο ΣΟΣ ΑΛΗΘΕΙΑ ΕΣΤΙΝ." *Journal of Theological Studies* 35 (1984): 104–17.

Sussmann, Yaakov. "The History of Halakha and the Dead Sea Scrolls: Preliminary Observations on *Miqsat Ma'ase Ha-torah (4QMMT)*." *Tarbiz* 59, no. 1–2 (Spring 1990): 11–76.

Swartz, Michael D. "*Alay Le-Shabbeaḥ*: A Liturgical Prayer in Ma'aśeh Merkabah." *Jewish Quarterly Review* 87, no. 2–3 (October–January 1986): 179–90.

Talmon, Shemaryahu. "The Emergence of Jewish Sectarianism in the Early Second Temple Period." In *Ancient Israelite Religion: Essays in Honor of Frank Moore Cross*, edited by Patrick D. Miller, Paul D. Hanson, and S. Dean McBride, 587–616. Philadelphia: Fortress Press, 1987.

Ta-Shma, Israel M. "The Origin and Place of 'aleinu le-Shabbeaḥ in the Daily Prayerbook: *Seder Ha-Ma'amadot* and Its Relation to the Conclusion of the Daily Service." In Hebrew. In *The Frank Talmage Memorial Volume*, vol. 1, edited by Barry Walfish, 85–98 (English précis 50–51). Haifa: University of Haifa Press, 1993.

Taylor, Joan E. *Christians and the Holy Places: The Myth of Jewish-Christian Origins.* Oxford: Clarendon Press and Oxford University Press, 1993.

Thompson, Leonard L. "The Martyrdom of Polycarp: Death in the Roman Games." *The Journal of Religion* 82, no. 1 (2002): 27–52.

Thornton, T. C. G. "The Stories of Joseph of Tiberias." *Vigiliae Christianae* 44 (1990): 54–63.

Thyen, Hartwig. "Das heil kommt von den Juden." In *Kirche. Festschrift für Günther Bornkamm zum 75. Geburtstag*, edited by D. Lührmann and G. Strecker, 163–83. Tübingen: Mohr Siebeck, 1980.

Tobin, Thomas H., S.J. *The Creation of Man: Philo and the History of Interpretation.* Catholic Biblical Quarterly Monograph Series, vol. 14. Washington, D.C.: Catholic Biblical Association of America, 1983.

———. "Logos." In *The Anchor Bible Dictionary* 4, 348–56. New York: Doubleday, 1992.

Torjesen, Karen Jo. *Hermeneutical Procedure and Theological Method in Origen's Exegesis.* Patristische Texte und Studien #28. Berlin: Walter de Gruyter, 1986.

Trevett, Christine. "Gender, Authority and Church History: A Case Study of Montanism." *Feminist Theology* 17 (January 1998): 9–24.

Troeltsch, Ernst. *The Social Teaching of the Christian Churches.* 2 vols. Translated by Olive Wyon. New York: Harper and Row, 1960.

Tropper, Amram. "*Tractate Avot* and Early Christian Succession Lists." In *The Ways That Never Parted,* edited by Peter Schaeffer. Berlin: Mohr Siebeck, 2002.

Turner, John D. "Sethian Gnosticism and Johannine Christianity." Conference presentation. Society of Biblical Literature. Denver, 2001.

Turner, John. "The Trimorphic Protennoia." In *Nag Hammadi Codices XI, XII, XIII,* edited by Charles W. Hedrick. Nag Hammadi Studies. Leiden: E. J. Brill, 1990.

Urbach, Ephraim E. *The Sages: Their Concepts and Beliefs.* 2 vols. Translated by Israel Abrahams. Jerusalem: Magnes Press, 1975.

Vaggione, Richard Paul. *Eunomius of Cyzicus and the Nicene Revolution.* Oxford Early Christian Studies. Oxford: Oxford University Press, 2000.

van der Horst, Pieter W. "The Birkat Ha-Minim in Recent Research." In *Hellenism-Judaism-Christianity: Essays on Their Interaction.* Contributions to Biblical Exegesis and Theology, 113–24. Leuven: Peeters, 1998.

Vermes, Geza. "Leviticus 18:21 in Ancient Jewish Bible Exegesis." In *Studies in Aggadah, Targum, and Jewish Liturgy in Memory of Joseph Heinemann,* edited by Jakob Josef Petuchowski, E. Fleischer, and Joseph Heinemann, 108–24. Jerusalem: Magnes Press and Hebrew Union College Press, 1981.

Vessey, Mark. "The Forging of Orthodoxy in Latin Christian Literature: A Case Study." *Journal of Early Christian Studies* 4, no. 4 (Winter 1996): 495–513.

———. "*Opus Imperfectum*: Augustine and His Readers, 426–435 A.D." *Vigiliae Christianae* 52, no. 3 (August 1998): 264–85.

Visotzky, Burton L. *Fathers of the World: Essays in Rabbinic and Patristic Literatures.* Wissenschaftliche Untersuchungen zum Neuen Testament 80. Tübingen: J. C. B. Mohr (Paul Siebeck), 1995.

Wallach, Luitpold. "The Colloquy of Marcus Aurelius with the Patriarch Judah 1." *Jewish Quarterly Review* 31 (1940): 259–86.

Weiss, Avraham. "On the Literary Development of the Amoraic Sugya in Its Formative Period." In Hebrew. In *Studies in Talmud,* 124–59. Jerusalem: Mossad Harav Kook, 1975.

Willett, Michael E. *Wisdom Christology in the Fourth Gospel.* San Francisco: Mellen Research University Press, 1992.

Williams, A. Lukyn, ed. and trans. *Justin Martyr: The Dialogue with Trypho.* Translations of Christian Literature. London: SPCK, 1930.

Williams, Michael Allen. *Rethinking "Gnosticism": An Argument for Dismantling a Dubious Category.* Princeton, N.J.: Princeton University Press, 1996.

Williams, Rowan. "Does It Make Sense to Speak of Pre-Nicene Orthodoxy?" In *The Making of Orthodoxy: Essays in Honour of Henry Chadwick,* edited by Rowan Williams, 1–23. Cambridge: Cambridge University Press, 1989.

Wilson, McL. R. "The Early History of the Exegesis of Gen. 1:26." *Studia Patristica* 1 (1957): 420–37.

Wilson, Stephen G. *Related Strangers: Jews and Christians 70–170 C.E.* Minneapolis, Minn.: Fortress Press, 1995.

Winston, David, trans. and commentary. *The Wisdom of Solomon*. Anchor Bible. Garden City, N.Y.: Doubleday, 1979.

———. *Logos and Mystical Theology in Philo of Alexandria*. Cincinnati, Ohio: Hebrew Union College Press, 1985.

Wolfson, Elliot R. *Along the Path: Studies in Kabbalistic Myth, Symbolism, and Hermeneutics*. Albany: State University of New York Press, 1995.

———. "God, the Demiurge, and the Intellect: On the Usage of the Word *Kol* in Abraham Ibn Ezra." *Revue des études juives* 149 (1990): 77–111.

———. "The Image of Jacob Engraved upon the Throne: Further Reflection on the Esoteric Doctrine of the German Pietists." In *Along the Path: Studies in Kabbalistic Myth, Symbolism, and Hermeneutics*, 1–62. Albany: State University of New York Press, 1995.

———. "Judaism and Incarnation: The Imaginal Body of God." In *Christianity in Jewish Terms*, edited by Tikva Simone Frymer-Kensky. Radical Traditions, 239–54. Boulder, Colo.: Westview Press, 2000.

———. *Through a Speculum That Shines: Vision and Imagination in Medieval Jewish Literature*. Princeton, N.J.: Princeton University Press, 1994.

———. "The Tree That Is All: Jewish-Christian Roots of a Kabbalistic Symbol in Sefer Ha-Bahir." In *Along the Path: Studies in Kabbalistic Myth, Symbolism, and Hermeneutics*, 63–88. Albany: State University of New York Press, 1995.

Yadin, Azzan. "The Hammer and the Rock: Polysemy and the School of Rabbi Ishma'el." *Jewish Studies Quarterly* 9 (2002): 1–17.

———. "*Shenei Ketuvim* and Rabbinic Intermediation." *Journal for the Study of Judaism in the Persian, Hellenistic, and Roman Periods* 33, no. 4 (2002): 386–410.

Young, Frances M. *The Making of the Creeds*. London and Philadelphia: SCM Press and Trinity Press International, 1991.

Young, Frances. "Did Epiphanius Know What He Meant by 'Heresy'?" *Studia Patristica* 17, no. 1 (1982): 199–205.

Young, Robert. *Colonial Desire: Hybridity in Theory, Culture, and Race*. London: Routledge, 1995.

Yuval, Israel Jacob. "Easter and Passover as Early Jewish-Christian Dialogue." In *Passover and Easter: Origin and History to Modern Times*, edited by Paul F. Bradshaw and Lawrence A. Hoffman. Two Liturgical Traditions, Volume 5, 127–60. Notre Dame, Ind.: University of Notre Dame Press, 1999.

———. "The Haggadah of Passover and Easter." In Hebrew. Tarbiz 65, no. 1 (October–December 1995): 5–29.

———. "Jews and Christians in the Middle Ages: Shared Myths, Common Language: Donatio Constantini and Donatio Vespasiani." In *Demonizing the Other: Antisemitism, Racism, and Xenophobia*, edited by Robert S. Wistrich. Studies in Antisemitism vol. 4, 88–107. Chur: Harwood Academic Publishers, 1999.

———. *Two Nations in Your Womb: Perceptions of Jews and Christians*. In Hebrew. Tel-Aviv: Alma/Am Oved, 2000.

———. *"Two Nations in Your Womb": Perceptions of Jews and Christians in the Middle Ages*. Berkeley and Los Angeles: University of California Press, 2003.

Zandee, Jan, ed. and trans. *The Teachings of Sylvanus (Nag Hammadi Codex VII, 4): Text, Translation, Commentary*. Egyptologische Uitgaven. Leiden: Nederlands Instituut voor het Nabije Oosten, 1991.

Zeitlin, Froma. "The Dynamics of Misogyny: Myth and Mythmaking in Aeschylus's *Oresteia*." In *Playing the Other; Gender and Society in Classical Greek Literature*, 87–119. Women in Culture and Society. Chicago: University of Chicago Press, 1996.

———. *Playing the Other; Gender and Society in Classical Greek Literature.* Women in Culture and Society. Chicago: University of Chicago Press, 1996.

Zhang, Longxi. *The Tao and the Logos: Literary Hermeneutics, East and West.* Post-Contemporary Interventions. Durham, N.C.: Duke University Press, 1992.

Žižek, Slavoj. "Introduction." In *Mapping Ideology*, 1–33. London: Verso, 1994.

Zuccotti, Ferdinando. *"Furor haereticorum" studi sul trattamento giuridico della follia e sulla persecuzione della eterodossia religiosa nella legislazione del tardo Impero Romano.* Milano: Giuffrè, 1992.

Zuckermandel, M. S., ed. *Tosephta: Based on the Erfurt and Vienna Codices, with Lieberman, Saul, "Supplement" to the Tosephta.* In Hebrew. Jerusalem: Bamberger and Wahrmann, 1937.

Index

Abbahu, Rabbi, 197–98, 223
Abraham, 15, 100–101
Abrams, Daniel, 138, 303 n.63
Abuya, Elisha ben, 142
Acts of the Apostles, 41, 54, 55, 213
Akavyah ben Mehalalel, Rabbi, 64–65, 178, 255 n.152
Akiva, Rabbi: and apostolic succession, 82, 83; and *hairesis*, 41; and Two Powers in Heaven, 56, 136, 139–45; and Yavneh legends, 165–66, 168–71, 173, 178–79
Alon, Gedaliah: and apostolic succession, 80, 268 nn. 28, 31, 32, 271 n.49; on curses, 258 n.163; and rabbinic historiography, 46–47, 244 nn. 43, 45; and Yavneh legends, 46–48, 259 n.172
Althusser, Louis, 9, 27
Amoraim, 151, 154
Amphilochius, 168
Anderson, Gary, 106–7
Antigonos of Sokho, 78
Antoninus Pius, 269 n.42
Aphrahat (Church Father), 156
Apocryphon of John, 110
Apologies (Justin Martyr), 100, 106, 114
apostolic succession, 30, 74–86; and Council of Nicaea, 196; and *diadoche*, 75–76, 85, 265 n.5; establishment of patriarchate, 82–83, 269 n.42, 270 n.43; and Hillel and Shammai, 78–82, 271 n.52; and influence of Christian heresiology/orthodoxy, 30, 74–76, 85–86, 265 nn. 5, 10, 272 n.60; and *paradosis*, 82–83, 85; and Pharisees, 42, 78, 83–84, 272 n.57; Rabbi Yehuda and Gamaliel-to-Yehuda line of succession, 79–83, 84–85, 269 n.42, 271 n.49; Torah

and, 74–75, 78–79, 83; Tractate Avot and succession list, 77–83, 84, 266 n.15, 271 n.52; women and, 60, 74, 78–79, 267 n.22; and Yavneh council, 196; and Yavneh legends, 76–77, 80, 81; Yohanan ben Zakkai and, 79–84, 271 nn. 49, 52
'Arakh, Rabbi El'azar ben, 180
Arcadius, 218
Arius Didymus, 115
Asad, Talal, 11, 15–16, 203, 204
Ashton, John, 286 n.2
Athanasius, 9, 42, 77, 160, 194–96, 255 n.152
Augustine, 72, 97, 194, 209
Avot of Rabbi Nathan, 60–61, 271 n.52

Baithuseans, 60–61
Bar Kokhba revolt, 91–92, 269 n.42
Barnard, L. W., 42
Barrett, C. K., 113, 132, 285 n.124
Basil of Caesarea, 161
Bauer, Walter, 3
Baumgarten, Albert: and apostolic succession, 82; on Jewish sectarianism, 50, 245 n.65, 246 n.76, 250 n.121; and Second Temple period, 45, 50, 243 n.40
Bavli. *See* Talmud, Babylonian
Beard, Mary, 21–22, 59, 215, 216
Ben Azzai, 143
Benjamin, Walter, 227
Ben Zoma, 143
Bereshith Rabba, 128, 240 nn. 15, 17
Berger, David, 13
Bhabha, Homi, 12, 15, 132, 208, 218, 234 n. 65
Bickerman, Elias, 265 n.10
binitarianism, Jewish: binitarian prayer in pre- and pararabbinic Judaism, 120–25;

binitarianism (*continued*)
and Logos theology, 120–27, 283 n.97,
295 n.89; and Metatron, 121–23; and
minim, 123; Mishna and evidence of,
123–24, 293 n.71; Targums and, 124,
125–27, 293 n.71; and Two Powers theology, 120–25, 131, 137, 138, 295 n.89, 305
n.76. *See also* Two Powers in Heaven
birkat hamminim, 67–73; and division of
Judaism and Christianity, 71–72, 261
n.90; Justin Martyr and, 67–68, 71,
72–73, 258 n.163, 260 nn. 174, 175; and
rabbinic heresiology, 67–73, 259 nn.
170–72, 260 n.175; and Yavneh, 68–69,
70, 259 nn. 170, 172
Black, Matthew, 42
Bloch, Marc, 46, 47–48, 208
Boccaccini, Gabriele, 52, 54, 247 n.93
Borgen, Peder, 94, 276 n.24
Boyarin, Chava, 77
Boyarin, Jonathan, 224–25
Brakke, David, 9
Brent, Allen, 30, 54, 85
Brown, Peter, 215
Brown, Raymond Edward, 99, 101, 110–11,
117, 278 n.46, 296 n.6
Buell, Denise Kimber, 324 n.19
Bultmann, Rudolf, and John's Gospel, 93,
98, 108–9, 118, 280 n.66, 281 n.73, 284
n.107, 285 n.118
Burns, Gerald, 224
Burrus, Virginia: on Athanasius and
fourth-century orthodoxy, 194–96; on
Gregory of Nyssa and
language/knowledge, 167; on language
and heresiology, 9; on Logos and Pla-
tonism, 115; on Logos theology, 93, 95,
275 n.18
Butler, Judith, 9

Castelli, Elizabeth, 205–6, 262 n.201, 325
n.25
Chesnut, Glenn, 307 n.104
Chidester, David, 13–14, 202, 204, 209
Christian empire: and creation of orthodoxy, 167–71, 192–96, 200, 321 n.147;
and crises of dissension, 160–61, 165,
167–71, 180–81; and dogmatism, 155–56;
and early rabbinic Judaism, 202–25;
new Christian heresiological discourse, 206–14; parallels/shared practices with rabbinic Judaism, 155–57,
160–61, 167–71, 192–200, 311 n.50; and
the Theodosian Code, 214–20. *See also*
Nicene Christianity; rabbinic Judaism
and Christian empire
Christian heresiology, 2, 10–13, 202–11;
and *birkat hamminim*, 67–73; Christianity and invention of religion, 11,
232 n.39; and creation of Christian
identity/self-definition, 2, 4–5, 66,
206–14, 230 n.4; and early rabbinic
heresiology, 5–6, 65–66; Epiphanius
and classification of heresies, 206–8,
211–14, 218, 327 nn. 70, 71; formal
anathematizing of heretics at Councils, 70–71; Gregory Nazianzen and,
203–5; Hellenistic/Roman society and,
202–11, 324 n.19; heresiological discourse, 2, 4–5, 66, 206–14, 230 n.4; and
ideological discourse, 26–27; Jewish
orthodoxy in reaction to, 213–14;
Judaism and, 71–73, 205–20, 262 n.201,
324 n.19; and Judaizing heretics, 207–14;
Julian and, 202–5, 209–10, 326 n.52;
and legitimation of rabbinic Judaism,
217–20, 329 n.102; and new definitions
of religion, 11, 203–6, 214–20; *religio*
and *superstitio*, 214–20; and semantic
shifts, 214–20; and the Theodosian
Code, 214–20. *See also* Justin Martyr
Church History (Eusebius), 91
Church History (Rufinus of Aquileia), 167
Clement of Alexandria, 264 n.3
Cohen, Shaye J. D., 5; and apostolic succession, 82, 266 n.15; and rabbinic
heresiology, 45, 243 n.42, 255 n.148, 263
n.204; on excommunication of
Eli'ezer, 174, 181–82; and Justin on
Pharisees and heresy, 42; and proto-
type semantics, 236 n.99; on Yavneh,
44–45, 76, 155, 180, 255 n.148
Constantine, 44, 243 n.36
Contra Apionem (Josephus), 53

Council of Antioch, 70
Council of Seleucia, 162
Culpepper, Alan, 282 n.86

Damascus Document, 51
Daniel and "Son of Man" passages, 136, 139–45
Dauphin, Claudine, 205
Davidson, Arnold I., 311 n.50
Davies, W. D., 286 n.130, 296 n.5
Day of Atonement, 186, 320 n.126
Dead Sea Scrolls, 49, 51. *See also* Qumran community
de Ausejo, Serafin, 111
Denzey, Nicola, 94–95, 276 n.31, 277 n.34
derasha: on pluralism/dissensus, 157–58, 185, 310 n.36; and Two Powers theology, 145
Derrida, Jacques, 1, 104, 115, 282 n.96, 316 n.99
Desjardin, Michel, 5–6
Deutsch, Nathaniel, 142, 305 n.76
diadoche, 75–76, 85, 265 n.5. *See also* apostolic succession
Dialogue with Trypho (Justin Martyr), 4, 28–29, 37–44; and *birkat hamminim* (curse of the heretics), 67–68, 71, 258 n.163, 260 nn. 174, 175; and Christian self-definition, 38–40, 238 n.2; *hairesis*, and Jews, 3–4, 40–44, 240 n.15, 241 n.18; on heresiology and apostolic succession, 265 n.5; and heresiology/ *hairesis*, 3–4, 39–44, 240 n.15, 241 n.18, 242 n.27; and Logos theology, 28–29, 38–40, 44, 106, 146; and Pharisees, 41, 42–43, 84, 241 n.19; on philosophy and *hairesis*, 242 n.27; writing of, 37–38, 238 n.2, 261 n.188
Díez Macho, Alejandro, 118–19, 131
Dionysius of Alexandria, 272 n.60
docetism, 293 n.75
Dodd, C. H., 111, 115, 280 n.66, 286 n.139, 296 n.3
Donnolo, Shabbatei, 293 n.73
Dormaskit, Rabbi Yose ben, 186
Dosa, Ḥanina ben, 319 n.116
Drake, Hal, 219, 243 n.36, 323 n.1

Dunn, James D. G.: on Bultmann, 109; and connection between John and first-century Judaism, 91, 93; on Jesus as *novum* of early Christianity, 105; on Sophia, 291 n.39; and Two Powers heresy, 306 n.90; on Wisdom Christology, 112

Ebionites, 207–10, 212–14
Edersheim, Alfred, 116–17
Edwards, Mark Julian, 106, 288 n.24
Eli‘ezer, Rabbi: excommunication of, 170, 173–74, 178, 181–82, 318 n.114; *minut* and arrest of, 221–22; reincorporation into community, 178–82; and Yavneh legends, 165–66, 168–74, 178–82, 186, 314 n.76, 318 nn. 110, 114
Eli‘ezer, Rabbi, son of Yose the Galilean, 129
Elm, Susanna, 202, 204
Elone Mamre, 14–15
Ephrem (Church Father), 156
Epicureans, 58, 249 nn. 115, 117, 118
Epiphanius: and Jewish *minim*, 71–72, 262 n.191; new definitions/classifications of heresy, 206–8, 211–14, 218, 327 nn. 70, 71
Epp, Eldon J., 93, 110, 281 n.79, 282 n.91, 286 n.131
Essenes, 52, 54, 59, 260 n.182
Eunomius, 166, 168, 321 n.147
Eusebius, 91, 205, 209–10, 272 n.60
Exodus angel, 121–23, 134–36

false prophets: and early rabbinic heresiology, 64–65, 255 n.152, 256 n.153; in Justin's heresiology, 51, 64–65, 246 n.75; pre-rabbinic sectarianism and Qumran, 51–52
Feldman, L. H., 272 n.57
feminist theory, 109–10
Finkelstein, Louis, 58
Fisch, Menachem: on dissension between Houses, 158–59, 163; and knowledge in rabbinic culture, 166; on rabbinic literature and pluralism/orthodoxy, 176, 314 n.79, 317 n.104; on Yavneh

Fisch, Menachem (*continued*)
    legends/Tosefta, 158–59, 309 nn. 30, 31,
    310 n.39, 314 n.76
Flusser, David, 259 n.171, 260 n.182
Fonrobert, Charlotte, 154, 181, 252 n.131,
    320 n.131
Foucault, Michel, 4, 311 n.50
Frankel, Zecharia, 152
Frend, W. H. C., 91, 232 n.39
Friedländer, Moriz, 56
Friedman, Shamma, 151

Gafni, Isaiah, 156–57
Gamaliel, Rabban: and apostolic succes-
    sion, 79, 83; death of, 181–82; and ex-
    communication of Eli'ezer, 173–74; and
    Yehoshua''s dissension, 185–89, 320
    n.127
Gamaliel, Rabban Shim'on ben, 79, 80,
    84
Gamaliel II, Rabban, 68, 79, 80, 259 n.172,
    269 n.42
Gamaliel III, Rabban, 79
Genesis: Justin and, 40; Prologue to
    Gospel of John and, 94–97, 100–101,
    103, 276 n.24, 277 n.34
Gieseler, J. K. L., 207
Glucker, John, 79–81, 82, 84
Gnosticism: and Justin, 4; and Logos the-
    ology, 93, 108–9, 285 n.118; and Pro-
    logue to Gospel of John, 94–95, 108–9,
    285 n.118; and rabbinic heresiological
    discourse, 56–57, 248 n.104; and Two
    Powers heresy, 56
Goodblatt, David M., 309 n.22
Goodenough, Erwin, 112, 289 n.27
Goodman, Martin, 45, 53, 55, 76, 258
    n.160, 266 n.11
Goranson, Stephen, 55, 213, 214, 327 n.70
Goshen-Gottstein, Alon, 180, 318 n.114
Gospel of John: Epiphanius and, 213; and
    Logos Incarnate superseding Torah,
    129, 296 n.6; and Logos theology in
    pre- and pararabbinic Judaism, 31,
    106–7, 114, 117–19, 126–27, 284 n.107;
    and Memra theology, 117–19, 126–27,
    284 n.107; Philo's Logos and, 114

Gospel of John, Prologue to, 31, 89–111;
    Christian kerygma and new focus on
    Jesus Christ, 104–5, 107, 283 nn. 97, 98;
    darkness and light in, 96, 98, 99, 114,
    126, 280 n.62; feminist approaches to
    Wisdom/Sophia and, 109–10; Gnosti-
    cism and, 94–95, 108–9, 285 n.118; and
    Hellenistic culture, 92, 274 n.13, 275
    n.15; and the incarnation, 98–100, 103,
    104–5, 279 n.57, 281 n.84; and John the
    Baptist, 99–100, 280 n.63; and Justin's
    Logos doctrine, 105–6; and Memra,
    108, 284 n.107; as midrash on Genesis,
    95–97, 100–101, 103; and movement
    from Logos theology to Christology,
    104–7, 283 nn. 97, 98; and the people of
    Israel, 100–103, 282 n.86; and problems
    in traditional reading as hymn, 109–11,
    285 n.124, 286 nn. 130, 131; as prologue
    to Genesis, 94–96, 276 n.24, 277 n.34;
    and relation to Judaism, 93–105,
    108–11; and standard Jewish rhetoric
    against Jews, 100–101, 280 n.70; and
    Targums, 96–97, 106–7, 284 n.107; and
    Torah, 104; verse-by-verse
    reading/analysis of, 98–105; and Wis-
    dom hymns/tradition, 93–98, 99–100,
    102, 108, 109–11, 277 n.34, 278 n.47, 281
    n.79, 285 n.124, 286 nn. 130, 131; and
    Wisdom's three attempts to enter the
    world, 100, 102, 104
Gospel of Matthew, 78, 104, 211, 213
Graham, William A., 171, 172, 315 n.85
Grant, Robert, 272 n.60
Gray, Patrick, 194
Gregory Nazianzen, 165, 166, 203–5
Gregory of Nyssa, 166–67
Guénoun, Denis, 11

Haenchen, Ernst, 111, 284 n.107
Ḥaggai, Rabbi, 177
Halbertal, Moshe, 316 n.96
Halivni, David, 151, 153, 154, 323 n.174
Hall, Jonathan M., 19, 20, 82
Halperin, David, 74
Hame'agel, Honi, 319 n.116
Hannah, Darrell, 113, 134

Harris, J. Rendell, 93, 95, 108, 251 n.124
Hasan-Rokem, Galit, 91, 267 n.22
Hasidim, 13
Haṣṣadiq, Rabbi Shim'on, 78
Havrelock, Rachel, 207
Hayes, Christine, 252 n.128, 255 n.152
Hayward, Robert: and Logos theology,
    116–17, 132; and Memra theology,
    116–17, 304 n.66; and Two Powers in
    Heaven, 123, 135, 136, 301 n.45
Heinemann, Isaak, 189
Heinemann, Joseph, 290 n.30
Hellenism and Christianity, 202–11, 324
    n.19
Hellenistic Jewish tradition: and *diadoche*,
    75–76, 85, 265 n.5; lexical influences, 55;
    Logos theology and first-century Ju-
    daism, 92, 274 n.13, 275 n.15; and Mid-
    dle Platonism, 114–15; and notion of
    ideological choice, 51–52; and Philo's
    Logos theology, 113–16, 289 n.27; and
    rabbinic heresiology, 51–52, 55
heresiology, Christian. *See* Christian here-
    siology
heresiology, rabbinic. See *minim/minut*
    and rabbinic heresiology; rabbinic
    heresiology
heresiology and theory, 2–27;
    Christian/Jewish identity and, 4–13,
    16–17; and creation/invention of reli-
    gion, 7–13, 232 n.39; heresiology as ide-
    ological apparatus, 26–27; heresy and
    orthodoxy, 2–3; hybridity and heresy,
    13–22, 234 nn. 54, 65; interpellation and
    creation of religions, 9–10; language
    and creation of religion, 7–11; language
    and hybridity, 17–22; Le Boulluec and,
    3–4; linguistics and dialect, 20–21, 24;
    and parallels in early Christianity and
    rabbinic Judaism, 2, 4–7, 29; prototype
    semantics, 22–24, 236 n.99, 237 n.101;
    wave theory account of Christian-
    Jewish history, 18–20, 26, 235 n.70
Herford, R. Travers, 56, 177, 197, 317 n.101
Herr, Moshe David, 51, 77
Hillel. *See* House of Hillel
Hippolytus, 303 n.59, 304 n.65

historiography, rabbinic, 46–49, 244 nn.
    43, 45, 47
Honorius, 218, 219
Hopkins, Keith, 155, 199, 309 n.21
Horbury, William, 259 n.170
Horner, Timothy J., 238 n.2, 241 n.18
Hoshaya of Caesarea, Rabbi, 128
House of Hillel: and apostolic succession,
    78; and issues of pluralism and dis-
    sensus, 158–60, 162–64, 315 n.89; and
    rabbinic heresiology, 61, 253 n.137; rela-
    tionship to Shammai, 61, 158–60,
    162–64, 253 n.137, 315 n.89
House of Israel, 52
House of Midrash, 169, 172, 189
House of Shammai: and apostolic succes-
    sion, 78; and issues of pluralism and
    dissensus, 158–60, 162–64, 315 n.89; and
    rabbinic heresiology, 61, 253 n.137; rela-
    tionship to Hillel, 61, 158–60, 162–64,
    253 n.137, 315 n.89
House of Study: and issues of pluralism
    and dissensus, 157–58, 161, 174–78,
    180–82, 186; and Logos theology,
    131–32; and rabbinic creation of ortho-
    doxy, 174–78, 180–82, 184–87, 320 n.127;
    and synagogues, 116, 290 n.30
Humfress, Caroline, 215, 219, 257 n.157
Hurtado, Larry, 119, 275 n.15, 283 n.97, 295
    n.89
hybridity and heresy, 13–22, 234 nn. 54,
    65

Idel, Moshe, 120, 285 n.118, 303 nn. 63,
    64
Idit, Rav, 120–22
Irenaeus, 77, 299 n.31
Ishmael, Rabbi, 190

Jacobs, Andrew, 202–3, 204–5, 208–9,
    210–11, 327 n.71
Janowitz, Naomi, 252 n.126
Jerome, 26, 71–72, 207–9, 262 n.191, 327
    n.70
Jerusalem church's flight to Pella, 62,
    91–92
Johannine community, 52, 256 n.155

John. *See* Gospel of John; Gospel of John, Prologue to

Johnson, Barbara, 282 n.96

John the Baptist, 99–100, 280 n.63

Josephus: and Jewish *hairesis*, 53–54, 55, 59; and Jewish sectarianism, 51, 53–54, 61–62, 85, 254 n.141; and Pharisees, 78, 83–84; on Sadducees, 59, 272 n.57

Julian, 202–5, 209–10, 326 n.52

Justin Martyr: and apostolic succession, 75, 76, 265 n.5, 269 n.42; application of *hairesis* to Jews, 3–4, 40–44, 240 n.15, 241 n.18; and *birkat hamminim*, 67–68, 71, 72–73, 258 n.163, 260 nn. 174, 175; and Christian self-definition, 17, 28–29, 38–40, 72–73, 238 n.2; and early heresiology, 3–4, 28, 39–44, 51, 64–65, 66, 137, 240 n.15, 241 n.18, 242 n.27, 265 n.5, 299 n.31; "false prophet" heresiology, 51, 64–65, 246 n.75; and first-century Hellenistic Jewish thought, 92, 274 n.13; and *hairesis*, 3–4, 39–44, 240 n.15, 241 n.18, 242 n.27; Le Boulluec on, 3–4, 28, 64–65, 75, 76, 242 n.23, 246 n.75, 265 n. 5; and Logos theology, 28–29, 38–40, 44, 105–6, 137, 146; and movement from Logos theology to Christology, 105–6; on Pharisees, 41, 42–43, 84, 241 n.19; on philosophy and *hairesis*, 242 n.27. See also *Dialogue with Trypho* (Justin Martyr)

Kahana, Menahem, 240 n.17

Kalmin, Richard, 221, 223, 319 n.116

Karaite schism, 63

Käsemann, Ernst, 98–99

Kelly, J. N. D., 146

Kimelman, Reuven, 261 nn. 187, 190

King, Karen, 28, 30, 56, 133, 230 n.4

King, Richard, 234 n.65

Kister, Menahem, 56, 107, 240 n.17, 248 n.104, 298 n. 20

Klawans, Jonathan, 260 n.179

Kline, Moshe, 78, 79, 271 n.52

Kraemer, David, 152

Krafft-Ebing, R. von, 211

Kronfeld, Chana, 22–23, 236 n. 99

Labov, William, 20, 24

Lakoff, George, 24, 25, 26

Laupot, Eric, 232 n.39

Le Boulluec, Alain, 133; and apostolic succession, 75, 76, 85, 264 n.3, 265 nn. 5, 10; on Christian heresiology, 3–4, 75, 76, 85, 230 n.9, 264 n.3, 265 nn. 5, 10; on Justin Martyr, 3–4, 28, 64–65, 75, 76, 242 n.23, 246 n.75, 265 n. 5; and study of heresiology, 3–4

Levine, Lee, 85, 217, 269 n.42, 272 n.60

Levi-Strauss, Claude, 207

Levy, Evonne, 170

Lieberman, Saul, 69–70, 81, 223

Liebes, Yehuda, 142

Lieu, Judith M., 6, 72–73, 238 n.3, 260 n.175, 262 n.199

Lightfoot, R. H., 281 n.73

Lim, Richard: on Christian orthodoxy, 153, 165, 167, 180–81, 193–94, 195, 196, 200, 314 n.78; on Nicene legends, 167–68, 170; on orthodoxy and elimination of dissensus, 153, 161, 165, 167, 180–81, 193–94

Limberis, Vasiliki, 202–3, 210, 323 n.1

Linder, Amnon, 217, 218

Loewe, Rabbi, of Prague, 271 n.52

Logos theology, rabbinic transformation of, 31–32, 128–47; and defining of Christianity and Judaism, 31–32, 38, 130–31, 132–35, 137–39, 145–47; Logos as heresy, 38, 130–39, 144–47; and Philo's Logos myth, 128; Sophia/Wisdom and Torah, 128–30, 296 nn. 3, 5; and Two Powers in Heaven as heresy, 31, 38, 56, 130–31, 133–47; and Two Powers in Heaven as Jewish theology, 134–39, 300 n.42, 301 nn.43–45. *See also* Logos theology in pre- and pararabbinic Judaism; Two Powers in Heaven

Logos theology and Gospel of John. *See* Gospel of John, Prologue to

Logos theology in pre- and pararabbinic Judaism, 31, 112–27; and the Christian incarnation, 124–25, 293 n.75; and connections between Logos, Word, and light, 114, 126; and Gospel of John, 31,

106–7, 114, 117–19, 126–27, 284 n.107; and Hellenistic Jewish tradition, 113–16, 289 n.27; and Jewish binitarian prayer, 120–25, 283 n.97, 295 n.89; language and the Divine, 115–16, 288 n.24; and mediation by the Logos, 114–15; and medieval exegesis of prayer texts, 124–25; and Memra theology, 108, 113, 116–19, 125–27; and Middle Platonism, 114–16, 288 nn. 19, 22, 24; and *minim*, 123, 292 n.63; Mishna and evidence of, 123–24, 293 n.71; and non-rabbinic Judaism, 113–16, 128; and synagogues, 116, 123–24, 289 n.28, 290 n.30; and Targums, 113, 116–19, 125–27, 289 n.28, 290 n.30, 291 n.40. *See also* Logos theology, rabbinic transformation of

Loomba, Ania, 7, 27

Lubavitch Hasidim, 13

Lyman, Rebecca, 92, 234 n.54, 263 n.202, 288 nn. 19, 22, 299 n.31

Macgregor, G. H. C., 281 n.73

Mack, Burton, 117

Maimonides, 117

Maldonatus, 101, 279 n.57

Manichaean heresy, 220

Marcion, 12, 17

Marcus Aurelius, 54

Markus, Robert, 9–10

Martyn, James Louis, 317 n.107

Martyrdom of Polycarp, 72–73

martyrology, 72–73, 238 n.3, 262 n.201

Matthew, Gospel of, 78, 104, 211, 213

McNamara, Martin, 117, 118, 126

Meir, Ofra, 272 n.60

Mekhilta d'Rabbi Ishmael, 41, 135, 139, 240 n.17, 241 n.18, 301 nn. 44, 45

Mekhilta of Rabbi Shim'on, 192

Melito of Sardis, 72, 146–47, 261 n.188, 300 n.42

Memra theology: and Gospel of John, 106–7, 117–19, 126–27, 284 n.107; and Logos theology in pre- and para-rabbinic Judaism, 106–7, 113, 116–19, 125–27; suppression/repudiation of, 131–32, 136–37, 139, 145–47; and syna-gogues, 116, 123–24, 289 n.28, 290 n.30; and Targums, 113, 116–19, 123–27, 289 n.28, 290 n.30, 291 n.40; and Two Powers in Heaven, 131, 136–37, 139, 145–47. *See also* Targums

Metatron: and pre-rabbinic binitarian prayer, 121–23; and Two Powers heresy, 138, 140–43, 303 nn. 63, 64, 305 n.76

Middle Platonism, 114–16, 288 nn. 19, 22, 24

Miles, Jack, 283 n.98

Milikovsky, Chaim, 249 n.115, 250 n.121

minim/minut and rabbinic heresiology, 29–30, 54–65; and *'am ha'areṣ* (pagan-ism), 59, 256 n.155; and Babylonian Talmud, 221–24; and *birkat hamminim*, 67–73; challenges to Jewish identity, 61–62; and excommunication of Akavyah ben Mehalalel, 64–65, 255 n.152; and false prophets, 64–65, 255 n.152, 256 n.153; and *gilyonim*, 58, 249 n.113; and Gnosticism, 56–57, 248 n.104; and *hairesis*, 55; and halakhic differ-ences, 60–61, 253 n.137, 256 n.153; Hellenic lexical influences, 55; and issue of authority, 60, 62–63; and Jewish self-identity, 66, 71–72; and Justin on hereti-cal Jews, 42–43; *minim* and idol worshippers, 57; *minim* defined, 2, 54–55; Mishna and, 55, 58–59, 60–63, 66, 252 n.128; parallels and coemergence with Christian heresiology, 29–30, 55, 65–67, 71–73, 261 n.185; and Pharisees, 58–59, 69–70, 251 n.125; and pre-rab-binic Logos theology, 123, 292 n.63; and pre-rabbinism, 54–55, 123, 292 n.63; and rabbinic legends, 177, 197–99; and rela-tionship between Hillel and Shammai, 61, 253 n.137; and Roman religion, 59–60; and Sadducees, 42, 58–59, 60–63, 252 n.129, 254 n.142, 255 n.146; and shift in meaning to Gentiles/Christians, 220–25; and Temple destruction, 62; and Two Powers heresy, 56, 131, 133, 137; women and female sexuality, 60, 62–63, 64, 252 n.131, 255 n.146. See also *birkat hamminim*; sectarianism, pre-rabbinic

Mischlinge, 208–9, 213

Mishna: apostolic succession in, 30, 60, 74–86, 267 n.22; Avot of Rabbi Nathan, 60–61, 271 n.52; and influence of Christian heresiology on nascent Judaism, 29–30; and Jewish binitarian prayer, 123–24, 293 n.71; Mishna Eduyyot, 64; Mishna Megilla, 123; and rabbinic invention of *minim*, 55, 58–59, 60–63, 252 n.128; Tractate Avot, 77–83, 84, 266 n.15, 271 n.52; Tractate Niddah, 63; Tractate Sanhedrin, 58, 252 n.128. *See also* apostolic succession

Modalism, 39, 133, 136, 137, 138, 146, 239 n.7, 305 n.76. *See also* Two Powers in Heaven

Monarchianism, 130, 133, 138, 146. *See also* Two Powers in Heaven

Moore, George Foot, 300 n.42

Morgan, Catherine, 20–21

Mosshammer, Alden, 166

Motyer, Stephen, 102, 245 n.58

al-Muqammiṣ, David, 289 n.29

Naeh, Shlomo, 65, 159–60, 162–63, 256 n.153

Nagy, Gregory, 48

Najman, Hindy, 275 n.17

Nazoreans, 207, 214

Nestorian Controversy, 321 n.147

Neusner, Jacob, 5, 71; on apostolic succession and Torah study, 83; on Eliʿezer legends, 179–80, 318 n.110; and rabbinic historiography, 47, 49, 244 n.47; on triumph of rabbinic Judaism, 219; on the two Talmuds, 151, 307 n.1; and Yavneh, 47, 49, 245 n.58

Newman, Hillel, 208

Nicaea, Council of, 167, 200, 312 n.57; and apostolic succession, 196; Athanasius and, 195–96; and formal anathematizing of heretics, 70; and Yavneh, 44–45, 193, 196–97. *See also* Nicene Christianity

Nicene Christianity: and creation of Christian orthodoxy, 167–71, 192–96, 200, 321 n.147; and creation of rabbinic orthodoxy, 167–71, 192–93, 195–96, 200; and defining characteristics of heresy/orthodoxy, 59, 251 n.124; legends of, 167–71, 193; and rejection of Logos theology, 139

Niehoff, Maren, 115, 295 n.2

Noetus, 303 n.59

Nomos, 147, 307 n.104

North, John A., 21–22, 59, 215, 216

Numbers, 129–30, 141

Numenius, 162, 288 nn. 19, 22

On the Infidelity of the Academy Toward Plato (Numenius), 162

Orestia (Aeschylus), 188, 320 n.131

Origen, 70, 191, 251 n.125, 269 n.42, 308 n.9, 311 n.45

paganism: Christian orthodoxy and hate speech regarding, 9–10; early rabbinic heresiology and ʿam haʾareṣ, 59, 256 n.155; Epiphanius and, 206; and ethnic designation, 324 n.19; and *minim*, 197, 322 n.169; and Prologue to Gospel of John and, 108–9; Theodosian Code on *superstitio* and, 215–16, 219

Pagels, Elaine, 4, 246 n.75

Panarion (Epiphanius), 211–14, 327 nn. 70, 71

paradosis, 85

Passover Haggada, 83

Paul, 51, 54, 103, 193, 250 n.119

Pearson, Birger, 283 n.98

Pharisees: and apostolic succession, 42, 78, 83–84, 272 n.57; curse on, 69–70; and early rabbinic heresiology, 58–59, 69–70, 251 n.125; and hand-washing ritual, 251 n.125; and heresy and orthodoxy, 41, 42–43, 58–59, 241 n.19, 250 n.119; Justin Martyr on *hairesis* and, 41, 42–43, 84, 241 n.19; and sectarianism of Second Temple period, 50, 52, 250 n.121; at Yavneh, 44–45

Philo: and Gospel of John, 96, 103, 114, 277 n.38; and *hairesis*, 230 n.9; and Hellenistic Jewish tradition, 113–16, 289 n.27; language and the Divine, 115–16,

288 n.24; Logos and Middle Platonism, 114–16, 288 nn. 19, 22, 24; and Logos theology, 96, 103, 112, 113–16, 128; and rabbinic heresy, 298 n.20

Pines, Shlomo, 249 n.113, 300 n.42, 322 n.169

Pionios, 72–73, 261 n.188, 262 n.201

Plato, 9, 162

Platonism, 114–16, 288 nn. 19, 22, 24

Plutarch, 307 n.104

Polycarp, 72–73, 261 n.188

postcolonial theory, 13–17, 234 nn. 54, 65

Pourkier, Aline, 262 n.191

Pratt, Mary Louise, 18

pre-rabbinic Judaism. *See* Logos theology in pre- and pararabbinic Judaism; sectarianism, pre-rabbinic

Price, S. R. F., 21–22, 59, 215, 216

Prigent, Pierre, 238 n.2

Proverbs, 93–94, 96, 128, 129–30

Pseudo-Clementine texts, 43

Pseudo-Dionysius, 165

Pseudo-Jonathan, 131, 290 n.30

Quartodeciman heresy, 220, 257 n.157, 330 n.115

Qumran community: as cult, 52; Essenes, 52, 54, 260 n.182; and "false prophets," 51–52; and Johannine community, 52; orthodoxy and heresy, 49–50, 51–52, 70; orthodoxy and sectarianism, 49–50, 51–52, 245 n.62, 253 n.137, 260 n.182

rabbinic heresiology: and apostolic succession, 74–86; and *birkat hamminim*, 67–73, 259 nn.170–72, 260 n.175; dating of, 67–70; and evidence for full notion of heresy, 58–63; and Jewish self-identity, 61–62, 66, 71–72, 213–14, 217–25; parallels and coemergence with orthodox Christian heresiology, 29–30, 55, 65–67, 71–73, 261 n.185; and rabbinic historiography, 46–49; Yavneh and originating moment of, 45, 46–49, 68–69. *See also* apostolic succession; Justin Martyr; *minim/minut* and rab-

binic heresiology; sectarianism, pre-rabbinic; Two Powers in Heaven

rabbinic Judaism and Christian empire, 202–25; and Christian heresiological discourse regarding Judaism, 206–14; and Christianity's role in Jewish self-definition, 61–62, 213–14, 217–25; and coemergence of heresiologies, 29–30, 55, 65–67, 71–73, 261 n.185; and Judaism's role in Christian self-definition, 205–20, 324 n.19; and legitimation of rabbinic Judaism as *superstitio*, 217–20, 329 n.102; and shift in meaning of *minut*, 220–25; terms *religio* and *superstitio*, 217–20, 329 n.102

rabbinic Judaism and creation of orthodoxy, 32–33, 151–201; *derasha* on pluralism and dissensus, 157–60, 185, 310 n.36; epistemic shifts, 33, 165–66, 167–71, 174–82, 316 n.96; Houses of Hillel and Shammai, 159–60, 162–64; and knowledge/power, 165–66, 167–71, 174, 314 n.78; language and hermeneutics, 189–92; *minim* and pluralism, 177, 197–99; parallels and shared practices with Christianity in, 155–57, 160–61, 167–71, 192–200, 311 n.50; pluralism, dissensus, and authority, 157–65, 168–71, 178–82, 310 n.36, 314 n.74; rabbinic literature and editorial pluralism, 182–89; and shifts in meaning of biblical texts, 177–78, 317 n.104; and the spoken word/the oral, 171–74, 315 n.85; and the theologization of indeterminacy, 183–92; and Yeshiva, 156–57, 309 n.22. See also *minim/minut* and rabbinic heresiology; Talmud, Babylonian; Yavneh legends

rabbinic literature: and apostolic succession, 77–83, 84, 266 n.15, 271 n.52; on dissension/pluralism and Yavneh, 157–58, 164, 168–71, 185; and editorial pluralism, 182–89; and epistemic shifts in meaning of texts, 177–78, 317 n.104; heresiology and rabbinic historiography, 46–49, 244 nn. 43, 45, 47; *minim* in, 177, 197–99; nascent heresiology in

rabbinic literature (*continued*)
    ante-Nicene, 5–6. *See also* Yavneh leg-
    ends; *specific rabbinic literature*
Rebillard, Éric, 194
Reiner, Elchanan, 290 n.30
Resh Laqish, 145
Ringe, Sharon, 102, 281 n.79
Robinson, J. A. T., 90
Rosch, Eleanor, 24
Roth, Gerald, 318 n.112
Rubenstein, Jeffrey L., 32, 153–54, 156–57,
    309 n.22, 320 n.128
Ruether, Rosemary Radford, 197
Rufinus of Aquileia, 167, 168–70
Runia, David T., 230 n.9, 239 n.11, 240 n.15

Sabellius, 146
Sachot, Maurice, 11, 214–15, 328 n.87
Sadducees: and heresy, 42, 58–59, 60–63,
    252 n.129, 254 n.142, 255 n.146; and
    Jewish sectarianism, 50, 52; Josephus
    on, 59, 272 n.57; Justin on, 42; women,
    60, 62–63, 252 n.131, 255 n.146
Saldarini, Anthony, 235 n. 73, 255 n.146,
    271 n.52
Samaritans, 62–63, 255 n.146
Schiffman, Lawrence H., 297 n.18
Schnackenburg, Rudolf, 278 n.47, 279
    n.52, 282 n.89, 296 n.5
Schremer, Adiel, 51, 246 n.72, 253 n.137
Schüssler Fiorenza, Elisabeth, 109
Schwartz, Seth: on apostolic succession, 269
    n.42, 270 n.43; on Christianization, 11,
    12, 202, 205; on Josephus and pre-
    rabbinic *hairesis*, 54, 254 n.141; on
    Neusner and rabbinic historiography,
    49; on rabbinic heresiology, 255 n.148;
    and systemic change in Jewish culture,
    16; on Theodosian Code, 218, 329 n.102
Second Temple period: and idolatry, 221;
    and Jewish sectarianism, 49–52, 65, 245
    nn. 62, 65, 250 n.121; and *minim*, 45,
    221, 223; rabbinism and heresiology,
    45, 243 n.40; transition from sectarian-
    ism to orthodoxy, 50–51. *See also* sec-
    tarianism, pre-rabbinic; Yavneh,
    council of

sectarianism, pre-rabbinic, 49–54, 65, 245
    nn. 62, 65, 250 n.121; difference from
    rabbinic heresiology, 61–62; and *haire-
    sis*, 53–54; parallel development of
    Jewish and Christian heresy, 52–53;
    Qumran community and, 49–50,
    51–52, 245 n.62, 253 n.137, 260 n.182;
    and transition to orthodoxy, 50–51
Segal, Alan: on Jewish rhetoric against
    other Jews, 280 n.70; on Logos and
    Christian incarnation, 293 n.75; on
    minim and pre-rabbinic Logos theol-
    ogy, 123, 292 n.63, 293 n.64; on rabbinic
    Judaism and orthodoxy, 130–13, 297
    nn. 11, 12, 298 n.20; on Two Powers
    theology, 136–37, 140–42, 144, 301 nn.
    43–45, 302 n.51, 304 n.72, 306 n.94
Shammai. *See* House of Shammai
Shapira, Haim, 187, 320 nn. 127, 128
Shemesh, Aharon, 49–50, 51, 52, 255 n.152
Shim'on, Rabbi, 192
Simon, Marcel, 41–42, 54, 241 n.19
Skarsaune, Oskar, 259 n.170
Smith, Jonathan Z., 133
Smith, Wilfred Cantwell, 11
Sophia/Wisdom: feminist approaches to
    Gospel of John and, 109–10; and
    Memra theology, 117; and rabbinic
    transformation of Logos, 129–30, 296
    n.5; as Torah, 128–29, 296 nn. 3, 5. *See
    also* Gospel of John, Prologue to
Sozomen, 14–15, 101
Stammaim and Babylonian Talmud,
    151–52, 153–57, 183–84, 198. *See also*
    Yavneh legends
Stammbaum theory, 18–19
Stemberger, Günter, 217, 289 n.28, 329
    n.100
Stern, David, 157–58, 161, 164, 185–85
Stove of Akhnai, 168–74, 186, 317 n.104
Stroumsa, Guy, 255 n.152
Studer, Basil, 90, 113
superstitio and Theodosian Code, 214–20
Sussmann, Yaakov, 55, 248 n.97, 253 n.137,
    254 n.142, 260 n.182
synagogues and Logos theology, 116,
    123–24, 289 n.28, 290 n.30

Talmud, Babylonian: and apostolic succession, 84; Baba Meṣia, 143; Berakhot,
185; differences from Palestinian
Talmud, 151–54, 191–92; and editorial
pluralism, 182–89; Ḥagiga, 143–44, 186;
history of evolution and canonization
of, 151–54; and issues of dissension and
unity, 32, 158–60, 161–65, 168–71,
178–82, 309 n.30, 310 n.36; and Jewish
binitarian prayer, 120–21; Ketubbot,
84; language and hermeneutics,
189–92; on *minut* and Christian gentiles, 221–24; and Nicene Christianity,
193, 196–97; pluralism and creation of
orthodoxy, 32, 151–89; redaction of, 32,
33, 154, 155, 156–57, 164–65, 183–84;
Sanhedrin, 65, 120–21, 190–92;
Shabbat, 190–91; and the Stammaim,
151–52, 153–57, 183–84, 198; and the
theologization of indeterminacy,
183–92; and Tosefta, 158–60, 309 nn. 30,
31, 310 n.36; and Yavneh legends,
168–82; Yoma, 143. *See also* Yavneh
legends
Talmud, Palestinian: Berakhot, 68; and
birkat hamminim, 68, 259 n.171; differences from Babylonian Talmud,
151–54, 191–92; Shabbat, 176–77;
Sukkah, 144; and Two Powers in
Heaven, 144–45
Tannaitic texts, 5, 55, 247 n.89. *See also*
rabbinic literature
Tarfon, Rabbi, 57
Targums: dating of, 118; and Gospel of
John, 96–97, 106–7, 284 n.107;
"Jerusalem Targum," 293 n.71; and
Jewish binitarian prayer, 124, 125–27, 293
n.71; and Logos theology, 106–7, 124,
125–26, 131–32, 284 n.107, 293 n.71; and
Memra theology, 113, 116–19, 123–27, 289
n.28, 290 n.30, 291 n.40; Palestinian,
96–97, 106–7, 118–19, 124, 125–26, 132, 293
n.71; Pseudo-Jonathan, 131, 290 n.30;
synagogues and, 116, 123–24, 289 n.28,
290 n.30; Targum Neofiti, 106–7, 118,
126, 139, 293 n.71; Targum Onkelos, 117,
131, 290 n.30; and Two Powers in

Heaven, 300 n.42. *See also* Memra theol-
ogy
Tartar, Helen, 243 n.37
Ta-Shma, Israel, 125
Taylor, Joan, 263 n.203
Tertullian, 66, 193
Theodosius, Emperor, 193–94, 219
Theodosian Code, 214–20
Tobin, Thomas, 118
Tosefta: and Babylonian Talmud, 158–60,
180, 309 nn. 30, 31, 310 n.36; and *birkat
hamminim*, 69–70; and *minut*, 221
Tractate Avot, 77–83, 84, 266 n.15, 271 n.52
Tractate Giṭṭin, 174–75
Tractate Ḥagiga, 84
The Trimorphic Protennoia, 94–95, 110, 276
n.31, 277 n.34
Tropper, Amram, 272 n.60
Trypho. *See Dialogue with Trypho* (Justin
Martyr)
Turner, John, 276 n.24
Two Powers in Heaven: and apostasy of
Rabbi Akiva, 56, 136, 139–45; and
Gnosticism, 56; heresy of, 38, 89,
130–31, 133–47; as Jewish theology,
134–39, 295 n.89, 300 n.42, 301
nn.43–45; and Logos conspiracy,
145–47, 306 n.99; and Metatron, 138,
140–43, 303 nn. 63, 64, 305 n.76; and
minim, 56; and "Son of Man" passages
from Daniel, 136, 139–45. *See also* binitarianism, Jewish

Vaggione, Richard, 168, 312 n.57
van der Horst, Pieter W., 70, 261 n.190
Vermes, Geza, 293 n.71
Vessey, Mark, 194
Vincent of Lerins, 194
"The Visions of Ezekiel," 141

Williams, Rowan, 10
Wilson, Stephen G., 68–69
Winston, David, 113, 300 n.42
Wisdom of Solomon, 300 n.42
Wisdom traditions. *See* Gospel of John,
Prologue to; Sophia/Wisdom
Wolfson, Elliot, 120, 124, 138, 293 n.75

women: exclusion from apostolic
succession, 60, 74, 78–79, 267 n.22;
Sadducees, 60, 62–63, 252 n.131, 255
n.146

Yadin, Azzan, 144–45, 190, 191, 288 n.24
Ya'ir, Pinḥas ben, 318 n.112
Yavneh, council of: apostolic succession
and, 196; and *birkat hamminim*, 68–69,
70, 259 nn. 170, 172; and Nicene
Council, 44–45, 193, 196–97; and originating moment of Jewish heresiology,
45, 46–49, 68–69, 260 n.180; pluralism
and dissension/unity, 44–45, 60,
157–58, 164, 168–71, 185; and rabbinic/
traditional historiography, 46–49. *See
also* Yavneh legends
Yavneh legends: and apostolic succession,
76–77, 80, 81; and Athenian mythmaking, 188; and curse against the heretics,
68–69, 70; Rabbi Eli'ezer and creation
of orthodoxy, 165–66, 168–74, 178–82,
186, 314 n.76, 318 nn. 110, 114; and epistemic shifts, 168–74, 178–82; Nicaea
and, 167–71, 193, 196–97; on origins of
Jewish heresiology and rabbinic historiography, 46–49, 260 n.180; on pluralism and orthodoxy, 157–59, 168–82;
power and knowledge, 165–66, 168–71,
174; truth and the spoken word/the
oral, 171–74, 315 n.85
Yehoshua', Rabbi, 158, 171, 182, 184–89
Yehuda, Rabbi, 64, 79–85, 269 n.42, 271
n.49, 271 n.52
Yerushalmi. *See* Talmud, Palestinian
Yeshiva, 156–57, 309 n.22
Yirmiah, Rabbi, 171, 317 n.104
Yoḥanan, Rabbi, 47, 91, 197–99
Yoḥanan ben Zakkai, Rabban: and "aban-
donment" of Jerusalem, 62; and Alon's
Yavneh legend, 46–47; and apostolic
succession, 79–84, 271 nn. 49, 52; and
Rabbi Eli'ezer, 180, 186, 318 n.10
Yose the Galilean, Rabbi, 140
Young, Francis, 313 n.69
Young, Robert, 15, 16, 18–19, 213
Yuval, Israel Jacob, 4–5, 267 n.18, 300
n.42

Acknowledgments

Since its earliest foundations, rabbinic culture has nurtured the concept that learning and scholarship are not individual but social practices. In particular the notion of the study pair, the *ḥavruta*, has been central to rabbinic study. Generous and critical study partners for me throughout this project have been Carlin Barton, Charlotte Fonrobert, Galit Hasan-Rokem, Karen King, and Dina Stein. Much of this book would simply not have happened were it not for my constant *ḥavruta* with Virginia Burrus throughout the last decade. She read two complete and countless incomplete drafts of this manuscript, helping me get closer and closer to my aspirations for the book. Ivan Marcus and Ishay Rosen-Zvi provided searching readings of a near-final draft that were unusually helpful. Adi Schremer's sharp (in both senses) critique enabled me finally to drop three chapters that needed to go. I would also like to thank Gil Anidjar, Carol Bakhos, Chava Boyarin, Almut Bruckstein, Sheila Delany, Paula Fredriksen, Erich Gruen, Christine Hayes, Ronald Hendel, Oded Irshai, Menahem Kahana, Catherine Keller, Chana Kronfeld, Lisa Lampert, Jack Levison, Evonne Levy, Rebecca Lyman, Harry O. Maier, Sharon Marcus, Jack Miles, Stephen D. Moore, Maren Niehoff, Elaine Pagels, Jeffrey Purvis, Seth Schwartz, Aharon Shemesh, and Azzan Yadin for reading early versions of several or all of these chapters and very helpfully commenting on them. I thank all of these and formally absolve them of responsibility for the failings of the book.

During the drafting of the chapters on the Logos, I had the privilege and pleasure to be a *Gastprofessor* of New Testament and Judaic Origins at the Harvard Divinity School, where I taught much of the material in this book. My students during that semester (spring 2000) were of enormous help in clarifying many of the issues treated here. My colleagues on that faculty, and especially Karen King, made the semester an intellectual and personal joy. I wish, in particular, to thank Elizabeth Busky, who made my visit at Harvard smooth and fun.

Special thanks to Carlin Barton for her help with my thinking, writing, and morale in moments of adversity during the making of this book.

Vincent P. (Bud) Bynack helped enormously in the process of transforming a draft into a book, and I am grateful to him.

Gratitude is due as well to Ana Niedermaier of East View Cartographic for her vital help in securing the cover art.

As ever, I am thankful to the funders of the Hermann P. and Sophia Taubman Chair of Talmudic Culture at the University of California, Berkeley, which makes my scholarly productivity possible.

A Berlin Prize Fellowship at the American Academy in Berlin in the fall of 2001 made it possible to finish the book. I wish to thank the director, Professor Gary Smith, and all of his wonderful staff for their hospitality and help.

I feel deeply privileged that the last stages of writing were completed in Rome at the Pontificia Universitas Gregoriana, amid the abundant material memories of the times, places, and peoples treated in this work.

Finally, I would like to thank Helen Tartar, the veritable Maxwell Perkins of scholarly editors. I am deeply indebted to her for all the effort she has shared with me over several years of working together and for the pleasure and profit I have derived. It was my hope and intention to publish this book with Helen at the Stanford University Press. With the unfortunate separation of individual from institution, my coeditors and I chose to move this book and the Divinations series of which it is part elsewhere. We are fortunate to have found a happy new home at the University of Pennsylvania Press, and I would like to thank Jerome Singerman, our new editor at Penn, for all of his exertions on behalf of the series and the book.